Jon Davies, Graham H
Wilfred Watson teach
Department of Religious Studies
in the University of Newcastle.

JOURNAL FOR THE STUDY OF THE OLD TESTAMENT SUPPLEMENT SERIES

195

Sheffield Academic Press

Words Remembered, Texts Renewed

Essays in Honour of John F.A. Sawyer

edited by
Jon Davies, Graham Harvey
and
Wilfred G.E. Watson

Journal for the Study of the Old Testament
Supplement Series 195

Published by
Sheffield Academic Press Ltd
Mansion House
19 Kingfield Road
Sheffield, S11 9AS
England

Typeset by Sheffield Academic Press
and
Printed on acid-free paper in Great Britain
by Bookcraft
Midsomer Norton, Somerset

British Library Cataloguing in Publication Data

A catalogue record for this book is available
from the British Library

ISBN 1-85075-542-6

CONTENTS

PREFACE

My friend, your mind is a river whose spring never fails
(from The Babylonian Theodicy)

For over a quarter of a century John Sawyer has been central to the life and work of the Department of Religious Studies in the University of Newcastle upon Tyne, where he has been successively and successfully, Lecturer, Senior Lecturer, Reader, Professor and Head of Department. A Scot, and son of the Manse, he grew up in Dunbar and Yarrow in the Scottish Lowlands; went to school and University in Edinburgh; and has worked, taught and examined at many universities in Britain and abroad. Both as scholar and Christian he has involved himself with the life of religious communities, both of the past and the present.

The dominant love of his *intellectual* life has been the study of Hebrew, the books of the Jewish Bible, and the culture and traditions of Judaism, ancient and modern. The dominant feature of his *public* life has been extensive and active involvement in the life and work of organizations such as the North East Council of Christians and Jews (of which he was for fourteen years Chairman), the Tyne and Wear Racial Equality Council's Inter-Faith Panel, of which he was also Chairman, and the Standing Advisory Committee on Religious Education of the City of Newcastle upon Tyne.

From this active public involvement John derived a kind of experiential hermeneutic which gradually drew him into a search not simply for the origin of the meaning of word and text but also for the many and strange ways in which word and text become transposed, re-oriented and often enough traduced by interests and purposes somewhat problematically, if at all, related to the interests and purposes of the 'original' authors. His students and colleagues have watched, with interest (and occasionally amusement) this drift towards things sociological, as all the skill of the linguist and biblicist are brought to bear on the question of the ways in which the present endlessly re-invents, and re-invigorates, the past. John's was the guiding hand behind the Newcastle Religious Studies Department's volume on *The Sociology of Sacred Texts*

(Sheffield Academic Press, 1993, edited by Jon Davies and Isabel Wollaston); and we all look forward to his forthcoming *The Fifth Evangelist: Isaiah in the History of Christianity*, foretastes of which have already indicated that in it we will find the full development of the repertoire of skills now so creatively deployed by John Sawyer. John's publications are recorded elsewhere in this volume. The range and scope of the many contributions are themselves ample evidence of the regard and affection in which he is held by colleagues and ex-students all over the world.

Jon DAVIES

Graham HARVEY

Wilfred WATSON

ABBREVIATIONS

AB	Anchor Bible
AfO	*Archiv für Orientforschung*
ANET	J.B. Pritchard (ed.), *Ancient Near Eastern Texts*
AnJapBibInst	*Annual of the Japanese Biblical Institute*
AOAT	Alter Orient und Altes Testament
AOS	American Oriental Series
ASJ	*Acta Sumerologica Japaniensis*
ATANT	Abhandlungen zur Theologie des Alten und Neuen Testaments
ATD	Das Alte Testament Deutsch
AuOr	*Aula orientalis*
BAGD	W. Bauer, W.F. Arndt, F.W. Gingrich and F.W. Danker, *Greek–English Lexicon of the New Testament*
BDB	F. Brown, S.R. Driver, and C.A. Briggs, *Hebrew and English Lexicon of the Old Testament*
BDF	F. Blass, A. Debrunner and R.W. Funk, *A Greek Grammar of the New Testament*
BethM	*Beth Mikra*
BETL	Bibliotheca ephemeridum theologicarum lovaniensium
Bib	*Biblica*
BKAT	Biblischer Kommentar: Altes Testament
BSO(A)S	*Bulletin of the School of Oriental (and African) Studies*
BT	*The Bible Translator*
BWANT	Beiträge zur Wissenschaft vom Alten und Neuen Testament
BZ	*Biblische Zeitschrift*
BZAW	Beihefte zur *ZAW*
CAD	*The Assyrian Dictionary of the Oriental Institute of the University of Chicago*
CBQ	*Catholic Biblical Quarterly*
CBQMS	*Catholic Biblical Quarterly* Monograph Series
ConBOT	Coniectanea biblica, Old Testament
CRINT	Compendia rerum iudaicarum ad novum testamentum
EstBíb	*Estudios bíblicos*
FRLANT	Forschungen zur Religion und Literatur des Alten und Neuen Testaments
GKB	Gesenius–Kautzsch–Bergsträsser, *Hebräische Grammatik*
HALAT	W. Baumgartner *et al.*, *Hebräisches und aramäisches Lexikon zum Alten Testament*
HAT	Handbuch zum Alten Testament
HKAT	Handkommentar zum Alten Testament

HSM	Harvard Semitic Monographs
HTR	*Harvard Theological Review*
ICC	International Critical Commentary
IDB	G.A. Buttrick (ed.), *Interpreter's Dictionary of the Bible*
JAOS	*Journal of the American Oriental Society*
JBL	*Journal of Biblical Literature*
JEA	*Journal of Egyptian Archaeology*
JJS	*Journal of Jewish Studies*
JNES	*Journal of Near Eastern Studies*
JQR	*Jewish Quarterly Review*
JSNT	*Journal for the Study of the New Testament*
JSOT	*Journal for the Study of the Old Testament*
JSOTSup	*Journal for the Study of the Old Testament* Supplement Series
JSS	*Journal of Semitic Studies*
JTS	*Journal of Theological Studies*
KB	L. Koehler and W. Baumgartner, *Lexicon in Veteris Testamenti libros*
KTU	Keilalphabetischen Texte aus Ugarit
MIO	*Mitteilungen des Institüt für Orientforschung*
NCB	New Century Bible
NICOT	New International Commentary on the Old Testament
NTS	*New Testament Studies*
NTT	Norsk Teologisk Tidsskrift
OBO	Orbis biblicus et orientalis
OLP	Orientalia lovaniensia periodica
Or	*Orientalia* (Rome)
OTL	Old Testament Library
RA	*Revue d'assyriologie et d'archéologie orientale*
REJ	*Revue des études juives*
RevSém	*Revue sémitique*
RHR	*Revue de l'histoire des religions*
SBLDS	SBL Dissertation Series
SBLMS	SBL Monograph Studies
SBS	Stuttgarter Bibelstudien
SBT	Studies in Biblical Theology
SJOT	*Scandinavian Journal of the Old Testament*
SUNT	Studien zur Umwelt des Neuen Testaments
TDNT	G. Kittel and G. Friedrich (eds.), *Theological Dictionary of the New Testament*
THAT	*Theologisches Handwörterbuch zum Alten Testament*
TRev	*Theologische Revue*
TZ	*Theologische Zeitschrift*
UF	*Ugarit-Forschungen*
VT	*Vetus Testamentun*
VTSup	*Vetus Testamentum*, Supplements
WBC	Word Biblical Commentary
WMANT	Wissenschaftliche Monographien zum Alten und Neuen Testament

WO	*Die Welt des Orients*
ZA	*Zeitschrift für Assyriologie*
ZAH	*Zeitschrift für Althebraistik*
ZAW	*Zeitschrift für die alttestamentliche Wissenschaft*

LIST OF CONTRIBUTORS

Francis Anderson, Fuller Theological Seminary, Pasadena

Philip Alexander, Oxford Centre for Hebrew and Jewish Studies, Yamton, Oxford

Graeme Auld, Department of Hebrew and Old Testament Studies, New College, Edinburgh

Calum Carmichael, Department of Comparative Literature, Cornell University, Ithaca, NY

Robert Carroll, Department of Biblical Studies, Glasgow University

David Clines, Department of Biblical Studies, University of Sheffield

Richard Coggins, Department of Theology and Religious Studies, Kings College, London

Jon Davies, Department of Religious Studies, University of Newcastle upon Tyne

Philip Davies, Department of Biblical Studies, University of Sheffield

James Dunn, Department of Theology, University of Durham

John Elwolde, Department of Biblical Studies, University of Sheffield

John Gibson, Department of Hebrew and Old Testament Studies, New College, Edinburgh

Graham Harvey, Department of Religious Studies, University of Newcastle upon Tyne

Peter Hayman, Department of Hebrew and Old Testament Studies, New College, Edinburgh

Dermot Killingley, Department of Religious Studies, University of Newcastle upon Tyne

Gerard Loughlin, Department of Religious Studies, University of Newcastle upon Tyne

Jonathan Magonet, Leo Baeck College, London

Robert Morgan, Linacre College, Oxford

Takamitsu Muraoka, Faculteit der Letteren, Rijks Universiteit Leiden, Netherlands

Christopher Rowland, The Queen's College, Oxford

Deborah Sawyer, Department of Religious Studies, Lancaster University

Clyde Curry Smith, Department of Religious Studies, University of Newcastle upon Tyne

Max Sussman, Department of Microbiology, Medical School, University of Newcastle upon Tyne

William R. Telford, Department of Religious Studies, University of Newcastle upon Tyne

Marc Vervenne, Faculteit Godgeleerheid, Katholieke Universiteit, Leuven

Wilfred Watson, Department of Religious Studies, University of Newcastle upon Tyne

Keith Whitelam, Department of Religious Studies, University of Stirling

Isabel Wollaston, Department of Theology, University of Birmingham

ALL THEY NEED IS LOVE: ONCE MORE GENESIS 6.1-4

Marc Vervenne

Piquant Stories

It seems as though the writers of the so-called 'Primeval History' in the book of Genesis engaged in muckraking. There are, as I noted elsewhere,[1] two particularly piquant stories set in the skilfully-shaped framework of the composition of the 'Noahite Generation' in Genesis 5 to 9. One story is found at the end of chapter nine, in vv. 20-27.[2] It reports an incident in the post-diluvian life of Noah and his sons Shem, Ham and Japheth. The story tells us about the ancestor who *begins* (ויחל) as a viniculturist but finishes up hitting the bottle. However, when the wine is in, the wit is out! Noah falls asleep and unknowingly exposes his genitals to the three sons. It is said, then, that Ham looks upon his father's genitals, whereas Shem and Japheth do not. Quite unexpectedly, the story culminates in the cursing of Canaan, 'the son of Ham', who has been catapulted into the text, while Shem and Japheth are blessed. I have argued that in Gen. 9.20-27, the narrator—or, more accurately, the Priestly redactor[3]—seems to condemn the enjoyment and idolization of sex in the fashion of the Syro-Canaanite world in which Israel lived.

The other bizarre anecdote, with which I am concerned here, occurs at the beginning of the sixth chapter of Genesis (vv. 1-4).[4] The text deals

1. Cf. M. Vervenne, 'What Shall We Do with the Drunken Sailor? A Critical Re-examination of Genesis 9.20-27', *JSOT* (forthcoming).

2. On Gen. 9.20-27, see P.R. Davies, 'Sons of Cain', in J.D. Martin and P.R. Davies (eds.), *A Word in Season: Essays in Honour of William McKane* (JSOTSup, 42; Sheffield: JSOT Press, 1986), pp. 35-56; W. Vogels, 'Cham découvre les limites de son père Noé', *Nouvelle Revue Théologique* 109 (1987), pp. 554-73. See also my contribution as mentioned in the preceding note.

3. See the Priestly key term ערוה (*'erwah*) in vv. 22, 23 and compare to Lev. 18 and 20.

4. Gen. 6.1-4 has been analyzed in six important monographs: G.E. Closen, *Die*

with 'the sons of (the) *'elohîm*' who, in the days when humankind *began* (החל) to increase and had begotten healthy daughters, made love to 'the daughters of humankind'. These bore them offspring in the days of the *nepilîm*, 'the heroes of old', 'the men of renown'. Against the reader's expectations, the heart of this story turns out to be a sort of penalty laid upon humankind for *benê ha'elohîm* and *benôt ha'adam* breaking rules. Moreover, like Canaan, who was catapulted into Gen. 9.20-27, the *nepilîm* are interjected into Gen. 6.1-4. However, unlike Canaan, who clearly serves a purpose in the context of the tale of 'Seeing the drunken father's genitals', *nepilîm* appears to be an erratic motif which is loosely woven into its context. Finally, the tension between eroticism (Gen. 9) or sex (Gen. 6), on the one hand, and

Sünde der "Söhne Gottes" Gen. 6,1-4. Ein Beitrag zur Theologie der Genesis (Scripta Pontificii Instituti Biblici; Rome: Pontifical Biblical Institute, 1937); F. Dexinger, *Sturz der Göttersöhne oder Engel vor der Sintflut? Versuch eines Neuverständnisses von Gen 6,2-4, unter Berücksichtigung der religionsvergleichenden und exegesegeschichtlichen Methode* (Wiener Beiträge zur Theologie, 13; Vienna: Herder, 1966); W. Schlißke, *Gottessöhne und Gottessohn im Alten Testament: Phasen der Entmythisierung im Alten Testament* (BWANT, 97; Stuttgart: Kohlhammer, 1973); J.L. Cunchillos, *Cuando los ángeles eran dioses* (Bibliotheca Salmanticensis, 14; Salamanca: Universidad Pontificia, 1976); R. Bartelmus, *Heroentum in Israel und seiner Umwelt. Eine traditionsgeschichtliche Untersuchung zu Gen. 6,1-4 und verwandten Texten im Alten Testament und der altorientalischen Literatur* (ATANT, 65; Zürich: Theologischer Verlag, 1979); H. Kvanvig, *Roots of Apocalyptic* (WMANT, 61; Neukirchen: Neukirchener Verlag, 1988), pp. 280-95. One should also refer to the analysis offered in C. Westermann, *Genesis* (BKAT, I; Neukirchen-Vluyn: Neukirchener Verlag, 1968), pp. 491-517.

The bibliographies found in Schlißke, Cunchillos and Bartelmus should be updated with a few contributions which appeared in the period 1971-1979 and are missing in these monographs: J.T. Milik, 'Problèmes de la littérature hénochique à la lumière des fragments araméens de Qumran', *HTR* 64 (1971), p. 349; M. Emanueli, '«בני האלהים לוקחים נשים מכל אשר בחרו». The Sons of God Took Wives Whomever They Choose (Gen 6,1-4)', *BethM* 20,1 (60) (1974-1975), pp. 150-52, 165-66; W. Vijfvinkel, 'De Bene Ha'elohim in Gen 6,1-4', *TRef* 17 (1974), pp. 181-94; L.R. Wickham, *The Sons of God and the Daughters of Men: Gen 6,2 in Early Christian Exegesis* (OTS, 19; Leiden: Brill, 1974), pp. 135-47; P. Weimar, *Untersuchungen zur Redaktionsgeschichte des Pentateuch* (BZAW, 146; Berlin and New York: de Gruyter, 1977), pp. 35-39. Since the text of Bartelmus, *Heroentum* (1979) basically reflects his 1976 dissertation, no reference is made to Cunchillos, *Cuando los ángeles* (1976). On the other hand, he does not refer to Cunchillos's article 'Los *bene ha'elohim* en Gén 6,1-4', *EstBib* 28 (1969), pp. 5-31. See below, note 7 for supplementary bibliographical data.

cursing (Gen. 9) or judgment (Gen. 6), on the other, is present in both textual units.

The Enigmas of a Text

There are three things about which scholars engaged in the study of Gen. 6.1-4 agree: (1) it is an eccentric story;[5] (2) it is a difficult text;[6] and (3) the literature on this text is extensive.[7] But here the consensus ends.

5. See, for example, N.M. Sarna, *Genesis* (JPSTC; Philadelphia: Jewish Publication Society, 1989), p. 45: 'The account given in these few verses is surely the strangest of all the Genesis narratives'.

6. Cf. Sarna, *Genesis*, p. 45: 'It is so full of difficulties as to defy certainty of interpretation. The perplexities arise from the theme of the story, from its apparent intrusiveness within the larger narrative, from its extreme terseness, and from some of its vocabulary and syntax.'

7. For the history of research, see, more particularly, C. Westermann, *Genesis 1-11* (Erträge der Forschung, 7; Darmstadt: Wissenschaftliche Buchgesellschaft, 1972), pp. 68-76.

Ever since the publication of Bartelmus's study, various contributions have been devoted to Gen. 6.1-4. In particular, the following articles and studies should be mentioned: D.J.A. Clines, 'The Significance of the "Sons of God" (Gen 6,1-4) in the Context of the Primeval History (Gen 1-11)', *JSOT* 13 (1979), pp. 33-46; L. Eslinger, 'A Contextual Identification of the *benê ha'elohim* and *benoth ha'adam* in Genesis 6.1-4', *JSOT* 13 (1979), pp. 65-73; D.L. Petersen, 'Gen 6.1-4, Yahweh and the Organization of the Cosmos', *JSOT* 13 (1979), pp. 47-64; A. Tsukimoto, '«Der Mensch ist geworden wie unsereiner»: Untersuchungen zum zeitgeschichtlichen Hintergrund von Gen 3,22-24 und 6,1-4', *AnJapBibInst* 5 (1979), pp. 8-44; J. Schreiner, 'Genesis 6,1-4 und die Problematik von Leben und Tod', in M. Carrez, J. Doré and P. Grelot (eds.), *De la Tôrah au Messie. Études d'exégèse et d'herméneutique bibliques offertes à Henri Cazelles* (Paris: Desclée, 1981), pp. 65-74; G.W.E. Nickelsburg, 'The Bible Rewritten and Expanded', in *Jewish Writings of the Second-Temple Period* (CRINT, 2.2; Assen: Van Gorcum; Philadelphia: Fortress Press, 1984), pp. 90-92; M. Black, *The Book of Enoch or I Enoch. A New English Edition, with Commentary and Textual Notes* (Studia in veteris testamenti pseudepigrapha, 7; Leiden: Brill, 1985), pp. 124-25; P.R. Davies, 'Sons of Cain' (1986), pp. 46-50; A.J. Greig, 'Genesis 6.1-4: the Female and the Fall', *Michigan Quarterly Review* 26 (1987), pp. 483-96; R.S. Hendel, 'Of Demigods and the Deluge. Toward an Interpretation of Genesis 6.1-4', *JBL* 106 (1987), pp. 13-26; G.J. Wenham, *Genesis 1-15* (WBC, 1; Waco, TX: Word Books, 1987), pp. 135-47; D. Dimant, 'Use and Interpretation of Mikra in the Apocrypha and Pseudepidgrapha', in M.J. Mulder (ed.), *Mikra* (CRINT, 2.1; Assen: Van Gorcum; Philadelphia: Fortress Press, 1988), pp. 402-406; J. Hong, 'Problems in an Obscure Passage. Notes on Genesis 6,1-4', *BT* 40 (1989), pp. 419-26; J.H. Sailhamer, 'Genesis', in *The*

Biblical scholars have dissenting opinions on the origin and meaning of this enigmatic compositional unit. Within the scope of this article, there is no need to go into the history of research, since the different problems and viewpoints are sufficiently well known. I will, therefore, confine myself to synthesizing the pertinent approaches to Gen. 6.1-4, with a view to re-examining the text in the next section.

Origin

In respect of the literary-historical origin of Gen. 6.1-4, one may distinguish between two positions, both departing from the observation that this passage is not a coherent unit within its present narrative context.[8] The first and most commonly defended position firmly adheres to the view that the passage is old and, therefore, is to be associated with the classical Davidic-Solomonic J tradition.[9] Moreover, some argue that the text resulted from the reworking by J (v. 3) of an archaic mythical tradition (vv. 1-2, 4).[10] Others, however, claim that the whole passage

Expositor's Bible Commentary. II. (*Genesis-Numbers*) (Grand Rapids, MI: Zondervan, 1990), pp. 75-80; R.S. Hendel, 'When the Sons of God Cavorted with the Daughters of Men', in H. Shanks (ed.), *Understanding the Dead Sea Scrolls. A Reader from the Biblical Archaeology Review* (London: SPCK, 1992), pp. 167-77; E. van Wolde, *Words Become Worlds: Semantic Studies of Genesis 1-11* (Biblical Interpretation Series, 6; Leiden, New York and Köln: Brill, 1994), pp. 61-74; C. Savasta, '"Figli di dio" e "giganti" (Gen. 6,1-4). Una proposta di identificazione', *Bibbia e oriente* 36 (1994), pp. 193-215; J.C. VanderKam, 'Biblical Interpretation in *1 Enoch* and *Jubilees*', in J.H. Charlesworth and C.A. Evans (eds.), *The Pseudepigrapha and Early Biblical Interpretation* (Sheffield: JSOT Press, 1993), pp. 96-125.

8. Cf. Sarna, *Genesis*, p. 45; E.A. Speiser, *Genesis. Introduction, Translation, and Notes* (AB, 1; New York: Doubleday, 1964), p. 45 ('Is what we have here an excerpt of a fuller account?').

9. See G. von Rad, *Das erste Buch Mose* (ATD, 2; Göttingen: Vandenhoeck & Ruprecht, 2nd edn, 1950), pp. 92-93; Speiser, *Genesis*, pp. 44-46; Cunchillos, *Cuando los ángeles*, pp. 145-46; Tsukimoto, 'Der Mensch'.

10. Cf. B.S. Childs, *Myth and Reality in the Old Testament* (Studies in Biblical Theology, 27; London: SCM Press, 1960), pp. 57-59; W.H. Schmidt, 'Mythos im Alten Testament', *EvT* 27 (1967), pp. 243-46; C. Westermann, *Genesis*, pp. 494-97, 500-505; Schlißke, *Gottessöhne*, pp. 20-32. Bartelmus maintains 'die Autorschaft des Jahwisten für Gen. 6,1.2.4 zumindest nicht auszuschließen' (*Heroentum*, p. 29, and see also p. 46 and H. Kvanvig, *Roots*, pp. 281-83) but considers v. 3 as a late addition.

stems from R^{JE} (after 750 BCE),[11] whereas still others relate it to the priestly tradition.[12]

The second, more provocative, position is that Gen. 6.1-4 is a late text which depends on a post-exilic, non-canonical tradition, more particularly, one which occurs in the so-called 'Legend of the Watchers' in the pseudepigraphic book of Enoch. This contention has been advanced by J.T. Milik and is followed by, *inter alia*, M. Black.[13] Contrary to the traditional conviction, that the myth of the angels and the daughters of humankind in Enoch originates from Gen. 6.1-4, it is claimed that the Enoch tradition is prior to the Genesis text. As a consequence, the author (or editor) of Gen. 6.1-4 is said to be borrowing from an existing 'Enochic document' (source-text) or 'Enochic tradition' (source-tradition). It is argued that the abridged and allusive formulation of the Genesis text suggests its relatedness to such a document or tradition. R. Bartelmus, though he defends as his main thesis that the author of Enoch relied on Genesis, contends that Gen. 6.3 is a late addition[14]

11. Cf. J. Schreiner, 'Genesis 6,1-4'; Weimar, *Untersuchungen*, pp. 35-39. Compare also H. Gese, 'Der bewachte Lebensbaum und die Heroen: zwei mythologische Ergänzungen zur Urgeschichte der Quelle J', in H. Gese and H.P. Rüger (eds.), *Wort und Geschichte. FS K. Elliger* (AOAT, 18; Kevelaer and Neukirchen-Vluyn: Verlag Butzon & Bercker and Neukirchener Verlag, 1973), pp. 83-85.

12. Cf. Dexinger, *Sturz der Göttersöhne*, pp. 56-58, who is of the opinion that Gen. 6.2 is either L or J, whereas vv. 3-4 are written by P. For a redaction of Gen. 6.1-4 by *der letzte Pentateuchredaktor*, a *Tradent* who appears to be familiar with the priestly tradition, see J. Scharbert, 'Traditions- und Redaktionsgeschichte von Gen. 6,1-4', *BZ* 11 (1967), pp. 66-78 (p. 74: 'zeitlich und räumlich nahe an P und Ez heranzurücken').

13. Cf. J.T. Milik, 'Problèmes de la littérature hénochique à la lumière des fragments araméens de Qumran', *HTR* 64 (1971), p. 349; *idem*, *The Books of Enoch. Aramaic Fragments of Qumrân Cave 4* (Oxford: Clarendon Press, 1976), pp. 30-32; Black, *The Book of Enoch*, pp. 124-25. The thesis of some sort of 'pseudepigraphic updating' in Gen. 6.1-4 is followed by Davies, 'Sons of Cain', pp. 46-49, but has been criticized in, *inter alia*, Nickelsburg, 'The Bible Rewritten', pp. 90-92; Dimant, 'Use and Interpretation', pp. 402-406; Kvanvig, *Roots*, pp. 95-96; VanderKam, 'Biblical Interpretation', pp. 103-107.

14. Bartelmus, *Heroentum*, pp. 25-28. Kvanvig only partly agrees with Bartelmus's thesis that v. 3 is a late insertion. More particularly, she casts doubt on the assumption that this verse originated in the second century BCE. According to her, one should '*not* place the composing of v. 3 (and v. 1) *too far from P* with regard to time and setting' (italics mine) (*Roots*, pp. 282-83). As stated above in note 12, J. Scharbert associates Gen. 6.1-4 with P and the final redaction of the Pentateuch. See, moreover, Dexinger, *Sturz der Göttersöhne*, pp. 56-58 (above, note 4).

which has probably been inserted under the influence of En. 6-11.[15]

Difficulties of Interpretation

Scholars also continue to argue about the meaning and function of Gen. 6.1-4. It goes without saying that the interpretations advanced depend largely on how one deals with the problematic issues inherent in this text. The passage Gen. 6.1-4 faces us with three types of difficulties.

1. To what extent is this segment a 'story' or 'narrative' with a plot? It appears to me that most scholars, including those who approach the text as the result of the interchange of an existing tradition and a redactional reworking (J, JE, P or a later editor), deal with it as if it were a narrative in the strict sense of the word.[16] Although most exegetes are put in an embarrassing position by the terse form and meandering structure of this portion of Gen. 6, it seems that they succeed in avoiding the difficulties by maintaining that the shortness of the present text 'is probably due to drastic abridgement by the original writer or later editors.'[17]

15. Bartelmus, *Heroentum*, pp. 192-93: 'Wenn man nun noch mit in Betracht zieht, daß der Autor von Hen. 6-11 auch die übrigen verwendeten Traditionen so genau wie möglich wiedergibt, erscheint es mir unwahrscheinlich, daß er ausgerechnet den Vers 3 aus Gen. 6 nur andeutungsweise und unter Verzicht auf die in seiner geistigen Welt durchaus vertrauten Begriffe 'Fleisch' und 'Geist' eingearbeitet hätte. Vielmehr legt ein umgekehrter Traditionsweg nahe: Zieht man die erfolgreiche Verbreitung der Textbearbeitung des Verfassers von Hen. 6-11 mit in Betracht, erscheint es durchaus denkbar, daß man unter den gegebenen politischen Umständen eine Korrektur im Sinne von Hen. 6-11 auch in den text der Genesis einfügte. Entsprechend der Struktur des Textes als mythische Ätiologie in äußerst geraffter Form wurde auch dieser Einschub im Stile einer Ätiologie formuliert. Drei wesentliche Gedanken aus Hen. 6-11 wurden dabei berücksichtigt: Zum einen die negative Wertung der sexuellen Verbindungen zwischen göttlichen und menschlichen Wesen—wenn auch in sehr dezenter Formulierung—zum anderen die Wertung des Handelns der Gottmenschen als Hybris und zum dritten die starke Tendenz, den Riesen bzw. Gottmenschen so weit wie möglich ihren Charakter als halbgöttliche Wesen zu nehmen. Dementsprechend wirkt Gen. 6,3 heute wie ein Strafbeschluß über die Menschen, deren Lebenszeit begrenzt werden soll -gemeint waren jedoch wahrscheinlich die Riesen, die der Urheber dieser Korrektur der Genesis so nahe wie möglich an menschliche Wesen rücken will. Ein weiteres Element, das explizit in Hen. 6-11 noch nicht zu finden war, fügt er zur Verstärkung der drei Gedanken noch zusätzlich ein—den bereits erwähnten Gegensatz Fleisch-Geist.'

16. See, for example, the brief description of the content of the *Texteinheit* in Bartelmus, *Heroentum*, p. 21. See also Van Wolde, *Words*, p. 65.

17. Hong, 'Problems', p. 420. See also Sarna, *Genesis*, p. 45: 'The passage cannot be other than a fragment of what was once a well-known and fuller story, now

Its literary setting, then, is determined as either a summary of the preceding section (ch. 5),[18] or a prelude to the Flood narrative,[19] or a textual unit which functions within a larger framework.[20]

2. The discussion of the meaning of Gen. 6.1-4 is especially concerned with the interpretation of a series of enigmatic expressions and motifs, such as בני האלהים, בנות האדם, נפלים, גברים, their mutual relationships and, finally, how these function within the framework of the literary section Gen. 6.1-4.[21]

With regard to בני האלהים, it is very likely that the Hebrew expression simply means 'the sons of the *'elohîm*', that is, the gods,[22] whereas the phrase בנות האדם points to 'the daughters of humankind', that is, women. In this respect, one can fall back on Deut. 32.8. The MT reads: 'When

etched in the barest outline'; Davies, 'Sons of Cain', p. 46: 'It is difficult to escape the conclusion that the meaning of these verses depends on a knowledge of matters not given in the text'.

18. Cf. Sailhamer, 'Genesis', pp. 75-76 and compare also Sarna, *Genesis*, p. 45.

19. Cf. Dexinger, *Sturz der Göttersöhne*, pp. 54-55; W. Brueggemann, *Genesis. A Bible Commentary for Teaching and Preaching* (Interpretation; Atlanta, GA: John Knox Press, 1982), p. 70; Childs, *Myth and Reality*, p. 58; Tsukimoto, 'Der Mensch', p. 18.

20. Cf. Bartelmus, who connects Gen. 6.1-4 with Gen. 4: '...in Gen. 4,20-22 finden sich drei Kurzätiologien. Letztere passen übrigens nicht nur formal mit der Ätiologie in Gen. 6,1.2.4 zusammen, sondern auch thematisch. Man kann alle vier Ätiologien unter einer gemeinsamen Frage zusammenfassen: Woher kommt die sozialfunktionale Gliederung der Menschheit in verschiedene Stände? Diese gemeinsame Frage wird dann in vier in sich abgeschlossenen Argumentationsgängen zu folgende Einzelfragen abgehandelt: Woher kommen die Nomaden (Gen. 4,20), die Musiker (4,21), die Schmiede (4,22) und die Heroen (6,1.2.4)?' (*Heroentum*, p. 29). Westermann, on the other hand, associates Gen. 6.1-4 with Gen. 3; 4.2-16 and 11.1-9: 'Seine [J] Absicht ist (...) die Vielfalt der Sünde in ihren Grundmöglichkeiten darzustellen. (...) Wohl aber kann der Ort von 6,1-4 bei J, also als eines der vier Beispiele der Verfehlungen und der Verderbnis der Menschen (Kap. 3. 4,2-16. 11,1-9), zum Verständnis von 6,1-4 helfen' (*Genesis*, p. 498).

21. For a summary of the discussion of these terms, see Westermann, *Genesis*, pp. 493-94, 501-503; Bartelmus, *Heroentum*, pp. 15-17; Hong, 'Problems', pp. 420-23, 425-26.

22. See, *inter alia*, B. Jacob, *Das erste Buch der Tora. Genesis* (Berlin: Schocken Verlag, 1934), pp. 170-72; Westermann, *Genesis*, pp. 502-503; Bartelmus, *Heroentum*, pp. 15-16; Hendel, 'When the Sons of God', pp. 168-73. See, moreover, P.S. Alexander, 'The Targumim and Early Exegesis of «Sons of God» in Genesis 6', *JJS* 23 (1972), pp. 60-71.

עליון gave nations (גוים) their inheritance, when he set the divisions of בני אדם/He fixed the boundaries of the peoples (עמים) according to the number of 'בני ישׂראל'. However, the reading בני ישׂראל is difficult, since it does not fit in with the context which, according to A.D.H. Mayes, 'is clearly concerned with Yahweh's actions on behalf of Israel'.[23] I would, therefore, follow the view that the fragment 4QDeut[q], which reads בני אל] (see also LXX: υἱῶν θεοῦ) instead of בני ישׂראל (MT), probably reflects a more original wording.[24] In Deut. 32.8, then, reference is made to a congregation of gods (עליון and אל: cf. Ugarit),[25] whereas v. 9 emphasizes in an adversative way (כי) that יהוה has Israel as his portion.[26] Moreover, בני אדם (human beings) is matched with בני אל[הים] (gods).

The word נפלים is more difficult to explain. The Masoretic form *nepilîm* as such only occurs in Gen. 6.4 and Num. 13.33. Ezek. 32.27 (MT), on the other hand, contains the phrase נפלים מערלים, *nopelîm me'arelîm*, in combination with גבדים (*gibborîm*) ('So they lie not down with the *mighty ones, fallen from the uncircumcised*'; compare to v. 21). W. Zimmerli, in his commentary on the book of Ezekiel, asserts that the LXX equivalent ἀπ' αἰῶνος for נפלים מערלים shows a more original reading מעולם, and may contain, together with *nopelîm*, a word play on the *nepilîm* of Gen. 6.4.[27] The Greek translation equivalent for נפלים in Gen. 6.4 and Num. 13.33 is twice γίγαντες (giants). This Greek

23. A.D.H. Mayes, *Deuteronomy* (NCBC; Grand Rapids, MI: Eerdmans; London: Marshall, Morgan & Scott, 1979), p. 384.

24. On this, see E. Tov, *Textual Criticism of the Hebrew Bible* (Minneapolis: Fortress Press; Assen/Maastricht: Van Gorcum, 1992), p. 269. Tov also refers to 4QDeut[j], which reads בני אלהים, considering this, together with LXX υἱῶν θεοῦ, as a secondary reading, though the broken textual fragment 4QDeut[q] would also allow for the longer reading אלהים. See, moreover, M. Lana, 'Deuteronomio e angelologia alla luce di una variante qumranica (4QDt 32,8)', *Henoch* 5 (1983), pp. 179-207. Compare also Hendel, 'When the Sons of God', pp. 169-72.

25. See S. Rummel (ed.), *Ras Shamra Parallels. The Texts from Ugarit and the Hebrew Bible*, III (Analecta Orientalia, 51; Rome: Pontificium Institutum Biblicum, 1981), pp. 19, 434-37. For the divine epithets *'il*/אל and *'lyn*/עליון, see M.C.A. Korpel, *A Rift in the Clouds. Ugaritic and Hebrew Descriptions of the Divine* (Münster: Ugarit-Verlag, 1990), pp. 273-80.

26. Mayes, on the other hand, argues that עליון (v. 8) and יהוה stand parallel (*Deuteronomy*, p. 385).

27. Cf. W. Zimmerli, *Ezekiel 2* (Hermeneia; Philadelphia: Fortress Press, 1983), p. 168. See also G.A. Cook, *A Critical and Exegetical Commentary on the Book of Ezekiel* (ICC; Edinburgh: T. & T. Clark, 1936), pp. 353-54; Kvanvig, *Roots*, pp. 284-86.

wording is also used for גברים in Gen. 6.4. In doing so, the Greek translator irons out the difficulties of the Hebrew syntax in MT (see below) and, thus, makes clear that the result of the union of the sons of the gods and human daughters are the 'giants' (*nepilîm*). Though the origin and meaning of the Hebrew word נפלים is definitely uncertain, the contexts of Gen. 6.4 and Num. 13.33 make it clear that *nepilîm* is 'a term not unlike the concept of bogeymen and hobgoblins'.[28]

3. A third difficulty in understanding the meaning of the passage Gen. 6.1-4 concerns the linguistic interpretation of the text. In particular, as mentioned before, the relationship between נפלים and גברים in v. 4 is not clear, since the אשׁר clause does not entirely fit into the syntactic pattern of the verse. This question will be discussed below. Moreover, the morphological clarification of the forms ידון (*yadôn*) and בשׁגם (*bešaggam*) in v. 3 is problematic. With respect to the former, I would claim that it is still the best solution to relate the *yiqtol* form ידון to Akkadian *danânu* ('to be strong') and Ugaritic *dnn* ('to be violent').[29]

As far as the phrase בשׁגם is concerned,[30] there are at least three interpretations put forward. To begin with, W. Gesenius discusses the form at length in his *Thesaurus*, and, more particularly, he suggests that the form בשׁגם, following several ancient manuscripts to be read as *bešaggām*, would be a construct infinitive of the verb שׁגג, 'to err, to go astray'.[31] In this proposal, however, the two pronominal morphemes (ם- and הוא) seem to be in conflict.[32]

28. R.B. Allen, 'Numbers', in *The Expositor's Bible Commentary*. II. (*Genesis-Numbers*) (Grand Rapids, MI: Zondervan, 1990), p. 812. Compare also Hendel, 'When the Sons of God', pp. 173-74.

29. Bartelmus, *Heroentum*, p. 19 and see also Kvanvig, *Roots*, p. 286. For a convenient overview of the discussion on ידון, see Jacob, *Genesis*, pp. 173-74; Closen, *Die Sünde*, pp. 36-40; Westermann, *Genesis*, pp. 506-507; Bartelmus, *Heroentum*, pp. 18-19; Kvanvig, *Roots*, pp. 286-87.

30. On בשׁגם, see A. Dillmann, *Die Genesis* (KHAT, 11; Leipzig: Hirzel, 3rd edn, 1892), pp. 121-22; Jacob, *Genesis*, pp. 174-75; Closen, *Die Sünde*, pp. 51-52; Westermann, *Genesis*, pp. 507-508; Cunchillos, *Cuando los ángeles*, pp. 143; Kvanvig, *Roots*, pp. 287-88.

31. W. Gesenius, *Thesaurus philologicus criticus linguae hebraeae et chaldaeae Veteris Testamenti*. Tomus tertius (Leipzig: Vogel, 1853), p. 1362. See also *BDB*, p. 993 and *GK*, §67p. Gesenius-Buhl, p. 807 is more reticent about the connection שׁגג–בשׁגם, whereas *KB*, p. 948 does not mention it any longer. *HALAT*, p. 1272 notes that this interpretation is 'weniger wahrscheinlich'.

32. Cf. F.E. König, *Historisch-comparative Syntax der hebräischen Sprache* (Leipzig: Hinrichs, 1897), §346p. Dillmann, *Genesis*, p. 122 avoids the conflict when

Secondly, D.J.A. Clines introduced the idea that בשגם might be built up with the morpheme ב and a noun cognate with the Akkadian root *šagāmu*, 'to roar, shout'.[33] This suggestion has been taken up again by Kvanvig, who, moreover, refers to the Akkadian nouns *šagīmu* and *šigmu* ('noise'). She claims that it would even be more probable since ידון in the same verse also seems to be derived from Akkadian.[34] Kvanvig then translates: 'My spirit shall not be powerful in man for everlasting time *because of the noise*. He is flesh and his days will be hundred and twenty years.' The main difficulty, however, is that such a derivation remains extremely hypothetical, since there is no evidence of any word whatsoever in the Hebrew language which can be related to a lexeme *šgm* and one, thus, creates a *hapax*. Moreover, the polarity רוח–בשר appears to be weakened by bringing in the idea of noise. In addition, the Mesopotamian motif of noise does not fit into the context of Gen. 6.1-4.

Finally, the most commonly used explanation is that בשגם is a morphosyntactic word consisting of the bound forms -ב and -ש and the free form גם, meaning 'because, since'. This linguistic interpretation occurs for the first time in LXX: διὰ (τὸ εἶναι) (see also TargOnq: בדיל). Though most contemporary scholars and translators understand the form בשגם in line with this explanation, many of them have doubts about its validity.[35] Westermann, for example, regards בשגם = 'because' as the only possibility, but at the same time he recognizes that the combination ב-ש-גם does not occur elsewhere in the Hebrew Bible. Moreover, he points to the fact that ש (*še*) is not used as a relative pronoun in the Pentateuch. Furthermore, he thinks that גם does not function in Gen. 6.3.[36]

Referring to Westermann's scepticism, Kvanvig concludes that there is 'no linguistic basis for the assumption' that ב-ש-גם means 'because'.[37] However, it appears to me that there is a lot to be said for the classical thesis that the morphosyntactic word בשגם in Gen. 6.3 resulted from the combination of the preposition ב (*be*), the relative pronoun ש (*še* or

he translates 'in Folge ihrer [= *benê ha' elohîm*] Verirrung ist er [= *he'adam*] Fleisch.'

33. Clines, 'The Significance', p. 40.

34. Kvanvig, *Roots*, p. 287.

35. See, for example, *GB*, p. 796: 'eine schwerlich intakte Stelle'; *HALAT*, p. 1272: 'Fragliches…'.

36. Westermann, *Genesis*, p. 507.

37. Kvanvig, *Roots*, p. 287.

ša), and the particle גם (*gam*).[38] The argument that שׁ does not occur as a relative pronoun in the Pentateuch is not convincing. It reveals, in fact, the assumption that שׁ is rather typical for late, post-exilic biblical writings, such as the books of Jona and Qoheleth, and, in consequence, cannot be part of an early (e.g., J) textual unit.[39] Sound linguistic research into the language of the Hebrew Bible, however, should deal prudently with literary-historical arguments, especially for those texts which are allegedly classified as early Hebrew texts. Furthermore, the very fact that בשׁגם is a *hapax* does not necessarily mean that it is grammatically impractical. Qoheleth 2.16, for example, includes the *hapax* בשׁכבר (*bešekebar*), which is compounded of -ב, -שׁ and the temporal adverb כבר ('already, past time'). The verse could be rendered, then, as follows: 'Indeed, the wise one is no more remembered than the fool, *because as in time past* both will be forgotten in days to come'.[40] In Jon. 1.7 we find the *hapax* בשׁלמי (*bešelemî*), which is a compound made up of -ב, -שׁ, -ל and the interrogative pronoun מי. Though it is hard to know how it functions, it 'is not likely to mean anything else but "on whose account"'.[41] Finally, it should also be noticed that the compound שׁגם is used three times in Qoheleth, namely in 1.17: שׁגם זה הוא רעיון רוח[42] and 2.15, 8.14: שׁגם זה הבל. Consequently, the combination of ב + שׁ + גם in Gen. 6.3 seems meaningful. The contention, then, that the word גם would not function in Gen. 6.3 can easily be weakened. This particle often denotes addition ('also'). However, in line with C.J. Labuschagne's well-known study on גם, we may claim that it can also express emphasis, certainty, reality, and could be rendered with 'indeed, really, of

38. Cf. Zorell, *Lexicon*, p. 810; C.H.J. van der Merwe, *The Old Hebrew Particle* GAM (ATSAT, 34; St. Ottilien: Eos Verlag, 1990), pp. 56, 57, 126, 137, 161, 187; E. Jenni, *Die hebräischen Präpositionen.* I. *Die Präposition beth* (Stuttgart, Berlin and Köln: W. Kohlhammer, 1992), p. 357; A. Schoors, *The Preacher Sought to Find Pleasing Words. A Study of the Language of Qoheleth* (Orientalia Lovaniensia Analecta, 41; Leuven: Departement Oriëntalistiek and Peeters, 1992), p. 54.

39. Schoors, *The Preacher*, pp. 54-56.

40. Cf. C.D. Ginsburg, *Coheleth, Commonly Called the Book of Ecclesiastes* (London, 1861 = New York: KTAV Publishing House, 1970), p. 293. See also Schoors, *The Preacher*, p. 189.

41. J.M. Sasson, *Jonah. A New Translation with Introduction, Commentary, and Interpretation* (AB, 24B; New York: Doubleday, 1990), p. 112.

42. Ginsburg, *Coheleth*, p. 274: 'I know *that even this* is striving after the wind' (italics mine).

course'.[43] An *ad sensum* translation of Gen. 6.3 could read as follows: 'My spirit shall not remain strong in humankind for ever, because he *really/indeed* is flesh'.

In respect of the origin of Gen. 6.1-4, it should not be excluded that the usage of the morphosyntactic word בשגם points to a rather late redaction. Though I fully agree with those scholars who maintain that the relative particle -ש is not *per se* a marker of Late Biblical Hebrew,[44] it is obvious, as we have already indicated, that ש occurs increasingly in post-exilic biblical writings. The fact that ש in בשגם is a *hapax* in the Pentateuch might even stress the late and unconventional character of its usage in Gen. 6.3.[45]

Text and Context

Gen. 6.1-4 is not a disorderly collage of ancient Near Eastern science fiction and fragments of Israel's religious traditions. To put it differently, one would misjudge the intention of its composer in regarding it as a bit of a scissors and paste job. The final shape of the Hebrew text, in its Masoretic form,[46] exposes a compositional unit embedded in the literary

43. C.J. Labuschagne, 'The Emphasizing Particle *GAM* and Its Connotations', in *Studia Biblica et Semitica Theodoro Christiano Vriezen* (Wageningen: H. Veenman & Zonen, 1966), pp. 193-203. See also T. Muraoka, *Emphatic Words and Structures in Biblical Hebrew* (Jerusalem: Magnes Press; Leiden: Brill, 1985), pp. 143-46; Schoors, *The Preacher*, pp. 129.

44. S. Morag states that 'the possibility that the two conjunctions [ש and אשר] originally belonged in the biblical period to different dialectal areas remains feasible' (see 'Qumran Hebrew: Some Typological Observations', *VT* 38 [1988], p. 161). See also Schoors, *The Preacher*, pp. 54-56.

45. Compare Schoors, *The Preacher*, p. 54: 'Being the shorter and more pliable form, ש must in the course of time have supplanted אשר in the language of the common people. But a literary prejudice against it seems to have remained even after BH had ceased to be a living speech. That explains its non-occurrence in Est and its scarcity in the work of the Chronicler. The same prejudice would be the reason for the scarce use of ש in the Qumran scrolls, where it is limited to CDC 15,11; 20,4. In MH אשר has disappeared altogether, except for biblical quotations and early liturgical language, which is conceived in an elevated and semi-biblical strain'.

46. The Greek text of Gen. 6.1-4 slightly diverges from MT. Apart from the linguistic interpretation of the words בשגם = δὶα τὸ εἶναι, נפלים = γίγαντες (v. 4) and גברים = γίγαντες (v. 4), which have been discussed above, a few other instances should be noted:

context of Gen. 1-11. C. Houtman appropriately designates it as 'a paragraph of a greater whole'.[47] This is not to say, however, that the passage is either easily written or that it reads smoothly. It is a *composition* in the truest sense of the word, which, moreover, acts extremely independently in its present context. This section of my analysis, then, aims to understand how the different parts and components of Gen. 6.1-4 are arranged to construct a unit. First, I will concentrate on the linguistic shape of the text; secondly, I will briefly examine the composition of the passage and its placement in the literary context.

Syntax

ויהי	1a
כי החל האדם	1aa
לרב על פני האדמה	1aaa
ובנות ילדו להם	1ab
ויראו בני האלהים את בנות האדם	2a
כי טבת הנה	2aa
ויקחו להם נשים מכל	2b
אשר בחרו	2ba

1) טבת = καλαί (v. 2). The Greek text suggests that the women selected by the gods are 'beauties'. The Hebrew word טוב in Gen. 6.2 can be compared with טוב in Gen. 1 and Exod. 2.2 respectively: God saw that what had been done was 'well-formed'—Moses' mother saw that her baby was 'well-formed'. To put it differently, it was perfect.
2) ידון = καταμείνῃ (v. 3). Did the Greek translators read ידור from דור, 'to dwell'? Sym reads the Hebrew form ידון as ידין, a form derived from דין = κρινεῖ, 'to judge'.
3) באדם = ἐν τοῖς ἀνθρώποις τούτοις (v. 3). LXX puts a limitation on the judgment. It does not affect humankind as a whole, but only these human beings who have been involved in this primeval love story.
4) הנפלים = οἱ δὲ γίγαντες (v. 4). Wevers notes that MT 'begins in an unusual fashion without a conjunction as though it was unrelated to the preceding text, but Gen [= LXX] has δέ to show change of subject.' (p. 77)

For helpful remarks on the LXX text of Gen. 6.1-4, see M. Harl, *La bible d'Alexandrie: la Genèse* (Paris: Éditions du Cerf, 1986), pp. 124-26 and J.W. Wevers, *Notes on the Greek Text of Genesis* (SCS, 35; Atlanta, GA: Scholars Press, 1993), pp. 75-78.

47. C. Houtman, 'Het verboden huwelijk. Gen 6,1-4 in haar context', *GerefTTs* 76 (1976), p. 72: 'De pericoop dient als een alinea in een groter geheel beschouwd te worden'.

ויאמר יהוה	3a
לא ידון רוחי באדם לעלם	3aa
בשגם הוא בשר	3aaa
והיו ימיו מאה ועשרים שנה	3ab
הנפלים היו בארץ בימים ההם וגם אחרי כן	4a
אשר יבאו בני האלהים אל בנות האדם	4aa
וילדו להם	4ab
המה הגבדים	4b
אשר מעולם	4ba
אנשי השם	4b

The linguistic shape of Gen. 6.1-4 is quite uncommon.[48] It appears to me that one can separate the unit into two distinct parts. The first part includes vv. 1-3. The temporally ordered story line of this section is constituted by four *wayyiqtol* clauses (1a: ויהי; 2a: ויראו; 2b: ויקחו; 3a: ויאמר). These clauses can be described as foregrounded, since *wayyiqtol* is the foreground form *par excellence*. They report on events belonging to the main story line (to begin to increase and have daughters, to see, to take, to speak). However, the introductory ויהי (1a) followed by a circumstance of time construction does not comprise an independent *wayyiqtol* clause, but functions as a protasis followed by an apodosis (2a). As a macro-syntactic marker,[49] it opens a new narrative segment, without

48. For the linguistic study of the text, see, among others, A. Niccacci, *The Syntax of the Verb in Classical Hebrew Prose* (JSOTSup, 86; Sheffield: JSOT Press, 1990); G. Hatav, 'The Aspect System and Foreground-Background Relation in the Biblical Hebrew Prose' (PhD dissertation, Tel-Aviv University, 1989); W. Richter, *Grundlagen einer althebräischen Grammatik. B. Die Beschreibungsebenen: III. Der Satz (Satztheorie)* (ATSAT, 13; St Ottilien: Eos Verlag, 1980); W. Groß, *Verbform und Funktion.* wayyiqtol *für die Gegenwart? Ein Beitrag zur Syntax poetischer althebräischer Texte* (ATSAT, 1; St Ottilien: Eos Verlag, 1976); R. Bartelmus, *HYH. Bedeutung und Funktion eines hebräischen »Allerweltswortes«—zugleich ein Beitrag zur Frage des hebräischen Tempussystems* (ATSAT, 17; St Ottilien: Eos Verlag, 1982). Compare the syntactic hierarchy offered in this essay with W. Richter, *Biblia hebraica transcripta. BH^t. 1. Genesis* (ATSAT, 33.1; St Ottilien: Eos Verlag, 1991), p. 55. Closen, *Söhne Gottes*, pp. 21-72 also achieves a detailed syntactic analysis, which, however, has to be revised in the light of recent developments in Hebrew linguistics.

49. Hatav, 'The Aspect System', pp. 67-80 discusses the usage of *wyhy* clauses in biblical Hebrew at length. More particularly, she distinguishes the 'predicative' (e.g., Gen. 5.3; Exod. 24.18) and the 'segmentational function' (e.g., Gen. 6.1; Josh. 3.1-2; 2 Kgs. 13.21). See also Niccacci, *The Syntax*, pp. 33, 48-60, 156-62.

indicating, however, a significant break.[50] More particularly, ויהי connects, though in an artificial way, the temporal circumstance with the main narrative thread which started in 5.2b. It thus avoids a disruption in the communication of the larger composition. In addition to the foregrounded events in 6.1-3, there is the backgrounded material, namely, the state of affairs described in 2aa (to be well formed) and the supporting events in 2ba and 3aa-ab (respectively to choose; a judgment). Here, we should distinguish between narrative and speech. On the narrated level (vv. 1-2), the background information is expressed by two types of clauses: a verbless clause (2aa) and a *(w-)x-qatal* clause (2ba). On the speech level (3aa-ab), the verbal forms *x-yiqtol* (3aa) and *wqatal* (3ab) are used. Within the speech segment, both forms function as foregrounded forms, whereas the verbless clause 3aaa (בשגם) serves as background.

The second syntactic unit in Gen. 6.1-4 consists of v. 4, which stands out clearly from the preceding sequential story line (vv. 1-3: *wayyiqtol*). The segment is built up of two main clauses. The first one is of the type *x-qatal* (4a), to which is added, by means of the anaphoric element אשר, a subordinate sentence consisting of two clauses of the type *yiqtol* (4aa) and *wqatal* (4ab) respectively. The second main clause is verbless and contains, moreover, an embedded אשר clause.

There are three syntactic problems to be discussed in this connection. To begin with, the narrative proper, which developed through a series of *wayyiqtol* clauses, is interrupted by the construction *x-qatal*—verbless (nominal) clause. This transition marks a shift from foreground to background, bringing an additional motif into the story, namely that of the *nepilîm*. As the initial *waw* is missing in both clauses, it may well be that the tense shift aims to place the emphasis on the subject, that is, הנפלים and המה respectively.[51] In the case of a verbless (nominal) clause the personal pronoun tends to come first when prominence is intended to be given to it.[52]

50. Hatav, 'The Aspect System', p. 78: 'When a new frame of time is established it is usually detached from the current discourse topic. (...) a shift in time (and a shift in place and topic) causes a switch in the scenario'. See also Niccacci, *The Syntax*, p. 48: 'The textual function of *wayehi* is to introduce a new element into the main narrative thread so that that element becomes an integral and important part of the account'.

51. See Niccacci, *The Syntax*, pp. 69-71.

52. P. Joüon and T. Muraoka, *A Grammar of Biblical Hebrew. Part Three: Syntax* (Roma: Editrice Pontificio Istituto Biblico, 1991), p. 568.

Furthermore, scholars are doubtful about the antecedent to which אשׁר in 4aa refers. Dexinger defends the quite complicated thesis that the אשׁר clause should be related to הנפלים, which, in turn, is to be connected with בני האלהים: the *nepilîm* came as *sons of gods* to *human women*.[53] Bartelmus, on the other hand, correlates אשׁר with בימים ההם.[54] In line with this view, one could even claim that the whole phrase בימים ההם וגם אחרי כן, the literary origin of וגם אחרי כן notwithstanding, is the antecedent of אשׁר in 4aa.[55] The usage of the verbal forms *yiqtol* (4aa) and *wqatal* (4ab) in this narrative segment can be explained as a frequentative *yiqtol* and a continuing *wqatal*.[56] Joüon says that the time value of these forms is to be derived from the context.[57] It is said that 'the *nepilîm* were on *hā'āreṣ* in those days, and even thereafter, *namely* (אשׁר) when the sons of gods *used to go* (יבאו) to the daughters of humankind who *then bore (children)* (ילדו) to them.'

Finally, it is not clear to whom the personal pronoun המה at the head of the noun phrase 4b is referring. Dexinger identifies בני האלהים, נפלים, גברים and אנשׁי השׁם with one another, thus relating המה to all these.[58] Bartelmus, on the other hand, associates the גברים with אנשׁי השׁם as the offspring (המה) of בני האלהים, making love to בנות האדם in the days of the נפלים.[59] Taking account of the parallel emphatic syntax of 4a and 4b, as

53. Dexinger, *Sturz der Göttersöhne*, pp. 44-46.

54. Bartelmus, *Heroentum*, pp. 20-21. See also Closen, *Die Sünde*, p. 68; Wenham, *Genesis*, p. 143; Sailhamer, 'Genesis', pp. 78-79. Childs, *Myth and Reality*, pp. 54-55 also understands אשׁר as a temporal particle, but claims, on the other hand, that once the later interpolation וגם אחרי כן has been removed, 'the causal meaning of אשׁר replaces the temporal': 'The giants were on the earth in those days *because* the sons of gods came in unto the daughters of men and they bore children to them'.

55. König, *Syntax*, p. 59 (§157) points to 2 Chron. 35.20a [אשׁר + אחרי כל זאת *qatal*] as a 'interessanter Gegensatz' to Gen. 6.4aa [אשׁר + וגם אחרי כן *yiqtol*].

56. GK, §107e and 112e. See also Westermann, *Genesis*, p. 493; Wenham, *Genesis*, p. 135: '*whenever* the sons of the gods went in to the daughters of man, they bore them children'. Compare, however, Bartelmus, *Heroentum*, p. 21 (n. 45), who claims that 4ab 'einen eigenen Hauptsatz bildet und so die Erzählung von V. 2 endlich zum Abschluß bringt.'

57. Joüon and Muraoka, *A Grammar*, §113e1: 'Therefore this yiqtol can only be used in a context which has been situated in the past beforehand'. See, moreover, §119uC.

58. Dexinger, *Sturz der Göttersöhne*, p. 45.

59. Bartelmus, *Heroentum*, p. 21: 'Somit ergibt sich, daß המה mit hoher Wahrscheinlichkeit auf die Kinder zu beziehen ist, die den Göttersöhnen geboren werden'.

described above, and the position of the אשר clause as well, there is reason to assume that the pronoun המה refers back to הנפלים: '*These* were the heroes of old, the men of renown'. In contrast to the first part of the story, which concentrated on בני האלהים and בנות האדם, the backgrounded information in v. 4 focuses particularly on the *nepilîm*.

In conclusion, careful syntactic analysis shows that Gen. 6.1-4 is a well-composed linguistic unit. Moreover, it seems as though this unit has been syntactically linked to its immediate context, and, more particularly, with the help of the initial verbal form ויהי. Within the framework of Genesis 1–11, the form ויהי mainly occurs as a regular narrative *wayyiqtol* of the verb היה.[60] On the other hand, there are seven instances where it is used as a syntactic marker (with temporal circumstance).[61] In Gen. 4.3 and 11.2, more particularly, ויהי comes at the beginning of an independent narrative, but only after it has been introduced by an antecedent (4.1-2 and 11.1 respectively). Taking account of the fact that 'segmentational' (Hatav) ויהי never opens a completely self-reliant narrative unit,[62] it is clear that the *wayehî–wayyiqtol* construction in Gen. 6.1-2, as already stated above, has to be linked with the main story line of Genesis 5. It appears to me that, from a linguistic viewpoint, the compositional unit Gen. 6.1-4 aims to resume the opening statement on the *'adam* in Gen. 5.1-5, and, through the latter, also the order to multiply (רבה) as mentioned in Gen. 1.28. At the same time, Gen. 6.1-4 functions as some sort of a summary of the state of affairs of the *'adam*'s descendants.[63]

Composition and Context

In the foregoing we have seen that Gen. 6.1-4 is not as rambling as one usually maintains. A brief examination of the composition and contextual fixation of the passage confirms this finding.

The text exposes a careful compositional technique. The unit is held together by a few key words and expressions (which are underscored in the hierarchically ordered text above). Verse 1 contains the passive construction *yulledû lahem* (*qatal*) with בנות as the explicit subject. These

60. Cf. Gen. 1.3, 5, 7, 8, 9, 11, 13, 15, 19, 23, 24, 30, 31; 2.7; 4.2, 17; 5.23, 31, 32; 7.12, 17; 9.29; 10.19, 30; 11.1.

61. Cf. Gen. 4.3, 8; 6.1; 7.10; 8.6, 13; 11.2.

62. See Niccacci, *The Syntax*, p. 60.

63. Cf. Sailhamer, 'Genesis', p. 75. Compare also the resuming and summarizing function of Exod. 1.7 (פרה, רבה, מלא).

בנות are subsequently modified as בנות האדם (2a), a phrase of which both components have been introduced in 1aa (האדם) and 1ab (בנות) respectively. So the daughters of humankind do not fall from heaven. In addition, האדם and האדמה are well-known motifs in the preceding context, whereas the noun בנות and the verb ילד have been a refrain in Genesis 5. On the other hand, בני האלהים in v. 2a is a completely new textual element, which is only identifiable for those readers who are familiar, for example, with the book of Job.

Verse 4 repeats the aforementioned key terms. In particular, the resumptive statement in 4aa-ab comprises the expressions of v. 1-2: ילד בני האלהים ,בנות האדם and ילד ל. By doing this, the composer of Gen. 6.1-4 has made a connection between the two parts of the 'story'. In fact, the syntactic analysis showed that the text has a bipartite structure. The first part, including vv. 1-3, focuses on the ardent love-making between *benê ha'elohîm* and *benôt ha'adam*, and, especially, on YHWH's intervention. The apparently unexpected limiting of *human* lifetime points to the nature of this part of the story, if not to the function of the whole unit. Gen. 6.1-3 obviously parodies the idea of the image of Elohim in humankind (see Gen. 1.27 and compare also 3.5)[64] and, against that background, the idea of multiplying on the earth (see Gen. 1.28 and compare also 1.22; 8.17; 9.1, 7; Exod. 1.7, 10, 12, 20). It is said that the *'adam* began to multiply,[65] but in contrast to Genesis 4 and 5, the human being only produces daughters. Moreover, the pattern ויראו את X כי טוב in v. 2 is very nearly a copy of the divine evaluation formula in Genesis 1. Furthermore, only Gen. 6.2 uses the verb בחר with respect to women. Taking account of the fact that the lexeme בחר predominantly operates in the Hebrew Bible as a theological term (YHWH/Elohim *bāḥar*),[66] it seems as though the statement בני האלהים לקח נשים מכל אשר בחרו in Gen. 6.2 is a parody of the common יהוה/אלהים בחר. In this sense, the sons of the gods having sex with human beings is presented as an act arising out of divine election. Finally, it is clear that the merging of the divine and human spheres is carried to extremes. In line with one of the main themes of Genesis 1–3, namely, the problem of humankind's likeness to God,[67] the composer of Gen. 6.1-4 is criticizing this

64. Compare Clines, 'The Significance', p. 37.

65. Within the context of the Primeval History, the verb חלל occurs with ל in Gen. 4.26; 6.1; 10.8; 11.6, and without ל in Gen. 9.20.

66. Cf. *THAT*, II, p. 277.

67. See, for example, YHWH'S concern in Gen. 3.22: חי לעולם, and compare

unacceptable 'hybridization'. The judgment YHWH passes on humankind in v. 3 emphasizes the marked contrast between the divine (רוח) and the human (בשר). This fundamental disparity is unmistakably expressed in Isa. 31.3: ומצרים אדם ולא אל/וסוסיהם בשר ולא רוח. Here it is said that 'flesh' (בשר) is opposed to 'spirit' (רוח) and humankind (אדם) to God (אל), just as mortality is opposed to immortality. The lesson of the Eden narrative is repeated in terms of dualism. The intended but utopian unity[68] is transmogrified into disunity.

Verse 4, which is clearly linked to the first part of the unit, marks a shift in the focal point of the story. Again, the composer introduces an entirely new textual element, which can be recognized only by readers who are familiar with the tradition in the book of Numbers (13.33). The *nepilîm* have taken the place of the sons of the gods. The text is not completely free of ambiguity, and, in particular, the phrase בארץ can be understood in more than one way. Within the context of Genesis 1–11, it may point to the 'earth' as a planet. Likewise, against the background of the Pentateuch traditions, it may refer to the 'land' as the area where the Israelites live (cf. Num. 13.33). Furthermore, in contrast to the earthly scene set up for the fatal attraction of *benê ha'elohîm* to *benôt ha'adam*, the second part of the story evokes a world of imagination, populated with fantastic bogeys. However, this section does not stand on its own. The phrase בימים ההם, referring to the past, produces a sequence.[69] It is suggested that the *nepilîm*, who are הגברים מעולם and אנשי השם, are the offspring of the relationship between the sons of gods and the daughters of humankind.

Post-redactional Expansion

Linguistic and literary investigation into Gen. 6.1-4 in its final form demonstrates that this short pericope is to be treated as a compositional unit. However, can we discover how and why this text was composed? This is a far more difficult task than simply describing the final (Masoretic) text as a compositional unit. As a matter of fact, Gen. 6.1-4 is such a strange story and displays such a great variety of motifs and wordings, that most scholars understand it as a composite of elements

this with לא ידון רוחי באדם לעלם.

68. See, for example, Gen. 7.15: מכל הבשר אשר בו רוח חיים, and compare Joel 3.1: אשפוך את רוחי על כל בשר.

69. Cf. S.J. DeVries, *Yesterday, Today and Tomorrow. Time and History in the Old Testament* (London: SPCK, 1975), p. 52.

drawn from several different traditions. The various attempts to resolve satisfactorily the question of the origin of our text have been briefly discussed in one of the previous sections of this paper. *Via trita via tuta*? The arguments put forward in the classical source-critical approaches (e.g. C. Westermann), as well as in the redaction-critical studies of the pericope (e.g. J. Scharbert, P. Weimar), are not really convincing, since they discover much more in the text than it can possibly contain. On the other hand, even though I would agree with J.C. VanderKam, when he observes that it 'has hardly been proved',[70] that Gen. 6.1-4 is a summary of a more ancient and non-canonical fuller account (cf. J.T. Milik), the idea of a relationship between the Genesis text and non-canonical traditions is attractive. Indeed, Gen. 6.1-4 is an eccentric text. But I would not go so far as to claim that those who shaped the 'story' relied solely on non-canonical traditions.

In line with the linguistic and literary analysis made above, I would argue that Gen. 6.1-4 is a carefully *composed* textual unit and that the *composer* drew on a variety of source texts and traditions. Consequently, the compositional unit Gen. 6.1-4 is certainly not the result of the disorderly juxtaposition of all sorts of elements. I would avoid, however, terms such as 'author' or 'redactor', since the text hardly fits in with any of the classical sources/traditions or redactions which can be distinguished within the Pentateuch. Again, it appears as though the composer of this unit carefully selected from among different sources.

First, it has been seen that various words and expressions are part of the immediate context.[71] It may well be that these have been collected from that co-text to function within a new framework. This is especially the case with the wordpair בשׂר–רוח, which now serves to introduce an explicit dualistic purport into the 'Noahite Generation' composition Genesis 5–9. The objection that the usage of the divine name יהוה points to the early, Yahwistic origin of v. 3, is not valid, since the composer of Gen. 6.1-4 might deliberately have picked it up from the larger context. As I have stated above, Gen. 6.1-4 is a parody of themes present in the 'Primeval History'. To that end the composer imitated the language and style of the literary context of this curious story. Secondly, it is very likely that the one who composed Gen. 6.1-4 also patterned the text

70. VanderKam, 'Biblical Interpretation', p. 104.

71. See, more particularly, בשׂר, רוח, ראה כי טוב, בנות, ילד, רבה על פני האדמה, אדם, ארץ.

according to biblical traditions outside Genesis. In particular, the motifs of בני האלהים and הנפלים should be related to the traditions in Deuteronomy/Job and Numbers respectively.[72] Finally, Gen. 6.1-4 also reflects non-canonical themes; in particular, a concern with extra-ordinary beings and dualistic world-views, as in the books of Enoch and Jubilees.[73] The seeds of dualism, are indeed already present in the Priestly portions of Gen. 1-11.[74] Apart from the aforementioned concepts of רוח and בשר in Gen. 6.17 and 7.15, reference should be made to the dualism of light/darkness in the creation liturgy of Gen. 1.1–2.4. Moreover, Genesis 5 introduces the person of Enoch, who is one of the prominent *dramatis personae* in the non-canonical traditions.[75] However, the presence of these pseudepigraphic motifs and themes does not necessarily mean that the biblical pericope provided the primary inspiration for the story of the heavenly angels in 1 Enoch 6–11. It may be argued that the composer of Gen. 6.1-4 drew on a late, non-canonical tradition which acquired its full literary form in 1 Enoch.[76] In other words, the one who composed the biblical story, on the one hand, and those who wrote the pseudepigraphic account, on the other, participated in a common tradition, which became prominent after the exile and grew more and more productive. In short, I would claim that Gen. 6.1-4 is an ultimate, post-redactional expansion in the light of novel ideas then in vogue. I call it 'post-redactional', since this case appears to be unique in the Pentateuch, and, in consequence, does not mirror a redactional reworking of a larger portion of Pentateuchal texts. Gen. 6.1-4 is a sort of parody which offers a new, and decisive key for reading and understanding the 'Noahite Generation' composition. The experience of a human world deviating from the original divine project, as it is said in Gen. 6.5 and, in particular, in vv. 11-13 (בשר), has led the writer of Gen. 6.1-4 to compose a story which shares the pessimistic ideas of the burgeoning stream of pseudepigraphical traditions. This literary activity

72. One should not exclude that the limitation of humankind's lifespan to 120 years (Gen. 6.3) alludes to the age of Moses in Deut. 32.7.

73. Cf. P. von der Osten-Sacken, *Gott und Belial. Traditionsgeschichtliche Untersuchungen zum Dualismus in den Texten aus Qumran* (SUNT, 6; Göttingen: Vandenhoeck & Ruprecht, 1969). See also above note 13.

74. Compare also Bartelmus, *Heroentum*, p. 25.

75. See also the close parallel between Noah and Enoch of whom it is said that 'they walked with God' (Gen. 6.19: התהלך את האלהים and compare 5.22, 24).

76. Black, *The Book of Enoch*, p. 125 explains the inter-relationship of Gen. 6.1-4 and the Enoch legend of the watchers as descending from a common literary ancestor.

resulted in a text which contains a dualistic view and sounds very apocalyptic.

Why was Gen. 6.1-4 composed and how does it function in the biblical text? These two basic questions were the point of departure for our investigation of the curious story on the edge of the Flood Narrative. It should be stressed that there is much more involved in the interpretation of this pericope than simply analysing it as a self-reliant text. Gen. 6.1-4 is part of a broad stream of ideas and convictions, all of which need to be taken into account. It has become clear that the question of the significance of the text is closely related to the matter of its origin. On the other hand, it makes no difference whether this passage reflects an old mythical legacy of the ancient Near East or is derived from late non-canonical traditions; it still makes biblical scholars and readers of the text theologically uncomfortable.[77] In this respect, the analysis offered does not aim to explain *the* original meaning of the text, but seeks simply to contribute to the understanding of an enigmatic composition. In his many challenging writings, Professor Sawyer has convinced me of the fact that biblical texts are inexhaustible. It is with gratitude and friendship that I dedicate this essay to him.

77. See, for example, Hong, 'Problems in an Obscure Passage', p. 426: 'The fact that most scholars today suggest the meaning of angelic beings has to be taken into consideration when a translation of the Bible is undertaken. However, for the sake of easily offended Christians, it may be advisable to provide the alternative meaning ("pious men" or "Sethites") in a note'; Speiser, *Genesis*, p. 45: 'The undisguised mythology of this isolated fragment makes it not only atypical of the Bible as a whole but also puzzling and controversial in the extreme'. See also a peculiar remark in Wenham, *Genesis*, p. 140: 'If the modern reader finds this story incredible, that reflects a materialism that tends to doubt the existence of spirits, good or ill. But those who believe that the creator could unite himself to human nature in the Virgin's womb will not find this story intrinsically beyond belief'. J. Scharbert marks Gen. 6.1-4 as a 'unorthodoxen Tradition' (*Fleisch, Geist und Seele im Pentateuch. Ein Beitrag zur Anthropologie der Pentateuchquellen* [SBS, 19; Stuttgart: Verlag Katholisches Bibelwerk, 1966], p. 35).

'TRADITIONS OF REMEMBRANCE': POST-HOLOCAUST INTERPRETATIONS OF GENESIS 22

Isabel Wollaston

> Why is this one of the first stories of our people? Why was it preserved in the Bible? I have read all sorts of interpretations and explanations of it, but this text does not leave me in peace: 'Take now, thy son, thine only son... and offer him as a human offering' (Friedlander 1979: 28-29).

What is it about the story of the Akedah (the binding of Isaac) in Genesis 22 that provokes such a reaction? The literary critic, Alvin Rosenfeld suggests that the answer lies in the narrative's inherent ambiguity: it is 'on the one hand, a tale of monumental faithfulness, on the other, one of the strangest and most problematic stories in the Bible' (Rosenfeld 1986: 243). As a result, the story is open to both 'positive' and 'negative' readings. Interpretations tend to fall into one of these two categories. A 'positive' reading interprets the Akedah as 'a tale of monumental faithfulness'; a 'negative' reading focuses on those qualities that make it 'one of the strangest and most problematic stories in the Bible'. The implication of Rosenfeld's statement is that such readings are mutually exclusive. However, there is a third possibility: the Akedah is 'a tale of monumental faithfulness' precisely because it is 'one of the strangest and most problematic stories in the Bible'. Such an interpretation is favoured by those writers (such as Mintz or Roskies) who argue that Jewish responses to catastrophe constitute a lamentation tradition.

The Lamentation Tradition

The lamentation tradition articulates public and private Jewish responses to catastrophe. A catastrophe is understood as a collective disaster that 'convulses or vitiates shared assumptions about the destiny of the Jewish people in the world' (Mintz 1984: 2). For Alan Mintz, a catastrophe is

> A national calamity that undermines the received paradigms of meaning concerning the relationship between God and Israel. The catastrophic potential in historic events can be gauged not by the quantum of pain, death and material destruction but rather by the degree of damage to the cognitive, theological frameworks that bind the people to their God (Mintz in Cohen and Mendes-Flohr 1988: 41).

The basic paradigm of meaning in Judaism is that of the covenantal relationship between God and Israel. This relationship is acted out in history, therefore historical events can be interpreted as a commentary on the covenantal relationship, as 'barometers of God's disposition towards His people' (Berger 1985: 1). Thus, Jewish history is understood as 'the record of the vicissitudes of a relationship acted over time' (Mintz 1984: 19). Such an understanding of history finds its classical expression in Deuteronomy, particularly in the Blessings and Curses (Deut. 27–30). According to the schema of Deuteronomy, prosperity and good fortune constitute God's blessing on covenantal faithfulness:

> If you obey the voice of the LORD your God, being careful to do all his commandments which I command you this day, the LORD your God will set you on high above all the nations of the earth. And all these blessings shall come upon you and overtake you, if you obey the voice of the LORD your God (Deut. 28.1-2).

Likewise, ill fortune and disaster arise from faithlessness:

> But if you will not obey the voice of the LORD your God or be careful to do all his commandments and his statutes which I command you this day, then all these curses shall come upon you and overtake you (Deut. 28.15).

The basic 'cognitive, theological framework' of Deuteronomy is therefore one which interprets catastrophe as punishment for sin (Deut. 30.15-20, see also Lev. 26; Lam. 2.5-8). The destruction of the Jerusalem Temple in 586 BCE stands as the 'primal event of national catastrophe' (Roskies 1989: 19). The response to it, notably the book of Lamentations, sets the pattern of response for subsequent catastrophes. Such responses often challenge the basic explanation of punishment for sin. Such challenges are to be found in the biblical text itself (for example, the book of Job).

Jewish self-understanding in the light of disaster comes to be articulated through reflection upon a series of key texts and archetypes (Genesis 22, Job, Lamentations, the woman and her seven sons, the Ten Hadrianic Martyrs, and so on). As a consequence, 'the traditional Jew sees his history through the lens of memory, for which all events are cyclical recurrences of ancient archetypes' (Biale 1987: 8). By interpreting subsequent events in terms of ancient archetypes, later events are absorbed into the continuing narrative of the covenantal relationship between God and Israel. Each successive generation retells and recasts the ancient archetypes in the light of its own experience. Thus, despite the fact that, in the biblical story, the sacrifice of Isaac never actually takes place, the Akedah becomes the archetype of martyrdom. Subsequent generations of martyrs—suffering at the hands of Antiochus Epiphanes, Hadrian, the Crusaders, Bogdan Chmielnicki, and others—interpret their fate in terms of the Akedah (see Mintz 1984: 84-154; Roskies 1984: 41-52; and Spiegl 1967).

David Roskies suggests that such an appropriation of ancient archetypes can take two forms: 'literal recall' or 'sacred parody' (Roskies 1984: 17). The literal recall of ancient archetypes—as in the modelling of dirges (*kinot*) on the book of Lamentations—serves to locate subsequent catastrophes in the continuum of covenantal history. Thus, a positive reading of the Akedah, one which interprets it as 'a tale of monumental faithfulness', serves as an example of literal recall. By contrast, sacred parody imitates 'the breach of God's promise in the parody of scripture' (Roskies 1984: 17, 20). Sacred parody employs the ancient archetypes, but subverts their original meaning (as in Chaim Nachman Bialik's 'In the City of the Slaughter', or Yitzhak Katzenelson's 'Song of the Slaughtered Jewish People'):

> by incorporating the anger, even the blasphemy, into the normative response to catastrophe, the language of sacred parody remains contained yet infinitely expandable; scriptural and liturgical texts can be appropriated while registering the enormity of the violation of central precepts (Ezrahi 1988: 141).

Thus, a negative reading of the Akedah might highlight the problematic nature of the story by offering alternative versions of it (see, for example the Akedah poems of Yehuda Amichai, Amir Gilboa, and Jacob Glatstein). However, such a strategy raises the question of whether 'the language of sacred parody' is, in fact, infinitely expandable'? To what extent can sacred parody remain 'contained'? When does it mark a break with, or the collapse of, traditional responses to catastrophe? Ezrahi suggests that, as a strategy, sacred parody comes to represent a precarious balancing act, particularly in modern times:

> for those who remain within the parameters of the tradition, the attempt to recreate the Holocaust in terms of its collective legacy is accompanied by

> the risk of exposing the ruptures, the discontinuities, and the cracks in the most fundamental codes of Jewish faith and conduct (Ezrahi 1980: 148).

Post-Holocaust Readings of the Akedah

In their discussions of the lamentation tradition, Ezrahi, Mintz, and Roskies stress how ancient archetypes inform the ways in which subsequent generations respond to catastrophe. They also point to the ways in which the experience of subsequent catastrophes informs the understanding of ancient archetypes. Did this symbiotic relationship between past and present continue in relation to the Holocaust? Or did the Holocaust expose 'the ruptures, the discontinuities, and the cracks' in traditional responses to catastrophe? The survivor, Elie Wiesel, suggests that it is only now, after the Holocaust, that the full meaning of the ancient archetypes becomes apparent:

> Only today, after the whirlwind of fire and blood that was the Holocaust, do we grasp the full range of implications of the murder of the one man by his brother, the deeper meanings of a father's questions and disconcerting silences. Only as we tell them now, in the light of certain experiences of life and death, do we understand them (Wiesel 1976: xiii-iv).

Thus, for Wiesel, the story of Cain and Abel is the first genocide, Isaac is the first survivor, Jacob is the first child of a survivor, Jeremiah is the first survivor-witness, and so on.

James Young suggests that in the Holocaust the ancient archetypes were found wanting and the event therefore became its own archetype: contemporary events were cited to explain other contemporary events. The literal recall of ancient archetypes was no longer considered to be a meaningful response given the magnitude of the catastrophe. Sacred parody continued to serve a purpose, but only to expose 'the ruptures, the discontinuities, and the cracks in the most fundamental codes of Jewish faith and conduct'. Rather than ancient archetypes informing contemporary responses to catastrophe, they are found wanting in the light of the experience of the present. Young illustrates his point by reference to Katzenelson's 'Song of the Slaughtered Jewish People'. Katzenelson explicitly distances himself from the ancient archetypes:

> Evoke not Ezekiel, evoke not Jeremiah...I don't need them!
> ...I don't compare myself to the prophets—
> But all the martyred Jews taken to their death, the millions murdered here—
> (Young 1988: 99).

When he does cite the ancient archetypes, 'it is almost always to mark their inadequacy as appropriate figures' (Young 1988: 102):

> A great throng, a huge crowd, O how huge!
> Far greater than Ezekiel's valley of bones.
> And Ezekiel himself would not have spoken to the murdered
> of trust and hope
> As in bygone days, but would have wrung his hands like me.
> Like me he would have cast back his head helplessly.
> (Young 1988: 102)

Post-Holocaust interpretations of the Akedah suggest that Young is only partly right: while the majority of writers employ the strategy of sacred parody, there are also those who continue to employ that of literal recall. The strategy of literal recall continues to understand the Akedah as 'a tale of monumental faithfulness'. As such, the Akedah is understood as the archetypal expression of trust in God and the covenant in the face of catastrophe. Eliezer Berkovits's reading of the Akedah typifies this approach. The more typical approach, that of sacred parody, is represented by Elie Wiesel.

Eliezer Berkovits

Berkovits offers a traditional reading of the Akedah, but it is a reading that takes care to address the challenge to faith posed by the Holocaust. He argues that the key to the Akedah lies in the recognition that it contradicts the divine promise to Abraham (Gen. 15.13; 17.1-21). The command to sacrifice Isaac was therefore the ultimate test to which Abraham could be subjected. For Abraham, the dilemma is whether to trust God in spite of the insoluble contradiction between the divine promise of an everlasting covenant with Isaac and his descendants (Gen. 17.19, 21), and the command of Gen. 22.2:

> Take your son, your only son Isaac, whom you love, and go to the land of Moriah, and offer him there as a burnt offering upon one of the mountains of which I shall tell you.

For Berkovits, this contradiction does not demand a leap of faith (*à la* Kierkegaard). Rather, it is to be understood as a question of trust (*emunah*) in the continuing validity of the covenantal relationship between God and Israel:

> the very essence of trust consists not in 'leaping', but in standing firm. Its moral value derives from its truthfulness in having the courage to face the irreconcilable, in seeing with open eyes that the sacrifice is a denial of the promise and yet continuing to trust. It is as if one said to one's 'Thou': 'In this situation I do not understand you. Your behavior violates our covenant; still, I trust you, because it is you and me, because it is us' (Berkovits 1979: 124).

The Akedah encapsulates the challenge constantly facing the Jew striving to live within the covenant: 'the unconvincing performance of divine providence in history' (Berkovits 1979: 127). God is a God who hides (Isa. 45.15). The divine presence in history is 'hidden' in order to allow humanity to exercise freedom. All too often such divine hiddenness is interpreted by the innocent as a lack of concern for their suffering (Ps. 44.23-26; 69.17; Berkovits 1973: 94-107). The story of the Akedah is found at the beginning of Israel's history because it indicates that 'to be chosen by God is to be chosen for bearing the burden of God's long suffering silences and absences in history' (Berkovits 1973: 124). The story is 'a tale of monumental faithfulness' precisely because Abraham maintains his faith in the covenant when confronted by the insoluble contradiction of the divine command to sacrifice Isaac. For Berkovits, such 'monumental faithfulness' is echoed in accounts of the faith of Jews in the ghettos and death camps. Such Jews continued to have trust in the covenant even when confronted by the Holocaust. In doing so, they gave expression to the 'ultimate in goodness' (Berkovits 1973: 84). As a consequence, Berkovits argues that the accounts of faith in the ghettos and death camps should be seen as 'a new collection of holy scriptures' (1973: 78).

Elie Wiesel

Whereas Eliezer Berkovits interprets the Akedah as 'a tale of monumental faithfulness', Elie Wiesel regards it differently. He suggests that 'of all the biblical tales, the one about Isaac is perhaps the most relevant to our generation' (Wiesel 1976: 96).

Wiesel draws a direct etymological link between the Akedah and the Holocaust. He points out that the Hebrew word translated as 'burnt offering' (vv. 2, 6, 13) is *ola*. In the Septuagint, this term is translated as *holokausten*, the root of the English word, 'holocaust'. In translating *ola* as 'an offering that has been totally consumed, a holocaust', Wiesel makes explicit the connection between the Akedah and his own experience (Wiesel 1976: 71; Abrahamson 1985, I: 203). The connection is made even more emphatically when he comments that 'when I think of Abraham, I think of a father and son during the Holocaust' (Cargas 1976: 107).

Read in the light of the Holocaust, the Akedah is a deeply ambiguous, even unsatisfactory text:

> the question is no longer whether Isaac was saved but whether the miracle could happen again. And how often. And for what reasons. And at what cost? (Wiesel 1976: 73).

Wiesel is acutely conscious of the gulf separating the Akedah as told in the biblical text, and the Akedah understood as the experiences of fathers and sons during the Holocaust. In many ways, *Night*, his memoir of his experiences in Auschwitz and Buchenwald, can be interpreted as a sacred parody of the Akedah. In the words of André Neher, 'if the Akedah had been real...then everything would have happened to Abraham and Isaac as is related in *Night*' (Neher 1981: 217; see also Rosenfeld 1986: 243-46). The theme of the testing of the relationship between fathers and sons runs throughout the narrative. On arrival at Auschwitz, a block elder advises the new inmates:

> don't forget that you're in a concentration camp. Here, every man has to fight for himself and not think of anyone else. Even of his father. Here, there are no fathers, no brothers, no friends. Everyone lives and dies for himself alone (Wiesel 1988: 121-22).

Night focuses in particular upon the relationship of Wiesel with his father after their arrival in Auschwitz. This relationship is, in turn, contextualized by a series of cameos depicting the relationship between other fathers and sons: there is Bela Katz, who, as a member of the *Sonderkommando* had to cremate his father's body; another son kills his father for a piece of bread; a third abandons his father on the death march from Auschwitz. Wiesel responds to this incident with the comment:

> And in spite of myself, a prayer rose in my heart, to the God in whom I no longer believed.
>
> My God, Lord of the Universe, give me strength never to do what Rabbi Eliahou's son has done (1988: 103).

However, after his own father's death in Buchenwald, Wiesel records his own response:

> I did not weep, and it pained me that I could not weep. But I had no more tears. And in the depths of my being, in the recesses of my weakened conscience, could I have searched it, I might perhaps have found something like—free at last! (1988: 123).

Thus, unlike the biblical Akedah, there is no 'happy ending', no voice from heaven to prevent the sacrifice taking place. In *Night*, it is the father (Abraham) who dies, while his only son (Isaac) survives, likening himself to a living corpse (1988: 126). In his essay, 'The Sacrifice of Isaac: A Survivor's Story', Wiesel makes the analogy explicit:

> We have known Jews who, like Abraham witnessed the death of their children; who like Isaac lived the Akedah in their flesh; and some who went mad when they saw their father disappearing on the altar, in a blazing fire whose flames reached into the highest of heavens (Wiesel 1976: 95).

Wiesel is not alone in interpreting the Akedah in the light of the Holocaust in this way. Increasingly, the Akedah motif is employed as a symbol of 'misguided and destructive' faith (Brown 1982: 111). The story is viewed almost exclusively from the point of view of Isaac, rebelling against his ordained role. Typical is the young Israeli soldier of 1967, cited by Saul Friedlander as saying: 'I refuse to be an eternal Isaac mounting the altar of sacrifice without asking or understanding why' (Friedlander 1979: 57).

Conclusions

The approach of Wiesel to the Akedah lends support to Young's contention that:

> experiences, stories, and texts of the ancient past remain the same in themselves; but their meanings, their echoes, causes and effects, and their significance all changed in the lives of these texts' interpreters (Young 1988: 109).

However, Berkovits's reading of the same biblical text suggests that this is not necessarily the case. It would therefore seem that Roskies's two categories of literal recall and sacred parody continue to be relevant. However, even while adopting a strategy of literal recall, Berkovits acknowledges the difference between Abraham's experience in the Akedah and that of subsequent generations. In the Akedah, God spoke directly to Abraham and 'the angel of the LORD' (Gen. 22.11-12) intervened to stop the sacrifice. Subsequent generations have no such direct experience of God, but are rather confronted by 'the unconvincing performance of divine providence in history'. As a result, the intimacy of the covenantal relationship confronted by the enigma of divine providence 'not only allows but, at times, requires the Jew to contend with the divine "Thou"' (Berkovits 1969: 128).

Such a concession by Berkovits suggests that perhaps Rosenfeld's two readings of the Akedah are not exclusive after all: the story is 'a tale of monumental faithfulness' precisely because it is 'one of the strangest and most problematic stories in the Bible'. Perhaps a post-Holocaust form of the lamentation tradition will only be meaningful if lamentation is understood in Mintz's sense of 'a record of man's struggle to speak in the face of God's silence' (Mintz 1982: 16). In defining lamentation in this way, he distinguishes between lamentation (human discourse) and consolation ('what is given from outside...God's word breaks through to man, ending the silence and confirming the persistence of the divine commitment' [Mintz 1982: 16]). Mintz argues that such consolation is increasingly rare, if not totally absent. He concludes that 'as man is left increasingly on his own whatever comfort he may get must come from himself' (Mintz 1982: 17). If the very different responses of Berkovits and Wiesel are understood as a record of their struggle to speak in the face of the absence of divine consolation, then perhaps the gulf separating them is not so wide after all.

BIBLIOGRAPHY

Abrahamson, I.
1985 *Against Silence: The Voice and Vision of Elie Wiesel* (3 vols.; New York: Holocaust Library).

Abramson, G.
1990 'The Reinterpretation of the Akedah in Modern Hebrew Poetry', *Journal of Jewish Studies* 41: 101-14.

Amichai, Y.
1988 *Selected Poems* (Harmondsworth: Penguin).

Berger, A.
1985 *Crisis and Covenant: The Holocaust in American-Jewish Fiction* (Albany: State University of New York).

Berkovits, E.
1973 *Faith after the Holocaust* (New York: KTAV).
1979 *With God in Hell: Judaism in the Ghettos and Deathcamps* (New York: Sanhedrin Press).

Biale, D.
1987 *Power and Powerlessness in Jewish History* (New York: Schocken Books).

Brown, M.
1982 'Biblical Myth and Contemporary Experience: The Akedah in Modern Jewish Literature', *Judaism* 31.1: 99-111.

Cargas, H.J.
1976 *Harry James Cargas in Conversation with Elie Wiesel* (New York: Paulist Press).

Cohen, A., and P. Mendes-Flohr (eds.)
1988 *Contemporary Jewish Religious Thought* (New York: Free Press).

Ezrahi, S.,
1980 *By Words Alone: The Holocaust in Literature* (Chicago: Chicago University Press).
1988 'Considering the Apocalypse', in B. Lang (ed.), *Writing and the Holocaust* (New York: Holmes and Meier), 137-53.

Fackenheim, E.L.
1973 *Encounters Between Judaism and Modern Philosophy: A Preface to Future Jewish Thought* (New York: Basic Books).

Friedlander, S.
1979 *When Memory Comes* (New York: Farrar, Straus, Giroux).

Gilboa, A.
1979 *The Light of Lost Suns: The Selected Poems of Amir Gilboa* (Menard Press).

Ginzberg, L.
1909 *The Legends of the Jews* (Philadelphia: Jewish Publication Society).

Glatstein, J.
1993 *I Keep Recalling: The Holocaust Poems of Jacob Glatstein* (New York: KTAV).

Jacobson, D.
1987 *Modern Midrash: The Retelling of Traditional Jewish Narratives by Twentieth Century Hebrew Writers* (Albany: State University of New York).

Mintz, A.
1982 'The Rhetoric of Lamentations and the Representation of Catastrophe', *Prooftexts* 2: 1-17.
1984 *Hurban: Responses to Catastrophe in Hebrew Literature* (New York: Columbia University Press).

Neher, A.
1981 *The Exile of the Word* (Philadelphia: Jewish Publication Society).

Rosenfeld, A.
1986 'Reflections on Isaac', *Holocaust & Genocide Studies* 1.2: 242-48.

Roskies, D.
1984 *Against the Apocalypse: Responses to Catastrophe in Modern Jewish Culture* (Cambridge, MA: Harvard University Press).
1989 *The Literature of Destruction: Jewish Responses to Catastrophe* (Philadelphia: Jewish Publication Society).

1994 'The Library of Catastrophe', in G. Hartman (ed.), *Holocaust Remembrance: The Shapes of Memory* (Oxford: Basil Blackwell), 33-41.

Spiegl, S.
1967 *The Last Trial: On the Legends and Lore of the Command to Abraham to Offer Isaac as a Sacrifice* (New York: Pantheon).

Wiesel, E.
1958, 1987 *Night* (Harmondsworth: Penguin).
1976 *Messengers of God* (New York: Summit Books).

Yerushalmi, Y.
1989 *Zakhor: Jewish History and Jewish Memory* (New York: Schocken Books).

Young, J.E.
1988 *Writing and Rewriting the Holocaust: Narrative and the Consequences of Interpretation* (Bloomington, IN: Indiana University Press).

WHAT BIBLICAL SCHOLARS MIGHT LEARN FROM EMILY DICKINSON

Francis I. Andersen

Introduction

In September 1993 the University of North Carolina Press published *New Poems of Emily Dickinson* (Shurr 1993). It remains to be seen whether the appearance of this book will be the literary event of the year, or a damp firecracker. The methodological principles that lurk in research of this kind raise issues for biblical studies. Those issues might be seen more clearly if we stand for a while in our field and look at workers on the other side of the fence.

The salient issue is, what is poetry? How can one tell the difference between poetry and prose, especially when a suspected poem is embedded in a piece of prose, such as a personal letter (in this case one of Emily Dickinson's) or a passage in the Hebrew Bible?

Are the 'New Poems' Poems?

Shurr and his co-workers claim to have added nearly 500 poems to the Dickinson canon by identifying hitherto unrecognized 'poems' in the poet's correspondence. The suggestion is not new: Johnson had already done this kind of thing in his standard *variorum* edition, but not on such a scale.

How can one tell? Two criteria validate the exercise: (1) When Miss Dickinson herself set out the poetic text in her letter in stichometric form, she knew (or thought) it was a poem, and she wanted her reader to know (or think) that it was a poem. (2) When the same text, although written in prose form in the letter, appears elsewhere in her papers in poetic form, she knew it to be a poem, but did not share this knowledge with the reader of that letter. In these two circumstances, according to Shurr, the poet declared the text to be a poem, and her perception is to be accepted. When neither of these clues is present, is it warranted to pick out a period or two from a letter that was written in prose format, arrange it in lines, and call it a poem? This is what Shurr has now done.

We have the same problem in biblical texts. The textual tradition of the Hebrew Bible has safeguarded the stichometric display of very few texts, not all of them poetic. There were two visual systems. One is described as 'half brick over whole brick and whole brick over half brick' (Exod. 15.1-18; Judg. 5.2-30; 2 Sam. 22 [but not when this poem is replicated in Ps. 18]), the other as 'half brick over half brick and whole brick over whole brick' (Deut. 32.1-43; also the list of the kings of Canaan [Josh. 12.9-24] and the list of the sons of Haman [Esth. 9.6-9]). But there are other poems in the Pentateuch, notably the *Blessing of Jacob* (Gen. 49) and the *Blessing of Moses* (Deut. 33) that are not required by the Talmud to be set out in either of these patterns; and the two lists of names are not poems.

The rabbis certainly knew the difference between prose and poetry; at least they devised two different systems of cantillation, one used only in the three main poetry books—Psalms, Job, Proverbs. This special pointing was not accompanied by a congruent stichometric display of the poetic units, even though the practice with the four poems in the Primary History showed that they knew how to do it. A notable exception is Psalm 119, displayed as one bicolon per line, in keeping with its acrostic pattern, already in the Qumran Psalms scroll. From Qumran until the Hebrew Bible was first printed, the manuscripts show some variation in the visual presentation of the poetry of the three books (Andersen 1995a). Some manuscripts of Job show one bicolon per line; but the system is often thrown out of sync by the occurrence of tricola. The Aleppo Codex attained some measures of order for some Psalms, but this soon deteriorated, as the disorder in the Leningrad Codex reveals.

The scribal tradition shows no awareness of the vast amount of poetic material in the prophetic corpus. Its presentation was indistinguishable from that of prose. As a result of his appreciation of *parallelismus membrorum* as the *sine qua non* of Hebrew poetry, Robert Lowth introduced the practice of printing translations of biblical passages he had identified as 'poetic' in stichometric form. This practice is now universal, and has even spread to editions of the Hebrew text, notably in *Biblia Hebraica*[3] and *Biblia Hebraica Stuttgartensia* (*BHS*).

In order to give instructions to the compositors, more is needed than the identification of a piece of poetry embedded in prose. The individual 'lines' (cola) have to be determined. The textual tradition is neutral in the matter of poetic theory. The stichometry of *BHS* is the outcome of modern critical theories about the structure of biblical Hebrew poetry.

Before returning to Emily Dickinson, a little more about Robert Lowth. Lowth identified and isolated a lot of little poems in the Pentateuch. These, and more, were set out as poems in BH^3. For example:

וַיִּבְרָא אֱלֹהִים אֶת־הָאָדָם בְּצַלְמוֹ	and God created the man in his image,
בְּצֶלֶם אֱלֹהִים בָּרָא אֹתוֹ	in the image of God he created him,
זָכָר וּנְקֵבָה בָּרָא אֹתָם	male and female he created them
	(Gen. 1.27)

This reverted to prose in *BHS*. I am not aware that the editors of *BHS* have ever given an account of their editorial policies and case-by-case decisions. Table 1 shows similar pusillanimity among nine English translations examined. Five of them print Gen. 1.27 as a three-line poem.

Table 1 summarizes the results of translators' and editors' decisions concerning 'poems' in Genesis. The inventory does not include all the passages that have been printed in these nine Bible versions as if they were poetry. First, we have not included the Testament of Jacob (Gen. 49.2-27), since there is complete agreement that it is a poem. Secondly, there are two versions that print some genealogical passages as if they were poetry. NAB prints Gen. 10.2-4, 10.6-7, and 10.22-23 in lines like poetry. NIV treats many more passages in the same way, namely Gen. 10.2-4, 6-7, 13-14, 22-28; 35.23-26; 36.10-29, 32-39, 40b-43; 46.8b-14, 16-17, 19-24. If the editors of these translations have anywhere explained and defended their policies in this matter, I have not come across the discussion.[1]

This leaves as many as twenty-nine places in Genesis where one or more of these nine versions has detected a poem.[2] Three different kinds of decisions have to be made in order to arrive at the published result.

1. Orlinsky states that the publication of the deliberations of the Jewish Publication Society represents 'the first time that a committee responsible for an official translation of the Bible has attempted a public and systematic exposition...of its labors and reasoning' (1969, p. 3). Even so the remarks about poetry are minimal.

2. The number of individual poems depends on whether we count a series of speeches, such as those of Yahweh God to the miscreants in Genesis 3, as one poem or several. Since the data do not warrant statistical calculations, the point is inconsequential.

First, the poem has to be identified; secondly, it has to be isolated; thirdly, it has to be scanned.

Of the alleged twenty-nine poems in Table 1, there are only two for which all nine versions are agreed in all three decisions. They are Gen. 4.23-24 and Gen. 25.23. The agreements of the versions in the first step, locating a poem, are shown in Table 1 as the 'Tally' in the right-most column. All nine agree in the detection of nine poems. In four cases (Gen. 8.22; 9.6; 16.11-12; 24.60) only RSV fails to detect a poem. In two cases seven versions agree, in three cases five, in one case four, in one case three, in five cases two, in four cases one. There is manifestly a gradient of confidence, ranging from complete (or nearly complete) agreement (thirteen poems recognized by eight or nine versions) to great uncertainty (nine poems recognized by only one or two).

Three kinds of judgment seem to have been at work. First, genre: all of the poems enjoying a high degree of recognition occur in dialogue and most of them are oracular pronouncements by God. There could be a prejudice in this diagnostic—it is considered likely that divine speech will be poetic (sixteen in Table 1), human speech less likely (eleven), while the narrator's voice will be prose (two poems recognized in Table 1). To make this distinction accessible, in Table 1 references for divine utterance are in roman, to human speech in *italic*, to narrative in **bold**.

Secondly, form: major reliance is generally placed on parallelism as the hallmark of Hebrew poetry. The more parallelism there is in a divine speech or in a solemn human pronouncement, the more votes there are likely to be for its being a poem. Yet some charming little bicola in narrative have not been identified as poetic, in spite of good parallelism; e.g., Gen. 11.30; 21.1; 24.16a; 29.16b; 29.17a; 37.24b.

Thirdly, metre: in addition to genre and parallelism, or even without them, some kind of metrical pattern is expected in poetry. The 'lines' (cola) of a poem should have a regular rhythm. And it is usually expected that the cola should be short (two or three beats supplied by stressed syllables). If length is measured by syllables rather than by stresses, typical two-beat cola have five syllables (perhaps four or six) and typical three-beat cola have eight syllables (perhaps seven or nine). In other words, cola might range in length from four to nine syllables; but one beat (or three or fewer syllables) is not enough and four beats (or ten or more syllables) would be too much for one colon, so far as most students of Hebrew poetry are concerned.

So much for the detection of a 'poem'. As for the delimitation of each poem, there is agreement about the boundaries of most of the poems in Table 1. In a few instances a continuous speech has been split into a poetry bit and a prose bit. Thus NJB says, in a note, that Gen. 27.40b is not part of the poem, because it is 'prose'; yet it includes Gen. 9.7 in the poem which others restrict to Gen. 9.6. Note also the lack of agreement as to how much of Gen. 12.1-3 is poetic.

A study of each case suggests that there is tacit reasoning that, when a part of a speech has been recognized (by parallelism and metre) as poetic, the whole speech is one poem, even if some of its lines are not very poetic, even if in other contexts they would be taken as straight prose. The criteria of parallelism and metre are set aside as the *sine qua non* of Hebrew poetry, but their absence from the text causes mischief when an attempt is made to scan the poem. Thus everybody is convinced that the speeches of Yahweh God in Gen. 3.14-19 are poetic; but there is much uncertainty about the individual cola. The same is true of Gen. 27.27b-29 (9, 10, 11, 12, or 13 cola) and Gen. 48.15-16 (as few as five, as many as ten cola).

While notionally scansion follows after the identification of a poem, in practice the analysis of verse forms (conspicuously parallelism and metre) already plays a major role in detecting a poem and charting its boundaries. All considerations come into play at the same time. In general terms, what we are looking for are (1) thematic matches between adjacent cola or thematic integrity within a bicolon; (2) metre, with two or three beats or five to nine syllables in individual cola that match (or have parallelism) or otherwise four to six beats (ten to twenty syllables) in individual bicola; (3) grammatically complete bicola and parallel cola that might be single clauses.

The least useful of the criteria is metre. This is not because we claim to know that Hebrew poetry did not have metre. We think it did. But, '[t]he most noticeable aspect of Hebrew metre when described in accentual terms (...) is that no single poem is consistently written in one metrical pattern' (Watson 1984a: 98).

The poem should be long enough to show that the tell-tale poetic features are sustained. The shorter the passage, the harder it is to snare it as a poem. Of the five suggested bicolon poems in Table 1, the only one that enjoys wide recognition is Gen. 48.20, and even then two versions read it as a tricolon.

In most cases, these diagnostics conspire to a unanimous result. Sometimes, however, they work against each other. In a limit case, one feature, if strong enough, is sufficient. And passages which, on their own merits, would not pass muster, might still be accepted as part of a larger composition, the rest of which is clearly poetic. Of course, every possibility must be allowed for, including the possibility that blemishes that make a poem seem inferior to us might be due to textual corruption. But it is precisely the enormous variety and lack of regularity in Hebrew prosody that makes it so hard to justify emendation to make a piece more acceptable as a poem.

The shorter the item, the harder it is to maintain that it is a 'poem', and not just a poetic flurry or flourish in a prose text. If a well-made poem is distinguished from prose by having some kind of *sustained* regularity in its form, then a two-line poem cannot be called 'sustained'. Such entities make a major contribution to Shurr's inventory of 'new' Dickinson poems. There are nearly two hundred two-line epigrams. One of the tests applied by Shurr is their possession of Emily Dickinson's favourite metre—14 syllables, 4:3 beats.

We need not get bogged down in argument as to whether a two-line epigram is a poem. Standing alone, it could be called a poem of minimum size. An epigram can also be an organic part of a flowing prose text, and Emily Dickinson's letters were rich with such epigrams.

Albright (especially in ch. 1 of the Jordan Lectures [1968]—'Verse and Prose in Early Israelite Tradition'), along with Cassuto (especially in 'The Israelite Epic' in 1975) and others, interpreted fragments like those listed in Table 1 as 'poetic substratum' from ancient epic texts. To debate this issue would take us too far afield. The main methodological point I wish to make is that the shorter the poem, the harder it is to prove that it is a poem. That is the first methodological moral from the new Emily Dickinson poems.

There is a flip side to this principle. If a pattern is sustained too consistently or for too long, it becomes mechanical and monotonous, and the artistic effect is ruined. Biblical poetry, with the continual variation in the length of cola (however we measure length, whether by beats, words, *moræ*, or syllables), is never in this danger. There are very few biblical poems (I have in mind pieces whose poetic character is not in doubt, notably psalms) that sustain the same rhythmic pattern throughout. Yet this pervasive feature of biblical Hebrew poetry, especially in prophetic compositions—the use of poetic cola of a wide range of lengths, however measured—has offended modern scholars, who expected poetry, including Hebrew poetry, to be 'regular'. And if it isn't—by golly!—

they will jolly well make it regular. Innumerable emendations—*metri causa*—have been proposed in the literature and many are suggested in *Biblia Hebraica Stuttgartensia*.

In the English tradition, even when regular line length is rigorously maintained, the better poets were able to vary the cadences. And some of the more adventurous poets varied the line length as well. Traversi says of Chaucer's prosody: 'At most the scansion pattern is a foundation, across which the emotional content may move with a very considerable degree of freedom' (1987: 22). George Frisbie Whicher says of Emily Dickinson's metrics: 'Emily Dickinson was both orthodox in her choice of meters,...and skillful in blending the fixed beat of the meter with the free cadences of speech' (1960: 240). In other words, she was a poet.

To my taste, the iambic tetrameter is the most dreary metre for English, especially when rhymed. The young Chaucer began with this form, imitating the French fashion of his day (Traversi 1987: 13). He was its last master. He was still using it in *The House of Fame*, where his maturity had brought it to its limits (Traversi 1987: 20). But, for the most part, he preferred the iambic pentameter, and this has dominated English epic and dramatic verse ever since. Yet it is misleading to say that Shakespeare and Milton wrote in iambic pentameters. Strictly speaking, this is a ten-syllable line; in natural speech such a line often has only four or even three beats. I speak 'The quality of mercy is not strained' with only three stresses—the two nouns and the verb. Of course a ten-syllable line can always be jingled into five iambs.

Having a trochee as the first foot in a line gives a strong onset and relieves the tedium of relentless iambic verse. The use of enjambment further overcomes the danger of monotony by setting the sense and syntax over the rhythm and rhyme (if the latter is used at all).

I will return to Hebrew metrics later. I suspect that the effectiveness of any particular metrical scheme is language-specific, and each language has to find its own best fit. Kemball's study (1965) of Alexandr Blok has made me appreciate the fact that it took a while for Russian poetry to break free from exotic conventions and take advantage of the natural amphibrach stress patterns of so many of the words in that language. We know that Sievers tried to fit Hebrew metrics to the fact that, *in massoretic pronunciation*, many Hebrew tri-syllabic words are anapaestic (1907). But we are dealing with a poetry that could come from a thousand years of literary tradition, and during that time the language

Table 1. Supposed poems in Genesis

References	RSV	NRSV	NASB	NIV	NAB	NJB	NEB	REB	NJPS	Tally[3]
1.27	x[4]	3[5]	x	3	3	3	x	3	x	5
2.23	4	4	4	4	4	4	5	5	5	9
3.14-19[6]	28	28	27	25	25	25	23	20	28	9
4.6-7	x	x	x	x	x	x	3[7]	4	8	3
4.23-24	6	6	6	6	6	6	6	6	6	9
7.11b	x	x	x	x	2	x	x	x	2	2
8.22	x	4	6	6	6	6	4	4	6	8
9.6(7)	x	4	6	4	4	6	4	4	4	8
9.13-14	x	x	x	x	x	x	5	5	x	2
9.25-27	7	7	9	8	8	8	9	9	9	9
12.(1-)3	x	x	11	8	8	4[8]	4	4	8	7
14.19-20	4	4	4	4	4	4	5	4	4	9
15.1	x	x	3	3	3	3	x	x	3	5
15.15	x	x	x	x	x	x	x	x	2	1
15.18	x	x	2	x	x	2	x	x	x	2
16.10	x	x	x	x	x	x	x	x	2	1
16.11-12	x	7	8	9	9	6	7	7	8	8
17.15[9]	x	x	9	x	x	x	x	x	x	1
21.6	x	x	x	x	x	2	x	x	x	1
21.7	x	x	x	x	x	3	x	x	3	2
24.60	x	4	4	4	4	4	2	2	5	8
25.23	4	4	4	4	4	4	4	4	4	9
26.24	x	x	4	x	x	4	x	x	x	2
27.27b-29	11	11	11	12	13	13	10	9	12	9
27.39-40	6	6	6	8	7	5[10]	6	6	6	9
35.10	x	x	3	x	3	x	3	x	3	4
35.11-12	x	x	7	x	10	x	6	6	9	5
48.15-16	5	5	7	10	10	5	8	8	7	9
48.20	2	2	2	2	x	2	3	3	x	7
Tally[11]	10	15	21	17	19	21	19	19	22	

3. The 'tally' in the right-most column is the count of versions that recognize a poem in this text.

4. An 'x' indicates that the version does not present the text as a poem.

5. The numeral indicates the number of cola recognized in this version.

6. There are three distinct speeches.

7. NEB presents 4.7b as one colon, in spite of the fact that it presents the similar unit in 3.16b as a bicolon.

8. Only v. 3; likewise NEB, REB.

9. A similar name-changing speech in Gen. 32.28 does not appear in the table, but the one in 35.10 does.

10. Verse 40b is not included in the poem.

11. The 'tally' in the bottom row is the number of poems recognized by each version.

itself evolved. The sound patterns available for a poet such as David were not the same as those used by the author of the *Lamentations*. Given all these variables, the identification of any portion of the text of the Hebrew Bible as (part of) a poem becomes even more problematic.

In what follows I study more closely the prosody of the alleged poems in Genesis. For consistency, but only as an experiment, I follow the stichometry of the New Jewish Publication Society Translation when they print the text as a poem.

Prosody, however, is not everything. In the case of Hebrew it has now been amply demonstrated that the mainstream of biblical poetry preferred a special kind of language—grammar as well as diction—marked by archaic usage of verb forms and especially by sparse use of the so-called 'prose particles': the definite article ה, the relative 'pronoun', אֲשֶׁר, and the *nota accusativi*, את, another archaic feature. There is detailed information in Andersen and Forbes (1983) and discussion by Freedman in Follis (1987).

Poetry in the Book of Genesis

	Beats	Words	Syllables
Gen. 1.27			
וַיִּבְרָא אֱלֹהִים אֶת־הָאָדָם בְּצַלְמוֹ	4	5	13
בְּצֶלֶם אֱלֹהִים בָּרָא אֹתוֹ	4	4	9
זָכָר וּנְקֵבָה בָּרָא אֹתָם	4	4	10

Only five of the versions studied recognized this poem. NRSV broke away from RSV in this matter. It was not recognized as poetic by NJPST. All agree on the scansion. The speech is certainly repetitive, formulaic, and artistic. The second colon repeats all the vocabulary of the first colon, except for האדם. The adjunct with ב (*beth essentiae*, making the adjunct a complement of the object) is in chiasmus. The syntactic sequence is the same in the second and third cola, and the match of בצלם אלהים with זכר ונקבה shows that the latter is another complement, explicating that צלם is manifest in male and female together. This plural phrase ('male and female') also matches the plural object אתם, showing that the singular אתו is collective and that its referent האדם is generic, not individual. The third colon is thus climactic. While each individual human is either male or female, it is together that they constitute the image of God. Poetic analysis refines exegesis. Having said this, I must now point out that the alleged poem is part of an unbroken narrative, the rest of which is indubitably prose. Furthermore, the language of Gen. 1.27 is that of prose, with the definite article used once, *nota accusativi* three times.

Gen. 2.23	Beats	Words	Syllables
זֹאת הַפַּעַם	2	2	3
עֶצֶם מֵעֲצָמַי	2	2	5
וּבָשָׂר מִבְּשָׂרִי	2	2	7
לְזֹאת יִקָּרֵא אִשָּׁה	3	3	7
כִּי מֵאִישׁ לֻקֳחָה־זֹּאת	4	4	7

Versions that read a quatrain take v. 23a as a bicolon of familiar kind. It has incomplete parallelism, and the syllable count gives balanced lengths. Note the use of זאת as *inclusio*. NEB, REB, NJPST read the first two words as a separate colon, as above.

Gen. 3.14-15	Beats	Words	Syllables
כִּי עָשִׂיתָ זֹּאת	3	3	5
אָרוּר אַתָּה מִכָּל־הַבְּהֵמָה	3	4	10
וּמִכֹּל חַיַּת הַשָּׂדֶה	3	3	8
עַל־גְּחֹנְךָ תֵלֵךְ	2	3	6
וְעָפָר תֹּאכַל	2	2	5
כָּל־יְמֵי חַיֶּיךָ	2	3	6
וְאֵיבָה אָשִׁית	2	2	5
בֵּינְךָ וּבֵין הָאִשָּׁה	3	3	8
וּבֵין זַרְעֲךָ וּבֵין זַרְעָהּ	4	4	8
הוּא יְשׁוּפְךָ רֹאשׁ	3	3	5
וְאַתָּה תְּשׁוּפֶנּוּ עָקֵב	3	3	9

The variations in the count of cola in this piece among the versions are the combined results of two different kinds of decisions. RSV takes all the words of the three speeches as poetic, the poetic portions gathering in, as it were, the more prosaic parts. NJPST excludes the introductory words of v. 17. REB excludes all of v. 14a as well, leaving only seven cola of poetry in the first speech. In the speech to the snake NASB and NJPST find eleven cola, RSV, NRSV ten. NIV and NJB have ten cola, because they exclude the first clause (as NJPST does in v. 17). NAB includes the first clause in the poem, but makes it part of the first colon. Apart from this detail, NIV and NJPST scan in the same way. NRSV reads v. 15a as a bicolon, with incomplete parallelism. Its judgment is similar to that made in 2.23. RSV is more consistent. NJPST recognizes such a bicolon in v. 14a. One colon is a complete clause; the other contains an echo of part of that clause. Good poetry. On these grounds it could be argued that the time reference at the end of v. 14 should not be a separate colon, since it goes equally with both the preceding verbal constructions. And this is precisely what RSV has done with the identical phrase in v. 17. There is, however, a prejudice against such a scansion, supplied by the theory that, while the cola of a bicolon can be unequal in length, the second should be the shorter. This principle is violated in Gen. 25.23a, where a longer second colon must be accepted, the verb doing retroactive double duty. Reading Gen. 3.14-15 in this way reveals larger symmetries. Long and short cola alternate in chiastic patterns. Each half of the poem is forty syllables long.

	Beats	Words	Syllables
Gen. 3.16			
הַרְבָּה אַרְבֶּה	2	2	4
עִצְּבוֹנֵךְ וְהֵרֹנֵךְ	2	2	8
בְּעֶצֶב תֵּלְדִי בָנִים	3	3	7
וְאֶל־אִישֵׁךְ תְּשׁוּקָתֵךְ	2	3	8
וְהוּא יִמְשָׁל־בָּךְ	2	3	5

The differences between NJPST and other versions in the scansion of v. 16 reflect the same kinds of options as we have already met in vv. 14-15. NJPST and NASB split the first clause into two bits, resulting in five cola. The others read a quatrain, each colon being a clause. The choice lies between grammatical structure and more uniform metre.

	Beats	Words	Syllables
Gen. 3.17-19			
כִּי־שָׁמַעְתָּ לְקוֹל אִשְׁתֶּךָ וַתֹּאכַל מִן־הָעֵץ אֲשֶׁר צִוִּיתִיךָ לֵאמֹר לֹא תֹאכַל מִמֶּנּוּ			
אֲרוּרָה הָאֲדָמָה בַּעֲבוּרֶךָ	3	3	12
בְּעִצָּבוֹן תֹּאכֲלֶנָּה	2	2	8
כֹּל יְמֵי חַיֶּיךָ	3	3	6
וְקוֹץ וְדַרְדַּר	2	2	5
תַּצְמִיחַ לָךְ	2	2	3
וְאָכַלְתָּ אֶת־עֵשֶׂב הַשָּׂדֶה	4	3	9
בְּזֵעַת אַפֶּיךָ	2	2	5
תֹּאכַל לֶחֶם	2	2	3
עַד שׁוּבְךָ אֶל־הָאֲדָמָה	4	3	8
כִּי מִמֶּנָּה לֻקָּחְתָּ	3	3	7
כִּי־עָפָר אַתָּה	3	3	6
וְאֶל־עָפָר תָּשׁוּב	3	2	6

NJPST (like BHS) does not recognize v. 17a as part of the poem. In the part of the speech that RSV (=NRSV) and NJPST agree is poetry, RSV has ten cola. NJPST has twelve cola, bisecting the clauses in vv. 17b and 18a. RSV agrees with NJPST in doing the same thing with v. 19aA; yet reading v. 19aA with v. 19aB as a bicolon gives a balance of 8 :: 8 syllables. NASB, NIV, NAB, NJB have eleven cola, reading v. 17b as a bicolon (with NJPST), but v. 18a as a colon (against NJPST). While REB generally follows NEB, in a few cases, as here, it has revised the stichometry in the direction of fewer (longer) cola. It has only nine cola in vv. 17b-19.

	Beats	Words	Syllables
Gen. 4.6-7			
לָמָּה חָרָה לָךְ	3	3	5
וְלָמָּה נָפְלוּ פָנֶיךָ	3	3	9
הֲלוֹא אִם־תֵּיטִיב	2	3	5
שְׂאֵת	1	1	2
וְאִם לֹא תֵיטִיב	3	3	5
לַפֶּתַח חַטָּאת רֹבֵץ	2	3	2
וְאֵלֶיךָ תְּשׁוּקָתוֹ	2	2	4
וְאַתָּה תִּמְשָׁל־בּוֹ	3	3	6

REB's quatrain is better than NEB's tricolon. NEB excludes the two opening questions, in spite of their excellent parallelism. NJPST has eight cola, two for each colon of REB. Some are quite short (one colon is just one word, not usually accepted as part of the Hebrew poetic conventions).

	Beats	Words	Syllables
Gen. 4.23-24			
עָדָה וְצִלָּה שְׁמַעַן קוֹלִי	4	4	10
נְשֵׁי לֶמֶךְ הַאְזֵנָּה אִמְרָתִי	4	4	9
כִּי אִישׁ הָרַגְתִּי לְפִצְעִי	4	4	8
וְיֶלֶד לְחַבֻּרָתִי	2	2	7
כִּי שִׁבְעָתַיִם יֻקַּם־קָיִן	4	4	7
וְלֶמֶךְ שִׁבְעִים וְשִׁבְעָה	3	3	7

All versions are agreed in the identification and scansion of this poem. For a full analysis see Gevirtz (1963: Study II).

	Beats	Words	Syllables
Gen. 7.11b			
כָּל־מַעְיְנֹת תְּהוֹם רַבָּה נִבְקְעוּ	5	5	11
וַאֲרֻבֹּת הַשָּׁמַיִם נִפְתָּחוּ	3	3	10

This 'poem' is recognized only by NAB and NJPST. Orlinsky (1969: 76) draws attention to the parallelism and inversion. I noted above that poetry is not often recognized in the narrative portions of Genesis. Below I shall point out more such parallel statements that might equally well be described as poetic.

	Beats	Words	Syllables
Gen. 8.22			
עַד כָּל־יְמֵי הָאָרֶץ	4	4	6
זֶרַע וְקָצִיר	2	2	4
וְקֹר וָחֹם	2	2	4
וְקַיִץ וָחֹרֶף	2	2	4
וְיוֹם וָלַיְלָה	2	2	5
לֹא יִשְׁבֹּתוּ	2	2	4

RSV alone among the versions consulted does not recognize a poem in this verse. The others read either four cola or else six, giving each pair of nouns one colon, as above. The latter seems preferable.

	Beats	Words	Syllables
Gen. 9.6			
שֹׁפֵךְ דַּם הָאָדָם	3	3	6
בָּאָדָם דָּמוֹ יִשָּׁפֵךְ	3	3	8
כִּי בְּצֶלֶם אֱלֹהִים	3	3	6
עָשָׂה אֶת־הָאָדָם	3	3	6

RSV is the only version consulted that does not recognize a poem here. The considerations are similar to those for Gen. 1.27, a companion piece. All recognize a quatrain. In addition, NASB and NJB include v. 7 in the poem, making six cola. Note the use of prose particles.

	Beats	Words	Syllables
Gen. 9.13-14			
אֶת־קַשְׁתִּי נָתַתִּי בֶּעָנָן	3	4	9
וְהָיְתָה לְאוֹת בְּרִית	3	3	8
בֵּינִי וּבֵין הָאָרֶץ	3	3	6
וְהָיָה בְּעַנְנִי עָנָן עַל־הָאָרֶץ	4	5	7
וְנִרְאֲתָה הַקֶּשֶׁת בֶּעָנָן	3	3	7

This item is recognized as a poem only by NEB and REB.

	Beats	Words	Syllables
Gen. 9.25-27			
אָרוּר כְּנָעַן	2	2	4
עֶבֶד עֲבָדִים	2	2	4
יִהְיֶה לְאֶחָיו	2	2	5

	Beats	Words	Syllables
בָּרוּךְ יְהוָה	2	2	4
אֱלֹהֵי שֵׁם	2	2	4
וִיהִי כְנַעַן עֶבֶד לָמוֹ	4	4	7
יַפְתְּ אֱלֹהִים לְיֶפֶת	3	3	6
וְיִשְׁכֹּן בְּאָהֳלֵי־שֵׁם	3	3	8
וִיהִי כְנַעַן עֶבֶד לָמוֹ	4	4	7

It is generally recognized that these oracular speeches are poetic. NASB and NJPST have three tricola as above. NIV, NAB, NJB read a bicolon in v. 26a. RSV, NRSV read bicola in vv. 25 and 26a. Once more we have competition between grammatical completeness in a colon (RSV) versus evenness of colon length (NJSPT).

	Beats	Words	Syllables
Gen. 11.30			
וַתְּהִי שָׂרַי עֲקָרָה	3	3	8
אֵין לָהּ וָלָד	3	3	4

This little bicolon has never been called a poem, so far as I know.

	Beats	Words	Syllables
Gen. 12.2-3			
וְאֶעֶשְׂךָ לְגוֹי גָּדוֹל	3	3	8
וַאֲבָרֶכְךָ	1	1	6
וַאֲגַדְּלָה שְׁמֶךָ	2	2	8
וֶהְיֵה בְּרָכָה	2	2	6
וַאֲבָרְכָה מְבָרְכֶיךָ	2	2	9
וּמְקַלֶּלְךָ אָאֹר	2	2	8
וְנִבְרְכוּ בְךָ	2	2	6
כֹּל מִשְׁפְּחֹת הָאֲדָמָה	3	3	8

NASB finds poetry (a quatrain) in v. 1, others only in vv. 2-3, some only in v. 3. Verse 3 is scanned either as a quatrain (NJPST, NAB), or a tricolon (NASB).

	Beats	Words	Syllables
Gen. 14.19-20			
בָּרוּךְ אַבְרָם לְאֵל עֶלְיוֹן	4	4	8
קֹנֵה שָׁמַיִם וָאָרֶץ	3	3	6
וּבָרוּךְ אֵל עֶלְיוֹן	3	3	6
אֲשֶׁר־מִגֵּן צָרֶיךָ בְּיָדֶךָ	3	4	9 (11)[12]

12. Here and often elsewhere in this exercise, the counting of syllables is indeterminate because of our limited knowledge of the syllabification of many words in biblical times, as distinct from massoretic pointing. While following massoretic

All are agreed that this is poetry. NEB differs in reading five cola.

	Beats	Words	Syllables
Gen. 15.1b			
אַל־תִּירָא אַבְרָם	3	2	5
אָנֹכִי מָגֵן לָךְ	3	3	6
שְׂכָרְךָ הַרְבֵּה מְאֹד	3	3	7

Versions that find a poem here agree that it is a tricolon.

	Beats	Words	Syllables
Gen. 15.15			
תָּבוֹא אֶל־אֲבֹתֶיךָ בְּשָׁלוֹם	4	3	10
תִּקָּבֵר בְּשֵׂיבָה טוֹבָה	3	3	8

NJPST is the only version that recognizes poetry here. It omits וְאַתָּה from the poem, making the bicolon more balanced.

	Beats	Words	Syllables
Gen. 15.18			
לְזַרְעֲךָ נָתַתִּי אֶת־הָאָרֶץ הַזֹּאת	4	5	7
מִנְּהַר מִצְרַיִם עַד־הַנָּהָר הַגָּדֹל נְהַר־פְּרָת	6	5	16

Only NASB and NJB recognize this poetic speech. Note the use of the prose particles.

	Beats	Words	Syllables
Gen. 16.10			
הַרְבָּה אַרְבֶּה אֶת־זַרְעֵךְ	3	4	7
וְלֹא יִסָּפֵר מֵרֹב	3	3	7

Only NJPST recognizes this bicolon. *Biblia Hebraica Stuttgartensia* does not recognize poetry in v. 10.

	Beats	Words	Syllables
Gen. 16.11-12			
הִנָּךְ הָרָה	2	2	4
וְיֹלַדְתְּ בֵּן	2	2	4
וְקָרָאת שְׁמוֹ יִשְׁמָעֵאל	3	3	8
כִּי־שָׁמַע יְהוָה אֶל־עָנְיֵךְ	4	5	8
וְהוּא יִהְיֶה פֶּרֶא אָדָם	4	4	7
יָדוֹ בַכֹּל	2	2	4

pointing for the most part, we allow for older pronunciation where we can, as with the monosyllabic status of segholates. The matter is complicated by the mixed orthography of the second person suffixes, as in the text above. The principles will be discussed in full detail in the forthcoming Anchor Bible commentary on the book of Micah.

	Beats	Words	Syllables
וְיַד כֹּל בּוֹ	2	3[13]	4
וְעַל־פְּנֵי כָל־אֶחָיו יִשְׁכֹּן	5	3	9

RSV does not recognize a poem here. All other versions did, recognizing from six (NJB) to nine (NIV) cola. The two quatrains of NASB, NAB, NJPST are acceptable. NJB's tricola have parallelism within two of the cola. NRSV gets seven cola by reading v. 11aB as one colon, in spite of the parallelism. NAB and NIV print v. 12a as a bicolon. Perhaps this is only a slip in typesetting.

	Beats	Words	Syllables
Gen. 17.1-5			
אֲנִי־אֵל שַׁדַּי	3	3	5
הִתְהַלֵּךְ לְפָנַי וֶהְיֵה תָמִים	4	4	11
וְאֶתְּנָה בְרִיתִי בֵּינִי וּבֵינֶךָ	4	4	12
וְאַרְבֶּה אוֹתְךָ בִּמְאֹד מְאֹד	4	4	10
אֲנִי הִנֵּה בְרִיתִי אִתָּךְ	4	4	9
וְהָיִיתָ לְאַב הֲמוֹן	3	3	8
וְלֹא־יִקָּרֵא עוֹד אֶת־שִׁמְךָ אַבְרָם	5	6	11
וְהָיָה שִׁמְךָ אַבְרָהָם	3	3	8
כִּי אַב־הֲמוֹן גּוֹיִם נְתַתִּיךָ	5	5	10

Only NASB takes this to be poetry. The solemn and stately lines are somewhat longer than is usual in classical Hebrew poetry. But the features are not unlike those which have been found sufficient in other places to detect poetry. One wonders why NASB stopped at the point they did, since the rest of the speech is in the same style.

	Beats	Words	Syllables
Gen. 21.1			
וַיהוָה פָּקַד אֶת־שָׂרָה כַּאֲשֶׁר אָמָר	6	5	13
וַיַּעַשׂ יְהוָה לְשָׂרָה כַּאֲשֶׁר דִּבֵּר	5	5	13

No one seems to have recognized poetry here, in spite of the parallelism. The language is admittedly that of prose, and the length of the piece is minimal. We are at the border-line between prose and poetry. But it is an abuse of method to cite an instance like this as proving that there is no difference between prose and poetry in the Hebrew Bible.

13. Three successive accented syllables in MT.

	Beats	Words	Syllables
Gen. 21.6-7			
צְחֹק עָשָׂה לִי אֱלֹהִים	4	4	8
כָּל־הַשֹּׁמֵעַ יִצְחַק־לִי	2[14]	4	7
מִי מִלֵּל לְאַבְרָהָם הֵינִיקָה בָנִים שָׂרָה	6	6	14
כִּי־יָלַדְתִּי בֵן לִזְקֻנָיו	4	4	9

Only NJB recognizes both parts of this double speech as poetic. NJPST found a bicolon in v. 7. In spite of its imbalance, the language of v. 7 is not that of standard prose. The syntax of the quoted speech—'she-suckled sons Sarah'—with the subject last, requires the first two words to be a predicate, nominalized without the benefit of the relative 'pronoun', אֲשֶׁר. *Sarah is [someone who] has suckled children.* If it is not poetry, it is at least a very artistic byword.

	Beats	Words	Syllables
Gen. 24.16			
וְהַנַּעֲרָ טֹבַת מַרְאֶה מְאֹד	4	4	10
בְּתוּלָה וְאִישׁ לֹא יְדָעָהּ	4	4	9

I am not aware of any suggestion that this comment is a poetic bicolon.

	Beats	Words	Syllables
Gen. 24.60			
אֲחֹתֵנוּ	1	1	4
אַתְּ הֲיִי	2	2	3
לְאַלְפֵי רְבָבָה	2	2	6
וְיִירַשׁ זַרְעֵךְ	2	2	5
אֵת שַׁעַר שֹׂנְאָיו	3	3	5

Not recognized by RSV. Most versions scan a quatrain. One school (NEB, REB) reads a bicolon (13 :: 10). NJPST reads the opening vocative as a distinct colon, and breaks the clauses into short cola. There is no parallelism to assist analysis. The one opportunity to use a prose particle has been taken.

	Beats	Words	Syllables
Gen. 25.23			
שְׁנֵי גֹיִים בְּבִטְנֵךְ	3	3	7
וּשְׁנֵי לְאֻמִּים מִמֵּעַיִךְ יִפָּרֵדוּ	4	4	14
וּלְאֹם מִלְאֹם יֶאֱמָץ	3	3	7
וְרַב יַעֲבֹד צָעִיר	3	3	6

14. Neither proclitic has a major accent in the Masoretic Text.

This unit is recognized unanimously as a quatrain. It has all the hallmarks of classical Hebrew poetry. The matching word pairs are conventional. The term לְאֹם is poetic diction, used only here and in Gen. 27.29 in the Primary History. The complete absence of the prose particles leaves many constructions structurally ambiguous. Is the prepositional phrase in the first colon a noun modifier, a predicate, or a verbal adjunct? A congruent and holistic reading of the bicolon requires the last parsing. This means that the verb dominates the whole bicolon, with retroactive double-duty functions in the first colon. In other words, the familiar incomplete synonymous parallelism is here inverted. The question even arises whether all the matches force the prepositions into synonymy, ב *from*. Since this insight (pointed out to me many years ago by Dr David Noel Freedman) has not found its way into any translation that I have seen, I must underscore the importance of accepting the use by Hebrew poets of double-duty items retroactively. O'Connor defines 'gapping' as 'the removal of the verb of the second clause, provided it is identical to that of the first' (1980: 123). Here the verb is 'missing' from the first clause. Freedman (1985) has pointed out an unimpeachable example in Isa. 1.3, where it is a noun that does retroactive double duty. The recognition of such 'backward gapping' has been hampered, not only by the expectation that 'incomplete parallelism' will occur only in the second colon, which cannot be longer than the first (the presupposition of Gordis and others, quoted above), but also by the theory—almost a dogma—that the Hebrew poetic bicolon consists of 'two brief clauses' (Kugel 1981: 1).[15]

It is expected that the first colon will be a complete clause. When it is not, instead of recognizing that the missing items are supplied in the second colon, a scholar is likely to take it upon himself (or herself) to supply something. In Ps. 70.2

	לְהַצִּילֵנִי	אֱלֹהִים
חוּשָׁה	לְעֶזְרָתִי	יְהוָה

something seems to be missing from the first colon. The usual remedy is to import רְצֵה from Ps. 40.14. *BHS* proposes further to delete יהוה 'm cs', presumably to recover Qinah metre, 3:2. Both cola are rewritten! It is only when the verb is supplied at the very end of the bicolon that the grammar of the whole bicolon falls into place. The trope

15. This starting point is a flaw in fundamental theory that invalidates much of what follows in Kugel's book.

is similar to that in Gen. 25.23. Giving the double-duty verb dominion over the first colon as well as over the second brings everything into line.

The chiasmus in the second bicolon, and the non-use of the *nota accusativi*, את, leaves the identity of subject and object enigmatic. It is only in hindsight that we know who won out. Here is poetry, without doubt. Furthermore, it requires the recognition of its companion piece in vv. 27-29 as another oracular poem, in spite of the difficulties in analyzing its prosody.

	Beats	Words	Syllables
Gen. 26.24			
אָנֹכִי אֱלֹהֵי אַבְרָהָם אָבִיךָ	4	4	12
אַל־תִּירָא כִּי־אִתְּךָ אָנֹכִי	5	4	9
וּבֵרַכְתִּיךָ וְהִרְבֵּיתִי אֶת־זַרְעֲךָ	4	4	12
בַּעֲבוּר אַבְרָהָם עַבְדִּי	3	3	8

Although recognized as poetic in only two of the translations, this quatrain is as good a poem as some of the others in Genesis. The personal pronoun is placed in chiasmus in the first bicolon. The two mentions of Abraham, with different titles, make an *inclusio*.

	Beats	Words	Syllables
Gen. 27.27b-29			
רְאֵה רֵיחַ בְּנִי	3	3	5
כְּרֵיחַ שָׂדֶה	2	2	4
אֲשֶׁר בֵּרֲכוֹ יְהוָה	3	3	7
וְיִתֶּן־לְךָ הָאֱלֹהִים	3	3	8
מִטַּל הַשָּׁמַיִם וּמִשְׁמַנֵּי הָאָרֶץ	4	4	12
וְרֹב דָּגָן וְתִירֹשׁ	3	3	7
יַעַבְדוּךָ עַמִּים	2	2	6
וְיִשְׁתַּחוּ לְךָ לְאֻמִּים	3	3	8
הֱוֵה גְבִיר לְאַחֶיךָ	3	3	8
וְיִשְׁתַּחֲווּ לְךָ בְּנֵי אִמֶּךָ	4	4	10
אֹרְרֶיךָ אָרוּר	2	2	6
וּמְבָרֲכֶיךָ בָּרוּךְ	2	2	8

While all recognize a poem here, the number of cola ranges from nine (REB) to thirteen (NAB, NJB). One can appreciate the difficulty of finding any breaks in v. 27b. It is one long clause; there is no parallelism. The relative 'pronoun', אֲשֶׁר, makes the construction heavy. REB excludes v. 27b from the poem altogether. NJB, NJPST find a tricolon, as above. Once again RSV, NRSV, NASB have a bicolon, preferring the longer, more integral construction for a colon, with the second longer than the first. RSV, NRSV, NASB, NIV, and NJPST recognize a tricolon in v. 28. They disagree in the identity of the three cola. NJPST has the parallel references to heaven and earth in the same colon, making the second longer than the first. This scansion is inconsistent with NJPST's treatment of the matching portion of Gen. 27.39b. The tricolon arrangement of the others displays a more conventional incomplete parallelism. NAB and NJB read a quatrain. All agree that v. 29 contains three bicola.

	Beats	Words	Syllables
Gen. 27.39-40			
הִנֵּה מִשְׁמַנֵּי הָאָרֶץ יִהְיֶה מוֹשָׁבֶךָ	5	5	14
וּמִטַּל הַשָּׁמַיִם מֵעָל	3	3	8
וְעַל־חַרְבְּךָ תִחְיֶה	2	3	7
וְאֶת־אָחִיךָ תַּעֲבֹד	2	3	7
וְהָיָה כַּאֲשֶׁר תָּרִיד	3	3	8
וּפָרַקְתָּ עֻלּוֹ מֵעַל צַוָּארֶךָ	4	4	12

Most versions read six cola. NAB has seven. NIV gets eight, reading v. 39b as a bicolon, and even v. 40b as a tricolon (unless the typesetting is faulty in my copy).

	Beats	Words	Syllables
Gen. 28.17			
מַה־נּוֹרָא הַמָּקוֹם הַזֶּה	3	3	8
אֵין זֶה כִּי אִם־בֵּית אֱלֹהִים	5	6	8
וְזֶה שַׁעַר הַשָּׁמָיִם	3	3	6

This rhythmic, impressive speech is as much a poem as many other items in Genesis that are widely accepted as poetic. Note, however, the use of the definite article.

	Beats	Words	Syllables
Gen. 35.10-12			
שִׁמְךָ יַעֲקֹב	2	2	4
לֹא־יִקָּרֵא שִׁמְךָ עוֹד יַעֲקֹב	5	5	9
כִּי אִם־יִשְׂרָאֵל יִהְיֶה שְׁמֶךָ	4	5	9
אֲנִי אֵל שַׁדַּי	3	3	5
פְּרֵה וּרְבֵה	2	2	5
גּוֹי וּקְהַל גּוֹיִם יִהְיֶה מִמֶּךָּ	5	5	10
וּמְלָכִים מֵחֲלָצֶיךָ יֵצֵאוּ	3	3	12
וְאֶת־הָאָרֶץ אֲשֶׁר נָתַתִּי לְאַבְרָהָם וּלְיִצְחָק	5	6	12
לְךָ אֶתְּנֶנָּה	2	2	5
וּלְזַרְעֲךָ אַחֲרֶיךָ	2	2	8
אֶתֵּן אֶת־הָאָרֶץ	2	3	5

NASB, NAB, NEB, NJPST recognize the two speeches as poetic. All read a tricolon in v. 10. The scansion of vv. 11-12 is problematic. NASB reads a bicolon, with good parallelism, as in v. 11b; but NJPST reads a tricolon. In v. 12 NJPST again opts for shorter cola. The ten cola of NAB are hard to match with the Hebrew text.

	Beats	Words	Syllables
Gen. 37.24			
וְהַבּוֹר רֵק	2	2	4
אֵין בּוֹ מָיִם	3	3	3

This passage has not been set as poetry in any of the versions examined. Some other small units, not discussed in detail, might equally well have been considered as poetic. See 31.1, 25b, 38; 34.14; 42.8.

	Beats	Words	Syllables
Gen. 42.8			
וַיַּכֵּר יוֹסֵף אֶת־אֶחָיו	4	3	8
וְהֵם לֹא הִכִּרֻהוּ	3	3	7

	Beats	Words	Syllables
Gen. 48.15-16			
הָאֱלֹהִים אֲשֶׁר הִתְהַלְּכוּ אֲבֹתַי לְפָנָיו אַבְרָהָם וְיִצְחָק	7	7	22
הָאֱלֹהִים הָרֹעֶה אֹתִי מֵעוֹדִי עַד־הַיּוֹם הַזֶּה	7	7	17
הַמַּלְאָךְ הַגֹּאֵל אֹתִי מִכָּל־רָע	5	4	11
יְבָרֵךְ אֶת־הַנְּעָרִים	3	2	8
וְיִקָּרֵא בָהֶם שְׁמִי	3	3	8
וְשֵׁם אֲבֹתַי אַבְרָהָם וְיִצְחָק	4	4	11
וְיִדְגּוּ לָרֹב בְּקֶרֶב הָאָרֶץ	4	4	9

The scansion of this poem yields a range from five to eleven cola. All versions recognize some long, stately lines. In RSV, NRSV, NJB the cola are 22, 17, 19, 19, 9 syllables long. This is unusual for biblical Hebrew poetry. They would not generally be accepted within the lyrical or cultic repertoire. No natural caesuras suggest themselves. NASB, NJPS have gained two more cola by splitting vv. 16aA and 16aB. The ten cola in NIV and NAB seem so arbitrary that one wonders whether the layout was intended to match the poetic structure of the Hebrew original at all.

	Beats	Words	Syllables
Gen. 48.20			
בְּךָ יְבָרֵךְ יִשְׂרָאֵל לֵאמֹר	4	4	9
יְשִׂמְךָ אֱלֹהִים כְּאֶפְרַיִם וְכִמְנַשֶּׁה	4	4	9

Most versions that recognize a poem here find a symmetrical bicolon.

Conclusion

The differences among these results have not been exhibited to disparage the work. I believe that each team of translators have done their best with real, perhaps insoluble problems. The problems indicate the need for more rigorous theory and more disciplined criticism of the material. I wish to distance myself from the approach that abdicates the task because of its difficulty, focusing on the texts in which poetry and prose merge, or in which the distinction is hard to maintain, concluding that in biblical Hebrew 'the distinction between "poetry" and "prose" is...not native to the texts' (Kugel 1981: 85). The problem becomes intractable when the pieces are of minimal length. As with the suspected poems of Emily Dickinson, so with many of the quotations from Genesis above, the smaller the piece, the harder it is to prove that it is a poem. It does not follow at all from this that Dickinson did not write her poems as poetry, her letters as prose.

There are poems in Genesis. The more indubitable ones are in speeches, but it needs at least four cola to secure unanimity in their recognition. The shorter pieces, especially in narrative, could be no more than a stylistic device, using seemingly redundant description or parallel expressions to underscore a point or to slow down the pace. The limited agreement among scholars as to whether these are little poems embedded in prose, or even archaic poetic substratum surviving as fragments in the story, does not change the fact that in other places the difference between poetry and prose is quite clear.

The poems in Genesis are not in the classic tradition. They are less regular; they show a much wider range of colon length; they are hardly different from their prose setting in diction; they do not present the archaic usage so commonly met in the main poetic works of the Hebrew Bible. To pursue the matter further, we would have to examine 'poems' in other narrative, and, more important, compare the oracular poems and the dialogue of the historical writings with the poetic forms of prophetic discourse in other parts of the Hebrew Bible.

BIBLIOGRAPHY

Albright, W.F.

1950 'The Psalm of Habakkuk', in *Studies in Old Testament Prophecy. Presented to Prof. Theodore H. Robinson* (ed. H.H. Rowley; Edinburgh: T. & T. Clark): 1-18.

1964 *History, Archaeology, and Christian Humanism* (New York: McGraw-Hill).

1968 *Yahweh and the Gods of Canaan: A Historical Analysis of Two Contrasting Faiths* (Garden City: Doubleday).

Alonso-Schökel, L.

1988 *A Manual of Hebrew Poetics* (trans. A. Graffy; Rome: Pontifical Biblical Institute).

Alter, R.

1987 *The Art of the Biblical Poetry* (New York: Basic Books).

1992 *The World of Biblical Literature* (New York: Basic Books).

Andersen, F.I.

1995a 'Linguistic Coherence in Prophetic Discourse', forthcoming in *David Noel Freedman Festschrift* (Winona Lake, IN: Eisenbrauns).

1995b 'The Scholarly Editing of the Hebrew Bible', in *The Scholarly Editing of Texts* (ed. D.C. Greetham; New York and London: Garland Publishing Co. for the Modern Languages Association): 31-57.

Andersen, F.I., and A.D. Forbes

1983 '"Prose Particle" Counts of the Hebrew Bible', in Meyers and O'Connor 1983: 165-83.

Andersen, F.I., and D.N. Freedman

1980 *Hosea: A New Translation with Introduction and Commentary* (AB 24; Garden City, NY: Doubleday).

1989 *Amos: A New Translation with Introduction and Commentary* (AB 24A; Garden City, NY: Doubleday).

forthcoming *Micah: A New Translation with Introduction and Commentary* (AB 24B; Garden City, NY: Doubleday).

Andersen, T.D.

1986 'Problems in Analysing Hebrew Poetry', *East Asian Journal of Theology* 4.2: 68-94.

Auld, A.G. (ed.)

1992 *Understanding Poets and Prophets. Essays in Honour of George Wishart Anderson* (JSOTSup 152; Sheffield: JSOT Press).

Avishur, Y.

1971–72 'Pairs of Synonymous Words in the Construct State (and in Apposition Hendiadys) in Biblical Hebrew', *Semitica* 2: 17-81.

1975 'Word-pairs common to to Phoenician and Biblical Hebrew', *UF* 7: 13-47.

1981 'Parallelism of Numbers in the Bible and in the Ancient Semitic Literature', *Proceedings of the Seventh World Congress of Jewish Studies. Studies in the Bible and the Ancient Near East* [Hebrew Section]: 1-9.

1984 *Stylistic Studies of Word-Pairs in Biblical and Ancient Semitic Literatures* (AOAT 210; Neukirchen–Vluyn: Neukirchener Verlag/Kevelaer: Verlag Butzon & Bercker).

Berlin, A.

1979a 'Grammatical Aspects of Biblical Parallelism', *Hebrew Union College Annual* 50: 17-43.

1981 'Motif and Creativity in Biblical Poetry', *Prooftexts* 3: 231-41.

1983a *Poetics and Interpretation of Biblical Narrative* (Bible and Literature Series 9; Sheffield: The Almond Press).

1983b 'Parallel Word Pairs: A Linguistic Explanation', *UF* 15: 7-16.

1985 *The Dynamics of Biblical Parallelism* (Bloomington: Indiana University Press).

1991 *Biblical Poetry through Medieval Jewish Eyes* (Indiana Studies in Biblical Literature; Bloomington and Indianapolis: Indiana University Press).

Bianchi, M.D., and A.L. Hampson (eds.)

1930 *The Poems of Emily Dickinson* (Boston: Little, Brown & Company).

Blok, A.

1981 *Selected Poems* (trans. A. Miller; Moscow: Progress).

Boling, R.G.

1960 '"Synonymous" Parallelism in the Psalms', *Journal of Semitic Studies* 5: 221-25.

Bronznick, N.M.

1979 '"Metathetic Parallelism": An Unrecognized Subtype of Synonymous Parallelism', *Hebrew Annual Review* 3: 25-39.

Brown, F.

1890 'The Measurements of Hebrew Poetry as an Aid to Literary Analysis', *JBL* 9: 71-106.

Cassuto, U.

1975 *Biblical and Oriental Studies. Volume 2: Bible and Ancient Oriental Texts* (trans. I. Abrahams; Jerusalem: Magnes Press).

Christensen, D.

1987 'Narrative Poetics and the Interpretation of the Book of Jonah', in Follis 1987: 29-48.

Cloete, W.T.W.

1988 'Verse and Prose: Does the Distinction Apply to the Old Testament?', *Journal of Northwest Semitic Languages* 14: 9-15.

Conrad, E.W., and E.G. Newing (eds.)

1987 *Perspectives on Language and Text: Essays and Poems in Honor of Francis I. Andersen's Sixtieth Birthday, July 28, 1985* (Winona Lake, IN: Eisenbrauns).

Cooper, A.

1987 'On Reading Biblical Poetry', *Maarav* 4: 221-41.

Cross, F.M. Jr

1974 'Prose and Poetry in the Mythic and Epic Texts from Ugarit', *Harvard Theological Review* 67: 1-15.

Culley, R.C.

1970 'Metrical Analysis of Classical Hebrew Poetry', in Wevers and Redford 1970: 12-28.

Dickinson, E.

1959 *Selected Poems and Letters of Emily Dickinson: Together with Thomas Wentworth Higginson's Account of His Correspondence with the Poet and His Visit to Her in Amherst* (ed. R.N. Linscott; Garden City, NY: Doubleday).

Fecht, G.
1990 *Metrik des Hebräischen und Phönizischen* (Ägypten und Altes Testament 19; Wiesbaden: Otto Harrassowitz).

Fisch, H.
1988 *Poetry with a Purpose. Biblical Poetics and Interpretation* (Indiana Studies in Biblical Literature; Bloomington: University of Indiana).

Follis, E.R.
1987 *Directions in Biblical Hebrew Poetry* (JSOTSup 40; Sheffield: University of Sheffield).

Freedman, D.N.
1960 'Archaic Forms in Early Hebrew Poetry', *ZAW* 72: 101-107.
1972 'Pottery, Poetry, and Prophecy: An Essay on Biblical Poetry', *JBL* 91: 5-26.
1980 *Pottery, Poetry and Prophecy: Studies in Early Hebrew Poetry* (Winona Lake, IN: Eisenbrauns).
1985 'What the Ass and the Ox Know—But the Scholars Don't', *Bible Review* 1: 42-44.
1987 'Another Look at Biblical Hebrew Poetry', Follis 1987: 11-28.

Gardner, J.
1977 *The Poetry of Chaucer* (Carbondale and Edwardsville: Southern Illinois University Press).

Geller, S.A.
1979 *Parallelism in Early Hebrew Poetry* (Missoula, MT: Scholars Press).
1982 'Theory and Method in the Study of Biblical Poetry', *JQR* 73: 65-77.
1983 *A Sense of Text: The Art of Language in the Study of Biblical Literature* (*JQR* Supplement: 1982; Winona Lake, IN: Eisenbrauns).

Gevirtz, S.
1963 *Patterns in the Early Poetry of Israel* (Studies in Ancient Oriental Civilization No. 32; Chicago: University of Chicago Press).

Gordis, R.
1978 *The Book of Job: Commentary, New Translation, and Special Studies* (New York: Jewish Theological Seminary).

Gray, G.B.
1915 *The Forms of Hebrew Poetry: Considered with Special Reference to the Criticism and Interpretation of the Old Testament* (London: Hodder & Stoughton).

Greenstein, E.L.
1983 'How does Parallelism Mean?', in Geller 1983: 41-70.

Grossberg, D.
1989 *Centripetal and Centrifugal Structures in Biblical Poetry* (SBLMS 39; Atlanta, GA: Scholars Press).

Hartman, C.O.
1980 *Free Verse: An Essay on Prosody* (Princeton: Princeton University Press).

Herder, J.G.
1782–83 *The Spirit of Hebrew Poetry* (trans. of *Vom Geiste der Ebraeischen Poesie* by J.M.Burlington [1782–83]: E. Smith, 1833).

Housman, A.E.
1933 *The Name and Nature of Poetry* (Cambridge: Cambridge University Press, 1933).
Hrushovski, B.
1980 'The Meaning of Sound Patterns in Poetry', *Poetry Today* 2: 39-56.
Jacobson, R.
1987 *Language in Literature* (ed. K. Pomorska and S. Rudy; Cambridge, MA/London: The Belknap Press of Harvard University Press).
Johnson, T.H. (ed.)
1960 *The Complete Poems of Emily Dickinson* (Boston/Toronto/London: Little, Brown and Company).
Jordan, R.M.
1987 *Chaucer's Poetics and the Modern Reader* (Berkeley, Los Angeles, London: University of California Press).
Kemball, R.
1965 *Alexander Blok: A Study in Rhythm and Metre* (Slavistic Printings and Reprintings XXXIII; ed. C.H. Van Schooneveld; The Hague: Mouton).
Kosmala, H.
1964 'Form and Structure in Ancient Hebrew Poetry', *VT* 14: 423-45.
1966 'Form and Structure in Ancient Hebrew Poetry', *VT* 16: 152-80.
Krašovec, J.
1984 *Antithetical Structure in Biblical Hebrew Poetry* (VTSup 35; Leiden: Brill).
Kugel, J.L.
1981 *The Idea of Biblical Poetry: Parallelism and its History* (New Haven: Yale University Press).
1991 *Poetry and Prophecy: The Beginning of a Literary Tradition* (Ithaca and London: Cornell University Press).
Labuschagne, C.J.
1982 'The Pattern of the Divine Speech Formulas in the Pentateuch', *VT* 32: 268-96.
1984 'Additional Remarks on the Pattern of the Divine Speech Formulas in the Pentateuch', *VT* 34: 91-95.
1985 'The Literary and Theological Function of Divine Speech in the Pentateuch', in *Congress Volume Salamanca 1983* (VTSup 36; ed. J.A. Emerton; Leiden: Brill): 154-73.
Landy, F.
1984 'Poetics and Parallelism: Some Comments on Kugel's *The Idea of Biblical Poetry*', *JSOT* 28: 61-87.
1992 'In Defense of Jacobson', *JBL* 111: 105-13.
Lowth, R.
1753 *Lectures on the Sacred Poetry of the Hebrews* (trans. G. Gregory; London: J. Johnson, 1787.
1868 *Isaiah: A New Translation; with a Preliminary Dissertation and Notes, Critical Philological and Explanatory* (London: William Tegg).

Maier, J., and V. Tollers (eds.)
1979 *The Bible in its Literary Milieu: Contemporary Essays* (Grand Rapids, MI: Eerdmans).

Meer, W. van der, and J.C. de Moor (eds.)
1988 *The Structural Analysis of Biblical and Canaanite Poetry* (JSOTSup 74; Sheffield: JSOT Press).

Meyers, C.L., and M. O'Connor (eds.)
1983 *The Word of the Lord shall go forth: Essays in honor of David Noel Freedman in celebration of his sixtieth birthday* (Winona Lake, IN: Eisenbrauns).

O'Connor, M.P.
1980 *Hebrew Verse Structure* (Winona Lake, IN: Eisenbrauns).

Orlinsky, H.M. (ed.)
1969 *Notes on the New Translation of The Torah* (Philadelphia: The Jewish Publication Society of America).

Pardee, D.
1988 *Ugaritic and Hebrew Poetic Parallelism: A Trial Cut ('nt I and Proverbs* 2) (VTSup 39; Leiden: Brill).

Petersen, D.L., and K.H. Richards
1992 *Interpreting Hebrew Poetry* (Minneapolis: Fortress Press).

Robertson, D.A.
1972 *Linguistic Evidence in Dating Early Hebrew Poetry* (SBLDS 3; Missoula, MT: Scholars Press).

Robinson, T.H.
1947 *The Poetry of the Old Testament* (London: Gerald Duckworth).
1953b 'Hebrew Poetic Form', in *Congress Volume: Copenhagen 1953* (VTSup 1; Leiden: Brill).

Segert, S.
1986 'Symmetric and Asymmetric Verses in Hebrew Biblical Poetry', in *Proceedings of the Ninth World Congress of Jewish Studies* (Jerusalem, August 4-12, 1985. Division A: The Period of the Bible. Jerusalem: World Union of Jewish Studies).

Shurr, W.H., A. Dunlap, and E.G. Shurr
1993 *New Poems of Emily Dickinson* (Chapel Hill/London: The University of North Carolina Press).

Sievers, E.
1907 'Alttestamentliche Miszcellen', *Berichte über die Verhandlungen der königlichen sächsischen Gesellschaft zu Wissenschaften* 59: 76-109.

Soden, W. von
1990 'Rhythmische Gestaltung und intendierte Aussage im Alten Testament und in babylonischen Dichtungen', *ZAH* 3: 179-206.

Stuart, D.K.
1976 *Studies in Early Hebrew Meter* (Harvard Semitic Monographs 13; Missoula, MT: Scholars Press).

Traversi, D.
1987 *Chaucer: The Early Poetry: A Study in Poetic Development* (Newark, DE: University of Delaware Press).

Watson, W.G.E.
1976 'Puzzling Passages in the Tale of Aqhat', *UF* 8: 371-78.
1977 'Reclustering Hebrew *l'lyd-*', *Biblica* 58: 213-15.
1983 'Further Examples of Semantic-Sonant Chiasmus', *CBQ* 45: 31-34.
1984a *Classical Hebrew Poetry: A Guide to its Techniques* (JSOTSup 26; Sheffield: JSOT Press).
1984b 'Allusion, Irony and Wordplay in Micah 1:7', *Biblica* 65: 103-105.
1988a 'More on Metathetic Parallelism', *WO* 19: 40-44.
1988b 'Some Additional Wordpairs', in Eslinger and Taylor 1988: 179-201.
1989 'Internal or Half-Line Parallelism in Classical Hebrew Again', *VT* 39: 44-66.
1990 'Abrupt Speech in Ugaritic Narrative Verse', *UF* 22: 415-20.
1993 'Number Parallelism in Mesopotamian Texts', *Maarav* 7/I: 241-52.

Watters, W.R.
1976 *Formula Criticism and the Poetry of the Old Testament* (Beiheft zur Zeitschrift für die alttestamentliche Wissenschaft 138; Berlin: de Gruyter).

Welch, J.W.
1981 *Chiasmus in Antiquity: Structures, Analyses, Exegesis* (Hildesheim: Gerstenberg Verlag).

Whicher, G.F.
1960 *This Was a Poet. A Critical Biography of Emily Dickinson* (Ann Arbor: University of Michigan Press).

Woodward, J.B.
1968 *Selected Poems of Aleksandr Blok* (Oxford: Clarendon Press).

Zevit, Z.
1990 'Roman Jakobson, Psycholinguistics, and Biblical Poetry', *JBL* 109: 385-401.

THE NAMES OF GOD IN BIBLICAL NARRATIVES

Jonathan Magonet

The power to bestow names is granted to Adam as a stage in the ordering of creation (Gen. 2.19). Each class of animal is defined by him in this way. But Adam takes this a step further. At first he names the creature who is formed to be his companion an *ishshah* because 'she has been taken from the *ish*' (Gen. 2.23), presumably treating her as part of the same species, like any female of any other animal. However after the episode with the forbidden fruit he gives her a very specific name as a way of identifying her uniqueness and establishing her nature or significance—the 'mother of all living' (Gen. 3.21). From then on each human being has a name which helps define their individuality and character.

Throughout Genesis much play is made on the naming of, or the changing of the name of, particular people, and it is possible to classify the different circumstances or reasons for these events (Motyer 1962: 810-11)—Abram/Abraham, Sarai/Sarah, Isaac, Jacob/Israel, Benoni/Benjamin, Joseph/Zaphenath-Paneah. But having established a person's name, the way it is used by others is also of significance. Most obvious are cases where someone is slighted or insulted by not using their proper name and referring to them instead, for example, as the son of their father (Isaiah's reference to 'Ben Remalyahu' [Isa. 7.4], or Saul's 'the son of Jesse' [1 Sam. 20.27, 30, 31; 22.7, 13]). Conversely, Korach's important status in Israelite society is emphasized by listing three generations of his genealogy (Num. 16.1). (For a broader perspective on the literary significance of names in the Hebrew Bible see Sternberg 1987: 328-31.)

Thus a distinction can be made between the significance of a name within Israelite society and culture in general and the specific utilization of someone's name within a particular biblical narrative context. That is to say the broader biblical context assumes the conventional Israelite values about the significance of a name, but the particular usage at any given point is dependent upon the overall narrative strategy of the author of that particular passage. For example, in Exodus ch. 1 the Egyptian ruler is referred to as 'Pharaoh' or as the 'King of Egypt'. Is the choice of name in a given case simply a 'stylistic variant' (in English we are taught never to use the same word twice if we can replace it with a synonym!) or does it have meaning as regards the particular idea being conveyed by the narrator? Thus it is the 'King of Egypt' who gives his secret orders, and then accuses the midwives (Exod. 1.16, 17, 18), but they respond to him as 'Pharaoh' (Exod. 1.19) as they try to appease and dupe him. If one approaches the episode seeking literary significance in such details, it might be argued that the title 'King of Egypt' emphasizes the full authority vested in him as he tries to persuade the midwives to do his bidding, whereas their courage in defying him is reflected in their addressing 'Pharaoh' when they resist his orders. Similarly what is the significance of the fact that Ruth is referred to at times simply by her name (Ruth 2.8), at other times explicitly as 'Ruth the Moabitess' (Ruth 2.21) (long after we, the readers, are aware of her place of origin) and, by Boaz's overseer, as 'the Moabite woman who came back with Naomi' (Ruth 2.6) when her name and relationship to Naomi is presumably known. In both these examples, from Exodus and Ruth, one may argue about the precise nuance implied by these changes but it is nevertheless important from a literary approach to the texts to recognize the fact of change and seek to find its relevance.

If we recognize both the significance of a particular name and the way in which that significance may be affirmed or undermined or interpreted in various ways, when it applies to a biblical character, the same approach should apply to the names of God. Insofar as 'God' is also a 'character' in the narratives, the particular designation used may have significance, especially when different names are used within the same passage or wider unit. Hence the 'meaning' or 'meanings' of the name should similarly be examined in terms of its function within the particular context. Thus there are a number of cases where the names YHWH and Elohim interchange within a given section and it is some of these instances that I wish to address in this study.

One preliminary observation is necessary. At the beginning of Exodus, when Moses confronts God at the burning bush, considerable play is made about the name of God, climaxing in a highly formalized definition of its ancient origin and eternal significance:

> YHWH the God of your fathers, the God of Abraham, God of Isaac and God of Jacob sent me to you: this is My name forever and this is My 'remembrance' from generation to generation (Exod. 3.15).

So definitive is this statement that echoes of it recur in various places in the Hebrew Bible:

> YHWH is Your name forever
> YHWH is Your 'remembrance' from generation to generation. (Ps. 135.13)
>
> But You YHWH dwell forever
> and Your 'remembrance' from generation to generation. (Ps. 102.13)
>
> YHWH is the God of hosts,
> YHWH is His 'remembrance' (Hos. 12.6).

In these passages *zekher*, 'remembrance' is parallel to *shem*, 'name', so the name is defined in terms of how it is to be remembered, what it stands for (compare Botterweck and Ringgren 1980: 76-77). The name reflects the nature of that which is named. But having thus anchored the name of Israel's God for all time, it is inevitable that there must be speculation about the nature of God as enshrined in this name.

One such attempt to define the qualities of God is also placed in the context of a dialogue between God and Moses in Exodus 33–34. The list of divine attributes that are given (Exod. 34.6-7) are similarly repeated and emended to serve a variety of purposes in other biblical texts, for example Num. 14.18; Joel 2.13-14; Jon. 4.2; Nah. 1.3; Pss. 86.5; 103.8-13. Since the name itself is fixed, it can be argued that the same name must serve a variety of functions within different narratives, functions that might otherwise have been expressed through different names, on the analogy of the variants 'Pharaoh/King of Egypt'. Sometimes specific alternative names of God appear, such as Naomi's use of *shaddai* in her complaint (Ruth 1.20-21); Isaiah's use of *adon* and *avir yisrael* in 1.24. The opposite process is that of 'assimilating' various names to YHWH as expressly illustrated in the dialogue between Abraham and Melchizedek with regards the name *El Elyon* whom Abraham specifically calls YHWH *El Elyon* (compare Gen. 14.18-20 with 21). Thus in each case the purpose of the particular designation of God is open to investigation.

The Burning Bush (Exodus 3)

Elsewhere I have examined in some detail the narrative of Exodus ch. 3 (Magonet 1975; 1983). I pointed out the technique present at the beginning of the chapter of using the verb *ra'ah* to see, in the *qal* and *niphal* forms within the same sentence to provide the reader with two different perspectives on the same scene. Thus in Exod. 3.2 the reader is informed that an 'angel of YHWH' '*appeared*' to Moses in a flame of fire in the midst of the bush, but, subjectively, Moses '"*saw*" and behold (the word *hinneh* itself emphasizing that we are seeing precisely what Moses could see), the bush was burning but was not consumed'.

The identical technique is used in Gen. 18.1-2 (where it is made even more explicit by the addition of the phrase in v. 2, 'and he lifted up his eyes and saw and behold...'). It reappears in a truncated form in other encounters with heavenly messengers: Josh. 5.13-14 (where Joshua has a similar experience to Moses); Judg. 6.12 (compare v. 22) to Gideon; Judg. 13.3 where, as we shall see below, Manoah's wife does seem to recognize the nature of her visitor, but her husband does not 'see' until the end (vv. 19-20). In all these cases the 'hero/heroine' is unaware of the divine nature of the figure he or she encounters at first, only discovering it in time or upon seeking to test it out.

In Exodus 3, having established these two perspectives, that of the reader and that of Moses, the narrative continues to switch between them, using the divine name YHWH to indicate to the reader the 'objective' reality of what is going on, and the name Elohim to indicate Moses' awareness of some sort of 'divine manifestation' or local deity. Eventually Moses comes to realize, as the reader has all along, that the 'Elohim' he has encountered is actually YHWH.

> Moreover Elohim said to Moses, Thus shall you say to the children of Israel: 'YHWH, the God of your fathers, the God of Abraham, the God of Isaac and the God of Jacob sent me to you...' (Exod. 3.15)

The point to make here is that the interchange between the two names serves a number of narrative purposes: it enables the reader to know more than Moses does and observe the process whereby Moses comes to understand. But it also dramatizes the problem of the distance between our own human limited perception of a revelatory event and the divine reality that it enshrines, a process that is similarly present in all the other examples where this technique is used—see the discussion below of Judges 13.

The Covenant at Sinai (Exodus 19–24)

At the risk of tackling too broad a subject, I would also like to argue that a similar 'subjective/objective' kind of effect is obtained in the event at

Mount Sinai. Here the people 'reproduce' Moses' experience—that is to say, throughout the episode it is evident to the reader that they are to meet with YHWH, but their subjective experience of this divine manifestation is repeatedly expressed in terms of the divine name Elohim.

Given this premise, the usages of the name Elohim fit logically into this structure. Thus:

> 19.3 And Moses went up to Haelohim and YHWH called to him from the mountain...
>
> 19.16 On the third day at dawn, there was thunder and lightning and a thick cloud upon the mountain and the sound of a horn extremely loud, and all the people in the camp trembled (v. 17). Moses brought the people out from the camp to meet Haelohim and they took up their stand beneath the mountain. (v. 18) and Mount Sinai was covered in smoke because YHWH came down upon it in fire, and its smoke arose like the smoke of a furnace, and all the mountain trembled (v. 19). The sound of the horn grew ever more strong, Moses spoke and Haelohim answered him with a voice.

Having established the perspective of the people, v. 20 then continues the narrative using the name YHWH from then on. It is the unit from 20.18-21, which describes further how the people were afraid and delegated Moses to speak on their behalf that once again reverts to the use of Elohim (v. 19) and Haelohim (vv. 20, 21).

> They said to Moses, 'You speak with us and we will hear, but let not Elohim speak with us lest we die'. Moses said to the people, 'Do not be afraid, because it is in order to test you that Haelohim came and so that the fear of Him be upon your faces so that you do not sin'. Then the people stood far off and Moses approached the thick darkness where Haelohim was.

There appear to be three stages in the covenant process. The first stage (Exod. 19.1-8) presents the general principles of the covenant to the elders and secures the general agreement of the people ('Everything that YHWH has said, we will do'). In the second stage (Exod. 24.1-3) Moses gets the detailed 'laws' which he recites to the people (v. 3), and all the people unanimously agree: 'All the matters which YHWH has said we will do'. The third stage, the actual sealing of the covenant, requires that blood be sprinkled on the two parties, beginning with the altar representing God (v. 6). This is followed by the reading of the covenant and the people's third and final affirmation: 'Everything which YHWH has said, we will do and we will obey' (v. 7). Then the rest of the blood is scattered on the people (v. 8).

When the narrative continues after the listing of the laws (21.1–23.33) with the third stage of the covenant process, the seventy elders are invited to join Moses, Aaron, Nadav and Avihu in God's presence. Once again the 'subjective' perspective is invoked:

> 24.10 And they saw the elohei of Israel and beneath His feet as it were a pavement of sapphire stone, like the very heaven for clearness (v. 11). And against the chief men of Israel He did not lay His hand, and they gazed upon Haelohim and ate and drank.

I would argue that here, as in the episode of the burning bush, the switching of the names of God serves primarily the narrative purpose of the author, maintaining the awe of the event in the eyes of the people, their difference from Moses who had a more intimate experience of God and the reality behind the outer forms, and the limited degree to which some of the elders were granted a vision, but not the reality, of God.

The Angel of YHWH Appears to the Wife of Manoah (Judges 13)

This story serves as a useful text for evaluating the suggestions made above about the 'two perspectives' utilization of the divine names. The pattern is again established by the use of the Niphal form of the verb 'to see':

> An angel of YHWH appeared to the woman... (Judg. 13.3).

The angel tells her that she will have a child despite her barrenness and that he will be a Nazir of Elohim (v. 5). The woman reports to her husband that a 'man of Elohim' appeared to her and his appearance was like that of an angel of Elohim (v. 6). She repeats that she will have a child who will become a Nazir of Elohim (v. 7).

Manoah's response is open to interpretation, but because of what follows, it seems to be one of considerable skepticism, if not downright suspicion, about what has transpired between his wife and this mysterious stranger. He prays to YHWH asking that the 'man of Elohim' reappear to explain again what to do with the child (v. 8). Elohim heard Manoah's voice and the 'angel of Haelohim' appeared again to the woman (v. 9).

She rushes off to fetch Manoah, now referring to the visitor as the 'man'. Manoah meets the 'man' and asks if he is the 'man' who spoke to his wife. Then the 'angel of YHWH' tells him to do all that he had said to his wife (v. 13).

When the instructions have been repeated (v. 14), Manoah invites the 'angel of YHWH' to eat (v. 15). The 'angel of YHWH' says he cannot but suggests instead that Manoah make a burnt offering to YHWH, because Manoah did not *know* that he was an 'angel of YHWH' (v. 16). Manoah asks the 'angel of YHWH' his name (v. 17). But the 'angel of YHWH' asks why (v. 18). Then Manoah makes the offering to YHWH (v. 19). As the fire rises to heaven, the 'angel of YHWH' rises with it, and Manoah and his wife fall on their faces (v. 20). The 'angel of YHWH' did not appear again to them, then Manoah *knew* that he was an 'angel of YHWH' (v. 21).

Manoah tells his wife that they will die because they have seen Elohim (v. 22). But with considerably more common sense, his wife points out that if YHWH had wanted to kill them He would not have accepted their offering or shown them all these things or given such instructions (v. 23). The woman gives birth, names the child Samson, and as the child grows he is blessed by YHWH (v. 24). The spirit of YHWH comes upon him (v. 25).

A narrative pattern seems to be established here again, one that plays on what Manoah *knows* and does not *know* about the divine manifestation before him. Thus v. 3 establishes that it is an 'angel of YHWH' who is acting. The wife reports to Manoah using the term Elohim throughout, including the common designation for a prophet ('man of Elohim'). Manoah prays to YHWH asking that this 'man of Elohim' reappear. The one seemingly inconsistent usage is v. 9 where it is Elohim who obeys Manoah and the 'angel of Elohim' reappears. However the response of Elohim would appear to be in keeping with Manoah's perception of what is going on, highlighting his disbelief in the divine origin of the visitor. From then on the term YHWH is used throughout until Manoah *knows* what is going on.

It is also possible that another factor reinforces this view. Manoah's request that the man come 'again' (v. 8), his coming 'again' (v. 9) and his not appearing 'again' (v. 21) highlight Manoah's implicit disobedience of divine commands clearly given to his wife and its consequences. He can pray to YHWH but cannot recognize a manifestation of YHWH when it is literally in front of his eyes. We will see a similar usage of a repeated 'key' or 'cue' word in our next section on Balaam.

Balaam (Numbers 22)

At the heart of the Balaam narrative (Num. 22–24) is a major contradiction. When Balak's visitors come to invite Balaam to curse Israel he consults with God and is told in no uncertain terms: 'You shall not go with them, you shall not curse the people, for they are blessed' (22.12). But when the second delegation comes, Balaam asks God a second time and receives the answer: 'If the men have come to summon you, arise, go with them, but only the matter which I shall speak to you, that shall you do' (22.20). God appears to have had a change of mind, permitting Balaam to go. And yet in the next verse but one, when Balaam heads off with them, we read: 'The anger of Elohim became hot because he was going, and an angel of YHWH stood in the way to obstruct him' (22.22). As events progress, the 'angel' nearly kills Balaam. Ironically Balaam will sum up his experience at the end of the chapter by telling Balak: 'God (El) is not man that He should lie, nor the son of man that he should change his mind!' (23.19).

So how do we account for this clear contradiction in the text—unless we have recourse to the clumsy editing of two separate traditions? (So, for example Noth 1968: 178). One approach is to accept the contradiction as an intentional and integral part of the story. Extraordinary though it is, it is no more extraordinary than the phenomenon of the talking donkey, and indeed it is no large step to recognize them as part of the same narrative strategy. So it was understood by Maimonides who placed the entire episode of the 'angel of YHWH' and the talking donkey within a prophetic 'vision' or 'dream' (Friedländer 1925: 237). A more directly literary solution, but one which similarly suggests a changed perspective at this point within the overall narrative, is offered by Franz Rosenzweig (see Jacobson 1956: 236-42). Using the theory of 'cue words', he notes that the verb *yasaf*, 'to repeat or resume', recurs several times in the chapter after Balaam goes to God a second time to ask permission: v. 15, Balak *resumes* sending messengers; v. 19, Balaam tells the messengers that he will see what YHWH will *resume* to say to him; v. 25, when the ass presses Balaam's leg against the wall, he *resumes* to strike her; v. 26, the angel *resumes* passing by and obstructing the way. That is to say that after Balaam *knows* that God has refused permission, and *resumes* asking God, he sets in train a series of actions of escalating violence which are leading to his potential death, all underlined or signalled by the repetition of this cue word. In

Rosenzweig's view, Balaam really wanted to curse Israel, despite God's refusal of permission, and by only telling the messengers of Balak a half truth ('God will not let me go'—and omitting to add 'God will not allow me to curse Israel'), he himself creates the problem. The contradiction does not lie in God, but within Balaam. Thus the experience with the angel and the donkey exists in some kind of parenthesis within the narrative framework, an inner state of mind equivalent to Maimonides' prophetic vision.

There is however another factor that reinforces such a literary approach to the story. The alternation of YHWH and Elohim would seem to reinforce the view that two sources have here been combined. However if we look at the way the two names function within this narrative the possibility emerges, once again, of a deliberate differentiation between them, though again it is possible to debate the precise effect or aim of this differentiation.

Let us look at the sequence of name changes:

v. 8	Balaam tells the first set of messengers he will ask what YHWH has to say.
v. 9	Elohim comes to Balaam and asks who the men are.
v. 10	Balaam replies to Haelohim.
v. 12	Elohim tells him not to go with them and not to curse Israel.
v. 14	Balaam reports to the messengers that YHWH has refused to let him go (but omits that he is also not allowed to curse Israel).
v. 18	To the second set of messengers he says, 'I cannot pass over the mouth of YHWH my God (Elohai).
v. 19	But then offers to see what YHWH has to say.
v. 20	Again Elohim comes to him: 'If they have come to summon you, go, but only do what I say.'
v. 22	It is Elohim who gets angry that he went and an angel of YHWH stands in the way.
v. 23	The donkey sees the angel of YHWH.
v. 24	The angel of YHWH stands in the way.
v. 25	The donkey sees the angel of YHWH.
v. 26	The angel of YHWH resumes standing in the way.
v. 27	The donkey sees the angel of YHWH.
v. 28	YHWH opens the donkey's mouth and the discussion with Balaam ensues.
v. 31	YHWH finally opens the eyes of Balaam and he sees the angel of YHWH.
v. 32	The angel of YHWH speaks to Balaam and explains.
v. 34	Balaam addresses the angel of YHWH.

v. 35	The angel of YHWH replies: 'Go, but only say what I tell you.' i.e. a variation on the permission formerly given by Elohim in v. 20.
v. 38	To Balak, Balaam says, I can only say what Elohim tells me.

How are we to understand these variations? When addressing the messengers, Balaam refers to YHWH, who is presumably known as Israel's God, and therefore the appropriate one to evoke for the sake of cursing Israel (vv. 8, 14, 18, 19). Throughout the angel/donkey sequence, the name YHWH is prominent in the phrase the 'angel of YHWH' (vv. 22, 23, 24, 25, 26, 27, 31, 34, 35); and it is YHWH who opens the mouth of the donkey (v. 28) and the eyes of Balaam (v. 31). However the name Elohim is used precisely at the points where Balaam has his personal conversation with the 'God' (vv. 9, 10, 12, 20 and 22), who tells him not to go or to curse (v. 12), but then allows him to go (v. 20) and becomes angry when he does so (v. 22). The transitional point is v. 22 when Elohim becomes angry and then an angel of YHWH stands in the way—a transition similar to the verse in Exod. 3.4 where YHWH sees that Moses has turned aside to see the bush and Elohim calls to him from the midst of the bush, or, at Sinai, where Moses goes up to Haelohim (the people's subjective impression) and YHWH speaks to him (Exod. 19.3). Could this episode be utilizing a variation on the same convention? The 'objective' reality is that YHWH is acting, but Balaam is subjectively addressing 'Elohim'?

There are, of course, other possibilities for understanding the distribution of these names. Perhaps they reflect an Israelite reluctance to have a heathen prophet like Balaam directly addressing YHWH, hence the use of Elohim as a more general term or the use of an 'angel' as an intermediary. Nevertheless, in line with Rosenzweig, it remains attractive to view the contradictory messages as coming not from God but as reflecting Balaam's own inner ambivalence. The word he receives from 'Elohim' is a projection onto God of his own desires. But God's word, once given, remains unchanged. As one who has the power to bless and curse, and who would seek to bend God's word to suit his own will, Balaam must learn that God's word is not to be manipulated in this way.

Jonah

Another prophetic narrative dramatizes the idea that God's word, once given, does not change but remains somehow present until it is fulfilled. When Jonah refuses to obey God's command to 'arise, go to Nineveh and call against it' (Jon. 1.2), the same call words recur in the mouth of the captain (1.6) and are expressly repeated, 'a second time', (3.1) when Jonah vows to offer sacrifices (2.10) rather than go to Nineveh (3.2).

In my doctoral dissertation on the book of Jonah I analysed the use of the names of God within the four chapters of the book (Magonet 1976: 33-38). I concluded that in chs. 1 and 3, a distinction is made between 'Elohim', which was used to depict the 'gods' worshipped by the sailors (1.5) and Ninevites (3.5), representing humanity at large, and 'Haelohim', 'the' One and Universal God that the captain of the ship recognized (1.6) and the sailors then identified with 'YHWH', Israel's God (1.10, 14, 16). Similarly, in ch. 3 the King of Nineveh hopes that 'Haelohim' will change His mind about destroying the city (3.9), but never makes the same identification with YHWH, that the sailors made—thus distinguishing two groups of 'pagans', those who, while recognizing a single God are willing to enter into the same relationship that Israel has, and those who are not so willing.

However in chs. 2 and 4, a different system takes over in the 'inner Israelite' discussion between Jonah and God. Here the clue lies in the different designation of God that are linked with the verb *vayyeman*, 'he appointed' (2.1; 4.6, 7, 8). These are in succession 'YHWH' (2.1); 'YHWH-Elohim' (4.6); 'Haelohim' (4.7); 'Elohim' (4.8). Similarly the question 'Do you well to be angry?' (4.4) is first posed by 'YHWH', whereas the variation 'Do you do well to be angry about the gourd' (4.9) is posed by 'Elohim'. I suggested that, given the precision with which the author uses his particular vocabulary, these differing designations are also deliberately chosen. The best explanation I could find for this distinction (Magonet 1976: 36-37 and n. 129, 35-36) is in line with that which was suggested by the Rabbis in according to the name YHWH the quality of the *middat harahamim*, 'the attribute of mercy', while to the name 'Elohim', they accorded the quality of *middat haddin*, 'the attribute of strict justice'. In the Jonah narrative, it is YHWH who 'appoints' the fish that saves Jonah's life; the combined name is used for the gourd which serves two purposes, emphasized by a pun in the Hebrew, *lihyot tzel al rosho l'hatzil lo mera'ato*, 'to be a shade upon his head to "shed" him of his evil'; similarly the worm, and the east wind, which are introduced by variations on the name 'Elohim', have a corrective or even punitive effect upon the recalcitrant prophet (cf. Strikovsky 1976).

Such an analysis suggests a purposive rather than purely arbitrary basis for the distribution of the different names. Attempts to divide up the story by 'sources' on the basis of the name changes were abandoned relatively early because of the obvious unity of the book (Magonet 1976: 125 nn. 106-108), apart from the debate about the 'Psalm' in ch. 2. Again the intended effect of this differentiation is open to interpretation, but some such distinction as suggested here is consistent with the narrative techniques of Jonah's author.

The Akedah, The Binding of Isaac (Genesis 22)

The above illustrations of different possible meanings to be associated with the names of God in contexts where the names interchange inevitably raises the question of the Binding of Isaac passage in Genesis 22. One of the striking features of this most striking of stories is the change in the designation of God that comes in the middle of it. It is Haelohim who 'tests' Abraham (Gen. 22.1), asking him to offer up his son, his only one, Isaac. Abraham set off to do so as 'Haelohim' has told him (22.3). When Isaac asks about the lamb for the burnt offering, Abraham replies that 'Elohim' will see to it (22.8). They reach the place that Haelohim had designated (22.9), but it is an angel of YHWH that calls to Abraham and stops him (22.11). Abraham names the place 'YHWH will see', as it is called to his day, 'on the mountain of YHWH it may be seen'. It is an angel of YHWH who calls to Abraham a second time (22.15) and informs him that YHWH has sworn that because Abraham has not withheld his son all God's promises will be fulfilled (22.16-18).

Why this change of designation half way through the story? Again it could be argued that this reflects two different sources, though the consistency of the narrative would argue against it. Speiser admirably notes the problem:

> On internal evidence, however, based on style and content, the personality behind the story should be J's. Since the crystallized version was such as to be cited and copied more often than most accounts, it is possible that a hand which had nothing to do with E (conceivably even from the P school) miswrote Elohim for Yahweh in the few instances involved, sometime in the long course of written transmission. The issue is thus not a closed one by any means (Speiser 1964: 166).

Benno Jacob identifies the term Elohim here with one of the 'servants' of God, like the Satan of the book of Job, that is designated for such difficult tasks. He likewise identifies the Elohim and the 'angel of YHWH' of the Balaam story as the same kind of creature. Hence the designation Haelohim, 'the divine servant' specified for this particular task (Jacob 1934: 492).

Surely a logical explanation would be to see in the two designations some kind of literary device in line with those indicated above. Is the author (or a sensitive editor) somehow distancing God from responsibility for making this demand upon Abraham to sacrifice his son? Does it follow the pattern in Jonah so that the use of Elohim in the opening section represent the 'judgmental' or 'punitive' aspect of God that is transformed into the 'merciful' aspect (YHWH) in the latter part of the story? Does it instead, as in the case of Balaam, reflect an inner process within Abraham himself that leads him to wish to kill his son in obedience to Elohim—perhaps to show loyalty to God, or because of his self-destructive despair, having just lost his son Ishmael? (I am grateful to my colleague Rabbi Alexandra Wright for this suggestion.) There are also psychoanalytic explanations that would likewise see in Abraham's initial wish to slay his son a deeper fear of the son's potential rivalry that might lead to murder were that urge not resisted (Elkan 1989/90). A more commonly held view simply sees it as an aetiological story that demonstrates an Israelite critique of child sacrifice.

However, what is important for this paper is once again the point that the change in the actions or demands of God are reflected in the changing designations of God. In the end, as with all the previous illustrations, one's judgment on this particular narrative depends on whether one's analysis of the text is determined by assumptions about the logic and structure of the narrative, or about the divine names as reflections of the prehistory of the text.

The Ark of the Covenant (1 Samuel 4–6)

One final illustration, however, offers a distinction between the possible 'meaning' of the divine names of a quite different order. In the story of the capture of the Ark by the Philistines there are frequent changes in the designation of God. Rather than simply list these variants, it is helpful to follow the narrative line and see what they are and where they appear.

When the Israelites find themselves losing against the Philistines, the elders ask why YHWH has let them be defeated (1 Sam. 4.3). They propose collecting the *aron brit YHWH*, 'the ark of the covenant of YHWH', from Shiloh and taking it into battle so that it can deliver them from their enemies. So they collect the *aron brit YHWH tzevaot yoshev keruvim* but there were the two sons of Eli with the *aron brit elohim* (v. 4).

Now when the *aron brit YHWH* came to the camp, the Israelites shouted so much that the earth shook (v. 5) and the Philistines were scared because the *aron YHWH* was in the Israelite camp (v. 6). They say that '*elohim*' has entered the Israelite camp (v. 7), then express their fears that those are the 'mighty *elohim*' (plural) who smote the Egyptians (v. 8). Nevertheless they rally and defeat the Israelites, the *aron elohim* is taken and Eli's two sons are killed (v. 11).

The messenger brings the report to Eli, who is terror-struck about the fate of the *aron haelohim* (v. 13) and eventually reports, as a climax to his message, that the *aron haelohim* has been taken (v. 17). When he mentions the *aron haelohim*, Eli falls from his throne and dies (v. 18). On hearing the news of the capture of the *aron haelohim* Eli's daughter-in-law aborts (v. 19). But the child survives and she calls to it *ee kavod*, 'there is no more Presence/glory', the Presence has been taken away from Israel because of the taking of the *aron haelohim* and the death of her father-in-law and husband (v. 21). This sentence is then virtually repeated as she says 'the Presence has departed from Israel because the *aron haelohim* has been taken' (v. 22).

Meanwhile the Philistines take the *aron haelohim* to Ashdod, where they place the *aron haelohim* in the temple of Dagon (1 Sam. 5.1-2). But the next morning the Ashdodites find that Dagon has fallen on its face before the *aron YHWH*, and the same thing happens the following day (also before the *aron YHWH*) and the two hands of the idol are broken off (vv. 3-4). But against the powerless 'hands' of the idol, the hand of YHWH proceeds to smite the Ashdodites (v. 6) so they say, let not the *aron elohei yisrael* stay with us (v. 7). So they gather all the leaders of the Philistines and ask what shall we do with the *aron elohei yisrael* and the representatives of Gath offer to take the *aron elohei yisrael* and indeed take the *aron elohei yisrael* (v. 8).

Again the hand of YHWH strikes (v. 9) and they move the *aron haelohim* to Ekron, but when the *aron haelohim* comes to Ekron the Ekronites protest that they have brought the *aron elohei yisrael* there to kill them as well (v. 10). So the Philistines gather again and decide to send the *aron elohei yisrael* back to Israel because of the destruction wrought by the hand of *haelohim* (v. 11). So the *aron YHWH* was with the Philistines for seven months (1 Sam. 6.1), and they summoned their priests and soothsayers to decide what to do with the *aron YHWH* (v. 2). They advise that if they are to send back the *aron elohei yisrael* they should send a guilt offering with it (v. 3). They propose making golden gifts and to give honour to the *elohei yisrael* (v. 5). They should also construct a special wagon to carry the *aron YHWH* (v. 8) and send it to the border. They do so and place the *aron YHWH* on it, (v. 11) with the gifts, and follow it to the border.

The reapers of Bet Shemesh see the *aron* and rejoice (v. 13), and the wagon is chopped up for its wood and the animals that drew it are sacrificed to YHWH. Then the Levites take the *aron YHWH* and more sacrifices are made to YHWH (v. 14). A postscript refers to the Philistine places which had stored the *aron YHWH* (v. 18) and describes the further damage inflicted by the *aron YHWH* on the people of Bet Shemesh for 'looking on' the *aron YHWH* (v. 19), so the *aron YHWH* is transferred to Kiryat Yearim (1 Sam. 6.21; 7.1).

It has been necessary to detail this story, to show the variations in the designation of the 'ark' throughout. When a named speaker or group uses one of the terms *aron YHWH* or *aron haelohim* it is not clear that this was the actual term used. More probably the usage is simply in conformity with the pattern that the narrator has established for his own concept. Thus what seems to emerge is that when the Israelites seek initially to use the ark on their own initiative as a weapon in their fight with the Philistines, without due and appropriate recourse to God, it is designated with the term 'YHWH' (1 Sam. 4.3-6), but from the moment it proves ineffective, the name 'Elohim' is used instead (1 Sam. 4.11–5.11). The Philistines refer throughout to the *aron elohei yisrael* and to the *elohei yisrael*, which are presumably their own 'technical terms' for this sacred object of Israel. But all the destructive acts against the Philistines, and even against the men of Bet Shemesh, are inflicted by YHWH or the *aron YHWH* itself. Thus *elohim* is used throughout either by outsiders or by Israelites when they are treating the 'ark' in much the same way as an idol—to be manipulated (ineffectively) for their own purposes. In such a context it is powerless. But that same ark that proved powerless against the Philistines when the Israelites were attempting to use it, is overwhelmingly powerful against the Philistines, and others, when it is left alone in alien hands or mistreated by the Israelites themselves—and here the name YHWH is invariably used.

It would seem that in this narrative the terminology is deliberately used to distinguish the living God of Israel acting autonomously with full power (YHWH) from that same God as perceived by the Philistines or 'misused' by the Israelites (Elohim).

Conclusion

It is obvious from this paper that my particular interest is in the synchronic approach to the texts in question. The variety of passages selected is not intended to be comprehensive but rather to present an approach that takes seriously the different designations of God when they vary within a particular context. It is logical within such an approach to treat the names of God as those of any other 'character' and to seek meaning in their variation. While suggesting possible explanations I do not wish to claim any ultimate value to them. Rather it is the phenomenon itself I want to explore and the opportunity for interpretation that it opens up. Moreover the frequency of the phenomenon suggests that an approach to it is needed that is more comprehensive, and raises again interesting questions about the literary conventions of the biblical authors and editors, the degree of their dependence on 'inherited' materials and their freedom to transmute them for their own purposes. To what extent did there exist a range of 'legitimate' or 'acceptable' interpretations of the names for God that were part of common currency?

Having raised these questions, perhaps it is appropriate to end with the rabbinic comment that we noted above in the case of Jonah regarding the meanings of the two divine names. Whether it represents a rabbinic attempt to read something into the texts before them or an ancient tradition about such a conventional differentiation, it does remind us of how far biblical names conceal as much as they reveal.

> Said Rabbi Aba bar Memel: The Holy One, blessed be He, said to Moses: You wish to know my name? I am named according to my actions. At different times I am called El Shaddai, Tzevaot, Elohim, YHWH. When I judge the creation I am called Elohim; when I wage war against the wicked I am called Tzevaot; when I suspend judgment for a person's sins I am called El Shaddai; and when I show mercy to my world I am called YHWH—for the term YHWH refers only to the *middat harahamim*, the attribute of

mercy, as it says 'YHWH YHWH a God of mercy and compassion' (Exod. 34.6). That is why it says: 'I am that I am' (Exod. 3.14)—I am named according to My actions (*Exod. R.* 3.6).

BIBLIOGRAPHY

Botterweck, G.J., and H. Ringgren
1980 *Theological Dictionary of the Old Testament* IV (trans. D.E. Green; Grand Rapids, MI: Eerdmans).

Elkan, J.
1989–1990 'The Binding of Isaac: A Psychoanalytic Perspective', *European Judaism* 22.2 (Winter/Spring): 26-35.

Benno, J.
1934 *Das Erste Buch Der Tora: Genesis* (Berlin: Schocken Verlag).

Friedländer, M. (trans.)
1925 *Maimonides Guide to the Perplexed* (2.42) (London: Routledge & Sons).

Jacobson, B.S.
1956 *Meditations on the Torah* (Tel Aviv: Sinai Publishing).

Magonet, J.
1975 'The Bush That Never Burned (Narrative Techniques in Exodus 3 and 6)', *The Heythrop Journal* 16: 304-11.
1976/1983 *Form and Meaning: Studies in Literary Techniques in the Book of Jonah* (Beitträge zur biblischen Exegese und Theologie; Bern and Frankfurt: Lang, 1976; repr. Sheffield: Almond Press).
1983 'The Rhetoric of God: Exodus 6.2-8', *JSOT* 27: 56-57.

Motyer, J.A.
1962 'Name', *New Bible Dictionary* (Leicester: Intervarsity Press; Wheaton, IL: Tyndale House): 810-11.

Noth, M.
1968 *Numbers* (OTL; London: SCM Press).

Speiser, E.A.
1964 *Genesis* (The Anchor Bible; Garden City, NY: Doubleday).

Sternberg, M.
1987 *The Poetics of Biblical Narrative: Ideological Literature and the Drama of Reading* (Bloomington: Indiana University Press).

Strikovsky, A.
1976/1977 'Divine Nomenclature in Jonah', *Niv. A Journal Devoted to Halacha, Jewish Thought and Education* (published by Friends of the Midrashia in Israel).

The Ten Commandments, Reading from Left to Right

David J.A. Clines

1. *Reading from Left to Right*

Almost any readings you will encounter of the Ten Commandments steadfastly read them from right to left—which is my metaphor for adopting the ideology inscribed in the text. Literally reading from right to left means falling in with the convention that Hebrew texts are read in that direction; as a metaphor, reading from right to left also signifies an acceptance of a convention. It means adopting the world of the text, the world and world-view of the author, and the original intentions of the text.

Most of our criticism of the Hebrew Bible lives in this right-to-left world. Historical criticism, form criticism and redaction criticism always read from right to left, asking as they do about origins, intentions and effects but never, in principle, critiquing them. So too does rhetorical criticism, with its concern for the words on the page and their articulation but with a studied unconcern for meaning or value. There is of course nothing wrong with reading from right to left; but it is a quantum leap from these approaches to one that directly confronts questions of value and validity.

For myself, I think that the only way of taking a text seriously is to ask whether I accept it, whether I buy it, whether I believe it, whether I want to call it 'true', whatever that may mean. I don't have to decide in advance that it *is* true in order to be taking it seriously; but it is only if I think that its 'truth' is an important issue, that it is worth arguing with—worth confronting, that is, from my own standpoint—that I give it any honour. It is the same with people, is it not? If I treat someone cordially but never argue with them, I probably do not take them very seriously. I probably do not really esteem them. It's not a great loss not to be esteemed by me, so no one should worry about it too much. But at least there is a reason why I find fault with so many people: I am trying to take notice of them.

2. *The Ten Commandments as Divine Law*

The first thing I observe when I try to take this text seriously, when I ask whether I believe it, when I consider whether I can buy its ideology, is its opening words, 'And God spoke all these words, saying' (Exod. 20.10), or, in its Deuteronomy version, its closing words, 'These words the LORD spoke to all your assembly at the mountain...and he added no more' (Deut. 5.22). Taking these words seriously, and not brushing them aside as some strange Hebrew idiom, I find myself asking: Did God (if there is a God) actually speak audible words out of the sky over a mountain in the Arabian peninsula in the late second millennium BCE? That is certainly what the text seems to be saying, and I seriously want to take it seriously. Now it is not for me to say what is and is not impossible, and I readily admit that the world is no doubt a more strange and wonderful place than I have personally experienced. But it will not shock the esteemed recipient of this volume, or many readers of these pages, if I say I do not believe that any such thing ever happened, and that I would be surprised if any scholarly reader did either. But, as I say, strange and wonderful things happen.

The point, indeed, may seem so obvious that some may wonder why or whether it needs to be made. It is because not a single commentator that I have found remarks on this datum of the text, not one confronts the claim of the text with their own personal refusal to accept its ideology, not one draws any conclusion about the status of the text once they have decided they do not believe some significant part of it.[1] Not one commentator remarks that, if God did not in fact say all these words and the text says that he did, the text is telling us lies and trying to deceive us, and that is a strange state of affairs in a text that is in the business of laying down ethical principles.

Commentators have their own ways of avoiding the issue, of course—which is to say, of not taking their text seriously. Method One is to tell us that someone else spoke the ten commandments, *without telling us that in so saying they are denying that God did.* J.P. Hyatt, for example, tells us that the commandments probably 'originated in the customs and regulations of the families and clans of pre-Mosaic times, as handed

1. It is not entirely surprising that the great majority of commentaries do not make even a single comment on the verse 'And God spoke all these words, saying' (Exod. 20.1). Not even the 659-page commentary of Brevard Childs on Exodus finds room for a single remark.

down by heads of families and clans, elders, and wise men' (Hyatt 1971: 210).[2] But he makes no remark whatsoever on v. 1, which says that these are the words of God.

Method Two is to change the subject, and to make the issue whether the ten commandments were spoken by *Moses* or not. R.H. Charles, for instance, writes: 'The two codes we are considering are ascribed both in Exodus and Deuteronomy to Moses' (Charles 1923: 28). This is of course not true; they are ascribed to *God*.

Method Three is to tell you how foolish you are if you think that 'God spoke all these words' was ever intended to mean that God actually spoke these words. Says James Barr, in a foreword to Eduard Nielsen's book on the ten commandments, 'Israelite law was not, as a superficial reading of the Old Testament might suggest, dropped complete from heaven, but grew and developed through various phases of the life of the Hebrew people' (Nielsen 1968: vii). So it is not that the Old Testament claims one thing and modern scholars think another. Let us have no criticism of the Hebrew Bible here. Let us rather put the blame on its readers, those superficial ones who cannot see that 'written with the finger of God' means what it has always meant to readers of any intelligence: 'developed through various phases of the life of the Hebrew people'.

Method Four is to pretend (or, talk as if) God did actually speak all these words, while at the same time making quite clear that you do not believe he did. Dale Patrick, for example, apropos the second commandment, says, 'It is intriguing to ask why Yahweh rejected images of himself' (Patrick 1985: 45). What the commentator really believes, I am sure, is that it was some human being who *said* that Yahweh 'rejected images of himself'. Whatever Yahweh thought about the matter, we have no first-hand knowledge about it. *We have only some human's word for it.* But the commentator makes it sound as if here in the ten commandments we have the *ipsissima verba* of Yahweh, as if here some question in the mind of Yahweh personally is being presumed and alluded to. The commentator simply does not confront the problem of the text's claim.

2. And here is Moshe Weinfeld: 'At the dawn of Israelite history the Ten Commandments were received in their original short form as the basic constitution, so to speak, of the Community of Israel. The words were chiselled or written on two stone tablets...' (Weinfeld 1990). Received from *whom*?, we are bound to ask. And chiselled by *whom*? But he does not say.

Perhaps it would not matter so much if the ten commandments were a less significant part of the Old Testament. The trouble is, the very commentators who refuse to take the text seriously—by buying its ideology uncritically—generally make a lot of noise about the importance of the text. Here is James Barr again:

> The Ten Commandments constitute beyond doubt the best known and most influential single passage in the whole Old Testament (Barr, in Nielsen 1968: vii).

And Eduard Nielsen takes up the strain:

> Of all the passages in the Old Testament the decalogue, 'the ten commandments', is presumably the best known to western civilization (Nielsen 1968: 1).[3]

Maybe this is true, maybe not. Maybe it seems more true if you are a Presbyterian like Barr or a Lutheran like Nielsen. Never mind. The point is that so-called critical scholars have been reading this unquestionably important text as if it contained divine words when what it really contains (and they know it) are human words, social and religious laws that their authors want to ascribe to God because they want other people to obey them. Let us not beat around the bush: reading from left to right, stepping outside the conventions and beliefs that the text wants to impose on us, which is to say, reading this text as a humanly produced text and not privileging it because we want to agree with it or want to affirm its divine origin, we have to say (do we not?) that it stands written in Exodus 20 and Deuteronomy 5 because it was in the interests of its framers to promulgate its contents.

All of us have interests. We have interests whether or not we know of them, even whether or not we are interested in them. Interests devolve from our personal, social, economic, ethnic, sexual (and so on) location.

3. Here are some more testimonials to the significance of the Ten Commandments, which we would do well to have in the back of our minds if we plan to study them critically: (1) 'the fundamental place of the Ten Commandments in human civilization as a revelation of eternal truths' (Urbach 1990: xi). (2) 'In their role as the fundamental demands made by the God of Israel on the Community of Israel, the Ten Commandments were familiar to every Israelite loyal to his heritage. They become the crowning point of his religious and ethical tradition...[I]t was only the Ten Commandments that Israel was privileged to hear directly spoken by the Deity' (Weinfeld 1990: 21). The reader is invited to decide whether Weinfeld is simply reporting the stance taken by the biblical texts, or whether he is speaking in his own voice, as a believer, and uncritically.

We do not have a lot of choice about what our interests are, for they are implicates of our identity. If I am rich, or if I am heterosexual, it is not in my interest to promote an egalitarian social order or to seek to outlaw heterosexual acts between consenting adults. I can of course act against my interests, whether recklessly or highmindedly; but I cannot act against interests I do not have. My interests are mine whether I like them or not; they are interests determined for me by where I fit into the web of social networks.

So when it comes to reconstructing the pattern of interests of people in societies long defunct (as I am trying to do in this paper), though we may be in the area of the contingent, we are not necessarily in the area of the speculative. Such an enquiry is, indeed, at the mercy of our historical knowledge or lack of it. But because it deals with social locations and social relations, and thus with typicalities, it is on rather firmer ground than we tread when we enquire after discrete historical 'facts'. And, being concerned with public and observable realities rather than private mental processes, it is on very much firmer ground than the common enquiry in biblical criticism after authors' intentions. All in all, I want to argue, the reconstruction of the interests that lie behind our biblical texts, though far from being an exact science, might well be more secure and foundational than much that has passed for biblical criticism in recent centuries.

3. *In Whose Interest Are the Ten Commandments?*

In whose interest?—that becomes the question for this paper. The ten commandments exist because it is in someone's interest for them to exist. In *whose* interest, then, are they? Since societies, even ancient Israelite society, are not homogeneous, I shall be asking, In which *group's* interest are these commandments? And since groups are usually in some kind of conflict with other groups, I shall be asking, What kind of *social conflict* is alluded to, or repressed, by this text? And since it is usually the victors in any social conflict whose texts get preserved, I shall be looking narrowly at *elites and powerholders* in Israelite society for the matrix of these laws.

So saying, I am already being controversial. For it is part of the accepted wisdom that the ten commandments do *not* serve a sectional interest, that they apply equally to everyone and promote the greater good of the community as a whole. Thus, for example,

Claus Westermann takes for granted that the commandment of monolatry applies 'to everyone and for all time' (Westermann 1982: 21; he presumably means all Israelites), and Walther Zimmerli that 'the law of Yahweh is addressed first and foremost to Israel as a nation' (Zimmerli 1978: 138). So too Brevard Childs: 'The Decalogue is not addressed to a specific segment of the population, to the priestly class, or a prophetic office within Israel, but to every man' (Childs 1973: 399-400).[4] Perhaps, indeed, the framers of the commandments did think, as innocently as Brevard Childs did when he spoke of every *man*, that they *were* addressing the whole community; we however can only gasp at the audacity of authors who manage with a word to suppress vast constituencies, whether the powerless in general or women in particular.

In the search for the interests represented by the ten commandments, however, it is a different question we find ourselves asking. It is not the question of the intention of the authors, not the question of whom they thought they were addressing, but rather a question about the text. It is, What does the text assume, and how does it function? With this question we deflect our attention from authors—who were real people once but are now unfortunately entirely inaccessible—and fall to discussing narrators and narratees—who, while they are nothing but mental constructs, are fortunately perpetually accessible, for they are embedded in the text, they are a function of the text.

Who *is* envisaged in the ten commandments, then? Who is the narratee supposed by the narrator? It is not at all difficult to profile that figure. Put together all the data we have in the commandments about who is envisaged, and what we find is: it is an individual, a male, an Israelite, employed, a house-owner, married, old enough to have working children but young enough to have living parents, living in a 'city', wealthy enough to possess an ox and an ass and slaves, important enough to be called to give evidence in a lawsuit. It is a man who is capable of committing, and probably tempted to commit, everything forbidden here—and likely to ignore everything enjoined here, if not commanded to observe it. It is, in short, one might say, a balding

4. Cf. also Weinfeld: 'By contrast with many laws and commands...the commands in the Decalogue obligate *everyone*. Every single individual, regardless of his condition or the circumstances in which he finds himself, is required to observe them' (Weinfeld 1990: 4). Weinfeld subsequently makes clear that by everyone he means every *Jew*, but he does not make clear whether he means every *male* Jew.

Israelite urban male with a mid-life crisis and a weight problem, in danger of losing his faith.

Everyone else is not so much ignored—for several other categories of persons are mentioned—as sidelined. Women, for example, are present, but they are not addressed. Apparently the work they do does not count as work, since they have nothing to rest from on the sabbath; presumably the daughters are out in the fields, Ruth-like, so they need a weekly rest like their brothers. Women's sexuality likewise passes without notice: they can be coveted by their husband's neighbour, but they themselves cannot covet their husband's neighbour—or even, for that matter, their neighbour's husband. Resident aliens are referred to; they are even required to observe the sabbath law. But they are not *addressed* as narratees. They are in the same position as cattle, obliged to obedience, but not the persons addressed. Likewise slaves, children, the unmarried, elderly parents, the disabled, beggars, the landless, the dispossessed, perhaps also peasants and the urban poor, are not the narratees.

The text screens these people out: they are not 'neighbours'. The text is busily pretending that the whole society is made up entirely of a group of 'neighbours', who are men of a certain income and social standing, men more or less equal to one another. It does not recognize the existence of those who are not the narratees, who are not 'neighbours'. Now we all know who it is who pretends that everyone in a society is equal, that everyone has the same chances: it is always the haves, for it is in their interest to maintain the fiction. It makes them more comfortable not to have to worry that their privilege may be the cause of other people's poverty; and, if the underprivileged can be made to believe in this equality, it lessens the chances of social friction. The poor, however, are not under the illusion that they are the brothers or neighbours or equals of the rich.

If, then, in the world of the text it is these urban middle-aged males who are the narratees, and it is (of course) Yahweh who is the narrator, the question for the real world of social relations now becomes: In whose interest is it to have a text telling these pillars of society what they should and shouldn't do, in the name of Yahweh? It will not be slaves or women or resident aliens; though they do indeed stand to benefit from some of the commandments—some of them finding it agreeable to live in a society where work is forbidden on the sabbath and others preferring the laws against theft or murder—most of the commandments leave them cold. The only group in the society that stands to benefit from observance of the commandments as a whole are those who have spent their lives in the enforcement of such commandments and who are consequently the only ones who have the authority to tell the addressees of the commandments that they must obey them, upon pain of... whatever. It is, in a word, the fathers of those addressed, that is, the old men of the society, who speak in the name of God and whose interests are represented in every one of the commandments. No word is breathed, naturally, of the inevitable tension between those who want these laws to be kept and those who do not, between those whose interests they serve and those whose interests they damage. But the moment we allow that the laws do not serve all the members of the community equally, at that moment we recognize a social conflict repressed by the text. The fathers are always *against* someone, some group, whenever they assert their own group's interests.

Now the interests of the fathers are of course principally represented by the fifth commandment, 'Honour your father and mother'. On this commandment, we might say, hang all the law and the prophets—to coin a phrase. Not only is the physical survival of the old men dependent on the observance of the law, but their self-esteem also will be measured by their ability to ensure that their sons maintain the family and national traditions. It is entirely in their interests to say that God demands you 'honour' your father, for that means you must make sure he doesn't die of hunger even though he has stopped being a productive member of the family and it also means that you must uphold all the values he has lived for. For it would be equally a dishonour to an old man to be left to rot by his son *and* to hear that his son is kicking over the traces. Now keeping the old folk alive may be a drain on the pocket, but it hardly does any harm to the younger generation. Or does it? Does it or does it not do harm to the younger generation if there is a pressure upon them, sanctioned with the name of God, to conform to the ideals of their elders, to be taught to regard their time- and culture-conditioned morals as divinely authorized?

If all goes well, from the father's point of view, the old men can hope that their sons will do exactly what they have done, and be exactly the kind of people they have been. To their mind, the commandments will have served their purpose well if no one can be quite sure whether 'you shall not' is a command or a prediction,[5] whether that turn of phrase

5. Henning Graf Reventlow is the only person I know who has suggested that

commands the younger generation how they should behave or whether it prophesies how in fact they will behave. The Hebrew, of course, allows either possibility. In reality, indeed, once the young have internalized the values of the old, what they are supposed to do will be the same as what they actually do—and the imperative will have been transmuted into an indicative. The fate of the younger generation is always to become the older generation, and the addressees of the ten commandments are, in the nature of things, destined to become one day their speakers—to the next generation.

So we ourselves do not need for the most part to distinguish between the older generation that is speaking and the younger generation that is being addressed. The fictive narratees of the ten commandments whom I have profiled above are very much the same as the real-life interest group whose benefit is being served by the commandments. But in the fifth commandment the exact group who author the commandments in their own interests step forward in their true colours. Honour thy father and thy mother, say the fathers—not because father and mother are on an equal footing where honour is concerned, but because a dishonour to the mother is a dishonour to the father. Honour thy father and thy mother, say the fathers, that thy life may be long in the land—which is when obedience to the commandment comes home to roost. If we have ever wondered why this should be the first commandment with a promise, as Eph. 6.2 has it (to be exact, it is the *only* one with a promise), we know now that it is because it is the commandment with the highest chance of benefiting both its authors and its addressees. If the younger generation will honour their elderly parents and ensure that their society supports this value, it is only a matter of time before they will be on the receiving end of the honour. It is just because they undertake to keep their aged parents alive that they have a chance of their own days being long.

4. *The Sabbath Commandment*

Let us take next the sabbath commandment. In whose interest is *this* commandment?

At first sight it is an easy question. The people who stand to benefit

any of the 'commandments' has a force other than an imperative: he argues that 'you have no other gods beside me' is an assertion of the current state of affairs (Reventlow 1962: 25-27).

from the commandment to sabbath rest are obviously those who are going to be desisting from work on the sabbath, paterfamiliases, their children, slaves, resident aliens and cattle. This is assuming of course that these people like working less than they like not working. Perhaps even in ancient Israel there were workaholics, who found the institution of the sabbath disagreeable and not in their own interest; but let us assume that in the ancient world as in the modern most workers preferred (strangely enough, say I) not to work. Is not the sabbath commandment in their interest, then?

Well, yes, it *is* in their interest. But I cannot accept that that is the *reason* for the commandment; I want to say it is only the side effect. This on two accounts. One is that that I am not disposed to believe that some of these commandments are in the interest of one group and others of other groups. At least, I will take some persuading about that, for that would mean that the ten commandments do not form a unity—from the interest point of view—and I think it is reasonable to suppose that they do. The second reason, though, has more weight. It is that children, slaves and resident aliens do not usually manage to have legislation effected that benefits them. Since they are never in a position of power in a society, they have no say in the rules the society makes. If they are benefited by a law, it will be coincidentally and accidentally, not through any design of theirs. No doubt it benefits the powerless to have a law forbidding murder, but it is not on account of the powerless that the law comes into being.

What, are there never any humanitarian or egalitarian impulses in a hierarchical society, which enact legislation on behalf of the needy? Are there never any demands for social justice that even the most self-interested rulers feel in sympathy with? Is it never possible for a powerful group to act selflessly against its own interests on behalf of a less privileged group? My response is that such questions arise only when we are working with a restricted definition of 'interest', such as a group's economic interest or its interest in maintaining its power. Ruling elites can also have an interest in their image as benevolent or as representative of all those they rule. The natural (not the cynical) assumption is that powerful groups do nothing against their interests; if they do, they threaten their own power.

In whose interest is it then to have a law forbidding work on the sabbath? Perhaps it will be easier to say in whose interest it is *not* to have such a law. I would imagine that those on the poverty line, who need to work all day every day to make a living, will be disadvantaged by this law. And those who have animals to look after will also find this law contrary to their natural advantage. Cows have to be milked every day, sheep have to be pastured, hens have to be fed. Presumably camels can be left to get on with it every Saturday, but even the most sabbatarian farmers of my acquaintance find themselves constrained to hold a (shall we say?) flexible interpretation of this commandment.

There is a better way still of answering this question, *Against* whose interest is the sabbath law? It is to ask, What evidence is there of what people actually wanted to do or tried to do on the sabbath but were prevented from doing by the law? Amos 8.5 has grain merchants wishing there were no sabbath; if they want to sell on the sabbath, we conclude, presumably their customers also want to buy. So the sabbath law is not in the interests of merchants or of cheatable little people[6] who need to buy their food daily and cannot afford weekly visits to supermarkets. Jer. 17.21-22 has the prophet insisting that people do not 'bear a burden' on the sabbath or 'carry a burden out of your houses'. People are unlikely to be carrying loads around Jerusalem for the fun of it, so we have to imagine what kinds of people, what kinds of loads, and for what purposes. Since they are carrying loads out of their houses and in by the gates of Jerusalem, we might well suppose that these are goods manufactured at home for sale in city markets. But the text is too unspecific for us to be sure. Neh. 13.15-16 is much more helpful. Here Nehemiah says he saw people in Judah treading wine presses on the sabbath, loading grain, wine, grapes and figs on asses and bringing them into Jerusalem. And Tyrian merchants resident in Jerusalem ran markets in fish and 'all kinds of wares' on the sabbath. So we can conclude that merchants, and perhaps home-based manufacturers, want to work on the sabbath, and are disadvantaged by the commandment. Perhaps, ironically, the only reason why they specially want to trade on the sabbath is precisely because there is a sabbath, on which most other people are free enough from work to go to the market. Nevertheless, the point is that traders would not be wanting to trade on the sabbath if it were not in their interest to do so; and being forbidden to do so must be against their interest.

If these are the people *against* whose interest the sabbath law is, *in* whose interest, then, is the sabbath law? It can only be those who stand to lose nothing by it, those who can afford it, those who can make the

6. The merchants are clearly envisaging doing business with poor people whom they can cheat, sell low quality produce to, and get into debt slavery (8.1-4).

income of six days last for seven, those whose income, that is to say, has a surplus of at least 17 per cent to daily requirements. So they are not little people, they are not the widows or the poor. They are probably not farmers or craftworkers, and, to judge by the evidence, they are not merchants. They are certainly not priests, since they *have* to work on the sabbath, perhaps harder than on other days, if the sacrificial list of Numbers 28 (note 28.9) is anything to go by. There are not many groups left in ancient Israelite society but the urban elite, administrators, officials and the wealthiest of traders.

All the same, in what sense could it be *in their interest*, or is it that it is no more than *not against their interest*? That is a question I need to defer for the moment, until I have looked at the commandments about worship.

5. *The Commandments about Worship*

Let us ask next in whose interest are the commandments enjoining monolatry and forbidding images and preventing certain uses of the divine name. It is not cynical to suggest that these commandments about the deity are not simply the result of religious experience or theological thinking. Religious people do have influence on how communities think, but the moment we have *laws* about religious beliefs, enforceable upon pain of sanctions, we are out of the realm of pure ideas and into the realm of social control. The moment someone tells me I must not make an image of my god and that I will be punished if I do, at that moment I know that that person has power over me or assumes power over me. (I also know that that person has something to lose if I do not obey, so I too have a kind of power of my own; but that is not quite the point here). Laws are a representation of a conflict of wills in a society, so I am asking here: Whose conflicting wills are in evidence?

Childs sets out the options in terms of a conflict between Israel and other nations. Either one can follow Eissfeldt, he says, arguing that the commandment is and always was an essential part of the Mosaic religion, or one can follow Knierim and derive the commandment from the covenant ritual at Shechem and the threat of rival Canaanite deities (Childs 1974: 404). But the commandment, addressed as it is to Israelites, witnesses rather to a conflict *within* Israel; it is not Canaanites who are being warned off Canaanite deities, but Israelites—*other* Israelites, Israelites who are not in the position of being able to tell their neighbours whom they are permitted to worship.

What these commandments, about monolatry, against images and improper use of the divine name—and enjoining sabbath observance as well—want to do is to make Israel different from other nations. They are markers of identity, they are distinctives, they are self-definitions of Israel, they are boundaries around someone's view of what is legitimately Israel. Who then are the people who care about Israel's identity, who are anxious that without laws, with sanctions, the identity they envisage for Israel may not exist? They are not the subsistence farmer trying to jog along peacefully with Philistines in the valley of Sorek, nor the itinerant potter who has always found a Canaanite shekel to be worth as much as an Israelite one; they are not the man and the woman in the street or in the suk. They are the wealthy at the apex of power in their society, whose position becomes precarious if social change is allowed to happen, if traditional forms of national identity are undermined. They are conservatives, and they are running scared.

These are the people who want to keep insisting that they are not autochthonous Canaanites, that they have been 'brought...out of the land of Egypt' (20.2). Why do they particularly want the god whose words they invent for these commandments to define himself as the one who brought them out of the land of Egypt? Because they need to define themselves as incomers, settlers, who do not have long-standing title to the land they occupy but are conscious of a different, more nervous, relationship to the land than their non-Israelite neighbours have. They want to keep alive a memory of arrival and settlement—even if it was, in historical actuality, from over the next hill rather than from Egypt—and they want nothing to change. Their own significance lies in the past when they were different from their neighbours because of their origins; they need to keep difference alive to preserve their identity and self-worth. In whose interest are these laws about monolatry, images, the sabbath? My answer is: these conservative old men who see themselves as inheritors of traditional ways of life.

6. *The Social Commandments*

Whose interests are being served by the other commandments, then?

Thou shalt not steal. Who needs laws against theft except those who have property to be stolen? Who wants to forbid coveting except those who have something worth coveting (whatever that means[7])? Those

7. Is it simply a mental act? See Jackson 1975: 202-34 (followed by Weinfeld, 1990: 9 n. 27).

who want to forbid coveting, and stealing also, presumably, are not the average Israelites in the street: they are, by their own admission, owners of male and female slaves, of oxen and asses, of houses. They are the grandees; they form the wealthiest stratum of the society.

Thou shalt not bear false witness against thy neighbour. Neighbours who have something to lose from false witness against them are the obvious originators of this law—because they are most benefited by it, it is in their interest. The kind of occasion envisaged may be that pictured in 1 Kgs 21.10-13, where two 'base fellows' (בני בליעל) are set (ישב hi.) by the elders of the city on Jezebel's instructions to testify falsely against Naboth. How do you 'set' false witnesses against someone, and how do you persuade 'base fellows' to waste their afternoon in a law court? Presumably money changes hands, and members of the lower orders find it worthwhile to lay false charges against a so-called 'neighbour', a member of the Volvo-driving, property-owning classes. Most references to witnesses in the Hebrew Bible are very generalized and do not evince this class differential, but when it gets down to a concrete example, isn't it interesting that *class* enters into it, that false witness is something men of property have to fear? It is noteworthy too that in Exod. 23.2 the injunction is 'not to bear witness in a suit, *turning aside after a multitude*, so as to pervert justice'. Is the law against false witness specially designed then to protect the interest of the elite against the plebs? It was never a law against lying, of course, and so it did not apply to the rank and file members of Israelite society. It was a law about a specific form of lying, lying in a law-court when property was at stake, apparently.

Thou shalt not commit adultery. Who is so worried about other men committing adultery with their wives as to want a divine commandment about it? It is a well-known fear of polygamous men that while they are occupying themselves with one wife, their other wives can be doing anything they like. And polygamy, we know, is largely a function of wealth. Again, it is likely to be the property-owning classes who are most anxious about property going out of the family as a result of illicit liaisons. They are the ones who stand to lose the most from adultery. No doubt every Israelite male thinks himself robbed by another who manages to sleep with his wife, but those who have landed property that goes with the offspring are the ones who want to have a law about it.

Thou shalt not kill. This is a difficult commandment, on any view. The verb (רצח) is most commonly used, in the legal material at any rate, of unintentional killing, manslaughter. So the commentators solemnly note, but they never remark that it is somewhat absurd to have a law forbidding unintentional acts. In the only concrete example we have in the Hebrew Bible of an act of רצח, we find a man cutting wood in the forest with a neighbour where the axe-head flies off the handle and strikes the neighbour dead (Deut. 19.4-5). This cannot be the sort of thing forbidden here, for no commandment, human or divine, is going to stop axe-heads flying off. Perhaps the clue lies rather in the practice of blood revenge, as Reventlow has argued (1962: 71-73). We would need to ask, Who is doing this killing that is forbidden in the commandment, and why are they doing it? It is not unintentional killing, for which there is no reason, and which anyone might do by accident, but the associated, subsequent killing by the avenger. רצח in fact refers both to the act of the manslayer *and* to the act of the avenger (in Num. 35.27 the גאל is said to רצח the one who has רצח'd, and in 35.30 the רצח is to be רצח'd on the evidence of witnesses). So the commandment seems to be directed against the practice of blood revenge. What precise group is practising this custom I do not know, but I can assume it is some *group* since blood revenge is, by definition, a socially condoned killing, not an act of private vengeance; and here in these commandments it is being outlawed by another social group with more power. And I assume that the ones outlawing it are the conservative fathers; for blood revenge makes for social instability, and the fathers stand for social cohesiveness and order; and they are the ones with power.

7. *Conclusion*

How goes the programme of reading from left to right, then? Ask any question that steps outside the framework of the text and you relativize the ten commandments. Somehow the standard questions, Are the ten commandments Mosaic?, What did they originally mean?, How were they reinterpreted in later Israelite literature?, have evaded the question of their value or 'truth'—or, enduring quality, or, continuing applicability. And the most sophisticated of historical scholars and redaction critics have gone on entertaining the most appallingly uncritical views about the ideological and ethical status of the ten commandments. Is there a chance that an analysis like the present one, that focuses on the sectional interests they support, will demythologize them—without at the same time bringing western civilization tumbling?[8]

8. It is a pleasure to record Heather McKay's stimulating contributions to the

BIBLIOGRAPHY

Charles, R.H.
1923 *The Decalogue* (Edinburgh: T. & T. Clark).

Childs, Brevard
1974 *Exodus. A Commentary* (OTL; London: SCM Press).

Hyatt, J. Philip
1971 *Commentary on Exodus* (New Century Bible; London: Oliphants).

Jackson, Bernard S.
1975 'Liability for Mere Intention in Early Jewish Law', in *Essays in Jewish and Comparative Legal History.*

Nielsen, Edward
1968 *The Ten Commandments in New Perspective. A Traditio-Historical Approach* (SBT 2/7; London: SCM Press).

Patrick, Dale
1985 *Old Testament Laws* (Atlanta: John Knox Press).

Reventlow, Henning Graf
1962 *Gebot und Predigt im Dekalog* (Gütersloh: Mohn).

Urbach, Ephraim E.
1990 'Preface', in *The Ten Commandments in History and Tradition* (ed. Ben-Zion Segal; Jerusalem: The Magnes Press).

Weinfeld, Moshe
1990 'The Uniqueness of the Decalogue', in *The Ten Commandments in History and Tradition* (ed. Ben-Zion Segal; Jerusalem: The Magnes Press): 1-44.

Westermann, Claus
1982 *Elements of Old Testament Theology* (trans. D.W. Scott; Atlanta: John Knox Press).

Zimmerli, Walther
1978 *Old Testament Theology in Outline* (trans. D.E. Green; Edinburgh: T. & T. Clark).

ideas of this essay, whiling away the hours on our journeys up the M6 from Sheffield to Scotland. We always notice Lancaster, as the Sawyer residence, though much of the rest is a blur.

THE SUFFERING OF WITCHES AND CHILDREN: USES OF THE WITCHCRAFT PASSAGES IN THE BIBLE

Graham Harvey

'Thou shalt not suffer a witch to live' (Exod. 22.17).
'Suffer the little children to come unto me' (Lk. 18.16).

In this article I explore some aspects of the relationship between the Bible and modern Paganism. While my specific concern with Paganism may be tangential with John Sawyer's interests, his work and perhaps obsessions have been influential on my own. For example, John's important contributions to semantics affect my considerations of the use (and not 'original meaning') of words like 'witch'. John's participation in inter-faith dialogue (in which he expresses both integrity and tact) have been inspirational in my own exploration of the relationship between Paganism and the other faiths of modern Britain. Here too John's Isaianic stress on justice, honesty and integrity, clear in his presentation of Judaism to his students, in his writings, in his participation in the Council of Christians and Jews and in his repeated stress that terms like 'Old Testament' should be avoided, demand both clarity about the differences between religions and hope that they might meet with respect at least. Finally, I hope that John will appreciate my concern that some practical good may come of our scholarship: in this case an ending of the suffering of witches and children caused in part by the use of some biblical texts.

By reading the two verses (Exod. 22.17; Lk. 18.16) together I deliberately play on the fact that both use a word, 'suffer' which has two entirely separate uses. Both are relevant here, though perhaps to point this out is as bad as trying to explain a joke. The refusal of permission to 'witches' to live and the encouragement to permit children to meet Jesus are both relevant to the (Satanic) ritual abuse scare which has caused much suffering to children, parents and other adults (some of whom have named themselves witches).

My aim in this article is to explore the biblical witchcraft passages in the context of the Bible (as 'scripture') and of the European witch-craze of the fifteenth to seventeenth centuries. I conclude by commenting on the suffering of witches and children in the contemporary ritual abuse scare.

Biblical Witches

Deut. 18.10-11 lists a number of terms for people engaging in various sorts of magical practices. To these can be added terms from elsewhere in the Bible to provide a survey of magical terminology (Kuemmerlin-McClean 1992: 468-69). I am particularly interested, here, in the brief declaration of Exod. 22.17, 'Do not permit a *mekaššefah* to live'.

What does *mekaššefah* mean? Does it refer to people defined by their doing of particular activities or their believing in particular ideas? Are they always and only female? Is it only the female ones who are not permitted to live while some other response is made to male ones? Why is the command expressed this way rather than, as with the following death penalty for bestiality or for sacrificing to any divinity but YHWH, 'A *mekaššefah* shall be put to death'? Nothing in the immediate context answers these questions. The commandment is preceded by a collection concerned with damages. There is no obvious reason for mentioning the *mekaššefah* at this point rather than elsewhere. Cassuto (1967) links bestiality with Ugaritic and Babylonian magical practices. It is not clear that the theme linking bestiality, sacrifices and the *mekaššefah* in the text as we have it is *foreign* practices. Sarna (1991: 136) states that the three offences are linked by being foreign, incurring the death penalty and being designated an abomination somewhere in the Bible. The latter two are derived from the text, but the former is an assumption.

Do other occurrences of the consonant sequence *kšp* answer these questions? Even if a listing of such occurrences does not answer these questions, at least it will make clear the kind of context in which such words occur and the kind of words with which they are associated.

1. Exod. 7.11: 'Then Pharaoh summoned the wise men and the sorcerers, *mekaššefim*, and they also, the magicians of Egypt did the same [as Moses] by their spells. For every man cast down his rod and they became serpents...'
2. Deut. 18.9-11: 'When you come into the land which YHWH your god gives you, you shall not learn to follow the abominable practices of those nations. There shall not be found among

you any one who makes his son or his daughter pass through the fire, any one who practises divination, a soothsayer, an augur, or a sorcerer, *mekaššef*, or a charmer, or a medium, or a wizard or a necromancer. For whoever does these things is an abomination to YHWH.'

3. 2 Kgs 9.22: 'And when Joram saw Jehu he said, "is it peace, Jehu?" He answered, "What peace can there be so long as the harlotries and the sorceries, *kešafeah*, of your mother Jezebel are so many?"
4. Isa. 47.9,12-13: 'These two things shall come to you [Babylon] in a moment, in one day; the loss of children and widowhood shall come upon you in full measure, in spite of your many sorceries, *kešafaik*, and the great power of your enchantments... Stand fast in your enchantments and your many sorceries, *kešafaik*, with which you have laboured from your youth; perhaps you may be able to succeed, perhaps you may inspire terror. You are wearied with your many counsels; let them stand forth and save you, those who divide the heavens, who gaze at the stars, who at new moons predict what shall befall you.'
5. Jer. 27.9: 'So do not listen to your prophets, your diviners, your dreamers, your soothsayers or your sorcerers, *kaššafekem*, who are saying to you, "You shall not serve the king of Babylon". For it is a lie...'
6. Mic. 5.11: '[Among other things such as cities, strongholds; horses, chariots; images, pillars] I will cut off sorceries, *kešafim*, from your hand, and you shall have no more soothsayers.'
7. Nah. 3.4: 'And for all the countless harlotries of the harlot, graceful mistress of sorcery, *kešafim*, who betrays nations with her harlotries and peoples with her sorceries, *kešafeah*.'
8. Mal. 3.5: 'Then [on the 'day of the coming of the messenger of the covenant'] I will draw near to you for judgement; I will be a swift witness against the sorcerers, *mekaššefim*, against the adulterers, against those who swear falsely, against those who oppress the hireling in his wages, the widow and the orphan, against those who thrust aside the sojourner and do not fear me, says YHWH of hosts.'
9. Dan 2.2: 'Then the king commanded that the magicians, the enchanters the sorcerers, *mekaššefim*, and all the Chaldeans be summoned to tell the king his dreams.' [While Daniel and his

companions are not among this group they are condemned to be killed along with the wise men until they come and Daniel, addressed as 'chief of the magicians' tells the dream's interpretation and is given authority over all the wise men of Babylon. See also Dan 2.10, 27; 4.4, 6; 5.7, 11, 15].

10. 2 Chron. 33.5-6: '[Manasseh] built altars for all the host of heaven in the two courts of the house of YHWH and he passed his sons through fire in the valley of the son of Hinnom, and practised soothsaying and divination and sorcery, *kiššef*, and dealt with mediums and with wizards. He did much evil in the sight of YHWH.' [Later] he 'knew that YHWH was god' (33.13) and among his other righteous actions he had 'seers who spoke to him in the name of YHWH the god of Israel'.

As these passages mention other types of magic worker or magical activity, passages in which other words from the semantic field of *kšp* should be noted too.

1. Gen. 41.8: '[Pharaoh] sent and called for the magicians of Egypt and all its wise men; and Pharaoh told them his dream, but there was none to interpret it to Pharaoh [until Joseph is remembered and brought from prison. Pharaoh tells him the dream and says,] "I told it to the magicians but none of them could explain it to me".'
2. Exod. 7.22; 8.3, 14, 15; 9.11: 'The magicians of Egypt did the same [as Moses and Aaron in turning water into blood] by their secret arts; so Pharaoh's heart remained hardened...The magicians did the same [as Moses and Aaron] and brought a plague of frogs upon the land of Egypt...The magicians tried by their arts to bring forth gnats, but they could not...The magicians could not stand before Moses because of the boils.'
3. Lev. 19.26: 'You shall not practise divination or witchcraft.'
4. Lev. 19.31: 'Do not turn to mediums or wizards; do not seek them out, to be defiled by them: I am YHWH your god.'
5. Lev. 20.6: 'If a person turns to mediums and wizards, playing the harlot after them I will set my face against that person, and will cut him off from among his people. Consecrate yourselves therefore and be holy for I am YHWH your god.'
6. Lev. 20.27: 'A man or woman who is a medium or wizard shall be put to death; they shall be stoned with stones, their blood shall be upon them.'

7. Num. 23.23: 'There is no augury in [or against?] Jacob, no divining in [or against?] Israel, Jacob is told at once, yea Israel, what god is planning.'
8. 1 Sam. 15.23: 'Defiance of him [YHWH] is like the sin of divination, defiance like the iniquity of terafim [idols or oracles?].'
9. 1 Sam. 28: '[Although] Saul had put the wizards and mediums out of the land, [after YHWH fails to answer his enquiries, by means of dreams, Urim or prophets, he] said to his servants, "Seek out for me a woman who is a medium, that I may go to her and inquire of her". And his servants said to him, "behold there is a medium at En-dor"...So Saul went and said to her, "Divine for me by a spirit and bring up for me whomever I shall name to you"...[Having gained assurance, on oath, that this is not a snare to bring about her death, the medium calls up Samuel. Then Samuel, disturbed at being brought up, tells Saul the outcome of the coming battle].'
10. 2 Kgs 17.17: 'They made their sons and daughters pass through the fire, and used augury and divination and gave themselves over to what was displeasing to YHWH, making him angry.'
11. 2 Kgs 21.6 (similar to 2 Chron. 33.6): '[Manasseh] burned his son as an offering, and practised soothsaying and divination, and dealt with mediums and wizards.'
12. Isa. 3.2-3: '[Among others being taken away from Jerusalem and Judah by YHWH are] the mighty man and the soldier, the judge and the prophet, the diviner and the elder, the captain of fifty and the man of rank, the counsellor and the skilful magician and the expert in charms.'
13. Isa. 8.19: 'When they say to you, "Consult the mediums and the wizards that chirp and moan"; should a people not consult their god? Should they consult the dead on behalf of the living.'
14. Isa. 44.24-25: 'Thus says YHWH..., "who frustrates the omens of liars and makes fools of the diviners, who turns wise men back, and makes their knowledge foolish, who confirms the word of his servants and performs the counsel of his messengers".'

15. Isa. 57.3: 'But as for you, come closer, you sons of a sorceress, *ᶜonnah*, you offspring of an adulterer and a harlot...[who are accused of insolence and making offerings to others than YHWH].'
16. Jer. 8.17: 'I will send serpents against you, adders that cannot be charmed.'
17. Mic. 3.6: 'It shall be night for you so that you cannot prophesy; and it shall be dark for you so that you cannot divine; the sun shall set on the prophets and the day shall be darkened for them. The seers shall be disgraced and the diviners shamed; they shall cover their lips because no response comes from god.'
18. Eccl. 10.11: 'If a serpent bites before it is charmed, there is no advantage to the charmer.'
19. Dan 1.20: '[The king found Daniel and his companions] ten times better than all the magicians and enchanters that were in all his kingdom.'

The major benefit of this second list of passages is that we discover that not only any woman labelled *mekassefah* but 'any man or woman in whom is an *'ob* or a *yidᶜoni'* is to be killed (Lev. 20.27). At least we know that gender is not always the central preoccupation of these laws. The bias in Exod. 22.17 needs to be explained in light of the fact that other passages do not assert that it is mainly women commit these abominations to YHWH. The two terms, *'ob* and *yidᶜoni* can be interpreted in different ways (Kuemmerlin-McClean 1992: 469; McCasland 1962: 223; Ahituv 1971: 114; Clines 1993: 148) but here presumably refer to some sort of possessing spirit. The method of execution, stoning, is specified—perhaps we should assume that Exod. 22.17 presupposes stoning too. Furthermore, those who consult with such despised people are to be 'cut off from among the people' (Lev. 20.6).

I have followed Bible translators in giving English equivalents for words whose meanings are debatable, but so too are the meanings of English words given. If a *mekaššefah* and her male equivalents are 'sorcerers' are we really any the wiser? What in modern Britain is 'a sorcerer'? The word 'witch' is not much better; perhaps it is worse in that our preconceived idea of a witch may not be remotely similar to that of the Bible. Certainly these texts tell us little about what these condemned people actually do, or believe, or wear, or whatever it is for which they are opposed. They are linked with people who 'pass children through fire' (Heider 1985; Day 1987; Levenson 1993: 18-24). They are linked to adulterers. Harlots and harlotry are often collocated with them. In places (Lev 20.6; 2 Kgs 9.22; Nah. 3.4) 'sorcery' and 'harlotry' almost gloss one another. Perhaps there is a deliberate ambiguity (Gordon 1992) here for which we could use the English equivalent 'charmer'. 'Charmer', however, does not have the sinister connotation required for translating a name for one condemned to death. Nor perhaps does it convey the Bible's disapproval of 'harlotry' which gains considerable strength as a metaphor from its opposition to the family metaphors used of the relationship between Israel and Israel's god. Nahmanides explains the strictness of the death penalty for the sorceress on the grounds that she misleads, ensnares or seduces people away from the right path. Seduction and sorcery also seem to be associated in 4Q184 (Baumgarten 1991: 143).

Also in the company of the condemned sorcerers are 'dreamers' and 'prophets'. Perfectly acceptable people could be called 'dreamers' and 'prophets' (Joseph and those expressing their disapproval here for example). At times Israelite heroes (e.g. Joseph, Moses, Aaron, Daniel) can be linked with magicians, astrologers, future-forecasters and so on. At times the 'abominations' look similar to acceptable practices such as using the Urim, listening to prophets or waiting for dreams.

If the majority of those referred to with the 'sorcerer' (assuming that to be at least as useful a word as *mekaššefah*) seem to have something to do with attempting to predict the future, this in itself is too general to be enough to deserve the death penalty. (Milgrom asserts that the sorcerer 'attempts to change the future' while the less-culpable diviner merely tries to predict it [1990: 471]. This distinction is not clear in the texts.) If it is the methods by which these people try to predict the future, it would have been of great help to us to be told what exactly they did. Later Jewish teachers (Nachmanides and Sforno, for example) say that the issue is being completely devout to Israel's god and only using acceptable means (Urim and prophets). Rashi, more radically, says that one should not even attempt to know the future. What did the acceptable oracles of god do that these people did not do? What is the difference between the astrology of the condemned and the signs in the heavens looked for by the righteous? Is this just a case of being on the wrong side of some long forgotten barrier in the same way that a 'terrorist' and a 'freedom-fighter' differ only in being on different sides of an ideological divide? Is this 'just semantics'?

Even when we consider the narratives in which magicians (by different names) are central we gain little information to help us know whether the 'sorceress'/'witch' of the Bible was specific to her own culture or somehow managed to survive. The medium of En-dor, the magicians of Egypt and Babylon and Queen Jezebel appear in such narratives. The 'witch of En-dor' calls up a spirit; her activities are those we associate with mediums, seances or with the Spiritualist Churches today. If she had cast lots, 'inquired of YHWH', dreamt, interpreted a dream of Saul or prayed would she have been in danger? The magicians of Babylon interpret dreams, offer insight and advice and try to establish their authority. Perhaps they were like therapists in the modern world: offering a range of counselling practices and sometimes in competition with other experts. In Egypt also the magicians interpret dreams but also do amazing things with staffs. Despite their undoubted wisdom they compete in what we are more used to considering as stage magic, mere entertainment and not state-craft. The medium at En-dor is unlike the magicians of Egypt and Babylon in not having an acceptable YHWH-inspired counterpart. The magicians do nothing that Joseph, Moses, Aaron, Daniel and others cannot do better.

Queen Jezebel is a rather different case. We are told nothing about 'magic', only that she was a foreigner who continued to honour Baal and Asherah, maintained their prophets, organized the false accusation and stoning of Naboth and 'painted her eyes and dressed her hair' before being defenestrated at the instigation of Jehu. Perhaps the make-up and tidy hair were meant to 'charm' Jehu, or was Jezebel 'putting on a brave face'? Certainly there is nothing obviously magical in her career.

Is the calling up of spirits the sole remaining identifiable taxic indicator of biblical witchcraft? Are all the laws, prophecies and writings against witchcraft now only applicable to those who act as mediums? This is clearly not what the Bible intends in giving an array of names for unacceptable people and practices. Even if we do not know exactly what most of them did or believed, or whatever it is exactly that they were condemned for, we must assume that a variety of roles or techniques are lost to us.

Before examining the way that this material has been used, I want to consider the possibility that there may never have been any clarity about what a *mekaššefah* was. Can we really be sure that the women condemned by Exod. 22.17 were a recognizable group? Is this a name that anyone would have accepted for themselves? Just as, presumably, no one uses 'harlot' (with its strongly negative connotations) as a self-designation but only as an insult, so perhaps with the Bible's use of many (if not all) of these words. Perhaps there was a cultural stereotype which would only fit actual people loosely, but could be used as a catch-all term for current scapegoats. Perhaps this too is true of the English word 'witch'.

There are many people today, women and men, who name themselves 'witches'. By this they mean something positive. The collocation 'white' is frequently added to the word 'witch' (by some of these people and the media for example) to distinguish them from evil 'black witches'. In most societies there is some equivalent to 'witch' in reference to people (often in marginal positions) who are perceived to be negative, dangerous, hostile and/or polluting (Douglas 1966: 94-113; Evans-Pritchard 1929 and 1937; Lewis 1989; Middleton 1987). The characteristics and activities of witches vary greatly, but, except in the self-understanding of modern Western self-identified witches, they are associated with 'evil' in some way(s). To be labelled a 'witch' in the traditional (negative) sense is not something welcomed and is only very rarely a self-designation (Douglas 1970: xxxiv; Lewis 1986: 51-62). What you had to do, or be believed to do, to be named a witch varied. There are, in the same societies as the 'witches', often people who engage in acceptable forms of 'magic'. 'Witch', except in modern western usage, is not a self-designation but an attack on others. What you have to do to be called a witch was rarely unambiguous and avoidable. The Monty Python film, *The Quest for the Holy Grail*, has a scene in which a village is attempting to lynch a woman for being a witch. When the patently false accusations and the stuck-on nose fail to convince the supposedly more rational knight, an equally preposterous test is instituted by the knight. On the grounds that witches are known to float on water and that they are therefore similar to ducks, the witch is weighed in a balance opposite a duck. The Monty Python team here explore the theme (to which they return in *The Life of Brian*) that religious conviction, especially where strongly held, often leads to irrational actions. If religion is (or can be) a 'licensed insanity' (Bowker 1987), not to mention bigotry, xenophobia, and intolerance, 'witchcraft' is a small and dangerous weapon in its verbal arsenal.

The Bible does not always distinguish between 'witches' and socially acceptable magic workers. It is not consistent and leaves us confused as to why Moses, Daniel and company are not punished for their conjuring tricks. Some later interpreters distinguish between the 'magic' of the magicians and the 'miracles' of Moses and Aaron, for example (e.g. *Exod. R.* 9.7). This distinction is not based on the texts but on the beliefs and context of the interpreters.

Exod. 22.17 and the other biblical passages do not tell us enough to be able to say, 'yes, our society has people like that too'. We cannot look over the shoulder of those who cast lots and see the difference between acceptable and unacceptable ways of doing it. We cannot watch Daniel to see the essential difference between him and the other wise men of Babylon. The witch of En-dor may well have considered herself a good Israelite; after all she did not say to her visitors, 'No I don't call up the spirits of prophets like Samuel, I only do non-Israelite loved-ones'. Even those who 'passed their children through the fire' probably did so as part of their worship of YHWH and his court (Levenson 1993). The Bible performs a sleight of hand when it outlaws divination as witchcraft but encourages the use of other divinatory systems such as the Urim. What these passages unambiguously tell us is that it was possible for some Israelites to level an accusation against other Israelites. They do not tell us how anyone could judge whether or not to stone or exile the accused.

Some 'magical' practices are both condemned and accepted in the Bible. Some are labelled 'sorcery' and portrayed as abominations to Israel's god. An attempt is even made to portray some of these things as 'foreign'. We cannot recognize these as a coherent form of spirituality, a counter-culture or a magical system. Nor can we identify what someone would have to do to be (or avoid being) labelled a sorceress or witch. The passage most concerned with proper responses to 'sorcery' is also the least helpful to us if we are searching for clear, unambiguous information on what this means. We might as well leave the word untranslated. It is, for precisely that reason, an immensely useful passage for those who want to oppose someone or something and need a license.

The Great Witch Craze

The great witch craze of fifteenth- to seventeenth-century Europe has been discussed in a vast number of books and articles. Almost every possible issue related to that period has provoked opposing evaluations, theories and emotions. My interest is in the role of the biblical witchcraft passages in two areas: the image of the witch and the requirement to execute the witch. One question can be addressed to both these areas: was the Bible responsible for the recognition and execution of 'witches' in Europe?

The Image of the Witch

What does a witch look like? What does she do? What does she wear? The questions already make one assumption clear: witches are female. This assumption derives from the modern stereotype, evidenced in children's books, horror films and Hallowe'en fancy dress costumes. Male magic workers, 'wizards', wear similarly pointed hats but are not necessarily bat-infested, cat-accompanied, broomstick-riding, infirm or elderly. Where do these stereotypes come from?

The modern stereotype was certainly current during the time of the great witch craze. Reginald Scott described the typical witch as 'commonly old, lame, bleare eied, pale, fowle, and full of wrinkles' and, of course, female (Scott 1584: Book 1, chap. 3 in Robbins 1978: 12). We are also familiar with the three witches of Shakespeare's *Macbeth*.

The Bible has nothing to do with this stereotype. It is not interested in the physical description of a witch, or assumes its readers/hearers share its stereotype. The nightmare hags of European witch-beliefs do have earlier ancestors, however. Classical Roman writers present an image that would be recognized as 'a witch' if she appeared in a modern horror film. In Lucan's *Civil War* a graveyard-inhabiting witch, 'knowing the abodes of hell', is described.

> Haggard and loathly with age is the face of the witch; her awful countenance, overcast with a hellish pallor and weighed down by uncombed locks, is never seen by the clear sky; but if storm and black clouds take away the stars, then she issues from rifled tombs and tries to catch the nocturnal lightnings. Her tread blights the seeds of the fertile cornfield, her breath poisons the air that before was harmless (Duff 1928: 341-45).

All that is missing is the dry ice, the howling wolf and the spine-chilling music. Or the paraphernalia of the torture chamber of those popularly, though not always accurately, named the Inquisition. Almost everything about the stereotype of 'the witch' in the medieval and early modern Europe can be found in Roman classical, pagan writers (Horace's *Epodes*; Lucan's *Civil War* vi.499-568; Apuleius's *Golden Ass* and *Apologia*) and indeed in other pagan sources (Flint 1991: chapter 2; Baroja 1964: 47-57). (I am grateful to Ronald Hutton of Bristol University for drawing my attention to these, the main sources for Shakespeare's witches. He also pointed out the perhaps the only contemporary, Elizabethan, idea here is the belief that witches cursed those who were inhospitable to them. Also see Dellasega 1990.) Did the Bible contribute anything to this? Probably not. Its 'witches' may be female but they are not described physically. In fact, very little is said about them or their actions.

It should be noted that despite the stereotype, those accused and executed (or lynched) as witches were not always female and/or elderly (Robbins 1978: 17). However, it must be significant that the majority of those accused and the majority of those executed were women (Barstow 1988). Gender is significant.

Neither the stereotype nor the actual accused witches were concerned with a fertility cult. For all the variety in their views of witchcraft neither the Romans nor the Inquisition nor the Bible were interested in a fertility cult. Ginzburg's *Benandanti* are not exceptions as their concern with agriculture was considered to be opposition to 'witchcraft' until the Inquisition decided their actions were also witchcraft (Ginzburg 1983). The classical Romans had their own techniques for ensuring the fertility of the land and the vitality of the state; they had their own magical and occult arts (Luck 1985), but were still able to execute 'witches' (*Lex Cornelia de sicariis et veneficiis*). This is true of other 'pagan' nations too (Flint 1991: chapter 3).

The Pact with the Devil

What is new in the witch stereotype of the Christian Europe and what is most significant for the understanding of the great witch craze is the belief in a pact with the devil. That the witch is 'dear to the deities of Erebus' is not, in itself, particularly problematic for Lucan. The deities of Erebus were honoured in ways that did not evoke fear or provoke hostility. The Christian devil, however, had no legitimate rites or rights. Changing beliefs in European Christianity allowed that the devil had the power to control people or things if god permitted him to do so. Where previously 'witches' had been accused as people (mostly women) who did harm to others, *maleficium*, now witches were people who had made a pact with/sold their soul to the devil. This seems to be a rare consensus in the study of witchcraft (e.g. Robbins 1978: 12, 17; Thomas 1971: 521; Russell 1987: 417). In 1580 a witch could be defined as 'one who knowing God's law tries to bring about some act through an agreement with the Devil' (Jean Bodin, cited in Robbins 1976: 17).

Belief in demons (and/or 'fallen angels') is ancient but the linking of *maleficium*, 'magical wrong-doing', to a pact or contract is the distinguishing factor, the taxic indicator, of the fifteenth- to seventeenth-century great witch craze. This element in itself inspired churchmen to great efforts to eradicate by burning and hanging what they might otherwise have fought with education and the techniques of the confessional. This, at least, is my reading of Ruth Martin's discussion on witchcraft in Venice (Martin 1989).

Was the pact derived from the Bible? Despite Noth's claim that biblical sorcery meant 'trafficking with strange divine powers' none of the texts noted above contains such an idea. However, just as interpreters distinguished between the 'magic' of the magicians and the 'miracles' of Moses and Aaron, so they refused the clear sense of 2 Samuel that the medium of En-dor called up Samuel. Instead they explained, or more often asserted, that a spirit appearing to be Samuel spoke. I cannot find any clear point at which the doctrine of the pact began or spread. Though its popularity may be due to Augustine, there are earlier texts, for example the story of Theophilus (see Flint 1991: 344-47). There is a consensus that the pact is a scholarly import into popular beliefs about witches. I suspect, though I cannot prove it here, that the origins of the pact are to be found in wider scholarly and theological sophistication in European Christianity. The pact is just one of the developments in the thinking of the Church. It rapidly became very popular and very deadly for many people, mostly women.

There are also indications that some aspects, at least, of the Church's attack on 'witches' gained much from its more general and more lasting opposition to Judaism. Witches gathered in regular 'sabbats', originally called 'synagogues', frequently on a Friday night, they mocked the Mass in particular and Christianity in general (Cohn 1975). Accusations of poisoning, child-sacrifice and cannibalism were made against the Jews long before (and after) the great witch craze. (These accusations are still being made; for example, in spring 1994, a letter repeating them was sent to many addresses in north London.) Again, such accusations (not only against Jews) are not unique to Christian polemics: the earliest evidence I can find is of Antiochus IV Epiphanes' accusation against the Jews (Russell & Wyndham 1976; Russell 1984: 48). But it is in Christian polemics that they found greatest authority and had their greatest, most devastating effect. This was possible as the more lurid accusations fit easily with the 'hard sayings' of foundational Christian texts, such as

Rev. 2.9-11; 3.9 and Jn 8.31, 44 (Jones 1993). What the Bible did contribute to this incitement to hatred of witches and Jews is support. Exod. 22.17 supports the popular stereotype of the witch as female.

The Requirement to Execute Witches

The Bible is not the source of the image of the witch, nor of the full doctrine of the pact with the devil. It is not the only source of the death penalty for witchcraft. It is, however, the ultimate authority referred to by those who were most enthusiastic about the hunt for and attempt to exterminate 'witches' in Europe. Unless I have accidentally skipped a page the 'classic' text of the great witch craze, the *Malleus Maleficarum* does not cite Exod. 22.17 in support of its claimed need to kill 'witches'. It refers rather to Deuteronomy 18 (going so far as to allege that this passage says, 'all wizards and charmers are to be destroyed') and Leviticus 19 and 20. The *Malleus Maleficarum* is certain too that women are more susceptible than men to the devil's seductions, not because Exodus stresses the gender of 'the sorceress' but because the Bible has convinced the writers that women were weaker in resisting temptation (and probably quicker in enjoying sin). In this non-usage of Exod. 22.17, however, the *Malleus Maleficarum* must be almost unique in its time.

When people doubted the existence of witches, or raised objections to some of the more outlandish accusations, the Bible was quoted against them as absolute proof that witches must be believed to exist. Denial of such belief, though dangerous, had to be couched as biblical interpretation (Filmer 1653; *Discourse* 1736). (I am grateful to Jonathan Thompson, a student in Newcastle University's Religious Studies Department, who let me see a copy of the *Discourse* which is a family heirloom.)

I should note, before concluding this section, that earlier Christian writers had read Exod. 22.17 very differently. Peters discusses the twelfth-century *glossa ordinaria* of the Bible in which the *maleficos* of Exodus are

> those who use the illusions of the magic art and of the devil. They are heretics. They should be separated from the community of the faithful, which is true life. They are to be excommunicated so that their error will die with them (Peters 1978: 68).

This, refusal of livelihood and spiritual death, may be the intention of Exod. 22.17 rather than, as read during the great witch craze, the 'extermination out of the land' (Childs 1974: 241) or crusade that was then attempted.

The Modern Satanism Scare

The contemporary satanism scare has caused considerable suffering to many people. It has cost the police and the courts considerable amounts of money and time. It has not uncovered any evidence to support the claims and allegations that there is an international conspiracy of child-abusing, child-sacrificing devil-worshippers who are engaged in a war against Christianity, god and decency. The most useful discussions of this issue are in the volume edited by James Richardson, Joel Best and David Bromley (1991). Jean La Fontaine has recently concluded her research into the allegations about satanic abuse in Britain (1994). Despite these (and other works) some people continue to assert that the satanic conspiracy does exist, that satanists and witches are abusing and murdering children and the homeless, and that society is being corrupted through the media, education, feminism and music among other means.

In my review of Richardson, Best and Bromley I wondered whether 'perhaps there are no real Satanists' (Harvey 1992: 290). I now know that there are indeed people in Britain who name themselves 'Satanists'. What they mean by this is, however, far from what most people, especially most evangelical Christians mean by 'Satanist'. My research into several of these groups (the Temple of Set, the Church of Satan and the Order of the Nine Angles) (Harvey forthcoming) notes again what I have said elsewhere (Harvey 1995): there is no evidence that these people or any others are involved in a satanic conspiracy or that the crimes alleged by believers in such a conspiracy have ever taken place.

Clearly child (sexual) abuse takes place. It happens most often in families: parents (usually fathers) or relatives (usually uncles or brothers) abuse their children (usually daughters, sisters or nieces). The semantics of abuse are interesting (though disturbing): what was once named 'incest' is now acknowledged to be 'abuse'. Jokes about 'keeping it in the family' are no longer so acceptable. There is also a problem with the word 'ritual' in this context. The phrase 'ritual abuse' is another way of saying 'satanic abuse'. As to the choice of which phrase to use, it seems to me that those who make the allegations have realized that trying to bring Satan into court is not necessarily going to help their case. The vague but sinister sounding 'ritual abuse' is far more effective. It has associations with all the long history of this sort of accusation. The nefarious activities of Jews, Communists, Catholics, Mormons, Masons and Witches are evoked. I hope it is not really necessary to note that not one of the many accusations of child-abuse and sacrifice alleged against any of these groups has produced evidence of the sort normally required by secular courts. We are dealing with scares and polemics not with real crimes.

What is the role of the Bible in all this? Once again it is ambiguous. The Bible permits, even demands, belief in demons, Satan, conflict between heaven and hell. It demands belief in the wickedness of humanity. It permits the demand for strong action against 'witches' and other malefactors. Never, however, does it describe exactly the same strange activities as the current accusers. The Bible alone would not lead us to examine LPs for backwards recorded subliminal messages. It would not lead us to expect Satan's prime objectives to include the manufacture of toys and films with 'occult' symbolism (as is alleged to be the case with the Smurfs, Care-Bears, Star Wars and many other seemingly innocent expressions of the modern world).

Perhaps we should not be surprised that feminism is implicated in the current scare. Here we return to the centralizing of gender seen in the Bible, Qumran, Rabbinic commentators and Christian Inquisitors. The link with idolatry (and perhaps 'foreignness') in biblical 'witchcraft' passages is explicitly present in some evangelical writings about the New Age and Inter-faith dialogue, both allegedly dependent on satanic inspiration (Gassmann 1991; Reachout Trust 1993). To speak of the divinity, even the Christian one, as 'mother' or 'goddess' or 'she' is an attempt to return the Church to the Pagan past. How much worse then is actual Paganism?

What is central to the modern scare is its stress on the family as the locus of satanic evil-doing. Neither the Bible nor previous witch-hunts demand this. It is arguable that the family is the place where all the tensions of the modern world are played out. The family (whatever that might mean exactly) is a place of tension because of the changes in society. If allegations of 'witchcraft' arise at times of tension and change then it is not surprising that they find their most emotive force in those places or institutions most privileged (emotionally, spiritually, culturally, financially) in any society. We do not want to admit that families are frequently places of danger, for women and children in particular, but we have discovered that child (sexual) abuse is far more common than we thought. Instead of dealing with this unpleasant fact, many people have found comfort in the belief that there is a satanically inspired attack on the family. It is not 'normal' parents who abuse their children because that is their source of sexual pleasure and/or the expression of their power, but 'strangers' with weird, 'occult' intentions. This can be seen in the speech of Geoffrey Dickens MP (Hansard 132: 485-88; 27 April 1989) and many of the books, tracts and speeches made by evangelical Christians.

Another factor that has enabled the current scare to spread has been the fact that a growing number of people name themselves 'Witches' and even more people use the self-designation 'Pagan'. A handful of people, with very different beliefs to Pagans and Witches, name themselves 'Satanists'. Child-abuse, sacrifice, anti-Christianity and other aspects of the scare picture of a 'witch' have no role in the spirituality of these people. There may, of course, be Pagans who abuse children, just as there are Christians who do so. This should not lead to the assertion that such abuse is part of the definition or expression of either spirituality.

Conclusion

The 'witchcraft' passages are among the texts of terror (Trible 1978), the 'hard sayings' (Jones 1993) of the Bible. At the centre of their power is the fact that they do not provide enough information to identify exactly what a 'sorceress' is, or does. They are not culturally or historically specific. They are applicable to any number of situations or people. The 'witch' of any society is a composite and complex stereotype, though always (except in the self-understanding of modern self-identified witches) a negative one. The biblical injunction to deny life to the 'sorceress' has predisposed many people to treat the accused in unheralded ways. In the sixteenth and seventeenth centuries it was permitted to torture accused witches, to listen to children's evidence against them, and to execute them on evidence considered inadmissible in other situations. In recent years children have been removed from homes in night raids on the evidence of a half-heard garbled report that a child has said something strange. Parents who wear pentagrams have had to explain themselves to unsympathetic if not hostile police officers. This is not because the Bible is the source for every police officer's understanding of crime. It is, however, one root of the predisposition of our society to believe in 'occult crime'. It is also central to the belief system of those people who are most interested in the allegations of satanic ritual abuse: those who make the allegations and organize the training courses. There is no evidence that their allegations are correct, but there was no evidence that Antiochus Epiphanes' allegations were correct. All they have is their belief, partly inspired and certainly supported by, the biblical passages against witchcraft which have caused so much suffering to 'witches' and, more recently, children. It is often said, 'there is no smoke without fire'. The question has to be asked, 'who is lighting the pyre?'

BIBLIOGRAPHY

Ahituv, S.
1971 'Divination', *Encyclopaedia Judaica* 6: 111-16.

Baroja, J.C.
1964 *The World of the Witches* (trans. N. Glendinning; London: Weidenfeld & Nicolson).

Barstow, A.L.
1988 'On Studying Witchcraft as Women's History: A Historiography of the European Witch Persecutions', *Journal of Feminist Studies in Religion* 4: 7-19.

Baumgarten, J.M.
1991 'On the Nature of the Seductress in 4Q184', *Revue de Qumran* 15: 131-43.

Berkhout, C.T., and J.B. Russell
1981 *Medieval Heresies: a bibliography 1960-1979* (Toronto: Pontifical Institute of Mediaeval Studies).

Bowker, J.
1987 *Licensed Insanities: Religions and Belief in God in the Contemporary World* (London: Darton, Longman and Todd).

Cashman, H.
1993 *Christianity and Child Sexual Abuse* (London: SPCK).

Cassuto, U.
1967 *A Commentary on the Book of Exodus* (Jerusalem: Magnes Press).

Childs, B.S.
1974 *Exodus* (London: SCM).

Clines, D.J.A.
1993 'ob', *The Dictionary of Classical Hebrew*, I (Sheffield: JSOT Press).

Cohn, N.
1975 *Europe's Inner Demons: An Inquiry Inspired by the Great Witch-Hunt* (London: Chatto-Heinemann).

Cohn, H.H.
1971 'Sorcery', *Encyclopaedia Judaica* 15: 163-64.

Dan, Y.
1971 'Magic', *Encyclopaedia Judaica* 11: 703-15.

Day, J.
1987 *Molech* (Cambridge: Cambridge University Press).

Dellasega, M.
1990 'Witches and Women: Performance Choices for Macbeth', *The Shakespeare Newsletter* 40.1: 9.

Discourse
1736 *A Discourse on Witchcraft occasioned by a bill now depending in Parliament.*

Douglas, M.
1966 *Purity and Danger: An Analysis of the Concepts of Pollution and Taboo* (1991 repr.: Routledge and Kegan Paul).

Douglas, M. (ed.)
1970 *Witchcraft Confessions and Accusations* (Ass. Social Anthropology Monogr., vol 9; London: Tavistock).

Duff, J.D. (ed.)
1928 *Lucan* (Loeb Classical Library; London: Heinemann).

Evans-Pritchard, E.E.
1929 'The Morphology and Function of Magic: A Comparative Study of Trobriand and Zande Ritual and Spell', *American Anthropologist* 31: 619-41.
1937 *Witchcraft, Oracles and Magic among the Azande* (Oxford: Clarendon Press, 2nd edn)

Filmer, R.
1653 *An Advertisement to the Jury-men of England touching Witches* (repr. 1975; Exeter: The Rota).

Fishbane, M., and E. Tov
1992 *'Sha'arei Talmon': Studies in the Bible, Qumran and Ancient Near East Presented to Shemaryahu Talmon* (Winona Lake, IN: Eisenbrauns).

Flint, V.
1991 *The Rise of Magic in Early Medieval Europe* (Oxford: Clarendon Press).

Gassmann, L.
1991 'Occultism, Eastern Religions and the New Age Movement', *Gospel* 1: 17-29 and 3: 65-83.

Ginzburg, C.
1983 *The Night Battles: Witchcraft & Agrarian Cults in the Sixteenth and Seventeenth Centuries* (London: Routledge and Kegan Paul).

Gordon, C.H.
1992 ' "This time" (Genesis 2.23)', in Fishbane and Tov 1992: 47-51.

Gruen, E.S.
1968 *Roman Politics and the Criminal Courts 149—78 BC* (Cambridge, MA: Harvard University Press).
1974 *The Last Generation of the Roman Republic* (University of California Press).

Harvey, G.
1992 Review of Richardson, Bromley and Best (1991), *Religion* 22: 290-91.

1995 'Ritual Abuse Allegations, Incitement to Religious Hatred', in *New Religions and the New Europe* (ed. R. Towler; Aarhus: Aarhus University Press), 154-170.

forthcoming 'Satanism in Modern Britain'.

Heider, G.A.

1985 *The Cult of Molek* (JSOTSup, 43; Sheffield: JSOT Press).

Jones, G.L.

1993 *Hard Sayings: Difficult New Testament Texts for Jewish-Christian Dialogue* (London: Council of Christians and Jews).

Kramer, H., Sprenger, J.

1486? *Malleus Malleficarum* (trans. M. Summers; London: Arrow Books, 1971).

Kuemmerlin-McClean, J.K.

1992 'Magic (OT)', *Anchor Bible Dictionary* 4: 486-71.

La Fontaine, J.

1994 *Extent and Nature/Organized and Ritual Abuse/Research Finding (Summary)* Department of Health

1994 *Extent and Nature/Organized Ritual Sexual Abuse of Children (Report)* Department of Health

Levenson, J.D.

1993 *The Death and Resurrection of the Beloved Son: The Transformation of Child Sacrifice in Judaism and Christianity* (New Haven & London: Yale University Press).

Lewis, I.M.

1986 *Religion in Context: Cults and Charisma* (Cambridge: Cambridge University Press).

1989 *Ecstatic Religion: A Study of Shamanism and Spirit Possession* (London: Routledge, 2nd rev. edn).

Luck, G.

1985 *Arcana Mundi: Magic and the Occult in the Greek and Roman Worlds* (Baltimore: Johns Hopkins University Press).

Luhrmann, T.

1989 *Persuasions of the Witch's Craft: Ritual Magic in Contemporary England* (Cambridge, MA: Harvard University Press).

Martin, R.

1989 *Witchcraft and the Inquisition in Venice 1550—1650* (Oxford: Blackwell).

Marwick, M. (ed.)

1970 *Witchcraft and Sorcery* (Harmondsworth: Penguin).

McCasland, S.V.

1962 'Magi', *IDB* 3: 221-23.

Mendelsohn, I.

1962 ''Magic', *IDB* 3: 223-25.

1962 'Divination', *IDB* 1: 856-58.

Merzbacher, F.

1966 'Witchcraft', *New Catholic Encyclopedia* 14: 977-79.

Middleton, J.

1987 'Magic', *Encyclopedia of Religion* 4: 81-89.

Milgrom, J.
1990 *Numbers: The JPS Commentary* (Philadelphia/Jerusalem: Jewish Publication Society).

Neusner, J., E.S. Frerichs, and P.V. Flesher
1992 *Religion, Science and Magic* (Oxford: Oxford University Press).

Noth, M.
1962 *Exodus: A Commentary* (London: SCM Press).

Palsson, G.
1991 'The Name of the Witch: Sagas, Sorcery and Social Context', in Samson 1991: 157-68.

Peters, E.
1978 *The Magician, the Witch and the Law* (Hassocks: Harvester Press).

Potter, H.
1993 *Hanging in Judgment: Religion and the Death Penalty in England* (London: SCM Press).

Rabbinowitz, L.I.
1971 'Divination', *Encyclopaedia Judaica* 6: 116-18.

Reachout Trust
1993 'The New Age'.

Richardon, J.T., J. Best, and D.G. Bromley
1991 *The Satanism Scare* (Berlin: de Gruyter).

Robbins, H.R.
1978 *Witchcraft: An Introduction to the Literature of Witchcraft* (Millwood, NY: KTO Press).

Russell, J.B.
1972 *Witchcraft in the Middle Ages* (Ithaca, NY: Cornell University Press).
1984 *Lucifer: The Devil in the Middle Ages* (Ithaca, NY: Cornell University Press).
1987 'Witchcraft', *Encyclopedia of Religion* 15: 415-23.
1980 *A History of Witchcraft, Sorcerers, Heretics and Pagans* (London: Thames & Hudson).

Russell, J.B., and M.W. Wyndham
1976 'Witchcraft and the Demonization of Heresy', *Mediaevalia* 2: 1-21.

Samson, R. (ed.)
1991 *Social Approaches to Viking Studies* (Glasgow: Cruithne).

Sarna, N.M.
1991 *Exodus: The JPS Commentary* (Philadelphia/Jerusalem: Jewish Publication Society).

Scott, R.
1584 *Discoverie of Witchcraft* (ed. M. Summers; London: Rodker, 1930).

Summers, M.
1928 *Introduction and translation of Malleus Maleficarum* (London: Rodker).

Thomas, K.
1971 *Religion and the Decline of Magic* (Harmondsworth: Penguin).

Trevor-Roper, H.R.
1969 *The European Witch-craze of the Sixteenth and Seventeenth Centuries and Other Essays* (Harmondsworth: Penguin).

Trible, P.
1984 *Texts of Terror: Literary Feminist Readings of Biblical Narratives* (Philadelphia: Fortress).

WHAT DOES 'DEUTERONOMISTIC' MEAN?

Richard Coggins

Half a century ago 'Deuteronomy' and 'Deuteronomic' were words applied in biblical studies either specifically to the book of Deuteronomy, or to the proposed Pentateuchal source D. In practice the difference between the two usages was not great, for in most versions of Pentateuchal criticism D was largely confined to the book of Deuteronomy. Even as recently as 1951 the well-known survey of current developments in Old Testament scholarship, *The Old Testament and Modern Study*, contained just one index reference to the Deuteronomic history work (Rowley 1951: 374).

Today all is changed. The additional adjective 'Deuteronomistic' has been coined, and its influence is all-pervasive. Elsewhere in this volume Graeme Auld refers to Deuteronomism (*sic*) as 'an internationally traded currency'. I myself wrote recently that 'the Deuteronomists have sometimes been praised or blamed for virtually every significant development within ancient Israel's religious practice', and tried to warn against the danger of 'pan-Deuteronomism' (Coggins 1993: 85). The problem has been steadily increasing. Not just the book of Deuteronomy and the Pentateuchal source D (if a four-document hypothesis relating to the Pentateuch is still accepted), but also the Former Prophets, Joshua–2 Kings, the editing of Jeremiah, the editing of other pre-exilic prophetic collections (?Amos ?Hosea ?Parts of Isaiah ?a major part of the book of the Twelve) can all be attributed to the work of Deuteronomists. In addition Deuteronomistic influence is claimed for or detected in practically every part of the Hebrew Bible, so that one may note with an element of surprise that the books of Job or Ecclesiastes are said to be free from, or perhaps are only rebelling against, Deuteronomistic influence or tendencies. When a word or a concept has taken over so much of our thought it seems only right to pause and explore its appropriate meaning; is it as pervasive as at first appears? Is the orthodoxy of ancient Israelite religion really laid down along Deuteronomistic lines, as has recently been claimed (Barker 1987: 142-60; 1992: 12-18)? What in practice do we mean when we use the term Deuteronomistic? In what follows a number of references will be made to recent authors and contemporary usage; it should be understood that these are intended only as illustrative, rather than as offering negative judgments upon the books and articles referred to. It is a pleasure to dedicate these rather puzzled reflections to John Sawyer, who throughout his professional career has been insistent on ensuring that the words we use really do mean what we think they mean and are not suffering from some hidden external system of judgment.

I

Deuteronomic and Deuteronomistic. One bone of contention can probably be removed quite quickly. There has been dispute as to whether we need two adjectives at all, and some scholars have suggested that 'Deuteronomistic' is an unnecessary coinage. But the sheer prevalence of the usage would suggest that two words are necessary, one to describe that which pertains specifically to the book of Deuteronomy, the other more general, to denote the influence or thought-forms associated with the work of the Deuteronomists and expressed more widely and diffusely in the literature. The usage followed in this essay will largely be dependent on that of the particular authors being referred to; no element of consistency can as yet be detected.

II

An issue that is often discussed, but from which no satisfactory conclusions are reached, is that of dating. Once again the conventional wisdom used to be relatively straightforward (Nicholson 1967: 58-82). Northern origins could be traced in Deuteronomy, through its sceptical view of kingship, its understanding of prophets as 'covenant mediators', its links with Hosea, and its use of 'love' terminology rather than the terminology associated with the Jerusalem tradition. It was thought likely, therefore, that, following the fall of the Northern Kingdom in 722/21, religious leaders had fled to the South, and had encapsulated their ideas in what would later become the book of Deuteronomy, but had been forced to hide the results because of the persecution under Manasseh.

Only in the new atmosphere brought about by Josiah's reform was it safe for them to bring those ideas out into the open. On such an understanding as this Deuteronomy—or at least its nucleus—was clearly pre-exilic: certainly no later than the seventh century, when the law-book was discovered, and perhaps significantly earlier, if the northern connection were taken seriously.

But then problems arose. The theory of a Deuteronomistic History, as the appropriate description for the books Joshua–2 Kings, first propounded by M. Noth in 1943 (ET 1991) has won all but universal acceptance, and this brings the dating down to the middle of the sixth century, since the last event referred to is Jehoiachin's restoration to at least partial favour at the Babylonian court (2 Kgs 25.27-30). Now we have to assume that the Deuteronomists survived for some 60 years at least after the discovery of the law-book under Josiah. For Noth the concept was still manageable, since he was convinced that one editor was responsible for the whole of the Deuteronomistic History, and he suggested that the final verses of 2 Kgs 25.27-30, were added by the Deuteronomist 'from his own knowledge' (Noth 1991: 117). But for the most part this view of unitary authorship is the one aspect of Noth's thesis which has not been accepted. Instead there have arisen various theories of levels of Deuteronomistic redaction which can be traced in the Deuteronomistic History, and that has led to proposed dates even further into the sixth century as the most likely background.

Two main types of proposal have been put forward. On the one hand, and largely in the USA, F.M. Cross and his pupils have suggested that the basic form of Joshua–2 Kings is pre-exilic, but that it underwent a further redaction during the period of the exile. Alternatively, and this time mainly in Europe, those who have followed R. Smend have taken the view that the whole work is essentially exilic, and that particular prophetic and 'nomistic' redactions (DtrP and DtrN) took place at a later stage. Thus, to give but one example of many that could be put forward, J. Vermeylen has claimed to detect three redactional levels which he identifies as 'Dtr 575', 'Dtr 560' and 'Dtr 525', the numbers referring to the dates of supposed activity (Vermeylen 1986: 123-27). (A very useful summary of the main views of the development of the Deuteronomistic History is provided by Provan 1988: 2-31.)

Difficulties have also arisen in assessing our knowledge of the earlier stages of this movement. In many reconstructions of the history of Israel, Josiah's reform and the discovery of the law-book have been taken as fixed points which could be relied upon where much else was controverted. But is this as firmly based as is sometimes assumed? We need not doubt that Josiah, rejoicing in new-found opportunities of showing his independence of Assyrian control, engaged in a religious reform which cleared his cultic places of what were deemed to be alien practices. But the story of the finding of the law-book, as has often been noted, fits somewhat awkwardly into the overall account. Could it be that this is an editorial construct, aimed in part at least at providing an acceptable contrast in behaviour over against the wicked Jehoiakim, who when he was confronted with a scroll rent the scroll (Jer. 36)? Josiah by contrast rent his garments and showed himself a model of deuteronomistic piety. Parallels also exist between the account of Josiah's reaction to the words of the Torah and the picture offered in Nehemiah 8 of Ezra reading from the Torah to the assembled congregation. How much in all of this is ideology and how much history must remain open to further scrutiny. The survey by Ahlström seems not to be wholly self-consistent, as the existence of a scroll at the time of Josiah appears to be sometimes affirmed, sometimes denied, but his work still offers a valuable introduction to the problems posed by the account in 2 Kings 22–23 (Ahlström 1993: 772-77).

Whatever conclusion we reach in these matters, the fact remains that the exilic and even post-exilic periods are now regarded as the age at which Deuteronomistic influence was at its height. Thus R.F. Person, writing on Zechariah 9–14, is concerned to show that 'the Deuteronomistic school', defined as 'a scribal guild active in the exilic and post-exilic periods' was responsible for the final redaction of those chapters, commonly regarded as among the latest additions to the prophetic corpus. He devotes the first part of his study, entitled 'Deuteronomic Redaction in the Post-Exilic Period', to establishing that traces of Deuteronomic redactional activity can be found in the post-exilic period, and affects books generally regarded as post-exilic in origin. His argument is based both on specific textual usage and on themes regarded as characteristically Deuteronomic (Person 1993: 40-78). This concentration on the 'post-exilic' period has been a feature of much Hebrew Bible study in recent years. Thus, for example, P.R. Davies's search for 'Ancient Israel' has led him to conclude that much of the material once regarded as embodying ancient traditions was the product of 'scribal schools' and may be as late as the third century. As he rightly sees, it then becomes almost meaningless to talk of a

'Deuteronomistic history', a usage which he suggests should be abandoned (Davies 1992: 131).

We thus find ourselves confronted with dates ranging from the eighth to the third centuries as the suggested period in which Deuteronomistic influence was at its height. (All this, of course, is purely within the range of critical scholarship; if we include within our consideration conservatives who claim to detect signs of traditions going back to Moses himself that will of course extend the range of possible dates still more widely.) Yet of so wide-ranging and influential a movement there is no external evidence of any kind; the whole history of tradition has to be worked out by inference. Deuteronomistic influence may be traced; but there is still no agreement as to who the Deuteronomists were.

III

It is scarcely possible, in an essay of this kind, to enter in detail into the discussions as to the identity of the Deuteronomists. As is well known three views have been particularly influential: that the Deuteronomists were Levites (von Rad 1953: 60-69); that they were part of, or heirs to, the prophetic tradition (Nicholson 1967: 58ff.); or that they were to be associated with wisdom schools (Weinfeld 1972: 260-74). It is noteworthy that all these theories were proposed in work from at least twenty years ago; more recently the tendency has been simply to take the Deuteronomists on their own terms, as it were, and to decline to identify them with some other group known to us in ancient Israel. Thus R.E. Clements (1989: 79) suggests that the most precise designation possible is to call them 'a "Reforming Party" with members drawn from more than one group'. The view of R.E. Friedman, that the Deuteronomist was an individual, either the Baruch of the book of Jeremiah, or 'a collaboration, with Jeremiah, the poet and prophet, as the inspiration, and Baruch the scribe' (Friedman 1988: 147), has not been taken up to the best of my knowledge, and is rebutted by Clements (1989: 77).

Reference to 'schools' has proved another potent source of confusion. Sometimes the 'Deuteronomistic School' is used in terms which imply something analogous to an institution, as in Weinfeld's reference to 'wisdom schools'. (Here again we have the problem of the complete lack of any direct reference to such 'schools'.) But often 'school' seems to mean little more than what we might term a 'school of thought'—a particular mode of expression, a particular theological stance, which is widely found and then described as 'Deuteronomistic'.

IV

Reference has just been made to the supposedly massive programme of redaction in which the Deuteronomists are supposed to have engaged. In what follows no attempt is made to be exhaustive; the quotations are given in an illustrative way, to show something of the range of alleged Deuteronomistic literary influence on the Hebrew Bible as it has come down to us.

One can begin at the beginning, with the Pentateuch. In the older days of the four-document hypothesis the amount of D redaction in the first four books was always regarded as minimal; S.R. Driver, for example, analysed the material in Genesis–Numbers, attributing sections to J, E and P, but without leaving any room for a significant input from D (Driver 1913). More recently, however, theories of a much more elaborate Deuteronomistic contribution have been put forward. Thus R. Rendtorff identifies a 'whole series of texts dealing with the events of the exodus from Egypt, Sinai, and the beginning of the occupation of the land which refer back to the patriarchal story, and especially to the promise of the land to the patriarchs'. All of these, in his view, are 'stamped with deuteronomic language' (Rendtorff 1990: 194-95). This understanding has been developed further by Rendtorff's sometime pupil, E. Blum, who claims that beneath the present form of the Pentateuch one can detect a Deuteronomistic level of redaction (K^D in his terminology, standing for D-Komposition). In this the different older traditions were shaped into a history stretching forward from Abraham. On Blum's view this was a product of the early post-exilic period (Blum 1990: 7-218).

Working in greater detail on a smaller block of material, W. Johnstone has isolated Deuteronomistic cycles of 'signs' and 'wonders' in Exodus 1–13 (Johnstone 1993: 166-85). This takes further an approach he had already adumbrated in outline in his earlier work, where a D version of Exodus was proposed and its characteristic theological concerns set out (Johnstone 1990: 105-10). Similarly L. Perlitt, in his investigation of the origins of the notion of covenant, had already identified a later part of Exodus, chs. 32–34, as essentially a Deuteronomistic composition (Perlitt 1969: 203-32). The whole theme has indeed been taken further by

S. Boorer, who explains in her introduction to the discussion of the theme of the promise of the land in the Pentateuch that she uses the symbol 'Dtr' to 'refer broadly and loosely to any text in Deuteronomic/ Deuteronomistic style' (Boorer 1992: 3). She also draws attention to the practice of Rendtorff, who, as we have seen, speaks of Dtr texts in Genesis–Numbers, without specifying their relation to Deuteronomy itself. Instead he spoke in more general terms of a 'Deuteronomistic school' or 'Deuteronomic-Deuteronomistic circles' (Boorer 1992: 31).

That the books Joshua–2 Kings owe their existing shape to Deuteronomistic editing, so that it is proper to describe them as forming a Deuteronomistic History, has now become part of the received wisdom of Hebrew Bible scholarship, and detailed support for this understanding need not be offered, though Davies's reservations, already mentioned, should be borne in mind. Similarly, among the prophets the presence of a substantial amount of Deuteronomistic editing in the present form of the book of Jeremiah is now widely accepted, and scarcely needs documentation. With the other prophetic collections this Deuteronomistic influence is less widely recognized, yet, as already noted in the introduction, has come to be quite widely proposed. Thus, for Isaiah, Vermeylen's detailed study of the growth of the whole Isaiah tradition, from the figure of the prophet himself down to the apocalyptic imagery of the later parts of the work, led him to find a significant place for Deuteronomistic editing. Many passages which had traditionally been considered as emanating from the prophet himself were regarded as later. Thus, the analysis of the 'Song of the Vineyard' in Isa. 5.1-7 is held to show features which are best explained as arising from a Deuteronomistic milieu at the time of the exile (Vermeylen 1977: 168).

Ezekiel, too, has entered into this discussion. Whereas much older scholarship was sceptical as to any links between Ezekiel and the broad stream of Deuteronomistic tradition, there have been recent writers who see closer links. Thus R.R. Wilson maintains that, while 'it is not possible to isolate a specifically Deuteronomic editorial layer', the theology of the book as a whole has 'Deuteronomic features' (Wilson 1980: 284).

When we turn to the Minor Prophets the issue of Deuteronomistic redaction is very much a matter of current debate. It has long been noted that the books of Hosea, Amos, Micah and Zephaniah all have similar introductory verses, in which the activity of the prophet is associated with the reign of a particular king or kings. Since we know of those kings mainly through the books of Kings, and since the books of Kings are part of the Deuteronomistic History, it is natural to regard these four books as having undergone Deuteronomistic redaction, offering them as an alternative and expanded version of the story being unfolded in the books of Kings, even though the lack of reference to them in 2 Kings remains an unexplained puzzle. This has been worked out in considerable detail by J. Nogalski, as part of his reconstruction of the editorial process underlying the complete 'Book of the Twelve'. While acknowledging the 'tentative' nature of this proposal of a Deuteronomistic corpus consisting of Hosea, Amos, Micah and Zephaniah, he nevertheless concludes that 'the language and perspective of this corpus bears signs of Deuteronomistic theology and the use of both Northern and Southern traditions in creating a historical compendium of prophecy' (Nogalski 1993: 278). This point is taken a stage further by T. Collins, in his redaction-critical study of the prophetic corpus. For him, it is not only that 'the theology of those responsible for producing [the final text of the Twelve] was broadly in line with that of the Deuteronomist writers', but also some of its later parts 'were written with an eye to the Deuteronomist theology in general, like Malachi, or to the Deuteronomist view of prophecy in particular' (Collins 1993: 62).

This perception of Deuteronomistic influence is not, however, confined to the introductory verses of these collections. In Hosea and Amos in particular, more detailed traces of deuteronomistic influence are often claimed. Thus, for Hosea, N.P. Lemche argues that 'the religious message of the book is not far removed from Deuteronomistic theology', and goes on to 'counter the accusation of "pan-Deuteronomism" by showing how the Deuteronomists themselves tried to monopolize the religious expression of early Judaism' (Lemche 1992: 255). The conclusion reached by G.A. Yee, in a detailed study of the way in which the book of Hosea reached its final form, is that the final redaction took place in Deuteronomistic circles. She traces two levels of redaction, the first 'very steeped in deuteronomistic ideology', the second also betraying a 'deuteronomistic orientation', but dating from a later period, when the exile had become a reality (Yee 1987: 308-309). The notion of being 'steeped in deuteronomistic ideology' is a point to which we shall need to return.

With Amos the emphasis has been on particular expressions as characteristically Deuteronomistic rather than larger claims for the whole thrust of the theology of the book. Thus, to give but two examples, the condemnation of Judah with its reference to the *torah* of Yahweh and his 'statutes' (*ḥuqqayw*) (Amos 2.4), and that to 'his servants the prophets' (3.7) are commonly held to be characteristic Deuteronomistic vocabulary.

V

Reference to 'his servants the prophets' invites consideration of yet another area in which the influence of the Deuteronomists in shaping our perceptions has been claimed. R.P. Carroll maintains that our understanding of prophets as those who speak the divine word, who must be listened to and obeyed, is essentially a Deuteronomistic one (Carroll 1992: 90). At this point it becomes difficult to be certain whether we are meant to think of a particular group of people, identifiable in principle as 'Deuteronomists', who successfully imposed this radical shift of perception, or whether the reference is rather in more general terms to the spiritual and intellectual climate of the period of early Judaism, when the search for identity and for the causes of the transformation which had affected the community could broadly be described as 'Deuteronomistic'. This is the same issue as that raised by the terms in which Yee describes the reaction of Hosea: her expression, it will be recalled, was that the process was 'steeped in deuteronomistic ideology', and this more naturally refers to a climate of thought than to a precise literary process of redaction. Similar questions arise with the well-known ascription by Perlitt of the importance of *b^{e}rith* (covenant) to Deuteronomistic influence; at times it is clear that he is engaged in precise analysis of distinctive vocabulary usage (Perlitt 1969: 8-30); elsewhere a much less specific ideological approach is more characteristic (Perlitt 1969: 54-128).

This uncertainty is what seems to me to underlie David Clines's judgment, expressed in a private communication, where he expresses doubts whether he believes in Deuteronomists at all. 'Maybe all the "Deuteronomic" language doesn't imply the existence of people called "Deuteronomists", but is just a kind of language', the kind that was thought especially appropriate for writing pompous religious prose. Parts of this are interestingly reminiscent of the argument used by J. Bright in his attempt to challenge the assumption of Deuteronomistic editorial activity in the shaping of the book of Jeremiah. Discussing the prose material in Jeremiah, he wrote that

> the style of these discourses, though indeed closely akin to that of the Deuteronomistic literature, is a style in its own right…; it is by no means glibly to be classified as 'Deuteronomistic'. It is moreover, not a late style, but a characteristic rhetorical prose of the seventh/sixth centuries (Bright 1965: lxxi).

The last point to raise relates to those parts of the Hebrew Bible where there are signs of revolt against the accepted norms of religious belief and practice; most obviously the books of Job and Ecclesiastes. Sometimes these works are seen as rebelling against the norms of the wisdom movement, as exemplified by the book of Proverbs. (And, of course, if the views of Weinfeld and others, that close links should be seen between Deuteronomy and Proverbs, are to be accepted, then what is implied is a rebellion against Deuteronomistic 'orthodoxy'.) But it has also not been uncommon to see Job's attitude to the question of suffering, in particular, as a rejection of 'the Deuteronomic doctrine of the rigid correlation of desert and fortune' (Rowley 1970: 22). Rowley saw this as an application at the individual level of what the Deuteronomists applied only to the nation, but it may be questioned whether a strictly individual reading of the book of Job is appropriate. Here once again we find belief in a generalized Deuteronomistic ideology shaping the character of Judaism's self-awareness. More generally, however, writers on Job and Ecclesiastes are cautious about defining what precisely is being rejected; instead, they concentrate rather on the viewpoint being expressed by their books, and only speak in more general terms about the Deuteronomistic character of Israel's understanding of its position before God.

VI

Perhaps enough has been said to illustrate the extreme diversity underlying contemporary scholarly usage of 'Deuteronomistic' and related terms. Reference was made at the beginning of this essay to *The Old Testament and Modern Study*. A contrast can be drawn between the views expressed there and those to be found in the successor volume, *Tradition and Interpretation*, in which the editor notes in his introductory essay that 'the range of its (Deuteronomy's) creative influence is seen as so extensive that it is not entirely out of place to speak of a pan-Deuteronomic phase in Old Testament study' (Anderson 1979: xix). In the same volume W. Zimmerli noted the urgency of the challenge 'to develop criteria more keenly developed for the phenomenon of "Deuteronomism", which certainly did not fall suddenly complete from heaven' (Zimmerli 1979: 380). J.R. Porter has raised important questions concerning the existence of a 'Deuteronomic school', as a notion which becomes 'more tenuous and vague' as its implications are examined in greater detail, and he goes on to identify as a danger 'the tendency to attribute almost all Israelite literary activity, from the period of Josiah to some time after the exile, to the Deuteronomic school, and thus to ignore the richness and variety of the religious expression in Judah during these years' (Porter 1989: 71).

The questions that Porter raises with regard to the specific question of the redaction of the prophetic collections can, it seems, be extended a good deal further. We need to balance his perfectly legitimate reference to 'richness and variety' with the recognition that there were ideological pressures at work to impose a particular view of Israel's past, of its relation with its God, of the meaning of the various events that had befallen it, culminating in the destruction of Jerusalem and the deportation of its leading citizens. It is obviously convenient to have some overall name by which to describe and refer to this ideological movement. Whether it is also convenient to describe it as 'Deuteronomistic' must be more open to question, for as we have seen there is then real danger of confusion. In short, it seems as if the use of the terms 'Deuteronomic' and 'Deuteronomistic' may have any one of at least three different implications. First, there is the long-established and traditional usage of that which relates to the book of Deuteronomy itself. Whether the theory of a Deuteronomistic History will continue to attract such widespread support, so that it can in effect be bracketed with this first usage, must be open to question: the points raised by Davies, suggesting a much later date of composition than has been customary, will need to be given fuller consideration than has so far been the case. Secondly, there is the much more disputed issue of Deuteronomistic redaction of other parts of the Hebrew Bible: possibly the remainder of the Pentateuch; more frequently substantial elements of the prophetic literature. Here Deuteronomistic influence is characteristically recognized because of distinctive vocabulary features, but as we have seen there is also a tendency to set down alongside this various ideological features which are regarded as distinctively Deuteronomistic. These should really be regarded as a third usage of the term.

That there is some linkage between these various usages is obvious enough; scholars have not simply applied the term 'Deuteronomistic' to them all in a wilful fashion without some justification. Nevertheless the question must be asked whether confusion is not being increased by applying the same description to what are essentially different phenomena. We need, it seems, to be clearer than we have often been in distinguishing between what can properly be said about a particular book and its immediately related congeners; what can be said by way of describing a literary process through which other pieces of literature reached their final form; and what can be said about an ideological movement which played a major part in shaping the self-understanding of Judaism. To use the same name for them all is to invite a breakdown in understanding.

BIBLIOGRAPHY

Ahlström, G.W.
1993 *The History of Ancient Palestine from the Palestinian Period to Alexander's Conquest* (JSOTSup 146; Sheffield: JSOT Press).

Anderson, G.W.
1979 *Tradition and Interpretation* (Oxford: Clarendon Press).

Barker, M.
1987 *The Older Testament* (London: SPCK).
1992 *The Great Angel* (London: SPCK).

Blum, E.
1990 *Studien zur Komposition des Pentateuch* (BZAW 189; Berlin: de Gruyter).

Boorer, S.
1992 *The Promise of the Land as Oath* (BZAW 205; Berlin: de Gruyter).

Bright, J.
1965 *Jeremiah* (AB 21; Garden City: Doubleday).

Carroll, R.P.
1992 'Co-opting the Prophets', in E. Ulrich, J.W. Wright, R.P. Carroll and P.R. Davies (eds.), *Priests, Prophets and Scribes. FS J. Blenkinsopp* (JSOTSup 149; Sheffield: JSOT Press).

Clements, R.E.
1989 *Deuteronomy* (Old Testament Guides; Sheffield: JSOT Press).

Coggins, R.J.
1993 'Prophecy—True and False' in H.A. McKay and D.J.A. Clines (eds.), *Of Prophets' Visions and the Wisdom of Sages. FS R.N. Whybray* (JSOTSup 162; Sheffield: JSOT Press).

Collins, T.
1993 *The Mantle of Elijah* (The Biblical Seminar 20; Sheffield: JSOT Press).

Davies, P.R.
1992 *In Search of 'Ancient Israel'* (JSOTSup 148; Sheffield: JSOT Press).

Driver, S.R.
1913 *An Introduction to the Literature of the Old Testament* (Edinburgh: T. & T. Clark, 9th edn).

Friedman, R.E.
1988 *Who wrote the Bible?* (London: Cape).

Johnstone, W.
1990 *Exodus* (Old Testament Guides; Sheffield: JSOT Press).
1993 'The Deuteronomistic Cycle of "Signs" and "Wonders" in Exodus 1–13', in A.G. Auld (ed.), *Understanding Poets and Prophets. FS G.W. Anderson* (JSOTSup 152; Sheffield: JSOT Press).

Lemche, N.P.
1992 'The God of Hosea', in E. Ulrich, J.W. Wright, R.P. Carroll and P.R. Davies (eds.), *Priests, Prophets and Scribes. FS J. Blenkinsopp* (JSOTSup 149; Sheffield: JSOT Press).

Nicholson, E.W.
1967 *Deuteronomy and Tradition* (Oxford: Blackwell).

Nogalski, J.
1993 *Literary Precursors to the Book of the Twelve* (BZAW 217; Berlin: de Gruyter).

Noth, M.
1991 *The Deuteronomistic History* (ET of *Überlieferungsgeschichtliche Studien* [1943], pp. 1-110) (JSOTSup 15; Sheffield: JSOT Press, 2nd edn).

Perlitt, L.
1969 *Bundestheologie im Alten Testament* (WMANT 36; Neukirchen–Vluyn: Neukirchener Verlag).

Person, R.F.
1993 *Second Zechariah and the Deuteronomic School* (JSOTSup 167; Sheffield: JSOT Press).

Porter, J.R.
1989 'The Supposed Deuteronomic Redaction of the Prophets', in R. Albertz, F.W. Golka and J. Kegler (eds.), *Schöpfung und Beifreiung* (Stuttgart: Calwer Verlag).

Provan, I.W.
1988 *Hezekiah and the Books of Kings* (BZAW 172; Berlin: de Gruyter).

von Rad, G.
1953 *Studies in Deuteronomy* (SBT 9; London: SCM Press).

Rendtorff, R.
1990 *The Problem of the Process of Transmission in the Pentateuch* (JSOTSup 89; Sheffield: JSOT Press).

Rowley, H.H. (ed.)
1951 *The Old Testament and Modern Study* (Oxford: Clarendon Press).

Rowley, H.H.
1970 *Job* (New Century Bible; London: Nelson).

Vermeylen, J.
1977 *Du prophète Isaïe à l'apocalyptique*, I (Paris: Gabalda).

1986 *Le Dieu de la promesse et le Dieu de l'alliance* (Lectio Divina 126; Paris: Cerf).

Weinfeld, M.

1972 *Deuteronomy and the Deuteronomic School* (Oxford: Clarendon Press).

Wilson, R.R.

1980 *Prophecy and Society in Ancient Israel* (Philadelphia: Fortress Press).

Yee, G.A.

1987 *Composition and Tradition in the Book of Hosea* (Atlanta: Scholars Press).

Zimmerli, W.

1979 'The History of Israelite Religion', in G.W. Anderson (ed.), *Tradition and Interpretation* (Oxford: Clarendon Press).

SOCIOLOGY OR HISTORY: TOWARDS A (HUMAN) HISTORY OF ANCIENT PALESTINE?*

Keith W. Whitelam

Introduction

The much vaunted paradigm shift in biblical studies has been attributed to two main factors: new literary studies and what has been described as the sociological approach.[1] The growing importance of social scientific approaches within biblical studies is testified to by the burgeoning literature, particularly handbooks, devoted to outlining its methods and applications: works such as J.W. Rogerson's *Anthropology and the Old Testament*, R.R. Wilson's *Sociological Approaches to the Old Testament*, A.D.H. Mayes's *The Old Testament in Sociological Perspective*, or the volume edited by R.E. Clements entitled *The World of Ancient Israel: Sociological, Anthropological and Political Perspectives*, along with countless articles in the major journals. Perhaps the most symbolic event of all was the election of Norman Gottwald to the presidency of SBL for 1992. It is tempting to suggest that all of this signals the movement of the so-called 'sociological approach' from the radical fringes of the discipline to a more central role in the creation of a 'new orthodoxy'.[2] It is precisely in the area of the reconstruction of Israelite history that this so-called sociological approach has had, perhaps, its most dramatic impact in recent years.[3] Despite the fact that it is

* This is a revision of a paper read to the Scottish-Scandinavian Conference in Glasgow, April 1993. I am grateful to Robert Coote and Niels Lemche for their constructive criticisms.

1. For the latest assessment of the paradigm shift and the role of social scientific approaches see Davies (1992: 11-16).
2. See Gunn's analysis (1987) of new literary studies as the 'new orthodoxy'.
3. See Mayes (1989) for a bibliography and assessment of social scientific approaches within biblical studies as a whole. The present paper, however, concentrates upon the impact of the 'sociological approach' for the reconstruction of Israelite history in particular.

generally recognized that the utilization of social scientific methods in biblical studies is not new but has a long history in the discipline with much of the pioneering work attributable to Scottish and Scandinavian scholars, such as William Robertson Smith, Sigmund Mowinckel, and Johannes Pedersen, among others,[4] the frequent use in recent works of phrases such as 'the sociological approach' or, on occasions, 'the sociological school' suggests a widely-held belief that there is something which distinguishes this approach from traditional approaches to Israelite history. The use of these labels, whether descriptively or pejoratively, also embodies the assumption that there are a group of scholars who fit such labels: a representative list of names taken from various recent studies often includes Mendenhall, Gottwald, Chaney, Flanagan, Frick, Hopkins, Coote, and Whitelam, among others. However, even though there are similarities in the works of these scholars, there are also considerable differences. Perhaps not always as extreme as Mendenhall's (1983) notorious review of Gottwald's *Tribes of Yahweh*, but significant differences nonetheless. For instance, the key question of the interpretation and utilization of biblical texts for the reconstruction of the pre-state period is handled strikingly differently by Gottwald (1979) and Chaney (1983) compared with Frick (1985) or Coote and Whitelam (1987). What does characterize the work of these scholars, and many others, is the concern with methodological issues in appealing to social scientific methods and data when trying to reconstruct Israelite history. It is perhaps the suspicion of theory by many biblical specialists, along with questions about the applicability of parallels from societies removed in time and space from ancient Israel, which marks out the separation and which has usually been the focal point of differences of approach.[5]

Sociology or History? A False Dichotomy

The widespread notion of a separation between standard and sociological approaches to Israelite history is based, I believe, on a false dichotomy between sociology and history. It is usually stated in terms of a

4. See Wilson and Mayes for a description of the uses of social scientific approaches in biblical studies throughout this century. See Whitelam (forthcoming b) for a comparison of William Robertson Smith with recent work on the history of Palestine.

5. Gottwald (1979: 3) refers to the 'scholarly and religious aversion to, and hesitancy in, conceiving ancient Israel as a social totality'.

distinction between the nomothetic approach of sociology and the particularistic approach of history: sociology, it is often said, is concerned with general laws relating to the ways in which society operates, while history is concerned with unique events, the particular.

Wilson (1984: 13), for example, provides a representative view that sociology is a generalizing science in which sociologists tend to operate at a fairly high level of abstraction and to deal with general types of social phenomena, specific examples of which can be found in a number of individual societies. He goes on to say that sociologists tend to ignore or neglect unique phenomena that do not fit their more general 'ideal types'. By implication then, the role of the historian is to deal with these phenomena, the unique. This is a very common understanding of the nature of the distinction between 'biblical historians' and those in recent years who have been particularly interested in trying to understand Israelite and Judaean history by incorporating the insights of the social sciences. However, what underlies this argument is a more fundamental question of the nature of history and the type of history which is appropriate to the study of ancient Israel.

One of the most contentious issues is that of the use of 'models' or 'heuristic theories' to try to interpret the fragmentary data about the past. Rodd (1981) has rightly cautioned against the dangers involved in this process. In particular, he notes that sociological theories are essentially predictions about what is likely to happen, other things being equal. Such hypotheses are tested by experimentation and participant observation. Therefore since this is not possible for historical sociology, such theories cannot be accepted as valid and so cannot be used to organize and interpret evidence from the past. The most that can be done, he argues, is to use models heuristically to suggest lines of research. The danger he sees (1981: 104-105) is that 'general theory simply states that in given circumstances certain developments tend to occur, other things being equal', while ignoring that other things are never equal, that is, that 'historical and geographical chance must not be ignored'.

Lemche (1988: 581) has extended these concerns further by voicing anxieties about the use of 'heuristic models' such as 'system's theory' or, what he terms, 'general system thinking' in the reconstruction of Israelite history. In particular, the use of theories and models drawn from the many studies of state formation is seen as assuming an evolutionary view of social development which is deterministic. However, Carneiro's circumscription theory or other studies of state formation (Cohen,

1978a; 1978b; Service 1978; Fried 1978; Claessen and Skalnik 1978) by no means presuppose a notion of unilinear social development nor are necessarily deterministic. Such studies, however, are seen to be useful in trying to explain why and how an Israelite state developed in the early Iron Age (see Frick 1985; Hauer 1986; Coote and Whitelam 1987).[6] The work of Cohen on state formation (1978a; 1978b) illustrates the point that there is not a necessarily unilinear movement from pre-state societies to state formations (Coote and Whitelam 1987). In light of the fact that some pre-state societies and chiefdoms eventually cross the threshold to statehood while others do not, it is important to try to account for the fact that Israel does eventually move towards greater centralization rather than fissioning into smaller units. The works of Frick (1985), Hauer (1986), and Coote and Whitelam (1987) try to provide such explanations for the rise of the Israelite state which question that it was either inevitable or that it was an alien development brought about by external pressure from the Philistines alone: unlike standard approaches which view the monarchy as inevitable yet 'alien', these studies consider a wide variety of factors including internal and external pressures as well as environmental pressures and limitations.[7] It is acknowledged that the move to statehood is by no means inevitable but when it does happen, as in the case of early Israel, then the historian needs not only to describe but to try to explain.

Models and theories are every bit as important to the historian as the social scientist: historical research is not possible without theory (Iggers 1979: 4-5; cf. Humphreys 1978: 29). It is at this point that I would disagree with the common assumption that there is a clear dichotomy between history and sociology. It is not a distinction which Weber or Durkheim recognized (Mayes 1989: 1), and it is certainly not accepted by historians such as Braudel. I would agree with Knauf (1991: 34) that there is no structural difference between the disciplines of the humanities and the sciences since both proceed by conjecture and refutation, and

6. It has to be admitted that these studies, though they questioned traditional reconstructions based upon biblical narratives, nonetheless assumed knowledge of the early Israelite state, drawn from these very same narratives, which now requires to be re-examined (Jamieson-Drake 1991; Davies 1992). This does not affect the central question here, however, of the use of models and theories drawn from anthropological studies of state-formation for understanding the eventual formation of an Israelite state whether we date this to the ninth, eighth, or seventh centuries BCE.

7. Finkelstein (1989: 43-74) has provided an assessment of these studies in the light of more recent archaeological data.

both result in theories that attempt to interpret historical reality.[8] Of course, it is not so easy to test historical hypotheses as it is for the scientist in the laboratory or the social scientist through participant observation, as Rodd notes. But this does not then mean that the historian should abandon attempts to reconstruct the various aspects of social reality which made up the ancient past. It is necessary to test hypotheses against all available data and to reformulate or abandon hypotheses where data do not fit or where new data come to light.

The objections to the use of models stem in large part from the view that such generalizations or 'laws' in history deny the creativity of human beings.[9] Here we have a contrast between traditional forms of history concerned with the unique individual and discrete events over against the view of history which looks at the recurrent and regular in which individuals and individual events are set. Thus it is possible to look at generalizations in political development or recurrent patterns of settlement in Palestine to see how specific events fit with these and are to be explained in terms of these regular patterns or, just as importantly, to try to explain why they deviate from some well-known pattern. The historian might then use available data on state-formation to see how applicable this is to understanding the known data about the rise of an Israelite state or might be concerned to understand why the Late Bronze–Iron Age transition differs from some periods of Palestinian settlement while it is similar to others.

The historian does not merely describe but attempts to understand and explain (contra Thompson 1992: 61). As Finley (1968: 61) points out:

> Unfortunately, the historian is no mere chronicler, and he cannot do his work at all without assumptions and judgements, without generalizations,

8. As Knauf (1991: 34) points out this does not mean that such explanations can be considered to be identical with that past reality.

9. Knauf (1991: 35) makes the point that:

> There remains the objection that there exist no 'laws' in history. Attempts to produce them have proven to be futile. However, this claim seems to be based on the naïve misconception of 'laws' in physics. Basically, laws are generalizations that lead to definite expectations, which in turn can be formulated as predictions.
>
> On the analytical level of generalizations and predictions, history is no different than the sciences. History works with generalizations, sometimes disguised as analogies. Generalizations about the process of political evolution, or the spread of a new religion (or, for that matter, a new brand of toothpaste) are possible. So are predictions.

> in other words. In so far as he is unwilling to discuss generalizations explicitly—which means he does not reflect on them—he runs grave risks.

The danger where models are not made explicit can be seen in the very strong model imposed upon Israel's past by nineteenth- and twentieth-century *biblical histories*. Israelite history has been conceived and carried out in the context of the rise of the European nation-state which has dominated the concerns and the investigations of the historian. However, this has not been made explicit—probably since most biblical historians have not been aware of this influence—until very recently. It has come to light in the context of a growing crisis faced by European nation-states: a situation which has led in turn to a radical reappraisal of early Israelite history.[10] The historian has no other choice than to investigate the past from the standpoint of the present. The social sciences have a vital role to play in the construction of the past since they provide parameters for understanding what is possible so that the past is not simply a prisoner of the present.[11] Yet the past and the present are inevitably linked in the continuous stream of events that go to make up the ebb and flow of history. History and sociology cannot be divorced: they are part of the same investigation in terms of both understanding ancient societies and the modern contexts in which such research is carried out. Finlay (1968: 70) notes that there is little difference in terms of procedure for historians interested in ancient or modern societies:

> Only in one respect, perhaps, does the ancient historian face a special, though not unique, problem. Gaps in the evidence send him (should send him more often than they do, I may say) to other societies and periods for guidance.

The historian must appeal to other societies and periods to see what is possible in human affairs if the ancient society under investigation is not to be condemned to being placed in the straight jacket of the present.

However, in order to provide the necessary and observable controls over such analogical reasoning, the appeal to other societies and periods, a consciously formulated research strategy becomes essential (Price

10. See Sasson (1981), Clements (1983), and Coote and Whitelam (1987: 173-77). This is explored much more fully in the recent unpublished dissertation of Kray (nd). The implications of this were explored in Whitelam (nd), a paper read to the Winter meeting of SOTS, 7 January 1993.

11. As Humphreys (1978: 19) points out, when historians avoid comparative studies they fall into the trap of assimilating the society they study to the only one they know, their own.

1980: 173; Coote and Whitelam 1987: 19-20). It is of little use simply to pile up more and more anthropological and sociological parallels or archaeological data without trying to analyze, categorize and interpret. Knowing more sociology, anthropology, or archaeology is of little use without a coherent interpretative framework in which to interpret data. The proviso that such a framework is useless without data is obvious (Thompson 1978: 11; Frick and Gottwald 1975: 177) but it is not a problem peculiar to those labelled as members of the so-called 'sociological school'. However, what I would repudiate, in the strongest terms, is the amazing criticism of Thompson (1992: 405):

> In using sociology for historical research, we investigate the known patterns that human societies have taken: not what is intrinsic to society but what characterizes it! What is amazing about the 'models' of Mendenhall and Gottwald (and one could easily add Coote and Whitelam here) is not that their theories were unsupported by evidence, but that these theories, lacking evidence, were ever proposed. Logic, discipline and method were never entertained.

One has only to read Gottwald's introduction to see that he has thought clearly about the methodological difficulties and issues. We might disagree about the approach to texts, the use of parallels, the domain assumptions, etc., in the light of new data and changed perspectives but it is an insult to claim that Mendenhall, Gottwald, and Coote and Whitelam never entertained 'logic, discipline and method'.[12] The ground-breaking work of Mendenhall and Gottwald, particularly their insight into the largely indigenous nature of Israel, challenged received ideas and allowed the impasse on the discussion of the origins of Israel to be broken. They, along with Alt, Noth, Albright and Bright helped set the stage for current research. It is important to bear in mind that all reconstructions of the past are contingent, since our vantage point continually changes (Whitelam 1986: 63-64; Elton 1983: 100). Scholarship is built on the foundations of the insights of those scholars who have gone before and the inevitable critique of our colleagues: to enter into debate with and offer criticisms is not a note of disrespect but one of regard. The accusation that our work is illogical, undisciplined, and lacking

12. Lemche (1985) has produced an extensive critique of Mendenhall and Gottwald, particularly in terms of their use of sociological and anthropological parallels. However, it is a critique which takes their work seriously in defining the debate on the emergence of Israel. For a response to Thompson see Whitelam (forthcoming a).

in method hardly advances the debate.

There is, however, a second important concern which arises out of the criticism of the use of models. Lemche has been particularly critical of the application of 'systems theory' as a 'heuristic model' for understanding ancient Israel. He states (1990: 86) that Coote and Whitelam 'summarily dismiss' the Old Testament sources 'as of no use at all when it comes to the early history of Israel'. He goes on to say:

> Their dismissal of any other written source for Palestine is, however, rather distressing and bears evidence of a narrowness of mind which can be the outcome of a pronounced use of system theory (1990: 86-87).

The complaint centres on the fact that the Amarna texts are not utilized to the extent he would like in *The Emergence of Early Israel in Historical Perspective*.[13] It is not correct to conclude that the Amarna letters are dismissed as immaterial, although this might appear to be the case in that they are not used 'extensively'. He suspects (1988: 583) that these texts are not discussed because 'the kind of information contained in the letters is difficult to reconcile with a fixed holistic theory as presented in this book'. However, they formed the background and were part of the evidence drawn on for the analysis; they were utilized in the discussion of *apiru*, and in particular, the assessment of Chaney's discussion of social banditry (Coote and Whitelam 1987: 92-4). All this is consistent with Liverani's view, cited by Lemche (1988: 582), that the Amarna letters, despite their fourteenth century BCE provenance, provide valuable evidence for political and social conditions throughout the Late Bronze Age. The opening chapter (Coote and Whitelam 1987: 11-26) sets out briefly the arguments for believing that the Hebrew Bible does not provide relevant source material for understanding the so-called emergence of Israel in Palestine. Coote and Whitelam are not alone in this belief; consider the following:

> The second issue will be how to understand ancient documents and texts, including the writings in the Old Testament...My first 'thesis' is that because written sources must be considered testimonies of themselves, i.e., they tell us more about the men who wrote them and about the age in which they were composed than about the events told by them, then biblical historical writings that originated in the middle of the 1 mill. BCE cannot possibly be important sources concerning the early days of the Israelite people. (Lemche 1991: 14)

13. Lemche (1988: 581-84) also highlighted this feature in his review of Coote and Whitelam (1987).

Not we might note the view of Coote and Whitelam, but that of Lemche in his paper to the New Orleans SBL meeting in November 1990, published in *SJOT* 2 (1991: 7-18).

However, the crucial complaint is that the 'shortcomings' of the 'systemic approach' (1990: 87) leave out the human factor:

> The Amarna letters tell us about the behaviour of human beings and that this behaviour is unpredictable is my major point in this lecture. Therefore the human factor can never form an important variable in systemic thought since it cannot be controlled.
>
> My point is that as long as the members of the school leave this human factor out of consideration and as long as their work is not based on a proper anthropology in the theological (or humanistic or even psychological) sense of the word, their work is of limited use. The method in question considers Man a kind of robot or automaton. (1990: 87)[14]

This is not the case: Coote and Whitelam do not consider human beings to be automata or leave out the human factor. In fact, it is possible to argue that the opposite is true: they take proper cognisance of the nature and variability of human society in its entirety. What is being argued against is the 'pyramid' view of society imposed by 'biblical history' on Israelite history where it has been standard simply to adopt the chronology and characterization of the biblical texts. The human beings that appear, for the most part, in these texts are the king and elite, mostly male. The kind of approach advocated here is not some determinative form of history. Far from it, Coote and Whitelam (1987: 81) argued that:

14. Similarly, in his earlier review (1988: 583), he suspects that the Amarna letters were ignored because they do not fit into the rigid theory that drives the book:

> If so, there is, of course, every reason to question the theoretical basis of the study as such, for the problem is perhaps that living beings appearing in it are all of human origin, and that it will always be difficult to limit the possibilities of the human race to act against the presuppositions of a fixed model for its behaviour.

Mayes (1989: 128) makes a similar, but qualified, criticism:

> The critique of materialism will aim to reincorporate the individual as a real actor on the stage of history. This reincorporation must, however, be within the parameters of a theoretical understanding of the nature of human action as sketched out by Giddens. History is made by men, but it is made in response to given environmental conditions and through the medium of contemporary conventions.

The important point here is that individual actions need to be understood in their social and environmental context. The historian cannot ignore the social and environmental limitations of a given period, limitations which are not easily transcended.

> Geographical constraints have a profound effect upon the history of Palestine, particularly by setting certain limitations on the history of settlement expansion and decline. It is the combination of outside powers with other internal factors that defines which possibilities will be realised.

Internal and external factors inevitably include the actions of human beings. They talk in terms of limitations and possibilities and not inevitabilities. In fact, in the passage just cited, it is Baly's notion (1984: 1-2) that Palestinian history is 'geographically determined' which is being questioned. A review of the interactions between the broad social groups and the environment of Palestine helps to illustrate the many different permutations possible. Which possibilities are realized at a given time are dependent upon a complex interaction of factors. The attempt was to try to understand why things happened in the way that they did, not to contend that they could only have happened in this way.

Mayes (1989: 120) makes a similar criticism of the materialist approaches of Frick and Coote and Whitelam:

> The biblical record is dismissed as deriving from individualistic bias and prejudice, with no significance for the historical and sociological analysis of ancient Israel, while reliable objective knowledge can be found in sociological models, and archaeological and other non-biblical sources which are thought to yield objective data for historical and sociological description.

This is not an accurate portrayal of their arguments since the biblical texts are rejected as providing reliable information on the so-called emergence of Israel in Palestine, not for all periods. Coote and Whitelam do not claim that archaeological data or sociological models are 'objective knowledge'. This is a common misunderstanding of the argument which may be due to the lack of clarity in argumentation, but is a misunderstanding and misrepresentation nonetheless. The biblical texts are seen to be important historical sources for the later periods in which they were composed and transmitted (Whitelam 1986; 1989; 1991) when read in light of the ideological and factional disputes of which they were inevitably a part.

The criticism that texts, which reveal human values, are ignored seems to presuppose that it is only written texts which reveal these values. But what of other forms fashioned by human hand, works of art, everyday artifacts, architecture and town planning, or the way the countryside is fashioned and shaped by the centuries of human history? Do these not also reveal human values, directly and indirectly? All of these and more are available as sources of Palestinian history, often when we have no written sources. To focus on these is not to consider human beings as robots or automata. Lemche is correct, of course, that texts reflect the values of men. But what he would also acknowledge, I am sure, is that our written texts from Palestine, whether the Hebrew Bible, the Amarna letters, the Arad ostraca, and so on, are the products of elite male society. The vast majority of the population of Palestine in antiquity were illiterate and were not involved in the production of the material in the Hebrew Bible or other extant Palestinian texts. Such texts do not reflect the values of the vast majority of society nor does this majority share in the values projected. Far from leaving human beings out of account, the kind of history advocated here is designed to include the whole of society. It is not a form of historical materialism as traditionally understood 'which assumes that the economy is the basic cause and motive force of all human existence' (Braudel 1990: 15-16). It is sociological in the widest sense: an attempt to come to terms with the system as a whole with its complexity of causes and consequences. As such, it is not a 'degradation of the human intellect' or a 'denial of "free will"' (Lemche 1988: 584). Of course, things may have happened differently, we admit that, but they did not. What we are trying to explain is why they happened in the way that they did—why does Late Bronze Age urban society decline in the way that it does? Why is there a growth in highland rural settlement during the Late Bronze–Early Iron Age transition? How are these connected, if at all? We are trying to tease out the *processes* involved and account for them—not just to describe but to try to understand.

Lemche's *Early Israel* is rightly recognized as one of the landmark studies in the discussion of Israelite origins not least because of the phenomenal resource it provides on social organization and in particular on nomadism. However, he inevitably talks of nomadism in general, in all its variability, not simply in terms of individuals but nomadism as a system, how it operates under different circumstances in different areas. There are important generalities here and we can usefully talk about collective human groups without denigrating humanity or human values. The type of history advocated here is closely allied with the social sciences concerning itself with the human masses and social groups at the expense of individual princes, heroes and leaders who have kept historians occupied for the last 2000 years.[15] Such a history cannot depend on

15. See Davies (1991: 12) for justification of sociological approach, especially in terms of social over against individual:

written records alone, even where we have them, but must pursue all possible sources in order to reconstruct the past in its complex variability. The history of Palestine envisaged is one which takes into account all elements of society, the vast majority, who have been denied a voice in history. As such it is a history of human beings in general rather than of human beings as individuals.[16] Such a conception is based upon Braudel's notion of different levels of historical time. The history of events and individuals, is an essential part of the conception of a regional history of Palestine, where we have sufficient evidence, but it is also the most difficult. It is difficult because it draws primarily upon written sources which are part of the social and political process: invariably they are forged in dispute and are subject to the 'strong passions' and myopia of all contemporary history (see Braudel 1972: 21). Such events and individuals are often only 'momentary outbursts, surface manifestations of these larger movements' and explicable only in terms of the longer-term processes at work. As Plumb (1969: 105) points out:

> The aim of history, I believe, is to understand men both as individuals and in their social relationships in time. Social embraces all of man's activities—economic, religious, political, artistic, legal, military, scientific—everything, indeed, that affects the life of mankind. And this, of course, is a not a static study but a study of movement and change. It is not only necessary to discover, as accurately as the most sophisticated use of evidence will allow, things as they actually were, but also why they were so, and why they changed; for no human societies, not one, have ever stood still.

> The premise of a sociological approach is the construction of the human subject as a *social* being, and a prescription to define and explain this being in terms of social consciousness and behaviour. This entails the study of the social system, in the broadest sense, including ecology, economics, politics, and ideology (which is where the biblical literature fits). It corresponds in fact very closely to what modern historians call what they do, and historical sociology, it might be argued, is the most productive way of conducting historical inquiry into ancient times, since the sources for the reconstruction of individuals (a form of history-writing inherited from antiquity, not yet dead in biblical studies) are inadequate and the nation-state, the object of historical inquiry inherited from the 18th and 19th centuries, is an anachronism for the biblical period (though again, perpetuated in the unreflected use of the term 'Israel' in biblical historiography).

16. As Michelet or Fustal de Coulanges would say—the object of history is human beings (Bloch 1954: 25; see also Febvre 1973: 31). Bloch (1954: 59) adds that some segments of history necessarily assume the rather anaemic aspect of a world without individuals.

He goes on to add (1969: 106) that the historian produces answers in the form of concepts and generalizations to fundamental problems of social change in the social activities of human beings. As generalizations, they can, of course, only be tentative: but this is true of the vast majority of historical research. They must be as accurate and as informed as possible which means that the historian has to educate herself/himself in the methods of all the social sciences.

The challenge to standard approaches has come from those scholars who have tried to explore the importance of the social sciences for understanding Israelite and Palestinian history drawing upon sociology, anthropology, demography, ethnology, politics and so on. This challenge is not limited to those usually labelled by the terms 'sociological approach' or 'sociological school' but includes Lemche, Thompson, Knauf, Davies, Otto, and many others. The importance of such an approach has been that it has allowed new questions to be formulated and new areas to be explored. This is not to underestimate the problems of trying to come to terms with the multitude of disciplines and approaches involved nor is it any more value-free than the dominant theological approaches that are the subject of its critique (see Jobling 1991: 175-82). But again I would appeal to Braudel who says:

> Even if in practice none of us is capable of the necessary tour de force, we are all under an obligation to speak in terms of the global, of 'historical totalization', to reaffirm that 'total history [is] the only true history', or as Michelet long ago put it, 'everything stands and falls together, everything is connected'.

A New Paradigm? Towards a (Human) History of Palestine.

The importance of recent reappraisals of Israelite history has now moved the discussion way beyond the original debate on the explicit use of social scientific approaches and data. The implications of some of the works with which we have been concerned is that they have begun to lay the groundwork for a significant shift in approaches to the history of the region. At times this has been conscious but for the most part it has been the largely unforeseen result of recent research which has contributed to the fracturing of the previous consensus on historical research in biblical studies. Davies (1991) has taken seriously newer work on the emergence of Israel and has tried to draw out its implications for the study of the Hebrew Bible. Yet the paradigm shift is not restricted to biblical studies but goes considerably beyond this. The powerful combination of the many aspects of newer literary approaches and the historical revisionism which has been taking place has significant implications for historical research. What we are witnessing is the growing recognition of the development of Palestinian history as a subject in its own right, a multi-disciplinary approach, increasingly divorced from biblical studies. In effect, a broad-based thematic conception of history concerned with the economy, demography, settlement, religions and ideologies of Palestine as a whole, a history of the region concerned with its various micro-environments set in the context of world history. The outcome of the research on the emergence of early Israel published from the mid- to late 1980s has illustrated, in retrospect, that the proposals were not radical enough. The various studies are misleading because they reveal nothing of the so-called emergence of Israel but are concerned with the settlement and transformation of Palestinian society in general: they have been misled by the search for the nation state in the guise of Israel imposed by the general context of biblical studies. Thompson has contributed to and articulates (1992a; 1992b) a number of these developments very well. He sees a strong influence from Chicago and Tübingen, but thinks that it represents more a confluence of scholars drawn from biblical, archaeological, and semitic studies, rather than a single approach.[17] Israelite history is a sub-set of such a Palestinian history rather than the dominant entity that it has been in biblical studies for the last century or more.[18] The study of the Hebrew Bible will need to draw upon such a history in order to provide the context for understanding the development of the literature. Obviously the two are connected, but I suspect that it is in the definition of the separation rather than the interconnections between the two areas, that is, the study of the Hebrew Bible and Palestinian history, that much future work will initially be concerned.[19]

17. He cites (1992a: 3) the work of Ahlström (1992), Lemche (1985), Coote and Whitelam (1987), Finkelstein (1988), H. Weippert (1988), Knauf (1988; 1989), among others. See Whitelam (1991; forthcoming) for a provisional statement on the need for a broad regional history of Palestine and the implications of research on the emergence of Israel published in the 1980s.

18. Thompson (1987: 36) similarly argues that 'Israel's history (understood as distinct from biblical historiography), and the history of Israel's origin, fall unquestionably and inescapably into the context of regional, historical geographical changes in the history of Palestine'.

19. The question will also need to be faced as to where such a history might be

The value of a broad social history of Palestine approach is that it opens up the variability of human society and organization which helps to suggest *possible* interpretations for our fractured data in trying to understand Israelite history in its regional context. Too much Israelite history has been written from the limited perspective of 'biblical history' which has taken for granted the uniqueness of its subject as told to it by that very same literature. Nineteenth- and twentieth-century conceptions of history have been dominated by unique individuals and events—the aristocratic view of history (cf. Iggers 1979: 1). Yet the fracturing of this model by the crisis of the modern nation-state has been a significant factor, I believe, in the radical reappraisal of Israelite history and the shift towards a regional Palestinian history. It is not a coincidence, in my opinion, that much of the research has come from Europe or from scholars who have close connections with Europe. Whether, of course, it is to be the Maastricht model of a federal union which is to prevail or a Danish-inspired conception of subsidiarity we will need to wait and see.

BIBLIOGRAPHY

Ahlström, G.W.
1993 *The History of Ancient Palestine from the Palaeolithic to Alexander's Conquest* (Sheffield: JSOT Press).

Bloch, M.
1954 *The Historian's Craft* (Manchester: Manchester University Press).

Braudel, F.
1972 *The Mediterranean and the Mediterranean World in the Age of Philip II*, I-II (London: Collins).
1990 *The Identity of France*. II. *People and Production* (London: Collins).

Chaney, M.
1983 'Ancient Palestinian Peasant Movements and the Formation of Pre-monarchic Israel', in *Palestine in Transition: The Emergence of Ancient Israel* (ed. D.N. Freedman and D.F. Graf; Sheffield: Almond Press): 39-90.

Claessen, H.J.M., and P. Skalnik
1978 *The Early State* (The Hague: Mouton).

taught. Departments of History have traditionally been suspicious of 'biblical history' while faculties of Theology are going to have less interest in the development of a Palestinian history increasingly divorced from biblical studies.

Clements, R.E.
1983 *A Century of Old Testament Study* (Guildford: Lutterworth).
1989 *The World of Ancient Israel. Sociological, Anthropological and Political Perspectives* (Cambridge: Cambridge University Press).

Cohen, R.
1978a 'Introduction', in *Origins of the State* (ed. R. Cohen and E.R. Service; Philadelphia: Institute for the Study of Human Issues), 1-20.
1978b 'State Origins: A Reappraisal', in *The Early State* (ed. H.J.M. Claessen and P. Skalnik; The Hague: Mouton), 31-75.

Coote, R.B., and K.W. Whitelam
1987 *The Emergence of Early Israel in Historical Perspective* (Sheffield: JSOT Press).

Davies, P.
1992 *In Search of 'Ancient Israel'* (Sheffield: JSOT Press).

Elton, G.R.
1983 'Two Kinds of History', in *Which Road to the Past* (ed. R.W. Fogel and G.R. Elton; New Haven: Yale University Press), 71-121.

Febvre, L.
1973 *A New Kind of History and Other Essays* (New York: Harper Torch).

Finkelstein, I.
1988 *The Archaeology of the Israelite Settlement* (Jerusalem: Israel Exploration Society).

Finley, M.
1986 *The Use and Abuse of History* (London: Chatto and Windus).

Frick, F.
1985 *The Formation of the State in Ancient Israel* (Decatur: Almond Press).

Frick, F., and N.K. Gottwald
1975 'The Social World of Ancient Israel', in *SBL Seminar Papers I* (Missoula, MT: Scholars Press), 165-77.

Fried, M.
1978 'The State, the Chicken, and the Egg; or, What Came First?', in *Origins of the State* (ed. R. Cohen and E.R. Service; Philadelphia: Institute for the Study of Human Issues), 35-47.

Gottwald, N.K.
1979 *The Tribes of Yahweh. A Sociology of Liberated Israel, 1250-1050 BCE* (London: SCM Press).

Gunn, D.
1987 'New Directions in the Study of Biblical Narrative', *JSOT* 39: 65-75.

Hauer, C.
1986 'From Alt to Anthropology: The Rise of the Israelite State', *JSOT* 36: 3-15.

Humphreys, S.C.
1978 *Anthropology and the Greeks* (London: Routledge and Kegan Paul).

Iggers, G.G.
1979 'Introduction: The Transformation of Historical Studies in Historical Perspective', in *International Handbook of Historical Studies: Contemporary Research and Theory* (ed. G.G. Iggers and H.T. Parker; London: Methuen), 1-14.

Jamieson-Drake, D.W.
1991 *Scribes and Schools in Monarchic Judah. A Socio-Archaeological Approach* (Sheffield: Almond Press).

Jobling, D.
1991 'The Text and the World—an Unbridgeable Gap? A Response to Carroll, Hoglund and Smith', in *Second Temple Studies 1. Persian Period* (ed. P.R. Davies; Sheffield: JSOT Press), 175-182.

Knauf, E.A.
1985 *Ismael: Untersuchungen zur Geshcichte Palästinas und Nordarabiens in 1. Jahrtausend v. Chr.* (Wiesbaden: O. Harrassowitz).
1988 *Midian: Untersuchungen zur Geschichte Palästinas und Nordarabiens am Ende 2. Jahrtaused v. Chr.* (Wiesbaden: O. Harrassowitz).
1991 'From History to Interpretation', in *The Fabric of History: Text, Artifact and Israel's Past* (ed. D. Edelman; Sheffield: JSOT Press), 26-64.

Lemche, N.P.
1985 *Early Israel: Anthropological and Historical Studies in the Israelite Society before the Monarchy* (Leiden: Brill).
1988 'Review of Coote and Whitelam, *The Emergence of Early Israel in Historical Perspective*', *Biblica* 69: 581-84.
1990 'On the Use of "System Theory", "Macro Theories" and "Evolutionistic Thinking" On Modern OT Research and Biblical Archaeology', *SJOT* 2: 73-88.

Mayes, A.D.H.
1989 *The Old Testament in Sociological Perspective* (London: Marshall Pickering).

Mendenhall, G.E.
1983 'Ancient Israel's Hyphenated History', in *Palestine in Transition: The Emergence of Ancient Israel* (ed. D.N. Freedman and D.F. Graf; Sheffield: Almond Press), 91-103.

Plumb, J.H.
1969 *The Death of the Past* (London: MacMillan).

Price, B.J.
1980 'The Truth is not in Accounts but in Account Books: On the Epistemological Status of History', *Beyond the Myths of Culture: Essays in Cultural Materialism* (ed. E.B. Ross; New York: Academic Press), 155-80.

Rodd, C.
1981 'On Applying a Sociological Theory to Biblical Studies', *JSOT* 19: 95-106.

Rogerson, J.W.
1984 *Anthropology and the Old Testament* (Sheffield: JSOT Press).

Sasson, J.
1981 'On Choosing Models for Recreating Israelite Pre-Monarchic History', *JSOT* 21: 3-24.

Service, E.R.
1978 'Classical and Modern Theories of Government', in *Origins of the State* (ed. R. Cohen and E.R. Service; Philadelphia: Institute for the Study of Human Issues), 21-34.

Thompson, T.L.
1978 'The Background to the Patriarchs: A Reply to William Dever and Malcolm Clark', *JSOT* 9: 2-43.
1987 *The Origin Tradition of Ancient Israel I. The Literary Formation of Genesis and Exodus 1-23* (Sheffield: JSOT Press).
1992a 'Palestinian Pastoralism and Israel's Origins', *SJOT* 6: 1-13.
1992b *Early History of the Israelite People. From the Written and Archaeological Sources* (Leiden: Brill).

Weippert, H.
1988 *Palästina in vorhellenistischer Zeit. Handbuch der Archäologie: Vorderasien II/Band I* (Münich: Beck).

Whitelam, K.W.
1986 'Recreating the History of Israel', *JSOT* 35: 45-70.
1989 'Israel's Traditions of Origin: Reclaiming the Land', *JSOT* 44: 19-42.
1991 'Between History and Literature. The Social Production of Israel's Traditions of Origin', *SJOT* 2: 60-74.
forthcoming a 'New Deuteronomistic Heroes and Villains: A Response to T.L. Thompson', *SJOT*.
forthcoming b 'The Identity of Early Israel: The Realignment and Transformation of Late Bronze-Iron Age Palestine', *JSOT*.
nd 'The Politics of History: Perceptions of Israel's Past' (paper read to the Winter meeting of the Society of Old Testament Studies, London, January 1993).

Wilson, R.R.
1984 *Sociological Approaches to the Old Testament* (Philadelphia: Fortress Press).

READING JOSHUA AFTER KINGS

A. Graeme Auld

John Sawyer's friendship I have appreciated for thirty years since he briefed me in 1964 before my first student visit to Jerusalem. It gives great pleasure to offer him these comments and questions as I turn back from some years with kings and prophets to prepare a large commentary on Joshua.

There seem to be at least two questions jostling under the deceptively simple 'what are we reading if we are reading the book of Joshua?'

How independent is the book of Joshua? In what sense is it 'a book' in its own right? And in what sense is it merely a part of something bigger—Former Prophets, Deuteronomistic History, Hexateuch, Primary History (from Genesis to Kings)? This question betrays only partially reconstructed interests: beyond *Rezeptionsgeschichte*—and Joshua has been 'received' and studied in all of these contexts—I also want to probe the wider writing context within which Joshua grew, was shaped.

What precisely is the 'book of Joshua' about which we are talking—whether or not it is a part or a whole? What is the extent, shape, and wording of this text? Attention is being drawn this time to the fact that Joshua is one of the several biblical books where the received (that word again!) Hebrew and Greek texts differ substantially in length, and—though to a lesser extent than some—in order; and where the still scanty evidence from Qumran both illumines and complicates the already familiar relationships. Leonard Greenspoon asked at the 1990 Manchester conference of the Qumran fragments of Joshua: 'Which puzzle are they part of, and where do they fit?' (1992).

In matters of wording and shape and extent, the question of Joshua is the same as the question of Daniel, or Esther, or Jeremiah—yet these three stand more clearly on their own as separate books. In matters of independence or inter-connectedness, the question of Joshua is more like the question of Leviticus. In the Pentateuch, a case for at least relative independence within the union has long been more readily urged for Genesis or Deuteronomy. Mary Douglas, in her fascinating account of Numbers, published as *In the Wilderness* (1993), invites us to read *bmdbr*—the book's title in the Hebrew Bible—strongly, and not just as what happens to be the first word of a merely conventionally divided-up portion of the Pentateuch. And I am certainly open to her persuasion that the middle fifths of the Torah also have their own integrity. And yet Leviticus is still the middle of something bigger. How far is that true of Joshua as well?

When the book of Joshua was the main focus of my attention some fifteen to twenty years ago, I covered some of the necessary groundwork for a larger commentary. However, quite a lot has happened since; and the relevant bibliography has swollen. This is nowhere truer than in the area of text-critical studies. A detailed study of the relationship between Masoretic text and Septuagint, and especially of Codex Vaticanus, remains the indispensable investment and has still many rich dividends to repay. But several new tools have become available in the intervening period. Kraft and Tov's computer-aligned text is very helpful in suggesting a retroversion of the LXX into Hebrew, although it is based on Rahlfs, and so on Alexandrinus rather than the more interesting Vaticanus. The long-lost fifth and concluding part of Max Margolis's magisterial edition of the Septuagint of Joshua—believed destroyed during the Second World War—has come to light, and its publication been undertaken by Emanuel Tov. Alex Rofé and Tov and several others have devoted various papers to particular chapters or issues. Leonard Greenspoon has published valuable studies of the LXX and of other ancient Greek versions of Joshua (esp. 1983). The Leiden Peshitta volume including Joshua has appeared (1991). And fragments from Qumran have been discussed by Greenspoon (1992), Tov (1992a), and Kempinski (1993)—and, as will shortly be indicated, they have still exciting surprises to spring. Joshua has plenty of stimulus to offer the textual critic.

Joshua may have rather less to offer the literary critic. Joshua is not Judges. There are fewer stories and more lists. The humour is, at best, less obviously omnipresent. And yet the newer literary criticism is sending out spies; and, who knows, it may be preparing to cross the river in force. However, the majority of contemporary readers will doubtless find they are treading less congenial territory than in Judges or Samuel. Robert Polzin's first volume on *Moses and the Deuteronomist*

(1980) drew our attention to synchronic strategies for coping with discrepant voices in the narrative; and offers a wealth of suggestive commentary. And Daniel Hawk's (1991) monograph-length study of 'contesting plots in Joshua', under the title *Every Promise Fulfilled*, has sought to extend the bridgehead. Well and good. But Polzin and Hawk—and Hawk as the longer and the more recent is also the more culpable—remain silent about the conversation between the Hebrew and Greek texts. This seems to be true also of Mitchell (1993), although that monograph does offer a very useful review of some of the key language of Joshua. In a recent SBL paper, Fewell presented an able deconstructionist reading of Judges, which reminded her hearers how Achsah, a young bride of the first generation in the land flowing with milk and honey, had to demand something as basic as water in her portion of the promised land. Poor Achsah had to make that disruptive demand not just once in Judges—she had already made it in Joshua as well. Literary criticism of the Bible has made resolute strides in the same fifteen-year period, even if its colonization of Joshua is still at a very preliminary stage.

Our historical assumptions—expectations—deductions—perturbations have also altered considerably. After Coote and Whitelam (1987), Garbini (1988), Lemche (1988), Davies (1992), Thompson (1992), and Ahlström (1993), some of us like, and some of us dislike, models and constructs and much denser social-historical theory than we were accustomed to in the old days of not so long ago, when we simply had to check not very sophisticated readings of Joshua against the current views of the archaeologists. But then the archaeologists too are discoursing in new ways—witness Finkelstein's *Archaeology of the Israelite Settlement* (1988). The historian of Israel's origins may have had to give up on Joshua's spies, and the walls of Jericho. But the town lists and border descriptions must have some information to impart, even if not about dispositions made by Moses' successor in his old age. And the question is still there on the table, why it is about Jericho and Ai and Hazor that Joshua tells its stories. There is no answer to that question in Mullen (1993). Mullen, like many before him, is interested in the several evidences of ritual re-enactment within Joshua. 'The compositional style of the deuteronomistic history creates a world of dialogue that involves the reader or hearer in the literarily constructed social world of the author as though the past were actually the present (or the present, past, depending on the perspective of the reader).'

There have been several commentaries published since 1980: by Woudstra (NICOT) in 1981; Boling's completion of George Ernest Wright's Anchor Bible volume in 1982; Butler (Word) in 1983. John Gray's New Century commentary appeared in a third edition in 1986, and the translation of Soggin in a second edition in the Old Testament Library in 1988. To judge from early reviews by Porter (1992) and Lemche (1993a; 1993b: 177), Ottosson's novel approach in his Swedish commentary of 1991 will repay close study—not least because of his fresh attention to the 'priestly' passages in the book: not inserted into, but taken over by the Deuteronomist. The latest commentary, from Volkmar Fritz (1994), is in the same series (HAT)—and indeed in much the same spirit—as that of Martin Noth. The most obvious advances on Noth's position are that the *Grundschrift*, behind which no literary history is possible, was the work of the Deuteronomistic historian; and that that first historian did include a report of the division of the land.

It is in fact the second edition of Noth's commentary, of 1953, that has dominated most academic work for some forty years. That re-edition was the culmination of some twenty-five years of effort on Joshua and related issues. His many topographical studies of the late twenties and earlier thirties, and his long-influential study of the 12-tribe structure of early Israel, informed the first edition in 1938. Its publication proved to be a stepping-stone to his magisterial *Überlieferungsgeschichtliche Studien* of 1943. And in the light of that commanding new account of a Deuteronomistic historical work, he produced in 1953 the thoroughly revised second edition of his commentary. Yet his amphictyony thesis is largely discredited. And a series of scholars have successfully contested his reliance on Margolis's resolute preference for the Masoretic text over the *Vorlage* of the Old Greek—that Old Greek which Margolis had laboured so successfully to recover.

But not all things have changed. The thesis of a Deuteronomistic historical work reigns supreme. His impulse. His name for it. But seldom now Noth's thesis. There may be intense debate about whether there was but one Deuteronomistic historian, or two or three or several. There may be deep disagreement whether the foundations of this historical enterprise were laid towards the end of Judah's monarchy, or only after its demise. But Dtr is an internationally traded currency, even if not accepted quite everywhere: most readers know that Joshua is but part of a connected narrative, however often expanded and rewritten, stretching at least from Deuteronomy to Kings. Noth's inheritance and its ongoing significance were explored, mostly sensitively, in several papers offered within interlinked sessions of the 1993 annual meeting of SBL in Washington, fifty years on.

There was of course little talk on that occasion about Pentateuchal matters, although Rendtorff reminded participants of his view that Noth would have done better to go on to treat the Tetrateuch as he had the Deuteronomistic History. However, one of the less stable elements in Noth's position on Joshua, to deduce at least from the *Rezeptionsgeschichte* of his work, is his denial of a Priestly contribution to the book of Joshua. I sought in my *Joshua, Moses and the Land* (1980) to render that denial even more plausible. Quite the most vigorous critique that work has received has been mounted by Enzo Cortese (1985; 1990), with the precise aim of rescuing the Hexateuchal 'Priestly' dimension in Joshua while adhering to Noth's Deuteronomistic thesis. (Not even the more recent work on Exodus by Blum [1990] and Johnstone [1990; 1993], and their view not of a P-source but of a P-rewriting of a D-work, would offer an adequate model in my view for talk of a P-contribution to Joshua.) There is a good deal of name-calling in Cortese's attempt to regain something of Mowinckel's 1964 position. His jibe against me (he would call it diagnosis of me!) I most enjoy is *Settantamania* (LXX-madness)—I suppose because I feel least vulnerable when arguing on the basis of real differences, objectively there, in a range of ancient texts.

So much for reading or re-reading Joshua. What about 'Reading Joshua after Kings'? My most recent tussle with Kings and Chronicles has persuaded me that Kings must be de-privileged (1994). The books of Kings are not after all the source of Chronicles; they are not the 'text' on which Chronicles is 'commentary'. In fact, exactly like Chronicles, Samuel–Kings are part commentary on, part radical extension of, a pre-existing narrative of the house of David. The material common to Samuel–Kings and Chronicles is an account of David's house, of the monarchy in Jerusalem, from the death of Saul to the fall of Jerusalem. That source document, therefore, must date from after Jerusalem's fall. It tells the story of the schism after Solomon's death, and mentions several of the subsequent kings of Israel who did impinge directly on the story of Judah. But the interleaved continuous, if rather formulaic, story of the kingdom of Israel—that story whose presence in the book makes Kings what it is, and distinguishes it from Chronicles with its (in some respects) more conservative focus on Judah alone—is a later addition.

To read Kings this way is certainly to read against the grain of the Deuteronomistic History.

The source which both Samuel–Kings and Chronicles have used for their account of the house of David from the death of Saul to the fall of Jerusalem can be almost entirely recovered: it is more or less the text which Samuel–Kings and Chronicles share. Both successor texts had reproduced the words of their source more or less faithfully. They supplemented these words extensively, and hence often effectively marginalized them; but they hardly ever omitted any of them. The textual evidence for these bold claims and some first corollaries can also be sampled in discussions of the Solomon chapters in articles dedicated to Smend and Malamat (Auld 1992; 1993).

In the remaining pages, I invite readers to curb their impatience to know more about Kings/Chronicles relationships, and/or suspend their disbelief, and consider with me some of the implications for a Deuteronomistic History and a commentary on Joshua. Have I trapped myself or liberated myself as commentator on Joshua by dealing radically in 2 Samuel and Kings with the Deuteronomistic hypothesis? At the very least I have pushed forward the dating of the earliest edition of Kings: that cannot any longer be late monarchic or early exilic, for it represents a substantial revision of a source which itself cannot be earlier than the exile at which it ends.

In Noth's classic thesis, the Deuteronomistic History was shaped and informed by a series of chapters penned by the historian himself: some ostensibly his own editorial comment (Josh. 12; Judg. 2; 2 Kgs 17), some in the form of speeches put into the mouths of the leader of the time (Josh. 23; 1 Sam. 12; 1 Kgs 8). Noth rightly—over against many of his successors—reckoned Nathan's dynastic oracle in 2 Samuel 7 as pre-Deuteronomistic. But, in his view, 1 Kings 8 (Solomon's prayer at the dedication of the temple) and 2 Kings 17 (the author's own peroration on the fall of the north) were penned by the same Deuteronomistic hand. In my view, Solomon's prayer in 1 Kings 8, and his visions at the beginnings of Chapters 3 and 9, belong for the most part with Nathan's oracle. They are all shared by Samuel-Kings and Chronicles, and so derive from the source on which both biblical books have drawn. None of these shared materials can be from the same stratum as special Kings material like 2 Kings 17 on the fall of the north. And of these two strata, only 2 Kings 17 could be considered Deuteronomistic, if it was the

Deuteronomists who were responsible for something like the present shape of Kings.

I did not work with Eep Talstra's Dutch thesis on 1 Kings 8 when developing my own views on the Solomon chapters in Kings and Chronicles; and its English translation has become available (1993) only since my work went to the printer. But of course I can now welcome for my own ends Talstra's patient demonstration that Solomon's prayer is far from conforming to Noth's or Weinfeld's (1972) pattern for a Deuteronomistic oration. And, much more important, I salute a study which offers a very attractive model for the integration of synchronic and diachronic approaches to texts. As a bonus, his careful discussion of passages in Deuteronomy and Joshua will greatly benefit any reader who is turning again from Kings to Joshua.

But back to the Deuteronomists: was it they, after all, who were responsible for the shaping of the books of Kings? And my question could be re-formulated in two ways:

1. Was there ever a connected narrative, starting with Israel's beginnings in her land, of which Kings represented the final part?
2. Granted that there are links in language and thought between Kings and Deuteronomy, in which direction does the influence mainly travel between them? Should we continue to think of a core of Deuteronomy whose standards have become those of a Dtr historian, properly so called? Or should we argue instead, or as well, that many of the principles now enshrined in Deuteronomy were deduced from portions of the story of the nation? Deuteronomy before, or after, or contemporaneous with Kings?—and that is a book of Kings rather later than we normally suppose.

Having started at the end, it may be safest if we work backwards. The first story which Samuel and Chronicles share recounts the death of Saul and his sons: those deaths which were the indispensable prelude to the reign of David and to the telling of it. The Chronicler preserves a somewhat shorter and more original version of Saul's death; and one of my recent graduates believes he can correlate its emphases with earlier traditions now overwritten in 1 Samuel (Ho 1995), a book which of course tells the story of Saul's life and what preceded it before it reports his death. But are we to continue to believe that the Chronicler knew but chose not to retell the Samuel/Saul story? Or should we begin to reckon with the possibility that 1 Samuel supplied a story which the source common to Samuel–Kings and Chronicles had not told?

It is with the completed books of Kings—not the common source, but the monarchical story including the northern Israel additions—that Judges and Joshua have most in common. In some respects, the issues are clearest with Judges. Close links have been noted, and explored again recently by Eslinger (1989), between the 'Deuteronomistic' preface to Judges in Judg. 2.11ff. and the peroration on the fate of northern Israel in 2 Kings 17. And then it is throughout Judges and throughout the Israel supplements to the monarchic story that we find repeatedly a dread pattern of 'doing evil in Yahweh's eyes': always 'evil' and never 'right'. Important editorial elements of Judges are congruent with Kings. But are those sufficient grounds to call Judges and Kings part of the same work? Are their relationships any closer than, say, between Kings and Jeremiah? Judges may even be later than the completed Kings. Several stories within Judges apparently know stories in Kings and offer parable-like commentary on them. I have argued (1989), for example, that a few of the elements in the Gideon-stories depend on Kings and are relatively late.

There are connections between Joshua and different layers of material in Kings:

1. We have Joshua's curse on any rebuilder of Jericho (Josh. 6.26) and the price—the life of his own son—paid by Hiel of Jericho according to 1 Kgs 16.34. We have also the note about Gezer and the dowry of the daughter of Pharaoh who became Solomon's wife, which appears in the LXX at the end of Josh. 16.10 and in the MT in 1 Kgs 9.16. Both of these Kings references are in special Kings material, not shared with Chronicles. But both give the impression of being occasional afterthoughts or cross-references between already completed books of Joshua and Kings, rather than structural links.
2. Many have noted the similarity in territorial conception between some of the topographical information in the second half of Joshua and the list of Solomon's districts in 1 Kgs 4; and have argued for the priority of the much briefer Solomonic arrangement. That list is often claimed to be archival and ancient. Perhaps—but we should note that it is not part of the Solomon story shared between Kings and Chronicles.

3. Then Joshua 9, like 2 Sam. 21, offers us background information about Gibeon—that sanctuary which, according to the shared source on Solomon, was the great *bamah* before the temple and altar at Jerusalem were constructed. And in Josh. 22 as well, especially if we are right to detect behind the repeated LXX *bomos* an original Hebrew *bamah* (not *mzbḥ* as in MT) of witness between the people east and west of the Jordan, the story of a shrine though not for sacrifice may be making its own contribution to explaining how a *bamah* frequented by Solomon might be legitimate.
4. The common monarchic tradition and—with somewhat different emphasis from each other—the successor books of Samuel–Kings and Chronicles associate the divinely granted 'rest' (*hnyḥ/mnwḥh*) with the golden age of David and Solomon: in particular, with the Davidic line and the Jerusalem shrine. But Joshua, and Deuteronomy as well, repeatedly portray the successful occupation of the land as that 'rest'—or at least the first step towards Yahweh's 'rest'.
5. Closer to Noth's own argument: there are several links between his Deuteronomistic chapters Josh. 23 and 2 Kgs 17.

All of these links between Kings and Joshua could be accommodated within a fresh account of a Deuteronomistic History. But should they be? Was it those who re-wrote Kings who also wrote Joshua and Judges? The first thing implied by reading Joshua after a de-privileged Kings is no longer being sure that Kings is the destined end of the Joshua story. And that is different from the question: Was Joshua written in the light of Jerusalem's collapse?

At the beginning of this paper, I identified two questions jostling under the deceptively simple 'what are we reading if we are reading the book of Joshua?': How independent is Joshua as a book? And which text of Joshua should we be reading? I want to suggest that the answers to these two questions in fact impinge on each other. But I pause first at the text-critical question.

Josh. 8.30-35 (MT) appears two verses later in LXX—after 9.1-2 (MT), rather than before. Which position for this paragraph is original? Possibly neither. Commentators have long remarked that neither the report in 8.30-35 that Joshua had duly performed Moses' instructions in Deuteronomy 27 about setting up plastered stones bearing a copy of the *torah* nor the observation in 9.1-2 that the kings of the land were now motivated to oppose Israel sits easily or well-connectedly in the book. That in itself might suggest that one or other paragraph is a latecomer—and the suggestion draws support from the different relative position of the paragraphs in MT and LXX.

What provides the old discussion with a new twist is that the end of this report on Joshua's diligence is preserved on a Qumran fragment. This was discussed by Greenspoon (1992: 173), who plausibly reconstructed a reference to the Jordan crossing in a small plus in 8.35; but declared he had 'not been able to identify the source of the longer addition at the close of this section'. That addition has been discussed in some detail by Kempinski (1993), who reconstructs the fragment as part of a text in which Josh. 8.34-35 led immediately into the beginning of Josh. 5.2. Kempinski's view is that the Qumran fragment preserves the original position within Joshua of the circumcision story—this was subsequently promoted on halakhic grounds to before the story of the first passover in Canaan. It is, however, more natural to assume that in a third version of the book the whole paragraph (8.30-35) appeared much earlier, in fact just after the crossing of the Jordan—so enabling in time the addition of the small plus discussed by Greenspoon within what I shall continue to call 8.35.

The first of two suggestions I want to make is that, if we have three different positions for it, it is in fact not original at all, but a latecomer looking for a suitable home. If Achsah has to campaign twice for water within the promised land of milk and honey, and Dan make two attempts to become settled, here we have a short text making three attempts to win an appropriate context in the book of Joshua. May that not suggest that the rest of the contents of Joshua are already relatively successfully settled?

That is a point worth pausing over. Albrektson (1993) has mentioned Tov with approval in his discussion in the Anderson Festschrift of the current official Swedish translation project in which he is involved. He urges that the Hebrew text to be translated should not be any of the received texts, obvious mistakes and all, but a reconstructed text. With Tov, he opts for the 'book' at the stage at which literary development finished and after which textual variation began. He takes as an example Jer. 48.4, where *ṣ'rh* (to Zoar) should be read with the LXX, rather than *ṣ'yryh* (its little ones) of MT. I find it easy to agree that LXX attests an earlier reading. I find it easy to agree that MT should not be translated where late alterations have crept into it. But how do you distinguish between re-readings that became normative within the very period that a shorter text more like the LXX *Vorlage* was being expanded and reshaped to become the proto-Masoretic text from re-readings which later distorted that proto-Masoretic text? Given the presence within the textual tradition common to LXX and MT in Jeremiah of two instances of the construct plural of *ṣ'yr* and one instance of the plural with suffix, I am far from clear how we exclude the possibility that *ṣ'rh* was already being re-read as *ṣ'yryh* before the longer text of Jeremiah was complete. I have considerable sympathy with a point my Edinburgh colleague Peter Hayman was making in a recent departmental seminar paper on the three extended families of copies of the Jewish mystical *Book of Creation*. From that complex textual situation, he found it hard to sympathize with Emanuel Tov (1992) defining the proto-MT as the stage at which the literary development of biblical books was complete and the textual history began.

But, if the commentator has evidence of an alternative criterion to Tov's, evidence of a book of Joshua already settled and unwelcoming without 8.30-35, should this paragraph be translated within a critical translation of Joshua, at one or other of its three attested positions, just because it is attested in all witnesses? Or should it be omitted, at least from the main text, because literary development had finished before various attempts to insert it were made? Happily it is easier for a large academic commentary to adopt a pluralistic approach than an official translation. And pluralism within a Joshua commentary is both possible, because the divergences are not too bulky, and necessary, because many of them preserve clues to the development of the book. Our most antique textual evidence is bearing increasing witness to textual pluralism. A large commentary has a responsibility to present and comment on the various texts to hand.

In its own way, Josh. 8.30-35 also bears on questions of inter-connectedness—of Joshua as a Deuteronomic book, or as part of a Dtr History. The paragraph has always been recognized as, in some sense at least, a Deuteronomic text. It obviously recounts the carrying out of the command reported in Deut. 27; though, as Polzin nicely shows, it extends or subverts—we could settle for 'interprets'—it interprets the command quite as much as it carries it out. However, its not-yet-stabilized position within Joshua would remove any or most of its potential value as evidence of a structured relationship between Deuteronomy and Joshua—unless we were to say that it was only within a relationship that such afterthoughts would occur. But I would be very resistant to assigning Josh. 8.30-35 to the same stratum as any of the material in Joshua whose attested position was constant according to all our available witnesses.

I mentioned already a LXX plus about Gezer as part of the dowry of the daughter of Pharoah who married Solomon at the end of a note in Josh. 16.10 about the relationship of the town of Gezer and its inhabitants to the people of Ephraim. The same information is given in a MT plus in 1 Kgs 9.16. Is this another late supplement, like Josh. 8.30-35? And, if so, might it suggest that Joshua–Kings, at the time of the supplementing, was regarded as in some sense a single text?

Let me close with an alternative, more speculative account of the Qumran variant—one which tends in a rather different direction from my comments above. If the fragment located the end of 8.30-35 just before the circumcision report beginning in 5.2, then presumably in the complete scroll its opening had immediately followed 5.1. Now several elements of Josh. 5.1 are repeated in Josh. 9.1-2, the verses which precede our errant paragraph in the LXX. Both open with the identical *wyhy kšm'*; but, while 5.1 has 'kings of the Amorites beyond the Jordan' and 'kings of the Canaanites by the sea' doing the hearing, 9.1 first offers more generally 'the kings beyond the Jordan' and then supplies detail in a couple of clichéd expressions: 'in the the hill country and in the lowland all along the coast of the Great Sea toward Lebanon', and 'the Hittites, the Amorites, etc'—though in different order in MT and LXX. Admittedly, *wyhy kšm'* opens Josh. 10.1 and 11.1 as well; but these verses constitute a distinct pair with only a single king doing the 'hearing'. I suggest that 8.30-35 may first have been located at the beginning of ch. 5. But when this paragraph, telling of blessing and cursing at Gerizim and Ebal, was re-located after the campaign at Ai in the central highlands, it brought with it elements of 5.1; and these were rebuilt rather clumsily as 9.1-2—and are to be found there still in the LXX before 8.30-35, although after it in MT where they function as a somewhat more relevant introduction to chs. 9–11 as a whole.

There are plenty fresh questions for yet another commentary on Joshua to discuss. Reading Joshua after Kings, indeed reading Joshua after reading Talstra on Solomon's prayer, makes it necessary to reargue the case for Deuteronomistic origins from the bottom up. It also encourages persevering in one's *Settantamania*—and adding a predilection for Qumran-fragments to the symptoms.

BIBLIOGRAPHY

Ahlström, G.W.
1993 *The History of Ancient Palestine* (Sheffield: JSOT Press).

Albrektson, B.
1993 'Grundtext och urtext: om underlaget för svenska översättningar av Gamla testamentet', in A.G. Auld (ed.), *Understanding Poets and Prophets: Essays in Honour of George Wishart Anderson* (JSOTSup 152; Sheffield: JSOT Press), 23-37.

Auld, A.G.
1980 *Joshua, Moses and the Land* (Edinburgh: T. & T. Clark).
1983 'Prophets Through the Looking Glass: Between Writings and Moses', *JSOT* 27: 3-23.
1986 *Kings* (Daily Study Bible; Edinburgh: St Andrew Press).
1989 'Gideon: Hacking at the heart of the Old Testament', *VT* 39: 257-267.
1992 'Salomo und die Deuteronomisten: eine Zukunftsvision?', *TZ* 48: 343-55.
1993 'Solomon at Gibeon: History Glimpsed', *Avraham Malamat Volume* (Eretz Israel 24): 1*-7*.
1994 *Kings without Privilege* (Edinburgh: T. & T. Clark).

Blum, E.
1990 *Studien zur Komposition des Pentateuch* (BZAW 189; Berlin: de Gruyter).

Boling, R.
1982 *Joshua* (Anchor Bible; New York: Doubleday).

Butler, T.C.
1983 *Joshua* (Word Biblical Commentary 7; Waco TX: Word Publishing).

Coote, R.P. and Whitelam, K.H.
1987 *The Emergence of Early Israel in Historical Perspective* (Sheffield: Almond Press).

Cortese, E.
1985 'Gios 21 e Giud 1 (TM o LXX?) e l'"abbottonatura" del Tetrateuco con l'Opera deuteronomistica', *Rivista Biblica* 33: 375-94.
1990 *Josua 13–21: Ein priesterschriftlicher Abschnitt im deuteronomistichen Geschichtswerk* (OBO 94; Freiburg, Schweiz: Universitätsverlag).

Davies, P.R.
1992 *In Search of 'Ancient Israel'* (JSOTSup 148; Sheffield: JSOT Press).

Douglas, M.
1993 *In the Wilderness: The Doctrine of Defilement in the Book of Numbers* (JSOTS 158; Sheffield: JSOT Press).

Eslinger, L.
1989 *Into the Hands of the Living God* (Bible and Literature Series 24; JSOT Supplement Series 84; Sheffield: Almond Press).

Finkelstein, I.
1988 *The Archaeology of the Israelite Settlement* (Jerusalem: Israel Exploration Society).

Fritz, V.
1994 *Das Buch Josua* (HAT I/7; Tübingen: Mohr).

Garbini, G.
1988 *History and Ideology in Ancient Israel* (London: SCM Press).

Gray, J.
1986 *Joshua, Judges and Ruth* (New Century; London: Marshall, Morgan and Scott, 3rd edn).

Greenspoon, L.J.
1983 *Textual Studies in the Book of Joshua* (HSM 28; Chico CA: Scholars Press).
1992 'The Qumran Fragments of Joshua: Which Puzzle are they Part of and Where Do they Fit?', in G.J. Brooke and B. Lindars (eds.), *Septuagint, Scrolls and Cognate Writings* (Septuagint and Cognate Studies 33; Atlanta GA: Scholars Press), 159-94.

Hawk, L.D.
1991 *Every Promise Fulfilled: Contesting Plots in Joshua* (Literary Currents in Biblical Interpretation; Louisville KY: Westminster/John Knox Press).

Ho, Craig Y.S.
1995 'Conjectures and Refutations: Is 1 Sam xxxi 1-13 really the source of 1 Chronicles x 1-12?', *VT* 45: 82-106.

Johnstone, W.
1990 *Exodus* (Old Testament Guides; Sheffield: JSOT Press).
1993 'The Deuteronomistic Cycles of "Signs" and "Wonders" in Exodus 1-13', in A.G. Auld (ed.), *Understanding Poets and Prophets: Essays in Honour of George Wishart Anderson* (JSOTSup 152; Sheffield: JSOT Press), 166-85.

Lemche, N.P.
1988 *Ancient Israel: A New History of Israelite Society* (The Biblical Seminar; Sheffield: JSOT Press).
1993a Review of M. Ottosson, *Josuaboken*, in *JBL* 112: 512-13.
1993b 'The Old Testament—A Hellenistic Book?', *SJOT* 7: 163-93.

Mitchell, G.
1993 *Together in the Land: A Reading of the Book of Joshua* (JSOTS 134; Sheffield: JSOT Press).

Mowinckel, S.
1964 *Tetrateuch-Pentateuch-Hexateuch: Die Berichte über die Landnahme in den drei altisraelitischen Geschichtswerken* (BZAW 90; Berlin: de Gruyter).

Mullen, E.T., Jr
1993 *Narrative History and Ethnic Boundaries: The Deuteronomistic Historian and the Creation of Israelite National Identity* (SBL Semeia Studies; Atlanta, GA: Scholars Press).

Noth, M.
1938 *Das Buch Josua* (HAT 7; Tübingen: Mohr).
1943 *Überlieferungsgeschichtliche Studien*, I.
1953 *Das Buch Josua* (HAT 7; Tübingen: Mohr, 2nd edn).

Ottosson, M.
1991 *Josuaboken. En programskrift för davidisk restauration* (Studia Biblica Upsaliensia I; Stockholm: Almqvist & Wiksell).

Polzin, R.
1980 *Moses and the Deuteronomist: A Literary Study of the Deuteronomic History*, Part 1 (New York: Seabury).

Porter, J.R.
1992 Review of M. Ottosson, *Josuaboken*, in SOTS Book List 1992, 83-84.

Soggin, J.A.
1988 *Joshua* (Old Testament Library; London: SCM Press, 2nd edn).

Talstra, E.
1993 *Solomon's Prayer. Synchrony and Diachrony in the Composition of 1 Kings 8,14-61* (Contributions to Biblical Exegesis and Theology 3; Kampen: Kok Pharos).

Thompson, T.L.
1992 *The Early History of the Israelite People* (Leiden: Brill).

Tov, E.
1992a '4QJosh[b]', in Z.J. Kapera (ed.), *Intertestamental Essays in Honour of Józef Tadeusz Milik* (Krakow: The Enigma Press).
1992b *Textual Criticism of the Hebrew Bible* (Minneapolis: Fortress Press).

Weinfeld, M.
1972 *Deuteronomy and the Deuteronomic School* (Oxford: Clarendon Press).

Woudstra, M.H.
1981 *The Book of Joshua* (NICOT; Grand Rapids, MI: Eerdmans).

'AHA, ASSYRIA! ROD OF MY FURY, VERY STAFF OF MY SENTENCING-CURSE'

Clyde Curry Smith

Introduction

Including the eight stray references in the Pentateuch and the related texts (Gen. 2.14; 10.11, 22 [paralleled by the late repetition in 1 Chron. 1.17]; 25.18; Num. 24.22, 24 [cf. Ps. 83.8 (v. 9 in MT)]), which call to mind obliquely but from another historical dimension, the oldest direct indication within the Hebrew Bible of an awareness of the might and power of Asshur/Assyria occurs in the book of the prophet Hosea. This book is internally dated to 'the days of Uzziah, Jotham, Ahaz, and Hezekiah, kings of Judah, and in the days of Jeroboam, the son of Joash, king of Israel' (Hos. 1.1), which we would understand to be the chronological period after 793/792 BCE, though if inclusive, until 687/686 BCE (dates of biblical kings regularly with Thiele 1951: 283), the entire eighth century BCE!

The eight explicit uses of Asshur/Assyria in Hosea (5.13; 7.11; 8.9; 9.3 [cj. 6]; 11.5; 12.2; 14.4) have the vagueness of poetic parallelism, made only reasonably specific by the analogy that 'all your [Israel's] fortresses shall be destroyed, as Shalman destroyed Beth-'Arb'el on the day of battle' (Hos. 10.14), which personal hypocoristic recalls a victory of some Shalmaneser, as Solomon Mandelkern (1846–1902) had already guessed in his *Concordance* (1895: 1524). While Albert Ten Eyck Olmstead (1880–1945) did not hesitate to insert the datum under his treatment of the reign of Shalmaneser III (Shulmanu-asharidu [858–824 BCE, dates of Assyrian kings regularly with Brinkman *apud* Oppenheim 1977: 343-46]), he made no effort to identify the actual event involving 'Beth-'Arb'el' (1923: 193), and *The New Oxford Annotated Bible* fifty years later still carried the disclaimer, 'the allusion is unknown and the text uncertain' (1973: 1097, footnote to the passage). The evidence and alternative best guesses are significantly weighed by William Rainey

Harper (1905: 358-59), Michael Astour (1971), Hans Walter Wolff (1974: 187-88), and Gösta Ahlström (1993: 593-94), with my preference going to Shalmaneser III's destruction of Irbid in Gilead during the Assyrian invasion of 841 BCE.

From 'the year that king Uzziah died' (740/739 BCE) (Isa. 6.1), an even greater voice turned his attention to the inner dynamics of Israelite religio-political history and its meaning, and the oracular portions of the book in the name of Isaiah, son of Amoz, provide twenty-one more instances of reference to Asshur/Assyria, including the usage which gives title, and gave stimulus, to this essay. The post-biblical tradition dated the death of this Isaiah to the reign of Manasseh (coregency 696/695–687/686, alone until 642/641 BCE; cf. Cogan 1974: 90, n. 136, with references), so that the comparable period given in Isaiah (1.1) is identical in its *terminus post quem* to that of Hosea.

The Deuteronomic historian, in compiling from his diverse sources a history of Israel and Judah, initiates reference to Asshur/Assyria with the military coming of Pul(u) (= Tiglath-pileser = Tukulti-apil-Esharra III [744–727]) against Samaria/Israel (2 Kgs 15.19) during the reign of Menahem (752–742/741). The narrative which follows (2 Kgs 15.19–23.29) accounts for forty-four citations, incorporating by specific naming three more kings of Assyria in addition to Pul; namely, Shalmaneser (2 Kgs 17.3, doublet 18.9; = Shulmanu-asharidu V [726–722]), Sennacherib (2 Kgs 18.13; = Sin-aḫḫe-eriba [704–681]), and Esarhaddon (2 Kgs 19.37; = Assur-aḫ-iddin [680–669]).

The Deuteronomic narrative is harmonized by the partial repetition of 2 Kings (18.13–20.11) in the book of the prophet Isaiah (chs. 36–39) so that nineteen instances of Asshur/Assyria find exact verbal usages. Similarly, the later Chronicler (in 2 Chron. 28–33) has abridgingly or expandingly parodied his Deuteronomic source (2 Kgs 16.2–21.9), accounting for thirteen more equivalent verbal reflections. Within the Hebrew Bible there remain but twenty-six other instances of Asshur/Assyria (Mic. 5.4, 5; 7.12; Jer. 2.18, 36; 50.17, 18; Ezek. 16.28; 23.5, 7, 9, 12, 23; 27.6, 23; 31.3; Nah. 3.18; Zeph. 2.13; Isa. 52.4; Zech. 10.10, 11; Lam. 5.6; Ezra 4.2; Neh. 9.32; 1 Chron. 5.6, 26) to complete the count of the biblical total of one hundred and thirty nine.

Of the some one hundred and twenty kings of Assyria who ruled throughout its total history of more than fifteen hundred years, or more particularly of the twenty kings of Assyria who ruled in the course of those three centuries of imperial expansion before its own destruction

(Smith 1969: 350; cf. Brinkman *apud* Oppenheim 1977: 343-46), the Hebrew Bible knows by name only seven (including, in addition to those named above, Sargon [Isa. 20.1; = Sharrukin II (721–705)] and Osnapper [Ezra 4.10; = Assurbanipal (668–627)]). While this may be explainable on the grounds that these few are the ones who contributed to the political destruction of the kingdoms of Israel and Judah, the fact remains strange considering that as early as Shalmaneser III (858–824), within the first generation of Assyrian imperial expansion westward, the kings of Israel and Judah become known within Assyrian royal inscriptions, thus references to Omri, Ahab, and Jehu (Smith 1977a).

Others have seen in these correlations or their absences—increasingly clarified since that first summary of them by George Rawlinson (1812–1902) in his Bampton Lectures of 1859 (1881), and reemployed and further revised in his successive refinements of his *Ancient Monarchies* (1862; 2nd edn, 1870)—not merely the possibilities of clarification related to the wars, destructions, and political connections, but also the basis for understanding something of the kinds of impact, religious and otherwise ideological, made by the one upon the other (Cogan 1974).

Clearly, something like a proverbial sense is found in the almost offhand phrase from the book of the prophet Isaiah by which this essay was entitled: 'Aha, Asshur/Assyria! rod of my fury, very staff of my sentencing-curse' (10.5). While one might wonder at the exact intonation of the initial *hoy* (ha!; aha!)—whether a mere fingering, or an indication of recognition, or a suggestion of derision—its usage, nevertheless, ascribes most uniquely, even if ambiguously, to Asshur/Assyria a most applied role as 'the rod of [divine] fury, the very staff in the hand of the [divine] sentencing curse [of coming punishment]'.

Like the later ascription of Messianic redeeming status to Cyrus, the king of Persia (Isa. 45.1; = Kurush II [538–530]), these quasi-poetic metaphors make clear both a philosophy of history and a theological or ideological perspective. Therein the greater powers of those particular epochs and their explicit human representative in the specificity of a named monarch, irrespective of these powers or monarchs own self-understanding or imperial ideology, serve instead in punishment, even of that same Israel and Judah, as well as in its redemption, as agents of the activity of YHWH, God of Israel. Nevertheless, that biblical perspective is kin to the same mode of thought of the Assyrian and not far from equally clearly expressed, for example, by the Deuteronomist in the words placed in the mouth of the Assyrian 'Rab-shakeh' (2 Kgs 18.19-35, esp. 33-35; cf. Cogan 1974: 111, n. 1), though more often recalled in the oft-repeated Assyrian phrases of the Assyrian kings (Grayson 1976).

Clearly, such notions carry a daring at the moment of expression—whether by 'the' Isaiah of ch. 10, or by the other, disciple, 'Isaiah' of ch. 45—that did not have to wait to see the partialities of outcome, never completely fulfilled one way or the other, but rather such notions had enough of an impression of both the power inherent in Asshur/ Assyria and that which the even Greater Power could employ. For the particularity of this essay we seek to identify what it is that might illustrate the kind of Asshur/ Assyria worthy of receiving the 'Aha!' that told its expressing poet this was indeed the usable rod or staff for divine chastisement of the very people whose 'mouthpiece' [*nabi'*] for the same divine that poet was.

We have come to understand the necessity of reading not only written words, but also the non-verbal, especially as expressed in decorative art (Smith 1977a; Winter 1981). With Lewis Mumford (1895–1990), this essay assumes and affirms that 'the buildings speak and act, no less than the people who inhabit them' (1966: 135). The Assyrian kings of the ninth century BCE brought into being with wall slabs (*agurru* or *askuppu*; *CAD* A1 160-163 or A2 334-335, respectively) engraved (*esēqu*; *CAD* E 331-332) in low relief (*asumu* or *ṣalmu*; *CAD* A2 348-349 or Ṣ 78-85) a mode of communication that provides exquisitely a place for us to determine the inner character of Asshur/Assyria, just before, and responded to by, the Hebrew prophetic tradition.

An Impression of Asshur/Assyria

1. *The Palace Complexes of the Capital*

Assyrian power, especially as directed towards the West, was relatively new, or at least newly consolidated, as one comes in upon the eighth century BCE. The significant name of the creator of that power is Aššur-naṣir-apli II (883–859; on whom, in the sense of mini-biography, see Smith 1988: 259-63). The expression of the achievement of that power can be seen in the creation of Aššur-naṣir-apli's great new palace within a newly reconstituted capital for his empire. That palace was begun by 875 BCE and dedicated in about 862 BCE on the occasion of a great banquet celebrated by a unique stele (Wiseman 1952; Brinkman 1968: 186-87, n. 1143; Grayson 1976: 172-76; Postgate and Reade 1980: 322; Reade 1985: 207).

In so far as that palace remained functional, though with some minor degrees of enlargement and/or repair and/or reorganization of internal use, until the reign of Sargon II (Reade 1985: 207), who finally went elsewhere to build a new palace in a new capital—never completed due to his death in battle and subsequent vilification, but nevertheless setting a pattern to follow for the last few great Assyrian monarchs, especially Sennacherib and Ashurbanipal, in their reconstitution of Nineveh with 'Palaces Without Rival' in the final phases of Assyrian history—we could do no better to grasp what it was that impressed the first Isaiah—whether from direct observation as a member of delegations from Jerusalem to the Assyrian capital, or merely by the kind of reporting that such delegations made back to Jerusalem—than to look closely at the great king's achievement. If justification for this choice be required, one should note particularly the Deuteronomic narratives (of Menahem [2 Kgs 15.19-20), Ahaz [2 Kgs 16.7-18], Hezekiah [2 Kgs 18.13-16; 20.12-15], or Manasseh [2 Kgs 21.3-9]) which tell of Israelite or Judaean royal visits of tribute, and their impressions of such visits, albeit with consequences condemned and dire, so as to warrant the threat that someone even more evil, as the king of Asshur/Assyria might indeed be considered, would indeed perform those functions which 'the rod of my fury' and 'the very staff in the hand of my sentencing-curse' implied and required. (See also Cogan 1974: chs. 4–5.)

The Assyrian capital city of Kalḫu was, like Nineveh, located on the east bank of the Tigris, near but not at the junction with the Greater Zab, some nineteen miles south. The overall site of Kalḫu is an irregular rectangle some 7,000 feet east–west by 5,500 feet north–south, enclosing thus an area of 884 acres or just under one-and-a-half square miles, originally encompassed by mud brick walls. Two citadels occupied respectively the SE and SW corners within these city walls. (See Mallowan 1956: 45-78; 1966; Postgate and Reade 1977; Reade 1982.)

Since the SE example will not concern us further in this essay, it may be dismissed quickly by identifying it as the *ekal mašarti*, or arsenal (*CAD* M1 358-359; Turner 1970: 71-72), of the capital, built by Shalmaneser III (858–824), and by briefly describing its size as again roughly rectangular, some 1,150 feet east–west by 825 feet north–south, amounting to 18 acres, 'at a level noticeably higher than that of the fields to the north and west' (Laessøe 1963: 108). Within this smaller rectangle's corner, forming the corner of the whole city, lay a palace complex about 330 feet wide (roughly east–west) by 300 feet long (roughly north–south), which sat at a height some 65 feet above the plains. Its internal area was thus over two acres.

Its throneroom (T1), measuring 139 feet by 32.3 feet, contained the carved throne dais showing Shalmaneser III 'shaking hands' with his Babylonian contemporary, Marduk-zakir-shumi I (ca. 845) (Brinkman 1968: 196, n. 1199; Brinkman 1989; Marcus 1987: 84-87). Outside room SE8 was an old, non-carved, but inscribed, throne dais of Shalmaneser III, which had presumably been transferred there after the creation of the newer carved variety, as a podium from which he could conceivably have sat upon a throne to watch his troops drilling. In T3 were the remains of the giant glazed brick panel above the doorway, which stood some 13.3 feet high. In the residential area to the west, chamber S5, probably another, older and smaller, throneroom was decorated with life-sized murals of processional officers.

All of these ingredients are interesting and the stuff of which many another palace or part thereof was decorated. But such materials must be dismissed if we are to concentrate upon the aforementioned 'wall slabs', and would not have been mentioned here were it not that 'Fort Shalmaneser' is but the newest great Assyrian palace to have been discovered. Its locus enables us to perceive the entirety of the capital city of Kalḫu which Shalmaneser III's father, Aššur-naṣir-apli II had built and which the son continued to develop. It illustrates a greater significance in the history of decoration played by Shalmaneser III than that for which he usually receives credit in the histories of Neo-Assyrian or even Mesopotamian art (Meuszynski 1976c). And it reminds us of all the significant elements in palace decoration upon which we cannot dwell by virtue of the immensity of the one matter alone. All of these other matters are there to come back to ultimately, and must needs be considered before one can say one has a final understanding of the not-unrelated 'wall slabs engraved in low relief'.

But for the present essay it is the other citadel at the SW corner of Kalḫu which receives our sole attention. Again, on a height some 65 feet above the plain, in its own NW corner, which rises to a conical peak of 100 feet (wherein the *ziqqurratu* [*CAD* Z 129-132] remains are found), there was this second, but older, even more irregular rectangle—irregular due to its abutment on its western edge along the original bed of the Tigris, which measures about 1,980 feet north–south by a maximum of 990 feet east–west providing a total acreage on the tell (called Nimrud) of some 45.5 acres.

To the south of the remains of the *ziqqurratu*, along this western edge of the tell, lay a huge palace complex (*ekallu*; *CAD* E 52-61), whose integrity was not easily recognizable by the earliest excavators, since an erosive ravine had over the centuries cut off the palace's northern chambers from its central core. It was the excavations begun by Sir Max Edgar Lucien Mallowan (1904–1978), in the period from 1949 to 1963, which reestablished the outline of the total palace area, which may be compared with that of Sir Henry Austin Layard (1817–1894) begun a century earlier in 1845. More recent work of restoration by the Iraqis, plus renewed Polish, and British Museum excavations, have clarified further the central core of chambers, especially in the area nearer the western slope of the mound. (See Meuszynski 1971; Meuszynski and Abdul-Hamid 1974; Sobolewski 1977; Reade 1985; Anonymous 1989 and 1991.)

The total size of the 'Northwest Palace of Aššur-naṣir-apli II', to give it with Layard a localizing position and the name of its builder, has thus been ascertained to be about 425 feet wide (east–west) by 650 feet long (north–south), thereby occupying some 6.5 acres of ground space. This palace was divided into three distinct regions.

At its northern end was an administrative wing (Mallowan's ZT [Ziqqurrat Terrace] Extension). While the ravine now disguises a great open court area, it also makes it impossible to determine the total area of this administrative wing. But herein were found the majority of cuneiform texts, of which it had previously been common to say that, in contrast to Nineveh, Kalḫu was unproductive. Mallowan notes, 'Room 4 contained a collection of over 350 tablets, the greatest number hitherto found in any one room at Nimrud (1966: I 172)—although they date from the later reigns of Tiglath-pileser III and Sargon II, both of whom still seem to have found all or parts of this palace complex available for occupancy or storage. A photograph (Mallowan 1966: I 173) shows what is said to be the 'scribal chamber' with its 'burnt brick bench which must have been used as a seat or table by the scribe whose "filing cabinets" lined with burnt bricks once filled with diplomatic archives' lay against the wall behind—probably the *girginakku*, or library (Smith 1977b: 27; *CAD* G 86-87).

At the southern wing were the domestic suites, including, says Mallowan, the harem. These are being further explored and then restored by the Iraqis. But in neither this southern wing, nor the aforementioned northern administrative wing, were wall relief slabs found.

Thus, again, interesting as these areas are in themselves, they need not detain us—except to perceive that we have identified the basic division for all Assyrian royal palaces (see Reade 1979–1980).

As even Layard's incomplete plan shows (Layard 1849: I facing p. 70), and as Richard David Barnett (1909–1986) has rightly summarized therefrom, the ground plan of the Northwest Palace, which may also be seen to be paradigmatic, 'consisted of a series of long, narrow rooms arranged longitudinally in two rows around the sides of a single square court open to the sky' (Barnett 1957: 3). Gordon Loud (1900–1971) demonstrated that Assyrian palaces are essentially arranged in this mode but about two rather than a single courtyard (1936: 153-60). This is what we see at the Northwest Palace, wherein, what Layard's ravine (1849: I plan facing p. 272) had demolished was the first or 'outermost courtyard' (in Akkadian *babanu*; cf. *CAD* B 7), to which the public had access and from which the public moved, when appropriate, into the formal ceremonial chamber or throneroom (Layard's 'B') within the palace.

Layard's court 'Y' was the 'inner courtyard' (in Akkadian *bitanu*; cf. *CAD* B 274-275), and around it the chambers with decorated wall relief slabs are arranged in the double row fashion—though only more recently has archaeology begun to discover something of the explicit character of the 'western reception wing' (Reade 1979: 58; 1985) in which it is said some 'narrative' reliefs originated, perhaps many of those which were transported by Esarhaddon (680–669 BCE) to the Southwest Palace where they were found, still stacked and not yet in place, also by Layard, who recognized them both from style and from inscription to have originated with Aššur-naṣir-apli II. (For a complete discussion, see Barnett and Falkner, 1962: 20-33, plus corresponding plates.) Beyond to the west of the wing was again an outer or open court facing the river, which must also have been another route of public access. Much here still requires clarification (but see Reade 1985).

Across the great courtyard, now ravine, which according to Mallowan's 'gues-timation' measured about 195 feet north–south, southward from the administrative wing, was the central ceremonial block, which opened impressively off this great courtyard through the two massive and magnificently decorated gateways, labeled 'D' (west) and 'E' (east), respectively entrance and exit, directly into the throneroom 'B', the largest single room within the entire palace, and, within all other palaces of the Neo-Assyrian period, with the exception of the throneroom at Kuyunjik (Nineveh)—built by Sennacherib in his 'Palace Without Rival' (Russell 1991: 47-50). Layard gave its dimensions as 154 feet (east–west) by 33 feet (north–south) (1849: I 123), which were confirmed by Mallowan. (Those of Sennacherib's throneroom are 167 feet by 40 feet!)

2. *The Wall Reliefs of the Palace*

That palace proper, whose wall relief decorations are the concern of this essay, is defined by the set of chambers which begin with entrance into throneroom 'B' and move therefrom by various series of gateways southward into or off this block's inner courtyard 'Y'. Of the 27 rooms of this central ceremonial core, which Layard originally identified—for which he used the letters 'A' through 'Z', plus 'AA' and 'BB', but without 'Q', of which 'Y', as already noted, designated the innermost courtyard of the complex, 13 rooms had no sculptured wall reliefs ['A', 'J', 'K', 'M', 'O', 'R', 'U', 'V', 'W', 'X', 'Y', 'AA', 'BB'].

While John Barker Stearns (1894–1973) has made this appropriate distinction based on relief decoration (1961: 59), it is to be noted from Layard's plan that 'M' was lined with twelve numbered slabs, which prompted another look at Layard's verbal description (1849: I 308-317, Appendix 1 to Plan 3). What we learn is that 'unsculptured' may yet imply the presence of 'Standard Inscription' even in the absence of relief art. And that is the case for the walls of rooms 'A', 'J', 'K', 'O', 'R', 'U', 'V', 'X', 'Y', and 'AA'. Layard is a bit ambiguous for room 'M', which he describes as 'precisely similar to chamber J'; and for 'W' he simply states 'unsculptured slabs' without his typical addition 'with usual inscription'. Of 'BB' he notes 'unsculptured slabs, the greater part destroyed'. One might hazard the guess, however, that for the Northwest Palace of Aššur-naṣir-apli II the 'Standard Inscription' was indeed standard (Olmstead 1916: 19-20, n. 5; Reade 1965; Grayson 1976: 164-67; de Filippi 1977).

In the remaining 14 rooms, two basic types of relief slabs have been found. Exclusively in 'B', 'I', and 'Z' were slabs with two registers of relief separated by a band of 'Standard Inscription'. From the other 11 rooms ('C', 'D', 'E', 'F', 'G', 'H', 'L', 'N', 'P', 'S', 'T') all slabs have a single large relief, cut across its middle, right over the figure(s), by the same band of 'standard' inscription. Whether this inscription over relief adds to or detracts from the object as art, the viewer must decide; the argument has gone both ways, though I side with Edith Porada (1912–), that the art is enhanced by the inscription, especially as becomes evident from the magnificently presented, detailed photographs of those relief slabs in the collection of the Metropolitan Museum of Art, New York, as shown in that rare volume *The Great King, King of Assyria* (1945).

Since the slabs removed from the Northwest Palace have become distributed worldwide, so that they have not been viewed in original location or in context with one another for some fourteen decades, it has become necessary to delineate on the basis of Layard's original notes and drawings, plus a careful examination by direct or photographic inspection, a number of criteria by which one may again sense how the items stood originally. It has been possible to observe the room origin of each slab (and probably simultaneously the date of its carving) from the number of lines (and minor variety of textual variations) which each inscriptional example exhibits. This criterion, aside from being verifiable on the basis of the old notes and drawings, as well as inspection of relief joins from contiguous slabs, also makes sense aesthetically, when we perceive that such a principle means for each room a continuous horizontal band created by the very visible lines of the inscription.

Reade seems the first to have noted this phenomenon (1965: 121); examples include: 18-line from 'D' and 'F'; 19-line from 'S'; 20-line from 'G' and 'P'; 26-line from 'H'. 'B' was an exception, but, as Reade affirms, it 'was an exceptional room': between doorways 'a' and 'b' (hence slabs, by Layard's numbering, 1-15) and doorways 'd' and 'a' (hence, slabs 30-32), slabs have 16 lines, while the remainder which survive (the entire wall from doorway 'c' to doorway 'd', with the exception of its last three slabs which were already missing at the time of rediscovery) have 18 lines. This subtle difference is probably not unrelated to the thematic variation within this room, to which I will subsequently return.

But before continuing with analysis within this central core of the palace, it is necessary to observe one other peculiar location. Beyond the administrative wing northwards, between itself and the *ziqqurratu*, was the Ninurta Temple (see now the plan in Meuszynski 1972: 66). Somewhat peculiarly, and quite exceptionally, some few and most unusual decorated wall slabs are also known from there. They also bear the Standard Inscription of Aššur-naṣir-apli II. Clarification of their number, original location, size and theme, had been accomplished by Janusz Meuszynski (1946–1976) of the Polish Centre for Mediterranean

Archaeology (see especially, 1972: 52-67) before he was prematurely slain.

While it is the case that at a few other palace centers, especially at gateways, one does find the carved colossi and with them their guardian 'genii', as far as I have been able to ascertain, within no other structure than a palace do carved wall reliefs occur. But then Aššur-naṣir-apli II was after all the first to decorate with carved wall reliefs, and it remains a moot question whether the stimulus came to him from 'Hittite' usage, since he as initiating extender of Assyrian imperial power came into their regions, or whether the Syro-Hittite area examples are not themselves a 'feedback' of the splendor which such tributaries came to see within his novel palace.

Be that as it may, there is no hesitation in observing that 'the great king, king of Assyria' outdid his rivals, even if they were the intermediaries in the transmission of the idea for carved wall relief slabs. And even if it were the immediate availability and accessibility of a plentiful and high quality alabaster (*gišnugallu*, *CAD* G 104-106; cf. Rawlinson 1870: I 219) or gypsum (*gaṣṣu*, *CAD* G 54-55; cf. Reade 1981) from the immediate region of the 'Assyrian Triangle' (Kinnier-Wilson 1962: 99), plus the infused capital and manpower from conquered territories, which made the prodigious dimensions of his effort possible and attainable, nevertheless, Aššur-naṣir-apli II did so at an extraordinary level of craftmanship, and, as observed just above, with a few unusually located emplacements.

At a second quantitative level of phenomenological description there is the matter and size of the wall reliefs in and from the Northwest Palace. While Layard provides some basic information and some general information on a room-by-room basis (1849: I 308-17), and in spite of the extraordinarily good state of preservation of the central core of this palace which he rightly attributed to its lower level and hence earlier 'burial' upon the citadel (1849: II 161-62), he did not describe all the slabs that he knew from wall dimensions to have originally been present, for a number of reasons.

Some were already missing from their original positions (accounted for only in part subsequently by the matter of the Central and Southwest Palaces of the same citadel; Barnett and Falkner 1962). Some were not in fact actually viewed by him (since his excavation method was essentially tunnelling). Some were merely repetitious in theme to others he had already described fully enough for his own satisfaction (variety, not *ad nauseam*, was the spice for Layard's life!). But as the numbers on his plan show, he accounted for 302 carved wall slabs: 'B' = 32; 'C'= 13; 'D' = 8; 'E' = 5; 'F' = 17; 'G' = 31; 'H' = 35; 'I' = 33 (there are two numbered '5'); 'L' = 36; 'N' = 19; 'P' = 3 (there is no number '1'); 'S' = 29; 'T' = 10; 'Z' = 10. To these are added into the total some few gateway figures (though I am here excluding the giant human-headed, animal-bodied, winged colossi = *lamassu*; *CAD* L 60-66): out of 'C' = 2; out of 'F' = 4; out of 'G' = 6; out of 'S' = 8; out of 'T' = 2.

It is said, because of the study of the Standard Inscription, that more than 270 examples are still extant, though this number includes the fact of fragments and the artificially divided double-register examples from room 'B', etc. Of this number 65 are identifiable in the British Museum, 50 in smaller collections in the United Kingdom, 70 in other museums of Europe, 60–70 in museums and private collections in the United States and Canada, with scattered others in Baghdad, Mosul, Istanbul, Bombay, and 'who knows where else'. Others are still *in situ* as contemporary Iraqi and Polish excavations and restorations have found, along with many of the fragments and inscribed sections which were cut off in the initial process of collection and preparation for distribution worldwide. (See Meuszynski and Abdul-Hamid 1974: 111-19.)

The prevailing size of these great slabs was 'ca 2,70 m [= 8' 9.5"] in height and ca 0,25 m [= 10"] thick'. 'The lowest half meter [= 20"] of the slab was sunk into the floor, and the remaining 2,20–2,30 m [= 7' 3"–7' 6"] was decorated with low relief' (Meuszynski and Abdul-Hamid 1974: 111). Typical British Museum examples range in width from 7' to 8' although the great throne relief ('B' 23 = BM 124531), met as it now is mounted for display in a niche-like fashion, still measures 6' 4" high by 14' 2" wide (Budge 1914: 11, pl. XI). The cut-down slabs, all save for three in Berlin found in the British Museum, and originally from throne-room 'B', range from 2' 10" to 3' 4" in height, so that inscriptional pieces some foot or more in height were removed and discarded, just as the lower foot and a half or so were sawn free and left *in situ*—a phenomenon that did not go without some sensitive protest at the time of their first removal (Bonomi 1848: 1152, *apud* Gadd 1936: 132-33). Yet considering that the material is gypseous alabaster (specific gravity = 2.317), the great weight per typical slab must have amounted to some 7,000 pounds; no wonder the thrifty Englishman literally 'cut corners'!

3. *The 'Reading' of Wall Reliefs*

At a third level of analysis there is the typology of thematic representation. Julian Edgeworth Reade (1938–) in his dissertation (written during 1962–1965, accepted at Cambridge in 1970 but only published in 1979–1980), divides wall decorative relief into 'five main categories of subject matter' which he distinguishes, in spite of the necessity of recognizing some obvious overlaps, in the following manner:

1. 'narrative, mostly consisting of small-scale action pictures';
2. 'formal, mostly consisting of large-scale pictures sometimes narrative in content';
3. 'apotropaic, mostly consisting of large-scale genies and colossi';
4. 'ornamental, which includes all repetitive painted friezes'; and
5. 'hieroglyphic, which is virtually confined to Sargon's temple façades' (1979: 28-29).

For our purposes, only the first three categories are relevant in general, by virtue of our exclusive focus on palace slab relief, and in particular vis-à-vis the Northwest Palace of Aššur-naṣir-apli II.

The mix of all three categories occurred in throneroom 'B'. For an example chiefly of category 3, with a minimum admixture of the king and his immediate ceremonial courtiers, room 'G' is satisfactory. Porada once commented that it was 'as if a giant roller with that design engraved upon it had been passed over the dada of the room leaving the imprint of an interminable frieze' (1945: 19). She specifically had in mind the cylinder seal as an obvious background to this kind of art impression. Paint was used on the reliefs originally—'traces of black have been found on the hair, beard, and pupil, white on the eyeball; the king's headdress was red and his sandals red and black' (Porada 1945: 19). But such comments only serve to remind us upon looking at a total room that Reade's typology leaves something to be desired as to the content of his categories.

'Narrative' may be self-evident, and sufficiently unique in each instance to defy further categorization. But in the Northwest Palace only room 'B' creates that problem for us (see Meuszynski 1975). To say something about the combinations which make up Reade's categories of 'formal' and 'apotropaic' requires further differentiation, though one look at room 'G' by way of examples makes it clear that the number of larger ingredients is in fact quite few. The work initiated by Stearns provides the next clue.

'Of the fourteen sculptured rooms eight contained portraits of the king (B, C, D, F, G, H, N, S), and six did not (E, I, L, P, T, Z)' (Stearns 1961: 50; cf. Paley 1976; Paley and Sobolewski 1981; Reade 1985). Including these 'portraits of the king', Stearns defined there to be eight basic kinds of relief species in one register (his type 'A'). His coding of these sculptures is of the schematic order, for example, 'A-I-a-i-1', etc. But of the eight basic kinds, his differentiation is based on costume, such that at the first level of visual inspection, only four kinds of 'figures' plus a 'sacred tree' appear. While more subtle differentiation, especially of accoutrements (Stearns' 'a'–'k', 'p'; with 'i' = facing right, and 'ii' = facing left; and the final number = the individual specimen), is ultimately in order, so that one might arrive at some understanding of the matter of the function of the figures portrayed, Stearns at best brings us no farther than an initial grasping of the larger dimensions of the problem.

I would even note, with Meuszynski, that Stearns has not been subtle enough, for he failed to distinguish whether winged figures have two or four wings (Meuszynski 1972: 27-70; and 1976b: 427-30 especially); also, with Reade, that Stearns omits varieties of figures that actually appear by his conflation of species (Reade 1979: 35-43). But Stearns remains the place to begin, and his five commonly represented categories, with their frequency on known reliefs, give our point of departure:

1. the king (*šarru*; *CAD* Š2 76-105) (Stearns's subtype 'I')—25 examples;
2. the winged, human-headed figure with beard (*ša ziqni*; *CAD* Z 126-27) (subtypes 'II', 'III')—103 examples;
3. the wingless, human-headed figure without beard (*ša reši*; 'eunuch'; cf. *CAD* Z 127) (subtypes 'IV', 'V', 'VI')—25 examples;
4. the winged, hawk-headed figure (*kuribu*; *CAD* K 559; using 'hawk' for Stearns's 'eagle', following Reade 1979: 39) (subtype 'VII')—21 examples;
5. the sacred tree (subtype 'VIII')—3 examples (though many more were left *in situ* or are to be found in half or lesser portions behind one of the previous figures on the slabs as cut and now found in museums).

Since there are many fewer two-register slabs (Stearns's type 'B'), except for the 'narrative' examples, which Stearns rather ambiguously includes or omits, chiefly on the basis of the presence or absence of the king respectively, there are also fewer representations, but by our coalescence of his types the same five possibilities. The distinctive characteristics of the subtype not requiring repetition, the tally may be summarized: of (1)—15 examples; of (2)—32 examples; of (3)—21 examples; of (4)—26 examples; and of (5)—1 example.

And in three registers (Stearns's type 'C'), exclusively from the entrance to the Ninurta temple (where they accompanied the very large colossi [*lamassu*] which guarded the doorway since the combined height of the three would be approximately 3 x 55" = 13' 9"—see Layard 1853: 348, reproduced in Meuszynski 1972: fig. 18), there are only subtypes (2)—3 examples, and (4)—1 example.

To these must be added a few rarer examples not clearly or not at all distinguished as subtypes by Stearns:

6. the winged human-headed female figure (*lamassatu*; *CAD* L 60). There is but one at the single register size, which Stearns mixed in with his bearded subtype! (BM 124578; Budge 1914: pl. XLI); and but two at the double register size, correspondingly confused by Stearns (both illustrated by Budge 1914: pl. XLII). These three examples—the one-register example from room 'L', and the two-register size, who stood as a pair on either side of a sacred tree from room 'I'—were each found in proximity to a drain, which they are assumed to have guarded (so Reade 1979: 36).
7. the fish-cloak-headed, human-faced figure (*apkallu*; *CAD* A2 171-73; Reade 1979: 38-39; Green 1985: 79; 1986). (Not in Stearns, nor illustrated in Budge; cf. Meuszynski 1972: fig. 23. The known example, BM 124573, came from the Ninurta Temple, and presumably had an oppositely facing mate.)
8. the winged, human-headed, scorpion-tailed, bird-footed creature (*girtablilu*; s.v. *zuqaqipu*, *CAD* Z 163-66; Reade 1979: 39; Green 1985). (Not in Stearns; cf. Meuszynski 1972: fig. 15. The known example, which originated from the Ninurta Temple, is in the Louvre, AO 19.850, although William Boutcher [1814–1900] had made a drawing of it on the spot of its discovery, which is in the British Museum, Or. Dr. I 17, now published by Meuszynski 1976c: pl. XIV. Remains of another example *in situ* appeared during the excavations in the central

area of the mound by the Polish expedition; cf. Meuszynski 1976a: 39.)

9. the lion-headed, winged, scaly creature (*ugallu*; Reade 1979: 39-40) and its 'pursuer' who is winged, human-headed with beard. (The British Museum possesses the single example of the subtype, BM 124571, and its 'pursuer' [which appears in Stearns as 'A–II–f–ii'], BM 124572, from the Ninurta Temple; cf. Budge 1914: pl. XXXVII; Meuszynski 1972: fig. 20; the pertinent comments by Jacobsen 1961: 270; and Reade 1979: 42-43.)

Additional varieties of what Reade would call these 'apotropaic' creatures would have to be added for later kings and their palace decorations, but for the present we have identified all types pertinent to the Northwest Palace of Aššur-naṣir-apli II. For the identification of all these latter non-human figures, that is, those with characteristics not part of human anatomy (though one may suppose humans could or did play the role in 'costume'), Reade (1979: 35-43) has gone back to cuneiform prophylactic texts, published initially by Sir Charles Leonard Woolley (1880–1980) and Sidney Smith (1889–1979) (Woolley and Smith 1926), and secondly with additional examples by Oliver Robert Gurney (1911–), for possible verbal equivalences (Gurney 1935). The correlations are suggestive, though incapable of thorough treatment here. More recent considerations appear in the work of Anthony Green (1983; 1985; 1986; 1988), and are noted above.

I may now summarize the situation prevailing in the various rooms:

'F' had one king; otherwise its walls were entirely decorated with 'sacred trees' flanked by alternately facing 'hawk-heads'. 'H' had only kings, winged bearded-heads, and trees in a repetitive pattern. 'L' had only winged bearded-heads and trees in a repetitive pattern, except for the unique 'female' at the drain. 'N' had one king, with winged bearded-heads in a repetitive pattern. 'S' had one king, with a mix of hawk-heads, bearded-heads, and trees, in a repetitive pattern; its location makes it the 'reception room' for the connection to the residential area.

The two-register complex in room 'I' had paired kneeling winged bearded-heads above, and paired standing hawk-heads below; in both instances the pairs flanked the sacred tree. The one instance of paired 'females' below, near the drain of the room, has already received comment. (Generally, the two registers are separated by the lines of the Standard Inscription, but there are some examples whereupon the inscription runs across and partially covers the pair from the lower register. If symmetry prevails, are such examples really from room 'I'; but if not, where from? Many such problems remain to be solved!)

Barnett thinks it possible to identify the function of many of these rooms. If the great hall 'B' be the throneroom, and 'F' its connecting-, but king's chamber-, linkage to the inner court, as discussed above in the general description of palace layout with double rows or rooms around a central court, then, says Barnett,

> Rooms H and G on the east side were banqueting halls. Behind them lay two small suites of rooms I-J and M-L, the walls of which were sculptured with winged figures and 'sacred trees'. The analogy of Tall Ahmar and Arslan Tash suggests they were sleeping rooms, and that the perforated stone slab in the floor of each is the drain for a washing place or toilet. Exactly the same arrangement of rooms was observed in the group to the south of the courtyard; and it was in the innermost of these rooms, in the sleeping chambers marked by Layard 'V' and 'W', that he discovered the main quantity of his ivories (1957: 3).

Barnett is inexact enough to be unclear, but from plans, and the phenomenology of wall decoration, what we discern him to be saying is this. The unsculptured, enclosed rooms 'J', 'M', 'V', and 'W', are called 'sleeping rooms', since the ivories found in the latter included much that could be bedstead decoration. It seems to me more probable that these would be closets, or storerooms, at best. Who might have slept in 'J' or 'M' certainly remains unclear. It is to be noted from the plan that both once had direct access to the large hall 'H' which was blocked off merely by a decorative slab facing into 'H'. 'I' and 'L' are strange L-shaped rooms, perhaps narrower north–south corridors from 'H' going around to the access for 'J' and 'M' respectively, but also around to 'bathrooms' proper—since the drains were in the far corners of the broader areas at 'I'-16 and 'L'-20 respectively. (For the Akkadian for 'lavatory' see *musatu*; *CAD* M2 234-35, whose cited texts also make reference to the 'demon of the lavatory' against which we may assume the protective 'female' genii guard?)

We come finally to the greater rooms 'G' and 'B'. But that brings us back to Reade's classificatory system of 'narrative', 'formal', and 'apotropaic'. In the period of Aššur-naṣir-apli II (and certainly subsequently), it is appropriate to note that Reade had said of 'narrative' that they were '*mostly* consisting of small-scale action pictures', leaving open the occasional (and subsequently frequent) possibility of 'large-scale action pictures' (the great lion hunts of Assurbanipal, in the sequences BM 124858–124870 and BM 124850–124857, each involving many slabs, come obviously to mind; see Barnett 1976: plates A, V-XIII). Moreover, Reade had also admitted 'some obvious overlaps' between his main subject categories, and here I would stress the subtle observation that at one level the difference between 'narrative' and 'formal' may lie in the perception of the beholder.

Yet it is also granted that if 'narrative' implies the capacity to correlate with textual inscriptions, then some specific scenes and kinds of scenes are much more obvious, while by the same criteria some scenes are apparently never mentioned in the texts, such as the king 'standing with arrows and bow' or 'standing with bowl and bow' (see examples from room 'G', slabs 6, 8, etc.), or uniquely 'sitting with bowl alone' (only 'G'-3; Stearns 'A-I-h-ii' = BM 124565). Such as these, and at the larger scale, might well be deemed 'formal' rather than 'narrative'.

Similarly, it also seems to me, that as room 'G' shows, this 'formal'–'narrative' mix spills over readily into Reade's 'apotropaic' category (Meuszynski 1971). In fact, it is subject matter not form which allows one to make the differentiation. Apotropaic is a 'turning away from', presumably to 'ward off', evil, etc. But 'apotropaic' figures are precisely 'formal' in stance, posture, persistence of costume, almost to the point of total identity or lack thereof. This is 'action stopped'. We would not know them to be distinct entities, were it not for the accoutrements. In fact, Stearns uses the term 'figure' to mean a human like ourselves, save for costume (of period, rank, and function), and the term 'genie' to encompass both varieties of 'winged-figures'—the 'bearded-heads' and the 'hawk-heads'.

But the former look as human as do his 'unwinged' figures, except for the presence of wings, from which 'hawk-heads' go otherwise only one quite obvious step further in transformation. Both of these latter are somewhat more restricted in terms of accoutrements held and thus 'employed' (if that be an appropriate term to use with respect to their stiff and unmoving posture). Yet the items held are material objects of this world, and so are their garments. There is no clear level of transcendence. What we at most see in such scenes as include such figures is what Thorkild Jacobsen (1904–1993) has called the 'metaphor of intransitivity', which is descriptive of that level of reality from which the divine, pertinent to all human civilization, has been responsively evoked. It is not yet the 'metaphor of transitivity' which emerges finally only within history, and then is led ultimately by the king, who can have become in form almost 'intransitive' in the process! (Jacobsen 1961: 267-78; 1976: *passim.*)

But I also had in mind some cases 'in between', which are 'formal' because they show the typical ceremonial posture or 'procession'—whether such be of the king and his court alone, or the king and his court receiving foreigners—normally 'tribute', occasionally in 'submission', sometimes (and increasingly so after Aššur-naṣir-apli II) as 'prisoners' or 'captives' of war (Smith 1977a: 80-91). The 'cast of characters' becomes much more difficult in these instances, and, as I have tried to suggest elsewhere (1977a: 80), await an indexing on the two 'microscopic' levels, wherein, on the first level, all appurtenances, costumes and paraphernalia would be symbolically coded, and, on the second level, one would look even closer to classify, for example, embroideries on the costumes, etc. Where possible on such a base those items coded would then be identifyingly correlated with textual details (Henshaw 1967–1968; 1969; 1980; Marcus 1981). The difficulty of this 'cast of characters' lies precisely in their representation of the variety of human actors in the historical drama with their assortment of material goods and the presence of animals both wild and domesticated. Individuality overcomes type!

At the level of 'small-scale action pictures', known only from throne-room 'B', the detail at these microscopic levels of 'cast of characters' and their detailed garb and the like, not only becomes harder to identify, but takes on the greater complexity of a stylized, quasi-photographic, yet actually chaotic-event—wherein the simplification process, which is the work of the human mind, attempts to transform such chaos of actual human and human-related interactives into some kind of digestible order and/or meaning (Liverani 1973: 185; quoted approvingly as 'postlude' by Smith 1977a: 99).

Clearly, as the little reliefs and relief-sequences in throneroom 'B' show, we have encountered at this level of meaning the fundamental 'ideology of the Assyrian empire' (Liverani 1979: 297-317), as expressed, perhaps initiated, by the court of Aššur-naṣir-apli II. It was this court, after all, who were the very ones most frequently to view the reliefs (on who saw palace reliefs, see Russell 1991: 223-40), and whom, we must conclude, appear among the human representations, including even the 'formal' or 'apotropaic' wingless, human-headed figures, with and without beards! Moreover, one suspects such persons also played the roles of the more 'costumed' apotropaic figures with wings as well! On the other hand, we need be prepared for some evolution in 'figures', their representation and their meaning, as we would proceed through later palace complexes (such as Sennacherib's, detailed by Russell 1991).

Conclusion

But to pause for the moment in conclusion of this essay, one soon senses that to have been descriptive was phenomenologically necessary and useful, but that one also remains a long way from an interpretative appreciation and understanding of what was really being represented on the palace walls by these carved slab reliefs, and of how such representations provide some kind of clue to the functional use of the chambers within and of the palace as a whole. Olmstead spoke of 'the calculated frightfulness of Ashur-naṣir-apal' (1923: 81-97) even before he came into 'the palace of the king' (1923: 98-109). He meant to refer to the military muscle, which, along with the king as hunter, is on display in throneroom 'B'. To this area certainly foreign visitors did come, usually with appropriate tribute—like that shown in the one huge register of very human figures and their material goods, albeit goods rather exotic like the several species of primates which appear. These figures 'move' (perennially!) in 'processional' style on the outer façades marked 'D' and 'E', along which these same kinds of visitors in the flesh passed in entering and exiting from the king's enthroned presence (Budge 1914: pl. XXVIII; Barnett and Falkner 1962: pls. CXXI, CXXIV-CXXV).

But when one moves on within the inner chambers, to which such tributary visitors never or seldom penetrated, one begins to wonder whether Olmstead's 'of' in his phrase 'calculated frightfulness of', ought not be possessive rather than ablative genitive? Was it Aššur-naṣir-apli II himself who perceived that all about him there was much that was in need of exorcism—the fearful things of the worlds of humans and gods? Empire is an awesome matter. It may already have appeared so, even to its creator.

But the die was cast. Assyria was committed to the task. And I would go along with Olmstead (1923: 645-55), who rewrote Lord Byron's famous poetic line, 'the Assyrian came down like a wolf on the fold', to say, Assyria 'was the shepherd-dog of civilisation' who stuck to his post till his death! In that same vein the poet of Israel was equally perceptive in calling Assyria, 'the rod of my fury, the very staff of my sentencing-curse!'

But such poetic stuff has digressed a long way from the phenomenology of palaces and their decorations. Yet surely the relief art was meant to speak; and in an era of a low degree of literacy, it must have been one of the most impressive modes of communication. That communication must have spoken in both directions: from within the palace out—and that is obvious in throneroom 'B'. But I would think we cannot fail to note the alternative direction as well: from within the palace in—and that is even more overwhelmingly obvious from the rest of the decorated rooms. But what these internal rooms were meant to say, and to whom, is much more difficult for us to discern, until the phenomenological indexing achieves some higher degree of adequacy. To that task, as well as to the other palace complexes of the Neo-Assyrian period which also show us decorated wall reliefs, we must henceforth turn. But for the moment that means laying this essay aside.

Yet to end with ambiguity brings us back to our point of departure, for there does indeed appear an ambiguity inherent within the Hebrew particle with which the poet-prophet introduced his subject and this essay—an essay dedicated to one whose long career sought clarification of just such minuscule points of syntax and grammar with respect to the written text, but who would be equally open to those same points applied to the non-verbal. *Hoy, 'Asshur*!

BIBLIOGRAPHY

Ahlström, G.

1993 *The History of Ancient Palestine from the Palaeolithic Period to Alexander's Conquest.* (With a contribution by Gary O. Rollefson; ed. D. Edelman; JSOTSup 146; Sheffield: JSOT Press).

Anonymous [Editor of *Iraq*]

1989 'Excavations in Iraq, 1987–88: Nimrud', *Iraq* 51: 259.

1991 'Excavations in Iraq, 1989–90: Nimrud', *Iraq* 53: 177-78.

Astour, M.C.

1971 '841 BC: The First Assyrian Invasion of Israel', *Journal of the American Oriental Society* 91: 383-98.

Barnett, R.D.

1957 *A Catalogue of the Nimrud Ivories* (London: The Trustees of the British Museum).

1976 *Sculptures from the North Palace of Ashurbanipal at Nineveh* (London: The Trustees of the British Museum).

Barnett, R.D., and M. Falkner
1962 *The Sculptures of Assur-naṣir-apli II (883–859 BC), Tiglath-pileser III (745–727 BC), Esarhaddon (681–669 BC) from the Central and South-West Palaces at Nimrud* (London: The Trustees of the British Museum).

Bonomi, J.
1848 *Nineveh and its Palaces: The Discoveries of Botta and Layard, Applied to the Elucidation of Holy Writ* (London: Bell & Daldy).

Brinkman, J.A.
1968 *A Political History of Post-Kassite Babylonia, 1158–722 BC* (Analecta Orientalia, 43; Rome: Pontificium Istitutum Biblicum).
1989 'Marduk-zakir-sumi', in *Reallexikon der Assyriologie und vorderasiatischen Archäologie* (ed. D.O. Edzard *et al.*; Berlin: de Gruyter), VII, 378-79.

Budge, E.A.
1914 *Assyrian Sculptures in the British Museum: Reign of Ashur-nasir-pal, 885–860 BC* (London: The Trustees of the British Museum).

Cogan, M.
1974 *Imperialism and Religion: Assyria, Judah and Israel in the Eighth and Seventh Centuries BCE* (Missoula, MT: Society of Biblical Literature and Scholars Press).

de Filippi, W.
1977 'The Royal Inscriptions of Assur-naṣir-apli II (883–859 BC): A Study of the Chronology of the Calah Inscriptions Together with an Edition of Two of These Texts', *Assur* 1/7: 1-47.

Gadd, C.J.
1936 *The Stones of Assyria: The Surviving Remains of Assyrian Sculpture, Their Recovery and Their Original Positions* (2 vols.; London: Chatto and Windus).

Grayson, A.K.
1976 *Assyrian Royal Inscriptions, Part 2: From Tiglath-pileser I to Ashur-naṣir-apli II* (Records of the Ancient Near East; Wiesbaden: Otto Harrassowitz).

Green, A.
1983 'Neo-Assyrian Apotropaic Figures', *Iraq* 45: 87-96.
1985 'A Note on the "Scorpion-Man" and Pazuzu', *Iraq* 47: 75-82 + plates.
1986 'A Note on the Assyrian "Goat-Fish", "Fish-Man" and "Fish-Woman"', *Iraq* 48: 25-30 + plates.
1988 'A Note on the "Lion-Demon"', *Iraq* 50: 167-68.

Gurney, O.R.
1935 'Babylonian Prophylactic Figures and Their Rituals', *Annals of Archaeology and Anthropology* 22: 31-95.

Harper, W.R.
1905 *A Critical and Exegetical Commentary on Amos and Hosea* (The International Critical Commentary; Edinburgh: T. & T. Clark).

Henshaw, R.A.
1967–68 'The Office of *šaknu* in Neo-Assyrian Times', *Journal of the American Oriental Society* 87: 517-25; 88: 461-83.
1969 'The Assyrian Army and Its Soldier, 9th-7th c., BC', *Kodaigaku* [Osaka, Japan] 16: 1-24.
1980 'Late Neo-Assyrian Officialdom', *Journal of the American Oriental Society* 100: 283-305.

Jacobsen, T.P.R.
1961 'Formative Tendencies in Sumerian Religion', in *The Bible and the Ancient Near East: Essays in Honor of William Foxwell Albright* (ed. G.E. Wright; Garden City, NY: Doubleday), 267-78.
1976 *The Treasures of Darkness: A History of Mesopotamian Religion* (New Haven: Yale University Press).

Kinnier-Wilson, J.V.
1962 'The Kurba'il Statue of Shalmaneser III', *Iraq* 24: 90-115.

Laessøe, J.
1963 *People of Ancient Assyria: Their Inscriptions and Correspondence* (trans. F.S. Leigh-Browne; New York: Barnes & Noble).

Layard, A.H.
1849 *Nineveh and Its Remains: With an account of a Visit to the Chaldaean Christians of Kurdistan, and the Yezidis, or Devil-Worshippers; and an Inquiry into the manners and arts of the ancient Assyrians* (2 vols.; New York: George P. Putnam).
1853 *Discoveries in the Ruins of Nineveh and Babylon, with Travels in Armenia, Kurdistan and the Desert: Being the result of a second expedition undertaken for the Trustees of the British Museum* (London: John Murray).

Liverani, M.
1973 'Memorandum on the Approach to Historiographic Texts', *Orientalia* 42: 178-94.
1979 'The Ideology of the Assyrian Empire', *Mesopotamia* 7: 297-317.

Loud, G.
1936 'An Architectural Formula for Assyrian Planning Based on the Results of Excavations at Khorsabad', *Revue d'Assyriologie et d'archeologie orientale* 33: 153-60.

Mallowan, M.E.L.
1956 *Twenty-Five Years of Mesopotamian Discovery* (London: The British School of Archaeology in Iraq).
1966 *Nimrud and Its Remains* (2 vols.; London: William Collins).

Marcus, M.I.
1981 'A Study of Types of Officials in Neo-Assyrian Reliefs: Their Identifying Attributes and their Possible Relationship to a Bureaucratic Hierarchy' (Unpublished MA thesis; Columbia University).
1987 'Geography as an Organizing Principle in the Imperial Art of Shalmaneser III', *Iraq* 49: 77-90.

Meuszynski, J.
1971 'Contribution to the Reconstruction of Interiors of the Northwest Palace in Kalhu (Nimrud)', *Etudes et Travaux* 5: 31-51.
1972 'The Representations of the Four-Winged Genies on the Bas-Reliefs from Assur-naṣir-apli II Times', *Etudes et Travaux* 6: 27-70.
1975 'The Throne Room of Assur-naṣir-apli II', *Zeitschrift für Assyriologie und vorderasiatische Archäologie* 64: 51-73.
1976a 'Some Reliefs from the North-West Palace at Nimrud', *Etudes et Travaux* 9: 29-45.
1976b 'Die Reliefs von Assurnaṣirapli II: Die Sammlungen ausserhalb des Irak', *Archäologischer Anzeiger* 4: 423-80.
1976c 'Neo-Assyrian Reliefs from the Central Area of Nimrud Citadel', *Iraq* 38: 37-43 + plates.

Meuszynski, J., and H. Abdul-Hamid
1974 'Ekal Assur-naṣir-apli: First Report on Relief: Rooms "B" and "L"', *Sumer* 30: 111-19 + figures.

Mumford, L.
1966 *The City in History: Its origins, its transformations, and its prospects* (Harmondsworth: Penguin Books).

Olmstead, A.T.E.
1916 *Assyrian Historiography: A Source Study* (The University of Missouri Studies: Social Science Series, volume III, number 1; Columbia, MO: University of Missouri Press).
1923 *History of Assyria* (New York: Charles Scribner's Sons).

Oppenheim, A.L.
1977 *Ancient Mesopotamia: Portrait of a Dead Civilization* (Chicago: The University of Chicago Press, 2nd edn).

Paley, S.M.
1976 *King of the World: Ashur-naṣir-pal II of Assyria 883–859 B C* (Brooklyn, NY: The Brooklyn Museum).

Paley, S.M., and R. Sobolewski
1981 'A New Reconstruction of Room Z in the North-West Palace of Assurnaṣirpal II at Nimrud (Kalhu)', *Iraq* 43: 85-99 + plates.

Porada, E.
1945 *The Great King, King of Assyria: Assyrian Reliefs in the Metropolitan Museum of Art* (Photographed by Charles Sheeler; New York: The Metropolitan Museum of Art).

Postgate, J., and J.E. Reade
1977–1980 'Kalhu', in *Reallexikon der Assyriololgie und vorderasiatischen Archäologie* (ed. D.O. Edzard *et al.*; Berlin: de Gruyter), V, 303-23.

Rawlinson, G.
1870 *The Five Great Monarchies of the Ancient Eastern World, or the history, geography, and antiquities of Chaldaea, Assyria, Babylon, Media, and Persia* (3 vols.; New York: Dodd, Mead & Company, 2nd edn).
1881 *The Historical Evidences of the Truth of the Scripture Records Stated Anew, with special reference to the doubts and discoveries of modern times in eight lectures delivered in the Oxford University pulpit, in the year 1859, on the Bampton Foundation. From the London edition*

with the Notes translated by Rev. A.N. Arnold (New York: Sheldon and Company).

Reade, J.E.

1965 'Twelve Ashur-naṣir-pal Reliefs', *Iraq* 27: 119-34.

1979–80 'Assyrian Architectural Decoration: Techniques and Subject Matter', *Baghdader Mitteilungen* 10: 17-110; 11: 71-87 (plus plates).

1981 'Fragments of Assyrian Monuments', *Iraq* 43: 145-56.

1982 'Nimrud', in *Fifty Years of Mesopotamian Discovery* (ed. J. Curtis; London: British School of Archaeology in Iraq).

1985 'Texts and Sculptures from the North-West Palace, Nimrud', *Iraq* 47: 203-14 + plates.

Russell, J.M.

1991 *Sennacherib's Palace Without Rival at Nineveh* (Chicago: The University of Chicago Press).

Smith, C.C.

1969 'Some Observations on the Assyrians and History', *Encounter* 30.4: 340-53.

1977a 'Jehu and the Black Obelisk of Shalmaneser III', in *Scripture in History and Theology: Essays in Honor of J. Coert Rylaarsdam* (ed. A.L. Merrill and T.W. Overholt; Pittsburgh, PA: The Pickwick Press), 71-105.

1977b 'The Birth of Bureaucracy', *Biblical Archaeologist* 40.1: 24-28.

1988 'Ashurnasirpal II', in *Great Lives from History: Ancient and Medieval Series* (ed. F.N. Magill: Pasadena, CA: Salem Press), I, 259-63.

Sobolewski, R.

1977 'Die Ausgrabungen in Kalhu (Nimrud) 1974–76', *Archiv für Orientforschung* 25: 230-38.

Stearns, J.B.

1961 *Reliefs from the Palace of Ashurnaṣirpal II* (Archiv für Orientforschung, Beiheft 15; Graz: Im Selbstverlage des Herausgebers Ernst Weidner).

Thiele, E.R.

1951 *The Mysterious Numbers of the Hebrew Kings: A Reconstruction of the Chronology of the Kingdoms of Israel and Judah* (Chicago: The University of Chicago Press).

Turner, G.

1970 'Tell Nebi Yunus: The *Ekal Mašarti* of Nineveh', *Iraq* 32: 68-85.

Winter, I.J.

1981 'Royal Rhetoric and the Development of Historical Narrative in Neo-Assyrian Reliefs', *Studies in Visual Communication* 7.2: 2-38.

Wiseman, D.J.

1952 'A New Stela of Assur-naṣir-pal II', *Iraq* 14: 24-44.

Wolff, H.W.

1974 *Hosea: A Commentary on the Book of the Prophet Hosea* (Hermeneia; trans. G. Stansell; ed. P.D. Hanson; Philadelphia, PA: Fortress Press).

Woolley, C.L., and S. Smith

1926 'Babylonian Prophylactic Figures', *Journal of the Royal Asiatic Society of Great Britain and Ireland*, 689-713 (plus plates).

God of Cyrus, God of Israel: Some Religio-Historical Reflections on Isaiah 40–55

Philip R. Davies

I

John Sawyer has made a reputation for boldness: his *Semantics in Biblical Research*[1] broke ground that has since been richly harvested; his *From Moses to Patmos*[2] preceded the fashion of canon criticism and far exceeded the imagination of virtually all of its practitioners. Latterly he has devoted much of his scholarly effort to prophecy in general[3] and the book of Isaiah in particular.[4] This essay is offered to him as a reflection of both his audacity and also his current interest, though its strong historical emphasis betrays more of my own inclination than his.

'Second Isaiah' or 'Deutero-Isaiah' (Isaiah 40–55) has, like the book of Deuteronomy, secured a time and setting blessed by a virtual scholarly unanimity: both compositions serve as literary beacons of respectively those linchpins of biblical history (and fermenting vats of literary productivity), the 'Josianic reform' and the 'Babylonian exile'. This essay is a contribution to recent efforts at dislodging Isaiah 40–55 from its assigned place, and in so doing will revise some traditional notions about the history of the cult of Yahweh and the religion of Judah in antiquity.

An appropriate starting point for this investigation are the most explicit of historical references in Isaiah 40–55, viz, the naming of Cyrus

1. *Semantics in Biblical Research: New Methods of Defining Hebrew Words for Salvation* (SBT 2/24; London: SCM Press, 1972).

2. *From Moses to Patmos: New Perspectives in Old Testament Study* (London: SPCK, 1977).

3. *Prophecy and the Biblical Prophets* (Oxford: Oxford University Press, rev. edn, 1993).

4. 'The "Daughter of Zion" and the "Servant of the Lord" in Isaiah. A Comparison', *JSOT* 44 (1989), pp. 89-107.

in 44.28 and 45.1-7. The relationship between these passages and the famous inscription of the Persian king now housed in the British Museum[5] has been invoked and examined many times. According to the *Cyrus Inscription* the 'lord of the gods' (Marduk), also 'protector of his people', searched for a 'righteous ruler to take his hand' and pronounced the name of Cyrus as future ruler of the world. Marduk 'beheld Cyrus's good deeds and upright heart', as a result of which Babylon was overcome without any battle, and subsequently 'all the kinds of the world brought tributes' to Cyrus, while the new ruler of the world rebuilt cities and sanctuaries. Similarly, in Isaiah 45 Yahweh 'grasps Cyrus's hand', to empower him to 'subdue nations' and 'open gates'; as a result, the wealth of Egypt and the Sabaeans will come to Cyrus.

These parallels, first noted almost a century ago[6] continue to be noted, but almost inevitably with the disclaimer that the writer of the Hebrew poems cannot have been dependent on the inscription; they must have been written before Cyrus's capture of Babylon. This assertion is often supported by the claim that the poetry constitutes genuine prediction (by virtue of being 'prophecy', or in a book of 'prophecy'). At all events, the similarities between the texts tend for the most part to be regarded as each dependent on either a 'Babylonian court style'[7] or, with greater form-critical precision, the genre of 'royal oracle'.[8] A more precise definition of the relationship has been offered by Morton Smith,[9] arguing that the parallels between the biblical texts and the inscriptional all involve only the first part of the inscription, which speaks of the king in the third person, and which, on Smith's view, represents propaganda from the Babylonian priesthood, *originating from before Cyrus's arrival in Babylon*, and paralleled only in Isaiah 40–48, whereas to the second part of the inscription there are 'almost no parallels in II Isaiah'.[10]

5. The text may be read in J.B. Pritchard (ed.), *Ancient Near Eastern Texts Relating to the Old Testament* (Princeton: Princeton University Press, 3rd edn, 1969), pp. 315-16 (translation by A.L. Oppenheim); D. Winton Thomas (ed.), *Documents from Old Testament Times* (London: Nelson, 1958), p. 92 (translation by T. Fish).

6. R. Kittel, 'Cyrus and Deuterojesaja', *ZAW* 18 (1898), pp. 149.**

7. H. Gressmann, *Der Messias* (FRLANT, 19; Göttingen: Vandenhoeck & Ruprecht, 1929), pp. 59-60.

8. Westermann, *Isaiah 40–66*, p. 154, alluding also to Psalm 2 and a 'number of smaller units' within the Hebrew Bible.

9. 'II Isaiah and the Persians', *JAOS* 83 (1963), pp. 415-21.

10. 'II Isaiah and the Persians', p. 415.

Smith's verdict on a close comparison of Isaianic texts and the inscription is that 'the parallels demonstrate literary dependence'.[11] However, since the statements of Second Isaiah about the capture of Babylon are inaccurate, they must, he concludes, have been written before the peaceful capture of that city. The lack of parallels with the second part of the inscription, which tells of the favourable treatment of Babylon by its new ruler, are claimed to support this contention. Thus, the sentiments of the author of the Hebrew text are the result of successful Persian propaganda. The poet must have been persuaded by agents of the Persian king, before Cyrus's arrival in Babylon.

Smith deduces further that contacts *of the same kind* might have led to the transmission of further Persian ideas, such as the creation of the world, a doctrine which (he claims) cannot be found in any Hebrew text whose origins we can securely date earlier than the sixth century. The extent to which Isaiah proclaims this doctrine, which he claims to have existed 'of old' (40.21, 28 etc.) testifies to its very novelty (a typically Smithian insight!). And finally, he offers us a parallel between some texts from Isaiah 40, 44 and 45 and *Yasna* 44, one of Zoroaster's Gathas. The parallel texts deal with the supreme deity as the source of justice, creation of the heavenly and earthly beings, of light and darkness, of wisdom. These parallels, which involve the same material as the parallels to the Cyrus inscription (chs. 40–48) suggest to Smith 'relationship to the same tradition'. Why such parallels might have been taken up by Second Isaiah is left by Smith deliberately unanswered.

I take note of Smith's suggestion because it raises the issue of whether the poetry of Isaiah 40–55 is influenced by the ideology of the Achaemenid empire, an issue that will resurface later in this discussion. Also, it seems to have been endorsed in large measure by Mary Boyce, who speaks of the 'exalted trust in Cyrus which the unknown Persian propagandist had instilled in the prophet',[12] and actually makes a complete circle out of Smith's case by arguing that since the Zoroastrian influence came from Achaemenid agents, Cyrus must have been a Zoroastrian.

11. 'II Isaiah and the Persians', p. 417.

12. *A History of Zoroastrianism* (Handbuch der Orientalistik; Leiden: Brill, 1982), II, p. 45.

II

There are two objections to Smith's thesis, one minor and one major. The minor objection is that the parallels with Second Isaiah in the Cyrus inscription are not restricted to the first part. Its final section includes the following:[13]

> All the kinds of the entire world from the Upper to the Lower Sea, those who are seated in throne rooms, (those who) live in other [types of buildings as well as] all the kings of the West land living in tents, brought their heavy tributes and kissed my feet in Babylon…

This may be compared with Isa. 45.14: 'The wealth of Egypt and the merchandise of Ethiopia, and the Sabaeans, men of stature, shall come over to you and be yours, they shall follow you; they shall come over in chains and bow down to you. They will make supplication to you...' There are differences between the two passages, but the parallel should not necessarily be excluded, even though the same sentiments are also present in the first part of the inscription.

The more important difficulty is that Smith's view requires Second Isaiah to have been in Babylon. This does not seem at first sight an insuperable objection, since this is where scholarly consensus places the poet. However, this consensus, having come about in a curious and rather uncritical way, has recently been coming under attack. An impressive review of the history of this consensus, and of the argumentation on which it is based, has been offered by Christopher Seitz,[14] who has added his weight to some recent doubts that Second Isaiah is to be located in Babylon. These doubts (as will presently be shown) seem to be increasing as the current scholarly interest in the redactional history of the contents of the book of Isaiah as a whole intensifies.

Seitz reminds us that for Bernhard Duhm, as well as for a number of other scholars earlier this century, there was no question of a Babylonian provenance for these poems.[15] Duhm in fact stated forcefully that the

13. The translation is taken from *ANET*.

14. C.R. Seitz, *Zion's Final Destiny. The Development of the Book of Isaiah. A Reassessment of Isaiah 36–39* (Minneapolis: Fortress Press, 1992).

15. Besides Duhm himself (*Das Buch Jesaja* [HKAT; Göttingen; Vandenhoeck & Ruprecht, 1892]), the list of older commentators includes G. Ewald (*Die Propheten des alten Bundes I* [Göttingen: Vandenhoeck & Ruprecht, 1867]); K. Marti (*Das Buch Jesaja* [KHAT; Tübingen: Mohr, 1900]); G. Hölscher, (*Die Propheten*

author of Isaiah 40–55 was definitely *not* to be located there.[16] More recently Arvid Kapelrud,[17] James D. Smart[18] and Hans Barstad[19] have also proposed objections against a Babylonian setting. Not all of the earlier scholars (including Duhm himself) opted for a setting in Palestine, though the more recent critics have been more in agreement. In Barstad's view, the reason for this difference is that until fairly recently scholarship merely accepted the biblical claim that Judah was virtually denuded of population, religion and culture after 586 CE, so that the notion of prophetic activity such as Second Isaiah implied was simply not considered.[20] Barstad points, however, to not only the existence of the book of Lamentations—which the scholarly consensus sets in Jerusalem—but its similarity in many respects to some of the ideas of Second Isaiah. (It may also be worth remembering that Martin Noth placed the composition of his 'Deuteronomistic History' in Palestine during the 'exilic period', a view surreptitiously abandoned by most of his successors.)

The exilic setting is also being to some extent undermined (though less obviously) by the current trend towards denying the original independence of 40–55 from 1–39 (in some form). This independence (and not a distinct geographical setting) was, of course, the foundation of Duhm's own argument for a 'Second Isaiah'. Several scholars now suggest that Second Isaiah is to be understood as commentary on a collection which corresponds to the present 'First Isaiah', deliberately expanding an existing Isaianic corpus by adding a series of poems. The implications of this view are, on the conventional dating of chs. 40–55, that First Isaiah was substantially developed before the end of the seventh century. Not all commentators are content with boxing themselves into this corner,[21] in

[Leipzig: Hinrichs, 1914]), p. 322; C.C. Torrey (*The Second Isaiah: A New Interpretation* [New York: Charles Scribner's Sons, 1928); S. Mowinckel ('Die Komposition des Deuterojesanischen Buches', *ZAW* 8 [1931], pp. 87-112, 242-60).

16. Duhm, *Das Buch Jesaja*, p. xviii.

17. 'Levde Deuterojesaja i Judea?', *NTT* 61 (1960), pp. 23-27.

18. J.D. Smart, *History and Theology in Second Isaiah: A Commentary on Isaiah 35, 40–66* (Philadelphia: Westminster Press, 1965).

19. H. Barstad, 'Lebte Deuterojesaja in Judäa?', *NTT* 83 (1982), pp. 77-87.

20. An analysis of this biblical ideology of the 'empty land' can be found in R.P. Carroll, 'Textual Strategies and Ideology in the Second Temple Period', in P.R. Davies (ed.), *Second Temple Studies 1. Persian Period* (JSOTSup, 117; Sheffield: JSOT Press, 1991), pp. 108-24.

21. One exception is H.G.M. Williamson 'First and Last in Isaiah', in

view of the considerable amount of analysis which—resuming Duhm's own agenda—identifies a good deal of post-exilic material in Isaiah 1–39.[22] The recent study by Jean Marcel Vincent[23] assigning the whole of 40–55, with the rest of Isaiah, to the postexilic Jerusalem priesthood, has been virtually ignored, though Ronald Clements accepts some of Vincent's arguments, and pursuing his own thesis that Isaiah 40–55 is developed consciously out of 1–39, observed that while a Babylonian setting remains likely for 'at least some of the material', a Palestinian origin is 'an increasingly probable deduction to make from so much of the recent research into the origin of these enigmatic chapters'.[24] The issue of single authorship *versus* redaction is, however, not one which can be taken up here, important though it is.[25] It is enough to comment

H.A. McKay and D.J.A. Clines (eds.), *Of Prophets' Visions and the Wisdom of Sages: Essays in Honour of R. Norman Whybray on his Seventieth Birthday* (JSOTSup, 162; Sheffield: JSOT Press, 1993), pp. 95-108. In asserting that Second Isaiah has a sixth-century Babylonian setting, yet was composed as an addition to First Isaiah, he finds himself impelled to date the creation of First Isaiah in the pre-exilic period (the inevitable Josianic setting!) and thus to cut a path (cul-de-sac?) in a different direction from that taken by most of his colleagues who see Second Isaiah as an integral part of the developing corpus of Isaiah as a whole—not to mention in defiance of O. Kaiser, who is not cited in this article.

22. E.g. J. Vermeylen, *Due prophète Isaïe à l'apocalyptique. Isaïe I-XXXV, miroir d'un demi-millénaire d'expérience religieuse en Israël* (2 vols.; Etudes bibliques; Paris: Gabalda, 1977–78), O. Kaiser, *Das Buch des Propheten Jesaja: Kapitel 1–12* (ATD, 17; Göttingen: Vandenhoeck & Ruprecht, 5th edn, 1981 [ET London: SCM Press/Philadelphia: Westminster Press, 1983]). See also the recent work of B. Gosse, who relates the redaction of the entire book of Isaiah to priestly circles, linking the process to elements in both the Psalms and Proverbs (e.g. 'Isaïe 1 dans la rédaction du livre d'Isaïe', *ZAW* 104 [1992], pp. 52-66; 'Isaïe vi et la tradition isaïenne', *VT* 42 (1992), pp. 340-49.

23. J.M. Vincent, *Studien zur literarischen Eigenart und zur geistigen Heimat von Jesaja, Kap. 40–55* (BETL, 5; Frankfurt/Bern: Peter Lang, 1977).

24. R.E. Clements, 'Thematic Development in Isaiah', *JSOT* 31 (1985), pp. 95-113 (110).

25. The recent study by R.G. Katz, *Kyros im Deuterojesaja-Buch. Redaktionsgeschichtliche Untersuchungen zur Entstehung und Theologie von Jes 40–55* (Forschungen zum Alten Testament, 1; Tübingen: Mohr, 1991), divides *Grundtext* from *Erweiterung* first in 45.1-7, then in the other Cyrus material (41.1-5; 21-29). The results are applied to an investigation of the growth of 40–55, seen as originally a collection of *rîbs*, salvation-oracles and oracles against the nations, whereby a greater role for Cyrus as world-conquering divine agent develops. The 'Servant Songs' and the anti-idol polemic emerge as the product of secondary layers. By contrast,

that once the unity of Isaiah 40–55 is broken, arguments for a Babylonian setting would have to be made for each unit, and certainly could not *all* be successful. Indeed, the redaction itself would surely have to be placed in the post-exilic period, effectively destroying the conventional figure of 'Second Isaiah' and relegating his poems to a minor source. The assumption of a single author of 40–55 as a series of poetic meditations on an existing Isaiah scroll does not necessarily contradict the view of a poet impelled into his outbursts by the prospect of a Persian deliverer, but it still alters significantly the understanding of why and how the poems were written. It is possible to imagine a series of poems conceived *both* as a direct response to the unique historical circumstances of an exiled poet-cum-prophet and *also* as a literarily sophisticated gloss on a scroll of prophecies, but such a feat perhaps exceeds the capacity of all but the most credulous. Why need a poetic *tosafist* actually live in Babylon? Or even personally experience exile?

Seitz has shown, in fact, how the notion of an exilic poet asserted itself independently of Duhm's carefully constructed arguments for an independent redactional history to chs. 40–55, and has also reviewed the arguments against a Babylonian exilic setting.[26] The most compelling of these arguments are as follows:

1. The opening call of 40.1-2 (and other places) addresses itself to Jerusalem and not to exiles.
2. The exiles to be gathered in are from all the parts of the world not just from Babylon (43.5-6).
3. Cyrus is depicted as coming 'from a far country' (46.11), which seems inappropriate for a Babylonian perspective.
4. The complaint about refusal to offer sacrifice (43.22-24) is invalid except in Jerusalem or some other sanctuary city.
5. The expression in 43.14 שלחתי בבלה is inappropriate if the setting is itself Babylon.
6. Israel as 'a people robbed and plundered...trapped in holes and hidden in prisons' is not an apt description of life in exile.

A. Laato, *The Servant of* YHWH *and Cyrus. A Reinterpretation of the Exilic Messianic Programme in Isaiah 40–55* (ConBOT 35; Stockholm: Almqvist & Wiksell, 1992) takes the view that Isa. 40–55 comprises a literary unit: traditional themes and language of royal ideology, from both Judah and Assyria, inform the 'Servant Songs' and are applied to Cyrus. Isa. 40–55 is, on his view, an attempt to adapt an exilic messianic programme to the early post-exilic period, when there was no royal figure.

26. *Zion's Final Destiny*, pp. 205-207.

Seitz adds that Zion itself is presented as in exile (49.21) without the sense of physical deportation. This is consistent with the well-known *topos* of exile as designating the state of Judah throughout the Persian and Graeco-Roman periods.[27] In short, the fate of Jerusalem and the promised return of its children is a theme which suits better a setting *in that city* rather than in exile communities, and the notion of exile in these chapters is ideological rather than concrete. The evidence of composition in Judah is stronger than the evidence for Babylonia; and the question of dating is open.

There are really only two possible indications of a Babylonian context for the poems. One is the reference to Babylonian gods, including specific mention of Bel and Nebo.[28] Barstad notes, however, that since Judah had been under the Babylonian yoke for several decades before the exile, and was administered by the Babylonians as a province until the advent of Cyrus, references to alien gods might naturally name Babylonian deities (he cites in support Jer. 50.22; 51.44).[29] The other piece of evidence is the inaccuracy of the prediction of Cyrus's bloody capture of Babylon. That suggests, the argument runs, that the poem was written when Cyrus's seizure of the city was imminent but before the *peaceful* surrender of the city to his forces—and this strongly implies Babylon as the place of composition.

This argument may be seized upon by defenders of exilic authorship, and so some discussion is called for here. One could, of course, fall back on the argument that while chs. 40–55 are *as a whole* later and non-Babylonian, there are one or two earlier poems. But multiple authorship ought to be argued for on linguistic and stylistic grounds, and not appealed to as a *deux ex machina*. In any case, it is unnecessary if, as has been argued, we ought to doubt the reliability of Cyrus's own propaganda about the event.[30] It is *his* view that the city was taken peacefully. But is that the truth of the matter?

27. See M.A. Knibb, 'The Exile in the Literature of the Intertestamental Period', *Heythrop Journal* 18 (1977), pp. 253-72.

28. The name 'Marduk' is nowhere mentioned, let alone denounced in the Bible, though present in the name 'Mordecai'.

29. 'Lebte Deuterojesaja in Judäa?', *NTT* 83 (1982), pp. 82-83.

30. See, for example, A. Kuhrt, 'Nabonidus and the Babylonian Priesthood', in M. Beard and J. North (eds.), *Pagan Priests, Religion and Power in the Ancient World* (London: Duckworth, 1990), pp. 119-55.

The argument for a Babylonian setting based on the inaccurate reference to Cyrus's activities is circular: it requires its conclusion as a premise. Thus, *if* the poet lived in Babylon at about the time of Cyrus, the inaccurate prediction of his destructive entry into Babylon establishes a date prior to 538! Yet, if the poet lived some way from the city, or indeed, lived at another time, the error is equally explicable. The inaccurate prediction may as well be an inaccurate record or memory. And if a record or memory, it may be either accidentally or deliberately inaccurate. Poets are allowed this sort of thing, though we could know in this case which alternative to choose. A half-century after Cyrus, Xerxes I razed the fortifications laid by Nebuchadnezzar, destroyed the *Esagila* and melted down the statue by Marduk.[31] From 482 onwards, Babylon could be deemed to have been destroyed—just as much as Jerusalem was claimed to have been destroyed in 586. Moreover, the event would doubtless be seen as poetic justice. Just as Cyrus was the Yahweh-elected liberator of the Judaeans, so was his successor the Yahweh-inspired avenger of the Judaeans in destroying the city that had destroyed Jerusalem and exiled some of its inhabitants. Just as for the Chronicler it was David who planned the Temple, so for this author Cyrus destroyed Babylon—whether himself or through his dynasty is not poetically important. In other words, once we have established the date of the poet we can ask why he wrongly attributed the destruction of Babylon to Cyrus. We cannot assume the date as premise and then argue from it back to our starting point. The 'error' is not evidence of any particular date.

The evidence of a Babylonian setting for the author of Isaiah 40–55 is so slight, then, as to be virtually absent. Where this paper goes beyond recent criticism is in suggesting that the question of date is also open. It is time to ask again: at what time and place does this collection of poems make best sense? If arguments for a Babylonian setting were dictated largely by romantic notions of an exilic herald (and fellow-sufferer) and the theological mileage to be gained from such a figure, what better arguments, if any, can be used to find the real historical context of Second Isaiah?

31. See, however, A. Kuhrt and S. Sherwin-White, 'Xerxes' Destruction of Babylonian Temples', in H. Sancisi-Weerdenburg and A. Kuhrt (eds.), *Achaemenid History II: The Greek Sources* (Proceedings of the Gröningen 1984 Achaemenid History Worship; Leiden: Nederlands Instituut voor het Nabije Oosten, 1987), pp. 69-78, who cast doubt on the reliability of the (Greek) accounts of Xerxes' activities in this respect.

III

The starting point for a search after historical context, as I stated earlier, must be the ideology of the collection of poems taken as a whole, not items picked randomly. Accordingly, the best opening step is backwards, to look at the scope of the poetry, the wood rather than the trees. From such a perspective some interesting features appear. But before looking at these, we ought to consider a feature that does *not* appear! This is the matter of returning exiles.

Cyrus's role as liberator in Second Isaiah concerns only marginally (at best) his release of deportees. In fact, such an act remains entirely to be inferred. He is proclaimed (see below) rather as world-conqueror and restorer of the fortunes of Judah and Jerusalem. The poetry expresses the aspirations, not of immigrants about to return from deportation but inhabitants of underpopulated, devastated cities awaiting a glorious future. This observation supports Barstad's argument that there is no 'second exodus' motif in Second Isaiah.[32] Barstad, however, believes that the poet of 40–55 wrote in the sixth century in Judah, and, while making occasional reference to the exiles in Babylon,[33] offered wider promises to Judah of deliverance from the Babylonian yoke under which Judah lay during most of the sixth century. With this view, as will be seen presently, I do not wholly concur, though it is an important step in the right direction.

The lack of prominence given to a return of exiles is worth stressing, since its prominence is so often taken for granted. Here I shall for the most part summarize Barstad's treatment. The poems, at any rate, make fairly little of the arrival of immigrants from Babylon. As Barstad argues, the opening proclaims the coming of Yahweh (דרך יהוה, 40.3; cf. הנה אלהיכם, v. 9), not of immigrants; this divine presence is then contrasted with human feebleness (כל־הבשר חציר, v. 6). The following image of the shepherd feeding and carrying the flock in v. 11 does not refer to a trek from Babylon to Jerusalem: there is no identifying of the flock

32. *A Way in the Wilderness: the 'Second Exodus' in the Message of Second Isaiah* (Manchester: University of Manchester, 1989).

33. Barstad allows that one text only, 48.20-22, might link an exit from Babylon with the exodus, though spoken from the perspective of Judah. Yet he is right to point out (as do several other commentators) that the call to 'flee' (ברח) does not suggest a return home, but the avoidance of a catastrophe (so Jer. 50.8; 51.6, 45). Perhaps exiled Judaeans are being addressed—but perhaps not.

with *exiles*: the nearest antecedent to the object pronoun here is the 'cities of Judah' (v. 9). Perhaps the image ought to be compared with that in Psalm 23. Nor is there a 'new exodus' to be seen in 41.17-20, which refers to the blossoming of the desert, a time of prosperity (cf. Amos 9.11-15, etc.). In all other references to 'leading' Barstad finds only the use of metaphorical language, of a kind paralleled throughout the Bible. The restoration promised by the voice, by the poet, does not have a return from Babylon especially in mind;[34] where the gathering of exiles is mentioned, a general return from all areas is mentioned (a point also noted, as mentioned earlier, by Seitz).[35]

Let us now look at the features that collectively characterize the theme and outlook of the poet. These are the creation of a world empire by Cyrus (including the punishment and degradation of Babylon); the gathering of the scattered nation of Israel from all corners of the world to Jerusalem and the rebuilding of the nation, with Jerusalem as the centre of worldwide worship of Yahweh; criticism of the use of idols as vain and Yahweh as the supreme and creating deity.

These elements coalesce into a vision of the new historical world discerned in the near future, in which under the one supreme god (naturally in a Hebrew text, named as the god of Judah) a single world order will be achieved and sustained, in which this god alone will be aniconically worshipped at his central temple in Jerusalem, and his own chosen people restored to a place of security and prominence. The

34. There are perhaps some hints of it, nevertheless. In 52.2-6 Zion is spoken of as 'captive'; this is followed by a reference to Egypt, then Assyria, suggesting a third, contemporary oppression by Babylon. Shortly afterwards (11-12) comes 'Depart, depart, go out thence, touch no unclean thing; go out from the midst of her, purify yourselves, you who bear the vessels (weapons?) of the LORD. For you shall not go out in haste, and you shall not go in flight [*contra* 48.20!], for the LORD will go before you, and the God of Israel will be your rear guard'. Here the reference to departing, and the use of חפזון (elsewhere only referring to the Exodus, Exod. 12.11, Deut. 16.3). However, Barstad's suggestion that the theme is one of holy war (יצא, כלי) is worth considering. There is no *context* of exit from Babylon; at best such an event could only be inferred.

35. Important parallels which Barstad does not cite are Jer. 31.10 ('Hear the word of the LORD, O nations, and declare it in the coastlands afar off; say, "He who scattered Israel will gather him, and will keep him as a shepherd keeps his flock"'), Mic. 2.12 ('I will surely gather all of you, O Jacob, I will gather the remnant of Israel; I will set them together like sheep in a fold, like a flock in its pasture, a noisy multitude of men').

'Servant' poems, to which great prominence has traditionally attached, perhaps by reason of a bias towards referentiality as well as because of its importance in New Testament studies and Christian theology, are quite difficult to specify referentially and may constitute a motif rather than a specific character. In part, they probably elaborate the role of Israel in bringing about the world order. The people will not achieve it themselves: rather, Yahweh and the Persians will, though the suffering of the Judaeans will have played a part in bringing this new order about. Passivity and obedience are an appropriate role for many in achieving the new world order.[36] This exegesis is not intended to exhaust the theme of the 'servant'.

The scenario which the poems collectively depict is not a particularly unusual one within the literature of the Old Testament/Hebrew Bible, and its details are represented in passages conventionally dated before and after the exile. The vision of a new world order is thus not an easily datable item. However, there are features of this particular expression of that theme which make it possible to suggest likely historical contexts.

Cyrus as World Ruler

The idea that the political future of the Judaeans would be under a Persian king is more significant for dating than is often recognized. There is no expectation of a future *native* dynasty hinted at here. With this view we may contrast texts which suggest some kind of national royal or non-royal dynasty or ruler (e.g. Ezek 34.23-24; Jer. 23.5; 33.15-17; Amos 9.11; Zech. 12.7-8). The poems here *take for granted* that the role of 'anointed' has passed not just to Cyrus but to the Persians, for the role of Jerusalem as a centre for the kings of the world to come to implies a world empire, and this can only be a Persian one. The fate of Jerusalem does not await the destruction of the Persian empire, but will be achieved within it. Jerusalem will be a city of the Persian empire, perhaps replacing Babylon as a religious and cultural centre. It is possible that this vision is an unusually percipient prognostication from the sixth century, not shared by any other Judaean writings from the period. More likely it comes from a time when such an empire was already well and securely established, and the expectation of a native dynasty

36. I am not insisting here on a single identity (or any identity) for the Servant, nor on a discrete collection of 'Servant Songs'. I simply suggest that they suggest that the purposes of Yahweh may be furthered by various types of 'service', from suffering to world-domination.

abandoned—and thus not in the time of Cyrus but of his successors.

There are other biblical texts in which this view of the historical world order is explicated. 2 Chron. 36.22-23 (= Ezra 1.1-2) reads:

> Now in the first year of Cyrus king of Persia, that the word of the Lord by the mouth of Jeremiah might be accomplished, the Lord stirred up the spirit of Cyrus king of Persia so that he made a proclamation throughout all his kingdom and also put it in writing: 'Thus says Cyrus king of Persia, "The LORD, the God of heaven, has given me all the kingdoms of the earth, and he has charged me to build him a house at Jerusalem, which is in Judah. Whoever is among you of all his people, may the LORD his God be with him. Let him go up."'

Whether it was Cyrus who authorized the building of the Temple is dubious: the building certainly did not take place until later, and the decree is of dubious authenticity,[37] but here we encounter an example of the tendency to assign sponsorship of the entire restoration programme to the founder of the Persian empire (just as Nebuchadnezzar became the archetypal haughty oppressor, supplanting Nabonidus in Daniel 4). Additionally we may compare the role of David as first temple builder (according to the Chronicler) with Cyrus's role as second temple builder, underlining the view that Cyrus and his successors are the truly chosen heirs of the native Davidic dynasty. The biblical literature displays an almost unanimously benevolent attitude towards Persian world rule. The book(s) of Esther also endorse the idea of a world order governed by the 'law of the Medes and Persians'—and thus permit a Judaean queen to be envisaged, and Jews protected, as well as threatened, by the law of the 'Medes and Persians'. Daniel, although tempered by the experience of oppressive (non-Persian) rule, retains in its older narratives (chs. 1–6) the idea of Yahweh the Lord of history assigning government of the entire world to non-Judaean kings, who in turn 'inherit' his 'kingdom' (2.37; 4.34ff.; 5.30).

In fact the idea of a universal world order decreed by Yahweh is retrojected into the Neo-Babylonian period. Jeremiah 27–29 represent

37. For a recent summary of the long debate on the authenticity of the decree ascribed to Cyrus in Ezra (and the rest of the Aramaic 'sources') see L.L. Grabbe, *Judaism from Cyrus to Hadrian* (Minneapolis: Fortress Press, 1992), I, pp. 32-36 (and the bibliography cited). The most recent authority to argue against the authenticity of Ezra 1.1-4 is J. Briend, in a paper given at the *Institut Catholique de Paris* on 15 December 1993, who denies that it resembles the form of an official document but reflects rather biblical prophetic idiom.

Nebuchadnezzar as allotted the world empire by Yahweh, and in the closing verses of 2 Kings Evil-Merodach (Amel-Marduk) frees Jehoiachin from confinement and sits him at the 'king's table' (25.29-30). Most commentators have detected here a hint of hope for the future of a Davidic dynasty; but it is equally likely that the hint is of the incorporation of the Davidic monarchy into the new world-empire: Evil-Merodach is here the inheritor of the 'Davidic covenant'. Indeed, Jer. 25.9, 27.6 and 43.10 refer to Nebuchadnezzar as Yahweh's 'servant' (the other two 'servants' in Jeremiah being Jacob and David).

What may be seen in all these texts is a Yahwistic ideology of world-empire, in which the Judaean national god ensures the well-being and triumph of his own nation by means of benevolent world empires which he controls. This ideology presupposes a certain political order, one which did not develop until the fifth century.

The Gathering of the Scattered Nation of Israel to Jerusalem

This idea is attested in several prophetic texts: Isa. 11.12 ('He will raise an ensign for the nations, and will assemble the outcasts of Israel, and gather the dispersed of Judah from the four corners of the earth'); Jer. 23.3 ('Then I will gather the remnant of my flock out of all the countries where I have driven them, and I will bring them back to their fold, and they shall be fruitful and multiply' [cf. v. 8, referring to the dispersion of 'Israel' in the 'land of the north']); Jer. 31.8 ('Behold, I will bring them from the north country, and gather them from the farthest parts of the earth, among them the blind and the lame, etc.'); Ezek. 11.17 ('Therefore say, "Thus says the Lord God: I will gather you from the peoples, and assemble you out of the countries where you have been scattered, and I will give you the land of Israel"'). Other such texts include Mic. 2.12; 4.6; Zech. 10.8-12.

The idea of a scattered Israel to be restored in the future can be found in texts from throughout the Persian period and into the Hellenistic (for example, Daniel 9, the *Damascus Document*, 11QMelchizedek, 1 Enoch, Jubilees).[38] In reflecting this idea (and not, as we have seen, the idea of

38. That the dispersion of Jews over the world is still presented as totally the result of forced deportation or exile (the term 'golah' conveys this) shows the power of the biblical myth over modern religious thought. Of course it is partly the result of unwilling and enforced migration, but just as much, especially in the ancient world, was it voluntary and undertaken for economic and other reasons. From the time of the

only a return from Babylon), Second Isaiah thus reflects a very common idea in the biblical literature. The poems of Isaiah 40–55 address the city of Jerusalem (and the cities of Judah) in promising this mother a return and increase of her lost children (49.20-25; 54.1), namely a population which comes from afar (49.22: 'nations', 'peoples'), brought from many places (49.23 'kings', 'queens'): a vision best (if rather loosely) described as 'eschatological'. Such a prospect may have been prompted by the *hope* of an act of repatriation by Cyrus. But it is just as likely, and perhaps more likely, to have been based on some concrete action. From a rapidly growing volume of research it is becoming clear that under the Persians a new social structure emerged in Judah, including an enforced (not a permissive) repopulation of areas previously uninhabited, the goal being economic regeneration—followed in the time of Xerxes by military strengthening. Judah became a province of some regional importance, and the inhabitants of Jerusalem may have felt encouraged to hope that Jerusalem would become the major city of the Persian empire in the satrapy; the biblical texts which speak of the extent of the land promised to Abraham and then embraced by David in his 'empire' come close to a definition of the satrapy 'Beyond the River'. At any rate, the cult of the god of Samaria (as Yahweh had been, according to the evidence of the Mesha stele and a Kuntillet 'Ajrud inscription) was established in Jerusalem (as well as perhaps in Samaria). This did not happen suddenly: the Elephantine papyri suggest that Jerusalem was not seen as the sole authority even on religious matters. Some antagonism between the two regions must have occurred.[39] But at all events, the vision of Jerusalem as a major religious centre, economically prosperous and populous is one which at least fits (we can say no more) the perceived policy of the Persian empire towards the province of Yehud; the actions being taken were steps toward those hopes which Isaiah 40–55 expresses.

Babylonian deportation onwards, the majority of emigrants have not in fact wanted to return to Judah.

39. We should probably understand the presentation of 'Israel' in the books of Joshua to Kings as a refraction of the claims of Jerusalem over Samaria and of Judah's claim to the title of 'Israel'. But the real history (by which I do not mean the treatment of Samaria in Nehemiah, which is probably a polemic to explain the priority of Jerusalem) underlying this ideological struggle in the Persian and Hellenistic period remains to be investigated—including when and why the temple on

Idols as Vain

The oft-expressed puzzle here (recognized too often to need citing) is that the invective against idols is so silly. Worshippers of deities that are represented in the form of idols do not make the mistake of thinking that these images are the gods. The puzzle is not intractable, once it is asked: for what kind of audience is the poet writing this polemic? What point is he actually trying to make? In the first place, there is little to be achieved by ridiculing images unless the hearers themselves have some attachment to them. Thus, the poet is not merely reiterating some ancestral abhorrence of Judaeans to images. Why do this? Not because his audience is in danger of worshipping other deities—such worship is not criticized; monolatry is not the issue. If the audience were in danger of adopting other gods, we would find the sort of rhetoric we get in Deuteronomy, which deals with other deities but makes less fuss about idols. The polemic is not directed against other gods *as such* but against gods *as represented by idols*. No: the issue here is whether gods are to be represented in material form, and in making this point the poet is attacking, not other deities, but the iconic worship *of the god Yahweh*. This attack is supported by the claim that Yahweh is the creator and cannot be created/made, and also by castigating the makers of idols (44.9-21)—this passage does not specify non-Judaean gods or idol-makers and I take it to refer primarily if not exclusively to Judaean craftsmen making images of Yahweh. The reason for the attack is given elsewhere: Yahweh cannot be represented in the form (40.18) because he is to be invisible (סתר: 45.15).

In what historical context is a ban on images of Yahweh most probable?

1. Iconic worship of Yahweh was not previously discouraged.
2. Yahweh is being perceived and represented as a creator deity, not a local national or royal one.
3. There is a precedent, or an occasion, for the banning of icons.
4. The ban presumably refers in the first place to a temple, where the issue would be public.

Whether or not all these conditions apply to the issue of Second Isaiah's invective, it is worth asking in what political, social and religious context they might all be represented. We can begin by suggesting that the iconic worship of Yahweh (and Asherah) was normal during the period

Mt Gerizim was built and how there is such a thing as a 'Samaritan Pentateuch'.

of the Israelite and Judaean monarchies (perhaps most commonly by a bull?) and continued until the Persian period. Possibly even into the Persian period, if the much-discussed drachma coin from Yehud[40] does in fact display how the Persian authorities imagined Yahweh to look, namely as a warrior in a chariot.[41]

If the political dimension of the vision of the poems is consonant with Persian policy of the economic and political revival of Yehud, and the role of Jerusalem as the centre of the cult of Yahweh the universal god consistent with Persian religious policy, then we may reasonably suggest that the presentation of Yahweh as aniconic is part of that development whereby the old local deity, probably still worshipped in Jerusalem during the sixth century, becomes identified with the high god of the Persian empire, elsewhere known under the names of Marduk and Ahuramazda. The latter, as is known, was worshipped aniconically (as opposed to Anahita). Whether the attempt claimed by Xerxes to suppress *daiva*-worship[42] is in any way connected with a move to reform certain local cults is dubious. But even without it, there is every reason to suppose, given the treatment of Persian kings in the biblical literature, that a tacit recognition of Marduk, Ahuramazda and Yahweh as the same high god was widespread in Judah, and that Second Isaiah gives us a glimpse into the process whereby the creation of the cult of the high god Yahweh was promoted in the temple city of Jerusalem so favoured, it seems, by the Persians.

IV

By way of a postscript, we may now return briefly to Morton Smith's wider interest in things Persian. The supposition of Persian, specifically

40. See conveniently Y. Meshorer, *Jewish Coins from the Second Temple Period* (Tel Aviv: Am Hassefer and Massada), 1967, pp. 36-38 and plate I, coin no. 4, and *idem, Ancient Jewish Coinage I: Persian Period Through Hasmonaeans* (New York: Amphora, 1982), pp. 21-28; cf. Grabbe, *Judaism* I, pp. 71-72.

41. It is probably significant that Ezekiel's vision (ch. 1) stresses the form of Yahweh as a human (or *like* a human: the force of the כ is uncertain), just as texts from the Hellenistic period also represent him as such, together with the other minor deities who carry out his instructions (cf. Daniel 7 and 8–12 *passim*). It is possible that in the wake of the aniconic reform Yahweh was conceived as human in form, even if not to be represented (and Gen. 1.27 appears to reflect this perception). But such remarks can only be suggestions until further research is done on the history of the religion of Judah based on principles other than rewriting the Bible.

42. See Boyce, *History*, II, pp. 173-77.

Zoroastrian, influence, on Judaism has, as is well known, been suggested many times.[43] The idea that Judaism was highly influenced by Zoroastrian doctrines was very popular at the turn of the century, but has become rather less fashionable as *Religionsgeschichte* has lost respectability. It was first mooted as early as the eighteenth century, and in this century Bousset and Bertholet were its chief advocates.[44] A number of scholars currently adhere to this opinion, but it would be fair to say that mainstream opinion does not favour the view. The claimed areas of influence are well-known, and include angelology, eschatology (including resurrection, judgment, heaven and hell), dualism, creation and, as Boyce claims, purity.[45] The obstacle to reaching a conclusion on this claim is the late date of most of the Persian sources. This difficulty is often used to deny or minimize the possibility of influence, but in fact it does no more than guarantee a good deal of doubt about any conclusion either way (for the question of Persian influence on the cult of Yahweh remains open regardless of what the religion of the Achaemenids actually was!). In any case, there are no indisputably earlier Hebrew texts to prove that the ideas just listed obtained in Judah before the Achaemenid period.[46]

It is inherently unreasonable to assume that Persian religious ideas had no influence at all on the religion of a province whose temple was built, according to its own writers, by Persian decree, and whose religious leaders came to Judah under Persian auspices. It cannot be denied, on the other hand, that in many respects Jewish doctrines differ from Zoroastrian ones. The question must be the extent to which the religion of Judah in the sixth (fifth?) century onwards was shaped according to the principles of Zoroastrianism. And such an evaluation will obviously

43. There is a convenient survey in E. Yamauchi, *Persia and the Bible* (Grand Rapids: Baker, 1990), pp. 458-66, though his assessment of the evidence is rather prejudicial; see below.

44. Wilhelm Bousset, *Die Religion des Judentums im späthellenistischen Zeit alter* (Tübingen: Mohr, 1902); Alfred Bertholet, *History of Hebrew Civilization* (ET: A.K. Dallas; London: Harrap, 1926).

45. *Zoroastrians*, pp. 76-77.

46. As, for example, Yamauchi, *Persia and the Bible*, p. 459, tries, by claiming that Genesis 1 and the levitical rules on purity are 'earlier'. He also claims that there are 'pre-Isaianic references to angels' but in this case, as in every other, refrains from citing the texts he is thinking of. These statements are, like the entire book, essentially apologetic and do not contribute to the debate in any serious way.

depend on one's estimate of the alternative influence—the religion of Judah in the preceding period.

That religion, as I have argued elsewhere, can be reconstructed, very partially, by artifactual and other archaeological criteria, or it can be rebuilt from texts whose present shape (at the very least) comes from Persian period Judah. Such considerations make the evaluation of the extent to which the Persian (and Graeco-Roman) religion of Judah was essentially a localized form of Zoroastrianism very difficult indeed to assess. Nevertheless, the question is one of fundamental importance to our understanding of the history of religion in general and of Judaism in particular.[47] I have no sought to address the question directly in this paper, but any attempt to reconstruct the evolution of the cult of Yahweh, with which this paper *does* deal, must confront this basic question sooner rather than later.

47. The thesis that Judaean religion in the Persian period represents a fusion of the local cultic traditions and the local deity Yahweh with a high god cult, such as Nabonidus and, later, the Achaemenids promoted, has been advanced by T.L. Thompson in his *Early History of the Israelite People From the Written and Archaeological Sources* (Leiden: Brill, 1992). I am grateful to Thomas L. Thompson, N.P. Lemche, and above all to Lester Grabbe for invaluable advice and criticism in the preparation of this essay.

REVISIONINGS:
ECHOES AND TRACES OF ISAIAH IN THE POETRY OF WILLIAM BLAKE

Robert P. Carroll

Every honest man is a Prophet
–William Blake[1]

The eye's plain version is a thing apart,
The vulgate of experience.
–Wallace Stevens[2]

One of John Sawyer's most important contributions to the business of biblical studies has been his insistence on taking into account the history of the text's interpretation. Such an emphasis on the reception of the biblical text (*Rezeptionsgeschichte* or *Rezeptionsästhetik*) helps to bridge the abyss between the time of the production of the 'original' text and our contemporary readings of it (cf. Sawyer 1989[a]).[3] As a celebration of John's sterling contributions to our discipline I would like to offer some reflections on the book of Isaiah in conjunction with the writings of one of the acutest readers of the Bible, the poet William Blake. The book of Isaiah chooses itself (i.e., is chosen by me) because it is perhaps the densest of all the books in the Hebrew Bible, certainly among the most interesting, one John Sawyer has done considerable work on, and, last but not least, the poetry of William Blake is full of echoes and traces of Isaiah.[4]

My own interest in offering such a meditation on Isaiah has to do with

1. Keynes 1969: 392.
2. 'An Ordinary Evening in New Haven' in Stevens 1984: 465.
3. I put the word 'original' in inverted commas in the light of Sawyer 1989a and because I think the search for 'original' meaning of an 'original' text may well be a quest for a chimera.
4. Cf. Sawyer 1984 and Sawyer 1986. I have long awaited the appearance of John Sawyer's book on the Christian interpretation of Isaiah under the provisional title 'The Fifth Gospel'.

a long-standing teaching involvement with the book of Isaiah in Hebrew and a consequent pondering of meaning in that complex collection of material. I have found it much easier to say what others have said about the meaning*s* of the text than I have been able to fathom meaning and reference in the text itself. Here the history of the interpretation of Isaiah has been an invaluable source for commentary on a text which I regard as being fundamentally indeterminate of meaning (where not underdetermined). In lectures on the English text of Isaiah to generations of unfortunate students I have plundered the literature of poets and preachers, writers and dramatists to illustrate possible meanings in Isaiah. Frequently coming to my aid has been the poetry of William Blake and my reflections in this article are an attempt to focus more directly on Blake's debt to the book of Isaiah by way of acknowledging a most diligent reader of Isaiah.

It would be unrealistic not to recognize explicitly that in combining two complex sets of texts, such as the book of Isaiah and the poetry of William Blake, I am setting myself a difficult exercise in *Rezeptionsgeschichte*, but a festschrift is an ideal place to be exploratory, imaginative, creative and difficult. Some of the difficulty lies in the very nature of the *Rezeptionsgeschichte* of the Bible. The Bible, being a large collection of ancient writings, has had a very long history of interpretation at many different cultural levels. Mapping *all* the levels and analysing *all* the distinctive interpretative treatments of the Bible is a task beyond the competence of most biblical scholars—it is certainly beyond the actual achievement of the guild of biblical studies—so the wise scholar must necessarily limit any attempt at studying the history of the interpretation of the Bible to what can reasonably be treated within the constraints of the possible.[5] Hence my opting to read parts of Isaiah in conjunction with Blake's reading of that book. Reading Blake reading Isaiah (reading what?) in terms of my own reading of both Isaiah and Blake provides some indication of the complexities of any *Rezeptiongeschichte* of the Bible. It is a Sisyphean activity, without beginning and without ending.

The lengthy scroll of Isaiah embodies a very complex collection of material loosely focused on Jerusalem and the Judean community and held together by a very complicated interweaving of themes and topoi. Within the interstices of the book are many other subthemes and

5. In Carroll 1992 I have attempted to demonstrate some of the range and difficulty of writing a reception history of the Bible. What determines 'the constraints of the possible' in any specific study of the matter is another set of judgments.

subtopoi, all of which add to the complexities of its interpretation. The book of Isaiah is inscribed as 'the vision of Isaiah' and traditionally ascribed to Isaiah of Jerusalem. More recently critical scholarship has tended to assign the book to more than one writer (at least three Isaiahs if the work of Bernhard Duhm and others is followed), but that consensus is fast fading in favour of reading the book as a totality without reference to an imagined author or authors. A central feature of Isaiah is the focus on vision, on seeing. Indeed, one very effective way of reading the book is to read it in terms related to vision, visioning, revisioning and their opposites. The phrase 'blindness and insight' would do as an overall troping of the dynamics of Isaiah.[6] This selective understanding of Isaiah allows me to move easily to the work of Blake who was one of the great (Christian) poets of vision, perception, insight and blindness. Both Isaiah (book of) and Blake share a number of essentially imaginative visionings of land and people and to such an extent was Blake influenced by reading and reimagining Isaiah that his poetry deserves to be read directly as a commentary on Isaiah in any serious treatment of Isaiah today.

I

The importance of Isaiah for Blake cannot be gainsaid. It is directly acknowledged in the poem he wrote to his friend John Flaxman, when thanking him for his inestimable friendship:

> Now my lot in the Heavens is this, Milton lov'd me in childhood & shew'd me his face.
> Ezra came with Isaiah the Prophet, but Shakespeare in riper years gave me his hand (Keynes 1969: 799).

Blake's use of Isaiah is not simply a reading of the book attributed to Isaiah by tradition, but an imaginative construction of the biblical prophets as companions and instructors of his own imagination. Steeped in the Bible, Blake internalized its tropes and values and then transformed them by his own mystical religio-philosophical political point of view. In his famous 'The Marriage of Heaven and Hell' (Keynes 1969: 148-58) he devotes one of his 'memorable fancy' sections to an imagined encounter with the prophets Isaiah and Ezekiel:

6. This phrase owes something to Paul de Man's collection of essays under this title (de Man 1971); see also Evans 1988 for an aspect of the seeing/not seeing topos as developed in the reception of Isaiah.

> The Prophets Isaiah and Ezekiel dined with me, and I asked them how they dared so roundly to assert that God spoke to them; and whether they did not think at the time that they would be misunderstood, & so be the cause of imposition.
> Isaiah answer'd: 'I saw no God, nor heard any, in a finite organical perception; but my senses discover'd the infinite in every thing, and as I was then perswaded, & remain confirm'd, that the voice of honest indignation is the voice of God, I cared not for consequences, but wrote.'
> Then I asked: 'does a firm perswasion that a thing is so, make it so?'
> He replied: 'All poets believe that it does, & in ages of imagination this firm perswasion removed mountains; but many are not capable of a firm perswasion of any thing.'
> [I omit Ezekiel's responses here as being irrelevant to my paper!]
> I heard this with some wonder, & must confess my own conviction. After dinner I asked Isaiah to favour the world with his lost works; he said none of equal value was lost. Ezekiel said the same of his. I also asked Isaiah what made him go naked and barefoot three years? he answer'd: 'the same thing that made our friend Diogenes, the Grecian.' (Keynes 1969: 153-54).[7]

I am no Blake scholar so I cannot say to what extent Blake is being ironical or otherwise, nor can I deduce the extent to which he is imposing his own theories of poetic inspiration on the biblical prophets. The Bible offers virtually no information whatsoever on how the prophets came by their poetic oracles, so it is open to any poet to speculate on the matter and to draw comparisons between the imagined inspiration of scripture and their own inspired utterances. While Blake has been criticized for cancelling the Bible and misrepresenting Isaiah by means of his own Christian mythology (cf. Bloom 1989: 123-25), such ruination of the sacred truths seems to me to be inevitable in any reading of the Bible. We read it, give meaning to it, necessarily by means of how and what we think, imagine, experience and know. It cannot be otherwise. The interpretation of the Bible, like the reading of anything must be in accordance with our own understanding of things and cannot be somebody's else's imagined reading. This is partly why any interpretation of

7. It is not always easy to read Blake's proverbs and fancies in 'The Marriage of Heaven and Hell' so as to discriminate between his heavenly and diabolical senses: cf. his observation 'we often read the Bible together in its infernal or diabolical sense, which the world shall have if they behave well. I have also The Bible of Hell, which the world shall have whether they will or no' (Keynes 1969: 158). This double reading of the Bible seems to me to be a very important recognition of discrete modes of reading that ancient collection of books.

the Bible incorporates part of the Bible's *Rezeptionsgeschichte* because we read the book in the light of how we have heard it read as well as in terms of how we ourselves read it.

In his 'A Vision of the Last Judgment' Blake has a wonderful echo of Isaiah in his concluding statement about his own notion of perception:

> 'What', it will be Question'd, 'When the Sun rises, do you not see a round disk of fire somewhat like a Guinea?' O no, no, I see an Innumerable company of the Heavenly host crying 'Holy, Holy, Holy is the Lord God Almighty'. I question not my Corporeal or Vegetative Eye any more than I would Question a Window concerning a Sight. I look thro' it & not with it. (Keynes 1969: 617).

That echo picks up Isa. 6.2-3 where the seraphim attend the divine being in the temple and chant to each other the memorable trisagion phrase 'holy, holy, holy is YHWH of hosts'. Blake infuses the text with his own meaning—as all readers of texts do, especially of the Bible—and equates the rising of the sun with the beatific vision of the holy one surrounded by the heavenly host. Nature, Bible and Blake's imagination map each other and become equivalences. What links Blake and Isaiah here is the power of the imagination to assert (describe?) the unimaginable. For Blake the experience of the poetic impulse *is* what the ancient prophets also experienced and he appears to draw no distinction between *what* is described and *how* it is described.

A comprehensive reading of the poetry of Blake would reveal a myriad echoes and traces of biblical texts, including many from Isaiah. But such a reading will have to be done by other readers because the very warp and woof of Blake's poetry is partly constituted by biblical allusion and the transformation of biblical language. Phrases, figures and tropes from the Bible are so constantly used by Blake that there would be little point to itemizing them all here. In some cases Blake directly acknowledges the influence of the book of Isaiah on him, but in most cases the alert reader needs to be very familiar with the Bible as well as with Blake's poetry. For example, in 'The Marriage of Heaven and Hell' Blake writes 'Now is the dominion of Edom, & the return of Adam into Paradise' to which he adds 'see Isaiah xxxiv and xxxv Chap.' (Keynes 1969: 149). Elsewhere these chapters of Isaiah, along with ch. 63, are married by Blake (cf. Erdman 1969: 209 n. 21) and the reader needs to know the biblical text in order to recognize what Blake is doing. 'Edom; and 'the Demon red' (see the poem 'America: a Prophecy' in Keynes 1969: 195-203) are phrases echoing Isaiah 34 and especially 63.1-6. To the biblical scholar Edom/red (*'dm*) easily conjures up the kinds of images in the book of Isaiah (echoed in Rev. 19.15). Apart from its contribution to the well-known 'Battle Hymn of the Republic', Isa. 63.1-6 affords images of redness, garments of red, wine presses, power, anger, vengeance, war and destruction. The biblical images are a fusion of military conquest terms and wine-making processes language (cf. Jer. 48.32-33). Blake uses them in a number of poems (especially in 'Milton': see Keynes 1969: 480-535), employing the biblical trope to reflect on the American and French revolutions of his day.

One other image drawn from the book of Isaiah will suffice to make my main point about Blake's use of Isaiah. In Isa. 62.1-5 the restoration of Jerusalem/Zion is described in terms which include the notion of the marriage of the land: 'for you shall be called Hephzibah (i.e. my delight is in her), and your land Beulah (i.e. married); for YHWH delights in you, and your land shall be married. For as a young man marries a virgin, so shall your sons marry you, and as the bridegroom rejoices over the bride, so shall your God rejoice over you' (vv. 4-5, RSV translation with variations). Blake uses the proper name Beulah from 62.4 in various poems and with varying meaning. Among the meanings he gives to Beulah are the territory of Palestine, the realm of the subconscious, and the place where contrarieties meet.[8] The following extract from 'Milton' will demonstrate Blake's use of the biblical term in his own poetry:

> There is a place where Contrarieties are equally True:
> This place is called Beulah. It is a pleasant lively Shadow
> Where no dispute can come, Because of those who Sleep.
> Into this place the Sons & Daughters of Ololon descended
> With solemn mourning, into Beulah's moony shades & hills
> Weeping for Milton: mute wonder held the Daughters of Beulah,
> Enraptur'd with affection sweet and mild benevolence.
>
> Beulah is evermore Created around Eternity, appearing
> To the Inhabitants of Eden around them on all sides.
> But Beulah to its Inhabitants appears within each district
> As the beloved infant in his mother's bosom round incircled
> With arms of love & pity & sweet compassion. But to
> The Sons of Eden the moony habitations of Beulah
> Are from Great Eternity a mild & pleasant Rest. (Keynes 1969: 518)

8. An indispensable source for understanding Blake's symbolical uses of language is Foster Damon 1988; see also Damrosch 1980 and Curran and Wittreich 1973.

Beulah is one of the most dynamic representations used by Blake and, although he owes the term to the book of Isaiah, its use by him illustrates very well the range of his creative and transformative imagination. The Bible gave him many images and much imaginative symbolism with which he constructed and clothed his own thinking. There is in his work a nicely judged marriage of word and image, partly reflecting his own visionary thought and partly derived from his reading of the Bible. Reading Blake is like reading a good commentary on the Bible.

II

More important than the use Blake makes of Isaiah and the influence of Isaiah on Blake is the transformative vision Blake brings to his reading of the Bible. Historical-critical scholarship has tended to think of readers of texts as inert subjects registering the text's meaning by submitting themselves to an Oxbridge philological unpicking of the text. On the contrary, reading is a dynamic activity in which readers bring to texts their own experiences, sensibilities and ideological makeup. The conjunction of excavative archaeological-philological construals of the text with well-defined ideologically situated modern readers contributes to the generation of meaning. There is here a subtle interplay of text and reader within a social-intellectual context which constructs and determines meaning. While I have no wish to join the fashionable disparagers of historical-critical readings of the biblical text—in the current climate of anti-Enlightenment reactionaries and fundamentalists waging war on reason it would be very unwise to join forces with an imagined medievalism from which the Enlightenment rescued us—I do feel that after about a century of the search for the 'original' (i.e., historical) meaning of the biblical text it is time to recognize that the hermeneutic task is more complex than may have been allowed for when the historical-critical method was first developed. It is not simply the failure of the method to unearth the 'original' meaning—I take much of the postmodernist reaction in theology and biblical studies to be indicative of such a failure (whether real or imagined must be left for individual readers to decide)—it is more a case of the growing realization that there may never have been an 'original' meaning there in the first place! A text such as Isaiah is too indeterminate to have such an imagined meaning, so any meaning for it must be constructed in dialogue with many other factors.

What Blake brought to his reading of Isaiah (and the Bible) was a very strong set of Christian beliefs and symbolic values. Not Christian in the traditional manner of organized religion whereby an ancient religion has been transformed into an incarnation of empire, state and the denial of all that Jesus stood for; no, Blake was a sectarian Christian whose symbol and value system went back to the seventeenth-century Muggletonians and all those Puritan sects which had opposed hierarchy, power and the exploitation of the common people (for background and introduction see the invaluable Erdman 1969; cf. Thompson 1993). In the late eighteenth century when Blake began to be active in poetry and printing he performed as a prophet against empire, state and church. He supported the work of Thomas Paine and the revolutions in America and France. It is difficult today for many contemporary biblical scholars to remember that the churches to which so many of them belong by ordination (as well as birth and allegiance) were powerful institutions of reaction and oppression until quite recently. The Bible maintained and preached in the state church was an instrument of exploitation and oppression, hence a Bible-believing Christian such as Blake claimed to be was necessarily against such an oppressive institution. For Blake 'State Religion' was 'The Abomination that maketh desolate...which is the source of all Cruelty' ('Annotations to Watson', Keynes 1969: 393). When I call Blake a 'Bible-believing Christian' I do not mean a fundamentalist or anything like so-called 'Bible-believers' today. On the contrary, Blake believed the Bible in the sense that he read in(to) it his own symbolic world, complete with his highly figurative understanding of his own world. The world of the Bible for him was the world of his England, then and there in the late eighteenth century.

Blake constructed his vision of his world out of a very sophisticated (yet I believe essentially simple) reading of his own times transformed by the imaginative power of the Bible as read according to his own beliefs. His poem 'And did those feet in ancient time' (the preface to 'Milton', Keynes 1969: 480-81), now known as 'Jerusalem', epitomizes his view of England.[9] He had his own imaginative point of view and that allowed him to read the Bible and transform its tropes and figures into a highly

9. For the sake of hermeneutic piety I shall not challenge here this romantic England representation of the Englishman Blake—as one of the Lord's prophets Blake may be allowed poetic licence. The famous prefatory poem to 'Milton' has appended to it the text 'Would to God that all the Lord's people were Prophets' (Num. 11.29).

creative representation of his own symbolic world. Blake was always his own man: as he wrote 'I must Create a System or be enslav'd by another Man's' ('Jerusalem', Keynes 1969: 629). He read the Bible in the light of his own system of beliefs, values and symbols. He held the Bible in high regard, as an inspired book. Inspired in the sense that every poetic vision is inspired. He had no time for the minutiae of who wrote what when or all the mind-numbing quibbles about detail regarding the Bible—in this regard he would have dismissed the whole institution of biblical scholarship as one more bad example of Newton's single vision!—but regarded the Bible as a 'book of Examples' and its beauty lay in the fact 'that the most Ignorant & Simple Minds Understand it Best' (Keynes 1969: 786). In the response to Bishop Watson's 'Apology for the Bible', in which Blake defended Thomas Paine against ecclesiastical attacks and dismissed the nonsense of the Mosaic authorship of the Pentateuch, he offers his own view of the Bible (Keynes 1969: 383-96). I will just cite one response from that defence of Paine and dismissal of Bishop Watson's attack on Paine, as offering a fair account of Blake's view of the Bible:

> I cannot concieve the Divinity of the books in the Bible to consist either in who they were written by, or at what time, or in the historical evidence which may be all false in the eyes of one man & true in the eyes of another, but in the Sentiments & Examples, which, whether true or Parabolic, are Equally useful as Examples given to us of the perverseness of some & its consequent evil & the honesty of others & its consequent good. This sense of the Bible is equally true to all & equally plain to all. None can doubt the impression which he recieves from a Book of Examples. If he is good he will abhor wickedness in David or Abraham; if he is wicked he will make their wickedness an excuse for his & so he would do by any other book. (Keynes 1969: 393)

The many points made by Blake in his 'Annotations to Watson' provide excellent evidence of what he thought of the Bible and also of how he read it. Again it is very difficult for contemporary readers who know only a highly polarized ideological world of fundamentalists and 'liberals' to appreciate the fact that Blake was always his own person and read the Bible according to his own system. Where the Bible is wicked Blake says so and rejects it: thus the Israelites' murdering of so many thousands (of Canaanites) 'under pretence of a command from God is altogether Abominable & Blasphemous' (Keynes 1969: 387). Blake believes the Bible, but only insofar as it agreed with his own moral, political and spiritual values. I cannot imagine that there is a more civilized approach to the Bible than that! Although Blake regarded the Bible as inspired (both testaments, both Moses and Christ), he did not like the Jews of London so there is much criticism of 'the Jews' in his writings.[10] Hence Christ came 'to abolish the Jewish Imposture' and was murdered because he taught that 'God loved all Men & was their father & forbad all contention for Worldly prosperity in opposition to the Jewish Scriptures, which are only an Example of the wickedness & deceit of the Jews & were written as an Example of the possibility of Human Beastliness in all its branches' ('Annotations', Keynes 1969: 387). Blake's representation of the Jews here reflects the New Testament as much as it represents his own double reading of the Bible. Heaven and Hell are married in Blake's work because he believes in a dualistic outlook which allows him to read something from either perspective (heavenly or diabolically). For Blake 'Christ died as an Unbeliever' (Keynes 1969: 387), so no modern reader should ever imagine that Blake was an 'orthodox' Christian. His Jesus performs no miracles: 'Christ & his Prophets & Apostles were not Ambitious miracle mongers' ('Annotations', Keynes 1969: 391-92). Reading William Blake on the Bible is like reading the Sermon on the Mount on traditional religious piety, a transformative experience. Blake is, in many senses, a primitive Christian enhanced by poetic imagination into a Christian prophet of the Napoleonic period.

Imagination is the fundamental value in Blake. Everything springs from the imagination, but it is imagination as a metaphysical concept. Blake has a Wordsworthian notion of the imagination and invariably describes it in very Blakean terms: 'Imagination (which is the Divine Body of the Lord Jesus, blessed for ever)' ('Jerusalem', Keynes 1969: 624). So his reading of the Bible will always be a thoughtful, thought-provoking transformative interpretation of that sacred text. Bringing to the Bible such a powerful imagination, so total a symbolic world and reading it by means of a most radical socio-political critique, Blake's Bible is a wonderfully transformed document of revolution and opposition. Yet there is an ordinariness about Blake's reading of the Bible

10. Again I shall not take issue with the cultural anti semitism implicit in Blake's Christian representation of the Jews. Perhaps as with Shakespeare's Shylock it is necessary to recognize that major poets reflect cultural factors without adequately transforming them. Blake equally despised organized Christianity, taking the view that 'The Modern Church Crucifies Christ with the Head Downwards' ('A Vision of the Last Judgment', Keynes 1969: 615).

which conforms to his own understanding of prophecy. Of prophets he writes:

> Prophets, in the modern sense of the word, have never existed. Jonah was no prophet in the modern sense, for his prophecy of Nineveh failed. Every honest man is a Prophet; he utters his opinion both of private & public matters. Thus: If you go on So, the result is So. He never says, such a thing shall happen let you do what you will. A Prophet is a Seer, not an Arbitrary Dictator. It is man's fault if God is not able to do him good, for he gives to the just & to the unjust, but the unjust reject his gift. (Keynes 1969: 392)

Like the Christ who does not perform miracles, the prophet also is not a wonder-maker. But 'every honest person is a prophet' (contemporary translation of Blake's observation).

The final point I wish to make about Blake and Isaiah has to do with this notion of the prophet as an honest person. In his own life and by means of his own work Blake acted as a prophet in the England of his time. He was a great prophet against empire (to use David Erdman's phrase) and, no doubt, read the biblical prophets as similar kinds of poets opposing the religion of their time.[11] But there is nothing special in an honest person's activities against the evils of the time. Any such person would speak out against injustice and wickedness, whether it be Isaiah, Christ, Blake or the average university lecturer (if honest person they be!). Reading the poetry of William Blake against the backdrop of his life and times (born 28 November 1757, died 12 August 1827) one can see and feel his burning passion against injustice, religion and empire. It is therefore very easy to read the biblical prophets, say Isa. 3, 5, Amos or Micah 1–3, as Blakean poets. Whatever the complexities of understanding the Bible *as text* (i.e., as literary constructions independent of an identifiable historical moment), an imaginative reading of the prophets allows for family resemblances to be drawn between the prophets and William Blake. Interpretation is as much (if not more) imaginative as it is scholarly decipherment. I have found in lecturing on Isaiah to large classes of students that a reading of a Blake poem can be a very good way into reading the prophets on the (however imagined) society of their time. The poem which usually has the most impact is Blake's 'Holy Thursday' from his 'Songs of Experience':

11. One form of reading the biblical prophets is to take them as radical social critics and to project on to them whatever the current political radical ideology may be. I think this is how liberation theology tends to read biblical prophecy.

Is this a holy thing to see
In a rich and fruitful land,
Babes reduc'd to misery,
Fed with cold and usurous hand?

Is that trembling cry a song?
Can it be a song of joy?
And so many children poor?
It is a land of poverty!

And their sun does never shine,
And their fields are bleak & bare,
And their ways are fill'd with thorns:
It is eternal winter there.

For where-e'er the sun does shine,
And where-e'er the rain does fall,
Babe can never hunger there,
Nor poverty the mind appall.
(Keynes 1969: 211-12)[12]

In the 1980s when I used to lecture to first-year students on Amos and Isaiah, that poem read in conjunction with Amos's outbursts against the mercantile class's oppression of the poor and Isaiah's denunciation of rulers' 'grinding the faces of the poor' (Isa. 3.14-15) and the landed gentry's joining of house to house (Isa. 5.8-9) invariably bestirred members of the class to reflect on the biblical text vis-à-vis their own society. We were all living in 'Thatcher's Britain' then and so many people in Scotland felt about the state such strong feelings that it would take an Isaiah or a Blake to give adequate utterance to them. Vestiges of the old Scottish democratic intellect were still capable of being aroused by that combined reading of Amos, Isaiah and Blake. So I do know what a good (i.e. transformative) reader of the Bible Blake was. Every honest person is a prophet. So reading Blake reading the Bible allowed people to give expression to how they felt about Mrs Thatcher's savaging of the economy and destruction of the industrial base of Britain in favour of enriching the faceless merchants of the South East of England. Whether the prophetic critique was an accurate or helpful one in its time I cannot say nor am I certain that Thatcher-bashing was a useful activity, but as an emotive reading of the prophets Blake helped us to give voice to our deepest feelings. A prophet then is an honest person who is

12. There is a very different 'Holy Thursday' poem in Blake's 'Songs of Innocence' (Keynes 1969: 121-22).

prepared to oppose state, empire and church in the name of the common people who are, inevitably, suffering greatly at the hands of the powerful. William Blake would have understood our reading of the prophets and would, no doubt, have stood with us in that reading. In his time he hated 'the abomination which makes desolate' (the state religion) and it is remarkable that in our time (the 1980s and 1990s) we hear so much talk from politicians about the need to teach Christianity in the schools again in order to make society moral. Blake would have recognized the voice of the Beast masquerading in that evasion of true morality by politicians. And what might true religion be? Why, as Isaiah or Amos, Jesus or Blake would have said: 'Religion that is pure and undefiled before God and the Father is this: to visit orphans and widows in their affliction, and to keep oneself unstained from the world' (Jas 1.27).

III

My meditation on Isaiah and Blake must conclude at this point. Space does not permit a fuller investigation into the Isaianic vision, Blake's vision and any subsequent modern vision derived from transformations of both prophetic visions. So much of the book of Isaiah is about vision and revisioning, the keeping alive of that ancient vision by its constant renewal and retroping. Blake in his time transformed and revisioned the biblical vision. It is more difficult to see how the vision might be revisioned today because we lack the poetic insight which can see in the rising sun the divine being worshipped by the heavenly host. It is not easy in the century of world wars, the death camps and gulags, Alzheimer and AIDS to catch sight of the vision anymore. We lack a Blake, we lack an Isaiah, we lack the capacity to generate vision or to renew insight. The long history of the interpretation of the book of Isaiah bears witness to the capacity of the original vision for generating the revisioning process (Qumran, the New Testament, Blake and so many others constitute a cloud of witnesses), but the forces ranged against 'the vision thing' (to use George Bush's inspired phrase) are considerable. Yet the vision persists. That vision, as I read Isaiah troped by Blake, has to do with justice, the maintenance of the right of the poor, the ending of war, the coming of peace, the proclamation of liberty to the prisoners, and, among so many other visionary hopes, the ultimate creation of new heavens and new earth and it remains to inspire all subsequent visionings. On the other hand, the sense of having achieved 'no salvation', of having given birth to wind remains very strong (cf. Isa. 26.18). We may take our place on the watchtower (Isa. 21.8), but the watcher's answer always seems to be obscure or broken (21.11-12).[13] The language of vision invites and inspires yet further visions, but reading the visionary moment can be an encounter with a sealed book (Isa. 29.11-12).

The revision of rewriting Isaiah's vision transformed by the Blakean vision into a revisioning of our local world today so that 'Juda becomes New Haven', to use Wallace Stevens's trope (Stevens 1984: 473) which modernizes Blake's vision of Jerusalem built in 'England's green and pleasant land', offers a reading programme combined with an imagined praxis which would continue the project of the history of the reception of the Bible. It would allow for that 'vulgate of experience' which is 'the eye's plain version' while building on the older visions. It would also, in my opinion, make some connections between biblical studies and what I understand to be the heart of much of John Sawyer's important work on Isaiah. The combination of Isaiah and Blake allied to the modern attempt at revisioning the world in which we live brings the Bible, as a player, into a more practical form of reading. A form of reading which entails as substantive a transformation of how we read the text as William Blake's reading of the book transformed it into a prophetic reading in a time of revolution.[14]

13. The Watchtower trope of Isaiah puts me in mind of Bob Dylan's song 'All Along the Watchtower' (Dylan 1988: 374) and reminds me that some admirers of that minstrel of the 1960s revolution regard Dylan as 'Isaiah with a guitar'! I am not convinced that the Isaiah allusion is quite justified, but I can detect a certain biblicism in the poetry of Dylan.

14. This contribution to the celebration of John Sawyer's work as a biblical scholar is at best a simple meditation on aspects of Isaiah and aspects of Blake and is offered as a trace of that *Rezeptionsgeschichte* of the Bible which the guild ought to be constructing as a map of a very complex interpretative world.

BIBLIOGRAPHY

Bloom, H.

1989 *Ruin the Sacred Truths: Poetry and Belief from the Bible to the Present* (Cambridge, MA: Harvard University Press).

Carroll, R.P.

1992 'The Discombobulations of Time and the Diversities of Text: Notes on the *Rezeptionsgeschichte* of the Bible', in *Text as Pretext: Essays in Honour of Robert Davidson* (ed. R.P. Carroll; JSOTSup. 138; Sheffield: JSOT Press), 61-85.

Curran, S., and J.A. Wittreich, Jr (ed.)

1973 *Blake's Sublime Allegory: Essays on the Four Zoas, Milton Jerusalem* (Madison, WI: University of Wisconsin Press).

Damrosch, L., Jr

1980 *Symbol and Truth in Blake's Myth* (Princeton, NJ: Princeton University Press).

de Man, P.

1971 *Blindness and Insight: Essays in the Rhetoric of Contemporary Criticism* (New York: Oxford University Press).

Dylan, B.

1988 *Lyrics 1962–1985* (London: Paladin).

Erdman, D.V.

1969 *Blake: Prophet Against Empire. A Poet's Interpretation of the History of His Own Times* (Princeton, NJ: Princeton University Press, rev edn).

Evans, C.A.

1988 *To See and Not Perceive: Isaiah 6.9-10 in Early Jewish and Christian Interpretation* (JSOTSup 64; Sheffield: JSOT Press).

Foster Damon, S.

1988 *A Blake Dictionary: The Ideas and Symbols of William Blake* (Hanover & London: University Press of New England for Brown University Press, rev. edn).

Keynes, G. (ed.)

1969 *Blake: Complete Writings with variant readings* (Oxford: Oxford University Press).

Sawyer, J.F.A.

1984 *Isaiah*, I (Daily Study Bible; Edinburgh: The St Andrews Press).

1986 *Isaiah*, II (Daily Study Bible; Edinburgh: The St Andrews Press).

1989a 'The "Original Meaning of the Text" and Other Legitimate Subjects for Semantic Description', in *Questions disputées d'ancien testament: Méthode et théologie* (ed. C. Brekelmans; BETL 33; Leuven: Leuven University Press, rev. edn), 63-70, 210-213.

1989b 'Christian Interpretations of Isaiah 45.8', in *The Book of Isaiah. Le livre d'Isaie: Les oracles et leurs relectures unité et complexité de l'ouvrage* (ed. J. Vermeylen; BETL 81; Leuven: Leuven University Press), 319-23.

1989c 'Daughter of Zion and Servant of the Lord in Isaiah: A Comparison', *JSOT* 44: 89-107.

Stevens, W.
1984 *The Collected Poems of Wallace Stevens* (London: Faber & Faber).

Thompson, E.P.
1993 *Witness Against the Beast: William Blake and the Moral Law* (Cambridge: Cambridge University Press).

HOSEA III IN THE SEPTUAGINT VERSION

Takamitsu Muraoka

These days one hardly needs to be apologetic about writing a commentary on a book of the Septuagint.[1] The jubilaeus of the present volume has consistently championed the position that the Bible can be profitably studied not only in its historico-critically reconstructed Ur-form, but also in its canonized form and likewise in the light of its subsequent interpretations.

(1) Καὶ εἶπε κύριος πρός με Ἔτι πορεύθητι καὶ ἀγάπησον γυναῖκα ἀγαπῶσαν πονηρὰ καὶ μοιχαλίν, καθὼς ἀγαπᾷ ὁ θεὸς τοὺς υἱοὺς Ισραηλ καὶ αὐτοὶ ἀποβλέπουσιν ἐπὶ θεοὺς ἀλλοτρίους καὶ φιλοῦσι πέμματα μετὰ σταφίδων.

And the Lord said unto me, 'Go again, and love a woman who loves wicked things and is an adulteress, as the God loves the sons of Israel, though they look away towards alien gods and take delight in cakes (stuffed) with dried grapes'.

וַיֹּאמֶר יהוה אֵלַי עוֹד לֵךְ אֱהַב־אִשָּׁה אֲהֻבַת רֵעַ וּמְנָאָפֶת כְּאַהֲבַת יהוה אֶת־בְּנֵי
יִשְׂרָאֵל וְהֵם פֹּנִים אֶל־אֱלֹהִים אֲחֵרִים וְאֹהֲבֵי אֲשִׁישֵׁי עֲנָבִים׃

ἀγάπησον] The aorist tense of the imperative contrasts with the present participle ἀγαπῶσαν describing the woman's attitude and disposition. The prophet is commanded to take action, though it has been debated by scholars exactly what kind of action is meant.[2]

καί[2]] According to the Massoretic cantillation the adverb עוֹד is to be

1. For a recent general and stimulating discussion of the issue, see Harl 1993. For earlier expressions of my view on the matter, see Muraoka 1983 and 1986. Now cf. also Wevers 1990 and 1993.

The Greek text used here is Ziegler 1967, and for the Hebrew Bible I use *BHS*. Elliger prepared the edition of the Twelve Prophets. The Massoretic cantillation signs, except the athnach, have been left out. The abbreviations used in textcritical comments on the Greek text are those used in the above-mentioned Ziegler's edition.

2. See a discussion in Wolff 1965: 75.

construed with the preceding verb. Hebrew עוֹד as well as Greek ἔτι are equally flexible as regards their position: e.g. 1.6 וַתַּהַר עוֹד καὶ συνέλαβεν ἔτι; 12.9[3] עֹד אוֹשִׁיבְךָ ἔτι κατοικιῶ; Zech. 11.15...עוֹד קַח לְךָ Ἔτι λάβε σεαυτῷ, where an athnach is found on the preceding Hebrew word. Thus there is no linguistic clue for settling the question.

The use of καί between the two imperatives in contrast to the asyndetic structure of the Hebrew text may be due to the fact that the translator thought that the imperative לֵךְ had its full significance, not a kind of interjection. This might also account for the choice of πορεύομαι instead of βαδίζω, which latter is much more idiomatic in such an asyndetic construction, e.g. 1.2 Βάδιζε λάβε σεαυτῷ γυναῖκα for...לֵךְ קַח לְךָ אֵשֶׁת. See also Amos 7.12, 15.[4]

ἀγαπῶσαν] The MT form אֲהֻבַת is generally revocalized in conformity to the LXX reading and the Peshitta/rāḥmā'/.[5] But it is not absolutely necessary to read אֹהֶבֶת, for a passive participle can also indicate a state as in Cant. 3.8 חֶרֶב אֲחֻזֵי 'holding a sword'.[6]

πονηρά] Our translator obviously read רַע; so the Peshitta, /bišāṯā'/. When the Greek word is used substantivally in the neuter, the plural is the rule: so also at 7.15, Amos 5.13, 15, Mic. 3.2, Nah. 1.11, Hab. 1.13; exceptions are Amos 5.14, Mal. 2.17. In all these places the Hebrew text shows the singular, רַע or רָעָה.

μοιχαλίν] for the more usual μοιχαλίδα.[7]

ὁ θεός] יהוה. If one excepts innumerable cases of κύριος ὁ θεός, Mal. 2.17 is the only other instance in which the tetragrammaton in the MT is rendered with ὁ θεός. Regarding Jer. 1.2, where the same equivalence is observable, Streane (1896: 27) writes: 'It is unlikely that O' would, without any apparent reason, violate their rule, carefully to distinguish the words for Lord and God.' Targum, Peshitta and Vulgate all apparently read יהוה. The rendering ὁ θεός may be due to the desire to contrast it with the following θεοὺς ἀλλοτρίους.

αὐτοί] 'they in contrast'.

ἀποβλέπουσιν], a verb recurring at Mal. 3.9. The prefix ἀπο- is indicative of apostasy. The v.1. ἐπι- may best be regarded as secondary

3. Where the chapter and verse number differs between the Hebrew and the Greek texts, I follow the latter's numbering.

4. See Muraoka 1993, s.v. βαδίζω.

5. See, e.g., *BHS*, *ad loc*., and Wolff 1965: 70.

6. See Joüon and Muraoka 1993: §121 *o*, and cf. also Simon, 1989: 45.

7. See Moulton and Howard 1919–29: 131-32.

arising from an attempt to harmonize the form of the verb with the following preposition.[8] For further cases of the figurative use of פנה, see Deut. 31.18 ἐπέσ τρεψαν ἐπὶ θεοὺς ἀλλοτρίους, 20 ἐπιστραφήσονται ἐπὶ θεοὺς ἀλ., Lev. 19.4 οὐκ ἐπακολουθήσετε εἰδώλοις.

θεοὺς ἀλλοτρίους] Also Mal. 2.11. The Hebrew collocation אלהים אחרים may be rendered θ. ἕτεροι as in Exod. 23.13.[9]

φιλοῦσι] on the semantics of this controversial verb, see esp. Swinn 1990, and Muraoka 1993: 1f., s.v.

As Keil (1866: 50) correctly points out, אהבי does not refer to idols, but is parallel to פנים,[10] which has been correctly captured by the LXX.

πέμματα] אֲשִׁישֵׁי. Note that the Greek word πέμμα is elsewhere in the LXX attested only in Ezekiel (11x), where it renders אֵיפָה. Otherwise, אֲשִׁישָׁה is rendered variously: ἀμόρα 'sweet cake' Cant. 2.5; λάγανον ἀπὸ τηγάνου 2 Kgs 6.19; ἀμορίτη 1 Chron. 16.3. Aquila (παλαιά) seems to have read יָשִׁישׁ 'aged, ancient'.[11]

> (2) καὶ ἐμισθωσάμην ἐμαυτῷ πεντεκαίδεκα ἀργυρίου καὶ γομορ κριθῶν καὶ νεβελ οἴνου
>
> *And I hired (her) to myself for fifteen (pieces of) silver and a homer of barley and a flagon of wine.*
>
> וָאֶכְּרֶהָ לִּי בַּחֲמִשָּׁה עָשָׂר כָּסֶף וְחֹמֶר שְׂעֹרִים וְלֶתֶךְ שְׂעֹרִים׃

ἐμισθωσάμην] אֶכְּרֶהָ, which must have been read as אֶכְרֶה or אֶכְּרֶה.[12] The absence of object is awkward.[13] Aquila's ἔσκαψα is a rendering of a homonym, כָּרָה 'to dig'.

LXX translators seem to have had some difficulty with this rather uncommon word. Even when it is parallel to שבר Qal in Deut. 2.6, where it is translated with a straightforward equivalent, ἀγοράζω, the synonymous כרה is rendered with a colourless λαμβάνω. Is our

8. See also Muraoka 1993: 23-24 s.v.

9. For nuances of the epithet ἀλλότριος, see Muraoka 1993: 9-10, s.v.

10. On the syntax of the participle in the construct state, see Joüon and Muraoka 1993: § 121 *k*.

11. The Hebrew word at 1Q pHab 6.11 probably means 'strong men'; see Nitzan 1986: 170.

12. On the dagesh of the Kaph, cf. König 1881: 545.

13. Ehrlich (1912: 171) maintains that the object suffix of the MT is indetermined: 'da mietete ich mir eine', for it could not possibly, in his view, refer to the prophet's wife. Such a use of a pronominal suffix, however, is unknown to me.

translator, with the choice of μισθόω, referring to a prostitute?[14] But Ehrlich (1912: 171) wishes to interpret the unusual dagesh of the Kaph in וָאֶכְּרֶהָ as indicating that the Massoretes wanted to read the form as וָאֶשְׂכְּרֶהָ.[15] He further refers to Gen. 30.16 for this peculiar use of the verb שָׂכַר, which the LXX translates with our verb, μισθόω. Whether our translator actually read ואשכרה or not, the general thought seems to be close to that of the Genesis passage.

γομορ] חֹמֶר. The same transliteration is to be found in Ezek. 45.11, 13, 14. The similarity in sound to the prophet's wife Γομερ must be noted. Though indeclinable just as the following νεβελ, γομορ must be understood as genitive of price.[16]

νεβελ οἴνου] שְׂעֹרִים. *Pace* Nyberg (1935: 23) and Wolff (1965: 70), there is no need to postulate a variant reading in the *Vorlage* of the LXX. The rendering is most probably due to the translator's ignorance of the word לֶתֶךְ, a hapax, and in order to fill in the lacuna which would otherwise have resulted, he freely supplied the stuff that is commonly combined with other kinds of food; for the combination of שְׂעֹרָה (κριθή) and יַיִן (οἶνος), see 2 Chron. 2.14.[17]

> (3) καὶ εἶπα πρὸς αὐτήν 'Ημέρας πολλὰς καθήσῃ ἐπ' ἐμοὶ καὶ οὐ μὴ πορνεύσῃς οὐδὲ μὴ γένῃ ἀνδρί, καὶ ἐγὼ ἐπὶ σοί.
>
> *And I said to her, 'You shall stay with me many days and shall not prostitute nor become (another) man's (woman), and I also (shall stay) with you'.*
>
> וָאֹמַר אֵלֶיהָ יָמִים רַבִּים תֵּשְׁבִי לִי לֹא תִזְנִי וְלֹא תִהְיִי לְאִישׁ וְגַם־אֲנִי אֵלָיִךְ׃

εἶπα] εἶπον *L*''-613 Th. Bas.N., a very common Atticistic correction; so also at Zech. 4.11-12.

πρὸς αὐτήν] The general pattern of equivalence seems to be אמר ל־ = + dative and אמר אל = + πρός τινα. The only exception in the Twelve Prophets is Hos. 14.3 אִמְרוּ אֵלָיו εἴπατε αὐτῷ. The former equivalence is attested at Hos.1.6; 2.1; 10.8; Amos 6.10; Jn 1.6 (the variant πρὸς

14. Cf. Wellhausen 1898: 105: 'dass Gomer in fremde Gewalt gekommen war, vielleicht gar in Sklaverei.'

15. This is also Ibn Ezra's alternative interpretation: Simon 1989: 272. *Contra* Simon, I am not sure that Ibn Ezra rejects this interpretation in his main commentary on Hosea. See also Andersen and Freedman 1980: 298-99 for a discussion of various exegetical possibilities.

16. See Mayser 1934: 218-23, esp. 221-22.

17. For a discussion of this unique rendition, see Muraoka 1991: 214-15.

αὐτόν in A is probably influenced by the preceding προσῆλθε πρὸς αὐτόν for וַיִּקְרַב אֵלָיו); and Zeph. 3.16.

καθήσῃ ἐπ' ἐμοί] תֵּשְׁבִי לִי. The sense of the verb may be defined 'to remain, and not move away or abandon'.[18] The preposition with dat. pers. indicates physical proximity.[19] Cf. Mic. 7.7 ὑπομενῶ ἐπὶ τῷ θεῷ.[20] The Hebrew lamed, however, probably has the force of *dativus commodi*.

Manifestly our translator took אל at the end of the verse as parallel to ל towards its beginning, mentally supplying אֵשֵׁב, although the collocation יָשַׁב + אל + person. is otherwise unknown. Ibn Ezra completes the elliptical clause as גם אני לא אבוא אליך, taking the preceding לא as double-duty negative,[21] whereas Wolff (1965: 77) would read אני לא אלך אליך.

καί[2]] om. Thph. = MT. The addition of the conjunction renders it impossible to construe לִי with the second verb תִהְיִי, which is perfectly possible in the Hebrew.

οὐ μή] on this forcible and solemn negation, see Muraoka 1993, s.v. οὐ, **g**.

ἀνδρί] Many witnesses add ἑτέρῳ apparently for the sake of clarity. Cf. Deut. 24.2 καὶ ἀπελθοῦσα γένηται ἀνδρὶ ἑτέρῳ (והלכה והיתה לאיש אחר) and Jer. 3.1 ἀπέλθῃ ἀπ' αὐτοῦ καὶ γένηται ἀνδρὶ ἑτέρῳ (והיתה לאיש אחר הלכה מאתו). The phrase γίνομαι ἀνδρί with a woman as subject means 'to enter intimate relationship with a man'. Thus Ruth 1.13 γενέσθαι ἀνδρί; Ezek. 16.8 ἐγένου μοι.

ἐπὶ σοί] The identity of construction (ἐπ' ἐμοί) suggests that our translator saw here a case of ellipsis: καὶ ἐγὼ [καθήσομαι] ἐπὶ σοί, thus אליך = לך. It also indicates that the verb to be understood is not אהיה.

(4) διότι ἡμέρας πολλὰς καθήσονται οἱ υἱοὶ Ισραηλ οὐκ ὄντος βασιλέως οὐδὲ ὄντος ἄρχοντος οὐδὲ οὔσης θυσίας οὐδὲ ὄντος θυσιαστηρίου οὐδὲ ἱερατείας οὐδὲ δήλων.

because many days will the sons of Israel remain without a king, and without a ruler, and without sacrifice, and without an altar, and without priesthood, and without means of divination.

18. Muraoka 1993: s.v. **2**. Wolff (1965: 77) defines ישב as: 'zu Hause bleiben und—statt herauszugehen—ganz den häuslichen Pflichten hingegeben sein'.

19. See Muraoka 1993: 87-88, s.v. II, **1**. Ibn Ezra apud Simon 1989: 272: עם and Old Latin: *aput me...aput te* (Dold 1940: 266).

20. For a remarkable reading of Symacchus προσδοκησεις με, see Ziegler 1943: 353.

21. Cf. also Wolff 1965: 77, where he mentions Amos 2.7 הלך אל.

כִּי יָמִים רַבִּים יֵשְׁבוּ בְּנֵי יִשְׂרָאֵל אֵין מֶלֶךְ וְאֵין שָׂר וְאֵין זֶבַח וְאֵין מַצֵּבָה וְאֵין אֵפוֹד וּתְרָפִים׃

οὐκ ὄντος...] a praiseworthy stylistic achievement. The genitive absolute, which is by no means frequent in the LXX,[22] often renders the Hebrew circumstantial clause. So, for example, Gen. 18.1 ὤφθη δὲ αὐτῷ ὁ θεὸς...καθημένου αὐτοῦ ἐπὶ τῆς θύρας τῆς σκηνῆς for וְהוּא יֹשֵׁב פֶּתַח הָאֹהֶל.

In Hellenistic Greek, μή is normal with the participle and infinitive.[23]

ἄρχοντος] always = שַׂר in the Twelve Prophets, except at Mic. 5.2, where it renders מוֹשֵׁל. The Greek noun ἄρχων often occurs in conjunction with βασιλεύς, and following it, which most likely indicates the former's humbler position in the hierarchy. See Muraoka (1993: 31a, s.v.).

οὐδέ[2]] οὐκ A-Q* etc., perhaps because the following pair is to be grouped differently from the preceding one (of persons).

θυσιαστηρίου] מַצֵּבָה, an equation attested only here in LXX. Even in Hosea (10.1, 3, both // θυσιαστήριον = מִזְבֵּחַ), στήλη renders the Hebrew word in question. So also at Mic. 5.12. The unusual rendering can be explained as due to the accompanying θυσία.[24]

ἱερατείας] אֵפוֹד. It is hard to decide whether this rendering is due to ignorance on the part of our translator or it is simply a free rendering. In XII this is the only occurrence of אפוד, and the equation is unique in the entire LXX, while ἱερατεία renders either כְּהֻנָּה or the Piel infinitive construct of כהן. The Hebrew word אפוד is usually translated with ἐπωμίς, for example Exod. 25.7 (23× in all), ποδήρης only at Exod. 28.31, στολή in 2 Kgs 6.14, and 1 Chron. 15.27, and also transliterated at Judg. 17.5 *et passim* (13×). Seeing that the Greek translators understood אפוד as a kind of garment, we might be permitted to regard the rendering ἱερατεία 'priesthood' as a free rendering, a case of metonymy.

The omission of οὔσης is rather natural with a noun which does not indicate a tangible material object.

δήλων] תְּרָפִים, which occurs also at Zech. 10.2 and is translated οἱ ἀποφθεγγόμενοι. Its other renderings in the LXX are: γλυπτά Ezek. 21.26; εἴδωλα Gen. 31.19, 34, 35; κενοταφία 1 Kgs 19.13, 16;

22. Cf. Soisalon-Soininen 1987: 175-80. None of the functions Soisalon-Soininen attributes to the genitive absolute in the LXX—temporal, conditional and concessive—seems to apply to our examples here: they are purely circumstantial in the true sense of the term.

23. See BDF § 430.

24. Likewise Vulg. *altar* and Pesh. *madbḥā'*.

and transliterated at Judg. 17.5; 18.14, 17, 18, 20; 1 Kgs 15.23; 4 Kgs 23.24. The translator of XII emphasizes the divining function of the Hebrew word.[25] The Greek word δῆλοι appears nowhere else in XII, while elsewhere in the LXX it renders either אוּרִים (Num. 27.21; 1 Kgs 28.6) or תֻּמִּים (Deut. 33.8; 1 Kgs 14.41). The combination of אפוד and תרפים occurs also at Judg. 17.5, 18.14, 17, 18, 20, each time transliterated in Codex A and B alike.

(5) καὶ μετὰ ταῦτα ἐπιστρέψουσιν οἱ υἱοὶ Ισραηλ καὶ ἐπιζητήσουσι κύριον τὸν θεὸν αὐτῶν καὶ Δαυιδ τὸν βασιλέα αὐτῶν· καὶ ἐκστήσονται ἐπὶ τῷ κυρίῳ καὶ ἐπὶ τοῖς ἀγαθοῖς αὐτοῦ ἐπ' ἐσχάτων τῶν ἡμερῶν.

After this the sons of Israel will return and seek the Lord their God and David their king and will be astounded at the good (deeds) of His at the end of the days.

אַחַר יָשֻׁבוּ בְּנֵי יִשְׂרָאֵל וּבִקְשׁוּ אֶת־יהוה אֱלֹהֵיהֶם וְאֵת דָּוִד מַלְכָּם וּפָחֲדוּ אֶל־יהוה וְאֶל־טוּבוֹ בְּאַחֲרִית הַיָּמִים׃

ἐπιστρέψουσιν] יָשֻׁבוּ. The change of tense, imperfect > perfect, indicates that the verb שָׁב does not have the typical adverbial force 'again', but is used in the sense of 'to return (in repentance)'. The Greek version, however, does not distinguish these two different uses of the Hebrew verb. Thus we find ἐπιστρέφω at Zech. 5.1; 6.1; Mal. 1.4 where the Hebrew verb means 'again': at Mal. 1.4 ἐπιστρέψωμεν καὶ ἀνοικοδομήσωμεν τὰς ἐρήμους the first verb is rather mechanically used, since the text does not mean a second rebuilding. For the rest of the Old Testament the following results may be given:[26]

(a) ἐπανέρχομαι + inf.—Job 7.7;
(b) ἐπαναστρέφω + inf.—Deut. 24.4;
(c) ἐπιστρέφω—Deut. 30.9 (+ inf.); 3 Kgs 13.33 (οὐκ ἐπέστρεψεν ἀπὸ τῆς κακίας...καὶ ἐπέστρεψεν καὶ ἐποίησεν...); 19.6 (ἐπιστρέψας ἐκοιμήθη); 4 Kgs 19.9; 21.3; 2 Chron. 33.3; Eccl. 1.7 (+ inf.); 4.1, 7; 9.11; 2 Esdras 9.14 (+ inf.); Neh. 9.28 (+ inf.);
(d) πάλιν—Gen. 26.18; 30.31; Judg. A 19.7; 2 Chron. 19.4; Isa. 6.13; Jer. 18.4; 43.28; Job 10.16;

25. Cf. Targum: מְחַוֵּי.

26. This enquiry is based on the list given in BDB, 998, s.v. שׁוּב, Qal. **8.** See also Muraoka 1993: 92, s.v. **3, b.**

(e) προστίθημι + καί and verb. fin.—4 Kgs 1.11; + inf.—4 Kgs 1.13.

ἐπιζητήσουσι] ζητήσουσι V *L*' '-613-764 *C*'-68. The simplex is far more frequent: in XII, ζητέω (14×), ἐπιζητέω (2×). So also with God as object: Hos. 5.15 ἐπιζητήσουσι [B-V+ ζ.] τὸ πρόσωπόν μου; Zeph. 1.6 τοὺς μὴ ζητοῦντας τὸν κύριον, and similarly Zeph. 2.3; Mal. 3.1. The composita is altogether rare in the LXX, occurring some 20 times. Its choice in our passage may have been influenced by the preceding ἐπιστρέψουσιν or it is an attempt to vary the style; see 7.10...לא־שָׁבוּ אֶל־יהוה...ולא בִקְשֻׁהוּ καὶ οὐκ ἐπέστρεψαν πρὸς κύριον...καὶ οὐκ ἐξεζήτησαν...

ἐκστήσονται] The same rendering is found in Mic. 7.17 ἐπὶ τῷ κυρίῳ θεῷ ἡμῶν ἐκστήσονται καὶ φοβηθήσονται ἀπὸ σου אל יהוה אלהינו יפחדו ויִרְאוּ ממֶּךָ. The peculiar construction of פחד with אֶל, which is attested elsewhere in LXX only[27] at Jer. 2.19 (פַּחְדָּתִי אליך) and 43.16 (פָּחֲדוּ אִישׁ אֶל רֵעֵהוּ), was not correctly understood: εὐδόκησα ἐπὶ σοί and συνεβουλεύσαντο ἕκαστος πρὸς τὸν πλησίον αὐτοῦ.

The equivalence ἐξίστημι = פחד Qal or Piel is found nowhere else, while פַּחַד is rendered with ἔκστασις in 1 Kgs 11.7 ἔ. κυρίου, and analogously at 2 Chron. 14.13; 17.10; 20.29. This semantic relationship between fear and astonishment[28] as reflected in the LXX is also testified by correspondences such as ἐξίστημι = חָרֵד (Qal, Nifal, adjective) (very frequent), חתת Ni. 1 Kgs 17.11, and יָרֵא Ezek. 2.6.

For the combination with ἐπί + dat., see Exod. 18.9 ἐξέστη ἐπὶ πᾶσι τοῖς ἀγαθοῖς; Judg. 11.16 ἐφ' οἷς ἐκστήσεται; Job 36.28 ἐπὶ τούτοις πᾶσιν οὐκ ἐξίσταταί σου ἡ καρδία; Wis. 5.2 ἐκστήσονται ἐπὶ τῷ παραδόξῳ τῆς σωτηρίας; Jer. 2.12 ἐξέστη ὁ οὐρανὸς ἐπὶ τούτῳ; Ezek. 31.15A ἐξέστησαν ἐπ' αὐτῷ πάντα τὰ ξύλα.[29] Rarely

27. Job 31.23 φόβος κυρίου represents a reading different from the Massoretic punctuation, פַּחַד אֵלַי.

28. Cf. BAGD, s.v. 2b: 'in our lit. more freque., and (as it seems) so far only in the Bible or words influenced by it, in the weakened or attenuated sense *be amazed, be astonished*, of the feeling of astonishment mingled w. fear, caused by events which are miraculous, extraordinary, or difficult to understand...' Symmachus' επαινεσωσιν τον κυριον is probably an attempt to improve on the LXX reading.

29. See Muraoka 1993: 88, s.v. ἐπί, **II, 2**, also with other verbs of mental attitude: αἰσχύνομαι 'to feel ashamed' Zech. 9.5; λυπέω 'to feel grieved' Jn 4.9; χαίρω 'to rejoice' Hab. 3.18: Johannessohn 1926: 313 'Gemütsbewegung'. Cf. also Lk. 2.47 ἐξίσταντο ἐπὶ τῇ συνέσει αὐτοῦ.

also with acc.: Judg. 12.16 ἐξέστη ἡ καρδία...ἐπ᾽ αὐτήν; 15.1 ἐξέστησαν ἐπὶ τὸ γεγονός; Isa. 52.14 ἐκστήσονται ἐπὶ σὲ πολλοί. Once with gen.: Sir. 43.18 ἐπὶ τοῦ ὑετοῦ αὐτῆς ἐκστήσεται καρδία. Thus our translator did not see here, as Qimhi and Keil do,[30] a pregnant construction, 'to fear (and go) to'.[31]

ἐπὶ τοῖς ἀγαθοῖς] see the above-quoted Exod. 18.9.

ἐπ᾽ ἐσχάτων τῶν ἡμερῶν] ἐπ᾽ ἐσχάτου τ. ἡ. V Q-26-407-*II* '613 *C*; the same variant also in Mic. 4.1, an attempt to reproduce the singular number of the Hebrew expression. This fixed formula recurs in Gen. 49.1; Num. 24.14; Deut. 4.30; Jer. 23.20 (ἐσχάτου: A -των); 37.24; 25.19 (ἐσχάτου BS pau.: τῶν rel.); Ezek. 38.16; Dan. 10.14 (LXX sing., Th. pl.).[32] Deviations are: Deut. 31.29 τὰ κατὰ ἔσχατον τῶν ἡμερῶν; Isa. 2.2 ἐν ταῖς ἐσχάταις ἡμέραις.

BIBLIOGRAPHY

Andersen, F.I., and D.N. Freedman
1980 *Hosea* (AB; Garden City: Doubleday).

Dold, A.
1940 *Neue St. Galler vorhieronymianische Propheten-Fragmente der St. Galler Sammelhandschrift 1398b zugehörig* (Texte und Arbeiten, I; Abt., Heft 31. Beuron).

Ehrlich, A.B.
1912 *Randglossen zur hebräischen Bibel* (Leipzig).

Harl, M.
1993 'La «Bible d'Alexandrie» et les études sur la Septante. Réflexions sur une première expérience', *Vigiliae Christianae* 47: 313-40.

Johannessohn, M.
1926 *Der Gebrauch der Präpositionen in der Septuaginta* (Berlin).

Joüon, P., and T. Muraoka
1993 *A Grammar of Biblical Hebrew* (Rome: Pontifical Biblical Institute Press).

Keil, C.F.
1866 *Biblischer Commentar über die zwölf kleinen Propheten* (Leipzig: Dörfeling und Franke).

30. Keil 1866: 54.

31. Ibn Ezra also understood the verb פחד here in the sense of 'to move, flow fast'.

32. The New Testament also offers examples for both numbers: sg. Heb. 1.2, pl. 2 Pt. 3.3.

König, F.E.
1881 *Historisch-kritisches Lehrgebäude der hebräischen Sprache* (Erste Hälfte; Leipzig: Hinrichs).

Mayser, E.
1934 *Grammatik der griechischen Papyri aus der Ptolemäerzeit* (Berlin and Leipzig: Göschen).

Moulton, J.H., and W.F. Howard
1919–29 *A Grammar of New Testament Greek*, II. *Accidence and Word-Formation with an Appendix on Semitisms in the New Testament* (Edinburgh: T. & T. Clark).

Muraoka, T.
1983 'Hosea IV in the Septuagint Version', *Annual of the Japanese Biblical Institute* 9: 24-64.
1986 'Hosea V in the Septuagint Version', *Abr-Nahrain* 24: 120-38.
1991 'Hebrew hapax legomena and Septuagint lexicography', in C.E. Cox (ed.), *VII Congress of the International Organization for Septuagint and Cognate Studies Leuven 1989* (Septuagint and Cognate Studies 31; Atlanta: Scholars Press), 205-22.
1993 *A Greek-English Lexicon of the Septuagint (Twelve Prophets)* (Leuven: Peeters).

Nitzan, B.
1986 *Pesher Habakkuk. A Scroll from the Wilderness of Judaea (1QpHab).* [Heb.] (Jerusalem: Bialik Institute).

Nyberg, H.S.
1935 *Studien zum Hoseabuche, zugleich ein Beitrag zur Klärung des Problems der alttestamentlichen Textkritik* (Uppsala: A.B. Lundequistska Boekhandeln).

Simon, U.
1989 *Abraham Ibn Ezra's Two Commentaries on the Minor Prophets. An Annotated Critical Edition*, I [Heb.] (Ramat Gan: Bar-Ilan University Press).

Soisalon-Soininen, I.
1987 'Der Gebrauch des *genetivus absolutus* in der Septuaginta', in *Studien zur Septuaginta-syntax* (Helsinki), 175-80.

Streane, A.W.
1896 *The Double Text of Jeremiah (Massoretic and Alexandrian Compared)* (Cambridge: Deighton Bell and Co.).

Wellhausen, J.
1898 *Die Kleinen Propheten übersetzt und erklärt* (Berlin: Von Georg Reimer).

Wevers, J.W.
1990 *Notes on the Greek Text of Exodus* (Septuagint and Cognate Studies 30; Atlanta: Scholars Press).
1993 *Notes on the Greek Text of Genesis* (Septuagint and Cognate Studies 35; Atlanta: Scholars Press).

Wolff, H.W.
1965 *Das Dodekapropheton 1. Hosea* (Biblischer Kommentar. Altes Testament; Neukirchen–Vluyn: Neukirchener Verlag, 2nd edn).

Ziegler, J.

1943 'Beiträge zum griechischen Dodekapropheton', in *Nachrichten der Akademie der Wissenschaften in Göttingen. Philologisch-Historische Klasse. Jahrgang 1943, Nr. 10* (Göttingen: Vandenhoeck & Rupecht).

1967 *Septuaginta Vetus Testamentum Graecum etc. XIII. Duodecim Prophetae* (Göttingen: Vandenhoeck & Ruprecht, 2nd edn).

Some Ancient Near Eastern Parallels to the Song of Songs

Wilfred G.E. Watson

The Song of Songs was chosen largely because it is a reminder of the series of joint seminars between the universities of Durham and Newcastle upon Tyne, arranged by John Sawyer several years ago. Over several weeks, this text was examined in detail and the discussions were generally instructive, quite often amusing and always enjoyable. The aspect selected here reflects John's own interest in ancient Near Eastern texts and languages, which has been common ground in our long years of friendship.

Introduction

It is no new observation that the Song of Songs has many parallels in ancient Near Eastern literature, especially in Egyptian and Sumerian love poetry (survey in Pope 1977: 252-88). There have been several separate studies on the relationship between the Egyptian material and Song (Halévy 1922; Fox 1983; 1985; Niccacci 1991; White 1978) and on the comparison between Mesopotamian love songs and Song (Kramer 1962; Cooper 1971; Sasson 1973). In addition, most commentaries on the Hebrew Song of Songs use comparative material from the ancient Near East (notably, Pope 1977 and Fox 1985). Garbini, though, considers these parallels as irrelevant: 'sotto qualsiasi cielo, quando s'incontrano un uomo e una donna la conversazione diventa inevitabilmente monotematica' (Garbini 1992: 13). He considers, instead, that Song of Songs depends on Theocritus, as already proposed by Grotius in the seventeenth century. There has been no general survey, however, of all the ancient Near Eastern material comparable to the Hebrew Song of Songs. Here, therefore, the main intention is to compare and contrast this work with a whole range of ancient near Eastern texts to highlight some of the differences as well as the similarities. A re-examination of this material is required because the accepted interpretations of some ancient Near Eastern texts have recently been brought into question (as is shown below) and also because a few additional texts are now available for comparison. Lexical items are not discussed here for lack of space and because otherwise this contribution would become too technical.

The two main bodies of literature for comparison with Song are from Mesopotamia (Sumerian love songs: Kramer 1969; Alster 1985, 1992, 1993) and Egypt (collections of love songs: Fox 1985: 3-81, 194-202, 345-50. Also: Simpson, Faulkner and Wente 1972: 296-326; Lichtheim 1976: 179-93). There are, in addition, some comparable texts in Babylonian (Goodnick Westenholz 1987; Black 1983) and Assyrian (Livingstone 1989: 35-37), and from ancient Syria, that is, the Ugaritic texts (Avishur 1974; Pope 1977; Pope and Tigay 1971; Fisher and Knutson 1969), but very little from Anatolia (in either Hurrian or Hittite; cf. Güterbock 1983: 155-64, esp. 157, and Hoffner 1987) and nothing from Phoenicia. In addition, it has been suggested that there are connections with Indian love songs (Rabin 1973).

The points of comparison are set out under a number of headings: (1) point of view; (2) literary form; (3) poetic techniques; (4) descriptions of lovers; (5) themes and motifs; (6) overt or covert eroticism. In the final section, (7), some incorrectly proposed parallels are discussed. The presentation here is indicative only and by no means exhaustive.

1. *Point Of View*

Before discussing such aspects as literary form and poetic technique a few comments on the different points of view reflected in such poems as the Song of Songs and various Egyptian and Mesopotamian love poems may be helpful. In general, there is some evidence that to a large extent the speaker was (or was portrayed as) a girl. This, in turn, may indicate that in some cases the author might also have been a woman.

In Egypt, women wrote the poems and in fact the writing of love poetry was 'chiefly a feminine profession. The reason for this phenomenon must have been a social one: the women served as singers, as we see in many Egyptian reliefs' (Goitein 1992: 61; see 60-61 for further references). In Mesopotamia, such poems were written from female point of view (Cooper 1989: 88). 'Some of the love songs can...be seen as poems in which the girl expresses her desire to be married' (Alster 1993: 18-19). Alster goes further and suggests that the girl had more than a passive role in match-making, and that this was expressed in the poems:

> There can be no doubt that under normal circumstances it was the girl's family that selected a man to whom the girl could be married... However...it is equally clear that, at least in the world of poetry, the girl was not prepared to accept the choice without discussion. In view of the formalized way in which this issue is phrased, there are good reasons to believe that this does in some way reflect reality (Alster 1993: 18).

Many scholars now accept that Song of Songs, too, was composed by a woman (e.g. Goitein 1993; cf. Falk 1982: 75 and 86; Brenner 1993) though not all would agree (e.g. Garbini 1992: 312 n. 16). Irrespective of authorship, however, it is remarkable that in such male-dominated societies, the feminine point of view is so forcibly yet delicately portrayed.

2. *Literary Form*

1. *Collections of Love Songs*

Already in ancient times Egyptian love songs were copied as several different collections (Lichtheim 1976: 181). In Mesopotamia, too, such anthologies were compiled. An example is the Manchester Tammuz, which appears to be 'a conglomerate or a collection of short songs of various origin' (Alster 1992a: 2). Whether the Hebrew Song of Songs is a collection of songs (e.g. Goulder 1986) or a single structured composition (Exum 1973; Murphy 1979; Fox 1985; Deckers 1993; Elliott 1989; etc.) is still a matter of debate which comparison with the ancient Near Eastern material cannot resolve (Fox 1985: 204-205), although it can provide some indications.

2. *Dialogue or Monologue?*

The Song of Songs is cast in dialogue form (the two main speakers are the lovers, male and female) interspersed with choruses spoken by women. The same allocation of speakers is evident in Sumerian love poetry, for example, the Manchester Tammuz. In some of these Sumerian love songs, only the girl and a chorus of women speak; in others, only the two protagonists. However, in three such songs it is only the girl who speaks (details are given in Alster 1985). It is to be noted that in the one surviving Babylonian ballad 'unsignalled switching from one speaker to another... is entirely understandable as an artistic device, particularly if the text is not regarded as a sequence of lines upon the printed page but as merely the libretto of a live musical performance' (Black 1983: 3).

In contrast, 'all Egyptian love songs are monologues' (Fox 1983: 220). The boy and the girl are separate and speak to an unidentified audience; 'their monologues are soliloquies' because the poets 'are presenting personality and emotion rather than a complete relationship. They create a variety of personalities...and study each one in isolation' (Fox 1983: 221). However, in the first cycle of *Papyrus Chester Beatty I* male and female speakers alternate (Lichtheim 1986: 181).

In the Song of Songs, however, 'not only do the lovers address each other and exchange words, they *influence* each other. They speak to and respond to each other' (Fox 1983: 221). In respect of dialogue, then, the Song of Songs is closer to Mesopotamian than to Egyptian love poetry.

3. *Dramatic Presentation*

In Sumerian and Egyptian love songs and in the Song of Songs, the presentation is dramatic in varying degrees. The speakers are not identified because the audience could easily do so from a number of clues. 'There was no need to identify the speakers, because it was evident that particular phrases suggested the easily identifiable roles of bride, the bridegroom, and the audience. This applies not only to this composition, but is a general characteristic of the Sumerian love songs' (Alster 1992a: 3). This is also the case in the Hebrew Song of Songs (Meier 1992: 38-40). Whether there was ever any actual dramatic performance remains unclear.

4. *Sacred or Secular? Ordinary or Royal?*

Here, two related but distinct aspects are considered: whether or not these songs belonged to the cult (especially to 'sacred marriage') and whether or not they were connected with the court. There is no doubt that the Egyptian love songs depict everyday situations, where the protagonists are neither royal nor connected with the cult (see Fox 1985: 292-94, on the 'Travesties'). 'The lovers in the Egyptian songs... seem to be in the same social class as the audience' (Fox 1985: 293). Nor are these songs related to sacred marriage (Fox 1985: 239).

On the other hand, it has long been accepted that most if not all the Sumerian material is connected in some way with the sacred marriage rite (Kramer 1969). Recently, however, this view has been questioned. Alster comments: 'In fact, the importance of a sacred rite in the love songs, whether related to the temple or to the royal court, or both, may have been largely overrated.' He suggests, instead, that the formalized character of these texts is evidence for 'a traditional set of marriage ceremonies', and further, 'although a king's name is mentioned in some love songs, his name may stand for any lover'. Similarly, although the female may be called the (goddess) Inanna, in fact, she may be any girl (Alster 1993: 16; for further references, cf. p. 16, n. 12). And purely secular songs from Babylon are now known to us where Ishtar is portrayed as a young girl 'cast as an infatuated but reticent young girl' (Black 1983: 30).

This is of direct importance for the Song of Songs because there Solomon is expressly mentioned (Song 1.1; 3.7, 11; 8.11, 12) as is the king (Song 1.4, 12) and the expression 'King Solomon' actually occurs once (Song 3.11). These references are probably to be understood in the sense suggested by Alster and not necessarily as later insertions or reinterpretations. (On the enigmatic 'Amminadab' in Song 6.12 see Mulder 1992 and Deckers 1993).

3. *Poetic Techniques*

A sample of poetic techniques common to some of the love-poems in question is discussed here.

1. *Number Parallelism*

In a late Babylonian composition, Ishtar is portrayed as indefatigable even after coitus with a large number of men (Von Soden 1991: 340, lines 15-16):

> Seven at her midriff, seven at her hips
> Rejoicing is indeed foundation for a city.
> Sixty and sixty are repeatedly gaining gratification at her nakedness.
> Rejoicing is indeed foundation for a city.
> The men became tired, but Ishtar did not become tired.
> Rejoicing is indeed foundation for a city.

Although nothing comparable is to be found in the Egyptian texts, in the Ugaritic texts, number parallelism also features in connection with 'love', for example

> *škb ᶜmnh šbᶜ lšbᶜm*
> *tš[ᶜ]ly ṯmn lṯmnym*
> He (Baal) lay with her seventy-seven times,
> she (Anath) was mounted eighty-eight times (KTU 1.5 v 20-21).

In the Hebrew poem, parallelism between numbers occurs once (Song 6.8):

> sixty queens are they.
> eighty concubines,
> girls without number

These numbers are used to show that the girl in the Song of Songs is only one, in fact, unique (Song 6.9a). In all these texts, then, number parallelism is used with reference to sexual activity, though the allusion is very veiled in Song of Songs. In the Manchester Tammuz, however, number parallelism is used very differently and indicates enormous wealth (Alster 1992a: 29), whereas in one set of Egyptian songs it refers to the length of time since the boy last saw his girl: 'Three days now that I pray to her name, five days since she went from me' (Lichtheim 1976: 184—fifth stanza).

2. *Metaphors*
In the descriptions of the lovers there is a wide-ranging use of metaphors in all these love-songs (for Hebrew cf. Alter 1985: 185-203) some very bold, others obscure except to the initiated. For example, in the Mesopotamian poems, 'apples' denotes breasts (cf. Song 7.8), the 'apple tree' refers to the male member (cf. Song 8.5) and 'lettuce' denotes pubic hair (Alster 1993: 20 and 21; cf. Alster 1992b). Other metaphors are used to depict various aspects of the body (eyes, neck, limbs, etc.) and not all are transparent. Comparison with kindred metaphors in ancient Near Eastern texts may be of help here. For example, the enigmatic imagery in Song 4.1 may mean 'Your hair is like a flock of goats, flowing in waves from Mount Gilead' in view of the use Ugaritic *glt* with reference to Baal (Tuell 1993).

4. *Motifs and Themes*

Again, only a selection can be discussed here.

1. *'Siblings' denotes 'Lovers'*
In the expression 'my sister, bride' (Song 4.9, 10, 11; 5.1), 'sister' is usually explained as a loose term for 'lover'. It is well known that this

usage is attested in the Egyptian love songs (Niccacci 1991: 81) and in those from Mesopotamia (Alster 1992a: 29). Alster comments: 'This mere figure of speech should not surprise us in view of the fact that exactly the same phenomenon can be observed in the Egyptian love songs. The reason for using the terms of the closer family members is obviously that under cover of modesty this allows the lovers to use expressions of tenderness which would not otherwise be suitable for unmarried people' and he refers to Song 8.1-2 (Alster 1993: 17).

2. *Search for Lover*

The motif of the girl looking for her lover (Song 3.1-3), which is successful (Song 1.4ff.) would seem to occur in the Ugaritic Baal Cycle, where the goddess Anath is searching for her consort, Baal. The difference is, though, that in the Ugaritic text Baal is dead.

3. *Sweet Lips*

Sweetness of lips is implied in *ḥkw mmtqym*, 'his mouth is sweet' (Song 5.16), and the term *ḥk*, literally, 'palate' is unequivocal. Comparable is

> *hn. špthm. mtqtm.*
> *mtqtm. klrmn[m]*
> See, their lips were sweet,
> sweet as pomegran[ates]

which occurs twice in a Ugaritic myth concerning procreation (KTU 1.23: 50 // 55). The same motif is used with rather more piquancy in Mesopotamian literature:

> Like her mouth her vulva [is sweet],
> Like her [vulva] her mouth [is sweet]

(Text: Alster 1985: 131). Egyptian parallels to Song 1.3 are discussed by Niccacci (1991: 83). It can be noted, too, that honey, mentioned in the Hebrew Song of Songs (5.1), seems to have had erotic undertones, and also occurs in love songs from Mesopotamia (cf. Lambert 1987 and Alster 1993: 16 n. 7).

4. *Strong as Death*

'For love is as strong as death' (Song 8.6). In the Ugaritic mythological texts, Death (Mot or Motu) is portrayed as indestructible, which makes the comparison in Song particularly apt (survey of opinions, Pope 1977: 668). In addition, the phrase *mtm ᶜz m'id*, 'Death is very strong', occurs in a Ugaritic letter with reference to plague or pestilence: KTU 2.10: 12-13 (cited by Pope 1977: 668). Pardee (1987: 69) comments: 'the link with Song of Songs 8.6 is almost uniquely lexical, as the two texts are different in genre, originate in different situations, and have entirely different points of reference (love vs. pestilence) in different syntactic constructions'. No such phraseology, though, occurs in either Mesopotamian or Egyptian texts (see Fox 1985: 243).

5. *Skin Colour*

> *peṣatima ki peṣallurt[i]*
> *mašku naqlat kima diq[ari]*
> She was white, like a gecko,
> Her skin was burnt, like a (cooking) pot
> (Text: Lambert 1975: 120)

As Lambert himself points out (Lambert 1987: 34), this also occurs in Song 1.5: 'I am black and/but comely...like the tents of Qedar, like the pavilions of Solomon' (for the meaning here see Lee 1971). Similarly, from the Egyptian Memorial Inscription for Mutirdis: 'Blacker her hair than the black of night, than grapes of the riverbank. [Whiter] her teeth than bits of plaster etc.' (Fox 1985: 349).

6. *Love in the Garden*

In all three traditions there are many references to love in the garden or in an orchard. This can be seen in the Manchester Tammuz, lines 1-7, 44-47, 52-53, for example line 5 'Into the garden of apple trees he brought joy' (Alster 1992a: 18-20). In fact, 'the lovers meeting each other in a garden is a frequent theme in the Sumerian love songs' (Alster 1992a: 27). It is also used in Assyrian, for example, 'My lord, put an earring on me, let me give you pleasure in the garden!' (Livingstone 1989: 36). The same motif occurs in Egyptian (Fox 1985: 283-87). The garden features in the Egyptian poem 'The Orchard' but is most prominent in 'The Flower Song' where it is the principal theme. The girl says:

> I am yours like the field
> planted with flowers
> and with all sorts of fragrant plants.

Passages from Song are: 4.12, 15, 16; 5.1; 6.2, 11 (cf. 8.13) and Niccacci comments 'The garden orchard is the setting of Song of Songs and of the Egyptian love poems. It ensures secrecy, the intimacy of meeting and the appropriate background of scent, freshness, life. The garden is the setting of love and also a symbol of the beloved (girl)' (Niccacci 1991: 73).

7. *Chariot*

The meaning of Song 6.12 'Before I knew it, my soul placed me (in) the chariots of Amminadab' is very obscure (Mulder 1992; Deckers 1993) but the connection between 'chariot' and love, or rather, marriage, is reflected in other ancient Near Eastern texts. In a Sumerian text dealing with a divine chariot (Civil 1968) the connection is very clear. As Pope explains: 'in the text treated by Civil, after the description of the construction of the splendiferous chariot... the god is represented as entering [the chariot] and embracing his consort' (Pope 1977: 590). As Pope also reminds us (1977: 591) in the Epic of Gilgamesh, the goddess Ishtar tries to seduce Gilgamesh and offers him a chariot:

> Come to me, Gilgamesh, and be my lover!
> Bestow on me the gift of your fruit!
> You can be my husband, and I can be your wife.
> I shall have a chariot of lapis lazuli and gold harnessed for you,
> With wheels of gold, and horns of *elmešu*-stone
> You shall harness *ūmu*-demons as great mules!' (translation, Dalley 1990: 77).

Further, in the 'Love Lyrics of Nabû and Tašmetu' (Matsushima 1987; Livingstone 1989: 35-37) there comes the line (spoken by the male): '[Let me pro]vide a new chariot for you [....]!' while the woman, rather intriguingly, says to him 'Bind and harness (yourself) thither (i.e. in the garden)'.

In the Egyptian texts, too, there is reference to a chariot, but as part of a description of the lover anxiously awaited by the girl: 'All stables are ready for him, He has horses at the stations; the chariot is harnessed in its place, he may not pause on the road' (Lichtheim 1986: 186). Also, in an Egyptian poem, a Late Egyptian ruler is compared to the components of a chariot (Dawson and Peet 1933). Unfortunately, in spite of all this comparative material, the precise meaning of Song 6.12 remains enigmatic although the Egyptian passage suggests that it may denote the girl's intense desire to be with her loved one.

8. *Scent, Smell*

In Babylonian tradition fragrance denotes attractiveness:

> There is no question that the frequent allusions to the 'fragrance' of a person were—at least in some cases—a metaphor for attractiveness. It was probably not restricted to the erotic sphere—it was but a natural extension of the 'garden' symbolism which they liked so much (Westenholz and Westenholz 1977: 216).

Much the same is true of the Egyptian material (cf. Niccacci 1991: 82-83). In the Song of Songs there are also quite a few references to scent, all of them positive (Song 1.3, 12, 13, 14; 2.17; 4.6b, 10, 11, 14, 16; 5.1, 13; 6.2; 7.9, 14; 8.14). By contrast, some Mesopotamian texts allude to the more disagreeable side of bodily aromas, for example, 'vulva from which urine comes', 'spittle-laden mouth' and 'armpits stinking of mushrooms' (see Westenholz and Westenholz 1977; Lambert 1975: 123) though here the allusion, if not comic, may have been to what nowadays is termed an exchange of bodily fluids.

9. *Embrace*

The embrace of Song 2.6 (// 8.3) is chastely expressed:

> His left hand under my head,
> and his right hand embraces me.

The same applies to Egyptian, for example 'Embracing her expels my malady'; 'my arms spread out to embrace her' (Lichtheim 1976: 185, 193). In Mesopotamian tradition, however, the description could be more explicit, for example:

> Your right hand you have placed on my vulva,
> your left hand you have stretched toward my head (Alster 1985: 145).

Similarly, from another love-song:

> reach forth with your left hand and stroke our vulva (Westenholz 1987: 423).

The left hand was usually reserved for impure acts (Civil 1983: 46-47).

10. *Shade*

Reference to 'shade' is found in all the three main traditions. In an Egyptian song the little sycamore speaks: 'Come spend the day in pleasure, (one) morning, then another—two days, sitting in (my) shade' (Fox 1985: 46).

In the 'Love Lyrics of Nabû and Tašmetu' (see above):

> The shade of the cedar, the shade of the cedar,
> the shade of the cedar, the king's shelter!
> The shade of the cypress (is for) his magnates!
> The shade of a sprig of juniper is shelter for my Nabû and my games!
> (Text: Livingstone 1989: 35, lines 9-11).

And in Song 2.3

> I delight to sit in his shade

(For a sexual explanation of 'shade' see Alster 1993: 20, n. 44.).

11. *Sickness of Love*

This motif, found in Hebrew, 'Sustain me...for I am sick from love' (Song 2.5; cf. 5.8) and Egyptian:

> I shall lie down at home
> and pretend to be ill
> (Fox 1985: 13; cf. Niccacci 1991: 62-65)

does not appear to be present in Mesopotamian songs. It was partly a ruse for the 'sister' to visit the lovesick person when he was alone. Not unconnected is an Old Babylonian incantation text against the pangs of a broken heart (Veldhuis 1990: 39-40).

12. *Seal*

The lover's wish, in one of the Egyptian songs, to be the seal-ring on his beloved's finger and so steal her heart, has been compared to Song 8.6

> Place me like the seal on your heart,
> like the seal upon your arm
> (Niccacci 1991: 83)

Comparable, too, is the Mesopotamian custom of wearing a cylinder seal around the neck or a stamp-seal dangling from the wrist. An Assyrian letter, in fact, includes the expression 'you placed him like a seal around your neck' (Hallo 1983: 12). In all three traditions these are graphic wishes for closer intimacy.

14. *North Wind*

In one Egyptian song there is a reference to the north wind—'The north wind [blows]...'—which, according to Fox, 'represents the power of revitalization and vigour' (Fox 1985: 32, 34). This may explain Song 4.16: 'Awake, O North wind, and come, O South wind!' Garbini sees an erotic allusion here (Garbini 1992: 228).

6. *Overt or Covert Eroticism?*

Generally speaking, the eroticism of love-songs is not overt (but see sections 4.3, 4.8, 4.9 above; also Cottini 1990). Exceptionally, the following lines from a Babylonian love letter from the goddess *Belit-balaṭi* ('Mistress-of-Life') are particularly frank:

> I have opened for you [my] vulva;
> Strike [my] clitoris!
> The Venus mound like a *pequttu*-plant [...]

Unfortunately, little more of relevance is preserved (Grayson 1983). On the other hand, 'the Egyptian love songs are deeply erotic without dwelling on the details of sexual activity. The sex act is never *described*, even euphemistically' (Fox 1985: 311). The most explicit reference is 'it (i.e. the hour of my joy) began when I lay with you' ('The Flower Song, no. 17—see Fox 1985: 311; see also 298-300). In Sumerian, there are lengthy poems of self-praise, especially those in praise of the vulva, for example

> The lady started to sing in praise of herself.
> The *gala*-singer [repeated it(?)] in a song.
> Inanna started to sing a song in praise of herself.
> She [sang] a song of her vulva:
> '(My) vulva, which is something...'

(Alster 1993: 22; for a longer song cf. Alster 1992a: 32-35).
By contrast, the simple couplet in Hebrew:

> I am a rose(?) of Sharon.
> a lily of the valley (Song 2.1)

is modest in every meaning of the word. (See, in general, Ullendorff 1979).

7. *Incorrect Ancient Near Eastern Parallels*

Several alleged parallels to the Song of Songs can now be proved incorrect. Some of the more significant are discussed in this final section.

Many scholars have compared an incantation in Ugaritic with the Song of Songs because it was thought to concern the goddess Anath and her 'brother', whom she wished to 'devour', a verb understood as having a sexual meaning (e.g. Astour 1963; Lipiński 1965; for bibliography see Del Olmo Lete 1992: 7, n. 1). However, it has now been shown that this text does not in fact mention Anath at all and has no sexual content, but is, instead, an incantation against the Evil Eye (Del Olmo Lete 1992; for Mesopotamia cf. Thomsen 1992). Accordingly, it should not be brought into the discussion of parallels with love poems.

Another text, this time in Babylonian, was thought to be a set of love incantations (Wilcke 1985), but has subsequently been described as 'a collection of sorcerous or quasi-sorcerous spells designed to give someone control over other persons' (Scurlock 1989–90: 112). This text, too, can be excluded from our discussion.

In addition, a set of poems which scholars have considered as connected with love—the so-called Babylonian Love Lyrics (Lambert 1959; 1966–67)—may, in fact, prove to be completely different in character: 'Ich fürchte, die "Love Lyrics" sind weder lieblich noch sehr lyrisch' (Edzard 1987: 58; though whether, as he suggests, they deal with ritual defaecation has yet to be demonstrated). Note that according to Finkel 'The...81-7-28 collection also includes two new important tablets... which restore much of the text of the so-called *Love Lyrics*, from the hand of a scribe called [...]-iddin' (Finkel 1991: 92).

Dressler points out that 'the terms "brother" and "sister" are terms of affection only in Sumerian and Egyptian love songs' (Dressler 1979: 216). 'Common to a number of the [Sumerian] songs is that the lover and the girl address each other as "brother" and "sister"' (Alster 1993: 17). '"Brother" and "sister" are frequent terms of affection and intimacy in the Egyptian love songs. The usage probably arose because siblings are the closest blood relations; only the closeness of that relationship is implied by the epithets' (Fox 1985: 8, note 1). Accordingly, the couplet spoken by the goddess Anat to Aqhat (KTU 1.18 i 24):

> *šm*^{c}*. m[*^{c}*. laqht. ǵ]zr*
> *at. aḫ wan. a[ḫtk]*
> Listen, ple[ase, O hero Aqh]at!
> You are my brother and I am [your sist]er

is not a marriage proposal but an invitation to join her hunting party as an equal (Xella 1984). Therefore, it should not be cited in connection with the Song of Songs.

The oft-quoted Ugaritic passage (KTU 1.11 i 1-2):

lyṯkḥ wyiḫd bqrb
ṯtkḥ wtḫd bušr
He was aroused(?) and seized [her] vulva,
she was aroused(?) and seized [his] penis

(where the meaning of *ṯkḥ* is uncertain—see Del Olmo Lete 1981: 641) is followed by some difficult lines. The first of these, [*b*]*^{c}l yabd lalp*, has been rendered '[Mighty B]aal copulated by the thousand' (e.g. Pope 1977: 382) but in view of the fact that in this text Baal is represented as copulating with Anat in the form of a heifer, here *alp* apparently does not mean 'a thousand' but may refer either to Baal himself (de Moor 1987: 116) or to his offspring (Del Olmo Lete 1981: 471). Therefore, it does not describe multiple coition (see above).

Conclusions

Only a selection of the similarities and differences between the Hebrew Song of Songs and its ancient Near Eastern counterparts could be discussed here. Since the subject matter (love between a boy and a girl) is, of course, common to all mankind, it is not surprising that there are similarities. However, even a more detailed comparison shows that there was to some extent a common tradition within the love songs that have reached us through these texts, although each particular culture retained its own individual way of handling that tradition. And comparison among the cultural variety of the ancient Near East may help to explain aspects that to our eyes seem unusual or obscure.

BIBLIOGRAPHY

Abusch, T., J. Huehnergard and P. Steinkeller, P. (eds.)
1990 *Lingering over Words. Studies in Ancient Near Eastern Literature in Honor of William L. Moran* (HSS 37; Atlanta, Georgia: Scholars Press).

Albright, W.F.
1963 'Archaic Survivals in the Text of Canticles', in Winton Thomas and McHardy 1963: 1-7.

Alster, B.
1985 'Sumerian Love Songs', *RA* 79: 127-59.
1992 'The Manchester Tammuz', *Acta Sumerologica* 14: 1-46.
1992 'Two Sumerian Short Tales Reconsidered', *ZA* 82: 186-201.
1993 'Marriage and Love in the Sumerian Love Songs with some notes on the Manchester Tammuz', in Cohen, Snell and Weisberg 1993: 15-27.

Astour, M.C.
1963 'Un texte d'Ugarit récemment découvert et ses rapports avec l'origine des cultes bachiques grecs', *RHR* 164: 1-15.

Alter, R.
1985 *The Art of Biblical Poetry* (New York: Basic Books).

Avishur, Y.
1974 [Stylistic Elements Common between Ugaritic Literature and Song of Songs] *BethMikra* 59: 508-25.

Black, J.A.
1983 'Babylonian Ballads: A New Genre', *JAOS* 103: 25-42.

Bonanno, A. (ed.)
1986 *Archaeology and Fertility Cult in the Ancient Mediterranean. Papers Presented at the the First International Conference on Archaeology of the Ancient Mediterranean. The University of Malta 2-5 September 1985* (Amsterdam: B.R. Grüner Publishing Co).

Brenner, A. (ed.)
1993 *A Feminist Companion to The Song of Songs* (The Feminist Companion to the Bible 1; Sheffield: JSOT Press).

Brenner, A.
1993 'Women Poets and Authors' in Brenner 1993: 86-97.
1993 'To see is to assume: Whose Love is celebrated in the Song of Songs?', *Biblical Interpretation* 1: 265-84.

Civil, M.
1968 'Išme-Dagan and Enlil's Chariot', *JAOS* 88: 3-14.
1983 'Enlil and Ninlil: The Marriage of Sud', *JAOS* 103: 43-66.

Cohen, M.E., D.C. Snell and D.B. Weisberg (eds.)
1993 *The Tablet and the Scroll. Near Eastern Studies in Honor of William W. Hallo* (Bethesda, MD: CDL Press).

Cooper, J.S.
1971 'New Cuneiform Parallels to the Song of Songs', *JBL* 90: 157-62.

Cottini, V
1990 'Linguaggio erotico nel Cantico dei Cantici e in Proverbi', *LA* 40: 25-45.

Dalley, S.
1990 *Myths from Mesopotamia. Creation, The Flood, Gilgamesh, and Others* (Oxford/New York: Oxford University Press).

Dawson, W.R. and T.E. Peet
1933 'The so-called Poem on the King's Chariot', *JEA* 19: 167-74.

Deckers, M.
1993 'The Structure of the Song of Songs and the Centrality of *nepeš*', in Brenner 1993: 172-96.

Dressler, H.H.P.
1979 'The Metamorphosis of a Lacuna. Is *at. aḫ. wan*...a Proposal of Marriage?', *UF* 11: 211-17.

Edzard, D.O.
1987 'Zur Ritualtafel der sog. "Love Lyrics"', in F. Rochberg-Halton: 57-69.

Elliott, M.T.
1989 *The Literary Unity of the Canticle* (European University Series XXIII—Theology 371; Bern: Peter Lang).

Falk, M.
1982 *Love Lyrics from the Hebrew Bible: A Translation and Literary Study of the Song of Songs* (Sheffield, Almond Press).

Finkel, I.L.
1991 '*Muššu'u*, *Qutāru*, and the Scribe *Tanittu-Bēl*', *AuOr* 9: 91-104.

Fisher, L.R. and F.B. Knutson
1969 'An Enthronement Ritual at Ugarit', *JNES* 28: 157-67.

Fox, M.V.
1983 'Love, Passion, and Perception in Israelite and Egyptian Love Poetry', *JBL* 102: 219-28.
1985 *The Song of Songs and Ancient Egyptian Love Songs* (Madison/Wisconsin/London: The University of Wisconsin Press).

Garbini, G.
1992 *Cantico dei cantici. Testo, traduzione, note e commento* (Biblica: Testi e studi 2; Brescia: Paideia Editrice).

García Martínez, F., H. Hilhorst and C.J. Labuschagne (eds.)
1992 *The Scriptures and the Scrolls. Studies in Honour of A.S. van der Woude on the Occasion of his 65th Birthday* (VTSup 49; Leiden Brill).

Gelb, I.J.
1970 'No. 8. Incantation invoking love magic', in MAD no. 5: 7-12.

Goedicke, H. and J.J.M. Roberts (eds.)
1975 *Unity and Diversity: Essays on the History, Literature, and Religion of the Ancient Near East* (Baltimore: Johns Hopkins).

Goitein, S.D
1957 'The Song of Songs: A Female Composition', in Brenner 1992: 58-66 (original: *Studies in the Bible* [Tel Aviv: Yavneh Press]: 301-307, 316-7 [Hebrew]).

Goodnick Westenholz, J.
1987 'A Forgotten Love Song', in Rochberg-Halton 1987: 415-25.

Gorelick, L. and E. E. Williams-Forte (eds.)
1983 *Ancient Seals and the Bible* (Ocasional Papers on the Near East 2/1; Malibu, CA: Undena).

Goulder, M.
1986 *The Song of Fourteen Songs* (Sheffield: JSOT Press).

Grayson, A.K.
1983 'Literary Letters from Deities and Diviners: More Fragments', *JAOS* 103: 143-48.

Güterbock, H.G.
1983 'A Hurro-Hittite Hymn to Ishtar', *JAOS* 103: 155-64.

Halévy, J.
1922 'Le Cantique des Cantiques et le Mythe d'Osiris-Hetep', *RevSém* 14: 248-55.

Hallo, W.W.

1984 '"As the Seal upon Thine Arm": Glyptic Metaphors in the Biblical World', in Gorelick and Williams-Forte 1983: 7-17.

Hibbert, P.M.

1984 'Liebeslyrik in der arsakidischen Zeit', *WO* 15: 93-95.

Hoffner, H.A.

1987 'Paskuwatti's ritual against sexual impotence (CTH 406)', *AuOr* 5: 271-87.

Kramer, S.N.

1962 'The Biblical "Song of Songs" and the Sumerian Love Songs', *Expedition* 5: 25-31.

1969 *The Sacred Marriage Rite: Aspects of Faith, Myth, and Ritual in Ancient Sumer* (Bloomington, IN: Indiana University Press).

Lambert, W.G.

1959 'Divine Love Lyrics from Babylon', *JSS* 4: 1-15.

1966–67 'Divine Love Lyrics from the Reign of Abi-ešuḫ', *MIO* 12: 41-56.

1969 'An eye-stone of Esarhaddon's Queen and other similar gems', *RA* 63: 65-71.

1975 'The Problem of the Love Lyrics', in Goedicke and Roberts 1975: 98-126.

1987 'Devotion: The Languages of Religion and Love', in Mindlin, Geller and Wansbrough 1987: 26-39.

Lee, G. M.

1971 'Song of Songs V 16, "My beloved is white and ruddy"', *VT* 21: 609.

Lichtheim, M.

1976 *Ancient Egyptian Literature*, II (Berkeley: University of California Press).

Lipiński, E.

1965 'Les conceptions et les couches merveilleuses de ᶜAnat', *Syria* 42: 114-5.

1986 'Fertility Cult in Ancient Ugarit', in Bonanno 1986: 207-16.

Livingstone, A. (ed.)

1989 *Court Poetry and Literary Miscellanea* (State Archives of Assyria III; Helsinki: Helsinki University Press).

Marks, J.H. and R.M. Good (eds.)

1987 *Love & Death in the Ancient Near East. Essays in Honor of Marvin H. Pope* (Guilford, CT: Four Quarters Publishing Company).

Matsushima, E.

1987 'Le rituel hiérogamique de Nabû', *ASJ* 9: 131-75.

Meier, S.A.

1992 *Speaking of Speaking. Marking Direct Discourse in the Hebrew Bible* (VTSup 46; Leiden: Brill).

Mindlin, M., M.J. Geller and J.E. Wansbrough (eds.)

1987 *Figurative Language in the Ancient Near East* (London: School of Oriental and African Studies, University of London).

Moor, J.C. de
1987 *An Anthology of Religious Texts from Ugarit* (Nisaba 16; Leiden: Brill).
Mulder, M.J.
1992 'Does Canticles 6,12 Make Sense?', in García Martínez, Hilhorst and Labuschagne 1992: 104-13.
Murphy, R.E.
1979 'The Unity of the Song of Songs', *VT* 29: 436-43.
'Song of Songs, Book of', in ABD 6: 150-55.
Niccacci, A.
1991 'Cantico dei Cantici e canti d'amore egiziani', *LA* 41: 61-85.
Olmo Lete, G. del
1981 *Mitos y leyendas de Canaán según la tradición de Ugarit* (Fuentes de la Ciencia bíblica 1; Madrid: Ediciones Cristiandad; Valencia: Institución San Jerónimo).
1991 '*Yarḫu* y *Nikkalu*. La Mitología lunar sumeria en Ugarit', *AuOr* 9: 67-76.
1992 'Un conjuro ugarítico contra el "mal ojo" (KTU 1.96)', *Anuari de filologia* 15: 7-16.
Pangas, J.C.
1988 'Aspectos de la sexualidad en la Antigua Mesopotamia', *AuOr* 6: 211-16.
Pardee, D.
1987 ' "As Strong as Death"', in Marks and Good 1987: 65-69.
Pope, M.H.
1977 *Song of Songs* (AB 7C; Garden City, NY: Doubleday).
Pope M.H., and J.H. Tigay
1971 'A Description of Baal', *UF* 3: 117-30.
Rabin, C.
1973 'The Song of Songs and Tamil Poetry', *Studies in Religion* 3: 205-19.
Rochberg-Halton, F. (ed.)
1987 *Language, Literature, and History: Philological and Historical Studies Presented to E. Reiner* (AOS 67; New Haven, CT).
Sasson, J.M.
1973 'A Further Cuneiform Parallel to the Song of Songs?', *ZAW* 85: 359-60.
Scurlock, J.A.
1989–90 'Was There a «Love-hungry» *Entu*-priestess Named Eṭirtum?, *AfO* 36/37: 107-12.
Segert, S.
1986 'An Ugaritic Text Related to the Fertility Cult (*KTU* 1.23)', in Bonanno 1986: 217-24
Simpson, W.K., R.O. Faulkner and E.F. Wente, Jr (eds.)
1972 *The Literature of Ancient Egypt* (New Haven: Yale University Press).
Soden, W. von
1991 'Ein spät-altbabylonisches *parum*-Preislied für Ištar', *Or* 60: 339-43.
Suys, E
1932 'Les Chants d'Amour du papyrus Chester Beatty I', *Bib* 13: 209-27.

Thomsen, M.-L.
1992 'The Evil Eye in Mesopotamia', *JNES* 51: 19-32.
Tournay, R.J.
1982 *Quand Dieu parle aux hommes le langage de l'amour. Études sur le Cantique des Cantiques* (Cahiers de la Revue Biblique; Paris: Gabalda,).
Tuell, S.S.
1993 'A Riddle Resolved by an Enigma: Hebrew גלש and Ugaritic *glṯ*', *JBL* 112: 99-121.
Ullendorff, E.
1979 'The Bawdy Bible', *BSOAS* 42: 425-56, esp. 441 and 447.
Veldhuis, N.C.
1990 'The Heart Grass and Related Matters', *OLP* 21: 27-44.
Westenholz, J. and A. Westenholz
1977 'Help for Rejected Suitors. The Old Akkadian Love Incantation MAD V 8', *Or* 46: 198-219.
White, J.B.
1978 *A Study of the Language of Love in the Song of Songs and Ancient Egyptian Poetry* (SBLDS 38; Missoula, MT: Scholars Press).
Wilcke, C.
1985 'Liebesbeschwörungen aus Isin', *ZA* 75: 188-209.
Winton T.D., and W.D. McHardy (eds.)
1963 *Hebrew and Semitic Studies presented to Godfrey Rolles Driver in celebration of his seventieth birthday, 20 August 1962* (Oxford: Clarendon Press).
P. Xella
1984 ' "Tu sei mio fratello ed io sono tua sorella" (KTU 1.18 I 24)', *AuOr* 2: 151-53.

COORDINATION BY *Vav* IN BIBLICAL HEBREW

J.C.L. Gibson

If the following quotation is anything to go by, a former generation of Old Testament scholars had no high opinion of the language they professed. It comes from an article by no less distinguished a representative of that generation than Sir George Adam Smith. On page 11 he writes

> That subordination of clause to clause in which the subtlety and flexibility of other languages appears is hardly found, but to the end, both in prose and poetry, the clauses are almost invariably strung together by the bare copulas *and* and *then* in a coordination which requires both skill and spirit to redeem it from monotony.

Sir George goes on to make the most of what he clearly regards as a bad business, praising eloquently the biblical writers' mastery of (p. 17)

> ...a medium of expression so defective in construction and flexibility as we have seen the Hebrew language to be

And there is of course some truth in his assessment. We can concede that Hebrew prefers coordination to subordination, and coordination by *Vav* to coordination by other conjunctions. (I am assuming that by *then* he is thinking of the common alternative to *and* in English translation, and not of a different Hebrew conjunction; he can hardly be referring to אז, which is relatively rare and rather means *then* in the sense of *at that time*.)

But Sir George is very wrong in implying that because Hebrew does not, like English and other western languages, use a fair number of different conjunctions as substitutes for *and*, nor often omit *and* altogether between clauses, nor employ participles or subordinate clauses to ring the changes on *and* clauses, it is deficient syntactically. This is simply not the case. Hebrew has diversity, but it expresses *its* diversity, not by avoiding, but by means of clauses beginning with *Vav*. There are several kinds of these, which are distinguished formally from each other and express a wide range of discrete syntactical relationships.

It is not at all to the credit of our traditional textbooks that those who study Hebrew do not sufficiently appreciate this fact. I would exempt John Sawyer's *Modern Introduction,* at least partially, from this criticism. He broaches the subject briefly on pages 146-148, where he distinguishes between clauses which begin with a verb and clauses which begin with a noun (in both cases usually following *Vav*), though he tends to explain the noun-initial ones too narrowly in terms of emphasis. When a noun, whether subject or object (or indeed an adverbial phrase) is placed immediately after *Vav*, there is generally some emphasis or focusing upon it; but there is a lot more to it than that, as this article hopes to show. It is based mainly on the treatment of coordination and related matters in my recent revision of A.B. Davidson's *Hebrew Syntax* (see its Index of Subjects). Other studies which I have consulted are listed in the Bibliography at the end of the article.

The broadest coordinating distinction made by Hebrew is between clauses beginning with *Vav* consecutive and clauses beginning with simple *Vav* in extended narrative or discourse. The first kind denote temporal sequence, while the second halt or suspend such a sequence to enable another kind of statement to be made.

This is what happens regularly in prose narrative. The *Vav* consecutive imperfect (more simply VAYYIQTOL) carries forward the main development of the story, whereas simple *Vav* with a noun, etc., and a perfect verb (QATAL) introduces a variety of off-line background statements or other comments. (A nominal clause may replace a clause with QATAL.) Verbal clauses with simple *Vav* include negative statements, which deny rather than advance a previous statement (e.g. Gen. 31.33 ולא מצא '*but he did not find them*'); story-initial background statements made through a circumstantial clause (e.g. Gen. 3.1 והנחש היה ערום '*now, the serpent was more cunning*', etc.); similar statements beginning a new episode within a story (e.g. Gen. 20.4 ואבימלך לא קרב אליה '*now, Abimelech had not approached her*'); clauses re-identifying a character after an absence (e.g. 2 Kgs. 9.1 ואלישע הנביא קרא '*thereafter Elisha the prophet summoned*'); clauses describing a noteworthy happening (e.g. Gen. 8.13 והנה חרבו פני האדמה '*and behold, the face of the ground was dry*'), and so on. These clauses are traditionally and rather lamely explained by the rule that if another word interrupts the *Vav* consecutive construction, coming between *Vav* and the verb, the verb reverts to its non-consecutive form.

That may be so, but it is not really an explanation; it does not mention that the consecutive and simple *Vav*s have quite different syntactical functions.

Within narrative we also find passages employing the other pair of consecutive and non-consecutive forms, namely YIQTOL and VeQATAL. The ones with *Vav* and a noun, etc., followed by YIQTOL also introduce a tangential statement, but this time indicating repeated action in the past; and it is continued, where necessary, by VeQATAL. Thus Gen. 2.6 ואד יעלה...והשקה '*but* a mist *used to rise* from the ground *and water*', etc. The noun may be an object, for example 1 Sam. 2.19 ומעיל קטן תעשה־לו אמו והעלתה '*now,* his mother *used to make* for him a little robe, *and take it up*', etc. The YIQTOL form has here what is called its frequentative (or iterative) meaning.

In passages of discourse and poetry set in the future it is this second pairing that is used, though YIQTOL in that time-frame ceases to have a frequentative sense. The same patterning appears as in narrative, VeQATAL advancing the discourse step by step and YIQTOL (after *Vav* and a noun, etc.) marking an off-line statement, as when a negative is used or as in Exod. 4.15 ואנכי אהיה '*while I will be* with your mouth'. In keeping, however, with the more heterogeneous nature of discourse, clauses with simple *Vav* are both more numerous and more varied in their functions than in narrative. Thus we find backward references (which use QATAL rather than YIQTOL); clauses with *Vav* followed by YIQTOL, which are coordinated with a previous clause on the same time-scale; clauses with *Vav* and a modal verb in which a second clause marks the consequence or intention of a first; clauses coordinated by apposition, which do not use *Vav* at all; and a number of (mainly) two-clause sentences which, through changes in one or the other, express different relationships like contrast or antithesis. Let us look further at the more significant of these constructions.

Simple *Vav* with QATAL repeats on the same time-scale or, it may be, slightly extends the reference of a previous QATAL, the clauses being more or less synonymous, for example Isa. 1.2 גדלתי ורוממתי '*I have nourished and brought up* children'.

This construction sometimes occurs in narrative where, however, it is sequential, and it is not easy to see why VAYYIQTOL was not used, for example 2 Kgs. 23.10 וטמא '*and* (next) *he defiled* the Topheth'. The passages involved are by no means all late, so it is questionable whether they are properly put down to the influence of Aramaic; they are more likely to be the result of some inner Hebrew development. In either case, they eventually led, in post-biblical Hebrew, to the abandonment of VAYYIQTOL and its complete replacement by simple *Vav* with QATAL (which then ceases to indicate aspect and becomes a true tense). Since it is a harbinger of major changes in the structure of Hebrew, it is perhaps wise not to include this usage in normal classical syntax.

Simple *Vav* with YIQTOL likewise joins together, in passages set in the present or the future, two events or situations which happen at or around the same time, for example Exod. 23.8 'a bribe יעור *blinds* officials ויסלף *and subverts*', etc.; Isa. 40.30 ויעפו 'even youths *shall faint* ויגעו *and be weary*'. This usage is also found in past settings, but only in poetry, for example Ps. 107.20 ישלח '*he sent forth* his word וירפאם *and healed them*'. YIQTOL is clearly not imperfective in this context, but is in fact the same as in VAYYIQTOL (and therefore perfective in aspect). For a discussion of the different aspects expressed by QATAL and YIQTOL, which questions the appropriateness of the traditional terms perfect and imperfect, see Gibson 1993.

Modal verbs are coordinated by simple *Vav* in two ways: often similarly to QATAL and YIQTOL (e.g. Isa. 56.1 שמרו משפט ועשו צדקה '*keep* justice *and do* righteousness'; Ps. 96.11 ישמחו השמים ותגל הארץ '*let* the heavens *be glad and let* the earth *rejoice*'); but more often logically to express consequence or purpose. Thus after an imperative, Gen. 27.4 הביאה לי ואכלה '*bring* to me *that I may eat*'; Ps. 128.5 יברכך '*may* Yahweh *bless you* from Zion וראה *and you then see* the prosperity of Jerusalem'; after a cohortative, 1 Kgs 1.12 איעצך '*let me give you counsel* ומלטי *that you may save* your life'. The same construction may follow a negative, a wish, or a question, which have modal implications, for example Num. 23.19 'God is not a man ויכזב *that he should lie*'; Jer. 8.23 'O that my head were waters, etc., ואבכה *that I might weep!*'; Amos 8.5 'when will the new moon be over ונשבירה שבר *that we may sell corn?*'

One of the commonest kinds of clause in which simple *Vav* is followed, not by a verb, but by a noun (usually the subject) is the circumstantial clause, already occasionally referred to. It can be either verbal or nominal. It is often translated into English by a *now*-clause when it is placed before the statement to which it refers and, though it is syntactically coordinating, by a subordinate clause with *while, when* or a nominal phrase with *with* when it comes after. Circumstantial clauses are essentially marginal to their context, functioning to give background or additional information of various kinds. They are found in poetry, but are more frequent in prose, especially introducing a narrative or episode within it. In this macrosyntactic role they often accompany a statement of time. Examples: Gen. 4.1 והאדם ידע את־חוה '*(and) the man had intercourse* with Eve his wife, and she conceived'; Gen. 2.4-6 ביום עשות יהוה אלהים ארץ ושמים וכל שיח השדה טרם יהיה 'in the day when Yahweh God made earth and heaven, *while there was as yet no plant of the field* in the earth', etc. (other circumstantial clauses follow, the narrative proper beginning at v. 7); Gen. 18.12 'shall I have pleasure ואדני זקן *when my husband is old?*'; Gen. 11.4 'let us build a tower וראשו בשמים *with its head in the heavens*'.

All the above constructions are well known and fully enough described in the textbooks. They are not, however, usually drawn together as here and treated as different modes of coordination, otherwise I doubt that Sir George would have said so confidently what he did. Less well known and certainly less well described are a number of (mainly) two-clause constructions joined by *Vav* which, by the ordering of the first or second clause or both, relate the clauses together in terms of several different syntactic functions. Strictly speaking, it is the clauses which specify the meaning, and the *Vav* serves as a non-committal conjunction, but it is always there.

Conjunctive sentences are the least specific of these. They simply coordinate by *Vav* clauses which are broadly symmetrical in their structure and similar in meaning. They may begin with a verb or another clausal element, or be nominal. Sometimes instead of the repetition of every element, ellipsis is used. Many of the cases of like conjugations or moods, linked by simple *Vav* and already discussed, are properly conjunctive sentences. Examples: Gen. 42.36 יוסף איננו ושמעון איננו '*Joseph is no more, and Simeon is no more*'; Exod. 23.8 כי השחד יעור פקחים ויסלף דברי הצדיקים '*for a bribe blinds officials and (a bribe) subverts the words of the righteous*'; Ps. 103.9 לא־לנצח יריב ולא־לנצח יטור '*he will not chide for ever, nor will he keep* (sc. his anger) *for ever*'. Conjunctive sentences may contain three or more similar clauses, for example, Gen. 31.43 (four clauses). When a nominal and a verbal clause are used together (e.g. Prov. 16.15) or when the parallelism of elements is not very precise (e.g. Prov. 11.2), it may be wiser to speak simply of loose sentences, or the term conjunctive may be stretched too far.

Chiastic sentences are, unlike conjunctive, strictly binary in structure. They are not simply for rhetorical effect, but have a distinct function. By reversing in the second clause the word order of the first, they tie the two clauses more closely together and make the events or situations of which they speak two sides of a single whole. The first clause may be worked into a prose sequence, in which case the second halts it; but the construction is also common in more independent sentences in prose discourse or poetry. Any clausal element—verb, subject, object, adverbial phrase—may be chosen for reversal. Examples: Gen. 1.5 ויקרא אלהים לאור יום ולחשך קרא לילה '*God called the light day, and the darkness he called night*'; Exod. 40.34 ויכס הענן...וכבוד יהוה מלא '*the cloud covered* the tent of meeting, *and the glory of Yahweh filled* the tabernacle'; Prov. 9.10 תחלת חכמה יראת יהוה ודעת קדשים בינה '*the fear of Yahweh is the beginning of wisdom, and knowledge of the Holy One is understanding*'.

Contrastive sentences, also binary, achieve their end by highlighting in initial position in each clause the two persons or other entities which are brought into opposition. The opposition is relatively mild, and English *but* need not always be used. Where it is, it has the sense of *on the other hand* rather than *on the contrary*. Examples: Gen. 3.15 הוא ישופך ראש ואתה תשופנו עקב '*he* will crush you in the head, *and you* will crush him in the heel'; Exod. 16.12 בין הערבים...ובבקר '*at twilight* you shall eat flesh, *and in the morning* you shall be filled with bread'. Contrastive sentences are common in poetry, especially in proverbial sayings contrasting God and man, the wise and the foolish, etc., for example Ps. 119.113 סעפים שׂנאתי ותורתך אהבתי '*double-minded men* I hate, *but your law* I love'.

Antithetical sentences work by using antonyms in the two clauses or, more often, by negation of either the first or the second clause. After a positive statement, the antithesis in the second clause is often strengthened by putting the subject first. Antithesis after a negative statement does not require this, though it sometimes happens. This kind of antithesis is common in narrative and future discourse and may be expressed by *Vav* consecutive, as indicating the next action or situation (it is negative statements, not positive, which halt the sequence). A preceding negative clause is sometimes suppressed (ellipsis). Antithesis is probably the most frequent of the relationships we have been examining, and it alone of them may use conjunctions other than *Vav*, notably כי and כי אם after a negative. Examples: Exod. 10.23 ויהי חשך־אפלה '*and there was thick darkness* in all the land of Egypt, *but* to all the children of Israel היה אור *there was light*'; Exod. 19.24 'Go down...והכהנים והעם אל־יהרסו *but* let not the priests and people break through'; with ellipsis, Ps. 27.10 '(my mother and father have not taken me up) ויהוה יאספני *but Yahweh* will take me up'; Gen. 40.23 'the chief butler did not remember Joseph וישכחהו *but* forgot him'; Isa. 11.4 'he shall not judge by what his eye sees...ושפט בצדק *but* he shall judge in righteousness the poor'.

Apart from *Vav* only a few other coordinating conjunctions are found in Hebrew: כי or כי אם, mentioned above, to express antithesis; או *or* to express disjunction; גם or אף *also, moreover* to express inclusion; רק or אך *except that, only* to express exclusion. Coordination of clauses may also be expressed without *Vav*, by apposition which, as between nouns, indicates some overlap of reference. (See on these matters Andersen 1974; Gibson 1994, Index). Our concern in this article has been, because of the quote by Sir George Adam Smith with which it began, with coordination by *Vav*.

I think it can safely be concluded that Sir George got it wrong. Far from lending itself to monotony, coordination of clauses through *Vav* is the chief avenue by which the syntax of Hebrew achieves variety and differentiation of constructions. We owe many debts to Sir George, a scholar to whom I constantly turned for inspiration as a student, but his estimate of the subtlety (or rather lack of it) of the Hebrew language is not one of them. I suspect that in reaching it he was seduced by the literal kind of translation we find in English, for example, in the King James version. The exigencies of English style made it impossible for even the AV to reproduce a distinction between *Vav* consecutive and simple *Vav* or to follow Hebrew word order, which plays so important a role in the many different constructions we have listed; but it kept most of the *ands*, and laid itself open to the misunderstanding which Sir George, and many before and after him, were unable to avoid.

BIBLIOGRAPHY

Andersen, F.I.

1974 *The Sentence in Hebrew* (The Hague: Mouton).

Gibson, J.C.L.

1993 'The Anatomy of Hebrew Narrative Poetry', in A.G. Auld (ed.), *Understanding Poets and Prophets: Essays in Honour of George Wishart Anderson* (Sheffield: JSOT Press), 141-48.

1994 *Hebrew Syntax* (Edinburgh: T. & T. Clark, 4th edn) (earlier editions by A.B. Davidson).

Muraoka, T.

1985 *Emphatic Words and Structures in Biblical Hebrew* (Jerusalem: Magnes Press/Leiden: Brill).

Niccacci, A.

1988 *The Syntax of the Verb in Classical Hebrew* (trans. W.G.E. Watson; Sheffield: JSOT Press).

Sawyer, J.F.A.

1976 *A Modern Introduction to Biblical Hebrew* (Stocksfield: Oriel).

Smith, Sir G.A.

1927 'The Hebrew Genius in the Old Testament', in E.R. Bevan and C. Singer (eds.), *The Legacy of Israel* (Oxford: Clarendon Press), 1-28.

Waltke, B.K. and M. O'Connor

1990 *An Introduction to Biblical Hebrew Syntax* (Winona Lake, IN: Eisenbrauns)

MOSES AND PATMOS: REFLECTIONS ON THE JEWISH BACKGROUND OF EARLY CHRISTIANITY

C. Rowland

John Sawyer has been a friend and colleague for twenty years. He was on the committee which appointed me to a lectureship in Newcastle, and we shared much intellectually and administratively as we together with Dermot Killingley sought to save a small department in the late seventies. In those days my approach to Christianity was determined by the study of the 'History of Religions', and I found it difficult then to comprehend why John was so concerned with the history of interpretation. I realize how much closer I have moved to his position in the last decade. In the light of this it may seem strange that I am offering him something in historical mode. It was Judaism and its biblical interpretation that was the subject of so many of our lunch-time conversations, in particular the contribution of it to the study of Christian origins and the importance of mysticism and apocalyptic. It is to these themes I want to return in this essay in gratitude for what we shared and for his pioneering contribution to biblical theology.

My purpose is to offer a sketch of early Christian (I will use that word as a shorthand to describe the movement which in its disparate parts maintained allegiance to Jesus) identity and suggest briefly that messianism and mysticism are contributory factors to Christianity ending up as a separate religion. Visionary authority by itself cannot be regarded as the reason for the break. It is after all central to Jewish tradition and experience. Nevertheless it could pose a problem to convention and authority when innovation in belief and practice (and particularly the latter) is recommended, based on mystical experience.

I realize that the account I am about to offer will give the impression that the Christian texts which are now extant exhibit a greater degree of homogeneity in faith and practice than may have been the case and that my study has been conditioned by the canon. The sources do make it difficult to give an adequate account of the emergence of the diverse patterns of Christian practice when we are so dependent upon the documents which form the canon of the New Testament. I do, however, believe that in their messianic convictions there was considerable overlap even if there was disagreement about the consequences of these convictions. There is a degree of concreteness about the expression of those beliefs about the future, in particular with regard to the character of the messiah, which is absent in many Jewish formulations which were less tied to convictions about specific persons and events. I consider that the earliest Christian texts are products of the stage of consolidation and institutionalization, though we can catch a glimpse from the New Testament of situations typical of messianic enthusiasm. As such as a collection they represent that attempt to consolidate a religion shot through with stories and ideas of subversion of convention alongside attitudes more supportive of the status quo.[1]

This essay will be more theological than I would like. Discussion of Christian origins should not neglect Marx's words from *The German Ideology*: 'men (sic) are the producers of their...ideas...as they are conditioned by a definite development of their productive forces and of the intercourse corresponding to these.' The problem for the student of Christian origins is that we know so little about the social and economic forces at work at the end of the Second Temple period. Equally, there is little information about the 'class' and background of the earliest Christian movement. Passages like Mk 1.20 and 6.3 are hardly enough to indicate that (as in other movements for change) the leaders did not emerge from the base of society.

Debate continues over the 'political' character of early Christianity. Precision over the exact reasons for Jesus' execution is lacking. That the last months of his life represented a challenge to the fragile balance between the semi-autonomous Temple state based in Jerusalem and the Roman colonial power (as hinted at in Jn 11.48), because of a popular following which might provoke disorder, seems to be the most plausible reason for his death. No doubt messianic hope and unconventional belief contributed greatly to that event, but by themselves they are probably not the only explanation. We may conjecture that if Jesus had not chosen to go up to Jerusalem he may well have been ignored by the

1. See the suggestive comments in K. Wengst, *Pax Romana and the Peace of Jesus Christ* (London: SCM Press, 1987).

authorities (unless, that is, Herod Antipas decided that Jesus like John was a figure threatening the good order of his regime), and the decision to go up to Jerusalem (which forms such an important component of all the gospel narratives) sealed his fate.

In one respect, however, there has been a welcome perspective introduced into discussion of the social setting of early Christianity. The move of Christianity from Palestine to the Diaspora and the cities of the Roman world brought about a change in the style of Christianity if not in the form those ideas took.[2] The urban character of Christianity was already a factor in Palestine as the rural Jesus movement accommodated itself to life in the capital of the Jewish world. In all likelihood the pattern laid down by Jesus and preserved in the communities' memories of him was probably not a practical possibility for the urban churches of the Greco-Roman world. Sadly, the information at our disposal allows us to say little of any certainty about the earliest adherents of Jesus' form of Judaism and their relationship to the specific social formation in which they found themselves. It would be fascinating to know whether in fact the rural movement based in Galilee survived alongside the centralized urban movement that the New Testament suggests Christianity became. Christianity's textual monuments offer us our only significant glimpses of the character of the movement, from which we have to make the most of scraps of information to get some impression of the social pressures which formed it.

In the last decades of the Second Temple there was probably greater possibility of religious and practical diversity within Judaism than was to be the case by the beginning of the second century. While I do not think that those Jews with whom Christians disagreed accepted the validity of many of the Christians' arguments for continuity with the tradition, the earliest Christian writers considered that what they believed and practised stood in line with that tradition and were allowed a freedom to exist and expand because of the lack of a powerful central governing authority. The New Testament texts are products of power struggles within Second Temple Judaism and tell the story of Christianity's accommodation to the prevailing values of the Greco-Roman world. They do not obviously reflect any dominant ideology whether Jewish or pagan. Indeed, the epistemological dualism arising out of their messianism suggests a counter-cultural concern which is less evident in the more

2. G. Theissen, *The First Followers of Jesus* (London: SCM Press, 1978) and W. Meeks, *The First Urban Christians* (New Haven: Yale University Press, 1983).

accommodating Hellenized Christianity of a later period when the messianic and apocalyptic spirit had diminished. We see in the attempts from the Gospel of Luke onwards the need to demonstrate the respectability of Christianity and to accommodate it to the prevailing culture. Apocalyptic confirmed Christianity in its alternative, minority status even if in later hands that apocalyptic dualism could serve an ideology more concerned to maintain established values and institutions.

Messianism and its Mutation

Christianity had its origins in a form of political messianism in Galilee and Jerusalem. It was what Ed Sanders has called Jewish restoration eschatology:[3] a pattern of religion which expected the restoration of Israel's fortunes, the coming of a reign of peace and justice on earth by means of a divinely appointed agent. As such it resembles, at least in general terms, several short-lived popular movements described by Josephus (e.g. *Ant.* 20.167-68).[4] Clearly Josephus has little sympathy with such movements as he makes clear in his curt dismissal of the deluded prophet who promised deliverance in the last moments of the siege of Jerusalem (*War* 6.281-82), though (if authentic) the *Testimonium Flavianum* (*Ant.* 18.63-64) offers a more sympathetic portrait of Jesus. In the passages where Josephus describes the crushing of popular prophetic movements there is no record of them having been led by someone who claimed to be messiah. From the brief comments made about their actions it is apparent that the leaders were claiming to repeat some of the distinctive actions which marked the formation and liberation of the people of God in the past: the crossing of the Jordan, the miraculous destruction of the city walls of Jericho, the desert experience, etc. While the accounts of Jesus' life suggest a reticence on his part to claim messiahship, there are many indications that his career should be understood within the wide parameters of ancient Jewish messianism. Indeed, it is unlikely that the early Christians would have so consistently claimed the messianic office for him if there had been no warrant for that in the memories of his life.

The main difference about early Christianity as compared with what we now know of these other movements is that this was a messianic

3. E.P. Sanders, *Jesus and Judaism* (London: SCM Press, 1985).

4. R. Gray, *Prophetic Figure in Late Second Temple Jewish Palestine* (Oxford: Oxford University Press, 1993).

movement which survived. There appears to have been a movement which revered the memory of John the Baptist (cf. Acts 19.1ff.), and this may have played some role within the early church's struggle for self-identification, but the hopes surrounding other groups mentioned by Josephus were probably short-lived.

With Christianity we are dealing with a much more complicated phenomenon (probably unique among the groups of Second Temple Judaism): an example of a self-consciously messianic group which had managed to survive (in whatever way) the trauma of the death of its leader and the rejection of his message to become a well-established group within the last decades of Second Temple Judaism. There is little in the extant literature which resembles the peculiar factors which determined the growth of Christianity. That is something which needs to be borne in mind as we study the contemporary Jewish texts. Often differences between the sources are to be explained by one set of sources being messianic (in the sense that they were written by those who believed that the messianic age had in some sense already arrived) and another which is non-messianic (in these the hopes for the future of the world remained hopes and were still merely a matter for speculation). The fact that the Christians believed that the messiah had come involved them in dealing with a range of issues which would hardly have affected those Jews who did not share their convictions: the character of daily life in the messianic age, the order of the fulfilment of eschatological events and the timetable for the consummation of all things. For most other Jews it would have remained a matter of theoretical interest only. For the first Christians it had become a matter of decisive importance as a necessary corollary of the coming of the messianic kingdom. That had some effect on the understanding of the messianic timetable as may be seen from Paul's letters. Here a conventional Jewish expectation of the coming of the messiah leading in due course to the conversion of the nations is altered.[5] In the light of rejection of the messiah the inclusion of a number of pagans into the eschatological kingdom is to precede the mystery of Israel's salvation (Rom. 11.25-26).

Early Christian writings never abandon the hope for future transformation of the world.[6] As that hope gradually diminished in importance,

5. A. Schweitzer, *The Mysticism of Paul the Apostle* (London: A. & C. Black, 1931).

6. On the importance of eschatology see C. Rowland, *Christian Origins* (London: SPCK, 1985).

greater concern was expressed with the internal struggle against the flesh and the limited radical transformation possible in the present. In a world where societal change seemed to be difficult, if not impossible, the quest for personal perfection and the struggle which takes place in the human person were means of giving effect to its messianism. The fulfilment of the eschatological hope became internalized and individualized. The tension between old and new became primarily a matter for the individual overcoming the passions of the flesh rather than the power of the new breaking down the old order in the wider world beyond individual and ecclesia. The early Christian writings represent an example of that process of accommodation with the wider world and the channelling of the charismatic vision in a way which would guarantee preservation. The hope for the transformation of the world was kept alive though it became increasingly accepting of many of the institutions of society while it looked forward to the messianic kingdom. Christianity did not reject Jewish political messianism and replace it with a doctrine of a spiritual messiah. The typical features of a Jewish this-worldly eschatology in the form of chiliasm remained an important component of belief until at least the end of the second century.[7]

Defining Boundaries

By the beginning of the second century Judaism and Christianity were largely self-contained religious entities. Much debate has gone on the reasons for that separation. Two issues have dominated discussion of the subject: the promulgation of the *birkath ha-minim* at Jamnia and Paul's advocacy of faith in the messiah as the basis for Gentile admission to the eschatological people of God.

It seems to have been the case that at some stage towards the end of the first century the synagogue liturgy was reformulated after the fall of Jerusalem and there was included in it a prayer which pronounces a curse on apostates, in one version of which there is a clear illusion to the Christians (*notzrim*). Whether that was widely used by the end of the first century and was influential in the formulation of Christian responses to Judaism such as the Gospels of John and Matthew is a matter of dispute. Nevertheless that process of exclusion is symptomatic either of a growing apart or of mutual antipathy whose roots may well

7. B. Daley, *The Hope of the Early Church: A Handbook of Patristic Eschatology* (Cambridge: Cambridge University Press, 1991).

go back to the claim to messianic authority on Jesus' part. What we have in the (for want of a better description) church/synagogue conflict is the classic example of the renewal movement's at times startling innovation being greeted with hostility and, perhaps more often, indifference by the parent body (though the reasons for this are not entirely clear and may well have varied from place to place). A messianic movement which survived and explored the implications of its messianism was bound sooner or later to throw up doctrinal and ethical problems which conflicted with prevailing practice. That situation was exacerbated because, as far as we can ascertain, much early Christianity did not shut itself off in any kind of introversionist way[8] like the Qumran community. Thus it did not keep its heterodox views away from the mainstream but insisted on practising its messianic convictions, particularly with regard to the admission of Gentiles to its sect. In the light of this it seems likely that what happened in the *birkath ha-minim* was merely the culmination of the conflict which the very survival of a messianic movement within Judaism ensured.

Having said this, we should point out that concrete information about antipathy between Jews and Christians depends on a particular reading of polemical material in the New Testament.[9] The use of the so called 'transparency method' when applied to literary texts like the Gospels allows us to read from them the historical situation of writer and readers and their opponents. This has become standard fare in biblical scholarship but needs to be subjected to critical scrutiny (essential if one is wanting to move from the texts to the evidence of human interaction which may lie behind them). Texts' relationships with their social formation are invariably complex, and it is naive to suppose that they merely reflect it. References to conflict or evidence of relationships in texts may tell us absolutely nothing about actual historical events. Jesus' conflict with the Pharisees in Matthew, for example, *may* tell us something about the evangelist's community and its relationship with Judaism but equally well the stories could have been merely a rhetorical device which tell us absolutely nothing about the life of the community and everything about the literary strategy of the author. An attempt to understand what the relationship between Jews and Christians was rather than merely outline

8. See the summary of this kind of position in R. Bocock and K. Thompson, *Religion and Ideology* (Manchester: Manchester University Press, 1985).

9. See now J.T. Sanders, *Schismatics, Sectarians, Dissidents, Deviants* (London: SCM Press, 1993).

the attitudes is entirely admirable in theory. The problem is, of course, that our evidence is largely of attitudes. There is hardly any literary evidence which speaks directly of relationships once Acts is excluded. Paul's problems were probably more with Jewish Christians (though 2 Cor. 11.23 is an exception) and though Ignatius may have been referring to actual relationships, how accurate his knowledge is, is unclear. So what are we left with? Virtually no evidence at all of any relationships unless we construe the Jesus/Pharisees debates as ciphers for continued interaction. We may presume that any Christian in the vicinity of Jerusalem must have had relations with Jews (which at times caused problems as 1 Thess. 2.14-15 and *Ant.* 20.200 indicate). The problem is that we have little or no access to it, nor can we be absolutely sure that the Jewish-Christians did not separate themselves in a way that restricted their contact with fellow Jews, like the members of the Dead Sea Sect.

The Torah

A central issue for the first Christians was their attitude to the Law of Moses in the light of their conviction that the messiah had come. The solutions they offered were various and yet fundamentally unified. At first sight Paul's espousal of what is often loosely referred to as a 'Law-free gospel' (though this is hardly a characterization which would have been favoured by Paul) seems far removed from Matthew's assertion of the continued validity of the Law and the suspicion of those who advocate its dissolution (5.18-19). Two things united all the Christian groups: a common adherence to the Jewish tradition together with a consequent need to make sense of their own ideas and practice in the light of it; and the need to define the boundaries of the community of people who accept the messiahship of Jesus. Matthew and Paul are at one in desiring to authenticate their religious position in the light of the scriptures. Their solutions may differ in certain respects, but they are at one in thinking that the scriptures support their belief that Jesus is the messiah foretold in them. The use of proof texts throughout Matthew's Gospel indicates this. Paul uses the figure of Abraham in Galatians 3 and Romans 4 as the type of the true believer who relies on faith rather than works of the Law. Paul may have relaxed circumcision as an entry rite for Gentile converts to Christianity and sat loose to Jewish food laws. Nevertheless formulating his 'Christian halakah' he is prepared to resort to scripture (e.g. 1 Cor. 9.9), as well as the demands of experience and emerging custom in the Gentile churches, to enunciate appropriate patterns of behaviour, a method not unlike that evident in the tannaitic literature. Indeed, in the articulation of the prosbul (*M. Sheb*. 10.3-7) to circumvent the demands of Deut. 15.1-11 we find a parallel to Paul's cavalier treatment of the detail of the Torah rooted in experience, albeit an approach more widely accepted than Paul's abolition of circumcision for Gentiles in the messianic age.

Galatians offers the typical features of Paul's response. It was written at the height of Paul's controversy with opponents of his practice of admitting Gentiles into the messianic community without circumcision. Paul's fault in the eyes of his opponents was not that he admitted Gentiles into the Jewish commonwealth. Any Gentile who accepted circumcision and obedience to the Law of Moses could become a member of the people of God. Paul believed that the messianic age had come and that there was a new dispensation available for a number of Gentiles. Thus, the issue for Paul was not that he was abrogating the rules of admission which had for centuries applied to those who espoused Judaism. Rather, he was convinced that the heavenly messiah had called him directly to be the emissary to the Gentiles to summon them to be inheritors of the messianic kingdom on the basis of faith in the messiah alone, thereby fulfilling a Jewish eschatological expectation that some Gentiles would share in the privileges of Israel in the Age to Come. Circumcision was no longer necessary as a sign of entry into the people of God in the messianic age. Whereas scripture makes it clear that belonging to Israel normally involves circumcision, it is more vague on the conditions attaching to the admission of that select body of Gentiles who became children of Abraham in the messianic age.[10] Paul disagreed with most of his contemporaries over this issue. They seem to have thought that the regulations governing the admission of proselytes still applied in the messianic age. Paul argued that faith in the messiah was sufficient to justify those Gentiles' participation in the messianic community. It is here that we find the basis for his hostile attitude towards the Law. Paul chose to innovate over a matter in which he found the majority of Jews ranged against him and to seek to persuade Gentiles to become part of Israel by means of his missionary activity. Paul did not think of himself as an antinomian (he clearly wants to

10. See E.P. Sanders, *Paul, the Law and the Jewish People* (Philadelphia: Fortress Press, 1983).

repudiate that suggestion in Rom. 3.31 and 6.1 though often he does seem to want to assert that the basis for moral action depended on no external authority but on the autonomy conferred by the divine spirit). He is prepared to call on the Law in support of the ethical positions he seeks to recommend. Ed Sanders has suggested that Paul rejected the Law as an entrance requirement into the messianic community but kept it as the general guide for conduct within that community.[11] That is, provided that its implementation did not lead to any threat to messianic conviction and the unity of the messianic people of God (there could be no fracturing of the community over the issue of food and table-fellowship, for example).

The other issue which in all likelihood brought Paul into conflict with his contemporaries was his conviction that he should *act* as the divine agent to bring in the Gentiles to share the messianic age. The view that a number of Gentiles would participate in this was probably widely held by Jews. Paul would not have been unusual in holding such beliefs. Where he does appear to have been unique is in his conviction that the Gentile participation in the last days was not something which God would achieve through a miracle but through the agency of one specially commissioned for this task (Gal. 1.12ff.). Despite the frequent assumption in Christian scholarship that mission and evangelism was central to early Christian identity, apart from Paul there is little evidence to suggest that there was a widespread attempt to *proselytize Gentiles* by other Christian leaders (Eusebius, *Ecclesiastical History* 5.107 is a solitary example). There may well have been Jewish-Christian missionaries apart from Paul but their role seems to have been to persuade other Jews of the rightness of their cause. What is more, Paul's letters are remarkable for their lack of missionary exhortation. Paul and his circle had an evangelistic role but that does not appear to have been central to the paraenesis Paul addressed to the various Christian communities established in the Eastern Mediterranean.[12]

The Quest for Holiness

In two respects the Pauline letters resemble the contours of much of Jewish literature: the quest for holiness and the practice of religion in an

11. Sanders, *Paul, the Law and the Jewish People.*

12. See further M. Goodman, *Mission and Conversion* (Oxford: Oxford University Press, 1994) and R. Lane Fox, *Pagans and Christians* (Harmondsworth: Penguin, 1986), p. 282.

alien culture. Although it is the author of 1 Peter who quotes the key verse from Lev. 19.2 ('You shall be holy as I am holy'), that also summarizes Paul's understanding of the life of the messianic community. The quest for holiness is one that is at the heart of Jewish religion. The Torah offered a distinctive attitude and style of life thus embodying an alternative culture to that of the nations. At the time of the Second Temple there were a variety of means enunciated in order to give effect to this.[13] At one extreme were the Qumran sectaries who lived in the desert and provided a holy environment which was fit for the holy angels to assemble and share their common life. Here was indeed to be found heaven on earth in the middle of the wilds of the desert. By contrast the priests who held power in Jerusalem (as opposed to those relegated to the desert because of their opposition to the order of things in Jersualem) concentrated on the preservation of a holy space at the heart of Jewish life in the holy city to maintain the pattern of worship they believed prescribed by God for that place. From the temple all that might defile the holy place was excluded. So the notice at the entrance to the temple made it clear that foreigners were not allowed to pass the point on pain of death. It was that issue which the Acts of the Apostles says led to the hostile reaction to Paul when he journeyed to Jerusalem for the last time. (Perhaps there is a hint of Paul's lack of political judgment in which hope triumphs over reality when he took Christians made holy by the Spirit of God into the holy environs of the temple—Acts 21.27?). The maintenance of the cult necessitated some kind of co-existence with the Roman authorities (cf. Jn 11.48). It was this priority for the preservation of this holy place which was highest on the agenda. Small wonder that with the destruction of that holy place the raison d'être of the Sadducean religion should perish with the sacrifices they were pledged to preserve.

The most significant pattern of religion in Palestine (at least as far as later developments in Judaism were concerned) was Pharisaism. Basically, this was pledged to the maintenance of a holy environment not in some special 'religious' place but in the midst of everyday life. This was to be done by the creation of a holy space around the religious person and affected every aspect of life, as scripture enjoins. The detailed regulations of the Mishnah bear witness to the seriousness of the endeavour to ensure the preservation of a holy space in all aspects of

13. For a comprehensive survey of the evidence see E.P. Sanders, *Judaism Practice and Belief 63 CE to 66 CE* (London: SCM Press, 1992).

existence, not just at those moments when there is engagement in religious activities. Religion becomes entirely secularized in the sense that it applies to the whole of life. The pharisaic vision is to maintain the holiness appropriate to priests ministering in the temple. That will include the most surprising and unpromising places of life. It is that vision which enabled Judaism to survive the destruction of its holy place in 70 CE and for Pharisaism to become the driving force of what was to emerge in the second century as rabbinic Judaism.

Something of that vision also enlivens the Pauline pattern of religion. Unlike the details of pharisaic halakah there is no extensive prescription of what must be done to ensure proper observance. The Christian communities are called to be holy, however (1 Cor. 1.2—*hagioi* is a favourite term of Paul to describe the church). Of course, the means by which holiness is achieved is different, but its roots are quite clear. Thus Paul talks of the Corinthian church as the temple of the Holy Spirit in 1 Cor. 3.16 and 6.19. He stresses both the need to replicate that holiness which characterizes the temple and asserts that the means whereby that holiness is achieved are through the spirit of holiness which is a mark of belonging to the messianic community (2 Cor. 1.22). In describing the Christians in this way Paul, like the Pharisees (of whom he was once a member), offers a way of being in the world while retaining distinctive patterns of behaviour. Exactly what that involved can be glimpsed in 1 Corinthians where Paul begins to work out a form of Christian halakah: primarily maintenance of the unity of the community (even if that meant infringing one's freedom as a child of the messianic kingdom), rejection of idolatry, sexual purity, and the sobriety which does not draw attention to Christianity's peculiarities. There is little enough in these early Christian texts to indicate what kind of pattern of behaviour might have constituted a holy life amidst the complexities of everyday existence. That should not surprise us as we are here only at a very rudimentary stage in the evolution of that process.

The similarities with Judaism may have been more marked in the non-Pauline churches. The Pauline solution was not universally favoured and may well have been a minority opinion in the early church. We know from Revelation that in an area which had seen a significant part of the Pauline mission, Asia Minor, there was a different understanding on what constituted appropriate behaviour over issues like the eating of idol meat (Rev. 2.14 and 2.20). In many respects at the level of ideas there is much in common between Revelation and the Pauline letters (the christology of Revelation is every bit as sophisticated as that of Col. 1.15ff. for example), yet there is a much more uncompromising attitude towards relations with society at large. This may possibly be because it is addressed to churches who have come to a comfortable and satisfactory accommodation with the surrounding culture and its values.

Whether Revelation can be invoked as an example of a community which espoused a more overtly separatist sectarian outlook may be doubted as its dualistic outlook may be partly the result of its apocalyptic genre and the experience of its writer. There is more substance to the view that the Johannine corpus (the Fourth Gospel and the 3 letters of John) may be the products of a group which did maintain a certain degree of detachment from the surrounding culture and exhibit an 'Essene' form of Christianity.[14] Their dualism, introversion and negative attitude towards the institutions of the cosmos and its wealth (particularly evident in 1 John 2 and 3) may offer a glimpse of that ascetic form of Christianity at this early period which was to play such a decisive role in understandings of community formation in succeeding centuries. The lack of concern for the future of the world in the Fourth Gospel is in part because of the concentration on those who are of the light rather than of darkness. The sectarian slant of its writing has given the dominant position to the concern for the elect group rather than the world. The world is still an arena of divine activity. But the inward-looking character of the writings testify to a dominant concern with the life of perfection in a group which feels itself increasingly alienated from a world which prefers darkness to light.

There is enough evidence in the Jesus tradition to suggest that an ascetic strand formed an important part of the behaviour of Christianity from the very earliest stage and may indeed have been part of the earliest stage of the Pauline gospel if 1 Corinthians 7 is anything to go by. Of course, such attitudes were not new to Christianity. We have evidence that special states of intimacy with the divine demanded patterns of renunciation (Dan. 10; 4 Ezra 9). John the Baptist in the desert eating locusts and wild honey would have been eccentric but by no means unique. The prophet Jeremiah had long before commended the ancient ascetics, the Rechabites, for their frugality of life and their obedience as compared with the disobedience of the people of God (Jer. 35), and that

14. See J. Ashton, *Understanding the Fourth Gospel* (Oxford: Oxford University Press, 1992).

frugality is evident in the Jewish-Christian Elchesaites, a group which contributed to the ascetical spirit which culminated in Manichaeism.

The Problem of Authority

It was Paul's conviction that God had revealed to him Jesus the messiah, and that he was God's agent, which is at the heart of his approach to the scriptures. The same is true for the author of the Gospel of Matthew who authenticates Jesus' messiahship by a genealogy and the series of proof-texts. In both cases the scriptures are now read in the light of the fact that the age of the Spirit has come. Christians in Corinth are told that passages in the Bible were in reality addressed directly to those fortunate to be alive when the decisive moment in history came about: 'Now these things happened to them as a warning, but they were written down for our instruction, upon whom the end of the ages has come' (1 Cor. 10.11). The present has become the moment to which all the scriptures have been pointing. Their meaning can only be fully understood with that intuition which flows from acceptance of the messiah. The point is made most clearly in 1 Pet. 1.11-12 which stresses the privileged position of the recipients of the letters in understanding mysteries which the angels themselves had for long desired to look upon (cf. Lk. 10.24). Those who accept the messiah can understand the true meaning of the scriptures and taste the goodness of God and the powers of the age to come. It is not that the scriptures are redundant but that they have ceased to be the primary source of guidance. The scriptures are a witness to and confirm the prompting of the indwelling Spirit of God. Like Jesus, Paul compares the present with the situation at the beginning of creation. He describes Jesus as the Second Adam who rectified the pervasive transgression of the first Adam and thereby opened the way to the renewal of creation. Men and women could share in the divine liberation. The Mosaic dispensation is thereby seen as an interim arrangement which is made obsolete when the messiah comes and the creation begins to return to the perfection which God always intended.

Paul argues that the scriptures themselves vindicate his position, and in both Galatians and Romans 4 he supports his views on the irrelevance of circumcision by reference to Abraham. This resort to the scripture indicates that Paul is no opponent of the Jewish tradition (rightly understood). It was not for him a case of abrogating the authority of the scriptures. What was important was to see those scriptures in the context of the fulfilment of which they themselves had spoken. What Paul offered his readers was the true meaning of those scriptural texts. Or as Paul puts in one of his more daring interpretations, the Jew who does not recognize Jesus as the messiah still has his spiritual sight veiled, just as Moses' face was veiled when he descended from the mountain. But when the Jew recognizes the messiah, the veil is removed. In 2 Corinthians 3 exegetical ingenuity is used to vindicate the messianic understanding of scripture as Paul stresses the superiority of his ministry as compared with that of Moses. This exclusive reading has its parallel in the remarkable biblical interpretation found among the Dead Sea Scrolls where the true meaning of prophetic oracles is vouchsafed to the divinely inspired teacher.

A radical attitude towards the Jewish tradition reached its culmination in the gnostic treatises of the second century. Here a reading of the tradition emerged whose intent was to undermine its validity and relegate it to the revelation of a lesser god. Christianity ultimately rejected this solution. Nevertheless in some of its orthodox exponents it exploited the contradictions of the story of the people of God to undermine the finality of the present Jewish religio-political system. Thus in the letter to the Hebrews the redundancy of the sacrificial system based on the levitical priesthood is argued on the basis of the superiority of Christ's priesthood and sacrifice. His priesthood is validated by Melchizedek and not by Levi and the place of his sacrifice involves him in entering the heavenly shrine rather than the earthly. This makes all that takes place in the earthly tabernacle obsolete. Even more extreme is the Epistle of Barnabas[15] with its utilization of polemical traditions from the Bible against sacrifice and as proof of the deep-rooted recalcitrance of the people of God. Such approaches are used to support the feasibility of Christianity's case that the order brought by the messiah involved radical change in practice on the structure of 'normal' Jewish life. The anti-Jewish tone may be nothing other than the polemics of internecine religious strife, what to an outsider might appear to be 'bickering about words and names and your Jewish law' (Gallio's words as reported in Acts 18.15). The origin of this is the attempt to legitimate the Christian position possibly in the face of some polemic from Jewish sources (if Mt. 27.64; 28.15 are anything to go by). The extreme polemical tone

15. See now J. Carleton Paget, *The Epistle of Barnabas* (Tübingen: Mohr [Paul Siebeck], 1994).

fuelled the fires of anti-semitism in situations where the separation between the two religions was complete. What makes that attempt seem so exclusive is that messianic conviction of finality which can conceive of little that is superior in a religious system whose sole role is to point to a future fulfilment and even its own supersession.

A word needs to be said about the extent of doctrinal innovation within early Christianity. I do not subscribe to the view that with regard to their doctrine of God the early Christians were very innovative. The roots of trinitarian doctrine are to be found in the sophisticated intermediary theology of Second Temple Judaism. This gave early Christians all the resources they needed to speak, at least initially, in binitarian terms about Christ's relationship with the Creator God. Nowhere does early Christianity lapse into the two power heresy known to us from the rabbinic sources.[16] Indeed, one might argue that the subordination of the Son to the Father in the most sophisticated christological portrait in the Gospel of John is a repudiation of the view that the Christian doctrine of Christ is guilty of the two power heresy.

Even if we suppose that the sophisticated intermediary theology was to be found on the fringes of Judaism (and there are good reasons for supposing that it was in fact more mainstream than that), heavenly representatives who bore the image of the divine or humans who became divine vicegerents are common enough to indicate the resources available to a movement which sought to glorify its messiah before he consummated the eschatological deliverance begun in his earthly life. The issue, of course, is that the Christians identified these exalted figures with Jesus of Nazareth. The problem was, not that they spoke of God sharing power with another but that God shared power with (this) man executed on a cross (cf. Gal. 3.13).

Visions, Prophecy and Authority[17]

Underlying Paul's attitude to scripture there is an issue which is endemic to Judaism: the problem of true and false prophecy. In the most autobiographical of Paul's letters Paul speaks about the centrality of the

16. A. Segal, *Two Powers in Heaven* (Leiden: Brill, 1978) and L. Hurtado, *One God, One Lord* (Philadelphia: Fortress Press, 1988).

17. See C. Rowland, *The Open Heaven* (London: SPCK, 1982) and D. Aune, *Prophecy in Early Christianity and the Ancient Mediterranean World* (Grand Rapids: Eerdmans, 1983).

divine revelation using the words *apokalypsis* and *apokalupto* (Gal. 1.12 and 16). His authority clearly is rooted in the moment of commissioning which he believes came directly from God. In the early Christian story other decisive moments are 'clarified' by visionary insight (Mk 1.10; Acts 10–11). In the case of Peter in Acts 10 the vision is used, in part at least as the basis of the new turn in Christian practice: the admission of the Gentiles into the people of God. Such a significant shift in opinion might be the subject of intense wrangling and discussion but is here seen as the result of some kind of supernatural validation. Such an appeal to visions might not matter if the subject matter was itself uncontroversial. When it becomes the basis for a significant new departure then it becomes problematic.

There are Jewish apocalypses (or at least parts of them) which use the concept of revelation to offer a definitive solution to human problems. So we find particularly in a work like *Jubilees*, which purports to be an angelic revelation to Moses on Sinai, a retelling of biblical history which conforms largely with what is found in scripture. At many points there are divergences and the significance of these is nowhere greater than when halakic questions emerge. This is evident when the calendar and sabbath observance is discussed (e.g. *Jubilees* 6.32ff.). With regard to the former the revelation makes it quite clear that the calendar laid down by this angelic revelation (which affects the days on which major festivals and holy days are celebrated) is not only different from what applies elsewhere but that deviation involves a complete repudiation of the Law of God. Here revelation is used to exclude and anathematize opponents and their way of behaviour. Such a use of apocalyptic which in effect denies the fallibility of the recipient also removes any possibility of discussion of the subject. Something similar can happen when final, authoritative interpretations of scripture are offered by means of revelation, such as we find, for example, in Dan. 9.23 and in the biblical interpretation at Qumran (see 1 QpHab 8).

Problems with regard to prophetic authority have a long history in Judaism. They are legislated for in the Torah (Deut. 13 and 18) and had a part to play in the confusion which accompanied the debates over the nature of appropriate response to the divine will during the period immediately preceding the Exile (e.g. Jer. 23.16ff.). The central role that prophecy played within early Christianity (as is evident from virtually every document in the New Testament) indicates the problems posed by claims to divine inspiration. When these involved controversial items of behaviour, they would have been very much to the fore in debates between adherents of messianism and those who dissented from these convictions. All this could have been lived with if there had not been a substantial difference of opinion over an area of halakah, just as later the Jewish mystics could be accommodated provided that they did not infringe the teachings of the Sages. When they did the excesses of mystical religion needed to be hedged around with restrictions (*M. Hag.* 2.1).

Religious authority claimed as a result of experience of God was something which had a continuing history within early Christianity. The Nag Hammadi texts indicate the extent of the influence of the apocalyptic genre and also at the level of ideas. Threats from individuals or groups who claimed divine support by means of visions and revelations seem to have been quite a pressing problem. The problem of wandering prophets is alluded to in *Did.* 11.3ff. and 16.3, and there is a repudiation of false spirits in 1 Tim. 4.1; cf. Jude 4ff. If Paul could claim authority on the basis of a vision as also did John of Patmos, what was to distinguish them from a Cerinthus or an Elchesai, where esoteric teaching is communicated bearing the garb of divine authority? The heart of early Christian self-understanding was its realized messianism authenticated by the apocalyptic insight. Eschatological conviction is the content of the message, but the means whereby individuals came to apprehend its meaning came through claims to visions from God. What we find in earliest Christianity is apocalyptic functioning as the basis of its messianic convictions.

In my concern with the apocalyptic and prophetic I would not want to suggest that this represents the sum total of the Jewish tradition's contribution to the development of ecclesiastical power and structure. Indeed, of more lasting importance were the debts to synagogue organization (manifested in the Pastorals),[18] apostleship, and even hints of the dynastic succession known to us from rabbinic schools and the zealot movement. The variety of ecclesial structure and of the exercise of power contributed to the struggles which went on among the earliest followers of Jesus as well as with other Jews. In this period a feature of those struggles seems to have been claims to authority which were authenticated by appeal to direct divine mandate, a feature which rapidly become more circumscribed in a later age which was more suspicious of the prophet and visionary.

18. J. Burtchaell, *From Synagogue to Church* (Cambridge: Cambridge University Press, 1992).

The Jewish origins of Christianity are now doubted by few historians. Where there is wide divergence is where (and when) Christianity left behind its Jewish milieu and became a socio-religious system (substantially) different from the parent religion. Here, of course, Paul's contribution has been the centre of attention. What happened to Paul was that he originally transferred from Pharisaic Judaism to 'messianic Judaism'. But his journey did not end there, for he went on to create a form of religion characterized not by ethnicity but by allegiance to Jesus Christ. This religion was in the end unable to accommodate itself within the broad parameters of Jewish practice particularly after 70 CE when the scope for diversity possibly decreased in emerging Judaism and Christianity and the pressure for uniformity increased (as is evident in the growing rabbinic authority and the differing ecclesial patterns evident in the Pastoral and Ignatian Epistles). The move to set up communities identifiably different from Jewish communities (whatever the extent of common membership there may have been at first) impelled separation and the formulation of differing conceptions of life. Christianity's growth, its extension into groups other than Jews and above all its survival involved innovations that were incompatible with the more gradual evolution tolerated by other forms of Judaism. The fact that it survived and sought to practise messianic convictions meant that, like the adolescent, it had to separate from its parent and live a life of its own in which the characteristics it inherited determined to a significant extent its shape and behaviour. From a relatively early time the two religions went their own way, and the pain of the separation evident in the hostility towards various types of Jews in Christianity's foundation documents may have ceased to be part of the community's experience when these traditions were committed to writing and probably did not reflect any substantial interaction in succeeding generations. But of that we cannot be sure, as our sources remain quiet on the precise detail of relations between Jews and Christians. The bulk of the Christian polemic against Jews has a rather hackneyed air hardly redolent of struggles contemporary with the texts and the communities which lie behind them but of dim memories which served to confirm the readers' religious superiority and define the community over against the group with the closest family resemblance.

It would be easy to use the phrase 'from Moses to Patmos'[19] in a

19. The title of John Sawyer's pioneering study *From Moses to Patmos* (London: SPCK) published in 1977.

fashion so typical of Christian apologetics and construe Christian origins as merely a reaction of the charismatic to the legal, an interpretative strategy with a long history in post-Enlightenment biblical study. Such a polarization has truth in it as a characterization of the theological enterprise that emerged in Christianity. Yet what we find in the New Testament is not the repudiation of Moses but the accentuation of that which links Moses and Patmos. Moses after all is the one who ascended the mountain (and so gained access to heaven according to Jewish tradition) and of him God said: 'When there are prophets among you, I the LORD make myself known to them in visions; I speak to them in dreams. Not so with my servant Moses; he is entrusted with all my house. With him I speak face to face—clearly, not in riddles; and he beholds the form of the LORD' (Num. 12.6ff.). In the emerging deconstructing of Judaism Pauline Christianity harked back to other features of the Moses tradition which presented him as the mystagogue par excellence. Just as Moses had beheld the LORD on Sinai, so too John of Patmos had been in the Spirit and seen the form of the LORD. In Paul's case the apocalyptic vision had devastating effects on his conventional assumptions and practice. As with Moses this led to a new covenant between God and the people, not merely a reaffirmation of what had gone before. As the one who outshone Moses, Paul presumed to have access to greater mysteries than were revealed to Moses. But he too eventually found that the claims to new revelation were deeply subversive and threatened the fabric of the definitive revelation of which he was the bearer. Paul and his successors could not countenance the notion of an ongoing revelation apart from Christ. And so the framework of law and custom shored up the primal vision in order that the glory of that vision could continue to shine out among the people of another age. They could thereby glimpse its mystery and respond to its agenda of renewal by using it as a resource for the subversion of institutional complacency.

WATER AND BLOOD: BIRTHING IMAGES IN JOHN'S GOSPEL

Deborah Sawyer

The text which forms the subject of this paper concerns the final moments of Christ's life as described by the Fourth Evangelist in Jn 19.34. However, in traditional theology it has come to signify birth as much as death, and it is this aspect that I wish to explore here. The picture of the dying Christ on the cross with water and blood pouring from his side displays a rich use of biblical language and imagery, and, in addition, it has a fascinating history of interpretation: a history which includes contemporary feminist theology. Both these aspects of language and interpretation reflect the main research interests of the recipient of this Festschrift up to the present day. Furthermore, the object of birth itself is something that has sealed my relationship with John, and its outcome, Joseph, continues to provide the focus of our mutual love.

From the time of the earliest Church Fathers the passage from St John's Gospel has been understood symbolically as the moment of birth for the sacramental life of the church.[1] The water and blood pouring from Christ's side, from the wound inflicted by the Roman soldier, are identified as the types for the eucharistic and baptismal elements. This interpretation is presented vividly in the medieval period as an image of birth, where Christ, the New Adam, gives birth to the Church from his side in the same way, it is presumed, that the first Adam gave birth to Eve.[2]

The identification of this moment of the dying Christ with the act of birth is supported on two counts. First there is the presence of water and

1. To illustrate this point, later in this paper I will be discussing the language used by the Vulgate for this passage and the comments made by St Augustine.

2. This evidence is clearly annotated by C. Walker Bynum in *Jesus as Mother: Studies in the Spirituality of the High Middle Ages* (Berkeley and Los Angeles: University of California Press, 1982), and *Fragmentation and Redemption* (Zone Books, 1991).

blood that are always present during the process when a woman's body gives birth to a baby. Secondly, the word used by the Fourth Evangelist in this verse to describe the place of the wound in Christ's body is *pleura*. In the Septuagint of Gen. 2.21 the same word, *pleura*, is used for the place on Adam's body where Eve was brought forth.

In order to elucidate whether the church has been justified in identifying this moment on the cross from St John's Gospel with the act of birth, we need first to examine that scene from Genesis and discover how that was understood at the time of the rise of Christianity. If we have evidence that Adam was understood to give birth to Eve, then it could be argued that the Fourth Evangelist takes that phenomenon as a type for the birth of the church at the crucifixion.

We have evidence from the middle of the first century CE to help us elucidate how this passage in Genesis describing the advent of Eve was understood: whether as a birth or an act of creation. In his correspondence with the community at Corinth Paul discusses the concept of Eve being made out of Adam. This evidence is found among the advice and comments St Paul delivers in 1 Corinthians and where in ch. 11 Paul gives his views on the practice of women leading worship in the community with their heads uncovered. This passage, 11.2-16, has attracted the attention of scholars, churchmen and churchwomen over the centuries, but in the last twenty years it has been put under further scrutiny in the context of the contemporary debate concerning women's status and authority in Christianity.[3] It is important in our context of attempting to throw some light on the figure of Christ on the cross in St John's Gospel.

A common theme in 1 Corinthians 11 is that of origins. In the first part of the chapter Paul rehearses the argument that a distinction must be made between the sexes in order to recognize the unique creation of the first humans by the hand of God. Namely, that woman was the product of man and not man of woman. The special attention given to women's head covering exists to register that unique event of divine action. One problem at Corinth lay in the disregarding of that distinction. Likewise, in the second half of the chapter, Paul addresses the situation of chaos that was manifest when the community met to celebrate the eucharist. Again the community was oblivious to the origin and

3. See, e.g., the discussion of this passage in E. Schüssler Fiorenza, *In Memory of Her: A Feminist Theological Reconstruction of Christian Origins* (London: SCM Press, 1983), pp. 226-33.

significance of this phenomenon: that it was not just a communal meal but the consummation and realization of Christ's body. In this chapter Paul pleads for order and decency by explaining that mundane practices, that is, style of dress and sharing of food, when practised in the context of a community 'in Christ', are translated onto a metaphysical and theological level: believers experience the New Age when they meet together. They are the new humanity, the new Adams and Eves of God's Kingdom, eating the messianic banquet. To be unaware of this new reality can have dire consequences.

It is important to look closely at the images Paul evokes in 1 Corinthians 11 so that we can discover whether he does understand that Adam gave birth to Eve, or whether her existence comes about as a result of God's creative activity, as was the case with Adam. Although the main point of the passage in 1 Corinthians 11 is to discuss the hierarchical distinction between men and women through the order of creation, now reflected in women's distinctive headwear, we can make the clear observation that Paul does not understand Adam to have 'given birth' to Eve. Nowhere in this passage do we find 'birthing' language used, and instead the verb we do have is *ktizō*. This verb, like the Hebrew *bārā*, is reserved in biblical Greek exclusively for God's creative activity. English translations are misleading when 1 Cor. 11.12 is given as: 'for as woman was made from man, so man is now born of woman...' By inserting the word 'born' which is not in the Greek the inference can be made that Eve too had been born from Adam. Instead Paul argues that God in his work of creation made Adam's body the source of Eve's existence, just as previously God had made the earth the source of Adam's existence.

Paul does maintain a tension in his argument. While maintaining that in covering their heads women symbolize a distinction between the sexes which reflects the order of creation, he also argues that male and female are mutually dependent, and that both men and women equally owe their origin to God. An alternative translation of 1 Cor. 11.11-12 could read: 'Nevertheless, in the Lord woman is not independent of man, any more than man is independent of woman: on the one hand the woman is from the man, but on the other hand man owes his existence to the woman. All are from God.'[4] This counter argument, or

4. This is the force of the preposition *dia*, alluding to Gen. 2.23. Here Paul's argument can be used in support of Phyllis Trible's contention that it is only at the point of Eve's creation in Gen. 2.22 that the genders are distinguished, that is, that

explanation of God's reality rather than the social convention of Paul's day reflects the early Christian communities' dilemma of having to live in the 'old' age while already enjoying the fruits of the spirit in the 'new'. The egalitarian maxim found in Gal. 3.28, 'for you are all one in Christ Jesus', reflects the latter rather than the former.

The complicated passage which forms the first half of 1 Corinthians 11 contains comments that have been repeated, interpreted, and misinterpreted since the time it was written. Within the New Testament itself texts, which many modern scholars believe to be written by disciples of St Paul rather than by, or at the dictation of, the apostle himself,[5] contain ideas that understand the comments in 1 Corinthians 11 in a certain way and cement that particular interpretation for future generations. This can be illustrated by Ephesians, for example: 'Wives, be subject to your husbands, as to the Lord. For the husband is the head of the wife as Christ is the head of the church, his body, and is himself its saviour...' (Eph. 5.22-23). Likewise 1 Timothy: 'I permit no woman to teach or to have authority over men; she is to keep silent. For Adam was formed first, then Eve; and Adam was not deceived, but the woman was deceived and became a transgressor. Yet woman will be saved through bearing children, if she continues in faith and love and holiness, with modesty' (1 Tim. 2.12-15).

Both these passages could be understood as further comments of clarification on a biblical passage. Both are linked to the text of 1 Corinthians in discussing the subject of gender hierarchy, and both interpret Paul's comment on the origin of the two genders outlined in 1 Corinthians in terms of the secondary nature of women. Furthermore, both indicate a secondary soteriological status for women, only being realized through their husbands and children respectively. For our purposes we can observe that in the earliest interpretations of 1 Corinthians 11 it is the order of *creation*, the order of God's work, that is significant, and not that Adam's superior status to Eve is a result of him having given birth to her. We may note also that Paul's comment in

female and male can be recognized. 'Adam', prior to this event was a creature of the earth, neither male nor female. Both male and female depend on God's action in Gen. 2.22 for gaining their identity. See Trible, *God and the Rhetoric of Sexuality* (Philadelphia: Fortress Press, 1989), pp. 94-105.

5. The arguments for and against Pauline authorship of Colossians, Ephesians and the Pastorals are well rehearsed; a standard account of them can still be found in W.G. Kummel's *Introduction to the New Testament* (London: SCM Press, 1977).

1 Cor. 11.11-12 explaining that 'in the Lord', or 'in Christianity', male and female are mutually dependent and equally from God is ignored by these writers, and subsequent commentators.

Paul's writings date from the middle of the first century CE; the Fourth Evangelist's work is usually dated a short time later, the last quarter of that century. Both writers are diaspora Jews of the first century with common interests and beliefs. If Paul understands the advent of Eve in terms of creation rather than birth, it would not be surprising if the author of John's Gospel did also. Adam Christology was popular with Paul, appearing explicitly and implicitly throughout his epistles: 'For as in Adam all die, so also in Christ shall all be made alive' (1 Cor. 15.22). It can be found also in the Gospels, for example, in the imagery of Luke's birth narrative; also, in Mark's portrayal of Christ as the obedient Son of God who sets the pattern for the new humanity. In St John's Gospel the opening phrase, 'In the beginning...', evokes the origin of the world and humanity. What these early writers were attempting to convey was that for the coming of Christ to have any significance it had to be understood cosmologically. This explains such early speculations concerning Christ as the new Adam.

It would not be unsympathetic to the text to interpret the figure on the cross with the pierced side in St John's Gospel as the New Adam. The significant linguistic point that the Greek word for 'side' (*pleura*) used by the author in 19.34 is the same unusual singular form that appears in the Septuagint of Gen. 2.21-22 where Eve is created from Adam's body has already been referred to. Just as the first Adam was used as material by God to create a counterpart, Eve, who together with Adam will create the human race, so the second Adam provides the material for the new humanity: the community of believers. Christ's body provides the matter for this in terms of the sacramental elements: water and blood, creating the foundations of Christianity. Just as Adam and Eve share the same physical make-up, so the church shares in Christ's nature: it is Christ's body.

It is when we turn to the work of the Church Fathers that we discover that Eve's creation has been transformed into a birth from Adam's flesh. This transformation in the understanding of the text is crucial, not only for gaining an insight into the meaning of the figure on the cross, but also for clarifying how Christianity understands the advent of woman. If Christ on the cross is understood as the New Adam giving birth to the Church as the first Adam had given birth to Eve, then we are saying that it is man and not God who is directly responsible for woman's existence, and that it is Christ himself rather than God's work in Christ who is responsible for the birth of the church.

In Augustine's theology the moment when water and blood flow from Christ's side is identified as the moment when the church's sacraments are poured into the world: 'He did not say "pierced through", or "wounded", or something else, but "opened", in order that the gate of life might be stretched wide whence the sacraments of the Church flow' (Augustine *In Jo.* cxx 2; *PL* 35: 1953). Taking the verb in this passage to mean 'opened' reflects Augustine's dependence on the Vulgate which translates *enyxen*, 'pierced' as *aperuit*, 'opened'. This could be the result of simply misreading the Greek *enyxen* as the much commoner word *ēnoixen*, or else a deliberate echo of Gen. 2.21 which describes God closing Adam's side after he has removed the rib.

Although explicit birth language is not used by Augustine, it is implied. The phrase 'gate of life' does bring to mind the image of an open womb, and 'stretching wide' can be understood in the context of the act of giving birth. We can infer that by the turn of the fourth century this icon of the cross has evolved into a picture of maternity which now also includes nurturing. Not only does Christ give birth to the sacramental church in this interpretation, but he feeds it as a mother feeds her child: from his body. Modern scholarship has become familiar with the image of Jesus as mother, largely as a result of the work of Caroline Walker Bynum who has made this diverse material readily available.[6] We can see frequent images of birthing and lactating Christs from throughout the history of Christian art, though most particularly from the medieval period. Much of this imagery has the depiction of Christ in Jn 19.34 as its starting point.[7]

Many contemporary theologians have found such images appropriate for theology today, arguing that they can provide a focus for developing a less androcentric picture of the Godhead than that provided by traditional theology. As Bynum herself comments: 'Not only was Christ enfleshed with flesh from a woman; his own flesh did womanly things;

6. See note 2 above and, with particular reference to the nurturing Christ figure, her book, *Holy Feast Holy Fast: The Religious Significance of Food to Medieval Women* (Berkeley: University of California Press, 1987).

7. Examples are included in G. Schiller's *Iconography of Christian Art*, II (London: Humphries, 1971–1972).

it bled, it bled food and it gave birth to new life.'[8] In a paper given recently by Janet Martin Soskice,[9] which takes into account the work of Bynum and develops it for a discussion concerning a theology for women's ordination, she comments on the striking female image of Christ that appears when this description from St John's Gospel is translated into the art of the medieval painters.

As we have noted, in this representation nurturing is also present when blood fills chalices or mouths held up to Christ's side. Examples of this in medieval art include Hildegaard of Bingen's Scrivitas where, in a miniature of the sixth vision of the second part, a woman representing 'church' or 'humanity' holds a chalice at the foot of the cross that is being filled by the blood pouring from Christ's side.[10] A more vivid example is Quirizio da Murano's fifteenth-century composition, *The Saviour*, where Christ is seated and dressed in a manner reminiscent of many paintings of the Madonna. A wispy beard is the only clue to the masculinity of the figure. The garment he wears is parted by his hand at the place of the wound on his side, but now this wound has moved to where his breast could be, again, reminding us of the Madonna. A nun is kneeling at his feet, and with his other hand he offers her a eucharistic wafer as if it had been taken from his breast.

Can images such as these form the basis of a less androcentric Christianity? Do they represent the female in the Godhead? Do they allow theologians a way forward in the debate as to whether women can represent Christ at the altar? I would suggest that this is not a female image at all that we encounter at this stage in the history of this passage's interpretation. Rather, it is an image of male priesthood.

In these types of representations of the wounded Christ, the water and blood that are described by the Fourth Evangelist not only become identified with the sacramental elements of the church, probably the original intention of the author, but are also given to the faithful in an essentially female manner in terms of birth and nurturing. Although unique to female experience this phenomenon is taken outside of women's experience by the church and appropriated by the male sacrificial cult. They become 'dewomanized' and are transformed into the elements and tools of the patriarchal cult. The image of Christ giving

8. Bynum, *Fragmentation*, p. 185.

9. 'Blood and Defilement', given at The Society for the Study of Theology Conference, Oxford, 1994.

10. Reproduced in Bynum, *Holy Feast*, plate 25.

birth, an obvious interpretation of this verse, and developed by Christian tradition, is stripped of any reality of female experience of birth. Christ does not become a woman in these representations, outward signs of masculinity are always maintained, and, instead, he assumes female functions while remaining a man. He becomes a type of superman figure who, in addition to his male identity, can do all that a woman can do, biologically speaking.

I would argue that such a figure reinforces androcentricity, and undermines the essential nature of women, subsuming it into maleness. What medieval theologians such as Aquinas recognized as defective male, that is woman,[11] in this image is now perfected in perfect male form. It is an articulation of the type of Christian thought that was current in that period. The 'female' Christ figure is not an alternative strand reflecting a less patriarchal Christianity, but a reinforcement of its misogyny. Woman subsumed into man cannot mean the inclusion of the female in the Godhead. Just as the male Christ in this image performs functions that pertain to a natural female role, so also does the male priesthood assume female functions every time the eucharist is celebrated. This has not led to the ordination of women in Christianity, but, rather, led to the development of, perhaps, the most androcentric institution in contemporary society. To have female functions appropriated by males cannot lead to a balanced understanding of humanity.

If we turn back to the original image in St John's Gospel, however, and look more closely at it in terms of Christ the New Adam whose body God uses to create his new humanity, his community of baptized believers, just as the first Adam had been used to create a distinct male and female human species, then we might discover a more convincing theological basis for a balanced, gender-integrated Christianity. If we focus on an image of Christ giving birth out of his side, the temptation is to turn back to the first Adam image and see that, too, in terms of a man giving birth. Again, this stands in the way of Christianity developing a balanced theology of the two genders' relationship with God. Mutuality is absent if one gender is believed to be created by the hand of God which then gives birth to the other: definitively the second sex.

We should understand the scene in Jn 19.34 in terms of creation imagery, building on St Paul's theology found in 1 Corinthians 11 where, as we have shown earlier, he sees in the account of Genesis 2 the

11. *Summa Theologica*, I, Q. 92, art. 1 (trans. Fathers of the English Dominican Province; London: Burns, Oates and Washbourne, 1922), IV, pp. 275-76.

story of Eve's creation by God. This moment in John's Gospel is the moment of the creation of the church, just as when Adam slept God chose that moment to create Eve. The author's language is chosen with deliberation to identify these two moments in salvation history. God creates the church as he had created Eve. Not to introduce some defective life form into a perfect world, but, on the contrary, to perfect and complete that world. In Christ he finds the substance to continue that creative work, and thus ensures a divine sacramental presence through the life of the Church.

THE MARRIAGE AT CANA OF GALILEE

Calum Carmichael

Renowned for his linguistic skills, John Sawyer unstintingly puts them at the disposal of those of us much less gifted than he. I, for one, have benefitted from them for some thirty years, three decennia having passed since he and I began our scholarly careers with James Barr who met with both of us on a weekly basis in the year before he left Edinburgh for Princeton. Barr was working on a critique of Thorleif Boman's book, *Das hebräische Denken im Vergleich mit dem Griechischen* (Göttingen, 1954), which resulted in his major work, *The Semantics of Biblical Language* (Oxford, 1961).[1] Continuing in the tradition of his teacher, John has made outstanding contributions to our understanding of the Greek and Hebrew languages of the Bible. He also moves with enviable ease between the Hebraic and Hellenistic cultural worlds. He has been especially alert to the richness of Judaism at the beginnings of the Christian Era and what it owes to its Hellenistic milieu. I trust he will treat with characteristic generosity the following attempt to illumine one of the most puzzling stories in the Fourth Gospel by my reading it in light of cosmological speculation that, long before the composition of the Fourth Gospel, had brought together the creation story of Genesis 1 with Hellenistic categories of thought. The Wisdom of Solomon (19.6-8), as David Winston well brings out, describes how at the time of the exodus from Egypt there was a refashioning of the whole creation in its original nature.[2] Philo of Alexandria presents another classic example of the merging of Hellenistic philosophical ideas with the creation story.[3] I shall argue that the author of the Fourth

1. David Daube has shown me his forthcoming contribution to the topic, 'Word-Formation in Indo-European and Semitic', in *Festschrift for Alan Watson* (ed. H. Hoeflich; Athens: University of Georgia Press).

2. *The Wisdom of Solomon* (AB: New York: Doubleday, 1979), pp. 9, 325.

3. See T.H. Tobin, *The Creation of Man: Philo and the History of Interpretation* (CBQMS 14; Washington: Catholic Biblical Association of America, 1983), p. 18.

Gospel extends this process of linking new ways of thinking about the world with the account of creation in Genesis 1.

To illustrate how close the author of the Fourth Gospel is to the Hellenistic Jewish world of Philo in particular, I select the story of the marriage at Cana of Galilee. That story is one in a sequence that constitutes a profound attempt on the part of John to present Jesus as the Word at creation—in line with Genesis 1—who is active again in the world. What happens in the lifetime of Jesus echoes in allegorical fashion what occurred at creation.[4] Hence, the write-up of the marriage at Cana has to be understood in light of John's treatment of the third day of creation. Here are the pertinent texts:

> Gen. 1.9-13: [9]And God said, Let the waters under the heaven be gathered together unto one place, and let the dry land appear: and it was so. [10]And God called the dry land Earth; and the gathering together of the waters called he Seas: and God saw that it was good. [11]And God said, Let the earth bring forth grass, the herb yielding seed, and the fruit-tree yielding fruit after his kind, whose seed is in itself, upon the earth: and it was so. [12]And the earth brought forth grass, and herb yielding seed after his kind, and the tree yielding fruit, whose seed was in itself, after his kind: and God saw that it was good. [13]And the evening and the morning were the third day.

> Jn 2.1-12: [1]And the third day there was a marriage in Cana of Galilee; and the mother of Jesus was there: [2]And both Jesus was called, and his disciples, to the marriage. [3]And when they wanted wine, the mother of Jesus saith unto him, They have no wine. [4]Jesus saith unto her, Woman, what have I to do with thee? mine hour is not yet come. [5]His mother saith unto the servants, Whatsoever he saith unto you, do it. [6]And there were set there six waterpots of stone, after the manner of the purifying of the Jews, containing two or three firkins apiece. [7]Jesus saith unto them, Fill the waterpots with water. And they filled them up to the brim. [8]And he saith unto them, Draw out now, and bear unto the governor of the feast. And they bare it. [9]When the ruler of the feast had tasted the water that was made wine, and knew not whence it was, but the servants which drew the water knew, the governor of the feast called the bridegroom, [10]And saith unto him, Every man at the beginning doth set forth good wine; and when men have well drunk, then that which is worse: but thou hast kept the good wine until now. [11]This beginning of miracles did Jesus in Cana of Galilee, and manifested forth his glory; and his disciples believed on him.

4. For the thesis see my forthcoming, *History as Allegory: Days of Creation in the Fourth Gospel* (Ithaca: Cornell University Press); also C.M. Carmichael, 'Marriage and the Samaritan Woman', *NTS* 26 (1980), pp. 332-46.

[12]After this he went down to Capernaum, he, and his mother, and his brethren, and his disciples; and they continued there not many days.

Unique to the Fourth Gospel, the miracle story of the water turned into wine has proved to be one of the most elusive to interpret. C.H. Dodd points out that on the face of it, the story appears to be a naive tale about a marvel at a village wedding.[5] He notes its realism. There is an eye for character and for seemingly trivial detail—the water-pots hold from seventeen to twenty-five gallons apiece—and there is the homely humour in the remark of the steward of the banquet: 'Everyone puts the best wine on the table first, and brings on the poor stuff when the company is drunk; but you have kept your good wine to the last' (Dodd's translation). We then find the typical Johannine comment that brings out his theological interpretation of a tale: 'This beginning of the signs did Jesus in Cana of Galilee, and manifested forth his glory.' The verse commonly cited in comparison is Jn 1.14 about how the Word became flesh and his glory was to be beheld. The Word is the agency that spoke at creation, the uttered speech of the creation story.[6] The miracle story in John is not to be taken at its face value, its true meaning lies deeper, but where that meaning lies has been difficult to fathom.

The usual approach of commentators is to contrast the new Christian order with the entire system of Jewish ceremonial observance.[7] The waterpots are there in accordance with the Jewish manner of purifying, and since this water is turned into wine we have the contrast between a religion which is lower than the new religion of truth.[8] In other words, to these critics the water represents the Judaism of Jesus's time which was characterized by ceremonial observance, and the wine represents a 'higher' form of religion which concentrates on spiritual matters. Yet we note that Jesus directed the servants to fill the pots with water. He did not break or discard these pots and thus the imagery used in the tale

5. *The Interpretation of the Fourth Gospel* (Cambridge: Cambridge University Press, 1965), p. 297.

6. R. Schnackenburg, *The Gospel According to St John*, I (New York: Herder and Herder, 1968), p. 336, n. 29, makes the observation that the notion of the glory of God that underlies the term *doxa* in the Hebrew Bible had reference to the experience of God associated with thunderstorms, a feature to be connected with the third day of creation.

7. It is hardly a proper comparison. The tendency to think of Judaism solely in terms of its ritual law is a strange prejudice. Ignored are the equally important areas such as private law, the law of procedure, family law, and the moral law.

8. See Dodd, *Interpretation*, pp. 297-300.

does not fit too well with such a broad and sweeping contrast between two religions. Nor is the contrast that the steward of the banquet makes between the old and the new wine all that strong. In fact it is quite benign. He even emphasizes that the drinkers of the second round of wine will hardly notice the difference. Usually, when interpreters resort to large perspectives, they are admitting, as Dodd does, the difficulties of breaking into the substance of the story.

An approach through the creation story might prove more illuminating. As in that story up to the third day, so in John up to this miracle story, water plays an important role. If we assume that the events at Cana somehow mirror the activity of day three of Gen. 1.9-13, much that is suggestive emerges for a great many details of the Johannine pericope. For example, the first time that a concern with fertility emerges in the Genesis creation story is on day three: the union of earth and water to bring forth the fruits of the earth. John's description of how Jesus uses water in the stone pots to produce the juice of the vine is the equivalent of the union of earth and water on day three of creation. We might note how the focus of the story is not on the bride and groom, but on the water that is turned into wine. In some rabbinic circles of John's time, in the cosmological speculation that is inspired by the creation story, the water of day three of Genesis represents the masculine, generative source of life and the receiving earth is female (e.g., *Gen. R.* 13.13, 14; *y. Tann.* 64b).[9]

Philo's understanding of the miraculous nature of what took place on the third day of creation—he compares the dry land to a fertile woman (*Op. Mund.* 38, 39; *Plant.* 15)—is directly pertinent to the miracle at Cana. Philo states, 'And after a fashion quite contrary to the present order of Nature all the fruit trees were laden with fruit as soon as ever they came into existence' (*Op. Mund.* 40). The author of 2 Esd. 6.43, 44 describes how on day three of creation God's word went forth, 'And at once the work was done. For immediately fruit came forth in endless abundance and of varied appeal to the taste.'[10] In the close parallel of

9. See H. Odeberg, *The Fourth Gospel Interpreted in its Relation to Contemporaneous Religious Currents in Palestine and the Hellenistic-Oriental World* (Uppsala: Almqvist and Wiksells, 1929), pp. 48-71. He attributes the rabbinic speculation to a time before John.

10. Winston, *Wisdom*, p. 325, persuasively argues that in Wis. 19.7 the 'leafy plain' that emerged when the Israelites crossed the Red Sea at the time of the exodus from Egypt is a continuation in this section of Wisdom 19 of the motif of a

John's story water has turned into a great abundance of wine—so much wine that its quantity is out of all proportion to the needs of a village wedding at which, moreover, they have already imbibed—without the intermediate processes involving the planting, watering, growth, and harvesting of vines. Philo's comment in *Op. Mund.* 40 (cp. *Quaest. in Gen.* 2.47) contrasts the ordinary way of things: 'For now the processes take place in turn, one at one time, one at another, not all of them simultaneously at one season.' Nothing in John's narrative suggests how the miracle was brought about: no act of Jesus other than his word is required, as is true again at Cana when he heals the nobleman's son (Jn 4.49-53)—and as was true at the creation of the world when, according to John, Jesus as the Word made all things (Jn 1.3).[11]

Water and wine are indeed associated with day three of creation when the waters under the firmament were gathered together into one place, and the dry land—and the fruit trees—appeared. The link between wine and the events of the third day of creation is explicit in the hymn to God the Creator in Ps. 104.14, 15: 'He causeth [on day three of creation] the grass to grow...and wine that maketh glad the heart of man.' In Philo's discussion of Noah as the first tiller of the soil, when he planted the first vineyard, he states that agriculture began with Noah—and on day three of creation (*Quaest. in Gen.* 2.66).

In the description of the third day of creation in 2 Esd. 6.42—a work that is generally dated around the time of the composition of the Fourth Gospel—the focus is on God's command to assign one seventh of the space to water and the remaining six parts to dry land. As Joan E. Cook points out, the coming forth of vegetation results from this command, but is not the result of a direct command.[12] Moreover, unlike the account in Gen. 1.12, 2 Esd. 6.44 specifies that the resulting plants had taste, colour, and scent. In the incident at Cana of Galilee Jesus' only command is that the waterpots be filled with water. What follows is that,

refashioning of the days of creation in Genesis 1, in this instance the third day (Gen. 1.11-13).

11. In producing the miracle, Jesus gives instructions to the servants at the wedding. For Philo parts of the universe were made to serve God's purpose in the way in which a slave ministers to a master (*Vit. Mos.* 1.202).

12. 'Creation in 4 Ezra: The Biblical Theme in Support of Theodicy', in *Creation in the Biblical Traditions* (ed. R.J. Clifford and J.J. Collins; CBQMS 24; Washington: Catholic Biblical Association of America, 1992), p. 133.

something having occurred indirectly to this water, it now has the taste of wine.

What is also worth pointing out in the Fourth Gospel is how Jesus had the water fetched and poured into the waterpots, and how the amount could be measured. According to *Gen. R.* 5.1 God used a standard of measurement for the waters that were gathered together into one place at creation (cp. Job 38.5-8; Isa. 40.12; 2 Esd. 16.57, 58). Equally interesting is the Rabbis' understanding of the miracle whereby God poured the water that had covered all the world into one place. To draw out exactly what the miracle was, the Rabbis used the following illustration with waterpots. Man empties a full waterpot into an empty one. God emptied a full waterpot into a full one. That was the nature of the miracle when the waters were gathered together. The Rabbis' thinking, presumably, is that after the second day of creation water was everywhere under the firmament. The next day God moved all of this water into a lesser area miraculously, without creating a deeper place to accommodate it all. The result was the dry land in one place and the water in another. It is as if a man takes a full pot of water and pours it into another full pot which is miraculously able to accommodate it. In the Rabbis' implicit metaphor, the resulting empty pot is the dry land of day three of creation.

I am suggesting that in citing waterpots in his story John uses a metaphor similar to the one used by the Rabbis to allude to day three of creation. John's text which explicitly draws attention to the fullness of the pots ('Fill the waterpots with water. And they [the servants] filled them up to the brim' [Jn 2.7]), is comparable to the Rabbis' explanation of the miracle of fullness on day three of creation. Full pots of water miraculously became full pots of wine.

The fact that there are six waterpots in John's account may reveal an interesting link to a view found in (and taken very seriously by Christopher Columbus) 2 Esd. 6.42: the waters that were gathered together into one place at creation came from six out of the seven parts of the entire area of water that was under the heaven.[13] In other words, six parts of water were poured into one already filled part and in the place of the six appeared land to be cultivated. Since the development occurred immediately ('For thy word went forth, and at once the work was done', v. 43), what had been water instantly became fruitful

13. The author of this section of 2 Esdras was a Palestinian Jew who, as I have indicated, wrote around the time of the composition of John's Gospel. For another comparison between a cistern and the sea, note Sir. 50.3.

abundance ('For immediately fruit came forth in endless abundance', v. 44).[14] We should perhaps understand that the pots used by Jesus already had water in them, as a literal reading of the Greek suggests (Jn 2.6), and that more water was poured into them. If so, the parallel might be with God's activity on day three when he poured water into water.[15]

It is always difficult to know when to cease imputing significance to details in John's narrative, but the location of the miracle at Cana of Galilee can be viewed as a place on dry land between two seas, the sea of Galilee and the Mediterranean. The name Cana, which Birger Olsson thinks is significant and which may derive from *qanah*, 'to create', might tie into this observation about Cana's location.[16] Cana, this 'created place', recalls how at creation dry land appeared. The symbolical significance attributed to places in John's topographical references by second-century exegetes of John's Gospel would suggest that these interpreters, for example, Heracleon, were extending a process already begun in the Gospel, for example, Jn 9.7.[17] As T.L. Brodie well states, 'While the theological dimension of John's cities is strong, their hold on history is often fragile'.[18]

Another line of interpretation also leads us to the theme of fertility that is the topic of the third day of creation. John comments that what happened at Cana is the first of the signs Jesus did by way of manifesting his glory and 'his disciples believed on him'. The sign is indicated in

14. Dr Milton Horne, William Jewell College, Missouri, drew my attention to this possible link between the six waterpots and the passage in 2 Esdras when he was a participant in a seminar for College Professors I directed for the National Endowment for the Humanities at Cornell University in 1992 on 'Law and Religion in the Bible'.

15. Commentators, for example, R.E. Brown, *The Gospel according to John I–XII* (AB; New York: Doubleday, 1966), p. 100, are puzzled by the use of the verb *antlēsate* in reference to drawing water from the pots. The verb is normally used to refer to drawing water from a well, that is, the water lodged in the earth. B.F. Westcott, *The Gospel According to St John* (Grand Rapids: Eerdmans, repr. 1954), p. 84, goes so far as to suggest that the water came from a well and not from the pots. The point is, I think, that the verb is employed because the water and the pots symbolize the water and earth of the created order.

16. *Structure and Meaning in the Fourth Gospel* (Lund: Gleerup, 1974), p. 26.

17. See E.H. Pagels, *The Johannine Gospel in Gnostic Exegesis: Heracleon's Commentary on John* (Nashville: Abingdon, 1973), p. 52.

18. *The Quest for the Origin of John's Gospel* (Oxford: Oxford University Press, 1993), p. 161.

the words of the steward to the bridegroom: how the latter gave first the good wine, but now he provides the best and not, as is the customary way of bridegrooms, the less good. The significance of the development is that Jesus himself is to be thought of as a bridegroom. He, after all, provided the outstanding wine. We should note that the notion of Jesus as a bridegroom is also found in the words of the Baptist in Jn 3.29: 'He that hath the bride is the bridegroom: but the friend [the Baptist] of the bridegroom, which standeth and heareth him, rejoiceth greatly because of the bridegroom's voice: this my joy therefore is fulfilled.' When John writes that the disciples believed in him, he is suggesting that Jesus, the bridegroom, and his disciples became one, along the lines of a marital union.

The symbolism of the vine permeates the account of the water turned into wine at Cana. In the Hebrew Bible the vine is a well-established symbol of a woman as a wife and mother, for example, a man's wife is a fruitful vine (Ps. 128.3).[19] When Jesus says to his mother, 'Woman, what have I to do with thee? mine hour is not yet come' (Jn 2.4), we are dealing with what John thinks of as the lower order of creation. She is his mother, a vine, that gave him birth, an act of lower, that is, earthly creation. The use of the designation, 'Woman', brings out the fundamental feature that she, a woman, gave birth to a son. This relationship of mother and son is even more explicit in Jn 19.26, 'Woman, behold thy son'.

In rabbinic thought the hour of a man is the hour of his birth,[20] and in Jn 16.21 this notion, with the mother's situation as the primary focus, is used in a context that discusses Jesus' forthcoming resurrection: 'A woman when she is in travail hath sorrow, because her hour is come: but as soon as she is delivered of the child, she remembereth no more the anguish, for joy that a man is born into the world.' The context is one in which Jesus assures his disciples that their sorrow over his death will be superseded by their joy when they see him again in his risen state. That joyful time will be his hour that was yet to be when he spoke to his mother at the wedding at Cana. Paul's remark in Gal. 1.15 is comparable to Jesus's remark to his mother about how his hour has yet to come (Jn 2.4). In discussing the history of his conversion, his

19. See C.M. Carmichael, *Women, Law, and the Genesis Traditions* (Edinburgh: Edinburgh University Press, 1979), p. 63.

20. See H. Strack and P. Billerbeck, *Kommentar zum Neuen Testament aus Talmud und Midrasch*, II (Munich: Beck, 1924), p. 401.

becoming newborn, Paul refers to how God 'separated him from his mother's womb'.[21]

In Jn 17.1-4 a sequel to the state of unity between Jesus and his disciples is that when his hour (of resurrection) has come he will be glorified 'with the glory which I had with thee [his father] before the world was'. Moreover, he will have glorified his father at that point because he will have completed the work—of re-creation, we might add—that his father had given him to do. John interpreted the transformation of the water into wine as: 'This beginning of miracles did Jesus in Cana of Galilee, and manifested forth his glory' (Jn 2.11). In Jn 15.1-8 John gives symbolic expression to the idea of the unity that exists between Jesus and his disciples when he has Jesus speak of himself as the true vine and his disciples as its branches.

In Jn 2.4, then, when Jesus converses with his mother about his new 'hour' he is implicitly contrasting it with the hour he experienced with her when she delivered him as her offspring. He is hinting that the old order of earthly creation is passing away. His hour, which was actually the hour of his birth, is, oddly, yet to come: he awaits his new or second birth, the resurrection.

The symbolism of Jesus' mother as the vine that produced him can be observed from another angle. When she points out to Jesus that the wedding company has no wine, his response, 'Woman, what have you to do with me, my hour has not yet come', seems impossibly disconnected. Why should a remark by a mother to her son about lack of wine prompt the son to talk about the topic of birth? If the meaning of his remark about his 'hour' has to do with reproduction, as seems certain, we can infer that her reference to wine triggers the underlying symbolism about the vine as a metaphor for human reproduction.

The mother of Jesus is the vine that produced him. She in turn anticipates that he will do something with the water, which he does—he produces wine. Just as she anticipates this sign, so the sign anticipates something significant to come—he is to be the vine that produces branches, his disciples. Jesus himself as a vine thus produces offspring.[22]

21. On this aspect of Paul's conversion, see David Daube, *Appeasement or Resistance and Other Essays on New Testament Judaism* (Berkeley: University of California, 1987), pp. 67, 68.

22. It follows that the disciples are both bride and offspring. Three comments might be made. One, John does present such contradictions, e.g., Jesus is both shepherd and gate to the sheepfold. See Dodd, *Interpretation*, p. 135. Two, a vine as a

The sign manifested his glory and, as C.H. Dodd claimed,[23] the statement in the prologue is recalled where Christ's glory is that of the only begotten of the Father. The sign at Cana points to the glory he will achieve because those who believe in him, as his disciples did, are begotten of him. We have a remarkable continuity of theme, namely, union and procreation, in all of these manifestly related texts in John.

The incident at Cana closes with a transitional statement about how Jesus went with his mother and brothers, and his disciples, to Capernaum. The statement becomes much more significant in meaning in light of John's interplay between the mother who produces sons and Jesus who produces disciples. The imagery of the vine as powerfully reproductive underlies the statement. The apparently simple description about Jesus, his mother, brothers and disciples constitutes a choice illustration of John's use of a literal statement to bear great meaning, also of a 'historical' detail that means so much more than meets the eye. A major interpretive key in comprehending John's Gospel is this merging of history and allegory.

The notion of the vine whose seed is in itself, as described for the third day of creation, may also play a role in John's thinking. In referring to the miracle of day three Philo states that, 'the fruit comes out of the plants, as an end out of a beginning, and that out of the fruit again, containing as it does the seed in itself, there comes the plant, a beginning out of an end' (*Op. Mund.* 44). It is tempting to see a similar kind of reflection applied by John to Jesus and his mother. He had a beginning with his mother, but his death will be an end that leads to a beginning, the resurrection. Philo's focus is not dissimilar because of his own particular interest in immortality: 'For God willed that Nature should run a course that brings it back to its starting-point, endowing the species with immortality and making them sharers of eternal existence' (*Op. Mund.* 44). In Jn 3.4 Nicodemus asks Jesus if a man can enter his mother's womb a second time.[24] He misunderstands the higher order of creation.

metaphor for a human relationship does permit this double significance. The branches can be thought of as part of the vine in the sense of united with it, as a wife to a husband, but they can also be thought of as the fruit-bearing part of the vine, hence as offspring of the vine. Three, Jesus, in his role as the Word, is the creator of the vine. From this perspective, just as the fruit-trees of day three of creation in Genesis appeared simultaneously both as fruitfulness and as fruit producing, so Jesus' disciples at the same time are both united with him and his offspring.

23. *Interpretation*, p. 297.

24. Not in the sense of returning himself, but as semen. 'The simile is not that of

In regard to Jesus and his mother, Jesus will again experience the hour of his birth and simultaneously, along the lines of what miraculously occurred at the first creation, reproduce his own kind, his disciples, who, to borrow Philo's language, will have immortality and share in eternal existence.

John does in act use a similar line of thinking to Philo's when he describes Jesus' response to some visiting Greeks who sought him out. He focuses their attention on his forthcoming death and re-birth: 'Verily, verily, I say unto you, Except a corn of wheat fall into the ground and die, it abideth alone: but if it die, it bringeth forth much fruit' (Jn 12.24).

an involution, but of a repetition of the evolution of birth', Odeberg, *The Fourth Gospel*, p. 48.

USING SCRIPTURE: COMMUNITY AND LETTERALITY

Gerard Loughlin

It is not possible to work in the same department as Professor John Sawyer without picking up something of his enthusiasm for the study of the Bible, for *how* the Bible has been and is studied. For John, the story of the reading of the Bible is as much a part of biblical studies as anything else. One might even say that the Bible *is* the story of its reading. John also teaches a care and sensitivity in the study of the Bible that extends to both text and context; to the writing, reading and readers of the book. He leaves one in no doubt that the study of the Bible raises questions of responsibility.[1]

The following essay is offered as a tribute to John's infectious enthusiasm, not only for the Bible and its interpretation, but for the communities, Jewish and Christian, who still read the Bible as if it matters. The essay seeks to explore what it might mean for the Christian church to read its Bible literally,[2] looking first at the present low repute of the literal sense, contrasting this with its higher estimation in the medieval period, and tracing the story that led from one to the other. The essay argues for the literal sense as the embodied *use* of the text in the life of the church.

*

1. See J.F.A. Sawyer, 'Combating Prejudices about the Bible and Judaism', *Theology* 94 (1991), pp. 269-78; and in reply, W. Moberly, '"Old Testament" and "New Testament": The Propriety of the Terms for Christian Theology', *Theology* 95 (1992), pp. 26-32.

2. As John Sawyer rightly reminds us, the church's Bible is altogether different from the Jewish Bible; not even the Christian 'Old Testament' is the same as the Jewish Scriptures ('Combating Prejudices', pp. 273-74).

The church has always understood its scripture to have many meanings. For Origen, Augustine and Aquinas, the scriptural sense was multiple. One thing signified another, one sense led to the next. From the literal one was led to the allegorical, anagogical and tropological; from the earthly to the spiritual, the heavenly and the moral.[3] But always the literal sense mattered most. It was the one upon which all the others rested. For Hugh of St Victor it was like the foundation of a house.[4] Today, however, the literal sense seems the most problematic. Like Hugh of St Victor we take the literal to be the historical, but unlike Hugh we find the historical incredible. The Bible refers us to the past only falteringly. Today we look to metaphor for our meaning. But for narrative theology meaning and truth are still to be found in the literal sense, when scripture is followed to the letter.[5]

Avoiding the Literal

Liberal theologians provide many examples of what can happen when one does not attend to the literal sense of scripture. In particular liberal bishops provide a rich source, of whom Bishop John Shelby Spong is a good example. In his book *Born of a Woman* (1992), Bishop Spong attempts to rescue women from the dire effects of a 'literalised' reading of the gospel narratives: 'literalisation guarantees death'.[6] However, I shall argue that in failing to attend to the letter of the text, Spong renders women more securely dependent upon men. He does not take the gospel texts literally and therefore he does not take their stories of inde-

3. G.R. Evans, *The Language and Logic of the Bible: The Earlier Middle Ages* (Cambridge: Cambridge University Press, 1984), pp. 114-22.

4. *The Didascalicon of Hugh of St Victor: A Medieval Guide to the Arts* (trans. J. Taylor, Records of Western Civilization; New York: Columbia University Press, 1991 [1961]), Bk VI, Ch 3, pp. 135-39; Evans, *Language and Logic*, pp. 67-71.

5. By 'narrative theology' I intend a form of theological attention exemplified in such authorships as Hans Frei and George Lindbeck, Stanley Hauerwas and Nicholas Lash. Above all, it is an attention to the discipline of a practice which is first and last the following of a story: the life, death and resurrection of Jesus Christ.

6. J.S. Spong, *Born of a Woman: A Bishop Rethinks the Birth of Jesus* (San Francisco: Harper Collins, 1992), p. 176. Bishop Spong's book is something of a period piece. It is redolent of 60s Bultmannism, as suggested by the now quaint contrast between the 'three-tiered universe' of first-century people and the cosmology of 'space-age people' (p. 10). Compare J.A.T. Robinson, *Honest to God* (London: SCM Press, 1963), pp. 11-18.

pendent women seriously; stories of women whose primary relations are not with men, in particular with husbands, but with God.

Spong finds the idea that a man was not responsible for the birth of Jesus so problematic that he departs from the letter of the text and speculates that Jesus was the issue of a rape. The narrative of Jesus's conception—a conception chosen by Mary and without male agency—is then a cover-up for the actual story: conception by male force—'an illegitimate baby born through the aggressive and selfish act of a man sexually violating a teenage girl'.[7] Spong thinks that if we take the story as it is written we will have to speculate about 'parthenogenesis, or postulate a spirit with sexual organs and fluids'.[8] Rather than this, Spong re-writes the story, violating the letter of the text and inserting a man where no man was previously to be found.[9]

It has been said that early tradition obscured the role of women in the church; but Spong suggests that the church 'has done Joseph a disservice by relegating him to near obscurity'. Spong suspects that Joseph was far more important in the early life of Jesus than we have been led to believe.[10] If we follow the letter of the text we are led to Mary; but Spong would have us find our way to Joseph.

In Spong's world women must be attached to men; they cannot be allowed to do their own thing. He tells us that in first-century Jewish society, a 'group of women who followed a male band of disciples had to be wives, mothers or prostitutes'. Consequently, Spong marries Mary Magdalene to Jesus. This speculation is said to reverse the calumny of the early church, which quickly developed the need to remove the 'flesh and blood woman who was at Jesus's side in life and in death, and to replace her with a sexless woman, the virgin mother'.[11] Rather than having Mary Magdalene a disciple in her own right—a woman who chooses to follow Jesus as much as the men have done, and who follows him more faithfully—Spong makes her a sexual chattel; part of the group that follows the band rather than part of the band itself.

7. Spong, *Born of a Woman*, p. 185.

8. Spong, *Born of a Woman*, p. 127.

9. Of course the choice is not between parthenogenesis or rape; it is between the story we have, which mentions neither, or some other story.

10. Spong, *Born of a Woman*, pp. 181-82. 'I think we must entertain the possibility that Joseph, whatever his physical ties were with his son Jesus, did in fact give Jesus a relationship of such substance and beauty that it shaped his very understanding of God' (p. 184).

11. Spong, *Born of a Woman*, pp. 191, 197.

Bishop Spong, of course, wants the church to have a balanced view of sexuality and of relationships between the sexes; he wants to overcome the 'historic negativity toward women that has been a major gift of the Christian church to the world'.[12] But in not reading the Bible literally he falls short of achieving his intention. Because he does not follow the letter of the text he does not find stories about women who are first of all independent women, whose relationships with God are not dependent on men, but who are themselves disciples, the prime exemplars of Christian faith.[13] He makes up a story about a woman who was raped, rather than follow the gospel story about a woman who chose to conceive and didn't need a man to do so;[14] and he makes up a story about a woman who followed Jesus because she was married to him, rather than the story we have about a woman who chose to follow Jesus because she loved him as a disciple.

Bishop Spong's reading of the Bible may be called 'allegorical' in the sense that it takes the biblical text as pointing towards a second text—that of historical speculation—where the truth is to be found.[15] Spong's 'allegorical' approach is instructive of a general diremption of the literal sense in the modern period: between the *literal-as-written* and the *literal-as-historical*. This diremption is no doubt irretrievable, and can now be signified only in writings such as this. Here it is signified by the idea of the *letteral* sense.[16] The letteral is the literal proper, the literal-as-written.

12. Spong, *Born of a Woman*, p. 198.

13. 'In Luke we find a woman [Mary] who is not only in charge of her own destiny...but also the destiny of humanity...the perfect radical model of Christian discipleship': D.F. Middleton, 'The Story of Mary: Luke's Version', *New Blackfriars* 70 (1989), pp. 555-64 (p. 563).

14. It is interesting to note that for Spong, Mary's faithful obedience to God in Luke's Gospel (1.35) is the action of a 'compliant Jewish peasant girl' in the face of 'divine sexual aggression', while her son's faithful obedience to God (Lk. 22.42) is an action of intense human integrity, of self-giving and life-giving love (p. 179). It is not Luke who so belittles the mother's part.

15. Spong argues that attempts to 'reconcile or to harmonise the differences between Matthew and Luke are based on the false premise that some historical, factual truth lies behind these birth narratives' (p. 60). Yet Spong's entire book is concerned with speculating about the 'historical, factual truth' that lies behind the gospel stories. For an account of similar 'allegorizing' in other liberal theologians see my articles, 'Telling the Story of Jesus', *Theology* 87 (1984), pp. 323-29; and 'Myths, Signs and Significations', *Theology* 89 (1986), pp. 268-75.

16. The 'letteral' is a term borrowed from Rachel Salmon and Gerda Elata-Alster. There are interesting similarities between the textual attention I intend by the term and

The idea of the *literal* can then be used, as it is used, in the (improper) modern sense: the literal-as-historical. That the latter is a modern use can be indicated by attending to the discussion of scripture's several senses in the *Summa Theologiæ* of St Thomas Aquinas (1224–1274).

Literal Figures

In the modern period we have been taught to contrast the literal with the metaphorical. Thus Spong argues that there is only one literal phrase in the historic creeds, one 'literal fact of history': 'He suffered under Pontius Pilate, was crucified, died and was buried.'[17] By contrast, the credal phrase 'He sitteth on the right hand of God' is not to be understood literally but figuratively. It is then very odd for the modern mind to find Aquinas making no such distinction between the literal and the figurative.

It is not that Aquinas would not recognize 'He sitteth on the right hand of God' as a figure of speech. On the contrary, he teaches that in holy scripture 'spiritual things' are delivered to us 'beneath metaphors taken from bodily things'. This is because scripture is to be used 'in common without distinction of persons'. The uneducated may also lay hold of spiritual things. For the same reason, holy teaching (theology) finds the use of metaphors indispensable.[18] The use of metaphors is also important because it reminds us that God cannot be directly signified.[19]

But for Aquinas, unlike Spong, metaphors and other figures of speech are found at the level of the literal sense.[20] As Fr Thomas Gilby notes, in

the midrashic reading outlined in their article, 'Retracing a Writerly Text: In the Footsteps of a Midrashic Sequence on the Creation of the Male and Female', in *Hermeneutics, the Bible and Literary Criticism* (ed. A. Loades and M. McLain; London: Macmillan, 1992), pp. 177-97. Indeed, Hans Frei suggests that Midrash (and *peshat*) is 'the nearest Jewish equivalent to Christian literal reading'. (H. Frei, *Theology and Narrative: Selected Essays* [ed. G. Hunsinger and W.C. Placher; New York & Oxford: Oxford University Press, 1993], p. 149). For further on Midrash see G.L. Bruns, *Hermeneutics Ancient and Modern* (New Haven & London: Yale University Press, 1992), pp. 104-23.

17. Spong, *Born of a Woman*, p. 177.

18. St Thomas Aquinas, *Summa Theologiæ*. I. Christian Theology (Ia. I) (trans. T. Gilby OP; London: Blackfriars, 1964), p. 35.

19. The use of 'figures of base bodies' reminds us that no figure can be 'taken in the proper sense of their words and be crudely ascribed to divine things', for what God is not is clearer to us than what God is (*Summa Theologiæ*, p. 35).

20. Aquinas, *Summa Theologiæ*, p. 41. For a succinct statement of Thomas's

Aquinas there is 'no depreciation of the literal sense as though it expressed just the flat and unimaginative significance of the words as they stand'.[21] For Aquinas the metaphorical or figural is a disposition of the literal.

Aquinas draws a basic distinction between the literal and the spiritual senses of scripture. Under the heading of the literal sense he places history, etiology and analogy. 'You have history when any matter is straightforwardly recorded; etiology when its cause is indicated... analogy when the truth of one Scriptural passage is shown not to clash with the truth of another'. Under the heading of the spiritual or allegorical sense he places the tropological, the moral and the anagogical. The tropological sense 'is brought into play when the things of the Old Law signify the things of the New Law; the moral sense when the things done in Christ and in those who prefigured him are signs of what we should carry out; and the anagogical sense when the things that lie ahead in eternal glory are signified'.[22]

Aquinas discusses metaphor and figure in discussing the parabolic sense which he says is contained in the literal sense. He writes that 'words can signify something properly and something figuratively; in the last case the literal sense is not the figure of speech itself, but the object it figures'.[23] This is because things as well as words signify.

> That God is the author of holy Scripture should be acknowledged, and he has the power, not only of adapting words to convey meanings (which men also can do), but also of adapting things themselves. In every branch of knowledge words have meaning, but what is special here is that the things meant by the words also themselves mean something.[24]

An example of this is provided by Hugh of St Victor in his *Didascalicon* of the late 1130s.

> The Scripture says: 'Watch, because your adversary the Devil goeth about as a roaring lion.'[25] Here, if we should say that the lion stands for the Devil, we should mean by 'lion' not the word but the thing. For if the two words 'devil' and 'lion' mean one and the same thing, the likeness of that

teaching see B. Smalley, *The Study of the Bible in the Middle Ages* (Oxford: Clarendon Press, 1941), p. 234.

21. T. Gilby, 'The Senses of Scripture', Appendix 12 in Aquinas, *Summa Theologiæ*, pp. 140-41 (p. 140).

22. Aquinas, *Summa Theologiæ*, p. 39.

23. Aquinas, *Summa Theologiæ*, p. 41.

24. Aquinas, *Summa Theologiæ*, p. 37.

25. 1 Peter 5.8.

> same thing to itself is not adequate. It remains, therefore, that the word 'lion' signifies the animal, but that the animal in turn designates the Devil.[26]

Aquinas was heir to this way of thinking, to a tradition of commentary that had, as Beryl Smalley puts it, 'groped' its way to the position 'that figures and metaphors belonged to the literal interpretation without quite understanding why.'[27] For Aquinas, figures and metaphors belong to the literal sense because the latter is the intention of the inspired writer. Thus the figural takes place at the level of the letteral, the literal-as-written, and points beyond itself.

> When Scripture speaks of the arm of God, the literal sense is not that he has a physical limb, but that he has what it signifies, namely the power of doing and making. This example brings out how nothing false can underlie the literal sense of Scripture.[28]

Thus, to use Spong's example, when it is said that Christ sits on the right hand of God, the literal sense is not that he sits to the right of God or, as Spong's joke has it, on God's right hand—so that God can use only his left hand—but that Christ is what it signifies, namely that Christ is one with God. And this is the literal sense of the phrase.

It is important to note that for Aquinas the literal sense is 'that which the author intends, and the author of holy Scripture is God who comprehends everything all at once in his understanding'. From this it follows, for Aquinas, that 'many meanings are present even in the literal sense of one passage of Scripture'.[29] The difference between Aquinas and Spong on the literal sense of scripture is the difference between supposing the historical to be but one part of the literal and supposing the historical to be all of it.

26. Hugh of St Victor, *Didascalicon*, Bk V, Ch 4, p. 122.

27. Smalley, *The Study of the Bible*, p. 234.

28. Aquinas, *Summa Theologiæ*, p. 41. Aquinas is concerned to establish the truthfulness of scripture against any suggestion of its falsity. Clearly this is what concerns Spong: that at the literal level certain passages of scripture are false. Allegory has often been understood as avoiding such a suggestion. Thus David Norton writes that in the ancient world, allegory 'is a primary road of escape from the literal text' (D. Norton, *A History of the Bible as Literature*. I. *From Antiquity to 1700* [Cambridge: Cambridge University Press, 1993], p. 55.) But here Norton reveals as much about the modern as about the ancient world, for he understands the figurative as an 'escape' from the literal. This is not what Aquinas understands, for whom the figurative takes us deeper into the literal sense of the text.

29. Aquinas, *Summa Theologiæ*, p. 39.

The Diremption of the Literal

During the early medieval period the literal sense of scripture was often described as historical, in the sense of telling a story: *historia*. Hugh of St Victor (1096–1141) notes in his *Didascalicon*, that 'it is not unfitting that we call by the name "history" not only the recounting of actual deeds but also the first meaning of any narrative which uses words according to their proper nature.'[30] However, as Gillian Evans notes, by the twelfth century there existed 'the germ of a distinction...between *littera* and *historia'*, and by the middle of the century, Gerhoch of Reichersberg could use *littera* and *historia* in distinct senses.[31] However, the diremption of the literal did not really take place until the rise of modern biblical criticism, beginning as early as the seventeenth century with Benedict de Spinoza (1634–1677).

For modern biblical criticism the historical sense is found only when a second step is taken. First, one steps not from the biblical story to history, but from the story to a critically constructed narrative, which in turn leads to the past. The historical sense is found not in the biblical stories, but in the narratives of critical historians. If you want to know who Jesus was and what he was like you go, not to the Bible, but to a historian's critical narrative about him; not to a gospel, but to a life of Jesus; not to Matthew, Mark, Luke and John, but to Strauss or Schweitzer, Crossan or Sanders.[32]

According to Hans Frei (1922–1988), this development was due to a number of related disjunctions or uncouplings: of the literal from the historical and of both from the figural; of history-likeness from history; of narrative from reality; and of meaning from truth.[33] All these disjunctions follow from the severance of the literal and the historical.

30. Hugh of St Victor, *Didascalicon*, p. 137.

31. Evans, *Language and Logic*, p. 68.

32. D.F. Strauss, *The Life of Jesus Critically Examined* (London: SCM Press, 1973 [1835]); A. Schweitzer, *The Quest of the Historical Jesus: A Critical Study of Its Progress from Reimarus to Wrede* (New York: Macmillan, 1968 [1906]); J.D. Crossan, *The Historical Jesus: The Life of a Mediterranean Jewish Peasant* (Edinburgh: T. & T. Clark, 1991); E.P. Sanders, *The Historical Figure of Jesus* (London: Allen Lane, 1993).

33. H. Frei, *The Eclipse of Biblical Narrative: A Study in Eighteenth and Nineteenth Century Hermeneutics* (New Haven & London: Yale University Press, 1974), p. 12.

'When the identity of literal sense and historical reference is severed, literal and figurative likewise no longer belong together'.[34] In the modern period history becomes an autonomous domain, accessible by routes other than the biblical. It can be narrated otherwise, by stories which are not merely history-like but historical-critical, scientific.[35]

> The real events of history constitute an autonomous temporal framework of their own under God's providential design. Instead of rendering them accessible, the [biblical] narratives, heretofore indispensable as means of access to the events, now simply verify them, thus affirming their autonomy and the fact that they are in principle accessible through any kind of description that can manage to be accurate either predictively or after the event.[36]

For Frei the biblical stories are characteristically realistic or history-like narratives. 'The distinctiveness is simply indelible and a significant feature the synoptic gospels share with large sections of the Old Testament'.[37] Frei contends that while this characteristic was widely recognized in the eighteenth century, it could be understood only in terms of historical reference.

> Commentators, especially those influenced by historical criticism, virtually to a man failed to understand what they had seen when they had recognised the realistic character of biblical narratives, because everytime they acknowledged it they thought this was identical with affirming not only the history-likeness but also a degree of historical likelihood of the stories.[38]

When the literal and historical are conjoined, when what Frei calls the explicative sense and the historical reference are one, so also are the literal and the figurative.[39] For the most part, Frei takes the figurative to be that of type and antitype. A historical event is rendered by a story, and this story-event figures another storied-event. This reading strategy permits the relation, both literally and historically, of otherwise separate stories and events, which are then both related and separate. They retain their own identities and yet at the same time partake in the larger identity of the temporal succession rendered by the figural coding. The

34. Frei, *Eclipse of Biblical Narrative*, p. 37.
35. Frei, *Eclipse of Biblical Narrative*, p. 52.
36. Frei, *Eclipse of Biblical Narrative*, p. 4.
37. Frei, *Eclipse of Biblical Narrative*, pp. 12-13.
38. Frei, *Eclipse of Biblical Narrative*, pp. 11-12.
39. Frei, *Eclipse of Biblical Narrative*, p. 28.

separate stories become part of a larger narrative. 'Figural interpretation...sets forth the unity of the canon as a single cumulative and complex pattern of meaning'.[40]

But when the literal is dirempted—between, on the one hand, the letteral, and on the other hand, the literal construed as the historical—the figural is required to relate actual events rather than written narratives; histories rather than stories. It then becomes difficult to see how one event can be the type of another. The figural pattern appears more like artifice than transcription. If the Bible has a unity it is only because the history it relates has one also, and if history does have a unity it must display it to historical science. Thus was developed the idea of a special history: *heilsgeschichte*—salvation history—the idea that 'the unitary meaning of Scripture is its reference to one special sequence of real events, from creation to the end of history, with their centre in Christ's incarnation, the whole sequence ambiguously related to other historical events'.[41]

As story and history unravelled, so also meaning and truth. Once upon a time the meaning of the Bible was the truth of the world. The biblical narrative rendered the significance of the world's history. But in the seventeenth and eighteenth centuries people increasingly began to look elsewhere for the truth of their condition. The Bible told stories, but reason rendered truth.

Universal reason teaches true religion, a divine law common to all. As Spinoza wrote in his *Tractatus Theologico-Politicus* (1670), reason teaches 'that there exists a God, that is, a Supreme Being, Who loves justice and charity, and Who must be obeyed by whomsoever would be saved; that the worship of this Being consists in the practice of justice and love towards one's neighbour'.[42] This is the Bible's truth also, but not necessarily its meaning. For the purpose of the Bible is to move people to the practice of neighbourly love and justice, and to this end it tells stories which may not always, or not in all their parts, be true.

> Scripture does not explain things by their secondary causes, but only narrates them in the order and the style which has most power to move men, and especially uneducated men, to devotion; and therefore it speaks

40. Frei, *Eclipse of Biblical Narrative*, p. 33.

41. Frei, *Eclipse of Biblical Narrative*, p. 46.

42. Benedict de Spinoza, *The Chief Works of Benedict de Spinoza*, I (trans. R.H.M. Elwes; New York: Dover Publications, 1951), p. 186.

> inaccurately of God and of events, seeing that its object is not to convince the reason, but to attract and lay hold of the imagination.[43]

Consequently one must distinguish between the meaning of the biblical stories and their religious significance. Biblical interpretation is concerned only with the first. As Spinoza taught, 'we are to work not on the truth of passages, but solely on their meaning'.[44] This limitation of the exegetical task, and the distinction on which it is based, further buttresses the dissociation of history from story.

We now have three accounts of meaning: literal, historical and religious. Firstly, there is the story; secondly, the history, to which the story wholly or partly refers; and thirdly, religious truth, which the story may or may not accurately portray. Only the third really matters, and increasingly it cannot be thought to depend on the other two.

In the work of the English Deist, Anthony Collins (1676–1729), Frei finds a moment in which the literal ceases to be the written as such, and becomes merely a modality of the actual, as the written form of the historical; merely and only representation. 'A proposition is literal if it describes and refers to a state of affairs known or assumed on independent probable grounds to agree or disagree with the stated proposition'.[45] In this Collins predates the positivists, for whom the meaning of a statement is the method of its verification.[46] The literal-as-written or letteral no longer presents but merely re-presents the actual. It is no longer the place of truth, but rather the sign of where such a place is to be found: the historical-empirical rendered by (scientific) processes of verification.

As the historical reliability of the biblical narrative became increasingly doubtful, there emerged what Frei describes as 'mediating' theology. This located the religious significance of the biblical narratives in their relation to general human experience; a universal human condition. The biblical story is to be fitted into the story of the world, rather than the world into the story of the Bible.[47] With this development the modern world of John Spong comes into view.

Following Frei's story into the twentieth century, we find that the significance of the biblical text is now thought to lie either behind or in

43. Spinoza, *The Chief Works*, p. 40.
44. Spinoza, *The Chief Works*, p. 101.
45. Frei, *Eclipse of Biblical Narrative*, p. 76.
46. Frei, *Eclipse of Biblical Narrative*, p. 77.
47. Frei, *Eclipse of Biblical Narrative*, p. 130.

front of it. The Bible's truth is to be found either behind it, in the history it possibly re-presents; or in front of it, in the truths of human self-consciousness, which are accessible by universal reason or phenomenological hermeneutics, and which the Bible quaintly discloses and expresses. Above all, the significance of the Bible is not to be found in the actual biblical stories themselves. It is Frei's project, in both *The Eclipse of Biblical Narrative* (1974) and *The Identity of Jesus Christ* (1975), to steer a course between the behinders and the in-fronters—between the critical historians and the 'proponents of the "second naiveté" of "restorative" hermeneutics'—to the written text itself, the letteral.[48]

Community and Letterality

Hans Frei is concerned to secure the religious significance of biblical narrative at the level of the history-like, without the necessity of its opening to the historical. He suggests that what the biblical stories are about and how they make sense are 'functions of the depiction or narrative rendering of the events constituting them—including their being rendered, at least partially, by the device of chronological sequence'.[49] Biblical meaning is a function of narrativity.

Frei can do without historical reference because for him, the biblical is not to be judged by its adequation to the historical, but the historical by its adequation to the biblical. Thus from Erich Auerbach's contrast of Homer with the Bible he takes the suggestion that the biblical narratives 'seek to overcome our reality'.

> We are to fit our own life into its world, feel ourselves to be elements in its structure of universal history...Everything else that happens in the world can only be conceived as an element in this sequence; into it everything that is known about the world...must be fitted as an ingredient of the divine plan.[50]

48. H. Frei, 'The "Literal Reading" of Biblical Narrative in the Christian Tradition: Does It Stretch or Will It Break?', in *The Bible and the Narrative Tradition* (ed. F. McConnell; New York: Oxford University Press, 1986), pp. 36-77 (p. 62).

49. Frei, *Eclipse of Biblical Narrative*, p. 13.

50. Frei, *Eclipse of Biblical Narrative*, p. 3; E. Auerbach, *Mimesis: The Representation of Reality in Western Literature* (trans. W.R. Trask; Princeton, NJ: Princeton University Press, 1953 [1946]).

Frei noted the similarity between his view of the biblical story and the standing of the autonomous literary text in 'Anglo-American "New Criticism"'. 'Both claim that the text is a normative and pure 'meaning' world of its own which, quite apart from any factual reference it may have, and apart from its author's intention or its reader's reception, stands on its own with the authority of self-evident intelligibility.'[51]

However, Frei argues that his understanding of the biblical narrative is not an instance of a more general, New Critical, theory; but that the latter is a generalization of a specifically theological understanding of the gospel narratives, dependent upon the doctrine of the incarnation. For belief in the incarnation is the basis in faith for understanding the biblical narratives as the locus and cohesion of meaning and truth. This understanding of the autonomous text is 'strictly in the mode of faith seeking understanding'.[52] 'The irony of New Criticism is to have taken this specific case and rule and to have turned them instead into a general theory of meaning, literature, and even culture, in their own right'.[53] The autonomous text makes sense in the Christian tradition in a way that it does not in a general literary theory.

> In that [Christian] tradition, the ascriptive literalism of the story, the *history-likeness* if you will, of the singular agent enacting the unity of human finitude and divine infinity, Jesus of Nazareth, is taken to be itself the ground, guarantee, and conveyance of the truth of the depicted enactment, its *historicity* if you will.[54]

The *sensus literalis* is thus for Frei a case-specific way of reading; specific to a 'sociolinguistic community' rather than to a 'literary ambience'.[55] One can then understand the literal sense of the Bible as the 'plain' meaning it has within the community for whom it is Scripture. Frei believes that this literal or plain sense follows three basic rules. First, that everything associated with Jesus in the biblical stories is to be ascribed to him and not to any other person or thing. Second, that the unity of the entire biblical narrative must be maintained, the unity—in traditional Christian nomenclature—of Old and New Testaments.

51. Frei, 'The "Literal Reading" of Biblical Narrative', p. 63.

52. For the Anselmian nature of Frei's project see K.J. Vanhoozer, *Biblical Narrative in the Philosophy of Paul Ricoeur* (Cambridge: Cambridge University Press, 1990), pp. 161-65.

53. Frei, 'The "Literal Reading" of Biblical Narrative', p. 65.

54. Frei, 'The "Literal Reading" of Biblical Narrative', p. 66.

55. Frei, 'The "Literal Reading" of Biblical Narrative', p. 53.

Thirdly, that other readings are permissible so long as they do not contradict the first two rules of Christian reading.

Frei's stress on the ruled reading of the Bible within the Christian community—which community is itself predicated upon its reading of the Bible—goes some way to meeting a criticism that has been directed at his account of the biblical text as subsuming world, and which he himself directs at the autonomous texts of the New Criticism: namely, that it is 'artificial and dubious to claim a purely external relation of text and reading, which in effect sets aside the mutual implication of interpretation and textual meaning'.[56] In other words, texts are never truly autonomous, for they only exist when they are read. Texts and readers are mutually implicated.

Using the Bible Literally

My earlier reference to Aquinas and his view of the literal sense of holy scripture as that intended by its divine author, should not be taken as endorsing a strictly recognitive hermeneutic, so that scripture means what it meant to its writers. Strictly speaking it is people, not texts, who mean things. Texts mean something only when they are used in some way by someone. When texts are used they become occasions of meaning, usually the meanings of their authors but also of their readers.

A text may be used by its readers as its author would use it or would have it used; but a reader may use it differently from how its author intended or imagined. Clearly, then, a text can be used in more than one way. However, this does not mean that a text can be used in just any way. For usage is always particular to a time and place; context conditions and constrains usage. There is little doubt that the church now uses the Bible somewhat differently from how it was used in the past, especially past use of the 'Old Testament'. Equally, different Christians have used and use scripture differently, and make scriptural uses the bases of their differences.

On this Wittgensteinian account of scriptural meaning as (churchly) use, the question of the *sensus literalis* becomes a question of literal usage. How does one use the Bible literally? By using it as it is commonly used within the Christian community. This answer renders in terms of usage the idea that the literal sense is the plain sense; the sense it is normally held to have within the church. This is a purely formal

56. Frei, 'The "Literal Reading" of Biblical Narrative', p. 64.

answer, since it tells us little about the 'material character' of the scriptural sense. Kathryn Tanner notes that when 'participants in a practice of appealing to texts talk about the plain sense, they need not...*mean* by that the sense that commands general agreement. They may mean instead..."the sense the author intended"...the "sense that God intends"'.[57] This comment returns us to the idea of Godly intention, and suggests, as an answer to our question, that to use scripture literally is to use it as God would have the church use it.

A question about the literal sense of scripture will then take the form: 'How does God, as the true author of Scripture, intend us to use this text in our present circumstances?' The question has to be put in contextual terms because scripture—as co-constitutive of God's revelation—is addressed not only to the time of its writers, but to all times and places; but not all times and places are the same. As Aquinas, after Augustine, noted, divine authorship suggests multiple usage: 'it comes not amiss...if many meanings are present even in the literal sense of one passage of Scripture'.[58]

Frei locates the significance of the scriptural narrative in its depiction of Jesus of Nazareth; its rendition of his identity. That identity is such that those who follow after him are invited to find their own identities in his. The scriptural text is used literally when the church seeks, in the circumstances of its time and place, to be conformed to the one whom the scripture depicts. A literal reading of the text is one that follows it to the letter; not in the sense of trying to discern the frailties of its historical reference; nor in seeking for the disclosure of the human condition within its interstices; but in the sense of making oneself over to its narrative in order to be made anew.

This making over in order to be made anew is a way of enacting or performing the scripture. As Rowan Williams has suggested, it is a telling or reading of the scripture in which the tellers or readers take a part in the story so that it becomes their story and they become characters in its narrative.

> Christian interpretation is unavoidably engaged in 'dramatic' modes of reading: we are invited to identify ourselves in the story being contemplated, to reappropriate who we are now, and whom we shall or can be, in

57. K.E. Tanner, 'Theology and the Plain Sense', in *Scriptural Authority and Narrative Interpretation* (ed. G. Green; Philadelphia: Fortress Press, 1987), pp. 59-78.

58. Aquinas, *Summa Theologiæ*, p. 39.

> terms of the story. Its movements, transactions, transformations, become ours; we take responsibility for this or that position within the narrative... our appropriation of the story...is an active working through of the story's movement in our own time.[59]

As Williams notes, the most obvious example of such dramatic reading in Christian life is the 'scriptural lectionary bound to the festal cycle', above all the paschal celebration which is 'evidently designed to bring our time and the time of the canonical narrative together'.[60] In such celebration the church's story clearly retells the story of Jesus as one and the same story.

Living the Christian life within the ecclesial community involves more than just liturgical enactments; it involves radically reimagining and resituating one's entire life within the story of Jesus, seeking to remove once and for all the line between acting and play-acting. This is why even the figure of play-acting, of performance, fails to grasp the risk and radical contingency, the open-endedness, of the play being enacted, the performance being given. The players 'are invited to "create" themselves in finding a place within...[the] drama—an improvisation in the theatre workshop, but one that purports to be about a comprehensive truth affecting one's identity and future...In Paul's terms, all may find themselves both prisoners of disobedience and recipients of grace (Rom. 11.32).'[61]

Reading Time

According to Rowan Williams the literal sense of scripture is to be read diachronically. He makes central to his understanding of the *sensus literalis* the narrativity or temporality of the text, the time of its telling. To attend to the literal sense of scripture is to insist upon 'there being some controlling force in the fact that meaning comes to light in a process of learning to perceive'.[62] This 'process of learning to perceive' is a matter of following through a written text in a 'single-time continuum, reading

59. R. Williams, 'The Literal Sense of Scripture', *Modern Theology* 7 (1991), pp. 121-34 (p. 125).

60. Williams, 'The Literal Sense of Scripture', p. 126.

61. R. Williams, 'Postmodern Theology and the Judgement of the World', in *Postmodern Theology: Christian Faith in a Pluralist World* (ed. F.B. Burnham; San Francisco: Harper Collins, 1989), pp. 92-112 (p. 97).

62. Williams, 'The Literal Sense of Scripture', p. 123.

it as a sequence of changes, a pattern of transformations'.[63]

Williams sets a literal, diachronic reading of scripture over against a non-literal, synchronic viewing of the text as a '"field" of linguistic material, of signs that refer backwards and forwards to each other in a system of interaction more like the surface of a picture than a performance of drama or music'.[64] When such a structuralist mode of reading is adopted, the text is situated, as it were, in space rather than in time; it is viewed at a glance, read all at once. For Williams this way of reading is decidedly unfruitful, and he argues for the primacy of the diachronic over against the synchronic; of time over space. The primary fact of the literal form of attention is that the reader takes time, living with or in the text.

> Concern with the literal, the diachronic, is a way of resisting the premature unities and harmonies of a non-literal reading (whether allegorical, existentialist, structuralist or deconstructionist), in which the time that matters is only the present of the reader faced with the 'spatial' expanse of a text cut off from its own inner processes and the history of its production.[65]

The non-literal, synchronic or spatial reading of text is unsatisfactory, Williams suggests, because it ignores the basic fact that for human life meaning is not something that comes all at once, but is unfolded over time, slowly discovered, explored and assimilated. 'So long as our humanity remains unintelligible except as a life of material change, irreversible movement, it is unlikely—to say the least—that we could establish non-diachronic modes of reading as primary.'[66]

Williams suggests that synchronic or spatial modes of reading which, as he rightly notes, are notoriously idealist, run up against the basic materiality of human existence. Thus it is that Christianity, itself unable to avoid human materiality, takes for granted the fact that, as Williams puts it, 'meanings are learned and produced, not given in iconic, ahistorical form'.[67]

Williams argues that a literal reading of scripture requires a point of focus if it is to have any sort of unity. He finds this point of focus in the story of Jesus and his cross. He suggests that all Christian communities

63. Williams, 'The Literal Sense of Scripture', p. 121.
64. Williams, 'The Literal Sense of Scripture', pp. 121-22.
65. Williams, 'The Literal Sense of Scripture', p. 123.
66. Williams, 'The Literal Sense of Scripture', p. 124.
67. Williams, 'The Literal Sense of Scripture', p. 125.

have found their corporate symbolic life centred in the death and resurrection of Jesus, such that they construe and enact their own lives, through baptism and eucharist, as participating in his death and its meaning.

> Reading Scripture in faith is reading it as moving towards or around a unifying narrative moment, the story of the work of Jesus: *how* it does so, how we are to carry through such a reading in points of detail, is constantly elusive; we know only that, as a matter of fact, the movement that is portrayed by the texts of Scripture had produced the identifiable and distinctive meanings of the Church.[68]

However, I think it is necessary to reinstate synchronic modes of reading as inter-constitutive with diachronic ones of literal reading. In setting the literal against the non-literal, the diachronic against the synchronic, time against space, Williams is in danger of distorting the diachronic character of the reading he seeks to delineate. For any (diachronic) reading must consist, at least in part, of successive synchronies, some of which will remain and some of which will give way to others.

Reading is in part constituted by a number of passing provisional patterns, through which both the shape and movement of the text is apprehended in a process of invention and discovery. The synchronic or spatial moment—when, as it were, the forward movement of the narrative is twisted out of time's flight and pinned flat upon the earth—is no more than the projection-perception of patterns in the text. This moment is repeated in time as the text is read. The patterns are both vertical and linear, in space and in time. We know them as projected expectations that enable us to grasp the movement of the story, to understand what has been by what we expect to come.

As we read a text in time we imagine how it will turn out. We look for patterns or synchronies. Often the excitement of a text in time is constituted by the defeat of our expectations, of the patterns we project upon it in advance of its completion. Thus the thrill of the book, play or film that subverts the genres it at first appears to encode. Simple pleasure is to be had by the confirmation of our expectations, as when the child insists upon the retelling of the tale he or she already knows by heart, word for word. The child is comforted by the repeated pattern of the text. A syntagmatic succession of patterns is constitutive for any

68. Williams, 'The Literal Sense of Scripture', p. 131.

diachronic reading attentive to the time of the text, and productive of meaning.

Christian believers who enact the story of Jesus' passion in yearly celebration live both in the diachronic moment and in the synchronic pattern. The pattern of the passion gives a meaning to Easter week and informs its performance. But performing the pattern takes time, and this duration, with its enacted expectations and confusions, its desperation and horror, its numbed silence and dawning hope, gives meaning to and informs the pattern.

*

The foregoing has sought to suggest an understanding of the literal sense of scripture which does not, on the one hand, reduce it to the historical, nor, on the other hand, to the merely self-referential. I introduced John Spong as exemplary of a liberal tendency to disparage the literal as the historical, and suggested that by failing to attend to the literal sense of scripture he sabotaged his own best intentions. Hans Frei was introduced, first to suggest how the literal sense of scripture was dirempted in the modern period between the written or letteral and the historical; and second, as exemplary of those who, uneasy of historical reference, locate the meaning of scripture within a world subtended by the narrative. While Frei resists the lure of locating scriptural significance in the expression of self-consciousness, he finally fails to overcome the modern diremption of the literal, simply choosing the letteral in opposition to the historical, which becomes merely putative or optional on his account. Finally, I have tried to suggest that the literal sense of scripture is locatable in the co-constitution of scripture and church, of text and reading-community. Here, I would suggest, the literal is rebound insofar as the church performs in history the letter of the text.

Historical Text as Historical Text: Some Basic Hermeneutical Reflections in Relation to the New Testament

James D.G. Dunn

1. *Introduction*

My concern in this paper is the very modest one of underlining the importance of a text's historical status, that is, as a product of a particular period and society in the past—in some cases we can even specify a particular person writing in a particular historical context and for a particular historical occasion. The texts I have in mind are those of the New Testament, my own area of specialism. I write with some hesitation, since I have not made a close study of the debates on hermeneutics of the last 150 years and am not deeply involved in the current discussion on the applicability of literary criticism (a large label) to biblical texts. However, in various discussions with students and researchers using these tools (I do not say how wisely or well) I have frequently been concerned that the character of the NT text under discussion as a historical text has been down-played or marginalized to a serious extent.

The basic point I wish to re-emphasize is that the historical context within which a historical text emerged determines and limits, in some degree at least, the meaning which may be read from that text. Of course historical texts differ in the degree to which they are context-dependent. Some texts are almost ahistorical in character, that is, not tied to any particular historical context—epigrams and aphorisms which function equally effectively in different cultures and periods, truly ageless wisdom—or stories/legends which likewise transcend historical particularities of time and place. Others again belong to such a lengthy historical context that their potency cannot be narrowly computed in terms of this century or that; such is the Vulgate or the Authorized (King James) Version of the Bible. But there are still others which are so locked into their historical time and/or space that apprehension let alone comprehension (understanding) of them cannot even begin until they have been treated as historical texts with all that that means in terms of their historical particularity.

My basic contention is that the NT as a whole and on the whole belongs to the last category. In underscoring this point I am well aware that I am focusing on only one dimension of the hermeneutical process. In reaction against some of the more extravagant claims of some reader-response critics, that meaning is the creation of the act of reading, or that the text itself is simply a function of the interpretative context in which it is read, or a deconstructionist claim that all texts are inherently unstable and transitory, I side with those who affirm, in contrast, that the typical NT text belongs within its own language game, that it has its own horizons and a stability of referential meaning, and that its range of potential meaning is limited by its historical context.[1] In saying this, however, I am well aware of the other dimensions in the hermeneutical process—the reader's linguistic competence, the hermeneutical circle, the role of pre-understanding, the interpretive community, and so on—all, indeed, that the 'science' of hermeneutics and 'art' of interpretation has been familiar with since Schleiermacher.[2] It may nevertheless be useful to restate what respecting a historical text in its historical otherness means for meaning in the case of the NT texts and to offer some illustrations which have brought the point home to me most forcibly in my own work.

2. *No Reading Without 'Lower Criticism'*

In a recent conference seminar one paper offering a literary critical perspective on a NT text seemed to have forgotten that the text in question had been written in ancient Greek, or to be more precise, in the common Greek of the eastern Mediterranean world in the first century of the common era. Perhaps the point, being so fundamental, was too obvious, but since so much hangs upon it, the obvious is the place where we have to start.

1. For review and critique of reader-response criticism in biblical studies see particularly S.D. Moore, *Literary Criticism and the Gospels* (New Haven: Yale University Press, 1989), chs. 7–8, and A.C. Thiselton, *New Horizons in Hermeneutics* (London: Harper Collins, 1992), particularly ch. 14.

2. See A.C. Thiselton, *The Two Horizons* (Exeter: Paternoster Press, 1980); K. Mueller-Vollmer, *The Hermeneutics Reader* (Oxford: Basil Blackwell, 1986).

To someone whose only language was English, the critical texts which we have of the NT writings might well at first appear to be composed merely of strange squiggles on the page. How can such persons know that there actually are meaningful words in front of them? How can the written 'signs' become significant?[3] Only by comparing the squiggles with words written in Greek. And how can such persons begin to make sense of these squiggles? Only by comparing these words with the same or similar words written in ancient Greek texts and inscriptions. And how can such persons begin to construe these words into syntactical units and meaningful sentences? Only by comparative study of the grammar and syntax of these other ancient texts.

Of course, all this has been done for modern students of the NT by the cumulative garnering of the fruit of myriad careful studies of countless philologists and lexicographers over the centuries. And modern students can readily give meaning to the otherwise strange squiggles/signs simply by consulting the Greek grammars and lexica which store that fruit in easily accessible form. But when doing so they need always to recall that they are in fact taking a short cut, and that such short cuts can be deceptive. For example, such lexica will often reveal that the word in question could be used with different meanings. A too casual consultation of the lexicon can therefore result in a reading of the word's meaning which fuller knowledge of the language would have shown to be misperceived. More to the immediate point, it is crucial that such students always bear in mind that however short the short-cut is, it is still an indispensable few steps on the way to making sense of whatever Greek NT text is to hand.[4]

All this is simply to make the point that a considerable amount of historical critical work on the Greek text of the NT is unavoidable if it is to be read with and for meaning. Simply because that work now comes in compressed form in critical texts with textual apparatus, lexica and technical commentaries does not mean that it can be either ignored or

3. Cf. Roman Ingarden in Mueller-Vollmer, *Hermeneutics Reader*, pp. 194-95.

4. In a festal offering to John Sawyer it is presumably unnecessary to make the further observation that insofar as meaning inheres in the words of the Greek text it does so not in the words as single units, but in the words as part of a larger syntactical whole. I refer to J.F.A. Sawyer, *Semantics in Biblical Research* (London: SCM Press, 1972); for earlier discussions see Schleiermacher in Mueller-Vollmer, *Hermeneutics Reader*, pp. 86-93; Ingarden in Mueller-Vollmer, *Hermeneutics Reader*, pp. 197-205, and J. Barr, *The Semantics of Biblical Language* (Oxford: Oxford University Press, 1961).

dispensed with. Larger questions regarding authorship, sources, circumstances of composition, and so on, may be obscure. And to make meaning depend on the answers given to these questions may leave the text in effect dumb or at least able to speak in only strangled tones. But if the squiggles/signs are to form a text in the first place, if they are to grant even the possibility of meaningful communication, then the work of historical philology is a *sine qua non*. Without such basic historical criticism, a historical text in an ancient language simply cannot be a text for us today.

It is also true that modern students can have resort to modern English translations. And for any community which bases itself on a particular translation, the regularity and immediacy of communication based on the text (for example, in preaching) will often be able to treat the translation as sufficient in itself. At the same time, however, the diversity of modern translations will often raise questions as to particular meaning and potential nuance and inference, questions which can never be solved at the level of the translations themselves. Such communities will always need to be able to call on members or specialists who are familiar with the Greek text—the critically reconstructed text which in relation to the translations can properly be called 'original'.[5]

The Greek itself, of course, will often allow variations of translation, but the primary question for the community concerned by disagreement among English translations would have to be whether the diversity among the English translations falls within the limits of the variations of translation allowable by the Greek. And again such a question could not be resolved without recourse to historical critical examination of the Greek phrase or sentence in relation to the usage and conventions of the time. A reading of an English translation of the NT which wholly ignored the issue of whether the meaning read from the *English* was derivable from the underlying *Greek* would be at best irresponsible. Apart from anything else it would be discourteous to the translators themselves, since it would have been the intention of the translators to re-express the meaning of the Greek. So far as any reading of a New Testament text in English is concerned, it must be significant and in

5. The standard texts are *Biblica Hebraica Stuttgartensia* (ed. K. Elliger and W. Rudolph; Stuttgart: Deutsch Bibelgesellschaft, 1967/77, 1984) and *Novum Testamentum Graece* (ed. E. Nestle, K. Aland, *et al.*; Stuttgart: Deutsch Bibelgesellschaft, 26th edn, 1979) or *The Greek New Testament* (ed. K. Aland, *et al.*; United Bible Societies, 3rd edn, 1975).

greater or less degree determinative that the text is wholly derivative (from the Greek) and that its writer (the translator) was constrained throughout to reproduce the sense and force of the Greek.

In short, the meaning read from the NT always depends to greater or less degree on it being read as a historical text.

3. *No Reading Without 'Higher Criticism'*

What has so far been touched on used to be called 'lower criticism'—the criticism which was concerned with reconstructing the basic text itself, dividing lines of letters into syntactical units, putting the markings on the page into units of meaning. But there was also the 'higher criticism'—the criticism which was concerned with reconstructing the historical circumstances out of which the NT writings emerged.[6]

Here we need to note the further obvious fact that the meaning of a historical text is dependent in some degree on its historical context. This follows from what was said earlier. For language and culture are intermeshed. Language is a primary vehicle of culture, is culture-laden. The task of constituting the squiggles/signs of Greek lettering into a readable text inevitably involves inquiry into Greek usage of the time, and that includes awareness of idiom and of technical terminology. There will be terms which lexica show to have been distinctively Christian, but others whose function was evidently to 'plug in' to wider philosophic usage or social concerns. Without awareness of these wider factors in the historical context of the text the reader will be cut off from this whole dimension of the historical text's meaning.

The historical text, in other words, is linked to its historical context as a plant is rooted in the soil which first nourished it. The words of the text are like the innumerable small roots and tendrils which attach it to that soil. To attempt to transplant that plant by ripping it clear from its native soil and shaking it free from that soil may work, but it is likely to kill the plant. The greater horticultural wisdom is to take the plant together with the soil in which it first grew and is still rooted. That way a transplant, even in a quite different soil, is likely to have a chance of preserving the plant alive. So with a historical text. The words of a historical text root it in the historical context out of which it first grew, and unless it carries with it something at least of that historical context it is

6. In P.A. Boeckh the distinction was between 'grammatical interpretation' and 'historical interpretation' (Mueller-Vollmer, *Hermeneutics Reader*, pp. 15-17).

unlikely to survive any transplant into a different (contemporary) context. It may transmute into a different text, but then it will not be the historical text with which we are concerned.

What then of the uncertainties of historical results and the disputes between historians as to their findings?[7] These are not to be gainsaid. But neither should they be exaggerated. Here a sense of proportion and of relativity becomes important. Of course the ideal of setting a historical text fully into its historical context can never be more than an ideal. But that would only be of great moment if the objective was to recover a historical meaning conceived absolutely or punctiliarly. If on the other hand the first objective is, as it were, to hear the text as it might (would) have been heard by the body of people for whom it was written, with all the ambiguities which that historical speech act entailed, then the objective is better defined as recognizing meaning within its historical parameters, that is, recognizing both the scope and the limits of meaning which the text's historical context determined.

As advocates of the historical critical method claimed from the beginning, there is a broad parallel here with scientific method. The fact that there is today considerable debate in the scientific community about the microcosmic and macrocosmic level of reality does not diminish the large measure of consensus on more basic matters of everyday science. So with most NT study. The disagreements come primarily at the level of the overarching paradigm or the nitty-gritty detail. But the range of most of the key terms in the NT has long ago been established by the philologist and lexicographer. The contemporary texts and data most relevant to illuminating NT usage are well-known and form a consensus syllabus for NT scholars. The different genres in the NT, and the broad details of the ministry of Jesus and the mission of Paul are a matter of wide consensus. The historical text set within its historical context still provides a framework within which the finer points of detail can be discussed. Or in terms of statistical probability, if we were to try to draw the graph of a NT text's meaning, that is, in relation to the axes of the two horizons (meaning plotted in relation to both), the resulting graph would in most cases be a standard distribution curve, with most readings

7. I refer to the 'crisis in the historical critical method'; see e.g. W. Wink, *The Bible in Human Transformation* (Philadelphia: Fortress Press, 1973); and the discussions in R. Morgan and J. Barton, *Biblical Interpretation* (Oxford: Oxford University Press, 1988), chs. 6 and 7; and S.M. Schneiders, *The Revelatory Text* (San Francisco: Harper, 1991), chs. 4 and 5.

bunching in and around the middle, but with the graph tailing off on either side into increasingly improbable, exotic or maverick readings.

Are these arguments an attempt unjustifiably to privilege 'the meaning of the Greek', to limit the freedom of the text by tying it to a particular historical context? No, they simply recognize that the NT is nothing if it is not first and foremost a series of documents written in the Greek of the first-century Mediterranean world. No more can Socrates be 'liberated' from his fifth-century BCE Greek world or Gandhi from his Indian context in the first half of the twentieth century. Contemporary meanings can certainly be drawn from both great men, but if these meanings are to claim the authority of their names, repeated reference back to their historical contexts simply cannot be avoided. Contemporary readings of the NT, be they translations or expositions, can no more be exempt from repeated reference back to the 'original' Greek in which the NT as such was written and the original contexts out of which the NT documents grew.

Nor are these arguments intended to deny the possibility and viability of diverse readings of the NT texts, or to deny the role of the contemporary reader and/or interpretative community (primarily 'the Church') in the derivation of contemporary meaning from these historical texts. Of course these texts have functioned in many other contexts than the ones which gave them birth. As Christian scripture they have themselves been part of the context for creeds and confessions, for doctrinal disputes and religious wars, for innumerable creative sermons and many theological and ecclesiastical systems. And in all these contexts the NT texts have resonated with diverse sound and effect. Nevertheless, the basic facts outlined above retain their force. For the goal in all these cases has been to be 'true' to these texts, and that 'truth' can never be separated from their character as historical texts. Of course other considerations, systems, pre-understandings, gurus, reading communities can predominate in producing an agreed reading, of the NT as of any other text. But when ecclesiastical or dogmatic readings have come under question, as has often to happen in a Church describing itself as *ecclesia semper reformanda*, the primary principle of criticism which has come more and more to the fore since the Reformation has been that of historical text read in historical context.[8] And when Christians have

8. The point has been acknowledged in recent Roman Catholic discussion on the tension between scripture and tradition—both together being normative, but the latter understood as derivative from the former, *norma normans*; see e.g. the statement of

become confused as to the meaning of particular texts of scripture, a proper response has been and still is to inquire after the meaning of the text in question within its historical context. That may not provide the final determinant of meaning in any particular case, but in a historical text it cannot but be a vital constituent of meaning and indicate the scope and limit for its meaningful use. Without that the text is ever in danger of functioning merely as a puppet or a plaything.

4. *Case Study (1): The Good Samaritan*

The importance of these hermeneutical principles can be readily illustrated from the NT. That is not to say they apply equally in every case. As already noted, the character of much wisdom and parabolic teaching has a timelessness about it; and that applies not least to the tradition of Jesus' teaching. Moreover, one of the early form-critical conclusions in regard to the Jesus-tradition was how much of it had been remembered in the earliest churches without any attempt to recall the time and place of particular sayings or events; contemporary meaning was not decisively let alone solely determined by original context. And to make the meaning of such as the Pastoral letters depend on their having been written by a particular author (Paul) would fly in the face of most of the same historical critical scholarship in reference to these letters. Nevertheless the principle of reading historical text as historical text, that is in relation to historical context, remains a firm rule and norm.

Let me take first the example of one of Jesus' parables, indeed one of the best known—the Good Samaritan (Lk. 10.30-35). The story has indeed a timelessness about it which allows it to cross cultural and historical boundaries with remarkable ease. The innocent traveller/victim, the uncaring passers-by, the compassionate stranger are universal components in a basic pattern reproduced many times over. Alternatively, one could note the wide variety of meanings which have been read

the Biblical Commission on *Scripture and Christology* (1985), particular §§ 1.2.1.1 and 1.2.2.1, with its clear distinction between the language of the creeds as 'auxiliary' language, and the 'referential' language of the inspired writers, which is 'the ultimate source of revelation' (J.A. Fitzmyer, *Scripture and Christology* [London: Chapman, 1986], pp. 19-20, 57); and Schneiders, *Revelatory Text*—'Tradition is the essential context for the interpretation of scripture, but scripture is the norm by which the true and living tradition is discerned' (p. 86). For an earlier example see the assessment of John Locke by H.G. Reventlow, *The Authority of the Bible and the Rise of the Modern World* (London: SCM Press, 1984), pp. 243-85 (particularly pp. 259-60).

from its details in the course of history.[9]

But there is more to it. The details are not endlessly flexible, but as part of the story itself exercise determinative constraints on the meaning which can be read from the story. The compassionate stranger is explicitly identified as a Samaritan. And implicit in the story is some contrast between this Samaritan on the one side, and the uncaring passers-by, priest and Levite (and presumably also the victim himself) that is, as Jews, on the other. Integral to the story, therefore, is a contrast whose significance only becomes apparent when the story is set against its context. Not so much the context of the occasion on which the story was told, but the context of the times assumed by the story, that is, the well-known suspicion and hatred between Jews and Samaritans by virtue of the political and religious tensions which had marked their relationship since the return to Judea of the exiles in Babylon. Without such awareness on the part of the reader much of the point of the story is lost: that the compassionate stranger is one despised by the people of the man he helped, despised as a racial half-breed and a religious apostate.[10]

The important factor to bear in mind here is that nothing of this significance is present in the story as it stands. It is present only in the story integrated into its historical context, where the lines of living connectedness would set the bells jangling in the minds of hearers. It is present in the story only because the one who first told the story could and did assume an awareness of the historical context of first-century Palestine on the part of his hearers. Many who re-tell the parable with more modern characters (reflecting similar contemporary political and religious tensions) assume that the significance of the implicit contrast (between Samaritan and Jew) is clear enough in the story itself. But that is only because they are heirs of a long tradition of interpretation into which awareness of the historical significance of the contrast has been built. It is important to grasp the fact that that historical significance is not something which has accrued to the parable in the course of history; rather it belongs to the parable itself in its original context.[11] Without the

9. Cf. e.g. F. Kermode, *The Genesis of Secrecy: On the Interpretation of Narrative* (Cambridge, MA: Harvard University Press, 1979), pp. 34-41.

10. The point is well made, e.g., by J.D. Crossan, *In Parables: The Challenge of the Historical Jesus* (San Francisco: Harper & Row, 1973), pp. 63-64, and R.H. Stein, *An Introduction to the Parables of Jesus* (Philadelphia: Westminster Press, 1981), pp. 75-77.

11. It is not clear from his comments (*Genesis of Secrecy*, pp. 40-41)

historical context of first-century Palestine the story alone would be trite, a pot-boiler of little merit and hardly worth remembering.

Moreover, within a first-century Jewish context the juxtaposition of temple (priest and Levite) and presumably bloodied, near-dead victim, would set some other bells jangling. For in Jewish ears temple spoke primarily of purity and holiness, whereas blood and corpse would speak at once of impurity. That is to say, set within its original first-century context, the story implies that a primary reason for both priest and Levite to ignore the injured man was the possibility of their contracting blood or corpse impurity. The point would be all the more poignant since the priest is described as 'going down from Jerusalem', that is, presumably, having completed his service in the temple, whereas it was primarily for participation in the temple cult that purity was required. The implication, in other words, is that even in these circumstances, the avoidance of blood or corpse impurity took higher priority for the priest than helping the injured man or even checking whether he needed help.

When read against this context, the context of purity concerns within late Second Temple Judaism, the story thus gains the further dimension of a criticism of those who put cultic fitness above mercy, personal purity above the imperative of good neighbourliness. Now this dimension of the story is open to more dispute than the first,[12] and less familiar to most contemporary interpreters, despite the fact that the two who are criticized both happen to be temple functionaries—an important, but neglected clue. The point is, however, that such a clue can only be elucidated, once again, by reference to the context of the times. In this case that means by drawing in information about the place of the temple within the lives of first-century Palestinian Jews, which would be enough to heighten awareness of purity issues for those who centred their lives and religious meaning on the temple. The fact that this dimension is so often missed simply indicates that this feature of the story-in-context has been largely forgotten or ignored, in contrast to the feature of the Jew/Samaritan contrast. Yet to miss this second (temple/purity) dimension may deprive the parable of some of its vital force and prevent re-tellings of the parable in more modern contexts from having their full effect.

that Kermode has fully recognized this.

12. J. Jeremias, *The Parables of Jesus* (London: SCM Press, 1963), pp. 203-204; B.B. Scott, *Hear Then the Parable: A Commentary on the Parables of Jesus* (Minneapolis: Fortress Press, 1989), pp. 195-97.

The parable thus illustrates an important feature of historical text in historical context. That is the extent to which full meaning of so many texts depends on the allusions and echoes within the text which will be audible only to those who are familiar with the text's context.[13] It is the character of a group of any coherency, whether social or religious or national, to have a level of discourse which is meaningful to itself but may be quite meaningless to those outside the group (the 'interpretive community'). At this level of discourse communication is achieved by allusion to what the group takes for granted. It is part of the bonding power of that discourse that it functions by means of allusion, as a kind of secret language; if the allusions had to be spelled out, their bonding power would be broken and the boundary between insider and outsider breached. In such a case only when the group's language has been informed by the traditions which constitute the group will that language communicate to those outside the group. So also in the case of a historical text which brings to expression in any degree the character of the group which formed it. Only when the taken-for-granteds and allusions integral to the text (or should we say, integral to the text in its native context) are heard can the full force of the text be appreciated. Which is to say, only when the text has been set as fully as possible within its historical context can it really be heard in the first place.

For all its seeming freedom from a particular historical context and adaptability to different times, settings and social contexts, then, the parable of the Good Samaritan is still a historical text whose power grows out of its close correlation with the historical context in which it was first told.

5. *Case Study (2): The Pauline Letters*

A second illustration is provided by the Pauline letters, the earliest of the NT writings, which in effect provide the heart of Christian theology. What makes them stand out from the other NT writings is the fact that they are letters, and letters from a known author, writing to churches which he had founded or many of whose members he knew well. We

13. Cf. already Schleiermacher: 'Allusions always involve a second meaning, and if a reader does not catch this second meaning along with the first, he misses one of the intended meanings...An allusion occurs when an additional meaning is so entwined with the main train of thought that the author believes it would be easily recognized by another person' (Mueller-Vollmer, *Hermeneutics Reader*, pp. 78-79).

therefore have the possibility of setting these writings much more closely into historical context and into the immediate historical context than in any of the other NT documents. Which is just as well, because as genuine letters, as distinct from collections of Jesus-tradition or more general treatises, they belong as texts much more closely to their historical context.[14] What this means becomes clear when we take into account two of the primary features of these letters.[15]

The first is the fact that they are personal letters, intensely personal letters. The first-person singular personal pronoun occurs in Romans, Corinthians, Galatians and Philippians alone more than 300 times. The personal testimony of such passages as Gal. 1.13-16, 1 Cor. 15.8-10 and 2 Cor. 12.1-10 gives invaluable insights into Paul's self-understanding. And the strong personal emotion of such passages as Rom. 3.7-8, 9.1-3, and Phil. 1.15-26 gives the letters an unsurpassedly poignant tone. This personal quality is part of the character of these letters and any attempt to 'liberate' them from their author would inevitably destroy something of that character.

An inescapable question for any hermeneutical treatment of these letters, therefore, is the extent to which the personal concerns and individuality of Paul's thought and style have shaped each letter. Fortunately the letters themselves give quite an amount of personal information about Paul himself. In individual cases that would, of course, lock us into a hermeneutical circle, where it would be impossible to get from assumed author to real author. But the fact that we have at least seven genuine letters (according to a widespread scholarly consensus), written at different times and to different churches and situations, enables us to gain a sort of triangulation 'fix' on Paul himself. And the degree of correlation between the letters and the account of Paul in Acts is sufficient to reassure us that the Paul of the letters is indeed the real Paul.

Among the most important of these personal issues was evidently Paul's self-understanding of himself as an Israelite called by God to fulfil Israel's mission as a light to the Gentiles, an eschatological apostleship without which God's purpose for Jew, Gentile and the world would not be fulfilled (see e.g. Rom. 1.5; 11.1, 13-15; 1 Cor. 4.9). But whatever the

14. It is significant that Moore's review of the impact of literary criticism (narrative criticism and reader response) in NT studies is limited to the Gospels and Acts.

15. For what follows see further my 'Prolegomena to a Theology of Paul', *NTS* 40 (1994), pp. 407-32.

precise details on such points, the basic point is beyond dispute: that Paul was both theologian and missionary, and that the two roles were symbiotic in his writing as well as in his life. Certainly it would be a mistake to treat the Pauline letters as dispassionate treatises on abstract theories and doctrines. For they are nothing if they are not the outpouring from the heart of one who was totally involved in and committed to his work and to his churches, and for whom the letters were an indispensable expression of these concerns.

The other inescapable feature of these letters is the fact that they were all written to particular churches, and written by one who knew them well (he had founded most of them). Moreover, they were written primarily as pastoral letters, to deal with issues and problems which had arisen within these churches or matters which were of major practical concern to the members of these churches—including Romans, the one indisputed Pauline letter written to a church which Paul had not himself founded. This means that they all reflect in one degree or other the historical circumstances, the tensions and concerns of these churches at the time of writing. More important, the letters all take something at least of their shape and content from these circumstances, or to be more precise, from Paul's appreciation of these circumstances and of the need to address them. But if that is so, then it follows at once that these letters cannot be fully appreciated unless the reader knows something of these circumstances, something at least of their historical context.

The Pauline letters, as genuine letters, are for us rather like a telephone conversation, where we can hear only one end of the conversation. Many of their remarks will in fact be replies to questions or points put from the other end which we have not heard, and whole sentences and paragraphs will be shaped in form and content to address these questions and points. In most cases we gain enough from the end of the conversation that we can hear to make sense of what we do hear. Not least of importance here is the fact that many of the key issues seem to have focused on how common heritage, particularly of Jewish and Christian tradition, should be interpreted—issues like God's way of 'righteousing' people, what apostleship involves, the Jewish law, what moral standards are to be maintained, and the coming of Christ. But we know something about these subjects from elsewhere in Jewish and Christian writings. In other words, we have a larger context which informs the more immediate context which brought these letters forth. The point is, however, that some degree of filling out that context is going to be necessary; we can only make sense of our end of the conversation by reconstructing something at least of the other end of the conversation.

Alternatively expressed, the Pauline letters can be treated as a sort of mirror, from which we can read the reflection of the situation addressed by the letter. Fortunately, the art of 'mirror reading' is now well developed and has been long practised; maverick reconstructions do not stand the test of time, and there is sufficient consensus on the main features.[16] Once again, however, the point for us is that if it were not for something of the sort, if we were totally to ignore their mirror-like character, their letter/conversation character, we would have to resign ourselves to many inexplicable jumps in the argument or be forced to fill these gaps in from our own, unhistorically formed imagination. Without hearing the Pauline letters with their original historical context in mind, we prevent ourselves from hearing them as what they claim to be—genuine letters.

In the case of such letters the allusions could be much more personal, echoes of what had been said on a previous visit, shared memories, common interests. Still more than in the parable of the Good Samaritan, the unspoken taken-for-granteds of friends and 'brothers' could fill out undeveloped references, a train of common associations could be triggered by a key word or phrase, the well of shared faith and aspiration could be drawn on by a partial citation of hymnic or credal formula. Only those who actually stood or sat in gatherings where the letters were first read out, those for whom the letters were actually written, will have been able to appreciate their full scope. Of course, many or most of these allusions will be unrecoverable for modern readers (who today can be sure what Paul meant in 1 Cor. 15.29 by 'baptism on behalf of the dead'). But some at least are recognizable by setting the letter in historical context, immediate context within broader historical context, and without some awareness of these contexts any reading of the letter is immeasurably impoverished. The point is that any search for intertextual echoes must not confine itself to literary texts or texts that happen to have come down to us. The primary 'text' for such echoes is the historical context of the original letters.

All this means that the exegete of the Pauline letters cannot escape the question of authorial intention. For as letters they are nothing if they are not Paul's attempt to influence the readers for whom they were written.

16. See, e.g., J.M.G. Barclay, 'Mirror Reading a Polemical Letter: Galatians as a Test Case', *JSNT* 31 (1987), pp. 73-93.

That is not at all to deny their literary character. On the contrary, an awareness of the rhetorical tricks and devices by which first-century speakers and writers gained the attention of their audiences (the letters were written, after all, to be read out to listening congregations) is also part of the historical context which informs a historical reading of such a text.[17] Nor is it to deny that within canonical scripture these letters have functioned in a different context and exerted influence such as Paul could never have imagined.[18] But it does mean that any reading of these texts which does not recognize their personal character, their idiosyncrasies, their directedness to particular church situations, and does not attempt some correlation between Paul's intended effect and the reading proposed is to that extent disqualified as a reading of a personal letter.

6. *Case Study (3): The Anti-Judaism of John's Gospel*

A third illustration comes from the Fourth Gospel. It relates to the today highly sensitive issue of whether John's Gospel is anti-semitic or anti-Jewish. Such a charge is very difficult to escape from if the Gospel is read as though unrelated to its historical context. Once historical context is ignored, any reading of the text conscious of Jewish sensitivities is almost bound to conclude that the text is anti-Jewish.

The problem is easily posed. There is throughout the Gospel a sustained polemic against 'the Jews', particularly from ch. 5 onwards: 'the Jews persecuted Jesus'; 'the Jews sought all the more to kill Jesus'; 'the Jews sought to kill him'; 'for fear of the Jews no one spoke openly of him'; 'the Jews answered him, "Are we not right in saying that you... have a demon?"'; etc. (5.16, 18; 7.1, 13; 8.48). Most horrific is Jesus'

17. The pioneering study of H.D. Betz, *Galatians* (Hermeneia; Philadelphia: Fortress Press, 1979) opened up a line of exegesis which is still being fruitfully pursued. Narrative criticism has also found somewhat unexpected scope, as evident particularly in R.B. Hays, *The Faith of Jesus Christ: An Investigation of the Narrative Substructure of Galatians 3.1–4.11* (SBLDS; Chico, CA: Scholars Press, 1983), and N.R. Petersen, *Rediscovering Paul: Philemon and the Sociology of Paul's Narrative World* (Philadelphia: Fortress Press, 1985). Less fruitful has been the attempt to apply structural analysis to Paul—D. Patte, *Paul's Faith and the Power of the Gospel: A Structural Introduction to the Pauline Letters* (Philadelphia: Fortress Press, 1983).

18. Particular mention should be made of B.S. Childs, *The New Testament as Canon* (Philadelphia: Fortress Press, 1984).

denunciation of the Jews in ch. 8: 'You are of your father the devil, and your will is to do your father's desires' (8.44). Indicative of the power of such texts has been their baleful influence in encouraging and justifying Christian anti-semitism for the last eighteen centuries. Or to be more accurate, that is the way they have been read for the last eighteen centuries. Be it noted, it was the text (John's Gospel) read without reference to original historical context which was so understood. The text understood canonically, within the context of the Christian canon, did not prevent it being read anti-semitically. The text read by the magisterium or within the context of the Christian church(es) did not prevent it both feeding and feeding upon a virulent strain of Christian anti-Judaism.

The problem is so serious, and the despair so profound over such a deeply entrenched reading of the Gospel, that many can see no solution other than radical, emasculating surgery. For some that means urging as a policy that texts like Jn 8.44 should be excluded from Christian lectionaries. Others, in penance for the centuries of Christian anti-semitism and continuing revulsion against the Holocaust, urge that 'the Jews' in passages like those cited above should no longer be translated as such but be put into English as 'the Judeans', or rendered with paraphrases which remove any possible inference that the Jewish people as a whole were in view.[19] But is the solution to a negative reading of such an important and foundational Christian text not to read it at all, or to modify the bits we don't like?

Part of the answer is provided by the text itself. For a careful reading of the text as a whole reveals that the phrase 'the Jews' is not in fact used with unrelieved hostility to the body so designated. On the contrary, there is an equally prominent motif where 'the Jews' denote an ambivalent, neutral group (also described as 'the crowd') in between Jesus and his opponents. And indeed, a major feature of the drama which the Gospel skillfully unfolds is the tug-of-war for the loyalty of 'the(se) Jews' (6.52; 7.11-13, 15, 31, 35, 40, 43; 8.31; 10.19-21; etc.). 'The [hostile] Jews' are evidently a group within the wider Jewish community. Most striking here is the fact that on several occasions those

19. See, e.g., N.A. Beck, *Mature Christianity: The Recognition and Repudiation of the Anti-Jewish Polemic of the New Testament* (London/Toronto: Associated University Presses, 1985), ch. 9, and the discussion by R.A. Culpepper, 'The Gospel of John as a Threat to Jewish-Christian Relations', in *Overcoming Fear Between Jews and Christians* (ed. J.H. Charlesworth; New York: Crossroad, 1992), pp. 21-43.

who are clearly Jews themselves, and who belong to 'the [ambivalent] Jews', are distinguished from 'the [hostile] Jews' (e.g. 7.13; 9.22).

So even a reading of John's Gospel sensitive to the literary character of the text (as an unfolding drama) should have cautioned against a straightforward anti-Jewish reading. However, it would appear that this caution has not been heard, not at least as the text was read through the centuries. Nor does it seem to have been picked up in contemporary readings whose primary objective has been to reflect the internal dynamic of the text. Which suggests that the integrity of the text in itself has not been sufficient to prevent anti-semitic readings. That could, of course, mean that the text itself is integrally anti-Jewish. But before that conclusion is drawn, with its devastating consequences for Christian self-understanding, the issue at the heart of the present paper needs to be posed: whether the text read within its historical context provides an effective alternative. I believe it does so.[20]

For one thing the historical context makes sense of the double strand of reference to 'the Jews'. There is a broad consensus in modern scholarship that the Gospel reflects a situation (most clearly in ch. 9) where the still largely Jewish Johannine church(es) were under pressure from local Jewish authorities to choose between their belief in Jesus as Messiah and their continuing membership of the synagogue community (9.22).[21] It is also evident from the Gospel itself that the make or break issue had become the growing Christian conviction of the deity of Jesus (1.14-18; 6.18; 10.33; 20.28). This situation first emerged in the period after the first Jewish revolt when nascent rabbinic Judaism began to draw the boundaries of Judaism more tightly so as to exclude other Jewish groups, not just Nazarenes (Christians), whom they regarded as *minim* (heretics). In this situation the tension between 'the [hostile] Jews' and 'the [ambivalent] Jews' is an *intra*-Jewish tension, and not yet between Christians (who no longer regard themselves as Jews) and the Jewish people as a whole. To read the Gospel in the latter way is to read it anachronistically and so to import tensions into it from another period.

20. For what follows see further my *The Partings of the Ways between Christianity and Judaism* (London: SCM/Philadelphia: TPI, 1991), ch. 8; fuller version in 'The Question of Anti-semitism in the New Testament Writings of the Period', in *Jews and Christians: The Parting of the Ways* AD *70 to 135* (ed. J.D.G. Dunn; Tübingen: Mohr, 1992), pp. 177-211.

21. The consensus has been expressed most influentially by J.L. Martyn, *History and Theology in the Fourth Gospel* (Nashville: Abingdon, 1968: revised 1979).

The other important point which emerges from the text being set within its own historical context is the light it sheds on the character and seriousness of the polemic used in the text. In times gone by, up until the Enlightenment in fact, and beyond, religious polemic was a good deal more black and white and denunciatory than those touched in any measure by a more liberal tradition find it easy to recognize. The Qumran covenanters denounced fellow Jews as 'sons of Belial' (4QFlor. 1.8). The Testament of Dan warns the children of Dan that 'your prince is Satan' (*T. Dan* 5.6). Jesus denounces Cephas/Peter as 'Satan' (Mt. 16.23/Mk 8.33). And Paul denounced other 'apostles of Christ' as 'servants of Satan' (2 Cor. 11.13-15). In other words, this is the language of internal as well as of factional disputation and exhortation. It is only when removed from that context, its own historical context, that it can become (misleadingly) absolutized. And it is only by being read within that context that the tensions of the literary (and, in the background, real life) drama can be retained in balance and the power of the drama, and of 'the Jews' within it, can be properly appreciated.

To read the Gospel as a denunciation of the Jewish nation, then, is not to read it autonomously but to read it against a later historical context when anti-Judaism as such had become rife within Christianity. The fact is that no text of the extent and character of John's Gospel can actually be read without some historical context, and in John's case, if not the historical context of the original document, then the context of later church tradition or that of the modern reader. It is not least to save a historical text like John's Gospel from being read surreptitiously against undeclared, anachronistic historical contexts that it is necessary to emphasize the integral importance of the original historical context. Given the uncertainties which inevitably attend any reconstruction of historical context, historical text within historical context is not going to be a sufficient safeguard against abuse of the text. But without continuous reference to its own historical context it is difficult to see how abuse of such a historical text can be avoided.

7. *Conclusion*

This, then, is my very basic thesis: that the bulk of the NT documents are historical texts which are, in differing degrees, so integrally related to their original historical contexts that they cannot adequately be understood without reference to these historical contexts. As historical texts their historical context is in a critical measure subsumed within the text, so that exposition of the text is bound to depend on some awareness of that historical context, of the light it sheds on word and concept, on meaning and usage, on syntax and idiom, on patterns of thought forms, on cultural and social assumptions, on the implicit taken-for-granteds and the deliberate allusions, on the traditions being echoed and promoted, subtly as well as openly, and the traditions being disputed and set aside, on the faith being proclaimed in the context of the times.

Apart from anything else, it is respect for text in historical context which makes it possible for a historical text to retain its otherness (its historical autonomy, we could perhaps say). For its otherness is primarily its historical otherness, the otherness which historical distance gives to a historical text. Its integrity as a text is not independent of its historical context, and will be insufficient in itself to prevent abuse from those who read it willy-nilly against another context. In short, the first and most important rule of exegesis of a historical text is that it be read as much as possible in reference and relation to the historical context within which and for which it was originally composed or put together.

Is this, the question may be asked once more, to privilege one possible meaning of such a text unfairly? No! Partly because incompleteness of historical information and the nature of historical method leave a degree of uncertainty as to a text's meaning and thus leave open a range of meaning. What it does mean is that text in context provides parameters of meaning beyond which the suspicion of hermeneutical abuse grows steadily stronger.

Alternatively, is this to privilege unfairly the historical exegete, the specialist in the language of the text, to make meaning of NT documents dependent on esoteric knowledge of Hebrew idiom and Greek syntax? No, not the historical exegete, but historical exegesis. For if I am right historical exegesis has indeed an indispensable role, as I hope I have made clear. But the whole point of lexica and technical commentaries is to disperse such specialist information more widely. If I am right, *everyone* who seeks to expound or use such a text responsibly needs to take account of text in context, in however modest degree, by using the tools which it has been for many decades the task of specialist scholarship to provide and which it is the ongoing task of specialist scholarship to update.

The importance of thus recognizing a historical text's historical otherness is that it helps maintain the character of the interpretative process as a dialogue, a dialogue between the text in its historical otherness and its subsequent interpreters. In this dialogue it is the task of the historical specialist to help the text speak for itself, to liberate it *not* by freeing it *from* its historical context, but by freeing it *within* its historical context, to speak in its own tone and terms, the tone and terms of its own time. Of course, that is only one side of the dialogue, and the outcome of the dialogue, that is, the way the text relates to or is used in reference to later or contemporary issues, is not settled thereby. In that sense the meaning perceived in a NT text in relation to any contemporary situation is not to be regarded as a contest of skills, but rather as a cooperative effort. The only point I wish to stress is that if that meaning is to be the outcome of genuine dialogue with a historical text, it must be with the historical text as a historical text.[22]

22. I am grateful to Terry Wright (Newcastle) and Tony Thiselton (Nottingham) for reading and commenting helpfully on a first draft of this paper. The persisting defects, of course, can be credited only to me.

THE NEW TESTAMENT IN FICTION AND FILM: A BIBLICAL SCHOLAR'S PERSPECTIVE

W.R. Telford

Introduction

The Literary and Cultural Influence of the Bible

In his magisterial work, *The Great Code: The Bible and Literature,* the Canadian literary critic Northrop Frye posed the following question with respect to the Bible: 'Why does this huge, sprawling, tactless book sit there inscrutably in the middle of our cultural heritage...frustrating all our efforts to walk around it?'(1982: xviii-xix). Frye himself supplies an answer to this question by extolling the imaginative energy which has flowed from the Bible to creative minds for centuries. That, for him, is the Bible's great legacy.

One such creative mind was D.H. Lawrence. Despite the ambivalent feelings he harboured towards the Bible, Lawrence acknowledged his considerable literary debt to it. In his *Apocalypse*, for example, he gives an account of his attitude to the Bible and in particular of the influence of the Revelation of John upon him.

> I was brought up on the Bible, and seem to have it in my bones. From early childhood I have been familiar with Apocalyptic language and Apocalyptic image: not because I spent my time reading Revelation, but because I was sent to Sunday School and to Chapel, to Band of Hope and to Christian Endeavour, and was always having the Bible read at me or to me. I did not even listen attentively. But language has a power of echoing and re-echoing in my unconscious mind...And so the sound of Revelation had registered in me very early, and I was as used to: 'I was in the Spirit on the Lord's day, and heard behind me a great voice, as of a trumpet, saying: I am the Alpha and the Omega'—as I was to a nursery rhyme like Little Bo-Peep! (1980: 54-55)

Both these examples suffice to reinforce the point that the Bible is part and parcel of our literary and cultural heritage (as well as our religious one) and account must, therefore, be taken of it.

The Aims of the Essay

Several years ago, *The Independent* featured an article intimating the forthcoming production of Jean Binnie's play, *Heaven and Earth*, at Battersea Arts Centre, London (3 Dec—12 Jan, 1992) (Hemming 1991). The play places its author in a long tradition of attempts to stage the Bible. Binnie, it was reported, found in the Old Testament a combination of the topical and the archaic: 'It keeps having resonances'. On the magnitude of the enterprise, however, she commented almost despairingly: 'When I finished the first draft I was still in Genesis!'

I can sympathize with both these sentiments having embarked on an ambitious topic 'The New Testament in Fiction and Film'. My aims in this essay (which was first given as a public lecture at the University of Newcastle upon Tyne, 28 October, 1993) will be threefold: (a) to comment on contemporary interest in the Bible (in particular the New Testament) in the area of fiction and film, and to note some current developments, both popular and academic, in the field; (b) to consider some key fiction and film texts which merit attention and (c) to offer some reflections from a biblical scholar's perspective on the value of this subject. I write, I should say, as one whose native approach to the New Testament is historical-critical but who has come lately to literary approaches to the Bible through my study of the Gospel of Mark. I should also confess my longstanding love of the cinema! It is a particular pleasure, moreover, to dedicate this essay to my colleague John Sawyer from whom I have learned that biblical scholars should be as much concerned with the cultural reception and use of the Bible as with the historical-critical analysis of the texts.

The Bible/New Testament in Fiction and Film: Contemporary Interest and Developments

The Bible and/as Literature in Recent Scholarship

Academic studies on the Bible as literature or on the Bible's influence on western literary tradition or culture are too numerous to mention but such works in the seventies as T.R. Henn's *The Bible as Literature* (1970), a book which was a development of an article in *Peake's Commentary on the Bible* (1962), and H. Schneidau's *Sacred Discontent: the Bible and Western Tradition* (1976) should be noted. In the last decade, the field has been enriched not only by Frye's *The Great Code* (1982), previously referred to, but also most recently by the work of scholars such as S. Prickett (compare, for example, *Words and 'the Word'* [1986]), R. Alter and F. Kermode (compare, for example, *The Literary Guide to the Bible* [1987]), D. Jasper (compare, for example, *The New Testament and the Literary Imagination* [1987]) and T.R. Wright (compare, for example, *Theology and Literature* [1988]), to mention but a few. Works illuminating the history of the subject, such as D.A. Norton, *A History of the Bible as Literature* (1993), or exploring intertextual links, such as D.L. Jeffrey (ed.), *A Dictionary of Biblical Tradition in English Literature* (1992) are already proving invaluable.

As evidence of a growing interest in this general area, a related development on the British scene is the establishment of a Centre for the Study of Literature and Theology, formerly based in Durham but now transferred to Glasgow under the direction of Dr David Jasper. The Centre runs an MA in the subject and has also sponsored since the spring of 1987 a journal, *Literature and Theology*. The experimental North American journal *Semeia,* which is devoted to new and emergent areas and methods of biblical criticism and is sponsored by the Society of Biblical Studies, also promotes interdisciplinary study of the Bible and literature. Following the lead provided by Glasgow, my own University of Newcastle has launched in 1994 an MA in Religion and Literature which is taught jointly by the Departments of English and Religious Studies.

The Gospels

1. *The Canonical Gospels (especially Mark).* For those of us who have been taught to ask historical questions first and foremost of the Bible and especially of the New Testament, and to seek to establish the original context and meaning of the biblical text, the revolution created in New Testament scholarship over the last twenty or thirty years by the application of the newer literary approaches has been remarkable. Many insights have been gained by treating the New Testament texts as literary compositions in the first instance rather than as historical documents. Nowhere has this been more apparent than in the study of the canonical Gospels where there has been a strong emphasis on the gospel text as story and a serious regard for its narrative qualities. The Gospels have been analysed with the same tools as are applied to works of fiction. Approaches to the Gospels from a literary perspective have emphasized, among other things, the story line, settings, characters and plot as well as the literary or rhetorical technique, point of view or effect upon the reader.

In the case of the Gospel of Mark, there has been a recent reappraisal of the aims, influences and achievements of Mark as a creative writer and theologian (Telford 1985; 1990; 1994). It is now not uncommon to treat the text as a unified narrative (Kelber 1979; Kermode 1979; Rhoads and Michie 1982), to view it as a mythic narrative or folktale (Drury 1987), or even, drawing upon our present century's fascination with the movies, to posit cinematic montage (i.e. the production of a rapid succession of images to illustrate an association of ideas) as a clue to the unravelling of its literary and theological composition and unity (Zwick 1989).

2. *The Apocryphal Gospels (including the Gnostic Gospels).* That our canonical Gospels may be as much a product of literary artifice and theological imagination as of sober history has not been always been generally acceptable, and yet when we consider that other body of gospel texts not included in the New Testament, the apocryphal Gospels, the conclusion that they are largely works of fiction has long been a common one. The study of these latter texts (Hennecke and Schneemelcher 1963; Robinson 1977; Pagels 1979) has thrown light on the remarkable degree of literary and religious embellishment which they evince, a creativity clearly produced by the operation of imagination upon received traditions. As proof of this, one might compare E. Moltmann-Wendel's use of these texts (1982) to review and analyse the traditions that have grown up around the women associated in the canonical Gospels with Jesus, especially Mary Magdalene (ch. 3). In this respect it is now more reasonable to question whether the differences between the apocryphal Gospels and their canonical cousins are really a matter of *kind* and not merely of *degree*.

One function of these texts was surely to make up for gaps in early Christian tradition and to satisfy a widespread desire for more information concerning the origins of the faith, of its founding members and of its principal cult figure who never, as far as we know, wrote anything (a lacuna which has been filled many times since, as the most recent attempt, J. Sarramango's *The Gospel according to Jesus Christ* [1993] attests). Something similar doubtless also explains contemporary popular interest in the discovery of new sources, whether actual (like the Dead Sea Scrolls) or putative, and with books or novels which purport to be based on such. Everyone, it appears, wishes to get into the act. One such example appeared in 1975 as *The Jesus Scroll,* a popular (non-fiction!)

attempt by D. Joyce which sought to argue, on the basis of a scroll allegedly written by Jesus himself and smuggled out of Masada, that the founder of Christianity did not die on the cross, saw his son crucified instead (the child of his marriage to Mary Magdalene) and lived on to join the Zealots in their last defiant stand at Masada. The author was described by his publisher as a radio and television writer by profession who 'builds eighteenth-century ship models, types with one finger and drinks Dewar's'. The plot of the book is familiar and, with variations, much repeated.

The New Testament and Fiction

1. *Recent Scholarship.* Biblical scholars have traditionally tended to view with disdain such popular and bowdlerized versions of their discipline and to draw a sharp line between the meaning of the Bible and the history of its interpretation, whether in literary or cinematic representation. A new book by L. Kreitzer, *The New Testament in Fiction and Film: On Reversing the Hermeneutical Flow* (1993) may be a harbinger of change, being one of the first attempts by a New Testament scholar to approach the New Testament through literature and film. Literary or film texts may either re-present the Bible or embody biblical ideas, themes or motifs and Kreitzer is concerned with both. The book treats *Spartacus*, *Ben Hur*, *Barabbas*, *Dr Jekyll and Mr Hyde* and *The Trial*, and its major claim is that the study of literature and film based on the New Testament can help 'reverse the hermeneutical flow' in that such a study opens up fresh perspectives and raises new questions which the exegete can take back to the text.

2. *Some Contemporary Novels.* The range of contemporary novels which deal in some fashion with the Bible is too vast to summarize, but three, on which we shall shortly be saying more, offer imaginative treatments of the canonical and apocryphal Gospels, viz. N. Kazantzakis, *The Last Temptation* (1961), G. Theissen, *The Shadow of the Galilean* (1987) and M. Roberts, *The Wild Girl* (1984). All three are serious works the study of which will repay the biblical scholar in terms of the 'fresh perspectives' and 'new questions' they engender.

In some cases the treatment of the New Testament by contemporary novels has been less than complimentary to sacred history. A noteworthy example is *Live from Golgotha* (1992), Gore Vidal's new classic of 'the greatest story never told'. *Live from Golgotha* is to the Christ novel what *Life of Brian* is to the Christ film. It is a spoof involving computer tapes of the gospel story which are threatened by a cyber-punk 'The Hacker'. The narrator is Timothy and it is his version of the story which is attempted. Here are presented familiar New Testament characters in unfamiliar guises or actions (Paul as a tap-dancing gay, Jesus as a brilliant businessman with a weight problem, Nero as the perpetrator of date rape against Timothy, etc.) The topical and the archaic interpenetrate as, for example, in the sending of a NBC TV crew to pre-record the crucifixion, *live from Golgotha*, in order to boost ratings. According to one reviewer, an Irish bishop, a Conservative British MP and the Vatican press have all denounced Vidal for blasphemy. 'He is ever the restless bull in the china shop of conventional wisdom' but being also 'a serious student of history... Vidal can lampoon the New Testament because he knows the Bible and Roman history' (Duffy 1992: 58).

The Bible/New Testament and Film

1. *Developments in the Academic Field*

(i) *Recent Scholarship.* Although it remains a minority interest, the area of film and its relation to the Bible, as well as to theology (Hurley 1970; 1978), religion (Butler 1969; Blake 1991; May 1992) or the church (Wall 1971), is beginning to attract a growing number of scholars. A multitude of aids are available for study of the cinema whether general reference works (Hochman 1974; Thompson 1975; Quinlan 1983; Halliwell 1985; 1988), books on film theory (Deleuze 1986) or specialized treatments of the transcendent in film (Schrader 1972; Jackson 1990). In the last decade, a number of useful tools or collections have appeared such as R.H. and M.R. Campbell's, *The Bible on Film: A Checklist, 1897–1980* (1981) or the series of essays in J.R. May and M.S. Bird (eds.), *Religion in Film* (1982). Some recent specialized treatments have dealt with the biblical epic (Forshey 1992) or the Christ film (Malone 1990). Prominent among these is B. Babington and P. Evans's newly published *Biblical Epics: Sacred Narrative in the Hollywood Cinema* (1993), the first major survey and analysis of the relationship between religion and film in the Hollywood cinema (including, in Part Two, the Christ film). The same year also saw the publication of R. Jewett's *Saint Paul at the Movies: The Apostle's Dialogue with American Culture* (1989; 1992; 1993), a fresh and interesting book analysing the way themes in Pauline theology are to be detected in a series of recent secular films (viz. *Star*

Wars, Amadeus, A Separate Peace, Tender Mercies, Grand Canyon, Tootsie, Ordinary People, Empire of the Sun, Pale Rider, Red Dawn, Dead Poet's Society).

(ii) *Film Courses.* The growing interest in the Bible and the cinema within academia is also a function of the popularity of film studies in general on campus. More and more universities, it seems, are presenting film courses for a generation of students who are film-literate in a way their predecessors were not. In Chicago, for example, Robert Jewett, together with his colleague, David Rhoads, offers a course entitled 'Biblical Interpretation and Contemporary Film'. According to its syllabus (Fall Quarter, 1992), this course makes a study of the hermeneutical method of relating New Testament texts to contemporary films and aims to help students to develop skills in the interpretation of film, with particular attention to theological and biblical dimensions. Dissertations on the subject are emerging (Crain 1991). Such an interest is also apparent at my own University of Newcastle upon Tyne where Film Studies is a popular option in our Combined Honours programme and two MAs have been launched, one devoted exclusively to the general subject and another, previously mentioned, on 'Religion and Literature', which has a religion and film component.

(iii) *Excavating Cecil B. De Mille.* One example, though perhaps a rather whimsical one, of the seriousness with which the subject of the Bible and film is now taken, appeared in a *Sunday Telegraph* article several years ago (Bygrave 1991). There it was reported that plans were underway to uncover Cecil B. De Mille's Egyptian city, Karnak. The city—a film set—was constructed in the sands of California for his silent epic *The Ten Commandments* (1923) and at that time was the largest film set ever built. A documentary was to be made of the dig which was to be supervised by academics of the University of California using the same techniques as would be used on any archaeological site. De Mille, who had the set buried, had himself made a playful reference in his autobiography to archaeologists digging up the set. When asked for comment on the enterprise, the documentary film-maker responsible for the idea, Peter Brosnan, declared: 'A lot of people think what we are doing is silly. Of course it's silly. We're excavating an Egyptian city in the middle of California...[but] we're trying to save a rare and precious piece of film history'.

2. *Popular Interest and the Media*

(i) *The Hollywood Biblical Epic.* The role of the Bible in the history of film has been, as this example also serves to remind us, a not inconsiderable one. Despite the scorn often directed at the biblical epic, this particular genre, as well as being popular, has been influential in the development of the cinema, particularly in the hands of its great practitioners like D.W. Griffith and Cecil B. De Mille. Herein lies the great value of Babington and Evans's *Biblical Epics* (1993). Both treat the genre with seriousness and expose the banality of what passes for criticism of it. Their interest lies 'in the social and intellectual functioning of religion' (p. 22) and they examine with sharp insight how ethnicity, sexuality and gender as well as religion have had their effect upon the genre. Three sub-types of the biblical epic are analysed: the Old Testament epic, the Christ film and the Roman/Christian epic with its presentation of early Christianity. The 'life and death' of the genre is traced and accounted for from its heyday in the twenties, its lapse in the thirties and forties, its recovery and 'golden age' in the fifties and its rapid decline thereafter. This decline may not be considered to be terminal, however, given the interest shown in the eighties in such films as Bruce Beresford's *King David* (1985), Martin Scorsese's *The Last Temptation of Christ* (1988) or Denys Arcand's *Jesus of Montreal* (1989). Indeed a recent issue of *Sight and Sound* reported that on 4 October, 1993, the sixty-two year-old Italian director, Ermanno Olmi (*The Tree of Wooden Clogs,* 1977, etc.), had begun work on yet another film version of the Bible—John Huston had embarked on a similar project when he was fifty-eight—with an episode appropriately entitled 'La creazione'. For the Passover/Easter season (1994), American television (TNT) screened a four-hour film epic, *Abraham* with Richard Harris as Abraham and Barbara Hershey as Sarah (Lambert 1994). A few years ago, too, the controversial director of such films as *Robocop* (1987), Paul Verhoeven, was reported as intending to make a film on Jesus based on the results of R.W. Funk's equally controversial Jesus Seminar.

(ii) *The Christ Film.* Within the genre of the biblical epic, the Christ film has always occupied a significant and popular place. The Hollywood Life of Christ (compare such films as De Mille's *King of Kings* [1927]; Nicholas Ray's *King of Kings* [1961]; George Stevens's *The Greatest Story Ever Told* [1965] and Martin Scorsese's *The Last Temptation of*

Christ [1988]) is characterized, according to Babington and Evans, by its directness of presentation (1993: 98). Other indirect but no less compelling forms, however, have been in evidence, such as the musical (compare Norman Jewison's *Jesus Christ Superstar* [1973] or David Greene's *Godspell* [1973]) or the modern allegory (compare Stuart Rosenberg's *Cool Hand Luke* [1967] or again Arcand's *Jesus of Montreal* [1989] or even, some suggest, Steven Spielberg's *E.T.* [1982]). The classic Christ film is of interest to the biblical scholar for all kinds of reasons some of which we shall touch upon later: for the sources used, and hence for intertextual analysis; for its use of music, art, locations, settings, etc., and hence for aesthetic analysis; for its depiction of sexuality, gender, ethnicity or religion, and hence for sociological analysis; for its plot, characterization, point of view, etc., and hence for narrative analysis. Like the Gospels themselves, it is important for its presentation of the figure of Jesus (compare the 1992 [April 20] Channel Four documentary *Jesus Christ Movie-Star* devoted to this subject) and, given its popularity, is arguably the most significant medium through which popular culture this century has absorbed its knowledge of the gospel story and formed its impression of Christianity's founder. It is perhaps instructive to recall, as Kenneth Wolfe points out (1991: 48), that at the very moment in 1977 when Don Cupitt and Peter Armstrong were airing on BBC2 their scholarly and open-ended investigation on the subject 'Who was Jesus?', Sir Lew Grade's ITV epic *Jesus of Nazareth* was giving a long, firm and traditional answer to much larger audiences!

(iii) *Other Films with Biblical/Religious Themes.* At no time in its history has film (and the cinema) arguably been as popular as it is today. People flock to new releases in comfortable, air-conditioned, multiplex cinemas or see films in their own homes on television, video or cable. Film review programmes such as that presented by Barry Norman on British television (BBC1) command wide audiences, and for those who share his love of the cinema, his *100 Best Films of the Century* (1992) is a useful selection. For a film-literate readership, there are sophisticated magazines like the British Film Institute's *Sight and Sound* or for film buffs regular film festivals like that held annually here in Newcastle, the Tyneside Film Festival. The most recent of these (October, 1993) included a *Faith* and film component in a programme which announced: '*Faith* is an overview, incorporating images of institutionalised religion (at its best and worst), Biblical epics, crisis of faith, notions of the afterlife and taking both serious and light-hearted approaches on board'. The films included were Terry Jones's *Monty Python's Life of Brian* (1979); William Friedkin's *The Exorcist* (1973); Abel Ferrara's *Bad Lieutenant* (1992); William Wyler's *Ben Hur* (1959); Anthony Minghella's *Truly, Madly, Deeply* (1990); Frank Capra's *It's a Wonderful Life* (1946); Gabriel Axel's *Babette's Feast* (1987); and Arcand's *Jesus of Montreal.*

Among the current crop of films popular with moviegoers, both here and in the States (Crumm and Gerstel 1994), are a number which explore moral, religious or biblical themes: for example, Richard Attenborough's *Shadowlands* (1993) on the Christian writer and Oxford don, C.S. Lewis and his theological as well as actual struggle with the nature of suffering; Mike Leigh's *Naked* (1993) expressing the rawer, philosophical and existential questionings of its alienated and unemployed central character; Steven Spielberg's *Schindler's List* (1993) and its brave and moving treatment of the Holocaust; James Ivory's *Remains of the Day* (1993) with its portrayal of a butler facing a Schindlerian dilemma in the entirely different context of the British stately home; Jonathan Demme's *Philadelphia* (1993) and Bruce Joel Rubin's *My Life* (1993), each, like *Shadowlands,* treating the sensitive subject of death by terminal illness, the first Aids, the other cancer; Frank Marshall's *Alive* (1992) and Peter Weir's *Fearless* (1993), each about the survivors of a plane crash and each in their different ways exploring issues of life and death.

Although these recent releases are particularly rich in religious themes, religion, theology and the Bible and the motifs and concerns related to them have been present in the cinema since its inception. Reference has already been made to the 'Christ' motif in such films as *Cool-Hand Luke*—one thinks, for example, of the famous egg-eating scene where its suffering but triumphant hero, played by Paul Newman, sprawls semiconscious on a table, in cruciform pose, having absorbed more, to the delight of his fellow convicts, than his opponent—or *E.T.*—with its Christ-like alien and its salvific overtones—but a variety of Christ-like figures have also appeared in such films as Berthold Biertel's *The Passing of the Third Floor Back* (1935), Frank Borzage's *Strange Cargo* (1940), John Ford's *The Fugitive* (1947), or Ingmar Bergman's *The Face* (1958) (Halliwell 1985: 216).

Where other biblical motifs are concerned, mention of Bergman calls to mind the apocalyptic elements of *The Seventh Seal* (1957), where death comes for a knight who engages him in a game of chess, and similar echoes of the book of Revelation are present in Francis Ford Coppola's *Apocalypse Now* (1979) with its theme of an avenging angel (Martin Sheen) in pursuit of a demi-god (Marlon Brando as a deranged colonel) and its famous 'Ride of the Valkyries' attack on a Vietnam village. The avenging angel in Clint Eastwood's *Pale Rider* (1985) is not a US captain or a fleet of helicopter gunships but a gun-wielding preacher and in this film, as in many westerns, biblical themes of wrath, violence, vengeance, justice and redemption are all strongly presented (Jewett 1993: 118-33).

Some films have dealt directly with religion and the religious as their content matter (compare Leo McCarey's happy-go-lucky *The Bells of St Mary's* [1945] or Richard Brooks's more sinister *Elmer Gantry* [1960] [Babington and Evans 1993: 18-21]). Others, some of which we have just noted, have secular subjects but are imbued with religious or biblical concerns, motifs or undertones (compare also, for example, Elia Kazan's powerful *On the Waterfront* [1954] with its ex-boxer ['I coulda been a contender'] stevedore, Marlon Brando, who takes on the Mafiosi; in a film renowned for its fine performances, it is hard indeed to forget Karl Malden's gutsy priest and his denunciation of a stevedore's murder as 'a crucifixion' [Norman 1992: 192-93]).

Some directors like Bergman or Luis Buñuel (compare *Viridiana* [1961] or *The Exterminating Angel* [1962]) are known for the way in which religion figures in different respects as an influence in their films. One such director is Martin Scorsese, a former altar boy who at one time wanted to be a priest (Leo 1988: 43). Scorsese's films throb with moral issues of good and evil, love and hate, truth and falsehood, revenge and forgiveness, salvation and destruction. With raw honesty and realism, he can depict hell on earth (in an urban context) as no other contemporary director can, and yet at the same time, in the midst of sordid squalor, corruption and filth, hint at elements of redemption. This ability is illustrated in *Mean Streets* (1973), a story of two small-time Manhattan hoodlums, the one (played by Robert De Niro) a wild romantic, the other, his devout and protective Catholic brother (played by Harvey Keitel) a realist, and also in *Taxi Driver* (1976) which tells of a campaign by deranged Vietnam veteran Travis Bickle (played by Robert De Niro) to clean up the streets (Norman 1992: 176-77, 240-41). Scorsese's *The Last Temptation of Christ* will be discussed shortly, but echoing some of these same Scorsesian themes is the recent harrowing film by Abel Ferrara (otherwise known unpromisingly for the 1979 'video-nasty' *Driller Killer*), *Bad Lieutenant* (1993). About a nun raped in church by young thugs with a crucifix, the theme is again redemption, this time that of a corrupt New York cop (played courageously by Harvey Keitel). According to one reviewer, 'If *The Last Temptation Of Christ* was *Mean Streets* in the desert, then *Bad Lieutenant* is a morality play set in the Bronx' (Beard 1993: 26).

The New Testament in Fiction and Film: Some Key Texts Considered

Fiction

1. Nikos Kazantzakis, *The Last Temptation* (1961). Having commented on contemporary interest in the Bible (in particular the New Testament) in the area of fiction and film, and having noted some current developments, both popular and academic, in the field, let me now go on to consider briefly three novels and three films which in my view merit special attention. The first is the novel by the Greek writer, Nikos Kazantzakis, *The Last Temptation* upon which the film by Martin Scorsese was based. Though born in Crete (in 1883), Kazantzakis spent a considerable part of his life living or travelling abroad. Educated at the universities of Athens and Paris, he was a prolific and gifted writer nominated repeatedly for the Nobel Prize. Three major influences helped to shape his thinking: revolutionary activism (that of his Cretan childhood and of Lenin), philosophy (particularly Henri Bergson, Friedrich Nietsche and William James) and religion (briefly Buddhism but predominantly Christianity and its ascetic tradition). Kazantzakis was driven, according to his biographers by 'a metaphysical (or existentialist) anguish', one critic describing him as 'an unquiet spirit, athirst for every sort of knowledge...tormented by anxieties and fundamental problems... And though a Nietzschean unbeliever...troubled by religious problems' (Politis 1973: 221, 222; see also Lee 1979). Another describes him, like Joyce (or Lawrence), as 'a priest of the imagination' (Bien 1961: 512).

This is borne out by the novel which ranks as a major one in the genre of fiction lives of Christ. Its plot begins with an unusual twist: Jesus of Nazareth, a carpenter, makes crosses for the Romans on which they crucify Jewish rebels. Racked by guilt for this—especially after a visit from Judas—and for the descent into prostitution of his childhood sweetheart, Mary Magdalene, he pays a visit to her and then to an

Essene monastery where he is recognized as the Messiah by its ailing leader before he dies. A later visit to John the Baptist and hallucinations in the desert confirm him in a mission to save the world, and die for its sins, by engineering his own crucifixion. Judas, under contract from the Zealots to kill Jesus but now a follower, is instructed to aid him in this task. In an entirely fresh and highly original way, the plot follows that of the traditional passion narrative and Jesus finds himself on the cross confronting his last temptation—a series of visions in which he is presented by his guardian angel with an alternative to his redemptive but suicidal mission, viz. the pleasures of the body, sex, procreation, home, wife, family, domestic bliss, and happy longevity, all mediated through the figures of Mary Magdalene, Mary and Martha. Faced with the consequences that avoiding his destiny would entail, both for himself and his disciples (whom he meets forty years later), he rejects these visions and wakes up, much relieved to find himself still on the cross.

The work is a work of fiction but, where sources are concerned, Kazantzakis has clearly drawn on the canonical Gospels. The correspondence is often very close (compare, for example, the biblical account of Jesus' meeting with the Samaritan woman [Jn 4.1-42] and that of Kazantzakis, pp. 226-29, especially p. 227]). In places he has also drawn upon the apocryphal Gospels (compare, for example, the reference on p. 158 to the boy Jesus' fashioning of a bird of clay and giving it life; this is to be found in *The Infancy Story of Thomas* 2.1 [Hennecke and Schneemelcher 1963: 392-93]). What impresses one, however, is not simply the knowledge and experience which have been drawn upon in this book but its sheer imaginative audacity. Kazantzakis gives vivid descriptions of Jesus, his family and his disciples which the Gospels do not give. He supplies interesting motivations for his characters which his sources do not supply. Familiar gospel narratives are retold, extended or interpreted in new and highly imaginative ways (compare Jesus' temptations in the desert [Mk 1.12-13 par.] and pp. 247-70 or the description of the raised Lazarus [pp. 381-82] and the subsequent attempt by Barabbas to murder him [pp. 423-24]). Jesus' dialogues with the characters of the novel (compare, for example, those with Matthew on pp. 401, 425) raise the kind of issues (historical, political, theological) which both delight and tease the mind. Some magnificent scenes have no parallel in the gospel texts (Jesus' visit to Mary Magdalene's brothel on pp. 85-102, for example) or are only loosely based on them (e.g. the disciples' visit to Simon the Cyrenian's tavern, pp. 287-300, where they are reluctantly made to feast on a pig's head on a platter after hearing of the death of John the Baptist!). Others have such a rich and deep symbolism that their effect is quite breathtaking (e.g. Jesus' final temptation, pp. 468-92).

Above all, however, it is Kazantzakis's Christ who grips us and holds our attention. Unlike the Markan Christ, this Christ is a truly human figure grappling with the possibility of the divine. He is a man struggling with his own neurotic, obsessive and masochistic tendencies and seeking to resolve these conflicts in an act of self-immolation. This Messiah wishes to free the soul from sin, rather than Israel from the Romans. It is his struggle, and finally his success which, at a deeper level, invites us to see Kazantzakis's Christ as a hero. As Peter Bien puts it, by freeing himself from the various temptations that threaten to enslave his spirit (his family, bodily pleasures, the state, his own fear of death) 'by force of will [he] achieves a victory over matter or, in other words, is able, because of his allegiance to the life force within him, to transmute matter into spirit' (Bien 1961: 307). In that respect, he is, for Kazantzakis, a salvific figure, 'a prototype of the free man', a saviour for a new age. In that respect, too, as his old friend, Albert Schweitzer (who visited him just before he died [Bien 1961: 518; Marshall and Poling 1971: 244-45]) would have recognized, he is an embodiment of Kazantzakis's own values!

2. Gerd Theissen, *The Shadow of the Galilean* (1987). Our next life of Jesus in fiction is unusual in that it is written not by a novelist but by a respected New Testament scholar, Professor Gerd Theissen. Born in Germany in 1943, Theissen was educated at the University of Bonn, graduating in 1968, the year of the student protest movement. He has held teaching positions at the universities of Bonn and Copenhagen and is presently Professor of New Testament in the University of Heidelberg. The author of a number of books on the New Testament, he is particularly interested in early Christian origins and known for his fresh approach to New Testament studies. Described by one of his peers as 'perhaps the most creative and fertile mind in biblical scholarship and interpretation today' (Morgan and Barton 1988: 150), Theissen believes strongly in the value of sociological and psychological approaches to the biblical texts. Like Kazantzakis, he is distrustful of pedantic intellectuals, particularly with what some would regard as the closed, unimaginative, overly sceptical world of traditional (Germanic) biblical scholarship,

exemplified in the pernickety Dr Kratzinger, to whom Theissen explains himself in the novel. Unlike Kazantzakis, the social aspect of his Christianity is far stronger than the personal or spiritual element. In one of his letters to Kratzinger, he states his fear that religion might withdraw again 'into the conversation between God and the soul' (p. 153). He is also interested in hermeneutics, the problems involved in interpreting texts, and particularly in the links between ancient texts like the New Testament and the contemporary reader.

These concerns permeate the novel. The plot revolves around Andreas, a wealthy fruit and grain merchant who is arrested, although innocent, at a political demonstration in Jerusalem against Pontius Pilate and released only after being blackmailed into acting as a spy (or 'adviser in religious affairs') for the Romans. His brief is to collect information about Jewish religious movements with possible political implications. He agrees to collect information on the Essenes, John the Baptist and (later) Jesus of Nazareth and to send a report to Pontius Pilate through Metilius, the interrogating officer. On a series of travels, which involve, among other things, being captured by Zealots, he gathers information from a variety of informants, including Baruch, an excommunicated Essene whom he rescues in the wilderness. Sympathetic now to revolutionary activism and especially to Jesus and his non-violent expression of it, he sends his report to Pontius Pilate together with the proposal that to defuse the growing political situation, he declare a general amnesty for Zealots, remit the financial debts of the poor, and resettle landless peasants. Pontius Pilate refuses but takes up the amnesty suggestion in a limited way by offering people the choice between Jesus and Barabbas. Jesus is crucified and Andreas resumes normal business life. He is drawn into the resurgent Christian movement, however, by Baruch, who has joined the Jesus sect, and by a vision (Daniel 7) in which he comes to belief in Jesus as the (truly human (Messiah).

While the aim of Kazantzakis's novel was devotional (to enable 'every free man' to 'love Christ' better [1961: 10]), that of Theissen is didactic. As stated in the first of his letters to Dr Kratzinger, it is 'to sketch in narrative form a picture of Jesus and his time which both does justice to the present state of scholarly research and is understandable to present-day readers' (1987: 1). He describes the novel as a piece of *narrative exegesis* which he defines as follows: 'the basic structure of narrative exegesis consists of historical reconstructions of patterns of behaviour, conflicts and tensions, and its superstructure consists of fictitious events on which historical source material is worked over in a poetic way' (p. 19). In his mission, Andreas is 'an embodiment of the adventure of historical-critical research' (p. 83).

Theissen's choice of the narrative form has also been dictated by his didactic intentions. Where the Gospel of Mark is written from the perspective of an 'intrusive omniscient third-person narrator' (Petersen 1978), Theissen's choice of a first-person narrator (Andreas) is made on ideological grounds. It is to emphasize that 'all history is experienced and shaped by human beings from a limited perspective' (p. 27). Theissen's Jesus, moreover—a prophet, philosopher and poet—does not appear in the novel at all (hence its title). Instead, he presents 'the Galilean' as he is seen through the eyes of a variety of individuals and groups: Zealots, Romans, Essenes, Pharisees, etc. His characters represent diverse classes, groups and interests within first-century (and modern) society and speak from clear ideological positions (Joanna, for example, the wife of Herod Antipas's steward Chuza, represents women and speaks with feminist concerns). It is this quality which makes his novel in some respects more contrived, less vital, even clinical in comparison with that of Kazantzakis. Narrative, as some critics have pointed out, has become subordinate to ideology (Neyrey 1988: 548; see also Taylor 1988).

3. Michèle Roberts *The Wild Girl* (1984/1991). Theissen's ideology, however, is tempered by his academic approach and concerns and by his desire to give voice to a diversity of views. Not so subtle is the point of view of our next novel, by Michèle Roberts, which presents its reader with a sustained feminist perspective on Christian origins. Born in 1949 and described by her publisher as 'one of Britain's most talented and exciting new writers', Roberts was educated at the University of Oxford and has pursued a varied career as part-time journalist, part-time teacher, counsellor, British Council librarian, etc. Poetry editor for *Spare Rib* (1974–76) and *City Limits* (1981–83), she was also writer in residence at the University of Essex in 1987–88. In addition to other novels (e.g. *The Book of Mrs Noah,* 1987), her work has included poetry, numerous short stories and essays, a play (*The Journeywoman,* premièred in Colchester in 1988) and a recent film script *The Heavenly Twins* for French TV and Channel Four. Since 1970, she has been involved in the woman's liberation movement and this influence is apparent in the novel for whose inspiration she thanks, among others, the women of Greenham Common.

The novel presents itself as Mary Magdalene's account of the teaching of Jesus and her relationship with him as revealed in a fifth Gospel discovered in the parched soil of Provence. Like Theissen's novel, it is written in the first-person narrator form. After a childhood in Bethany, the 'stubby-nosed' and 'long-backed' Mary records how she ran away from home at the age of fifteen, suffers gang-rape and travels to Alexandria where she is befriended and instructed in the art of 'conversation and dalliance' (pp. 19-20) by the gentle and civilized *hetaira* Sibylla, who also takes her to bed. After returning to her home and family, at Sibylla's expense, she supports the delinquent Lazarus and the responsible Martha by (discreetly) plying her trade. Lazarus introduces her to Jesus who strikes her as 'quite ugly, with a lined face and a big nose, a slightly hunched back...[and]...utterly feminine' (pp. 33-34). Mary joins his mixed company of free and equal spirits and the two become lovers, much to the disapproval of the ascetic and misogynist Peter, who is later to become head of the church. A series of Mary's dreams and revelations are described against the backdrop of the familiar gospel story. When Peter organizes the Christian mission after the resurrection, Mary is excluded despite her prophetic gifts and her intimate knowledge of Jesus. The women decide to conduct a mission of their own to Alexandria but end up in Provence where they establish a community. Some years later Mary's account of all this is discovered by her grand-daughter.

Radical as this 'fifth Gospel' appears, its depiction of Mary Magdalene, of Jesus, of Peter and of certain aspects of the early Christian movement is not simply a product of Roberts's creative imagination *per se* but a result of that imagination operating on an amalgam of sources. These sources include not only the canonical Gospels but also the apocryphal Gospels, in particular the Nag Hammadi texts. In common with later Christian tradition (to which she is also in debt for legendary material [Moltmann-Wendel 1982: 61-90]) her Mary Magdalene is a composite of three biblical figures: the canonical Mary Magdalene (cf. Mk 15.40, 47; 16.1 par.; Lk. 8.2; Jn 20.1-18), the anonymous woman who anoints Jesus (Mk 14.3-9 par.; Lk. 7.36-39) and Mary of Bethany (Jn 12.1-8). Certain of the Gnostic texts (Robinson 1977; Pagels 1979) have inspired her depiction of the physical relationship between Jesus and Mary (compare *The Gospel of Philip* 63.32–64.5), the rivalry between Mary and Jesus' male disciples, especially a misogynistic Peter (compare *The Gospel of Mary* 17.18–18.15; *Pistis Sophia*

36.71 and again *The Gospel of Philip* 63.32–64.5), the revelations to Mary and the prominence given to her (compare *The Dialogue of the Saviour* 139.12-13; *The Questions of Mary* and again *The Gospel of Mary* 17.18–18.15) and even her song (p. 64) with the mother of Jesus (*The Thunder, Perfect Mind*). These sources she has embellished under the impetus of a feminist ideology.

This then is a politically correct version of early Christianity, 'the story of the liberated woman Mary Magdalen became in the Eighties' (Haskins 1993: 385). Echoing the work of some recent biblical scholars (Fiorenza 1983) on the egalitarian nature of early Christianity, she emphasizes equality between the sexes and celebrates female spirituality. The novel champions the values of sisterhood and brotherhood (e.g. p. 113) and espouses the notion that the man and woman within us have become separated (p. 110). 'We have lost the knowledge of the mother', says Mary, relaying the risen Jesus' words to his disciples (p. 111), and in a later dream (pp. 165-79) the tragic consequences for mankind for excluding the female from the gender of God—or even from the priesthood (pp. 127-34)—are recounted. Jesus' earthly mission indeed was to reconcile and reunite maleness and femaleness and to restore the knowledge of God as Mother (pp. 110-11).

Film

1. Pier Paolo Pasolini, *The Gospel according to St Matthew* (1964). Turning now to our three films, we begin with that by Italian director, Pier Paolo Pasolini. That a Marxist should undertake a film on the life of Christ makes *The Gospel according to St Matthew* for that reason alone unusual in itself. In a series of interviews with Oswald Stack (Stack 1969), however, Pasolini stated: 'I not a believer' (p. 83) but 'my vision of the world is religious (p. 77)...I am not interested in de-consecrating: this is a fashion I hate, it is petit bourgeois. I want to re-consecrate things as much as possible, I want to re-mythicize them' (p. 83). Indeed, in deference to his Catholic friends, he reinstated the investiture of Peter which had been removed after the first editing (Stack 1969: 96). While he admits, in connection with his treatment of the supernatural, that 'the miracles of the loaves and the fishes and Christ walking on the water are disgusting pietism' (Stack 1969: 87), 'he is able', in the words of Babington and Evans (1993: 104), 'to stage the miracles...without reservation, because his film announces itself as the recitation of shared cultural history but not belief in it...'

The film is also unconventional in that, while popular, it did not have the same rich 'production values' that we associate with the typical Hollywood biblical epic. It was made in black and white, has striking but not lavish sets and its camera-work is rough and intimate, at times close to that of a documentary. The director is fond of lingering facial close-ups, especially of Jesus whose animated persona is in sharp contrast to the passive acting, silent stares, looks of awe, etc. from the supporting cast. The film was shot in southern Italy, its actors were unknown non-professionals and all its minor characters were from the agricultural and pastoral proletariat there (Stack 1969: 77, 82). Pasolini himself describes it as 'a violently contradictory film, profoundly ambiguous and disconcerting, particularly the figure of Christ' (Stack 1969: 87). This leading role is played by a young Spanish student, Enrique Irazoqui. His thin, emaciated face, with its prominent forehead, piercing eyes, stubbly beard and sorrowful expression, creates a memorable impression as, dressed in a white robe and black shawl, he makes his vehement delivery of the Matthean text.

Where sources for Pasolini's angry young prophet are concerned, the film is a startlingly visual rendering of the biblical text upon which it is based. While our canonical Matthew is the sole Gospel employed, Pasolini allowed himself the liberty of using Isaiah (e.g. at Jesus' death) but justifies this on the grounds that it was also Matthew's source (Stack 1969: 95-96). Two other sources, however, should be mentioned. The first of these is the music accompanying the film and here Pasolini is in debt to a wide tradition. The arresting musical score features different styles and techniques (from Bach to Billie Holliday) with classical and religious music (e.g. chant, choral music, the Congolese Missa Luba), negro spirituals (e.g. 'Sometimes I Feel like a Motherless Child'), rhythm and blues and the haunting tones of the flute. The second of these is the western tradition of art. The film has numerous references to painting: 'I wanted to do the story of Christ plus two thousand years of Christianity' and to an Italian like himself, 'painting...is the major element in the Christological tradition' (Stack 1969: 91). Both these additional sources superimpose upon the presentation of the written text—and this is one of the distinctive strengths and capacities of an audiovisual medium like film—further layers of association, emotion and interpretation.

2. Martin Scorsese, *The Last Temptation of Christ* (1988). Pasolini's *Matthew* was one of the influences on our next film, *The Last*

Temptation of Christ by Martin Scorsese (Babington and Evans 1993: 150, 152). With its atmospheric 'world music' soundtrack by Peter Gabriel and its exotic Moroccan locations (as well as its painterly allusions), it too gives an air of strangeness to what is otherwise a familiar story. In interview, Scorsese has offered his reasons for filming Kazantzakis's book: 'through the Kazantzakis novel I wanted to make the life of Jesus immediate and accessible to people who haven't really thought about God in a long time' (Thompson and Christie 1989: 124). To aid him in this task, he employed as screenwriter Paul Schrader, 'the most obsessively religious director in the contemporary American cinema' (Babington and Evans 1993: 14). Coming from a rural Calvinist background in Grand Rapids, Michigan, Schrader had at one time studied for the ministry and his screenplays (cf. *Taxi-Driver, American Gigolo, Mishima, Cat People, Patty Hearst, Raging Bull, The Comfort of Strangers*) are 'harsh and anguished, full of metaphors for imprisonment, preoccupied with vengeance and the thirst for redemption' (Jackson 1990: x). For Schrader 'the great hook of [Kazantzakis's] *The Last Temptation* is the idea of the reluctant God' and he describes the resultant film as 'a psychological film about the torments of the spiritual life...a tortured human struggle about a common man possessed by God and fighting it' (Jackson 1990: 135-36).

Like the novel, the film begins with Jesus' mission (compare Mark's Gospel), ends with his crucifixion and declines to depict the discovery of the empty tomb and his subsequent appearances. Schrader departs from the novel, however, in certain respects. 'There are two elements in the book', he states. 'One is a kind of Nietzschean superman struggle, and the other is more Eastern, more mystical. Because of my background, I slewed it towards the Nietzschean and Calvinist and away from the mystical' (Jackson 1990: 137). He added, moreover, one scene that was not in the book, a dramatic gesture, with Catholic overtones, in which Jesus reaches into his chest, pulls out his bleeding heart and holds it up for his apostles to gaze upon. Paul (as arch-persecutor of the church) and not Barabbas is the murderer of Lazarus. Later, on the cross and in his visions, Jesus' Satanic guardian angel is played, not by a young man, but by a little girl. In this selfsame climactic scene, care was also taken to lend realism and historical verisimilitude to the film by drawing upon the most recent and accurate information about Roman methods of crucifixion (Wilson 1984: 126-30; Graham 1993: 8). In common with the biblical epic genre (Babington and Evans 1993: 10), use is also made throughout of contemporary American accents (though English is reserved for Satan and the Romans, including David Bowie's laconic Pontius Pilate) and this, one critic suggests, 'can be viewed as a substitute for Kazantzakis' use of the "demotic" language of the Greek peasantry' (Rosenbaum 1988: 281).

The film is sustained by two central performances, those of Willem Dafoe (Jesus) and Harvey Keitel (Judas) as well as by Barbara Hershey, who first introduced Scorsese to the novel and who plays an intensely sensual Mary Magdalene. Struggling between his own humanity and divinity, Scorsese's Christ is a weak, dithering individual who only gradually comes to see himself as the Messiah, a neurotic, even psychotic person torn between a violent but significant destiny and a peaceful, if bland domesticity. Here, according to Pam Cook, we have 'the exploration of masculinity in crisis' which was begun in *Taxi Driver* and *Raging Bull* and which Scorsese and Schrader have now taken to new extremes (1988: 288). A prominent role is given to the angry, bullish and streetwise Judas who, as Jesus' alter ego, (advocating redemption by violence rather than by love) and as one himself betrayed, ironically secures the future of Christianity by persuading Jesus to return to the cross and accept his final suffering 'like a man' (Rosenbaum 1988: 281; Babington and Evans 1993: 161-62). The last temptation—to enjoy sex, marriage and children with Mary Magdalene—is resisted and the Christ achieves his victory.

Sadly it is the controversy surrounding the film (Cook 1988: 288; Jenkins 1988: 352-53; Leo 1988; Rosenbaum 1988; Babington and Evans 1993: 149-50; Graham 1993: 7, 11-12), especially its depiction of a Jesus so fully human as to experience sexual desire, that has diverted attention from the real merit of this film (as also of the novel). As is well known, *The Last Temptation of Christ* sparked off, even before it was released, one of the most vehement religious disputes in years. It stirred up issues of blasphemy and censorship, of democratic rights to artistic expression versus religious toleration. The film was even seen as an attack upon religion itself (*Sunday Telegraph*, 21 February 1992). It inspired an organized letter-writing campaign by the American religious right (one example from a letter sent to the chairman of Gulf and Western, the parent company of the film's backers Paramount: 'The material it contains is straight from the pit of hell. We may as well destroy our country with the nuclear bomb as show this film. It's as destructive' (Jenkins 1988: 353). As one perceptive commentator noted, however, 'the use of females throughout to signify only motherhood and temptation (of the male) suggests that if anyone should be objecting to this film, it is women of all denominations rather than fundamentalists of both sexes' (Rosenbaum 1988: 281). The last word, in my opinion, however, should be left with *Time* magazine's film critic, Richard Corliss who wrote:

> By jolting the viewer to reconsider Hollywood's calcified stereotypes of the New Testament, Scorsese wants to restore the immediacy of that time, the stern wonder of that land, the thrilling threat of meeting the Messiah in the mean streets of Jerusalem...he believes in the power of cinema to rethink traditions, to make Jesus live in a skeptical age. And those willing to accompany Scorsese on his dangerous ride through the Gospels may believe he has created his masterpiece (1988: 44).

3. Denys Arcand, *Jesus of Montreal* (1989). Our final film, *Jesus of Montreal,* is by the French-Canadian director, Denys Arcand, who was relatively unknown until he made *The Decline of the American Empire*. Brought up in childhood by Carmelites, though not himself now religious, he later trained as a historian before becoming a film-maker. The film is a modern allegory on the Jesus story. In an interview with Adam Barker, Arcand said that the idea had come to him when he met an actor who was employed to play Jesus in a passion play for a shrine which was a tourist attraction in Montreal (Barker 1990: 4). This encounter led him to speculate how actors might undertake and revolutionize a commission of this kind in such a way that the story engaged sharply and meaningfully with a modern audience and society. The film, in Barker's words, is 'an impeccably post-modern version of the greatest story ever told', the passion play becoming 'for Arcand, as for his latterday Messiah...a form of contemporary satire' (Barker 1990: 4). In 1989, the film was nominated for an Academy Award for Best Foreign Film and gained Canadian Oscars for Best Picture, Best Director and Best Actor (Luthaire Bluteau).

Bluteau plays the part of the talented but unemployed actor, Daniel Colombe, who is recruited to play Jesus in the passion play. This play had been performed annually for some thirty-five years at a Catholic shrine on a mountain top overlooking Montreal and Colombe's brief is to give it fresh life. From different quarters, Daniel gathers together a group of fellow actors to form the cast: Constance, who works in a soup kitchen; Martin and Tony who do voice-overs for pornographic movies and Mireille, a model. Daniel's role as Jesus begins to pass from the stage to real life. In one of the film's most powerful scenes, Daniel accompanies Mireille to an audition for a television commercial where the director asks her to take off her clothes. Daniel objects and, in the ensuing action, drives the television company out of the building after overturning and damaging their equipment. Although the play is a great hit with the public, Father Leclerc, the priest who commissioned Daniel (and who is also having an affair with Constance) is scandalized by its revisionist treatment of the passion story and cancels the show. Daniel and his group continue to perform, however, despite the ban. The police are sent and Daniel is injured in an accident when the cross to which he is fastened collapses and he is crushed. After an initial visit to hospital for suspected concussion, he insists he is all right and leaves but, on the way home, begins to act like a demented prophet. He eventually collapses and dies whereupon his organs are removed to give sight to a blind woman and a new heart to a sick man. The media entrepreneur, Richard Cardinal, who had earlier enticed Daniel to exploit his acting talents commercially, then proposes to the other actors that a theatre company be set up to commemorate him. All but Mireille accept the commission.

As the plot suggests, the film exhibits a number of interesting themes and raises no few social, historical, philosophical and theological issues. These are handled, for the most part, in a subtle and unforced way. As an allegory the film operates on several levels, having something to say about society, the media and the modern church. It offers biting criticism of both the business world and organized Christianity. Arcand is concerned about the nature of truth and falsehood, of belief and unbelief, especially in relation to the media machine that dominates modern-day perceptions of reality. This was borne in on him after the success of *The Decline of the American Empire*: 'I was thrown into this maelstrom of media attention and I also wanted to reflect on that' (Barker 1990: 4). The film challenges the values of the world of advertising and the mass media, raising, for example, as the audition scene suggests, the feminist issue of sexual exploitation. The relation of the Jesus of history to the Christ of faith is also a prominent motif, the film offering comment on the institutional church and the way it preserves and promotes its traditional image of Jesus. For Arcand, 'Jesus was a visionary, a prophet, and a magician', and his picture of Jesus as a subversive in the movie is one that is also reflected in current studies of the historical Jesus (Willett 1991; Telford 1994). As with Scorsese in *The Last Temptation of Christ*, historical accuracy is sought by the director in the depiction of the crucifixion (Willett 1991: 14), as well as in the background information supplied by the actors for their audience.

'The Bible is such an old and mysterious book', states Arcand, '...that you can use it anyway you want' (Barker 1990: 4). In *Jesus of Montreal*, the use made of intertextual allusion is rich and striking. Some of the parallels are obvious. The gathering of the cast mirrors the calling of the disciples (especially from some unsavoury activities), their shared meals, innocent idealism and sexual equality echoing that of Jesus' first followers. Daniel's fame spreads as does that of Jesus and in a 'Temptation' scene, set in a very high office overlooking the Montreal cityscape, Cardinal promises him the world. The Catholic authorities embodied in Father Leclerc are the Pharisees, the audition the 'Cleansing of the Temple', the media the money-changers of modern life. The organ transplant after Daniel's death functions as both resurrection and miracle tradition combined and the experimental theatre company in commemoration of him as the early church. Some parallels are more subtle. In the opening scenes, Daniel (whose surname 'Colombe' means 'dove') receives recommendation from another more senior actor, so calling to mind the testimony of John the Baptist (compare also the psychologist's verdict on Daniel as 'better adjusted than most of the judges in court'). In his later apocalyptic ravings, there are echoes of Mark 13 ('Not one stone...').

Certain ironies tease the mind. His death is occasioned by a cross ('doing tragedy is dangerous') and he is turned away by a Christian hospital (St Mark's) and finds himself at death, a man with no family, in the caring hands of a Jewish one. Small suggestive details reinforce the effect of the plot (the creation imagery in René's dubbing of a programme on the 'Big Bang'; Daniel's being offered, at lunch with Cardinal, a 'Virgin Mary' and a 'Magdalen lobster'; his descent of the Metro escalator a reverse image of the Ascension; his expiration on a life support system in cruciform pose) and humour enlivens it (his being arrested on the cross and being read his rights). Parallels with certain other characters are also developed, such as Mireille who, as Susan Haskins points out, represents Mary Magdalene (selling her body in a commercial for scent; being rescued by Daniel/Jesus; a *vanitas* figure; washing/'anointing' Daniel while he takes a bath; supporting his dead body in her lap; walking away from the other actors after they accept the theatre commission to commemorate Daniel) (Haskins 1993: 385-86).

The New Testament in Fiction and Film: A Biblical Scholar's Perspective

Exploring the Intertextual Links

Finally let me draw things together and offer some reflections from a biblical scholar's perspective on the value of this subject, and on the ways the biblical scholar can both approach, benefit from and contribute to it. I have already touched on the question of value in connection with our discussion of the Christ film. There, among other things, I touched upon the topic of intertextuality and intertextual analysis. I also began with a reminder that the Bible is part and parcel of our literary and cultural heritage, and as we have seen, biblical texts, in quotation or allusion, or biblical characters, motifs or concepts, have influenced our literature and our films in substantial ways. I have commented on various ways in which writers have used their canonical and extra-canonical sources (compare, for example, Kazantzakis or Roberts) and the above examination of Arcand's *Jesus of Montreal* has revealed a wealth of intertextual allusion. Some Christ films have based themselves solely on one canonical Gospel (e.g. Pasolini's *The Gospel according to St Matthew*), most on all four (e.g. Stevens's *The Greatest Story Ever Told*). Some have drawn on the apocryphal Gospels (cf. for example De Mille's *King of Kings* where the tomb is sealed with seven seals, a detail drawn from *The Gospel of Peter* 8.33), or on Josephus (compare the opening scenes of Ray's *King of Kings*) or on fictional novels (compare Henry Koster's *The Robe* [1953] and Frank Borzage's *The Big Fisherman* [1959], both based on the novels of Lloyd C. Douglas, or Fred Niblo's *Ben Hur* [1926] on that of Lew Wallace or, of course, Scorsese's *The Last Temptation of Christ* or that of Kazantzakis).

Establishing, exploring and analysing the intertextual links, therefore, is one of the first tasks to confront us and one for which the biblical scholar, as well as the literary critic, is well suited. Indeed, such investigation, though important in itself, may well provide fresh insights into traditional aspects of New Testament study, for it may help us to appreciate the various ways sources can be used and so illuminate the compositional and redactional processes as well as the phenomenon of intertextuality at work within the Bible itself. A similar suggestion is made by Kreitzer who asks: 'might our understanding of the redactional forces (the editor's own concerns and interests) underlying the production of certain NT texts be enhanced by a consideration of both the novel and the film versions of the story?' (Kreitzer 1993: 46) I have also already mentioned in this connection the notion of cinematic montage as a compositional model for the Gospel of Mark.

Recognizing the Literary and Religious Imagination
In discussing the study of the apocryphal Gospels, I commented on the remarkable degree of literary and religious embellishment which they evince, a creativity clearly produced by the operation of imagination upon received traditions. Such creativity was also observed in the various ways the six writers and directors reviewed in this essay have adapted their canonical and extra-canonical sources to produce their respective works of fiction and film. It reminds us of the thin line that exists between fact and fiction. It exposes the power of the literary and religious imagination to formulate ostensibly 'authentic' constructions of reality, including a fictional Christ. The representation of Christ in fiction and film is based on the representation of Christ in the Gospels, as is the scholar's Christ. Indeed it is based on no less than *four* such representations. Is the Markan Christ, or the Matthean Christ, or the Lukan Christ or the Johannine Christ to be considered any less a 'construction' than the Kazantzakis Christ? Even when the search for 'the Galilean' is conducted with all the scholarly precision of a Gerd Theissen, the fact that our knowledge of Jesus is after all based on such *literary* sources and representations should gives us pause when seeking the answer to historical questions, and make us consider all the more keenly the part played by the imagination in the creation of so-called 'historical tradition'. Indeed, recognizing the power of the literary and religious imagination, as these studies lead us to do, serves to expose the relative subjectivity of all our efforts to secure facts in areas like religion.

Establishing Ideology and the Social Context
One aspect of our examination of the New Testament in fiction and film was the way it demonstrated the influence upon the genre of a particular writer's (or director's) ideology and personal values. This was observed nakedly in the case of Roberts's *The Wild Girl*, with its re-reading of Christian origins through feminist eyes, but it was also seen more subtly in the social interpretation of Jesus' message in Theissen's *The Shadow of the Galilean.* Contrasting with Theissen, on the other hand, was the inward or spiritual Christ of Kazantzakis's novel, or the intensely psychological treatment of him presented in Scorsese's film. A

second aspect to present itself was the importance of social context for the interpretation of these texts, and how they lend themselves readily to sociological analysis. Babington and Evans's work on the Hollywood biblical epic is proof of this for they show, as I have said, how ethnicity, sexuality and gender as well as religion have had their effect upon the genre. As with the Gospels themselves, these films (and reactions to them) reveal much about Jewish-Christian relations (the book reflects, for example, on the irony of Jewish producers bringing Jesus to Christian audiences in a secular age [Babington and Evans 1993: 33-41]), sexual politics and the treatment of the miracles (Babington and Evans comment in particular on how they treat the sacred in a profane world) as well as raising issues of censorship. Such studies of fiction and film, then, sensitize us to the influence of ideology and social context and reinforce its importance as a factor in interpreting our texts.

Correcting the Historical Perspective

As I noted above, film is arguably the most significant medium through which popular culture this century has absorbed its knowledge of the gospel story and formed its impression of Christianity's founder. The point is reiterated both by Kreitzer, who emphasizes the importance of Hollywood in helping to shape the popular imagination with regard to the New Testament (Kreitzer 1993: 151), and by Graham who observes that 'very often the Jesus of the constructing or deconstructing scholarly guild is not the Jesus of popular piety' and that it is 'the "popular" Jesus [who] has a profound cultural and religious influence on people' (Graham 1993: 13). On the other hand, fiction and film can also help correct popular misconceptions. This was the purpose after all of Theissen's book. Where film is concerned, we have also noticed the desire, especially on the part of post-war directors, to achieve historical accuracy (as in the opening history lesson, from Josephus, in Ray's *King of Kings* or those in dramatic tableaux in *Jesus of Montreal)* or verisimilitude (as in the details of the crucifixion in *The Last Temptation of Christ* or again *Jesus of Montreal)*. Novels and films, albeit fictional, can also help sharpen the critical sense. Even spoofs such as *Live from Golgotha* or *Monty Python's Life of Brian* can raise historical questions and powerfully expose, through satire, the weakness of traditional answers ('What have the Romans ever done for us?'...'Well, there are the aqueducts'). One is reminded of the words of Albert Schweitzer, that great iconoclast of lives of Jesus:

> There is no historical task which so reveals a man's true self as the writing of a Life of Jesus. No vital force comes into the figure unless a man breathes into it all the hate or all the love of which he is capable. The stronger the love, or the stronger the hate, the more life-like is the figure which is produced. For hate as well as love can write a Life of Jesus, and the greatest of them are written with hate... [for] their hate sharpened their historical insight' (Schweitzer 1981: 4, 5).

Presenting the Historical and Theological Issues

This last point touches upon the very nature of fiction and film as art forms. As Graham again remarks, 'while art is informative, it is also and always exegetical and interpretive. And this means that it has an amazing capacity to shock or disturb' (Graham 1993: 13). Fiction and film, as we have seen, can capture that sense of the strangeness of the biblical world which the scholar is also seeking to recover. It can re-present our otherwise familiar texts in unfamiliar ways. But it also 'dares to explore the "untouchables" of scholarship' (Graham 1993: 6). Both media can present or reflect historical and theological issues in ways which, although they are not historically accurate, nevertheless reach us with greater impact.

This is particularly the case with Kazantzakis's *The Last Temptation.* Of the novel as a whole, Kreitzer asks: 'might not Kazantzakis's story help us better understand the meaning of Hebrews 4.15, which, speaking of Christ, notes that he "has been tempted in every respect as we are, yet without sin"?' (Kreitzer 1993: 152) A single scene can also serve as an example. One persistent and much-debated issue concerns the Jesus of history versus the Christ of faith, and in the field of Christian origins or Pauline studies, the question of the relation between Jesus and Paul, or more precisely between Jesus' message and Paul's kerygma (proclamation). One side of this issue (the view that Paul invented Christianity) is presented dramatically in both the novel and the film, and in a way that carries more force than countless scholarly treatments of the subject. In one of his visions, Jesus has an encounter with Paul whom he denounces as a liar for claiming that he was the Son of God. 'True or false—what do I care!', replies Paul. 'It's enough if the world is saved!' (Kazantzakis 1961: 488) In the film version, Paul is played (by Harry Dean Stanton) as a born-again American evangelist who claims that his resurrected Jesus is a more powerful figure than the human figure appearing before him (Babington and Evans 1993: 167-68). It is his Jesus who will conquer the world—and such is the power of the scene that the audience is inclined to agree with him!

Reversing the Hermeneutical Flow

In reviewing recent scholarship, I referred to the claim by Larry Kreitzer that the study of literature and film based on the New Testament can help 'reverse the hermeneutical flow' in that such a study opens up fresh perspectives and raises new questions which the exegete can take back to the text. Our investigation may be said to bear out this claim. Allowing for the differences between ancient texts like the Gospels and modern texts, it can help us, if we may sum up, to appreciate the various ways that sources can be used and so illuminate compositional and redactional processes and the phenomenon of intertextuality at work within the Bible itself. Such study also assists us to recognize the creative power of the literary and religious imagination, even when operating upon sources, and so helps us to make more allowance for this factor in our literary and historical studies. It can refine our appreciation of the influence of ideology and social context and reinforce our awareness of its importance as a factor in interpreting our texts. Novels and films, albeit fictional, can also help sharpen the critical sense and can present or reflect historical and theological issues in ways which, although historically inaccurate, nevertheless engage, stimulate or provoke us with greater force.

Conclusion

There are, as is often pointed out, certain similarities between religion and literature or between theology and film. 'Faith', one film critic observes, 'consists not in knowledge but in disavowal, the willing suspension of disbelief which is also at work in the fictionalising processes of myth or, indeed, literature and cinema' (Cook 1988: 288). Likewise there are resemblances between our canonical Gospels and the works of fiction and film that are based upon them. The Gospels used sources but also creatively embellished them by means of their literary imagination, in line with their ideology and in response to their contemporary context. In their own way, to varying degrees and in certain respects, they sought to achieve historical accuracy or verisimilitude. To a greater extent, they are works of narrative theology, reflecting a wealth of theological ideas and religious beliefs. The new approaches of recent years have taught us to view the Gospel texts as literary compositions *in the first instance* rather than as historical documents. Such studies remind us that the Gospel writers, in presenting their picture of Jesus, were therefore subject to the limitations imposed by a *literary* enterprise as well as by a historical one.

In offering a biblical scholar's perspective on the New Testament in fiction and film, let me emphasize, in conclusion, that this form of study is also important *for its own sake*, as well as for the light it may shed on the original texts. The New Testament in fiction and film is part of the history of interpretation and, as John Sawyer has never ceased to remind us, biblical scholars should be as much concerned with the cultural reception and use of the Bible as with the historical-critical analysis of the texts. As biblical scholars, our study of the Bible is conducted in a world in which biblical ideas or texts, however they are understood, have had and continue to have real effects upon our heritage and culture. In the words of the scholar to whom this collection of essays is dedicated:

> the view that the history of interpretation is an integral part of biblical studies, and should not be left entirely to theologians or church historians [*and here we ourselves may add* 'or literary critics, for that matter'], is now widely held...If biblical scholarship is more than history and philology, it must take account of the context of the Bible, not only the original Sitz im Leben of separate literary units, but also its continuing 'contextualization' in the religious communities [*and here we may further add* 'and in secular culture as represented by fiction and film'] that have preserved it and for whom it makes sense' (Sawyer 1990: 316, 319).

BIBLIOGRAPHY

Alter, R. and F. Kermode (eds.)
1987 *The Literary Guide to the Bible* (London: Collins).

Babington, B. and P.W. Evans
1993 *Biblical Epics. Sacred Narrative in the Hollywood Cinema* (Manchester: Manchester University Press).

Barker, A.
1990 'Review (with interview) of D. Arcand's *Jésus de Montréal*', *Monthly Film Bulletin* 57: 3-4.

Beard, S.
1993 'The Power and the Gory', *Spectator: the Arena Review* (March) 26-28.

Bien, P.

1961 'Translator's Note', *The Last Temptation* (London: Faber and Faber), 509-18.

Blake, R.A.

1991 *Screening America: Reflections on Five Classic Films* (New York: Paulist Press).

Butler, I.

1969 *Religion in the Cinema* (New York: A.S. Barnes & Co).

Bygrave, M.

1991 'My name is Cecil, King of Kings', *Sunday Telegraph* (February 3), 13.

Campbell, R.H. and M.R. Pitts

1981 *The Bible on Film: A Checklist, 1897-1980* (Metuchen: Scarecrow).

Channel Four

1992 (April 20) *Jesus Christ Movie Star.*

Cook, P.

1988 'Review of M. Scorsese's *The Last Temptation of Christ*', *Monthly Film Bulletin* 55: 287-88.

Corliss, R.

1988 'A Critic's Contrarian View', *Time* (August 15), 44.

Crain, J.

1991 'The Communal Meal as Sacrament: "Babette's Feast", 1 Corinthians 11, and the Church Today' (M.T.S. Thesis, Garrett-Evangelical Theological Seminary, Chicago).

Crumm, D. and J. Gerstel

1994 'Moviegoers flocking to films that explore spirituality', *News-Press* (Fort Myers, Florida), 9G.

Deleuze, G.

1986 *Cinema 1: The Movement-Image* (London).

Drury, J.

1987 'Mark', in *A Literary Guide to the Bible* (ed. R. Alter and F. Kermode; London: Collins), 402-17.

Duffy, M.

1992 'A Gadfly in Glorious, Angry Exile', *Time* (28 September), 56-58.

Fiorenza, E.S.

1983 *In Memory of Her: A Feminist Theological Reconstruction of Christian Origins* (London: SCM Press).

Forshey, G.E.

1992 *American Religion and Biblical Spectaculars* (Westport, CT: Praeger).

Frye, N.

1982 *The Great Code: The Bible and Literature* (London: Routledge & Kegan Paul).

Graham, D.

1993 'Popular Interest in Jesus: The Scholar and the Media' (unpublished paper given at the British New Testament Conference Jesus Seminar, University of St Andrews, 18 September).

Halliwell, L. (ed.)

1985 *Filmgoer's Companion* (London: Paladin Grafton Books).

Halliwell, L.
1988 *Film Guide* (London: Paladin Grafton Books).

Haskins, S.
1993 *Mary Magdalen* (London: HarperCollins).

Hemming, S.
1991 'Staging Acts of God', *The Independent* (Wednesday, November 27).

Henn, T.R.
1962 'The Bible as Literature', *Peake's Commentary on the Bible* (ed. M. Black; London: Thomas Nelson and Sons).
1970 *The Bible as Literature* (London: Lutterworth Press).

Hennecke, E. and W. Schneemelcher (eds.)
1963 *New Testament Apocrypha* (London: SCM Press).

Hochman, S. (ed.)
1974 *American film directors: with filmographies and index of critics and films* (New York: Ungar).

Hurley, N.P.
1970 *Theology Through Film* (New York: Harper & Row).
1978 *The Reel Revolution: A Film Primer on Liberation* (Maryknoll, NY: Orbis Books).

Jackson, K. (ed.)
1990 *Schrader on Schrader and Other Writings* (London: Faber and Faber).

Jasper, D.
1987 *The New Testament and the Literary Imagination* (London: Macmillan).

Jeffrey, D.L. (ed.)
1992 *A Dictionary of Biblical Tradition in English Literature* (Grand Rapids, MI: Eerdmans).

Jenkins, S.
1988 'From the Pit of Hell: the Making of *The Last Temptation of Christ*', *Monthly Film Bulletin* 55: 352-53.

Jewett, R.
1989 'Sin and Salvation: Amadeus in the light of Romans', *Ex Auditu: An International Journal of Theological Interpretation of Scripture* 5: 159-69.
1993 *Saint Paul at the Movies: The Apostle's Dialogue with American Culture* (Philadelphia: Westminster/John Knox).

Jewett, R. and J.S. Lawrence
1992 'Rambo and the Myth of Redemption', in *Transforming Texts: Classical Images in New Contexts* (Lewisburg: Bucknell University Press).

Joyce, D.
1975 *The Jesus Scroll* (London: Sphere Books).

Kazantzakis, N.
1961 *The Last Temptation* (London: Faber and Faber).

Kelber, W.H.
1979 *Mark's Story of Jesus* (Philadelphia: Fortress Press).

Kermode, F.
1979 *The Genesis of Secrecy: On the Interpretation of Narrative* (London: Harvard University Press).

Kreitzer, L.
1993 *The New Testament in Fiction and Film. On Reversing the Hermeneutical Flow* (Sheffield: JSOT Press).

Lambert, B.
1994 'It's a miracle. Harris is in a biblical epic', *St. Paul Pioneer Press* (2 April) (St. Paul, MN).

Lawrence, D.H.
1980 *Apocalypse and the Writings on Revelation* (Cambridge: Cambridge University Press).

Lee, J.F.
1979 *Kazantzakis: The Politics of Salvation* (Alabama: University of Alabama Press).

Leo, J.
1988 'A Holy Furor', *Time* (15 August): 42-44.

Malone, P.
1990 *Movie Christs and Antichrists* (New York: Crossroad).

Marshall, G. and D. Poling
1971 *Schweitzer. A Biography* (London: Geoffrey Bles).

May, J.R. (ed.)
1992 *Image and Likeness: Religious Visions in American Film Classics* (New York: Paulist Press).

May, J.R. and M.S. Bird (eds.)
1982 *Religion in Film* (Knoxville: University of Tennessee Press).

Moltmann-Wendel, E.
1982 *The Women around Jesus* (London: SCM Press).

Morgan, R. and J.W. Barton
1988 *Biblical Interpretation* (Oxford: Oxford University Press).

Neyrey, J.H.
1988 'Review of G. Theissen, *The Shadow of the Galilean*', *Catholic Biblical Quarterly* 50: 548-49.

Norman, B.
1992 *100 Best Films of the Century* (London: Chapmans).

Norton, D.
1993 *A History of the Bible as Literature* (Cambridge: Cambridge University Press).

Pagels, E.
1979 *The Gnostic Gospels* (London: Weidenfeld and Nicolson).

Petersen, N.R.
1978 ''Point of View' in Mark's Narrative', *Semeia* 12: 97-121.

Politis, L.
1973 *A History of Modern Greek Literature* (Oxford: Clarendon Press).

Prickett, S.
1986 *Words and 'the Word': Language, Poetics and Biblical Interpretation* (Cambridge: Cambridge University Press).

Quinlan, D.
1983 *The Illustrated Guide to Film Directors* (London: Batsford).
Rhoads, D. and D. Michie
1982 *Mark as Story. An Introduction to the Narrative of a Gospel* (Philadelphia: Fortress Press).
Roberts, M.
1984 *The Wild Girl* (London: Methuen).
Robinson, J.M. (ed.)
1977 *The Nag Hammadi Library* (Leiden: Brill).
Rosenbaum, J.
1988 'Raging Messiah. The Last Temptation of Christ', *Sight and Sound* 57: 281-82.
Sarramango, J.
1993 *The Gospel according to Jesus Christ* (London: Harvill Press).
Sawyer, J.
1990 'Interpretation, History of', in *A Dictionary of Biblical Interpretation* (ed. R.J. Coggins and J.L. Houlden; London: SPCK; Philadelphia: Trinity Press International): 316-20.
Schneidau, H.N.
1976 *Sacred Discontent: The Bible and Western Tradition* (Berkeley, Los Angeles and London: University of California Press).
Schrader, P.
1972 *Transcendental Style in Film: Ozu, Bresson, Dreyer* (Berkeley, Los Angeles and London: University of California Press).
Schweitzer, A.
1981 *The Quest of the Historical Jesus* (London: SCM Press).
Stack, O. (ed.)
1969 *Pasolini on Pasolini: Interviews with Oswald Stack* (The Cinema One Series 11; London: Thames and Hudson).
Taylor, R. J.
1988 'Review of G. Theissen, *Shadow of the Galilean*', *New Blackfriars* 69: 410-12.
Telford, W.R.
1990 'Mark, Gospel of', in *A Dictionary of Biblical Interpretation* (ed. R.J. Coggins and J.L. Houlden; London: SPCK; Philadelphia: Trinity Press International): 424-28.
1994 'Major Trends and Interpretive Issues in the Study of Jesus', in *Studying the Historical Jesus: Evaluations of the State of Current Research* (ed. B.D. Chilton and C.A. Evans; Leiden: Brill), 33-74.
Telford, W.R. (ed.)
1985 *The Interpretation of Mark* (Issues in Religion and Theology 7; London: SPCK; Philadelphia: Fortress Press).
1995 *The Interpretation of Mark* (Studies in New Testament Interpretation; Edinburgh: T. & T. Clark, 2nd expanded edn).
Theissen, G.
1987 *The Shadow of the Galilean. The Quest of the Historical Jesus in Narrative Form* (London: SCM Press).

Thompson, D.
1975 *A Biographical Dictionary of the Cinema* (London: Secker & Warburg).

Thompson, D. and I. Christie (eds.)
1989 *Scorsese on Scorsese* (London: Faber and Faber).

Tyneside Cinema
1993 'Tyneside Film Festival Programme (October 8-21)', Newcastle upon Tyne, Tyneside Cinema.

Vidal, G.
1992 *Live from Golgotha* (London: André Deutsch).

Wall, J.M.
1971 *Church and Cinema: A Way of Viewing Film* (Grand Rapids, MI: Eerdmanns).

Willett, M.E.
1991 'Jesus the Subversive: Jesus of Montreal and Recent Studies of the Historical Jesus', *Centerquest Adult Resource* VII (July): 13-20.

Wilson, I.
1984 *Jesus: The Evidence* (London: Weidenfeld & Nicolson).

Wolfe, K.
1991 'The Bible and Broadcasting'. *Using the Bible Today* (ed. D. Cohn-Sherbok; London: Bellew Publishing Company): 47-67.

Wright, T.R.
1988 *Theology and Literature* (Oxford: Basil Blackwell).

Zwick, R.
1989 *Montage im Markusevangelium. Studien zur narrativen Organisation der ältesten Jesuserzählung* (Stuttgart: Katholisches Bibelwerk).

On the Unity of Scripture

Robert Morgan

> If biblical scholarship is more than history and philology, it must take account of the context of the Bible, not only the original *Sitz im Leben* of separate literary units, but also its continuing 'contextualization' in the religious communities that have preserved it and for whom it makes sense.

John Sawyer's thesis lies at the end of a provocative article on the history of biblical interpretation.[1] The argument runs deeper than the occasional insights which church history undoubtedly yields. Assuming as self-evident that biblical scholars are *interpreters* of the texts, not merely collators of manuscripts or students of language and ancient history, the question is what *kinds* of interpretation they are engaged in. Different issues are raised by the different aims and interests which guide different interpreters. Historians and linguists and even literary critics may sit lightly to the history of interpretation, whereas theologians, including protestant theologians, exemplify the hermeneutical significance of the church's tradition as they explain what they think the Bible is saying.

Not long ago it was widely taken for granted among biblical scholars that the Bible was telling them the truth about God. The larger hermeneutical question of what it was all about could then give way to a concentration on minutiae. Important gains in understanding the Bible were made. But now that the larger questions are both disputed and urgent in a pluralist culture divided by religious and quasi-religious conflicts, and threatened with moral anarchy, it seems irresponsible for specialists to ignore them. A scholar may reject some of the ways believers read these texts, and deplore some of the consequences, but narrowing the focus and excluding such questions no longer seems right.

For many biblical scholars today the once much-debated question of

1. J.F.A. Sawyer, 'Interpretation, History of', in R.J. Coggins and J.L. Houlden (eds.), *A Dictionary of Biblical Interpretation* (London: SCM Press, 1990), pp. 316-21.

the unity of the Bible is not a live issue. For one thing it is far from clear what the phrase means. It could mean several things, and most of these seem questionable to historically sensitive readers. The topic looks suspiciously like a product of theologians invading the field and making a mess of it, obscuring the richness and diversity of the texts themselves. Specialists are likely no doubt whether such a varied collection can be called a unity in any significant way.

That impatient reaction is correct in sensing that such theories are the province of theology rather than exegesis, and tend to abstract from the particularities of the texts in a way that goes against the grain of biblical scholarship. But this is what makes them interesting for anyone persuaded by John Sawyer's general thesis. These theories arise out of the ways the biblical texts are used in communities of faith, and therefore shelter under John Sawyer's large umbrella, whatever we personally think of them. Our topic is one of the areas in which historical study and religious interest in these texts seem to conflict, and has therefore been a preoccupation of biblical theology and hermeneutics, the disciplines which aim to manage any conflict between faith and biblical scholarship. One does not have to be a biblical theologian to see the cultural importance of how believers read the Bible any more than one has to be religious to recognize the historical, social, and psychological significance of religion.

As our topic is widely ignored within biblical scholarship it is necessary first to recall why it has seemed important for much Christian theology. Not all the ways the Bible is used in Christianity demand it. If the Bible is read by Christians as no more than an anthology of religious texts providing inspiration and instruction, but not dictating the fundamental shape of Christian belief, the question of its unity need not arise. Some parts are plainly more valuable than others and we naturally pick and choose, using our own judgment. The charm of anthologies can lie in their variety.

What makes matters different for traditional Christian understanding and use of the Bible is the assumption that its religious meaning and truth lie in the whole, not merely in (some of) the parts, and that this whole is in some sense definitive for Christianity. That does not, however, point necessarily to the 'unity' of the Bible. Those who speak of the Bible as a 'source and norm' of Christian faith and theology are selective in their use of it, and weight different parts of it very differently. They work with some idea of its 'centre' but do not need a strong sense of its unity. One may therefore wonder whether this whole idea of a unity is not the residue of a biblicism better discarded.

Some accounts of the unity, inspiration, and authority of the Bible have been rightly discarded. It is no use pretending that all the witnesses agree in what they say. Even if (as many believe) they were all inspired by God, the different historical situations in which they discerned God's will and guidance have led to different demands and formulations. That precludes one kind of theological use of the Bible found in some seventeenth- and eighteenth-century protestantism: the biblical theology that constructed a normative dogmatics out of biblical statements.[2] But that was only one way of construing the significance of the Bible for Christian faith. Abandoning that explanation need not involve abandoning the claim that gave rise to it: that the Bible is somehow definitive of Christianity, and so can function as a doctrinal norm.

What the collapse of pre-critical uses of the Bible in Christian theology makes plain is that it is not the Bible as such that defines Christianity or functions as a doctrinal norm, but the Bible as interpreted. Other elements enter the equation, including some later tradition and some of the contemporary knowledge and experience of those interpreting the Bible and seeking to clarify and communicate the faith of the church. But that does not mean that doctrinal norms are unavailable, or that the Bible is unable to provide them and no longer foundational for Christian theology except in a historical sense. A religion without boundaries would soon lose its identity, and what Christians have always asserted about God and the world directs us to the Bible as a source and norm of their faith, and does so on the assumption that given the right keys to interpret it, a basic clarity and perspicuity about Christianity can be found here.

Before arguing in favour of this assumption and proposing a hermeneutical key that will epitomize both the unity of the Christian Bible and the identity of Christianity it is well to recognize that their relationship is disputed. Some who take a stringent view of the identity of true or authentic Christianity base this (as they think) on the Bible, or (in fact) on their interpretations of the Bible. Others give more weight to the subsequent tradition and some add to that a strong emphasis on the teaching authority of the contemporary church, the magisterium. Some Christians give more weight to contemporary experience in defining

2. R. Bultmann, *Theology of the New Testament*, II (London: SCM Press, 1955), p. 237.

Christianity and these theologians are usually open to a greater variety of authentic forms of Christianity. The truth of the mystery is after all beyond all our formulations.

That is a salutary warning against absolutizing any of our theological proposals. Nevertheless, and quite apart from any ideas of the Bible as 'inspired' or containing 'revelation', Christians need to be able to identify their religion, and the way they read their scripture is likely to play an important part in this. One function of theories about the unity of the Bible is to provide quite general guidance as to how it should be read. They do this by providing a sense of what the Bible is all about, and the shape of the whole. That is relatively unproblematic. But such theories may be compatible with conflicting versions of Christianity. The harder question is whether any theory will allow the Bible to function as a *doctrinal norm*, which can exclude some versions of Christianity as inauthentic.

Any such critical judgments will of course be directed at particular *theologies*, not at the persons who hold them, and whose relationship to God (a) is invisible, and (b) may well be more profound than their theory about it. The most that even a Church can say is that certain mistaken formulations are untrue to Christian experience and may endanger the relationship to God of those who hold them. But recognizing that proposals about the unity of scripture are theological proposals about how it should be read by Christians involves a readiness to criticize what are judged inauthentic accounts of Christianity.

Approaching our topic in this way suggests that an account of the unity of scripture may have a hidden polemical function. It will also have to be general enough to avoid the contradictions among the witnesses. That in effect excludes the use of individual texts in isolation to settle (or rather to substitute for) a moral or theological argument. When an individual text is cited it is seen as epitomizing a larger strand of the biblical witness. The contingent historical character of scripture excludes its use as a quarry for proof-texts. If it has any kind of normative force this will have to derive from the whole or at least large parts of the biblical tradition, and that is what accounts of its unity are attempting to make intelligible.

The common-sense assumption that such theories are simply read out of the texts themselves will not stand up. The variety of possible proposals shows it is questionable. It is surely an expression of the strong residue of biblicism understandably found in much biblical theology.

Even after critical scholarship has discredited older views of inspiration and inerrancy, the strong belief of Christians in the givenness of the revelation of God in Christ continues to pull them in a biblicist direction, especially in protestantism where the sense of tradition and the magisterium are less strong than in catholicism. By 'biblicism' is meant here not a high regard for the importance of scripture for Christian faith and theology, which is to be strongly endorsed, but an attitude to it which minimizes the contribution of the theological interpreters who are seeking to make sense of it. Calling this 'biblicism', and avoiding pejorative words like bibliolatry and fundamentalism, acknowledges the legitimacy of its concern. Christianity asserts a revelation of God that is prior to faith, and is heavily dependent on the witness of scripture in identifying this. Interpretation is a dangerous business. It gives power to the interpreters, including the power to disregard some of the textual data. Christian theological interpretation of scripture, or the attempt to clarify and communicate the Christian message through reflection upon scripture, is bound to be selective and this opens a wide door to subjectivity. The witness of biblicism may be valued for recalling us to forgotten aspects of the biblical data.

Nevertheless, interpretation is what is going on in all Christian reading of scripture, and the contribution of the interpreters themselves to this process needs to be clarified. This is disputed among literary theorists, so theologians will have to make up their own minds, and say what view of textual meaning they take.

If they want scripture to function as any kind of a norm they are bound to resist textual indeterminacy. A scripture that can mean anything will not serve as any kind of a norm. On the other hand, limiting themselves to the judgments of exegetes and historians also proves inadequate for Christian use of the Bible, including Christian theological use of the Bible, for reasons already given. It is true that theology is more bound to literary and historical meanings than liturgy and devotion, but theology also needs a view of the whole which exegesis as such does not provide. Theories of the unity of the Bible aim to provide this without conflicting with the historical and exegetical meaning of the individual texts. They are constructed by interpreters and tested by the textual data.

The challenge taking shape is to construct a theory which will not only give general guidance on how Christians should read their scripture, but which will also function as a doctrinal norm and give some specific guidance about what is authentic Christianity and what is not.

Whether or not that proves possible it is important to recognize that constructing such a theory is an interpretative move made for specific theological purposes. It stems from the position of the Bible in Christianity and reinforces that.

Christian use of the Bible requires stable meanings from individual texts, such as historical exegesis strives to provide (not always successfully, but the ideal serves well as a guiding beacon). It also requires a view of the whole which is flexible enough to allow Christians to see some correspondence between their contemporary faith and their scriptures. Theories of the unity of scripture answer this latter need while allowing biblical scholarship to answer the former. Without that mechanism for guiding a Christian reading of scripture operating at the high level of generality found in theories about the whole there would be a constant pressure to squeeze Christian meanings out of particular texts, as happens in pre-critical exegesis. If the question of the Christian meaning of scripture can be satisfactorily answered at a level remote from the particularities of the texts the temptations to distorting exegesis can be avoided.

Whether it is possible to make a proposal which is both true to the texts and able to function as a doctrinal norm remains to be seen, but that is our aim. The danger of a very general account of the unity of the Bible is that it will lack cutting edge. Some theories are so vague as to licence contradictory accounts of Christianity. An account of the unity that can function as a doctrinal norm will have to be doctrinally specific as well as flexible. It will have to embrace the biblical diversity and the legitimate theological pluralism of Christianity, while excluding what the proposer thinks (and can make a case for saying) are inauthentic forms of Christianity.

A particular proposal about the unity of the Bible can clarify what is going on *in all such interpretative moves*, regardless of whether anyone is persuaded by the particular suggestion. In what follows I would like to persuade other Christian theologians about how best to epitomize the identity of Christianity and what their scriptures are essentially all about. That substantive proposal should be of interest to theologians and students of Christianity. But the broader aim of this essay is not dependent on the plausibility of that proposal. The attempt itself, as an act of interpretation, is designed to support John Sawyer's contention that biblical scholarship can extend beyond history and philology, essential as both these disciplines remain, and that the history of interpretation should not be consigned to the dustbin of church history. Biblical scholars should surely strive to be *interpreters* of one kind or another. Theological interpretation is one kind of biblical interpretation which has, by influencing the development of Christianity, had a massive cultural effect. It still has a massive cultural potential, both inside and outside the churches, and a responsible biblical scholarship cannot ignore this.

'Interpretation' implies literary study, both practical criticism and the theory which accompanies and sometimes outruns it. Some literary theory is more than faintly reminiscent of theological hermeneutics. The history of biblical interpretation makes visible a number of theoretical questions which intersect with recent developments in the study of texts. It also makes interpreters more self-conscious about their own goals and social locations, and sometimes more willing to appreciate other perspectives instead of brusquely dismissing them as 'pre-critical'. John Sawyer has contributed significantly both to the history of interpretation and to the emergence of new methods in biblical studies. Whether or not he would call himself a biblical theologian, he has illuminated the hermeneutical field which was once the province of theologians and is now shared with other theorists. It is therefore appropriate to honour a scholar who has encouraged us to step outside the purely historical camp without forgetting what we learned there by exploring an interpretative principle which has been a major topic in biblical theology ever since critical historical study cracked the earlier dogmatic framework of this discipline. We shall take our topic out of the mainly historical frame of reference in which it has usually been considered over the past 150 years and into a framework which makes greater allowance for the interpreter's subjectivity. The aim, as in all biblical theology, will be to provide some guidance to the communities of faith which read, mark, learn and inwardly digest the Bible as their scriptures, and beyond that to find a doctrinal norm for Christianity which can be said to be true of the biblical witness which is read by Christians as a coherent whole. Our choice of the word 'scripture' rather than (more neutrally) 'the bible' signals the theological and ecclesial interest which has usually and rightly guided discussions of this topic.

*

The Christian Bible as a unity of two testaments was forged in the struggles against gnosticism and Marcion. Guaranteed by the doctrine of inspiration it was read in Christian liturgy, theology, and culture from the late second to the eighteenth century and beyond as a unified whole. Neither God who inspired it nor church doctrine based on it were considered incoherent. The Bible's account of the world and humans' place in it from creation to the end of time centred on the incarnation and justified the church's spiritual and intellectual domination of Europe in the centuries which followed. Biblical myth and history provided a vision of reality untroubled by minor tensions and contradictions in the constituent parts of the overarching narrative.

Over the past 300 years, by contrast, the Bible has come to be seen in purely human terms as a diverse collection of literature, the product of a long and varied history. This new perception was and is part of the revolutionary changes in Western ways of understanding the world and human life. Modern biblical scholarship owes more to European rationalism than to its older roots in Christian humanism. It destroyed traditional ideas of the inspiration and unity of the Bible, and in the present century has proved equally destructive of modern attempts to reinstate biblical authority at least for theology, if no longer for the whole culture. This underlying concern of the 'biblical theology movement' of the 1940s and 50s led to a new emphasis upon 'the unity of the Bible'. The 1960s reaction against it has left the topic in some disrepute.

But those conservative biblical theologians were right in thinking that maintaining the authority of the Bible for Christian life and doctrine requires some theory of its unity. Christians who see scripture as merely a valuable or stimulating anthology of religious texts can rest content with the diversity, but faced with a variety of sometimes contradictory voices, those who still look to the Bible for some kind of doctrinal norm have needed to explain how such a diverse collection can be normative for them. The modern question of the unity of the Bible is a theological response to the perception of literary, historical, and theological diversity within the canon. Such a response was a necessity for believers who saw scripture as a source and norm of Christian faith. Not all believers see scripture in this way, but those who do so need some account of its unity and coherence.

One strategy, current over the 200 years since J.P. Gabler, has been to preserve the normativity of scripture by finding that part which could serve (in Käsemann's phrase) as a 'canon within the canon'.[3] The Enlightenment, liberal, and kerygmatic types of theology disagreed about both the content of authentic Christianity and the criteria for identifying it, but they agreed in taking a *firm* stand on *part* of the biblical witness. They also recognized the element of subjectivity in theological interpretation.

All their different suggestions about which parts of scripture should be selected as normative for Christianity have seemed arbitrary to their opponents. Hans Küng's attempt to counter Käsemann's proposal with an insistence on the *whole* of scripture[4] can be criticized for failing to see the necessity of *Sachkritik*. Any proposal which refuses to challenge aspects of the biblical witness by appeal to the heart of the matter is a form of biblicism. But even if Küng missed the subtleties of Reformation and neo-Reformation biblical interpretation,[5] he rightly expressed unease with a selectivity that excludes so much of the biblical witness. Granted the impossibility of a pre-critical biblicism which claims to take the whole Bible as equally normative for Christian faith, a more positive form of the selectivity strategy has been to look for a 'living centre of scripture'. This construction of a shape or pattern from the biblical data allows parts to be come peripheral or even subject to theological criticism (*Sachkritik*) in the light of the 'centre',[6] but is less likely to undermine the credibility and centrality of the Bible for Christian faith. It preserves the witness of the Bible as a whole, while in practice admitting that some parts are more important to the Christian religion than others. It combines a positive attitude to the scriptures, and attention to the whole, with a theory that highlights what is important.

Determining the unity of scripture is an even more cautious form of

3. E. Käsemann (ed.), *Das Neue Testament als Kanon* (Göttingen: Vandenhoeck & Ruprecht, 1970); I. Lönning, *Kanon im Kanon* (Oslo and Munich: Kaiser, 1972); S. Schulz, *Die Mitte der Schrift* (Stuttgart: Kreuz, 1976). Further bibliography in *Jahrbuch für biblische Theologie* 1 (1986).

4. H. Küng, 'Der Frühkatholizismus im Neuen Testament als kontroverstheologisches Problem' (1962), reprinted in H. Küng, *Kirche im Konzil* (Freiburg: Herder, 1964) and in Käsemann (ed.), *Das Neue Testament als Kanon*.

5. For this see G. Ebeling, '"Sola scriptura" und das Problem der Tradition', in Käsemann (ed.), *Das Neue Testament als Kanon*; translated in G. Ebeling, *The Word of God and Tradition* (London: Collins, 1968).

6. Cf. W. Schrage, 'Die Frage nach der Mitte und dem Kanon im Kanon des neuen Testaments in der neueren Diskussion', in J. Friedrich *et al.* (eds.), *Rechtfertigung* (Tübingen: Mohr, 1976), pp. 415-42.

the same interpretative move. It sounds even more positive about scripture as a whole, yet in practice introduces a similar process of discrimination. Instead of attacking biblicism head-on, and in the process weakening biblical authority, it can argue that biblicism is but one theory of the unity of the Bible, and that other theories are more true to what the texts say and to what Christianity is or should be, and to how the Bible is actually used in Christianity.

The similarity of these three moves becomes clear when Christians say that Christ is (in some sense) the unity of scripture, or the living centre of scripture, or that what matters is 'what proclaims Christ'—and that what fails to proclaim Christ is subject to *Sachkritik*—criticism in the light of the essential *matter* of scripture. Because Christians find in Jesus Christ crucified and risen the decisive saving revelation of God the central importance of scripture for them consists in its witness to him as that.

This common Christian answer to the question of the unity of Christian scripture is clearly formulated from the theological standpoint of the interpreter, not simply read out of scripture in a neutral or objective way. A purely historical and exegetical study of the New Testament might reasonably reach the same conclusion, and this has encouraged the biblicist tendency in New Testament theology which underestimates the contribution of the interpreters, but Christian scripture includes the Old Testament (and for some the Apocrypha), and hermeneutical proposals which absolutize historical exegesis to the exclusion of other considerations risk downgrading the scriptural status of the Old Testament because it is historically pre-Christian.

On the other hand we have seen good reason to value the controls provided by historical exegesis. They make for the relatively stable meanings which are needed if scripture is to function as (among other things) a doctrinal norm. But this needs complementing by a more general theory which will guide Christian reading of these mainly pre-Christian texts. Seeing them as pointing to Christ provides a criterion for excluding from the Christian norm aspects which contradict this without despising the weaker and more shameful parts of this fallible yet wonderful human witness to the faith of Israel. The Christian import of the whole, without which the New Testament might easily become vacuous, rests in its identifying who God is, the God and Father of our Lord Jesus Christ. Beyond that it has inestimable value as religious literature; but its scriptural status rests on its making the revelation in Jesus Christ recognizable as a revelation of God. There is apparently no knowledge of God independent of a prior religious tradition. In that case the Jewish tradition and especially its scriptures are as indispensable for Christian faith as they presumably were for Jesus himself.

Our christological answer to the question of the unity of Christian scripture, including as that does the Old Testament, makes clear that such theories originate in the mind of the reader. That is less subjective than it sounds because the Christian mind has itself been largely shaped by these texts, and the New Testament writings are more dependent on the Old Testament than is often realized. My point is that this is as it should be, given the interactive way in which scriptures function for religious communities. That is not to underestimate the givenness of the revelation of Christ, its priority to any believer's response, or the informational component to scripture. But it recognizes that revelation 'happens', if at all, in the present moment of disclosure, when the foundational event becomes alive for a believer, and the person who is said to be the revelation of God is confessed as 'alive' and Lord of the living and the dead. The alternative views of revelation which emphasize the text or the history behind it at the expense of the present event of faith with its dimension of hope for the future risk identifying the revelation of God with the Bible itself in a biblicist fashion, or with a part or the whole of human history in historicist fashion. Both are idolatrous.

The phrase 'the unity of scripture' admittedly has an almost biblicist ring, directing attention firmly to the texts themselves, as though the interpreter has simply to point out what is inherent in them. Attempts have therefore been made to establish the unity of scripture by critical historical methods[7] without acknowledging how far the creative contribution of interpreters goes beyond the legitimate differences of historians. The correct intuition within this misconceived approach is that the religious tradition, on the basis of which the revelation of God has happened and continues to happen, is already 'given', not spun out of each interpreter's imagination and preferences. But the interpreters' vision and discernment do play a part in the apprehension of God and the continuing life of the tradition and community.

All reflection on 'unity' is a function of the mind that sorts out and arranges the data.[8] It is a way of making sense of a diversity, respecting

7. E.g., F. Mildenberger, 'Biblische Theologie als kirchliche Schriftauslegung', *Jahrbuch für biblische Theologie* 1 (1986), p. 157.

8. So D. Stacy, *Interpreting the Bible* (London: SPCK, 1976), p. 34.

what is given but thinking about it and organizing it without doing it violence. There are many ways of construing the unity of the Bible, and all of them involve interpreters doing more than simply repeating what the texts are saying, while remaining subject to the constraints of a relatively objective historical exegesis. That exegetical task is essential, but judgments about the unity of the whole are synthetic judgments by interpreters who bring their theological interests and beliefs to the texts, not analytic judgments arising out of scholarly exegesis alone. They are proposals about the meaning of the whole collection of texts and reflect the interpreter's own perspective.

Proposals which find the unity of Christian scripture in Jesus Christ seen as the decisive revelation for all, of God who is known in the religion of Israel, depend on some historical and some doctrinal information. Christians expect to find in the Gospels enough historical information to identify Jesus of Nazareth and in the biblical literature enough transmitted of Israel's faith and experience to say who God is: the one God, the Creator, who is known in Judah and Israel (Ps. 76.1). But these two components do not add up to Christianity as understood by the New Testament writers or their successors. They are therefore on their own insufficient for a proposal about the unity of scripture which might serve as a doctrinal norm. Where, if anywhere, can that be found?

Just as the early church found the biblical references to God and Jesus insufficient to interpret either in a way which would exclude misunderstanding, so the christological proposal about the unity or centre or point of scripture has to be made more specific. Once we are free from the biblicist assumptions which have dominated and discredited much biblical theology and which implied that this definitional point must be drawn from within scripture itself, we can look elsewhere, and most naturally to the subsequent Christian doctrinal tradition. What is proposed will have to be tested by reference to the biblical data, and not be incompatible with that, but need not be drawn from it directly. It will be drawn from it only indirectly insofar as the doctrinal tradition itself claims to be interpreting scripture in the light of on-going Christian experience and reflection.

Neither need it be drawn from the history behind the texts, important as this aspect of the subject-matter of scripture may be. Recent theories of meaning recognize the contribution made by the interpreters themselves, and that corresponds to our claim that proposals about the unity of their scripture are made by theologians from the perspective of their own convictions about what is central to their religion, convictions shaped by a tradition itself governed by the texts but also responding to other experience and developing in ways deemed faithful to both.

The doctrinal specification which an orthodox Christian will want to add to the christological proposal about the unity of scripture is that Jesus Christ, the crucified and risen Lord, is rightly understood as truly human and truly divine. The reason for proposing this is that it corresponds to what Christianity has generally asserted about God and Jesus from New Testament times, and therefore (unless there is sufficient reason to deny it) would seem to be indicative of authentic Christianity.

Even that formula will require conceptual clarification and supporting historical argument because it is not self-evident what 'truly divine' means—or that it can be defined in a way that embraces all the New Testament witnesses and all subsequent Christians generally considered orthodox. The formula does not have to embrace the Old Testament beyond asserting that it is the same God who is spoken of in both testaments. Christians value the Old Testament and see in it a prerequisite for understanding the New, but do not identify their faith by reference to it or base their christologies on it beyond that essential claim about who the God made known in Jesus is. The unity Christians find in the Old Testament writings is not so much their historical and literary relationship to one another as their relationship to Christian faith expressed in the New Testament. Obviously Jewish worshippers will determine the unity of the Hebrew Bible very differently, relative to their own faith, even if both parties are keen to respect the integrity of the individual texts. They work from different centres, while both being theocentric, because they locate the revelation of God differently. The central Christian witnesses lie outside the Old Testament.

The conceptual clarification by which the early church affirmed and restated its central conviction, that in having to do with Jesus it had to do with God, involved asserting that the man Jesus has also to be confessed as truly God, not some inferior being, and that God has to be thought of as triune. This conceptual clarification cannot be found in the New Testament because no New Testament writer, not even the Johannine evangelist at 1.1-3 and 20.28, was answering the question with which trinitarian theology was to wrestle: how Jesus could be called God without abandoning monotheism. Neither were they asking how Jesus could be both human and divine. The justification for having recourse to the Chalcedonian *vere deus, vere homo*, which states the conditions of any orthodox christology without solving the problems, is that this formula expresses the conviction of all the NT writers that in the human person Jesus we find a saving revelation of God.

John's revelational theology makes this most clear and explicit within the New Testament, but there is no reason to doubt that all the New Testament writers shared that basic christological faith. They did not all express it in the same ways, or through incarnational theology or myth, but it is not John's incarnational theology that we see as constituting the shared faith of all these writers. That is simply one contingent set of terms by which this faith was expressed. If Christians assume the pre-existence of the Son that is not because John's mythical language is obligatory for them but because their belief in his divinity implies his transcendence of time.[9] It is in the actual faith in Jesus as the revelation of God, which John's metaphorical and even on occasion mythic language expresses,[10] that we find the unity of the New Testament writers. The christological definition is purely formal until filled out with theological content (e.g. the language of natures and person), but it specifies the shape of Christian belief and excludes some christological proposals and solutions. It insists on making what we believe about Jesus constitutive for belief in God and vice versa.

Reading scripture through the lens of this doctrinal definition does not commit us to any of the particular christologies through which believers have made their faith intelligible in different social and intellectual milieux. Even the language of 'two natures' in the Chalcedonian formula, and 'substance' in the Nicene creed is excluded from our proposal because these are particular christologies, whereas it is only the structure of Christian faith itself which we wish to specify. Theological elaboration is inescapable when anyone tries to articulate Christian faith, but considerable diversity is possible in responsible theological articulation.

This legitimate theological diversity and pluralism is a fact. But the christological definition sets limits to what has been considered authentic Christianity. It was intended to exclude docetism, apollinarianism, and arianism for example, and it continues to exclude ebionism, adoptionism and some other heresies. In particular it rules off-side some versions of Christianity which understandably became popular in eighteenth-century

9. I owe this phrase and much else to Professor C.F.D. Moule.

10. I have argued this in 'St John's Gospel, the Incarnation, and Christian Orthodoxy', in D. Ford and D. Stamp (eds.), *Essentials of Christian Community* (Edinburgh: T. & T. Clark, 1995).

Europe and still enjoy some currency: those which deny the divinity of Christ. These denials were sometimes motivated by a healthy desire to cut through the tangle of tradition and recover the simple gospel. Pruning is always needed, and new insights are sometimes authentic expressions of the old faith. But here elements were excluded which the first generation and subsequent sixteen centuries found essential. Many of these denials are misunderstandings based on wooden ideas about what divinity must mean, but those who persist in denying that Jesus himself is the decisive saving revelation of God part company with the New Testament and classical Christian tradition in a fundamental way.

Our proposal to find the unity of scripture in the *doctrine* of the incarnation (not any particular mythical expression or theological elaboration of that bald heading, but the purely formal doctrinal rule) is thus a polemical theological move, and as such unlikely to commend itself to all theological interpreters. Can it be defended?

It is no help to show that it is a better proposal than certain others, because those who dislike it are likely to deny that any doctrinal unity can be found in the Bible. The first task is to show that for all the theological diversity of the New Testament, visible in its christological pluralism, there is also a Christian doctrinal unity, encapsulated in some words from Chalcedon. To do that would be to write a New Testament theology, constructed in such a way as to incorporate enough Old Testament theology to identify the God of Israel as the God in Christ of whom the New Testament speaks. Of course it is possible to claim only that the Chalcedon doctrinal belief is *implicit* in the christological faith of the New Testament writers. They had not yet faced the conceptual problems inherent in their Christian faith. But if what they wrote and how they responded to Jesus implies the traditional religious evaluation of the risen Lord that is sufficient to justify our proposal.

There is no need even to argue that all the early Christians were as 'orthodox' (to speak anachronistically) as the New Testament writers themselves. It is not those hypothetically reconstructed figures who are said to be normative for Christianity, but the New Testament documents. It is possible to surmise that a source or even an early version of John's Gospel may have been less clear about the humanity of Jesus than the canonical version.

If our claim about the New Testament witnesses can be sustained (and since some are so short that means in practice that our claim is *not falsified* by historically critical exegesis) then the proposal can be said to be indirectly drawn from the scripture and not imposed upon it heteronomously. The Fathers' claim to be interpreting scripture through their conciliar decisions can be defended, even though these were not the only possible ways of reading scripture. Christians' assumption of the truth of the christological formula is based on its fruitfulness over centuries, and if that sounds too pragmatic an account of religious truth it is hard to see any alternative at the level of doctrinal framework. Most theological proposals have more content and can be tested more rigorously, but the general doctrinal shape of Christianity expressed in that formula has become axiomatic. Its rationale is that it seems to be what all orthodox Christians everywhere have always, at least implicitly, believed.[11]

This relatively loose version of traditional Christianity makes room for a legitimate theological pluralism without abandoning doctrinal boundaries as some forms of this religion do. Our discussion has wandered into what is clearly theological and ecclesial territory in order to support the initial claim that this is where discussions of the unity of scripture belong. They are not exegetical proposals, but have to be conducted within earshot of the historical and exegetical debates. Even though proposals about the unity of scripture reflect contemporary religious and theological interests they are also proposals about these texts and must therefore avoid doing violence to them, indeed must be seen to make a kind of sense of them—if not the only possible sense.

It is this combination of historical exegesis at the level of particular texts, with a theory of the unity of scripture as a whole which is not drawn directly from these texts themselves, that allows both the flexibility needed in Christian readings of scripture and the controls provided by a mass of texts whose meaning is still determined by the linguistic and literary conventions they employ. So long as critical exegesis continues alongside proposals about scripture as a whole, and the possibility of these being challenged by that is recognized, there is no real danger of theological interests either distorting exegesis on the one hand or subverting the capacity of scripture to challenge later tradition on the other. The challenge of particular texts read afresh with whatever scholarly methods seem appropriate need not be inhibited by a general theory about scripture which surveys and makes sense of the whole.

11. Vincent of Lerins is here being re-interpreted along the lines of Schleiermacher and Troeltsch, among others, on 'the essence of Christianity'. See S.W. Sykes, *The Identity of Christianity* (London: SPCK, 1984).

Proposals about the unity of scripture may stem from the interpreters' theological interests, but are tested by reference to the texts and can be expected to illuminate them. If they do so their validity will be confirmed and the suspicion that they have been imposed and are at odds with these diverse witnesses will be allayed. That the Old Testament speaks (however imperfectly) of the God that Christians worship has been confirmed by the experience of many generations. That all the New Testament witnesses identify Jesus (however gropingly) in terms compatible with the summary provided in the later doctrinal formula will have to be argued in detail in a New Testament theology.

Like interpreters of the law theologians depend on a tradition and are answerable to a community, but unlike the law we expect engagement with these texts to generate new insights. In this respect theological interpretation has more in common with literary criticism than with the law. But it resembles legal interpretation in ruling some judgments out of line with the normative texts and the tradition of interpretation deriving from these. Our formula of unity sets limits to what count as authentic Christian interpretation of any writing. These are generous, and need not exclude more than the heresies already enumerated, because they must not allow the tradition to extinguish the spirit Christians believe can work through biblical interpretation. Those who think our Chalcedonian proposal a good example of old wine-skins burst by the spirit of Jesus in a new age must be referred to the mystery of the resurrection on which the traditional doctrinal definition depends. If their spirit of Jesus does not depend on that divine event their Christian humanism, however admirable, is not that of the New Testament and Christian scripture.

In their private devotional uses of scripture believers may play all kinds of tunes on this instrument, but in theology they are more constrained by what is given. Our proposal has attempted to identify and define what is given in a way which is true to Christianity, can guide Christian reading of scripture, and can exclude (for certain purposes) readings which Christians have generally agreed miss the Christian point that God is known in the crucified and risen Lord Jesus. If that norm seems too loose and general for some, it will doubtless seem too restrictive to others. But there is much to be said for a *via media*.

We may doubt whether historical exegesis, essential as it is, can do full justice to the potential of a single text. Much less can it give clear directions about the meaning of the whole. Frameworks are inevitably brought by interpreters, and if this process was largely invisible within a unitary religious culture, it is no longer so today. That is liberating and exhilarating. But the conflict of interpretations can easily degenerate into a chaos of interpretations. That too is exciting for some, but intolerable for church theologians. Their definition of a unity in scripture builds a dam which allows the reservoir to gather depth and irrigate the valley. It also provides a standpoint for surveying the whole scene. Gathered in a canon of scripture, historically shallow streams gain a new significance. Dams, like canons and interpretative lenses, are constructed by humans, but the rain which streams into the lake to be preserved and made available for new purposes comes from above. A modified doctrine of inspiration remains possible. The notions of both a canon and the interpretation of scripture imply co-operation between human and divine agency.

A bomb was placed by modern European rationalism under the dam which both circumscribed the canon and taught believers how to read it. The great lake of scripture, perceived as a unity from the doctrinal standpoint of traditional Christianity, was released by enlightened dam-busters and replaced by the isolated streams of scripture running freely through a cultural valley once submerged in religious meanings. These have a beauty and a freshness of their own, and apparently satisfy the needs of some religious individuals, if not of churches which need boundaries, or societies which need authorities.

If inspiring writings are all we possess we shall have to learn to live on such mean rations. It seems inconceivable today that the old dam can be rebuilt and the depth of the old reservoir regained and the culture permeated by it. But a more modest construction is possible, allowing these texts to gather into a new slim-line scripture sufficient to meet the reduced doctrinal needs of a religious community that sees the importance of co-operating with other sources of energy. The new and shallower lake still provides Christians with their religious identity, found in the same Lord and God that they worship in much the same way, holding much the same faith and hope and love, with all the faults and failures that remain par for the human course.

The simple construction that has here been presented as the doctrinal norm of Christianity, and accordingly the essential unity of Christian scripture, is less vulnerable to the terrorist activities of historians and exegetes than the earlier imposing structures of biblical theology. It provides a consensual platform for Anglicans who see in the creeds an interpretative key to scripture, and Presbyterians like John who have learned from Jean Calvin that John's Gospel is the key to Christian scripture, and for such less doctrinaire Roman Catholics as those to whom John Sawyer dedicated his splendid book.

'A SIXTIETH PART OF PROPHECY': THE PROBLEM OF CONTINUING REVELATION IN JUDAISM

Philip S. Alexander

It appears to be an axiom of the historiography of Judaism that the Jews are 'a people of the book'. By this is usually meant that central to Judaism as we know it today is a closed canon of sacred literature—the Torah of Moses and the other writings of the Hebrew Bible—which are the ultimate authority and court of appeal on all matters of belief and practice. Prophecy came to an end some time after the Babylonian exile and with its demise direct revelation from God ceased. Thereafter the will of God was to be discerned only indirectly through the text of Scripture, which was seen as fixed, self-contained and valid for all time. With the end of prophecy and the formation of a canon of sacred Scripture a new type of religious authority emerged in Judaism: the prophet, the direct bearer of the word of the Lord, was supplanted by the scribe, the expert interpreter of holy writ.

The view that the history of Judaism can be divided into biblical and post-biblical, or prophetic and scribal periods, pervades the scholarly literature and is reflected to a large measure in the articulation of the academic discipline of Jewish studies. Yet this view can hardly be said to be based on an objective analysis of the historical facts. Rather it has been taken over uncritically from certain Jewish sources, in which it functions as an article of faith and as a fundamental element of a particular world-view. The most influential of these sources are the classic writings of rabbinic Judaism—the form of Judaism which has been normative from late antiquity to modern times. The social structure and religious authority of the rabbinate are predicated on the assertion that prophecy has ceased: God no longer speaks directly to humanity; the Sages now determine his will by applying their rational faculties to the elucidation of sacred texts.

A paradigmatic statement of this position is found in the well-known story in the Babylonian Talmud, *Bava Meṣia'* 59a-b, about the dispute among the Sages over the oven of Akhnai:

> We learnt elsewhere: If it was cut up into rings and sand put between each ring, then Rabbi Eliezer declared it clean, but the Sages declared it unclean. This was the oven of Akhnai. Why of Akhnai? Rav Judah said in Samuel's name: 'Because they surrounded it with arguments like a snake (*'akhna*) and proved it unclean'.
>
> It was taught: On that day Rabbi Eliezer brought forward all the arguments in the world, but they refused to accept them.
>
> He said to them: 'If the halakhah agrees with me, let this carob tree prove it'. The carob tree was uprooted from its place a hundred cubits (some say: four hundred cubits). They said to him: 'No proof can be brought from a carob tree'.
>
> Again he said to them: 'If the halakhah agrees with me, let this stream of water prove it'. The stream flowed backwards. They said to him: 'No proof can be brought from a stream of water'.
>
> Again he said to them: 'If the halakhah agrees with me, let the walls of the schoolhouse prove it'. The walls started to lean as if about to fall. Rabbi Joshua rebuked them. He said to them: 'If the pupils of the Sages are disputing about halakhah, what business have you to interfere?' The walls did not fall, for the sake of Rabbi Joshua's honour, nor did they become upright again, for the sake of Rabbi Eliezer's honour. And they are still standing in the inclined position.
>
> Again Rabbi Eliezer said: 'If the halakhah agrees with me, let it be proved from heaven'. A heavenly voice (*bat qol*) went forth and said: 'Why do you dispute with Rabbi Eliezer, seeing that in every case the halakhah agrees with him?' Rabbi Joshua stood to his feet and said: 'It is not in heaven!' What did he mean by, 'It is not in heaven!'? Rabbi Jeremiah said: 'He meant: The Torah has already been given on Mount Sinai, so we pay no attention to a heavenly voice, since you wrote long ago in the Torah at Mount Sinai: "After the majority you must incline" (Exod. 23.2)'.
>
> Rabbi Nathan met Elijah. He said to him: 'What did the Holy One, blessed be he, do in that hour?' He said to him: 'He laughed and said, "My sons have defeated me, my sons have defeated me!"'

This story gives vivid expression to the fundamental rabbinic dogma that the Torah was given once for all, and that decisions as to its meaning lie solely within the competence of the collectivity of the Sages, relying on argument and persuasion. Rabbi Eliezer's attempt to gain acceptance for his ruling goes through three distinct phases. First he tries argument. Then he invokes miracle, presumably as an indirect sign of divine approbation for his opinion. Finally, he calls for direct divine intervention in the form of a heavenly voice (a *bat qol*). The Sages rule both miracle and new revelation out of court: neither, they assert, has any part now to play in the process of deciding the law. When Rabbi Eliezer's arguments failed that should have been the end of the matter. By appealing to miracle and direct revelation Rabbi Eliezer was transgressing a basic principle of rabbinic Judaism: he was anachronistically and inappropriately seeking prophetic forms of validation for his halakhic position. The story implies that there *is* halakhah in heaven. Behind this is the belief that there exists a *Beit din shelema'alah*—a heavenly law-court where God himself sits and decides cases. This widespread rabbinic tradition was used at a theological level to legitimate rabbinic authority by showing that the Rabbis in their courts and schools on earth were engaged in an *imitatio dei.*[1] But at a legal level it was fraught with danger, for the question naturally arises as to what was the relationship between the upper and the lower courts. The *bat qol* announces that Rabbi Eliezer's view is the same as that of the celestial *Beit din*. But the Rabbis rule that the writ of the heavenly court does not run on earth.

They support their case by appealing to two texts. The first is Exod. 23.2, 'You shall not turn aside after the multitude to pervert justice'. This was taken to mean that one *should* follow the multitude (i.e. the majority) to *establish* justice (i.e. to decide cases). The second proof-text to which they allude, Deut. 30.11-14, speaks for itself:

> For this commandment which I command you this day, is not too hard for you, neither is it far off. It is not in heaven, that you should say: 'Who shall go up for us to heaven, and bring it down to us, and make us hear it, that we may do it?' Neither is it beyond the sea, that you should say: 'Who shall go over the sea for us, and bring it to us, and make us hear it, that we may do it?' But the word is very near you, in your mouth and in your heart, that you may do it.

Rabbi Joshua's, 'It is not in heaven!', is not intended to deny that there is halakhah in heaven. Rather, it is meant to assert the irrelevance of that celestial halakhah on earth. He could, perhaps, just as effectively have quoted Deut. 29.28, 'The secret things belong unto the Lord our God;

1. On the rabbinic concept of the heavenly law-court see P.S. Alexander, '3 Enoch', in J.H. Charlesworth, *The Apocrypha and Pseudepigrapha of the Old Testament* (New York: Doubleday, 1983), I, pp. 244-45.

but the things that are revealed belong to us and our children for ever, that we may do all the words of this law'. The Rabbis could, in principle, have set up a legal system in which knotty legal problems were decided by oracular means. Such systems are not unknown. Early in the history of Israel the *urim* and *thummim* may have performed this function (see, e.g., Num. 27.21). Trial by ordeal, as in the case of the suspected adulteress, the *soṭah* (Num. 5.11-31), also involves divine intervention in the decision of cases. Or, the Rabbis could have consecrated one of their number who, when speaking *ex cathedra* like the Pope, could have definitively resolved matters of doctrine and practice. But they reject all such expedients. They cannot admit divine intervention in legal disputes. They will not tolerate any blurring of the distinction between prophetic and scribal functions and authority.

The ending of the tale is highly ambivalent. Despite their brave show of scriptural proof-texts, the Rabbis still seem to feel that they need direct confirmation from heaven itself of their view that the heavenly court's writ does not run on earth. Through the agency of the prophet Elijah they learn that God has conceded defeat. Whether or not this is a late addition to the story, it serves our present purposes by reminding us of a profound paradox at the heart of the rabbinic position, namely that although there *is* truth in heaven, and although direct channels of communication still exist (much used in the past) by which that truth may be discovered, it should not be sought out. We should rest content with what has already been revealed in the Scriptures. This paradox, as we shall see, was to trouble Judaism right down to modern times.

Here, then, we have a ringing affirmation of the rabbinic doctrine that prophecy has ceased.[2] The statement is fundamentally theological and prescriptive in character: it asserts what *ought* to be the case. It claims that prophecy cannot now exist within Israel, and it implies that should prophetic phenomena occur they cannot by definition be accepted as valid. But is the statement also descriptive? As an actual fact was prophecy absent from Judaism? Did everyone agree that there was no longer any possibility of fresh, direct revelation from God? The answer to these questions must be an emphatic negative. Even within rabbinic

2. For a discussion of the various rabbinic views as to when precisely prophecy ceased see the important survey by E.E. Urbach, 'Matai paseqah ha-nevu'ah', *Tarbiṣ* 17 (1946), pp. 1-11; further Urbach, *The Sages: Their Concepts and Beliefs* (Jerusalem: Magnes Press, 1975), pp. 576-79. See also the bibliography cited in note 23 below.

Judaism prophetic phenomena constantly manifested themselves, direct revelations were received from God, and the very authorities who promulgated the end of prophecy embraced at the same time doctrines which, in effect, taught that revelation was open-ended and continuous.

The Rabbis concede that certain elements of prophecy survived even in their own day. One of these was the *bat qol*, 'the heavenly voice'. 'From the death of Haggai, Zechariah and Malachi, the holy spirit was removed from Israel. Nevertheless they could make use of a *bat qol*' (*Tos. Soṭ.* 13.2; *B. Soṭ.* 48b; *Yom.* 9b; *Sanh.* 11a). This phenomenon, according to some, was not simply a faint, residual echo of prophecy: the *bat qol* had been heard also back in biblical times. For example, a *bat qol* had confirmed Solomon's judgement in the case of the disputed child (see *B. Mak.* 23b). It was a genuine prophetic form of communication which had persisted down into the post-prophetic era. The *bat qol* was, indeed, ruled out of court in *B. B. Meṣ.* 59a-b, but its existence is not denied. So, too, dreams—a major form of prophetic communication in the biblical period—are acknowledged as still having some kind of prophetic power: 'a dream is a sixtieth part of prophecy' (*B. Ber.* 57b). Again there is an attempt to play down the significance of the phenomenon: a sixtieth part of anything is the minimal amount that counts. Yet the reality of the phenomenon is not totally denied. And there were other experiences which were also recognized as in some sense direct communications from God. Thus, 'Rabbi Yoḥanan said: If at the moment of rising from sleep a verse of Scripture comes [unprompted] into one's mind, this is a minor kind of prophecy (*nevu'ah qetannah*)' (*B. Ber.* 57b).

Moreover, the fundamental rabbinic concept of Oral Torah can be regarded, at least in some of its formulations, as involving a doctrine of continuous revelation. It is true that the Oral Torah is traced back to Moses on Sinai and presented as a clarification of the Written Torah. But the Rabbis seem to concede that at least *some* of the content of the Oral Torah has only emerged with time: there is an on-going process of unfolding in which the latent meaning of the Torah is revealed. God has always more light to break forth from his word. This view is famously expressed in the story in *B. Men.* 29b, which tells of how Moses visited the school of Rabbi Aqiva and found himself unable to follow the halakhic discussion. 'However, when they came to a certain topic and the students said, "Master how do you know this?" and Aqiva replied, "It was given as halakhah to Moses from Sinai", Moses' mind was set at rest'. The suggestion appears to be that the halakhah has so evolved since the time of Moses that, were he to come back, he would not recognize it. This is continuing revelation in all but name.[3]

Allied to the doctrine of the Oral Torah is the belief that, although the holy spirit no longer inspires individuals, it resides in the *collectivity* of the Sages, who stand in a tradition of ordination going back to Moses: 'from the day that the [first] Temple was destroyed prophecy was taken from the prophets and given to the Sages' (*B. B. Bat.* 12a). As a group the Sages are endowed with the power to determine correctly the meaning of the Torah: they have been granted a kind of *collective* inspiration which ensures that they will finally reach the truth. Set against

3. The rabbinic doctrine of Oral Torah is immensely complicated and once we go beyond the simple *credo* that two Torahs were given to Moses on Sinai consensus as to its meaning begins to break down. Some did assert that the *whole* content of the Oral Torah (including the Mishnah and the Gemara) was given to Moses at Sinai (see *B. Ber.* 5a; Sifra, *Be-ḥuqqotai* 8). This view is difficult to maintain, since many of the traditions are clearly cited in the names of later scholars. *Pes. K.* 4.7 offers a defence by appealing to divine foreknowledge: Moses, when he ascended to heaven to receive the Torah, found the Holy One reciting those later traditions verbatim in the name of the scholars who would later promulgate them. *Exod. R.* 26.6 takes a rather different line: the souls of the later authorities (in this case the prophets) were actually present at Sinai and heard the words which they were later to speak. The idea seems to be that they recalled them in a kind of Platonic *anamnesis*. This position ties in with the model of the tradition which sees the task of the student as simply to pass on verbatim the words of his teacher (see, e.g., *B. 'Eruv.* 54b; further, Birger Gerhardsson, *Memory and Manuscript: Oral Transmission and Written Transmission in Rabbinic Judaism and Early Christianity* [Lund: Gleerup, 1961], which remains a valuable and accessible discussion of this question). But such a highly static and conservative model of the tradition is intensely problematic, and it is significant that in the middle ages, when attempts are at last made to articulate a fully coherent doctrine of Oral Torah, many of the theologians follow the *B. B. Men.* 29b line. For example, Joseph Albo, *'Iqqarim* III, 23, maintains that, if we exclude the category of halakhot designated *halakhot le-Mosheh mi-Sinai*, then the Oral Torah given to Moses at Sinai consisted essentially of the hermeneutical norms (*middot*) by which the Torah is to be elucidated. The application of these *middot* may result in differences of opinion, which can only be resolved by following in each generation the opinion of the *majority* of the Sages. Only the Sages' opinions are to be followed, since they alone have been endowed by God with wisdom (which is here the scribal analogue of the prophetic holy spirit). For a useful analysis of the classic rabbinic texts on the Oral Torah, see P. Schäfer, 'Das "Dogma" der mündlichen Torah im rabbinischen Judentum', in P. Schäfer, *Studien zur Geschichte und Theologie des rabbinischen Judentums* (Leiden: Brill, 1978), pp. 153-97.

these other rabbinic ideas the rabbinic doctrine of the cessation of prophecy begins to look much less absolute than might at first sight appear.[4]

Even within the halakhic tradition the fundamental rabbinic dogma that Torah is not in heaven was from time to time directly challenged. Two cases will serve to illustrate briefly how direct that challenge could be. The first is well known and involves Joseph Karo (1488–1575), who, as the author of the *Beit Yosef* and the *Shulḥan 'Arukh*, is counted as one of the great legal luminaries of Judaism. According to tradition Karo was visited by a heavenly mentor known as a *maggid*. The visitations of this *maggid* were recorded in the mystical diary known as the *Maggid Mesharim*. The following is a typical entry:[5]

> No sooner had we studied two tractates of the Mishnah than our Creator smote us so that we heard a voice speaking out of the mouth of the saint [i.e. Karo], may his light shine. It was a loud voice with the letters clearly enunciated. All the companions heard the voice, but were unable to understand what it said. It was an exceedingly pleasant voice, becoming increasingly strong. We all fell on our faces and none of us had any spirit left because of our great dread and awe.

We are clearly here in the presence of ecstatic, charismatic phenomena—some form of automatic speech, possibly even glossolalia. From the Second Temple period this type of 'possession' was associated in Judaism with an influx of the holy spirit and hence with prophecy. For the most part the *maggid*'s utterances take the form of rather generalized paraenesis, but some touch on halakhic issues, and are preceded by a formula such as: 'Thus it has been decided in the heavenly *Beit din*, and the Holy One, blessed be he, together with the members of the *Beit din*, has sent me to tell you things hitherto unrevealed'.[6] These attempts to reopen direct lines of communication between God and man were not confined to Karo. According to reliable sources, Moses Cordovero,

4. Ordination was seen not simply as the formal and symbolic transfer of authority from the master to the pupil, but as a passing on in some sense of the 'spirit' in a kind of apostolic succession. See A. Rothkoff, 'Semikhah', *EncJud* 14, cols. 1140-42.

5. I quote the translation given in Louis Jacobs' useful anthology of texts, *Jewish Mystical Testimonies* (New York: Schocken Books, 1977), p. 100. R.J.Z. Werblowsky, *Joseph Karo: Lawyer and Mystic* (Oxford: Clarendon Press, 1962) puts Karo's mystical experiences in their historical context. See especially his richly informative chapter on 'Spiritual Life in Sixteenth-century Safed: Mystical and Magical Contemplation' (pp. 38-83).

6. Jacobs, *Jewish Mystical Testimonies*, p. 114.

Solomon Alkabetz and other mystics in Safed belonging to the circle of Karo, would go on the eve of Sabbath and prostrate themselves at the graves of the saints in the vicinity of Safed, in the belief that they would receive communications from the heavenly law-court.[7] The similarity of this practice to an incubation oracle hardly needs mentioning. The idea presumably was that the saints who had died had graduated to the celestial *Beit din*, from which they might be induced to return in a dream or vision to reveal that court's decisions.

The second case involves the curious work entitled *Responsa from Heaven* (*She'eilot u-teshuvot min ha-shamayim*), composed by Jacob of Marvège sometime during the twelfth or thirteenth centuries. This consists of a collection of halakhic questions which Jacob submitted to the celestial *Beit din*, together with the heavenly responsa which came back. Jacob's technique appears to have been to write out his question before he went to sleep, and then to receive an answer in a dream. The *Responsa from Heaven* generated a considerable degree of puzzlement and debate among halakhists, some of whom saw clearly that it breached a fundamental principle of halakhah to appeal, not, as was common practice, to a great legal authority on earth, but direct to heaven. Some, however, were prepared, under certain circumstances, to condone the practice. There is evidence to suggest that Jacob was by no means the only halakhist to appeal directly to the *Beit din shelema'alah*.[8]

These cases come from the main-line halakhic tradition, where the constraints on prophetism are extremely strong. It is hardly surprising, then, that in the mystical tradition, where the constraints are much weaker, prophetic phenomena abound. Prophecy and mysticism are, of course, commonly distinguished, and there are, indeed, differences between them. It is often alleged that while the prophets have a strong sense of mission and feel called upon to proclaim a public message, mystics show little sense of being commissioned to perform a public role: they tend to keep their experiences secret and to concentrate on

7. Jacobs, *Jewish Mystical Testimonies*, p. 99.

8. For a translation see Jacobs, *Jewish Mystical Testimonies*, pp. 74-78. For discussion see G. Scholem, *Origins of the Kabbalah* (Princeton: Jewish Publication Society/Princeton University Press, 1987), p. 240 and note 88; I. Ta-Shma, 'She'eilot u-teshuvot min ha-shamayim', *Tarbiṣ* 57 (1987), pp. 51-66; N. Danzig, 'Teshuvot ha-ge'onim sha'arei teshuvah u-she'eilot u-teshuvot min ha-shamayim', *Tarbiṣ* 58 (1989), pp. 21-48.

personal spiritual development.[9] Prophecy and mysticism, narrowly defined, belong to different periods in the history of Israel and reflect very different societies. The two phenomena cannot simply be equated. Yet it would be wrong to overplay the differences. Both claim direct contact with the transcendent divine world; both claim to receive direct revelation. For our present purposes this is the crucial point. The mystics are at some pains to deny for themselves a public role, but we should not take their protestations too seriously. Many of them have a very definite message for Israel (and a radical one at that), and they have recorded it a length in large tomes: Jewish mystical literature is many times greater in bulk than prophetic literature. And in all sorts of ways, both direct and indirect, the mystics indicate that they see themselves as heirs of the ancient prophets. Even if their understanding of the nature of biblical prophecy is historically defective (as it undoubtedly is), that does not affect our argument here. What is important for us is their belief that prophecy has not ceased, that God may still be contacted directly and revelations received.

Merkavah mysticism, the earliest documented mystical movement within rabbinic Judaism, clearly reflects this belief. The Merkavah mystics were interested not simply in expounding the vision of Ezekiel, but in replicating it: they wanted to see for themselves what Ezekiel had seen. Some of the adepts ascended in trance to heaven, and had a vision of God seated on his throne. They communed with God, were shown secrets, and the treasuries of the heavenly Torah were opened and bestowed upon them. Such heavenly ascents are not a striking feature of the biblical narrative (the rapture of Elijah and, possibly, of Enoch, despite their later use by the mystics, hardly count). However, it was widely held in post-biblical tradition that Moses not only ascended Mount Sinai but went up into heaven itself to receive the Torah. The parallel between Moses' ascent and the mystics' ascent is explicitly played upon in the Merkavah literature. They were following in his footsteps; their experience was a 'Sinai' experience. The barrier between heaven and earth was penetrated not only by the mystics' ascent from earth, but by the descent of powerful angels from heaven. One of these angels—the Prince of Torah (*Śar Torah*)—was, as his name suggests, in some sense the custodian of the Torah, who was able to disclose its

9. See, e.g., M. Verman, *The Books of Contemplation: Medieval Jewish Mystical Sources* (New York: State University of New York Press, 1992), p. 5, appealing to A.J. Heschel, *The Prophets* (New York: Harper and Row, 1962), II, pp. 141-42.

secrets. The Merkavah mystics were not simply contemplatives. There is in Merkavah mysticism a strong element of theurgy. Many of the mystics believed that they possessed the spells to compel heaven to open and to bend divine agencies to do their will.[10]

A similar picture emerges when we examine the mediaeval Qabbalah. The Qabbalists were theosophists, intoxicated with the drama of the inner life of God. But how did they gain access to this most secret and impenetrable of worlds. The short answer, which they themselves routinely offer, was that they had received this secret knowledge by tradition (*qabbalah*) from hoary antiquity. The implication is that the secrets go back, like the Oral Torah, to the prophetic era, and originated then. But historically speaking this was not the case. The Qabbalah, though it draws on earlier texts, is a creation of the middle ages. It has a variety of sources, one of which is direct visionary experience. It is not ncessary to look far into qabbalistic literature to discover that prophetic, ecstatic phenomena were common in the circles of the *mequbbalim*.

These ecstatic phenomena are, perhaps, most explicit in the writings of the school of the thirteenth-century Qabbalist, Abraham Abulafia. Again, the theurgy of the texts is noteworthy. Abulafia claimed to teach his disciples how to attain a state of prophecy through manipulation of combinations of the Name of God. In a famous passage he writes:[11]

> Prophecy is a mode of the Intellect. It is the expression of 'the Lord our God, the Lord is one'. It is well known that those who love prophecy love God and they are beloved of God. Undoubtedly these are sages and prophets. Observe and realize that the numerical value of the word 'lovers' (*'ohavim*) is the same as that of the word 'prophecy' (*nevu'ah*), and by 'lovers' I mean 'beloved prophets'. This stage of prophecy is itself the worship of God in love. Appreciate that whoever knows the name of God has the spirit of God, the holy spirit, within him. That holy influence, descending by virtue of divine grace, will bestir, move and incline a man to strive to attain the knowledge of God, so as to sanctify him and declare his name to all the earth. Know and realise that those who prophesy by virtue of their knowledge of God are beloved by God.

10. The bibliography on Merkavah mysticism is now very extensive. Particularly relevant to our present theme is P. Schäfer, *Der verborgene und offenbare Gott* (Tübingen: Mohr-Siebeck, 1991).

11. Jacobs, *Jewish Mystical Testimonies*, p. 57. On Abulafia see further, M. Idel, *The Mystical Experience in Abraham Abulafia* (Albany, 1988); *idem*, *Studies in Ecstatic Kabbalah* (Albany, 1988).

One of Abulafia's disciples vividly describes the effect of applying his master's method as follows:[12]

> I practised this method for about a week. During the second week the power of meditation became so strong in me that I could not manage to write down the combinations of letters (which automatically spurted out of my pen), and if there had been ten people present they would not have been able to write down so many combinations as came to me during the influx. When I came to the night in which this power was conferred on me, and midnight—when this power especially expands and gains strength whereas the body weakens—had passed, I set out to take up the Great Name of God, consisting of seventy-two names, permuting and combining it. But when I had done this for a little while, behold the letters took on in my eyes the shape of great mountains, strong trembling seized me and I could summon no strength; my hair stood on end and it was as if I were not in this world. At once I fell down, for I no longer had strength in any of my limbs. And behold, something resembling speech emerged from my heart and came to my lips and forced them to move. I thought: 'Perhaps this is, God forbid, a spirit of madness that has entered into me?' But, behold, I saw it uttering wisdom. I said: 'This is indeed the spirit of wisdom'. After a little while my natural strength returned to me; I rose very much impaired and still did not believe myself. Once more I took up the Name to do with it as before and, behold, it had exactly the same effect on me. Nevertheless I did not believe until I had tried it four or five times.

This testimony has psychological truth written all over it. It is a remarkable account of the onset of glossolalia—a phenomenon which, as we noted earlier, has been associated in Judaism since the first century with prophecy.

The Zohar tends to be more restrained and contemplative, but it too seems to allow that a state of prophecy can be attained. For example, its doctrine of the three levels of consciousness—*nefesh*, *ruaḥ*, *neshamah*—is analogous to the Merkavah doctrine of the ascent of the soul to heaven. As the adept, through study and *askesis*, rises to ever higher levels of consciousness, his knowledge and insight expands, and he penetrates ever further into the sefirotic world of the godhead. This notion of states of consciousness appears to have been borrowed from philosophy. There is, of course, a great deal of contemplative writing in the Zohar, and, indeed, speculative argument that is philosophical in character. But there are also elements in the qabbalistic world-view which can only be attributed to some form of 'inspiration'. As much was acknowledged by

12. Jacobs, *Jewish Mystical Testimonies*, p. 67.

the Qabbalists themselves. Note how in a comment on the *Berit Menuḥah* of Abraham ben Isaac of Granada (? fourteenth century) Moses Cordovero effortlessly slips from the standard claim that the Qabbalah is ancient tradition to the claim (which one suspects represents his real view) that Qabbalah is newly revealed from heaven:[13]

> It is certain that the contents of this book have been handed down from mouth to mouth [i.e. they are Oral Torah], or else they have been imparted by an angel, since these are not subjects to be grasped as a result of profound speculation and subtle reasoning, but can only be the fruit of wondrous comprehension by the aid of the holy spirit.

For the mystics, then, prophecy to all intents and purposes had not ceased. But did it lead to fresh revelation? The answer to this question, is, at first sight, rather unclear. And for a very good reason: the Rabbis, with their halakhah, succeeded in so dominating Judaism from the talmudic period onwards, that few attempted to challenge them openly. Any challenge tended to be oblique: it was presented in traditional categories and was often ostensibly aimed at strengthening rather than challenging the halakhah, or negating the *miṣvot*. The challenge was nonetheless real and radical. It can be seen in the powerful antinomian tendencies which lie at the heart of the mystical tradition. Just how radical those tendencies could be may be illustrated from the *Ra'ya Meheimna* and the *Tiqqunei ha-Zohar*, two immensely influential sections of the Zohar, written a little later than the body of the text by a disciple of the main author.

Fundamental to these two documents, as to the Zohar as a whole, is the idea that there are basically two levels of meaning in the Torah—an outer, literal sense (*peshaṭ*), and an inner, mystical sense (*sod*). The inner, mystical sense gives the true meaning of the Torah: the literal sense is only the black, outer garments of the Shekhinah. Contempt is poured on those who remain at the level of the literal sense:[14]

> Alas for those fools whose minds are closed and whose eyes are shut, of whom it is said, 'They have eyes but they do not see' (Ps. 115.5) the light of the Torah! They are animals, who do not see or know anything except the straw of the Torah, which is the outer husk or the chaff, of which it is said: chaff and straw are exempt from the tithe. The sages of the Torah, the mystics, throw away the straw and chaff, which are without, and eat the wheat of the Torah, which is within.

13. Jacobs, *Jewish Mystical Testimonies*, p. 87.
14. *Tiqqunei ha-Zohar*, *Tiqqun* 69, 114a (trans. Tishby).

Here, typically, the 'new' Torah is represented as the 'true' sense of the old Torah, but this is largely window-dressing and should not be taken too literally. The mystical sense of Scripture is so deep that it can only be achieved by some form of inspiration, or by direct inspection of the archetypal Torah in heaven. It is tantamount to fresh revelation.

Significantly the despised literal sense of the Torah is identified closely in the writer's mind with the halakhah. He writes:[15]

> It is for this reason that Moses was buried outside the Holy Land, and his grave is the Mishnah, 'and no man knows his grave to this day' (Deut. 34.6). His grave is the Mishnah that rules over the consort, who is a tradition (*qabbalah*) going back to Moses...and the consort is separated from her husband. Consequently, 'For three things the earth quakes [and for four it cannot endure]: for a servant when he reigns'—this is the well-known servant Meṭaṭron; 'for a handmaid that is heir to her mistress'—this is the Mishnah; 'and a churl when he is filled with food' (Prov. 30.1-2)—this is the mixed multitude.

Elsewhere the halakhah is compared to a pool of stagnant water, in contrast to the qabbalah, which is a well of living water. The scholars who study halakhah are derided as 'the asses of the Torah', who make life hard for Israel with their pilpulistic arguments. Their wanderings from Yeshivah to Yeshivah in search of instruction are compared to the wanderings of exile. By way of contrast, the mystics sit contentedly at home, meditating on the secrets of Torah and communing with the Shekhinah.[16]

Potentially even more radical is the writer's distinction between a Torah of Emanation (*Torah de-'aṣilut*) and a Torah of Creation (*Torah di-veriah*), identified respectively with the Tree of Life, and the Tree of the Knowledge of Good and Evil. The Torah of Emanation (= the Tree of Life) is, in some sense, an ideal Torah which exists, beyond space and time, in the world of emanation, the world of the Sefirot. The Torah of Creation (= the Tree of Knowledge) is the Torah as we know it, as it exists physically in the created world. The mystic is able somehow to catch a glimpse of the splendours of the Torah of Emanation, in part through its imperfect representative, the Torah of Creation. The Torah of Creation is unquestionably a diminished Torah, since it reflects the

15. Zohar I, 27b-28a (*Tiqqunim*) (trans. Tishby).

16. See I. Tishby, *The Wisdom of the Zohar: An Anthology of Texts* (trans. D. Goldstein; Oxford: Littman Library/Oxford University Press, 1989), III, pp. 1090-91.

deformed conditions of our broken world: it is concerned with the forbidden and the permitted, with the clean and the unclean. To live at this level is to live at a level of spiritual impoverishment.

The radical, antinomian possibilities of this doctrine are obvious and have occasioned fierce debate. Scholem has argued that the Torah of Emanation represents, in effect, a utopian, eschatological aspect of Torah.[17] We cannot live at this level here and now in the present aeon, but only at the level of the Torah of Creation with all its *miṣvot*. In favour of this interpretation is the undoubted fact that the concept of the Torah of Emanation is linked in the mind of our author with the question of what the Torah was before man sinned. It cannot have been the same as the Torah after the Fall, since it addressed a totally different world. This question naturally leads to speculation as to what the Torah will be when, at the end of history, the Fall is reversed and paradise regained. Scholem seems to see our author as picking up in his own way earlier rabbinic speculation on Torah in the messianic age, according to which Isa. 51.4, 'A Torah will proceed from me', was interpreted as announcing that a *new* Torah would be promulgated when the Messiah came (*Lev. R.* 13.3). Scholem also links the ideas of the *Ra'ya Meheimna* and the *Tiqqunei ha-Zohar* with the contemporary doctrine of the *shemiṭṭot*, according to which, as classically expounded in the *Sefer ha-Temunah* (composed in Catalonia around 1250), the whole history of creation can be divided into seven cosmic cycles, or *shemiṭṭot*, each governed by its own Torah, and by its own divine attribute. Our present *shemiṭṭah* is governed by the attribute of justice, and its Torah reflects that fact. The previous *shemiṭṭah* was governed by the attribute of grace, and its Torah reflected that fact. Setting the *Ra'ya Meheimna* and the *Tiqqunei ha-Zohar* in this context encourages us to see the relationship between the Torah of Emanation and the Torah of Creation essentially as chronological. This saves our author from outright antinomianism. He becomes a reluctant conformist. He may look forward to the time when the present Torah, with its laws of forbidden and permitted, of clean and unclean, will be set aside, but he is prepared to knuckle under to those laws for the time being.

Tishby, however, restating with more precision a position advocated by Graetz, strongly contests Scholem's reading of the *Ra'ya Meheimna*

17. G. Scholem, 'The Meaning of the Torah in Jewish Mysticism', *Diogenes* 14 (Summer, 1956), pp. 36-47; 15 (Fall, 1956), pp. 65-94; reprinted in Scholem, *On the Kabbalah and its Symbolism* (New York: Schocken Books, 1969), pp. 32-86.

and the *Tiqqunei ha-Zohar*.[18] He does not deny that there is an eschatological aspect to the Torah of Emanation, and that in the messianic age there will be 'a great upsurge of mystical repentance' which will allow the majority of Jews to 'penetrate the depths of the Torah of the Tree of Life' and to be 'liberated from the yoke of the Torah of the Tree of Knowledge', but he argues that our author believed that it was possible, even now, to live at the level of the Torah of Emanation. The mystics, 'the sons of the palace (*benei heikhala*)', the privileged few, are able to cling to the Tree of Life, and to break the yoke of the Tree of Knowledge and live in the mystical-spiritual freedom that the Torah of Life offered them. He writes:[19]

> Those passages which oppose the teachings of the halakhah and reject its literature and its way of thought are not simply Messianic in character, reflecting a desire for change in the distant future. These hopes can be realized here and now. They represent the contemporary mystical opposition to the nature and authority of rabbinic Judaism.

Anyone with even a superficial knowledge of the history of religions will recognize a familiar pattern here, namely, the desire of an elitist group of *illuminati* to live at a level of spiritual freedom above the ignorant masses.[20]

The doctrine of Torah in the *Ra'ya Meheimna* and the *Tiqqunei ha-Zohar*, as, indeed, in the mystical tradition as a whole, is immensely complex and even self-contradictory. It is impossible to do it justice in the present brief account. Yet enough has been said to show that its

18. Tishby, *Wisdom of the Zohar*, III, pp. 1092-1108.

19. Tishby, *Wisdom of the Zohar*, III, p. 1108.

20. The influence of the *Ra'ya Meheimna* and the *Tiqqunei ha-Zohar* on Shabbatean literature and thinking is well documented. Given this ideological underpinning, there is an inner logic to Shabbateanism. The Shabbateans believed that a new *shemiṭṭah* had been inaugurated with the arrival of Shabbatai Ṣevi, and with it a new spiritual Torah, which abrogated the old Torah of Creation, had come into effect. This led them conspicuously to break the *miṣvot*, in accordance with the principle that 'the abrogation of the Torah is the fulfilment of the Torah' (*biṭṭulah shel ha-Torah zehu qiyyumah*). The followers of Jacob Frank were to carry this antinomianism to even more bizarre lengths. See G. Scholem, *Sabbatai Sevi: The Mystical Messiah* (Princeton: Princeton University Press, 1973). It is a pity that no-one seems to have followed up W.D. Davies pioneering and rather daring discussion of the similarities between the origins of Christianity and the origins of Shabbateanism: see his essay, 'From Schweitzer to Scholem: Reflections on Sabbatai Sevi', in W.D. Davies, *Jewish and Pauline Studies* (London: SPCK, 1984), pp. 257-77.

radical antinomianism calls into question the classic rabbinic view that the Torah, given once-for-all to Israel at Sinai by the hand of Moses, will never be abrogated. Some mystics clearly saw the Torah to Moses on Sinai as provisional—one day to be superseded by fresh revelation to which they had direct, if limited access, here and now. For such thinkers prophecy, to all intents and purposes, cannot have come to a definitive end early in the Second Temple period.[21]

I have analysed the problem of the cessation of prophecy in terms of the classic rabbinic texts of late antiquity and the early middle ages. There are certain advantages in this approach. When the canon of Scripture was finally closed is still a matter of intense debate,[22] but there

21. A.J. Heschel, ''Al ruaḥ ha-qodesh bimei ha-beinayim', in *Alexander Marx Jubilee Volume*, Part 2 (Hebrew Section) (New York: Jewish Theological Seminary, 1950), pp. 175-208, provides an excellent survey of Jewish prophecy in the middle ages. See further, Verman, *Books of Contemplation*, pp. 5-20. Considerations of space prevent me from discussing the theories of prophecy in Jewish philosophic literature. Suffice to say that some mediaeval Jewish philosophers adopted rationalist views of prophecy which seem to allow that prophecy was still attainable in their days.

22. It has become rather fashionable to deny that the concept of canonicity in any strict sense of the term has any revelance to Judaism in Second Temple times. What we have at that period is simply a loosely defined collection of texts which were widely revered. In my view this is mistaken. The same body of literature is appealed to as authoritative right across the whole spectrum of early Judaism—by Alexandrian Jews, by the Dead Sea Sectarians, by the Christians, and by the Rabbis (and hence, one assumes, by their forerunners the Pharisees). Different parties, to be sure, wanted to add to that core of sacred texts, but all were agreed on what belonged to the large and diverse core. It seems implausible to claim that this situation was reached simply by a natural growth of consensus. At some point these texts must have been declared as authoritative by competent religious authority. The only authority with the prestige to achieve such a result in the Second Temple period was the Jerusalem priesthood. Canonization may have been accompanied by the deposition of master copies of the sacred texts in the Temple. Just when all this happened is not recorded, but that it did happen is a reasonable inference from the observable facts. Some who correctly note the continuation of prophetic activity in the Second Temple period seem tempted to argue that this fact further reinforces the view that the canon was not yet closed. But this conclusion does not follow. Canonization and the cessation of prophecy do not necessary go hand in hand. After all, the first canon of sacred Scripture, the Pentateuch, was created long before anyone started claiming that prophecy had come to an end. For contrasting treatments of this problem see J. Barr, *Holy Scripture: Canon, Authority, Criticism* (Philadelphia: Westminster Press, 1983) and Roger Beckwith, *The Old Testament Canon of the New Testament Church and its Background in Early Judaism* (London: SPCK, 1985).

can be no doubt that by the talmudic period the Rabbis had a fixed canon, and the corollary of this was for them the belief that prophecy had ceased. Yet the Rabbis themselves advocated doctrines which unquestionably imply that revelation in some sense continued, and prophetic phenomena continued to manifest themselves in abundance in the rabbinic milieu.

A similar situation obtains in the Second Temple period. Then, too, there was a widely held conviction that prophecy was a thing of the past. Yet in all sorts of ways prophecy persisted.[23] And if we go back

23. The cessation of prophecy is already proclaimed in the (? scribal) postscript to the second division of the canon (Mal. 4.4-6): prophecy has departed from Israel and will not return again until the end of history and the coming of the day of the Lord. 1 Maccabees speaks as if prophets were very rare, if not totally absent, in its day (see 4.46 and 9.27). *4 Ezra* 14.44-47, by stating that Ezra was responsible for finally collecting the sacred books and closing the canon, seems to imply that prophetic inspiration came to an end with him. The frequent pseudepigraphic attribution of Second Temple texts to figures from the 'biblical' period points to a common belief that prophecy had come to an end, as does the Christian claim that the outbreak of charismatic and prophetic phenomena in Christian circles was evidence that the messianic age had arrived (see e.g. Acts 2.14-36). Yet, it does not take much searching to find prophecy in the Second Temple period—individual prophetic figures and movements (such as Christianity), prophetic literature (e.g. the apocalyptic texts), as well as 'inspired' interpretation of Scripture (in Philo, the Dead Sea Scrolls and the New Testament). For a recent discussion of prophecy in the Second Temple period, see R. Gray, *Prophetic Figures in Late Second Temple Jewish Palestine: The Evidence from Josephus* (New York: Oxford University Press, 1993), especially pp. 7-34. Further, R. Meyer, 'Prophecy and Prophets in the Judaism of the Hellenistic-Roman Period', *TDNT*, VI, pp. 812-19; W.D. Davies, *Paul and Rabbinic Judaism* (London: SPCK, 2nd edn, 1955), pp. 208-16; W. Foerster, 'Der Heilige Geist im Spätjudentum', *NTS* 8 (1961-62), pp. 37-49; R. Leivestad, 'Das Dogma von der prophetenlosen Zeit', *NTS* 19 (1972-73), pp. 288-99; T.M. Crone, *Early Christian Prophecy: A Study in its Origin and Function* (Baltimore: St Mary's University Press, 1973); P.W. Barnett, 'The Jewish Sign Prophets—AD 40-70: Their Intentions and Origin', *NTS* 27 (1980-81), pp. 679-97; M. Hengel, *The Charismatic Leader and his Followers* (Edinburgh: T. & T. Clark, 1981); D.E. Aune, *Prophecy in Early Christianity and the Ancient Mediterranean World* (Grand Rapids, MI: Eerdmans, 1983); R. Beckwith, *Old Testament Canon*, pp. 369-76; R. Horsley and J. Hanson, *Bandits, Prophets and Messiahs: Popular Movements at the Time of Jesus* (Minneapolis: Winston Press, 1985); R. Horsley, '"Like One of the Prophets of Old": Two Types of Popular Prophets at the Time of Jesus', *CBQ* 47 (1985), pp. 435-63; *idem*, 'Popular Prophetic Movements at the Time of Jesus: Their Principal Features and Social Origins', *JSNT* 26 (1986), pp. 3-27; J. Barton, *The*

still further in time we never seem to reach a decisive point or period which can be said to mark the transition from the biblical to the post-biblical, from the prophetic to the scribal era. The reason is quite simple: no such transition in fact ever took place, at least as far as an end of prophecy is concerned. The cessation of prophecy is a historical fiction. The Rabbis and others who proclaimed the end of prophecy had a strong tendency to homogenize the biblical period: *all* the writers of the Hebrew Bible were 'prophets'—not only Isaiah and Jeremiah, but Moses, David and Solomon as well. This notion was simply the mirror image of the view that we now live in a post-prophetic, scribal era. This theological schema does not correspond to historical reality. It is perfectly clear that *scribes* played a significant part in the creation of the literature of the Hebrew Bible. For example, scribal activity has been detected in the elaboration of biblical law: earlier laws were explained and extended by a process which has been appropriately compared with later rabbinic midrash.[24] The Rabbis themselves, in some of their pronouncements, tend to play down the freedom and originality of the prophets. Moses was the supreme prophet, who uniquely spoke with God 'face to face'; the prophets who followed after him exercised a lesser form of prophecy and did not introduce any innovations but merely clarified and reinforced the Torah given to Moses on Sinai (*B. Shab.* 104a; *Meg.* 14b). This concern to curtail prophetic innovation retrojects onto the biblical period some of the deepest concerns of the Rabbis' own days, but at the same time it blurs the distinction between the later prophets and the sages: *both* become bearers of the Oral Torah. The biblical and post-biblical eras are thus put on the same continuum: there is no qualitative difference between them.

Only one conclusion can reasonably be drawn from the foregoing analysis. It is that we should be extremely wary of allowing the doctrine of the cessation of prophecy too much weight in our historiography of Judaism, or lean too heavily on it in articulating the discipline of Jewish studies. To do so involves identifying ourselves more closely than we

Oracles of God: Perceptions of Ancient Prophecy in Israel after the Exile (London: Darton, Longman and Todd: 1986); F.E. Greenspahn, 'Why Prophecy Ceased', *JBL* 108 (1989), pp. 37-49; R.J. Bauckham, *The Climax of Prophecy: Studies on the Book of Revelation* (Edinburgh: T. & T. Clark, 1992); *idem*, *The Theology of the Book of Revelation* (Cambridge: Cambridge University Press, 1993), pp. 1-12.

24. The classic discussion of this question is M. Fishbane, *Biblical Interpretation in Ancient Israel* (Oxford: Clarendon Press, 1985).

should with a highly tendentious and prescriptive point of view from within Jewish tradition. Rather we should recognize that in Judaism, as in many other religions, two fundamentally opposed types of religious authority co-existed side by side—the prophet and the scribe, the charismatic and the scholar. The tension between these two types is a constant theme of Jewish history right from biblical times to our own days. Scribes have always tended to occupy the centre ground in Jewish society (even in the biblical period). This is hardly surprising, since as a class they are orderly, easily institutionalized and for the most part supportive of the *status quo*. They belong to, or aspire to be part of, the establishment and are backed by the political authorities and the powers that be. By way of contrast prophets and charismatics are frequently anarchic and are perceived of as a threat to the existing order: they often function as dissidents on the margins of society. The dominance of the scribes means that from time to time prophetism has been effectively driven underground, and has been forced to express itself obliquely, in categories borrowed from, or acceptable to, scribalism. It presents itself in the form of exegesis of the canonic texts, or it tries to suggest that its form of prophecy is quite different from that of the revered prophets of antiquity. There may, indeed, be differences, but often the claim is camouflage and should be seen as such.

The scribes saw clearly the potential dangers of prophetism and did their best to circumscribe and contain the phenomenon. The mystical tradition was declared esoteric, to be studied, if at all, only by the chosen few, and then not until they had mastered the intricacies of the halakhah (see e.g. *M. Hag*. 2.1). Yet there was a serious weakness at the heart of the scribal position. How, faced with the uncompromising prophetic claim to direct revelation from God, could the scribes assert the authority of *their* traditions? The Rabbis answer to this problem was ingenious. They claimed that their traditions too originated in direct prophetic revelation from God: they based themselves on a canon of sacred texts which they themselves categorized as 'prophetic'. But they then avoided any problems which this might engender by introducing the factor of time. They chronologized the relationship between prophetism and scribalism: prophets belong to the past, scribes to the present. Authority is now vested in the scribes who have the right to determine the meaning even of the prophetic utterances contained in the sacred texts. The theological and apologetic nature of this claim should be transparent. In actual fact the history of Judaism cannot be divided neatly into a biblical and a post-biblical era, at least if such a division involves denying or neglecting the phenomenon of *post*-biblical prophecy. It should be recognized that even within rabbinic Judaism—that most scribal of traditions—prophecy has continued to flourish in various forms and guises right down to modern times, and the on-going tension between prophetism and scribalism has constituted one of the central dynamics in the evolution of Jewish tradition.

THE 'ORIGINAL TEXT': A SCHOLARLY ILLUSION?

A.P. Hayman

This paper is a meditation on the problems of producing a critical edition of a Jewish text from the period of late antiquity. I have been working for some considerable time on producing an edition of the Hebrew text of the Jewish mystical/magical/philosophical text *Sefer Yeṣira* (henceforth *SY*). This text is first attested in manuscripts from the tenth century, but Saadya Gaon, the most important Jewish scholar of the time, wrote a commentary on it about 931 (Saadya 1891, 1972) and he regarded it as a very ancient text, possibly written by Abraham. The core of the text may well go back to around 300 CE though many of the ideas in it can be traced much earlier than this.

There are a very large number of manuscripts of this text in existence. Over one hundred and twenty are listed in the catalogue of the Microfilm Centre of the Jewish National Library in Jerusalem. It has been recognized since the last century that *SY* has been handed down to us in three main recensions whose existence is attested already in the first half of the tenth century. These have been named the Long, the Short, and the Saadyan recensions, the latter after the version which seemed to lie before Saadya as he wrote his commentary. The Israeli scholar Ithamar Gruenwald produced a 'A Preliminary Critical Edition of *Sefer Yezira*' in 1971 and he used fifteen manuscripts, the ones he regarded as containing 'a more or less acceptable text' (Gruenwald 1971: 134). The format of his edition seems to presuppose that a critical edition can be used to recover the 'original text' of the work, though in his introduction he eschews any attempt to solve 'the riddles of *SY*, especially the question, which of the three recensions is the more original' (Gruenwald 1971: 132). Occasionally the differences between the recensions are such that Gruenwald lays out the text of the Long and Short Recensions in parallel columns though he always subsumes the readings of the Saadyan recension in those of the Long Recension.

Gruenwald's textual apparatus is very difficult to read; for example, §48 has eight lines of text followed by a whole page for the critical apparatus.

Is there something wrong with both the assumptions underlying critical editions like these and the scholarly effort to produce books that hardly anyone finds possible to read and use? These are questions that have been widely aired in recent years by scholars working on Jewish texts in the period of late antiquity. The *bête noire* of this debate has been the German scholar Peter Schäfer. He has more or less proclaimed the death of the so-called 'critical edition' but has also challenged the notion of regarding Jewish texts of this period as 'texts', that is, as works consciously shaped by authors which can be studied by techniques applicable to modern literary works (Schäfer 1988). He has argued that this concept of the text ignores the reality of the textual evidence we have for nearly all Jewish texts from this period. Most of them are attested in medieval manuscripts mainly from Europe and they contain a bewildering variety of text types. How can we know that these texts were not put into their present shape by the scribes of these medieval manuscripts? Schäfer's approach to textual criticism was enshrined first in his ground-breaking *Synopse zur Hekhalot-Literatur* (1981) and now in his *Synopse zum Talmud-Yerushalmi* (1991–). Schäfer provides no critical apparatus in these works but just lays out the text of the most important manuscripts in synoptic form. He leaves it to scholars using his works to make what comments they like on the text and, if they so wish, to engage in the futile task of reconstructing an original text which never existed. The extent of Schäfer's scepticism can be gauged from the introduction to his synopsis of the Jerusalem Talmud where he claims that the most that can be achieved is to reconstruct the text as it existed in the thirteenth to eighteenth centuries. This is bad news for the scholar who wants to use the Jerusalem Talmud as evidence for rabbinic Judaism in the centuries before 400 CE when the text is supposed to have been completed. Especially is it bad news for New Testament scholars who frequently plunder the Yerushalmi for parallels to the NT.

In his own books on the *Hekhalot* texts Schäfer has given up referring to them as 'texts'. He prefers the term 'macroform' for the agglomerations of material which exist in the manuscripts and which have been traditionally known by names like III Enoch, Hekhalot Rabbati, Hekhalot-Zutarti, etc. Schäfer is confronting head on the major shift in biblical and Jewish studies in the present generation, namely, the move from the so-called source and historical criticism towards, first of all, redaction criticism and now literary criticism. This present generation is marked by a reaction against what is seen as the atomizing tendencies of earlier generations of scholars and so has shifted its attention to the so-called 'final form' of biblical and Jewish texts, looking for the signs of the theological and literary strategies of the person or persons responsible for the canonical or classical forms of the documents. But Schäfer is arguing that the scholars who have been swept along by these current trends have been by-passing the hard work of textual criticism and failing first of all to establish the existence as coherent literary works of the texts on which they are commentating. Perhaps the ultimate example of the absurdity of the sort of work he criticizes is the current rash of books in New Testament studies on the intentions and literary strategies of that non-existent text Q!

Schäfer's views have been the subject of fierce debate in many conferences on Jewish studies in recent years. The emotional atmosphere can get quite tense at times in these debates since he threatens a lot of the academic enterprise—all those endless numbers of books (many of which start out as PhD theses) applying the latest in structuralist and deconstructionist criticism, discourse analysis, feminist criticism, phenomenological criticism, poststructuralism etc, etc, to what Schäfer regards as the errors and blunders of medieval scribes. I have a lot of sympathy for Schäfer's position. It is very easy to see over a period of time that modern critics are no better than ancient commentators at avoiding describing the reflections of their own faces in the mirror of the texts they are reading. However, I am not so pessimistic as he is over the possibilities of using textual criticism at least to reconstruct earlier forms of texts than are attested in the manuscripts we have. Hence the layout of my edition of *SY* will be a compromise between that of Gruenwald and that which would be suggested if I followed Schäfer's procedures in his synopses.

Appendix One contains the first draft of page one of my proposed edition. The aim of this edition will be to present the evidence for the textual history of *SY* in as clear a fashion as possible. Therefore the text of the three main recensions is printed in parallel columns, each with its own textual apparatus. Manuscript K (Parma De Rossi 1390, fols. 36b-38b) in the left hand column serves as the base text for the Short Recension, manuscript A (Vatican 299(8), fols. 66a-71b) in the middle column serves as the base text for the Long Recension, and manuscript

C (the Geniza Scroll of *SY*) in the right hand column serves as the base text for the Saadyan recension. Where the text of any other manuscript diverges too far from the base manuscript in its recension to make collating its variants useful, I will print its full text in the relevant column. Thus, for example, manuscript D (Florence Pluteo II 5/9, fols. 227a-230a) which often hovers between the Long and the Short Recensions in its readings is printed in full below the text of manuscript A.

But in laying out my edition in the order §1, §2, §3 etc. am I not, with Gruenwald, almost unconsciously creating a text which never existed? For no manuscript, not even Vatican 299 which Gruenwald uses as his base text, has precisely this order. Appendix Two presents a table of what parts of *SY* are attested in the manuscripts I will use for my edition. One might be tempted, looking at this list, to draw some immediate conclusions on the history of the text. The three recensions clearly identify themselves by what they have in and what they leave out. For example, the Saadyan Recension leaves out §§11, 21-22, 27-31, 42-43b, 60b, and 64. The Short Recension leaves out the large block of material in §§52-57 as well as smaller blocks at §§11, 35-36, 43b-44, 46. If we look more closely at the omission of §§27-31 in the Saadyan recension, we notice that §§23-31 all begin with the same words: 'Three matrices—Aleph, Mem, Shin'. Could the omission have happened by homoioteleuton on the part of a careless scribe back in the chain of transmission before this recension took shape? At this level of investigation, using the traditional techniques of textual criticism, it would certainly seem possible to reconstruct an early form of *SY* from which all the manuscripts descend, if not the original text itself.

Unfortunately, what seems to be a relatively comprehensible situation becomes anything but when we look, not at the actual contents of the various manuscripts, but at the order in which the paragraphs appear in each manuscript (Appendix Three). All the manuscripts begin with §1 but that is about as much as they agree on! The Saadyan Recension in particular has a radically different ordering of the material than the other recensions. There are good reasons for thinking that this is not the original shape of the text, but the very existence of the recension shows the amount of licence scribes permitted themselves with a text which was traditionally ascribed to Abraham. How do we know that the whole history of this and other Jewish texts (including the Bible) is not littered with similarly creative scribes who, while keeping the basic material intact, yet shaped and reshaped the whole text according to their own predilections? And where then is the creative author whose interests and literary skills shaped the final form of the text?

At the micro-level of the individual paragraph our task is no easier. Gruenwald states that 'the three recensions differ from each other mainly in the length of the text and in the inner organisation of the material. The differences of reading between the three recensions are not as many as is generally assumed' (Gruenwald 1971: 133). But let us look at §1 (Appendix One). Manuscript Q has 13 words, P 15, D 26 while the rest have 28 or 29. Has the longer text evolved out of the shorter, or has the shorter text, as Gruenwald seems to suggest, arisen from an attempt to resolve the syntactical problems of the longer form of the text (Gruenwald 1973: 481-82)? Problems like these confront me constantly as I attempt to write a commentary on this text. But what is the 'original text' on which I should attempt to comment—manuscript Q or KACZ? There seem to be rather a lot of 'authors' at work here.

It is very easy to get bogged down in the technical problems of sorting out the textual history of a block of material like *SY* §1. So I turn now to the question: is the situation that confronts me in editing *SY* unique in the history of Jewish literature or just typical? What light can be thrown on my dilemmas by other similar texts or even by very different texts which were yet created by the same people? Here space limitations dictate selectivity in choosing texts for comparison. I have already mentioned Schäfer's work on the Hekhalot texts which nearly all present similar problems to *SY*. Indeed, *SY* is invariably found in large manuscripts which also contain a selection of these other texts. In discussion with other scholars Schäfer has conceded that some Hekhalot texts have a better 'redactional shape' than others and therefore reflect more of an authorial intention on the part of the scribe or scribes who transmitted them. Philip Alexander, the translator of *3 Enoch* in the Charlesworth translation of the Pseudepigrapha (Alexander 1983) feels that Schäfer's views do not quite match the reality of the text as he has worked on it. Jim Davila in the USA is preparing a new edition of Hekhalot Rabbati because he disagrees with Schäfer's view of how this text took shape and that something closer to a traditional critical edition is worth attempting. But by and large I have to concede that we can read this literature only as it was shaped in early medieval Germany.

What about the rabbinic texts of late antiquity? Here the situation is very similar to that in *SY*. We have a huge amount of free-floating material which is shaped and re-shaped into many different texts. What is more, the same rabbinic saying may be ascribed to many different authors as we move from text to text. At the level of the manuscripts this situation gets even worse. Some trends can be discerned like the increasing tendency to ascribe ever larger amounts of material to great rabbinic heroes like Aqiva; *SY* was even ascribed to him by some medieval commentators. On the basis of the manuscript evidence I have no confidence that we can safely say that any of the Rabbis said anything ascribed to him in the texts. One can nearly always find a manuscript ascribing the saying to someone else! Early in his career Jacob Neusner wrote books on the work of Rabbis like Eliezer ben Hyrcanus but soon gave this up. The real Eliezer is irrecoverable. Scholars still write books on the contribution of Rabbis like Aqiva to the shaping of rabbinic Judaism but increasingly such books have diminishing credibility. Neusner has written a mass of books on the redactional shaping of nearly all the rabbinic texts but he almost invariably ignores the text-critical data and translates and comments on the texts basically as they have been transmitted in the early printed editions. How do we know that the final redactional shape of the Babylonian Talmud was not achieved sometime in the Middle Ages? After all the earliest complete manuscript (the Munich Codex) dates from 1343. One scholar even goes as far as stating that the Babylonian Talmud 'reached its present state only in the last century' (Strack and Stemberger 1991: 225]. Many years ago I used to teach the text of *Pirke Aboth* (*PA*), very often to New Testament students anxious for material to parallel with the sayings of Jesus. But what a nightmare is revealed when we dig below the level of editions like that of Herford (1962) which seem almost designed to keep their readership ignorant of the real situation. *PA* like *SY* exists in three separate recensions in which both the text and the order of the material vary. At the level of the individual manuscripts there is even more variation. One can make comments on the history and development of this text and the rabbinic values which it reveals but the search for the 'original' *PA* is doomed to failure. There never was one—just an ever-growing collection of rabbinic sayings attached to the end of the Mishnah in order to encourage people to study it.

The closest parallel to the phenomena which greet the scholar when studying texts like *PA* and *SY* is actually the Synoptic Gospels, for there we have a large mass of sayings which reveal a bewildering mixture of both order and disorder while yet quite clearly having a common origin. I cannot rehearse now the various theories which have arisen to explain the material in the gospels. What I would say is that such theories have often been expounded by scholars who are rather ignorant of comparable material also produced by Jews in not too distant periods. The fact that there are so many books written on the redactional intentions of the gospel authors which all happily disagree with each other is proof enough for me that somebody is seeing things which are not there. But the level of intention and the authorial control presupposed by these studies is just not supported by the evidence of the comparable Jewish material or, I would argue, the textual data itself. I am very much inclined to agree with my colleague John O'Neill that 'Matthew, Mark, and Luke as we have them are the end product of three lines of scribal tradition. They are not the work of three authors who looked across at unified sources and made hundreds of changes on each page at their authorial will' (O'Neill 1991: 500). As for Q, I await the discovery of the first manuscript containing it!

And now, finally, to the Hebrew Bible. There is no scope here to go into the whole issue of 'the original text' of the Bible, but what I do want to do is to show that, in principle, the text-critical situation I have described for later Jewish texts also applies to the Hebrew Bible. I want to do this by way of some critical remarks on the latest, and most important, book on the subject, namely, Emmanuel Tov's *Textual Criticism of the Hebrew Bible* (1992). This is now likely to become the standard work on the subject. However, it was dissatisfaction with some of the arguments in this book which gave me the idea for writing this paper. Tov has an enviable grasp of the details of the textual tradition of the Bible and of the proper way to practise textual criticism but when, as he constantly does, he comes to discuss the issue of the 'original text' and the distinction between textual and literary criticism he gets into a muddle and even into self-contradiction.

In his section on the original shape of the Hebrew Text (Part B of chapter 3, 164-97) he first of all describes the two older models which have been favoured by earlier critics. The first model, traditionally ascribed to Paul de Lagarde, is that we can reconstruct the original form of MT from all existing Hebrew manuscripts; we can do the same for the LXX; then, by comparing them both we can reconstruct the original shape of the biblical text. There is one 'original text' from which all existing copies ultimately descend. The second model, to which the name of Paul Kahle is now conventionally attached, is what is called the theory of 'parallel texts'. On this view there is no 'original text' but the texts we have have crystallized out over time into the MT, LXX and the Samaritan version. No one uniform text will emerge if we follow the procedure recommended by Kahle because plurality preceded not followed uniformity. These two theories both assume and support the specialization among Old Testament scholars into text-critics and literary critics. But they also assume that scribes know whether they are authors or copyists, that there is a point at which we can say the literary formation of the text stopped and the period of textual transmission began, and that those involved knew which period they were in.

However, the emergence of the Dead Sea Scrolls and the consequent revision of the value of the LXX and Samaritan versions has put in question these older theories of how the biblical text may have evolved. So Tov discusses a third theory, namely, the view that the textual transmission of the Hebrew Bible started before the stage of literary formation was completed. Tov marshalls a mass of evidence from the Scrolls, LXX and the Samaritan versions to show that this was the case. It is the only conclusion one can draw from the different versions we have of such books as 1 and 2 Samuel, Jeremiah, Ezekiel, Daniel, Esther, Proverbs, etc. It is when he attempts to evaluate this third view that Tov gets himself into a muddle because his arguments and the evidence he marshalls leads to this third view but in his heart he is still with de Lagarde: 'the evidence shows how phenomena operative at the compositional level continued to be influential at the transmission stage, but the areas should nevertheless be separated as much as possible' (Tov 1992: 266, n. 36).

Why should they be separated according to Tov? The answer turns out to be highly traditional:

> Since only one finished literary composition is in our mind when we deal with textual issues, textual criticism aims at that literary composition which has been accepted as binding (authoritative) by Jewish tradition, since textual criticism is concerned with the literary compositions contained in the traditional Hebrew Bible. This implies that the textual criticism of the Hebrew Bible aims at the literary compositions as contained in MT, to the exclusion of later (midrashic) literary compositions such as the Hebrew text behind several sections in the LXX, viz, sections in 1-2 Kings, Esther, and Daniel, and earlier and possibly parallel compositions, such as the LXX of Jeremiah, Joshua, Ezekiel, and sections of Samuel.' [Tov 1992: 177]

Since the final literary composition is MT, Tov is arguing that 'textual evidence, which is mainly taken from LXX (such as the short text of Jeremiah), is not taken into consideration in the reconstruction of elements of the original text' (Tov 1992: 178). What a neat way of ruling out of court all the new evidence that might undermine the older theories! You just define it out of existence; the original text is the Masoretic text. Tov digs himself deeper and deeper into a hole as he attempts to maintain the distinction between the period of the literary formation of the text and its textual transmission. This can lead to his contradicting himself within a few lines. On p. 189 he says: 'our description corresponds, therefore, with the accepted view in research of one original text, albeit in a more moderate formulation, for it takes into account the possibility of earlier, written stages.' Five lines later we get: 'the period of relative textual unity reflected in the assumed pristine text(s) of the biblical books was brief at the best, but in actual fact it probably never existed, for during the same period there were also current among the people a few copies representing stages which preceded the completion of the literary composition.' Tov yearns for this 'pristine' 'original text' but he cannot find it except by reaffirming arbitrarily the choice of one text (MT) made by the Rabbis after the destruction of the Temple in 70 CE.

But why should scholars be bound by the choice made by the Rabbis? I do not know Tov so I do not know whether his choice may be made on the grounds of religious authority. But it seems possible to me that his choice is almost determined by the structure of what Professor Robert Carroll (in a paper recently delivered at Edinburgh University) called 'the guild' of Old Testament scholars. Since Old Testament scholars have traditionally seen themselves as either literary or textual critics, even though we now know that the division makes no sense and that every good scholar has to be both, the division lives on after the time when it did seem to make sense. Such a situation is not unknown in the history of bureaucratic institutions. The subject matter gets defined in such a way as to preserve the structures and the self-understanding of those who have an economic stake in the system. New evidence must not be allowed to undermine this.

A few conclusions from this rather wide-ranging discussion:

1. The search for an 'original text' in the kind of literature with which we are dealing is likely to be fruitless. It represents the transference of a false analogy with the circumstances of literary creation in our society to those of a very different society in the past. Nearly all the works with which we deal are communal products, shaped by many hands sometimes over

many centuries. The process of formation of these texts stopped, not because they had reached an ideal literary shape, but usually from sheer historical accident. The Dead Sea community were wiped out by the Romans in 68 CE and so their form of the biblical text ceased to be transmitted. The same happened to the Alexandrian Jewish community in the diaspora revolt of 115-117. Only rabbinic Jews and (to a lesser extent) the Samaritans survived, so, until recently, theirs were the only forms of the biblical text we have. Things could have been different. Only the invention of printing stopped the evolution of texts like *Sefer Yesira* and the Babylonian Talmud—in the case of the latter, not even that. The so-called 'final form of the text' is a historical accident.

2. Textual criticism can be used to reconstruct earlier forms of the text than those witnessed to in the available manuscripts but it has to go hand in hand with literary criticism. Contrary to Tov's declarations, textual criticism cannot confine itself to the accidental errors of scribes but has always to take into account that scribes did not belong to the 'guild' of academic scholars; they did not know that they had to be either textual or literary critics. They were participants in a communal enterprise of both handing on and shaping their community's traditions. Even when it became impossible for them actually to alter texts like the Bible they got round this by inventing 'midrash' or 'exegesis' which has precisely the same effect.
3. I am sceptical about the value of applying to ancient Jewish texts literary techniques evolved from the study of modern literary works unless full attention is paid to all the text-critical data. Undoubtedly, such techniques can sometimes bring to our attention features which are in the text and enhance our comprehension of it, but all too often they assume the presence of a literary craftmanship and intention which is simply not borne out by what we know of the circumstances under which our texts were created. I remain convinced that the bedrock qualifications for pursuing our discipline are a knowledge of Hebrew, Greek, Aramaic, Syriac, etc. and not of Jacques Derrida's French. Textual criticism remains prior to, but not separable from, literary criticism.

BIBLIOGRAPHY

Alexander, P.

1983 '3 (Hebrew Apocalypse of) Enoch', in *The Old Testament Pseudepigrapha* (ed. J.H. Charlesworth; New York: Doubleday), I, 223-315.

Gruenwald, I.

1971 'A Preliminary Critical Edition of Sefer Yezira', *Israel Oriental Studies* 1: 132-77.

1973 'Some Critical Notes on the First Part of Sefer Yezira', *REJ* 132: 475-512.

Herford, R.T.

1962 *The Ethics of the Talmud: Sayings of the Fathers* (New York: Schocken Books).

O'Neill, J.C.

1991 'The Lost Written Records of Jesus' Words and Deeds Behind our Records', *JTS* 42: 483-504.

Saadya Gaon

1891 Saadya b. Yusuf al-Faiyumi, *Commentaire sur le Sefer Yesira ou livre de la création* (ed. M. Lambert; Paris: Émile Bouillon).

1972 Y. Kafach, *Sefer Yeṣira im Perush ha-Gaon Rabbenu Saadya* (Jerusalem: הועד להוצאת ספרי רס"ג).

Schäfer, P.

1981 *Synopse zur Hekhalot-Literatur* (Tübingen: Mohr).

1988 *Hekhalot-Studien* (Tübingen: Mohr).

1991- *Synopse zum Talmud-Yerushalmi* (Tübingen: Mohr).

Strack, H.L. and G. Stemberger

1991 *Introduction to the Talmud and Midrash* (Edinburgh: T. & T. Clark) .

Tov, E.

1992 *Textual Criticism of the Hebrew Bible* (Minneapolis: Fortress Press; Assen/Maastricht: Van Gorcum).

APPENDIX ONE

Sefer Yeṣira §1

K

בשלשים ושתים נתיבות פלאות חכמה חקק יה יהוה צבאות אלהי ישראל אלהים חיים אל שדי רם ונישא שוכן עד וקדוש שמו. ברא את עולמו בשלשה ספרים[1] בספר וספר וספר.

1. דברים K^{mg}

A

שלשים ושנים נתיבות פלאות חכמה חקק יה ייי צבאות אלהי ישראל אלהים חיים אל שדי רם ונישא שוכן עד וקדוש שמו. ברא את עולמו בשלשה ספרים בספר וספר ומפר

C

[בשלשים ושתים] נ[תיבות] פלא[ות חכמה חקק יה יוי] צבאות אלהי ישראל אלהים חיים אל שדי קדוש ונורא שמו שוכן עד. ברא את עולמו בשלשה ספרים בספר וספר וסיפור.

P

בשלשים ושתים נתיבות פלאות חכמה חקק יה יהוה צבאות שמו בג' ספרים ספר וספר וספור.

D

בשלשים ושתים נתיבות פלאות חכמה חקק יה יהוה צבאות אלהים חיים אלהי ישראל אל שדי רם ונישא שוכן עד וקדוש שמו בשלשה ספרים סֶפֶר סְפָר וסִפּוּר.

Z

בשלשים ושתים נתיבות פלאות חכמה הקק יה יוי צבאות אלהי ישראל אלהים חיים אל שדי רם ונשא שוכן עד וקדוש שמו. ברא את עולמו בשלשה ספרים בספר וספר וסיפור.

Q

בשלשים ושתים נתיבות פליאות חכמה חקק יי צבאות בשלש ספרים בספר וספר וסיפור.

LMNSFIR collated to K:

פליאות [פלאות .I שלשים [בשלשים MNFIR. אלהי ישראל] om LMN. אלהים חיים...וקדוש] om L. חיים] add ומלך עולם MN. אל שדי...שמו] om MN. וסיפור [2° וספר LS, וספור MNFIR, add והוא חשבון לב F.

B1B2GH collated to A:

פליאות [פליאות B1B2GH. ושתים [ושנים G. וסיפור [2° וספר B1B2GH.

E collated to Z

פליאות [פלאות E.

Sefer Yeṣira §2

K

עשר ספירות בלימה ועשרים ושתים אותיות יסוד. שלש אמות כפולות ושתים עשרה פשוטות.

A

עשר ספירות בלימה ועשרים ושתים אותיות יסוד.

C

עשר ספירות עשר[ים] ושתים אותיות שלש אומות שבע כפולות [ושתים] עש[רה] פשוטות.

D

עשר ספירות בלי מה עשרים ושתים אותיות יסוד שלש אמות שבע כפולות ושתים עשרה פשוטות.

Z

עשר ספירות בלימה עשרים ושתים אותיות שלש אמות שבע כפולות ושתים עשרה פשוטות.

LMNSFPIQR collated to K:

נתיבות [ספירות .I יסוד] om MNI. כפולות] ושבע כפולות L...R

§2 in the Long Recension occurs only in Mss A and D.

E collated to Z:

עשרים ושתים ,*עשר...אמות] om E אותיות יסוד, E^{mg}. בלימה] om E.

APPENDIX TWO

The Attestation of the Paragraphs in the Manuscripts

* = paragraph is present in the manuscript

	Long Recension						Saad Recens			Short Recension									
Mss.	A	B1	B2	G	D	H	C	Z	E	K	L	M	N	S	F	P	I	Q	R
§																			
1	*	*	*	*	*	*	*	*	*	*	*	*	*	*	*	*	*	*	*
2	*				*		*	*	*	*	*	*	*	*	*	*	*		*
3	*	*		*			*	*	*	*	*	*	*	*	*	*	*	*	*
4	*	*	*	*	*	*	*	*	*	*	*	*	*	*	*	*	*	*	*
5	*	*	*	*	*	*	*	*	*	*	*	*	*	*	*	*	*	*	*
6	*	*	*	*	*	*	*	*	*	*	*	*	*	*	*	*	*	*	*
7	*	*	*	*	*	*	*	*	*	*	*	*	*	*	*	*	*	*	*
8	*	*	*	*	*	*	*	*	*	*	*	*	*	*	*	*	*	*	*
9	*	*	*	*	*	*	*	*	*	*	*	*	*	*	*	*	*	*	*
10	*		*		*	*	*	*	*	*	*	*	*	*	*	*	*	*	*
11	*	*	*	*		*													
12	*	*	*	*	*	*	*	*	*	*	*	*	*	*	*	*	*	*	*
13	*	*	*	*	*	*	*	*	*	*	*	*	*	*	*	*	*	*	*
14	*	*	*	*	*	*	*	*	*	*	*	*	*	*	*	*	*	*	*
15	*	*	*	*	*	*	*	*	*	*	*	*	*	*	*	*	*	*	*
16	*	*	*	*	*	*	*	*	*	*	*	*	*	*	*	*	*	*	*
17	*	*	*	*	*	*	*	*	*	*	*	*	*	*	*	*	*	*	*
18	*		*		*	*	*	*	*	*	*	*	*	*	*	*	*	*	*
19	*	*	*	*	*	*	*	*	*	*	*	*	*	*	*	*	*	*	*
20	*	*	*	*	*	*	*	*	*	*	*	*	*	*	*	*	*	*	*
21	*	*	*		*	*				*	*			*		*	*		*
22	*	*	*		*	*				*	*	*	*	*	*	*	*	*	*
23	*	*	*	*	*	*	*	*	*	*	*	*	*	*	*	*	*	*	*
24	*	*	*	*	*	*	*	*	*	*	*	*	*	*	*	*	*	*	*
25	*	*	*	*	*	*	*	*	*	*	*	*	*	*	*	*	*	*	*
26	*		*	*	*		*	*	*	*	*	*	*	*	*	*	*	*	*
27	*	*	*	*	*					*	*	*	*	*	*		*	*	*
28	*	*	*	*	*					*	*	*	*	*	*	*	*	*	*
29	*	*	*		*	*				*	*	*	*	*	*		*	*	*
30	*	*	*	*	*	*				*	*			*	*	*	*	*	*

Mss.	A	B1	B2	G	D	H	C	Z	E	K	L	M	N	S	F	P	I	Q	R
31	*	*	*	*	*	*				*	*	*	*	*	*	*	*	*	*
32	*	*	*	*	*	*	*	*	*	*	*	*	*	*	*	*	*	*	*
33	*	*	*	*	*	*	*	*	*	*	*	*	*	*	*	*	*	*	*
34	*	*	*	*	*	*	*	*	*	*	*	*	*	*	*	*	*	*	*
35	*	*	*	*	*	*	*	*	*										
36	*	*	*	*	*	*	*	*	*										
37	*	*	*	*	*	*	*	*	*	*	*	*	*	*	*	*	*	*	*
38	*	*	*	*	*		*	*	*	*	*	*	*	*	*	*	*	*	*
39	*	*	*	*	*		*	*	*	*	*	*	*	*	*	*	*	*	*
40	*	*	*	*	*	*	*	*	*	*	*	*	*	*	*	*	*	*	*
41	*	*	*	*	*	*	*	*	*										
42	*	*	*	*	*	*				*	*	*	*	*	*	*	*	*	*
43a	*	*	*	*		*				*	*	*	*	*	*	*	*	*	*
43b	*	*		*		*													
43c	*	*	*	*	*	*	*	*	*										
44	*	*	*	*	*	*	*	*	*										
45	*	*	*	*	*	*	*	*	*	*	*	*	*	*	*	*	*	*	*
46	*	*	*	*	*	*	*	*	*										
47	*	*	*	*	*	*	*	*	*	*	*	*	*	*	*	*	*	*	*
48a	*	*	*	*	*	*	*	*	*	*		*	*		*	*	*	*	*
48b	*	*	*	*	*	*	*	*	*	*	*	*	*	*	*	*	*	*	*
49	*	*	*	*	*	*				*	*	*	*	*	*	*	*	*	*
50										*	*	*	*	*	*	*	*	*	*
51										*	*	*	*	*	*	*	*	*	*
52	*	*	*	*	*	*	*	*	*										
53=43c			*	*	*		*	*	*										
54	*	*	*	*	*	*	*	*	*										
55	*	*	*	*	*	*	*	*	*										
56		*	*	*	*	*	*	*	*										
57	*	*	*	*	*	*	*	*	*										
58	*	*	*	*	*	*	*	*	*	*	*	*	*	*	*	*	*	*	*
59	*	*	*	*	*	*	*	*	*	*	*	*	*	*	*	*	*	*	*
60a	*	*	*	*	*	*	*	*	*										
60b	*	*	*	*	*	*				*	*	*	*	*	*	*	*	*	*
61	*	*	*	*	*	*	*	*	*	*	*			*	*	*	*	*	*
62	*	*	*	*	*	*	*	*	*	*									*
63	*	*	*	*	*	*			*	*									*
64	*	*	*	*	*	*				*	*	*	*	*	*	*	*	*	*

APPENDIX THREE

The Order of the Paragraphs in the Manuscripts

	Long Recension						Saad Recens			Short Recension									
Mss.	A	B1	B2	G	D	H	C	Z	E	K	L	M	N	S	F	P	I	Q	R
	1	1	1	1	1	1	1	1	1	1	1	1	1	1	1	1	1	1	1
	2	4	4	3	2	4	2	2	2	2	2	2	2	2	2	2	2	3	2
	3	5	5	4	4	5	3	3	3	3	3	3	3	3	3	3	3	4	3
	4	6	6	5	5	6	7	7	7	4	4	4	4	4	4	4	4	7	4
	5	7	7	6	6	7	9	9	9	7	7	7	7	7	7	7	7	8	7
	6	8	8	7	7	8	23	23	23	8	8	8	8	8	8	8	8	6	8
	7	9	9	8	8	9	37a	37a	37a	6	6	6	6	6	6	6	6	5	5
	8	3	3	9	10	3	45	45	45	5	5	5	5	5	5	5	5	10	6
	9	11	10	11	12	10	58a	1	58a	10	10	10	10	10	10	10	10	12	10
	10	12	11	12	9	11	59a	58	59	12	12	12	12	12	12	12	12	13	12
	11	13	12	13	13	12	4	59	4	13	13	13	13	13	13	13	13	14	13
	12	14	13	14	14	13	8	4	8	14	14	14	14	14	14	14	14	15	14
	13	15	14	15	15	14	24a	8	24a	15	15	15	15	15	15	15	15	16	15
	14	16	15	16	16	15	38	24a	38	16	16	16	16	16	16	16	16	9	16
	15	17	16	17	17	16	46	37b	46	9	9	9	9	9	9	9	9	23	9
	16	19	17	19	18	17	47	38	47	19a	26	23	23	17	23	17	23	26	17
	17	20	18	20	19	18	18	46	18	17	17	17	17	18	26	18	17	17	19a
	18	21	19	23	20	19	58b	47	58b	18	18	18	18	19	19a	19	18	18	18
	19	22	20	24	21	20	5	18	5	19b	19	19	19	20	17	20	19	19	19
	20	23	21	25	22	21	6	58	6	20	20	20	20	21	18	21	20	20	20
	21	24	22	26	23	22	9	5	9	21	21	22	22	22	19b	22	21	22	21
	22	25	23	27	24	23	25	6	25	22	22	23	23	23	20	23	22	23	22
	23	27	24	28	25	24	26	9	26	23	23	24	24	24	22	24	23	24	23
	24	28	25	30	26	25	24b	25	24b	24	24	27	27	26	21	28	24	27	24
	25	29	26	31	27	29	37b	26	37b	26	27	28	28	27	22	30	26	28	26
	26	30	27	32	28	30	48a	24b	48a	27	28	29	29	28	23	31	27	29	27
	27	31	28	33	29	31	40	37b	40	28	29	31	31	31	24	32	28	30	28
	28	32	29	34	30	32	56	48a	56	29	30	32	32	29	26	33	29	31	29
	29	33	30	35	31	33	57	40	57	30	31	33	33	30	27	34	30	32	30
	30	34	31	36	32	34	10	56	10	31	32	34	34	32	28	37	31	33	31
	31	35	32	37	33	35	12	57	12	32	33	37	37	34	29	38	32	34	32
	32	36	33	38	34	36	17	10	17	34	34	38	38	33	30	39	34	37	34

Mss.	A	B1	B2	G	D	H	C	Z	E	K	L	M	N	S	F	P	I	Q	R
	33	37	34	39	35	37	19	12	19	33	37	39	39	37	31	42	33	38	33
	34	38	35	40	36	40	20	17	20	37	38	42	42	38	32	40	37	39	37
	35	39	36	41	37	41	12	19	12	38	39	40	40	39	33	43a	38	42	38
	36	40	37	42	38	42	13	20	13	39	42	43a	43a	40	34	42	39	40	39
	37	41	38	43a	39	43a	14	13	14	40	40	42	42	43a	37	45	42	43a	42
	38	42	39	43b	40	43b	15	14	15	43a	43a	45	45	42	38	47	40	42	40
	39	43a	43a	44c	41	43c	16	15	16	42	42	47	47	45	39	49	43a	45	43a
	40	43b	40	44	42	44	32	16	32	45	45	49	49	47	42	48a	42	47	42
	41	43c	41	45	43c	45	33	32	33	47	47	48a	48a	49	40	50	45	49	45
	42	44	42	46	44	46	34	33	34	49	49	27?	27?	50	43a	51	47	48a	47
	43a	45	43c	47	45	47	35	34	35	48a	50	50	50	51	42	58	49	50	49
	43b	46	44	48	46	48	39	35	39	50	51	51	51	58	45	59a	48a	51	48a
	43c	47	45	49	47	49	41	39	41	51	58	58	58	59a	47	25	50	58	50
	44	48	46	52	49	52	43c	41	43c	58	59a	59a	59a	25	49	26	51	59a	51
	45	49	47	43c	52	54	48	43c	48	59a	25	25	25	59b	48a	59b	58	25	58
	47	52	48	54	43c	55	52	48	52	25	59b	26	26	60b	50	60b	59a	26	59a
	48	54	49	55	54	56	43c	52	43c	59b	60b	59b	59b	48b	51	48b	25	59b	25
	49	55	52	56	55	57	62	43c	62	60b	48b	60b	60b	61	58	63	26	60b	59b
	52	56	43c	57	56	58	36	62	36	48b	61	48b	48b	64	59a	61	59b	48b	60b
	54	57	54	58	57	59	44	36	44	61	64	64	6		25	64	60b	61	48b
	55	58	55	59	58	60	54	44	54	62			64		26		48b	64	61
	57	59	56	60	59	61	55	54	63	63					59b		61		62
	58	60	57	61	60	62	59	55	55	64					60b		64		63
	59	61	58	62	61	63	60a	59	59						48b				64
	60	62	59	63	62	64	55	60a	60a						61				
	61	63	60	64	63		61	61	61						64				
	62	64	61		64														
	63		62																
	64		63																
			64																

ISAAC ISRAELI AND HIS *SEFER HASHETEN*: GLASGOW MS HUNTER 477*

Max Sussman

From the biblical period to the present day, medical subjects have been an important stimulus for Jewish literary activity. The interpretation of some of the sources continues to exercise scholars and to this Professor John Sawyer has made an important contribution.[1] This brief preliminary and, so far, incomplete study of MS Hunter 477, a Hebrew medical manuscript in the Hunter Collection at Glasgow University Library, and its author Isaac Israeli, seems an appropriate tribute to a Scottish scholar with broad interests who has contributed much to the understanding of Hebrew biblical literature.

Isaac Israeli[2]

Isaac ben Solomon was a native of Egypt, is said to have lived to the age of more than a hundred, and died in Kairouan in what is now

* I wish to express my gratitude to the Librarian, Glasgow University Library for access to Glasgow MS Hunter 477 and for permission to reproduce here pages 61v-62v. My sincere thanks are also due to Mr David Weston of Glasgow University Library for his unfailing help and courtesy during my visits to the library and for paginating the codex. It is a very special delight here to acknowledge my very dear friends Dr Berl Cutler and Dr Sam Lazarus, both of Glasgow, for drawing my attention to the above MS in the first place. I wish also to record my thanks to the late Dr Haskel D. Isaacs of the Taylor-Schechter Geniza Research Unit, Cambridge University Library for his invaluable assistance in deciphering parts of the MS and for his help in translating many of the plant and drug names.

A bibliography of books and articles about Issac (*sic*) ben Solomon al-Isra'ili up to 1971 is to be found in R.Y. Ebied, *Bibliography of Mediaeval Arabic and Jewish Medicine and Allied Sciences* (London, 1971).

1. See J. Sawyer, 'A Note on the Etymology of Ṣara'at', *VT* 26 (1976), pp. 241-45.

2. See A. Altman and S.M. Stern, *Isaac Israeli* (Oxford, 1958).

Tunisia. The dates of his life are not known with certainty; the best available evidence suggests that he died in about 955 CE, which puts his birth in about 855 CE. The name Israeli derives from his Arabic name Abu Ya'qub Ishaq ibn Sulayman al-Israī'lī, which also gave rise to the name Isaac Judaeus used in the Latin translations of his works.

Isaac Israeli began his career, probably still in Egypt, as an oculist. He emigrated to Kairouan in 907 CE and became court physician to the Aghlabite prince, Ziyadat Allah. Some years later he became physician to 'Ubayd Allāh al-Mahdī, the founder of the Fatimid dynasty in North Africa (reigned 910–934 CE). It is said that Israeli composed his medical writings in Arabic at the request of the Mahdi.

According to Ibn Juljul, the Andalusian author of *Generations of the Physicians*,[3] Israeli remained unmarried. When asked whether he would have liked to have a child, he replied that he had a better thing in his *Book of Fevers*, by which he appears to have meant that he would be better remembered by that book.

Though Israeli appears to have practised as an opthalmologist while still in Egypt, in Kairouan he became a pupil of the physician Ishaq ibn 'Imran al-Baghdadī. In turn Israeli became the teacher of the noted physician Ibn al-Jazzar (c. 924–1004 CE). It is interesting to note that al-Jazzar's *Kitab zad al-musafir wa-qut al-hadir* (*Provisions for the traveller and the nourishment of the settled*) was translated into Latin in Italy by Constantinus Africanus under the title *Viaticum peregrinatis* and by Moses ibn Tibbon into Hebrew under the title צדת הדרכים.

Israeli's Writings and Influence

Israeli's philosophical work has received detailed attention[4] and will be mentioned here only in passing. He was a Neoplatonist, whose sources are to be found in al-Kindi, the first great Islamic philosopher of the first half of the ninth century, and a lost pseudo-Aristotelian work that has been reconstructed.[5]

Israeli's influence as a philosopher was considerable. According to one of his pupils, Dunash ibn Tamīm, he was in correspondence in Kairouan with Saadya Gaon (882–942 CE), while the latter was still in

3. Edited by F. Sayyid (Cairo, 1955), p. 87. Cited by Altman and Stern, *Isaac Israeli.*

4. See Altman and Stern, *Isaac Israeli.*

5. See Altman and Stern, *Isaac Israeli*, p. 95.

Fayyum before departing to the gaonate in Babylonia.[6] It is possible that some aspects of Saadya's philosophy are derived from Israeli's opinions. A number of Jewish philosophers, including Moses ibn Ezra (*c.* 1060–1139 CE), Joseph ibn Ṣaddiq (d. 1149) and Solomon ibn Gabirol (Avicebron, *c.* 1021–*c.*1058), made use of Israeli's writings and his philosophical works were also highly regarded by Muslim and Christian authors.

Among mediaeval Christian scholars, Israeli was known as *eximius monarcha medicinae*.[7] To judge by the very large number of his extant medical MSS in Arabic, Hebrew and Latin, his writings were extraordinarily influential. Israeli's collected writings were translated into Latin by Constantinus Africanus of Carthage (1020–1087 CE), who claimed them for himself. It was not until the translations were republished in 1515[8] that they were correctly attributed to their true author.

Israeli's most influential medical work was his *Kitab al-Ḥummayat* (*Book of Fevers*, ספר הקדחות).[9] In its Latin translation this was used as a textbook in several European universities, including Paris and Oxford until the seventeenth century.[10] Other works include the *Book on Foods and Simple Remedies* and the *Book of Urine*.[11] In 1861 Soave discovered a MS entitled *Sefer Musar Harofim* (ספר מוסר הרופאים).[12]

6. See H. Malter, *Saadia Gaon: His Life and Works* (New York, 1926, reprinted 1969).

7. See Malter, *Saadia Gaon*, p. 47.

8. *Omnia Opera Ysaac* (Lyon, 1515).

9. A translation of the *The Third Discourse: On Consumption* has been published by J.D. Latham and H.D. Isaacs (Arabic Technical and Scientific Texts: Volume 8; Cambridge Middle East Centre, Pembroke Arabic Texts; Cambridge, 1981).

10. See B. Cutler and S. Lazarus, 'The Isaac Israeli Manuscript', *Glasgow University Gazette* 77 (1975), pp. 4-5.

11. See H. Friedenwald, 'Manuscript Copies of the Medical Works of Isaac Judaeus', *Annals of Medical History* NS 1 (1929), pp. 629-39.

12. Tübingen, MS Orient. 4⁰836. Several translations have been published: D. Kaufmann, 'Isak Israeli's Propädeutik für Aerzte', *Magazin für die Wissenschaft des Judentums* 11 (1884), pp. 97-112 (German); S. Jarcho, 'Guide for Physicians (Musar Harofim) by Isaac Judaeus (880?–932?)', *Bulletin of the History of Medicine* 15 (1944), pp. 180-88; A. Bar-Sela and H.E. Hoff, 'Isaac Israeli's Fifty Admonitions to the Physicians', *Journal of the History of Medicine* 17 (1962), pp. 245-57. The authorship of this interesting text has been disputed but the present consensus appears to be that it is a genuine Israeli text.

The Book of Urine (ספר השתן, *De urine*)
Attempts to employ visual observation of the urine for diagnostic and prognostic purposes reach back into hoary antiquity. In the Greek medical tradition of Hippocrates and Galen, observation of the urine appears to have been as important as other diagnostic aids. Israeli's *Book of Urine* belongs to this tradition. It has not been systematically studied and, in common with the *Book of Fevers*, it must have been much valued if one is to judge by the many MSS still extant.[13] It describes the formation of the urine, its examination by observation (uroscopy) and the significance of the appearances for the diagnosis and prognosis of disease.

According to Steinschneider,[14] the *Book of Urine* 'belongs to the most famous of its kind'. It was originally written in Arabic and later translated into Latin and Hebrew. This led to its being known by a number of names. Its short Arabic name is *Kitab al'bawl*. According to Steinschneider[15] MS Vatican 310, which is in Arabic but in Hebrew script, bears a longer title that is generally consistent with that of the Hebrew versions:

> בתאב מגמוע מן אׄקאויל אלאואיל פי מערפה אלבול ואקסאמה
>
> 'Compilation of the words of the Ancients about the knowledge of the urine and its types.'

In translation, the title of MS 477 reads 'Book compiled from the words of the Ancients about the knowledge of the urine (בידיעת השתן), and its deposits (ובהפרשיו, lit. separations) and signs (ואותותיו) which Isaac the son of Solomon Israeli the physician determined to compile and it consists of ten chapters (שערים)'. The similarity of the titles of MS 477 and MS Vatican 310, and the appearance in MS 477 of many Arabic words, suggests that our MS is a translation from the Arabic.

13. The Hebrew and Arabic MSS are incompletely listed by M. Steinschneider, *Die Hebräischen Übersetzungen des Mittelalters und die Juden als Dolmetscher* (Graz, 1956) (reprint of 1893 edition). Glasgow MS Hunter 477, the subject of this paper, and a Hebrew translation of the Latin version, that appeared in a sale at Sotheby's, London, on 19 April 1990, were unknown to Steinschneider. A list of Latin MSS, probably also incomplete, is provided by Johannes Peine, in his doctoral thesis submitted to the University of Leipzig, 1919.

14. Steinschneider, *Hebräischen Übersetzungen*.

15. Steinschneider, *Hebräischen Übersetzungen*.

Glasgow MS Hunter 477

A brief account of this interesting codex was published by Cutler and Lazarus.[16] It is a Hebrew translation of Israeli's treatise on uroscopy first written by him in Arabic. The entry in the Hunterian Museum Library Catalogue reads as follows:

> *Isaac Judaei, Liber de Urinis Cognoscendis*: Paper $7\frac{1}{2}$ inches by $5\frac{1}{4}$ inches, ff. 62, written in single columns of 24 lines, each $5\frac{3}{8}$ inches by $3\frac{1}{2}$ inches, marginalia (in Hebrew), marginal drawings of vasa urinalia. Binding: Millboards, covered spattered calf, gilt-tooled panelled back, red edges, title, on lowest panel but one and inverted gilt on crimson morocco shield: LIBER | MED | MSS. HEB. Contents: Ishak ibn Sulaimana'l Israili's Treatise on the Diagnosis of Urines.

Cutler and Lazarus noted that the MS is bound upside down. They suggested that it is written on paper of the fourteenth century (but see below) and that the fly leaf is of the eighteenth century. This suggests that it was bound or rebound at about the time it entered Hunter's library. How the codex reached the collection of William Hunter (1718–1783)[17] is unknown. The MS is said to be in an Italian script[18] but as has been noted[19] the Hebrew writing has North African characteristics.

Examination of MS 477 revealed that what appears to be a colophon (page 62v, see text below), in fact reads, 'These last three pages are prescriptions that I have found and they are not from the book. Finished and completed, praise to the Lord of the world.' The colophon of Israeli's book, in fact, appears on page 61r of the MS and reads:

> נשלם הספר בעזרת האל וטובת עזרו שחברו יצחק הישראלי הרופא זצל על
> ידי רפאל הרופא ג ימים לחדש אדר רמט

> Completed is the book, with the help of the Lord and the goodness of his assistance, that was compiled by Isaac Israeli the Physician, may the

16. See Cutler and Lazarus, 'The Isaac Israeli Manuscript'.

17. William Hunter (1718–1783) was the elder brother of John Hunter (1728–1793). He was educated at Glasgow and Edinburgh Universities and at St George's Hospital, London. He was an anatomist, physician extra-ordinary to Queen Charlotte, 1764 and first professor of anatomy, Royal Academy, 1768. His portrait was painted by Reynolds and his museum was acquired by Glasgow University (from *The Concise Dictionary of National Biography* [Oxford University Press, 1992]).

18. Dr B. Richler, Jerusalem, personal communication, 1992.

19. Cutler and Lazarus, 'The Isaac Israeli Manuscript'.

memory of the righteous be for a blessing, by the hand of Raphael the Physician, third day of the month of Adar 249.

Unfortunately, the copyist does not give his patronymic, nor does he indicate where the copy was made. However, the year of completion must be 5249 AM, which corresponds with 1489 CE. This makes it unlikely that the codex is written on fourteenth-century paper.

The MS has certain interesting characteristics. The margins contain several drawings of flasks used for the examination of the urine, showing the meniscus of the urine. The urine is clear in the drawing on page 5r, while it appears to be turbid on page 27v. In the margins of a few pages (e.g. 8r and 9r) there are drawings of a pointing finger. These indicate references to Galen and Hippocrates but not all such references are indicated in this way. The repeated references, particularly to Galen, would make it interesting to carry out a detailed comparison of Galen's and Israeli's teachings on the urine.

Occasionally, Hippocrates is referred to as 'The Pious' (החסיד e.g. page 27v). On page 25v there is reference to a man called Paleononis, who it is suggested was a patient of Hippocrates. Beginning on page 29v there is a case history of a 20-year-old man, Ruh ibn Ruh Hatmimi, with a severe fever, seen by Israeli.

There are a number of marginal notes throughout the MS. They are written with a finer pen, in a script similar to that of the MS as a whole and appear to be by the scribe of the MS. They include translations of Arabic words and very brief explanations of the text. On page 1v there is a reference to the 'bowel of the twelve fingers' (המעי שנים עשר אצבעות—duodenum).

Beginning on page 5r are detailed instructions on how the urine is to be taken and examined. On page 9v mention is made of urine that is 'sweet' (מתוק), clearly a reference to diabetes mellitus.

As we have seen, the *Book of Urine* ends with the colophon on page 61r. Examination of the final pages (61v–62v) shows that they contain a series of prescriptions of medicines for the treatment of a variety of common diseases. This is consistent with the final 'colophon', on page 62v, where they are referred to as רציטי (?rece[p]te).

A transcript of the Hebrew text of the prescriptions and a partial translation are presented below. These prescriptions raise interesting questions. If the MS was copied in Italy, what is the origin of the prescriptions? It is known that Israeli was the originator or transmitter of many medical prescriptions. Were these prescriptions originally Israeli's?

If so, how did the Castilian terms enter the text? Some of these problems may be soluble with the examination of MS texts extant in various libraries. In the meantime, this Italian MS with its Castilian traces may be a surviving silent witness to the persecution of the Jews in the Iberian peninsula during the fifteenth century and its resulting emigration.

Text[20]

61 v

פליריס קונטיריון יפה לקדחת רביעית והוא מנוסה. קח עצי אסרא בקרא. עץ אהלים מא' א' דרח'. גרמא של קיטראן א' דרח'. פושטקיי ופיניי מנוקים ד' אונק' בין שניהם. קנמון טוב ומובחר ב' אונק' זנגביל* טוב ב. אונק'. גרופולי א' אונק' וחצי. גלנגי מאצי מא' חצי אונק' עצי מוסקטא חצי אונק'. יוכתו ויעורבו היטב ביין יפה ולבן ויעמדו שם שעה. ואח'כ ייבשם לצל ועשה ליטובריאן עם ב' ליט' צוקרו לבן. התפישה ממנו יהיה בשעור אגוז בבקר ובערב ובליל הקדחת לא יאכלנו. וישמר מכל ירק כגון כרוב ושאר ירקות. ומכל מאכל ומשתא קר. ויעשה הדיאיטא כמו ד' או ח' ימים קודם שיתחיל לתפוש זה הליטובריאן וכ'ש שצריך לעשות הדיאיטא ג'כ כשיתפוש הליטובריאן תמיד מבשר סריס. ופולשטרי. ומכל מאכל טוב. וישמר מן המאכלים רעים

משיחה לגרב שבשוקים והרגלים. קח א' אונק' שמן רוסטן. חלב סריס נקי. מיץ פלנטיני. לבוה זכה. ליטריירו מזהב צרוסא מא' א' אונק'. שעוה לבנה ב' אונק' ועשה תחבושת.

קרישטירי לכאב הכולנקי. קח קולוקוינטידא חצי אונק'. צינטוריאה חצי מטפולו. קרוא. זרע פינוקלו. אניסו. צימיט מא' חצי אונק' דבש. שמן זית מא' ג' אונק'. בינידיטא פשוטה חצי אונק' מעט מלח ויועיל בעה'ש.

קרישטירי לכאב הכולנקי ולחולי הרינילא. קח פרחי קממילא . פרחי מלילוטו זרע אפיו זרע אלטיאה. זרע פשתן פינגריקו. לוישטיקו. קרואי. זרע פינוקלו. אמיאוס. זרע אניסי. זרע אניטו. זרע פיטרוסיטלו. תאני' יבשי' מיץ בליטי. מי סובין. קטריטיקו. אמפריאלי. מא' אונק' שמן אניטו ד' אונק' ויועיל בעה'.

20. Words underlined in the text are Castilian Spanish, while those marked with an asterisk are Arabic.

62 r

משיחה לפונטורא[21]

קח זפת גריקא ג' אונק'. טריבינטינא ג' אונק' שעוה חצי ליט' אופורביאו ג' אונק' לאכול הבשר הרע ולהגליד החבלות

זפת גריקא א' ליט'. שעוה ח' אונק'. שמן ב' אונק' אוליבנו א' אונק' חומץ א' ליט'. ויטריאולו ב' אונק'

משיחה לבנה לגרב שבשוקים והרגלים והיא מנוסה וטובה מאד ונפלא. קח שמן רוסטו ג' אונק'. צירוסה ליטריירו מזהב מא' חצי אונק' לבונה זכה בי דרח'. חלב סריס ב' אונק'. מיץ פלנטייני א' אונק שעוה לבנה ב' אונק'. ועשה תחבושת והוא יפה מאד ומנוסה למה שזכרנו ולכל גוטא מלוחה.

משיחה טפה מלוחה שבשוקים והיא טובה ומנוסה. קח שעוה חדשה. וראוה דפיני. טריבינטינא מא' ב' אונק'. חצי כוס יין ישן. ותתיך על אש מגחלים בלתי שלהבת תוך קדרה מחרש משוחה ושועה באבר ונענע בכף תמיד ואחרי' כן תסירם מעל האש ונענע בכף וכשיתחיל להיתקרר תשים מעט חומץ חזק ואח'כ סככהו ותניחהו להתקרר ותעשה חוד באמצעיתו והפוך אותה על פניה כדי שיצא ממנה החומץ ומשח לרפואה אמן.

משיחה אחרת מועיל לגרב כמו הנז'. קח צירוסא וליטריירו מזהב מאט בשוה וערבם בשמן רוסטו ונענעם יחד בטיב ואחכ' משח בכל מקום שיש בו גרב. והוא מנוסה.

62 v

ליטובריאו יפה לחולי הכוליקי והאבן והרינילא. ויש אומרי' גם לטחולין קח סיליאו קסיאה. קלמינטו. פלפל לבן פלפל אריך. ציפרי סקינטו. פיליטרו. דאנקו איריאוס. אמומו פוליאו אסרי מא' א' סקרופט. קמידריאוס. זנגביל*. קנמון. גלנגא. מרטרי הוא זרע פינוקלו. קארוא מא' א' סקרופט וטו' גראני. ריגוליציאו מסטיצי מא' ב סקרופט וה' גראני. אניסי. גראני אסולי. מא' ב' דרח' וטו' גרני ספיקו נרדו. כרפס. גומא רביקא. זרע אניטו. גומא דרגנטי. קלמו ארומטיקו קוביבי* גרופולי. קרפו* בלסאמו. לווישטיקו הוא זרע פירולא אלסדרי הנק' פיטרוסינילו. מצידוניקו. ייניפרי. סיליאו. הוא זרע אצי פינטפילון. שרש ספריצי. זרע ספריצי. קליפות אתרוג. אמיאוס. אקורי ריאוברברו. דיאפונטיקו. אגוז מוסקטו. עץ אלואי. זרע בסיליקו.

21. ‘Puntura’ is Italian for ‘sting, ‘prick’ or an ‘insect bite’.

ססופריקא. זרע ציטרולי קלופי'. זרע מלוני קלופי'. זרע קוקומרי. קלופי' . זרע קיקיצא קלופי'. זרע סקרולא. זרע פיטרוסיטלו. ביאימי לבני' ואדומי' שטורצי קלמיטא. קרדמומן מא' טו גראני. פטטי חצי אונק' וב' סקרופט. צוקרו קפטי? ב' ליט' וחצי. ולאחר בשול הצוקרו ישים בו כל העניני' כת[...]. ויתפוש ממנו ב' דרח' עם יין מזוג שיהיה מבושל באותם המים עשב הנק' לינגווא צירוונא היא סקולופינדריא ויתפוש ממנו בבקר או בערב משהולך לישן ב' או ג' פעמי' בשבוע חצי אונק' בכל פעם.

קרישטירי לכאב הכולוקי ולחולי הרינילא. קח צינטואווריאה חצי מטפול. זרע אניס. זרע פינוקלו. זרע אפייו. קרואי. לויסטיקו מא' חצי אונק' כמון א' אונק'. קולוקווינטירא ב' דרח'. קשורה במעט סטרטוט. סאליימא ב' דרח'. בטריטא צמא א' אונק'. דבש ד' אונק'. שמן אניטו. שמן רוטא מא' ג' אונק' ועשה קרישטירו ויועיל בעה'

השלושה דפים האלה האחרונים הם רציתי מצאתים ואינם מן הספר

תם ונשלם תהילה לש' עולם

Translation[22]

61v

(1) Centaury pill good for quartan fever and it is tried. Take wood of valerian

(2) עץ אהלים, 1 dr. of each, juniper gum one drachm. clean pistachio

(3) and pine seeds, together 4 oz., good choice cinnamon 2 oz.

(4) good ginger 2 oz., גרופולי 1 oz. and a half, galanga, מאצי of each half an oz.

(5) wood of muscat half an oz. Beat and mix well with good white wine and allow them to stand

(6) for one hour. And then allow to dry in the shade and make ליטובריאן with 2 lit. of sugar [that is]

(7) white. The dose of it shall be the measure of a nut. In the morning and the evening and the night of the fever

(8) he shall not take it. And he shall avoid [eating] all vegetable, such as cabbage and other vegetables and all food

(9) and cold drink. And he shall take the diet about 4 or 8 days before he starts

22. In the following partial translation, the untranslated words are reproduced rather than left as lacunae. The measures ‘dr.’, ‘oz.’ and ‘lit.’ are merely approximations to the abbreviations in the original. Their exact meaning and scale value are, as yet, undetermined.

(10) to take this הליטוברי׳אן and though he must take the diet, so also when he takes
(11) הליטובריאן always מבשר סריס ופולשטרי and of all good food
(12) and he shall refrain from bad foods.

(13) Ointment for eczema of the legs and feet. Take 1 oz. oil of רוסטן, חלב סריס [that is]
(14) pure, plantain juice, pure frankincense, grated gold, white lead
(15) of each 1 oz., white wax 2 oz. and make a bandage

(16) מרישטירי for colic. Take scolopendrion half an oz., centauria half
(17) מטפולי quarrua, foenoculum seeds, anise, צימינו of each half an oz.
(18) honey, olive oil, of each 3 oz., plain benedictus half an oz.
(19) a little salt and it will be effective with the help of God.

(20) קרישטירי for colic and for diseases of the kidney. Take camomile flowers, meliloto flowers
(21) opium seeds, altea seeds, linen seeds, fenugreek, levistico, quarrua, seeds of
(22) fennel, ammi majus, aniseed, aneth seeds, parsley seeds, dry figs
(23) bellota juice, bran water, קטריטיקו אמפריאלי of each an oz. aneth oil
(24) 4 oz. and it will be effective with the help of God.

62r

(1) Ointment for insect sting
(2) Take agaricum tar 3 oz. turpentine 3 oz. wax half a lit.
(3) euphorbion 3 oz.

(4) To remove bad flesh and to cicatrise wounds
(5) agaricum tar 1 lit., wax 8 oz., oil 2 oz. אוליבנו
(6) 1 oz. vinegar 1 lit. vitriol
(7) 2 oz.

(8) White ointment for eczema of the legs and feet and it is tried and very good

(9) and marvellous. Take oil of רוסטו 3 oz. white lead, gratings of gold, of each
(10) half an oz. pure frankincense 2 dr., חלב סריס 2 oz., plantain juice
(11) 1 oz., white wax 2 oz., and make a bandage and it is very good
(12) and tried for what we have mentioned above and for all גוטא מלוחה.

(13) Ointment לטפה מלוחה of the legs and it is good and tried. Take
(14) new wax and pine resin, turpentine of each 2 oz.
(15) half a cup of old wine, and place it on a fire of embers without a flame in a pot
(16) of [? glazed] terracotta. ושועה באבר and shake by hand continuously and after this
(17) remove from the fire and shake by hand and when it begins to cool add
(18) a little strong vinegar and after this cover it and place it to cool and make
(19) a point in its centre and turn it upside down so that the vinegar may drain
(20) and apply the ointment for a cure, Amen.

(21) Another ointment effective for eczema like the one mentioned. Take white lead and gratings of gold
(22) ? [מא' בשוה] and mix with oil of רוסטו and shake well together and then spread
(23) on all places where there is eczema, and it is tried.

62v

(1) Good ליטובריאו for sufferers from colic and stone and the kidney, and some say also for sufferers from diseases of the spleen.
(2) Take silvanus, cassia, wild thyme, white pepper, long pepper, ציפרי סקינטו,
(3) פיליטרו, wild carrot, איריאוס אמומו פוליאו אסרי, of each 1
(4) scruple, comedrio, ginger, cinnamon, galanga, מרטרי that is seeds of
(5) fennel, quarrua of each 1 scruple and 15 grains, ריגוליציאו מסטיצי
(6) of each 2 scruples and 5 grains, anise, grains of אסולי of each 2 dr. and 15 grains

(7) spikenard, lettuce, gum of רביקא, aneth seeds, gum of dragoneta, calamo
(8) aromatico of qufi גרופולי, bark of balsam tree, levistico that is the seeds of פירולא
(9) of Alexandria called petroselinon of Macedonia, juniper, silvanus that is seeds of אצי
(10) פינטפילון, root of ספריצי, peel of ethrog, ammi majus, אקורי
(11) ריאוברברו (? rhubarb), דיאפונטיקו, nut of muscat, wood of aloes, basil seeds
(12) saxifrage, peeled citron seeds, peeled melon seeds, cucumber seeds
(13) peeled, peeled קיקיצא seeds, סקרולא seeds, parsley seeds, ביאמי
(14) white and red, שטורצי קלמיטא, cardamon, of each 15 grains, פטטי half
(15) an oz. and 2 scruples, sugar (.)קפטי 2 lit. and a half. After cooking the sugar
(16) put in it all the items (...)כת, and he should take of it 2 dr. with wine diluted [with]
(17) water in which there has been cooked the grass called lingua cieroona that is סקולופינדריא
(18) and he shall take of it in the morning or the evening when he goes to sleep 2 or 3 times a week
(19) half an oz. each time.

(20) קרישטירי for colic and diseases of the kidney. Take centaurea half מטפול,
(21) aniseeds, fennel seeds, opium seeds, קרואי, levistico, of each half an oz.
(22) (?מיין) 1 oz. wild cucumber 2 dr. bound with a little סמ(.)טוט סאליימא
(23) 2 dr., בטריטא צמא 1 oz., honey 4 oz., aneth oil, oil of רוטא,
(24) of each 3 oz., and make קרישטירי and it will be effective with the help of God.

(25) These last three pages are prescriptions that I have found and they are not from the book
(26) Finished and completed praise to the Lord of the world.

THE *MAḤBERET* OF MENAḤEM—PROPOSALS FOR A LEXICOGRAPHIC THEORY, WITH SAMPLE TRANSLATION AND NOTES

John F. Elwolde

1. *Introduction*

Ever since 1854, when Herschell Filipowski published *The First Hebrew and Chaldaic Lexicon to the Old Testament by Menahem ben Saruk the Spaniard* (London: James Maden/Leipzig: K.F. Köhler), western scholarship has known about the *Maḥberet* (literally, 'fascicle', hence 'Dictionary in fascicles') and its author, Menaḥem ben Jacob ben Saruq (born Tortosa c. 910–920; died after 960). The level of acquaintance with this work has, however, been low. Although Filipowski provided an English translation of parts of the *Maḥberet*, these tend towards abridgment, paraphrase, and summary (for example, the entry אולי takes up only six lines in Filipowski's translation but fifty-five in the translation provided below). Moreover, Filipowski's 'critical' edition was based not only on the relatively few manuscripts available to him but also on mid-nineteenth century text-critical perspectives. Only recently has the lack of a reliable critical edition and study of the *Maḥberet* been overcome through the labours of Angel Sáenz-Badillos (*Menaḥem ben Saruq: Maḥberet. Edición Crítica e Introducción* [Granada: Universidad de Granada, 1986]), but, although his work contains an excellent introduction of 142 pages, this is mostly in Spanish, and there is no translation—into Spanish or English—of the Hebrew text.

The purpose of the present article is to help draw more attention to the *Maḥberet*, first, in Section 2, by proposing (part of) a theoretical framework for Menahem's lexicographical work, and, secondly, by giving a short sample translation of the *Maḥberet* itself (Section 3, an earlier draft of which Professor Sáenz-Badillos very kindly looked through and to which he suggested a number of improvements; several of the points touched upon in Section 2 are also treated—sometimes at length—in Professor Sáenz-Badillos's edition, although not in the theoretical context in which I have placed them). Following the translation are some notes on the entries translated (Section 4).

I hope in a small way to reflect and pay homage not only to John Sawyer's contribution to scholarship by his application to Hebrew of the techniques of general linguistics, but also to his valuing of Jewish traditions of biblical and linguistic learning, both for their intrinsic scholarly worth and as a facet of John's commitment to the breaking down of barriers between Jews and Christians.

2. *Towards a Lexicographical Theory for the* Maḥberet

a. *A Distributional Theory of Meaning*

The most obvious linguistic fact of the *Maḥberet* is that it is a Hebrew-to-Hebrew dictionary in an age when Arabic was not only the dominant language of the major centres of Jewish culture, in Babylonia and Andalusia, but also the language in which previous attempts at the lexicography of Hebrew had been composed (by Saadiah Gaon, mentioned once in the *Maḥberet*, and by David al-Fasi). One of the reasons for Menaḥem's choice of Hebrew for explaining biblical vocabulary is, clearly, his high regard for biblical Hebrew not only as 'the language of holiness' but also as a language of beauty to be conserved and cherished for its intrinsic aesthetic merits. In the introduction to the *Maḥberet*, Menaḥem claims that Hebrew (he varies between *leshon ha-qodesh* 'language of holiness' and *lashon Yehudit* 'Jewish language') is 'the language of excellence, the choicest form of expression and most beautiful of tongues, the language refined in the crucible, exalted over every other language inherited by human beings'. It is also clear that there is a subtext here, to do with religious and cultural point-scoring: Hebrew—and the Bible—is at least as good and as holy as Arabic—and the Koran. From this perspective, then, it could also be argued that the exclusion of Arabic—*qua* language of Judaism at a relatively late stage in its development—is part of Menaḥem's alleged philo-Caraism, with its rejection of the post-biblical religious corpora and the language(s) associated with them.

However, while such cultural, aesthetic, and polemical aspects might have a rôle to play, I would claim that they are secondary to—or, in some sense, by-products of—Menaḥem's theory of language—his general linguistic theory, we might say—namely, that a language should be explicable from within itself, and does not need to be mapped onto a second—target—language. Or, put another way, a language can provide its own metalanguage. Within this theoretical framework, not only is a 'target' language (Arabic) excluded in principle, but so also is the appeal to Arabic or other 'comparative' languages, also rejected by Menaḥem, but espoused by his Arabic-writing predecessors.

In fact, however, the *Maḥberet* goes much further, by doing away not merely with target language 'definitions' but with 'definitions' altogether; it is, we might say, radically formal—almost solipsistic—so that meaning is nothing more than a by-product of form and distribution, without any ontological status in its own right. Menaḥem's pure structuralist semantics, in which meanings are conveyed merely through the contrastive distribution of texts, is reflected in the immediate impression of the *Maḥberet* as being long on examples but short on analysis.

Typically, Menaḥem will begin an entry with the phrase *mitḥalleq li-shne fanim* 'divided into two [etc.] senses (literally 'faces')' or simply *mitḥalleq li-shte maḥleqot* 'divided into two [etc.] divisions', with each of the constituent parts then introduced by *ha-eḥad/at* 'the first', *ha-sheni/nit* 'the second', etc. Where there is only one 'division' registered under a lemma, this is contrasted, implicitly, with all the other lemmata in the dictionary. Thus, rather than 'giving' the different meanings of words—and especially homographs—attached to a particular lemma, Menaḥem simply distributes the texts exemplifying the various meanings among different sections. What is in section one is not in sections two or three, what is in section two is not in sections one or three, etc. This essentially *is* Menaḥem's semantic analysis. He does not say that word *a* conveys sense *x*, but simply that word *a* means. *What* it means is, in principle, sufficiently represented by listing it separately from other words. It means what the other words—and specifically its homographs—do not mean.

In this distributional/taxonomic/inductive approach to semantic description, Menaḥem's 'formalism' appears even purer than that of a pre-Chomskyan structuralist, as it is not just semantic entities that are discounted, but morphological ones as well, for Menaḥem's analysis is based on graphic form, or letter-combination, alone. Menaḥem does come close to a morphological theory based on the triliteral root (see especially אזר), and even if he is no longer regarded as the teacher of Ibn Janāḥ, he is at least an intellectual precursor. But Menaḥem's analysis is still graphic, or 'pre-radical', as is clearly seen in the case of the entry אח, where not only does Menaḥem, foreshadowing Lane's Arabic lexicon, include under the same lemma words that today would be regarded as homonyms (similarly, for example, under אדן, both אָדוֹן 'lord' and אֶדֶן 'base' are registered), but also words that happen to include the same sequence of consonants although they are from other 'roots' entirely.

b. *Deviations from the Theory*

What I have presented is a 'theory of lexicography' to which Menaḥem might be regarded as consciously adhering or by which at least he is unconsciously guided (perhaps of relevance here is the intention expressed in the introduction to the *Maḥberet: le-faresh toṣe'ot 'inyanim le-maḥleqotehem*, 'to explain the results of meanings in accordance with their divisions'). It does, I believe, account for and throw light on the bulk of Menaḥem's analysis. Nonetheless, in the practical realization of Menaḥem's distributional theory of meaning, there are many exceptions to the rule, and a great deal of subtle shifting and widening of linguistic goal-posts in order to save the appearance of the theory, and without which the theory could hardly function in practice.

1. Perhaps the most important of these is the assumption that the readership already knows biblical Hebrew quite well, albeit as a second (or third) language. In the case of the lemma אח, for example, Menaḥem commences by simply listing two examples of the common word אָח 'brother'. He makes no comment whatsoever on it, because he can assume that it is well known to his readers (note, however, that the second example, 'is not Esau Jacob's brother?' expresses a practical definition-by-example of what an אָח is, of some poignancy to the Jews of Muslim Spain). On this assumption, Menaḥem is then able to present a further three sections of less well-known words containing אח, 'defining' each one not only by grouping together its biblical references, but also by setting each group as a whole in contrast to אָח 'brother'. Through this distributional technique, Menaḥem indicates that the אח represented by this group of texts is not the same as the אח of the first group—what this second (or third or fourth) אח actually means is deducible from the texts grouped together. In practice, in the case of אח 2–4, Menaḥem also adjoins short explanatory comments to help his readers (see below, 3–4). But in principle, the only semantic information provided is via distribution—the אח in this group of texts means something that is distinct from the אח in the other groups. His pedagogic technique in essence, then, is to 'nudge' his readers into expanding their

knowledge of lesser-known Hebrew vocabulary, by showing its links with the biblical Hebrew that was already well known to them. Returning to an earlier point, we can say that the reason why the *Maḥberet* is long on examples but short on analysis is because analysis is unnecessary in the face of the readers' direct appropriation of contextualized—and hence meaning-laden—vocabulary, facilitated by Menaḥem's gentle 'nudging'.

2. Menaḥem's success in describing lesser known biblical Hebrew vocabulary from within biblical Hebrew itself depends in part on his readers' knowledge of Rabbinic/Mediaeval Hebrew, which was still 'alive' to them, at least from the perspective of literary consumption and production, and on the unspoken assumption that this later Hebrew is an integral part of the language of the Bible itself—there is no 'target' language, because the target language is the same as the 'source' language. This should not be overstated, however—in support of Menaḥem's theoretical consistency, non-biblical Hebrew is only used extensively in the strictly non-lexicographic discourses of a morphological, grammatical, or exegetical nature, scattered through the first nine letters of the *Maḥberet* (and well-represented in our sample translation); the lexicographic descriptions proper are usually so brief that they require only the use of biblical Hebrew vocabulary, albeit vocabulary that is common to later Hebrew as well. Although Menaḥem will very occasionally mention the 'language of the Mishnah' or quote the Talmud, he mentions 'Aramaic' (as an integral part of the language of the Bible; see below, 7) much more often. Indeed, Menaḥem has a strong consciousness of the Hebrew of the Mishnah in particular as being quite distinct from that of the Bible: *bi-lshon Mishnah we-lo' ba-lashon 'Ivrit*, 'in the language of (the) Mishnah but not in the Hebrew language' (towards the beginning of Alef).

3. Within any given entry, Menaḥem will often add a brief explanatory comment. Generally speaking, Menaḥem's analyses may be divided into three broad types: (a) mere quotation of texts; (b) quotation of texts, followed by the expression *ke-mashma'o* (and variants), 'as its meaning is (normally understood to be)'; (c) linking of words in one or more texts to a 'definitional' word in another text or texts, preceded by the preposition *kemo*, '(this is) like'. Each of the last two categories may also include wording of the sort, *ke-'inyano* (and variants), 'according to its context', which, of course, makes explicit the grounding of Menaḥem's analysis in the source language.

4. Moreover, on some occasions, Menaḥem will lapse into straight-

forward description of referents, as for example in the case of אֵזוֹב 'hyssop', אֶזְרָח 'native (tree)', אָח 'brazier', and אָחוּ 'reed(s)'. But note that this information only comes *after* the relevant texts, as secondary explanations designed to emphasize or clarify what the mere distribution of the texts is supposed to reveal sufficiently by itself. Even though at times it can appear that Menaḥem simply provides a definitional gloss, before the citation of texts, as in the case of מֹאזְנַיִם 'scales', under אזן, or after, as in the case of אֲזִיק 'chain' or אֵזֵא 'heated' (see also the second paragraph of אזר), on closer inspection, these 'definitions' turn out to be not components of a metalanguage, but abbreviated citations of biblical texts.

5. We can often detect inconsistency in Menaḥem's application of formal techniques. Thus, frequently, a word is listed under more than one lemma or not listed under the lemma where we might expect it to be. It is odd, for example that under the lemma זק Menaḥem includes אֲזִיק 'chain' (Jer. 40.8), even though under the lemma אֲזִיק, the obvious connection with זֵק 'fetter' is only found in one manuscript. Similarly, אָחוּ 'reed(s)' is listed under the lemma אח, but not under the lemma אחו, which Menaḥem reserves for the verb חוה pi. 'declare' and the Hebrew and Aramaic noun אַחֲוָ(י)ה 'declaration'—the fact that Menaḥem includes here the form יְחַוֶּה 'he will declare', where the alef of the lemma is absent, is a clear indication of his awareness that the 'root' does not include alef, despite the lemma, which might explain the exclusion of אָחוּ, where, perhaps, Menaḥem felt the alef to be more radical than servile. In the case of אוּלַי 'perhaps', rather than separating into three 'sections', Menaḥem sensitively distinguishes three separate 'subsenses' that have developed, as he says, from a single word with originally just one meaning. Both of the last two examples reflect the way in which Menaḥem's linguistic insights—into triliterality and the (diachronically-based) distinction between polysemy and homonymy, for example—are ahead of the letter-based formality of his lexicographic super-structure, which appears morphologically, diachronically, and semantically naïve. But like any good lexicographer, Menaḥem ensures that the theory is made for Menaḥem, not Menaḥem for the theory!

6. Other ways in which Menaḥem 'cheats the system', that is the theory—or at least the framework—of his own making, have to do with the absence of a target language. We have already noted some sleight of hand in connexion with the use of Rabbinic/Mediaeval Hebrew. But also, as already mentioned, Menaḥem does not write his explanatory

material in Arabic. However, since the last century, it been argued that the stock-phrase *ke-mashma'o*, which we have rendered, in accordance with normal custom, 'as its meaning is normally understood to be', does not mean this but rather 'as the meaning of its cognate', namely in Arabic, presumably of the Classical or the Andalusian variety. Thus, for example, when Menaḥem uses this expression in connexion with *az* 'then', we should understand him to be referring to the Arabic *idh*. Although there is no really firm evidence for this interpretation, some support is provided by the entries for אַדְרַזְדָּא 'correctly' and אֵפֶר 'dust', where three manuscripts have a text which makes explicit reference both to the Arabic language and to a *non-cognate* Arabic vocable. Thus, it might be argued, just as Menaḥem *overtly* refers to Arabic when a non-cognate target language equivalent is required, so he *covertly* alludes to it when the target language equivalent is cognate with the Hebrew word being interpreted. This understanding of Menaḥem's analysis could account for the brevity of his entries; if correct, it would of course, have considerable negative implications for what we have said about Menaḥem's 'intra-linguistic' or 'non-target language' approach.

In fact, however, it seems that this is yet another example of Menaḥem having his cake and eating it. On the one hand, for whatever reasons, the appeal to cognate languages is excluded in principle from his lexicographic arsenal; on the other hand, Menaḥem realizes that in practice Arabic is known to his intended readership and will clearly be of use to them in understanding biblical Hebrew. So he uses the deliberately vague expression 'as its meaning is', knowing that some readers, true to the apparent spirit of Menaḥem's lexicographic theory, will fill this out by 'normally taken to be', while others will fill it out by 'in Arabic', contravening the spirit but certainly not the letter of Menaḥem's theory. But on a couple of occasions, he lets the cat slip out of the bag, and Arabic appears quite explicitly. It seems to me that this is the only way in which we can both maintain a coherent theory of lexicography in Menaḥem and display a responsible attitude to the references to Arabic, few though they may might be, in the manuscript tradition, for if we adhere, like Sáenz-Badillos, to what might be called a 'radical' exclusion of Arabic in Menaḥem, we then have to explain how it came about that references to Arabic were *inserted* in manuscripts originating from non-Arabic-speaking areas.

7. Our conclusions here are borne out by Menaḥem's treatment of Aramaic. *Maḥberet* is a dictionary of both biblical Hebrew and biblical

Aramaic, and forms from both languages will often appear under one lemma (as in the case of אַחֲוָה mentioned earlier, or, under אזן, of מֹאזְנַיִם 'scales'), and Menaḥem will select with equal ease forms from biblical Aramaic or biblical Hebrew to elucidate Aramaic, at the level of semantics, as with אזא 'be hot' (Aramaic) and יקד 'burn' (Hebrew), or morphology, as with אֶשְׁתּוֹמַם 'he was desolated' (Aramaic) and שְׁמָמָה 'desolation' (Hebrew; for both examples see the entry אֲזָא). At one level, then, for Menaḥem a word is not really Aramaic or Hebrew, simply biblical. But there is a certain disingenuousness in this attitude, and Menaḥem quietly and creatively exploits the distinction between the theoretical sameness of Aramaic and Hebrew and their practical differentiation in the minds of his readers. We see this in the entry אזל 'go', where after listing—almost exhaustively—the Hebrew examples of this verb, Menaḥem states 'all of them (represent) a term for "going", and whenever "going" occurs in Aramaic, it is the same as this: וַיֵּלֶךְ אִישׁ "now a man went" (Exod. 2.1) (is rendered by Onkelos as) וַאֲזַל גַּבְרָא; אֲזַלוּ בִבְהִילוּ לִירוּשְׁלֶם "they went in haste to Jerusalem" (Ezra 4.23), אֲזַל וְכֵן אֲמַר־לֵהּ "he went and said thus to him" (Dan. 2.24).' Here then, by adding the two biblical Aramaic references, Menaḥem is able to sustain the fiction that he is simply 'explaining meaning by listing', while at the same time in practice confirming/justifying his interpretation of אזל in Hebrew as 'go' by appeal to a cognate language, where the equivalent word is more common. The crux of his analysis is the text of Exod. 2.1 with its Targumic counterpart. The use of the Targum, as an integral part of Jewish sacred literature and liturgy, frees Menaḥem, albeit on a technicality (the language of the Targum presumably classes as a *lashon Yehudit*, 'Jewish language') from the charge of breaking his own ground rules about appealing to languages or literatures outside of the Bible. So here, as in the case of Arabic, Menaḥem will let his theoretical rigour slip just enough to allow his users to draw the obvious practical conclusions, but not so much that he can be condemned of radical theoretical inconsistency.

Good lexicography requires above all the prioritization of users' needs, an underpinning theory that is transparent in the framework of the dictionary, and, perhaps most of all, a sense of serendipity which can invisibly stretch the theory to accommodate readers' needs. Menaḥem may have lacked consistency and a sophisticated morphology, but a sense of serendipity he possessed in good measure.

3. *Sample Translation of the* Maḥberet

The following preliminary translation is of the text included in pp. 31*–35* of Sáenz-Badillos's edition ('S-B' in notes), although with the entries re-arranged in alphabetical order. Apart from the first entry, אולי, no translation of this material appears in Filipowski ('F' in notes). For purposes of explanation, I have usually vocalized the text of Menaḥem ('M' in notes); I have usually quoted biblical references directly from *Biblia Hebraica Stuttgartensia*, ignoring differences between this and Menaḥem's text in respect of *scriptio defectiva/plena*, and I have added the translation of the *Revised Standard Version* (sometimes with very minor adjustments), even where it goes against Menaḥem's own interpretation, except in cases marked by an asterisk after the chapter and verse reference, which I have attached to each translation. Round brackets enclose 'periphrastic' wording in the translation, while square brackets contain the original Hebrew text, textual comments, etc. The lemma is vocalized if it relates to just one word, with a standard gloss provided in brackets; otherwise, I leave the lemma unvocalized, and list the various words treated under it in brackets. (Other abbreviations: Kt [Ketiv], L [Codex Lenigradensis], ms(s) [manuscript(s)], MT [Masoretic Text], Qr [Qere]).

אולי (אוּלַי 'perhaps', לוּ 'if')
אוּלַי יִרְאֶה י׳ בָּעֳנִי 'it may be that the LORD will look upon my affliction' [Qr (L): עֵינִי 'my eye'; Kt (L): עֲוֹנִי 'my iniquity'; (biblical) mss, F: עָנְיִי] (2 Sam. 16.12), אוּלַי יֵשׁ חֲמִשִּׁים צַדִּיקִם 'suppose there are fifty righteous' (Gen. 18.24), אוּלַי יִשְׁמַע י׳ אֱלֹהֶיךָ 'it may be that the LORD your God heard' (Isa. 37.4). There are certain words in the holy tongue that are shaped according to their (common) paradigm [קְצוּבִים בִּגְזֵרָתָם; ms: קְבוּצִים 'grouped'], but are not similar in their interpretation, (as for example, with): אוּלַי יִרְאֶה י׳ בָּעֳנִי [M: וְא׳] 'it may be that the LORD will look upon my affliction' (2 Sam. 16.12), וְאוּלַי יְמֻשֵּׁנִי [M: וְא׳] 'perhaps he will feel me' (Gen. 27.12), and אוּלַי נָטְתָה מִפָּנַי [M: וְא׳] 'if she had not turned aside from me' (Num. 22.33), where the three (instances of the word) do not have similar meanings, as this is one of those words for which different contexts [עִנְיָנִים] draw them away from having just a single meaning [עִנְיָן אֶחָד]. אוּלַי יִרְאֶה י׳ בָּעֳנִי is to be interpreted as a term of request (i.e. 'would that the LORD look'), but the interpretation of אוּלַי יְמֻשֵּׁנִי אָבִי is different, for its meaning is '(beware) lest [פֶּן] he feel me'; similarly with

אוּלַי לֹא־תֹאבֶה הָאִשָּׁה '(beware) lest the woman be not willing' (Gen. 24.5*); and a third meaning is (found in) אוּלַי נָטְתָה מִפָּנַי, where the sense is לוּלֵי אֲשֶׁר נָטְתָה מִפָּנַי 'except that she had turned aside from me'.

And like this word there are many—similar in appearance but different in meaning, for the contexts draw them on and after them they incline. Compare the following.

(1.) לוּ יִשְׁמָעֵאל יִחְיֶה לְפָנֶיךָ [S-B: יִהְיֶה] 'oh that Ishmael might live in thy sight' (Gen. 17.18), אַךְ אִם־אַתָּה לוּ שְׁמָעֵנִי 'if you will, hear me' (Gen. 23.13), לוּ יְהִי כִדְבָרֶךָ 'let it be as you have said' (Gen. 30.34), לוּ־מַתְנוּ בְּאֶרֶץ מִצְרַיִם 'would that we had died in the land of Egypt' (Num. 14.2), לוּ גָוַעְנוּ בִּגְוַע אַחֵינוּ 'would that we had died when our brethren died' (Num. 20.3), לוּ הוֹאַלְנוּ וַנֵּשֶׁב 'would that we had been content to dwell' (Josh. 7.7), לוּ אַבְשָׁלוֹם חַי 'if Absalom were alive' (2 Sam. 19.7 [Qr]), לוּ־אִישׁ הֹלֵךְ רוּחַ וָשֶׁקֶר כִּזֵּב 'if a man should go about and utter wind and lies' (Mic. 2.11), לוּ־יֵשׁ נַפְשְׁכֶם תַּחַת נַפְשִׁי 'if you were in my place' (Job 16.4). In connection with its interpretation, לוּ here is like מִי יִתֶּן־לִי שֹׁמֵעַ לִי 'Oh, that I had one to hear me' (Job 31.35 [S-B: 31.25]).

2. לוּ חָפֵץ י׳ לַהֲמִיתֵנוּ 'if the Lord had meant to kill us' (Judg. 13.23), לוּא הִקְשַׁבְתָּ לְמִצְוֹתָי [M: לו] 'O that you had hearkened to my commandments' (Isa. 48.18), לוּ עַמִּי שֹׁמֵעַ לִי 'O that my people would listen to me' (Ps. 81.14), לוּ שָׁקוֹל יִשָּׁקֵל כַּעְשִׂי 'O that my vexation were weighed' (Job 6.2), לוּ אָנֹכִי שֹׁקֵל עַל־כַּפַּי 'even if I felt in my hand the weight of' (2 Sam. 18.12 [Qr]), לוּ־חַיָּה רָעָה 'if wild beasts' (Ezek. 14.15), לוּ־קָרַעְתָּ שָׁמַיִם יָרַדְתָּ 'O that thou wouldst rend the heavens and come down' (Isa. 63.19 [Qr]), לוּ חָכְמוּ יַשְׂכִּילוּ זֹאת 'if they were wise, they would understand this' (Deut. 32.29), אַף כִּי לוּא אָכֹל אָכַל הַיּוֹם הָעָם [M: לו] 'how much better if the people had eaten freely today' (1 Sam. 14.30), לוּ יֶשׁ־חֶרֶב בְּיָדִי 'I wish I had a sword in my hand' (Num. 22.29), לוּ הַחֲיִתֶם אוֹתָם 'if you had saved them alive' (Judg. 8.19). In connection with its interpretation, לוּ here is like אִלּוּ חָיָה אֶלֶף שָׁנִים פַּעֲמַיִם 'even though he should live a thousand years twice told' (Eccl. 6.6).

3. לוּ יִשְׂטְמֵנוּ יוֹסֵף 'it may be that Joseph will hate us' (Gen. 50.15). There is no further (text) in this meaning (of לוּ) [mss: although some have interpreted it, according to its context (כְּפִי עִנְיָנָהּ), as '(beware) lest' (פֶּן) Joseph hate us'].

All three are from the same underlying form [מִגְזָרָה אַחַת F: מִגְזֶרֶת אַחַת], but through usage [לְעֵת מִקְרֵיהֶם; ms: לְאַחַת 'through one of their usages'] they become distant from one another and have undergone changes in meaning. And there are many similar examples.

אָז ('then')

אָז אָמְרָה חֲתַן דָּמִים לַמּוּלֹת 'then it was that she said, You are a bridegroom of blood, because of the circumcision' (Exod. 4.26), אָז יָשִׁיר־מֹשֶׁה 'then Moses sang' (Exod. 15.1), וּמֵאָז בָּאתִי אֶל־פַּרְעֹה 'for since I came to Pharaoh' (Exod. 5.23), אֲזַי חַיִּים בְּלָעוּנוּ 'then they would have swallowed us up alive' (Ps. 124.3), אֲזַי הַמַּיִם שְׁטָפוּנוּ 'then the flood would have swept us away' (Ps. 124.4), אֲזַי עָבַר עַל־נַפְשֵׁנוּ 'then over us would have gone' (Ps. 124.5). (To be taken in) their usual meaning [כְּמַשְׁמָעָם].

The interpretation of אָז אָמְרָה חֲתַן דָּמִים לַמּוּלֹת (Exod. 4.26) is as follows. At first, she (Zipporah) said כִּי חֲתַן־דָּמִים אַתָּה לִי 'surely you are a bridegroom of blood to me' (Exod. 4.25), and afterwards she said חֲתַן דָּמִים לַמּוּלֹת 'a bridegroom of blood, because of the circumcision' (Exod. 4.26). This was because before she had brought her son to the statute of the blood of the covenant, God had come upon him (Moses) and sought to kill him (Exod. 4.24). Zipporah did not know why he had been set upon, but said to herself, Some (supernatural) harm [אָסוֹן] has befallen him. Therefore, she said, You are a bridegroom of blood to me, (that is) a bridegroom (of blood) who is (to be) put to death [חֲתַן דָּמִים מוּמָת אַתָּה; mss, F: חתן מומת אתה 'you are a bridegroom [to be] put to death'; ms: חתן דמים אתה מומת 'O bridegroom of blood, you are (to be) put to death'; ms (F): חֲתַן דָּמִים וָמָוֶת אַתָּה 'you are a bridegroom of blood and death'] because of me. And when she had finished circumcising the foreskin of her son, she saw that the harm had departed from him. When she saw this, she was amazed; she understood and realized that what had befallen him had only happened because of the foreskin of her son. Therefore she said, when the angel had let him go, A bridegroom of blood, because of circumcision; because of this I know that nothing has befallen Moses except through (lack of) circumcision. And the usage of the lamed here (in לַמּוּלֹת) is like (that of) the other lameds that have already appeared in their appropriate section at the beginning of the book (i.e. in p. 10* of M's introduction), for example וְאָמַר פַּרְעֹה לִבְנֵי יִשְׂרָאֵל [S-B: פרעו] 'for Pharaoh will say of [לְ] the people of Israel' (Exod. 14.3).

אֵזֵא ('heated')

אֵזֵא יַתִּירָא [MT: אֵזֵה] 'very hot' (Dan. 3.22). Its interpretation, according to its context, is (as follows): אֵזֵא 'hot' is like מוֹקֵד 'furnace' (Ps. 102.4) [S-B does not recognize the reference; F: אֵזֵא כְּמוֹ יְקֹד 'hot, like יְקֹד "fire" (Isa. 10.16)']. The majority of alefs written in Aramaic are not (part of the) basic form [עִקָּר] (of the words in which they appear). Thus, אֵזֵא יַתִּירָא

is related to [מִן passim] דִּי חֲזֵה לְמֵזְיֵהּ '(that which) it was wont to be heated' (Dan. 3.19), אִתְגְּזֶרֶת אֶבֶן 'a stone was cut' (Dan. 2.45) is related to גָּזְרִין 'astrologers' (Dan. 2.27; 5.11), אֶשְׁתּוֹמַם 'he was dismayed' (Dan. 4.16) is related to שְׁמָמָה 'devastation' (Exod. 23.29, etc.), אֲקִימֵהּ בְּבִקְעַת דּוּרָא 'he set it up on the plain of Dura' (Dan. 3.1) is related to לְצֶלֶם דַּהֲבָא דִּי הֲקֵימֶת 'to the golden image which I have set up' (Dan. 3.14), and אֶשְׁתַּנִּי [Qr, F; S-B: אִישְׁתַּנּוּ; ms: יִשְׁתַּנֵּי] 'was changed' (Dan. 3.19) is related to דִּי־עִדָּנָא יִשְׁתַּנֵּא [S-B: עדינא, perhaps: עִדָּנַיָּא] 'that the times change' (Dan. 2.9). And there are many similar examples.

אַזְדָּא ('sure')
מִלְּתָא מִנִּי אַזְדָּא 'the word from me is sure' (Dan. 2.5). Its interpretation is according to its context [פתרונו כפי ענינו; mss, F add: (כמו) נֶעֶלְמָה '(like) "hidden" (Job 28.21)'; reference not recognized by F, despite commenting on this interpretation].

אֵזוֹב ('hyssop')
אֲגֻדַּת אֵזוֹב 'bunch of hyssop' (Exod. 12.22), תְּחַטְּאֵנִי בְאֵזוֹב וְאֶטְהָר 'purge me with hyssop, and I shall be clean' (Ps. 51.9); עַד הָאֵזוֹב אֲשֶׁר יֹצֵא בַּקִּיר 'to the hyssop that grows out of the wall' (1 Kgs 5.13). It is one of the plants of the earth. Scholars [אַנְשֵׁי סְבָרָא] have not established its (exact) interpretation.

אֲזִיק ('chain')
אֲזִקִּים 'chains' (Jer. 40.1.4) [F: מִן־הָאזִקִּים אֲשֶׁר עַל־יָדֶךָ 'from the chains on your hands' (Jer. 40.4)]. Like רְתֻקוֹת 'chains (of)' (Isa. 40.19) [S-B and F do not recognize this as a (partial) quotation—however one ms gives a fuller text; another ms adds: לֶאְסֹר מַלְכֵיהֶם בְּזִקִּים 'to bind their kings with chains' (Ps. 149.8)].

אזל ('go')
אָזְלוּ־מַיִם 'waters fail' (Job 14.11), וְאֹזֵל לוֹ אָז יִתְהַלָּל 'but when he goes away, then he boasts' (Prov. 20.14), אָזַל מִכֵּלֵינוּ 'has gone from our vessels' (1 Sam. 9.7*), אָזְלַת יָד 'power is gone' (Deut. 32.36). All the examples represent a term for 'going' [הִילּוּךְ]; and whenever 'going' occurs in Aramaic, it is the same as this: וַיֵּלֶךְ אִישׁ 'now a man went' (Exod. 2.1) (is rendered by Onkelos as) וַאֲזַל גַּבְרָא; אֲזַלוּ בִבְהִילוּ לִירוּשְׁלֶם 'they went in haste to Jerusalem' (Ezra 4.23), אֲזַל וְכֵן אֲמַר־לֵהּ 'he went and said thus to him' (Dan. 2.24).

אזן (אזן 'hear', אֹזֶן 'ear', מֹאזְנַיִם 'scales', אָזֵן 'tool')

Divided into three. 1. אִזֵּן וְחִקֵּר 'he listened intently and researched' (Eccl. 12.9*), יַאֲזִין זֹאת 'he will give ear to this' (Isa. 42.23), הַאְזֵנָּה אִמְרָתִי 'hearken to what I say' (Gen. 4.23; Isa. 32.9), הַאֲזִינוּ וְשִׁמְעוּ 'give ear, and hear my voice' (Isa. 28.23), אָזְנַיִם כָּרִיתָ לִּי 'ears thou hast dug for me' (Ps. 40.7). All of them are (in their reference the same as) הַשְׁמָעוּת אָזְנַיִם 'informing of ears' (Ezek. 24.26) [M appar. הַשְׁמָעַת 'hearing of'; ms הַשְׁמָעוּת, as in the clear citation under שמע; reference not recognized by S-B or F].

2. מֹאזְנַיִם 'scales' (Isa. 40.15, etc.), מֹאזְנֵי צֶדֶק 'just balances' (Lev. 19.36), תְּקַלְתָּא במאזניא [MT, F: תְּקִילְתָּה] 'you have been weighed in the balances' (Dan. 5.27)—a term to do with weight [לְשׁוֹן מִשְׁקָל].

3. עַל־אֲזֵנֶךָ 'upon your tools' [L: אֲזֵנֶךָ 'your tool'] (Deut. 23.14*). These are [ms: The context shows them to be (עִנְיָנוֹ יוֹרֶה עָלָיו)] instruments from among the weapons of war. [ms: This is like 'your weapons' (זֵינֶיךָ) (in reference to) weapons of war.]

אזר (אזר 'gird', אֵזוֹר 'girdle')

אֲאַזֶּרְךָ 'I gird you' (Isa. 45.5), אָזְרוּ חָיִל 'they gird on strength' (1 Sam. 2.4), אֱזָר־נָא כְגֶבֶר חֲלָצֶיךָ [S-B: כנגד] 'gird up your loins like a man' (Job 38.3 40.7), כַּאֲשֶׁר יִדְבַּק הָאֵזוֹר 'as the waistcloth clings' (Jer. 13.11), וַתְּאַזְּרֵנִי חַיִל 'for thou didst gird me with strength' (Ps. 18.40). The interpreters found וַתַּזְרֵנִי חַיִל 'for thou didst gird me with strength' (2 Sam. 18.40 [||Ps. 18.40]), and thought that the word lacked an alef; in fact it is structured regularly [סְדוּרָה כְּמִשְׁפָּט]—whereas וַתְּאַזְּרֵנִי is morphologically related to [מִגִּזְרַת] אֵזוֹר 'girdle', וַתַּזְרֵנִי is morphologically related to זֵר זָהָב 'circlet of gold' (Exod. 25.11,* etc.). Hence, (both) the words are found to be complete (i.e. without elision [שְׁלֵמוֹת]), but (although the forms are distinct) their meanings are the same.

And thus they also treated וַיְרַפּוּ אֶת־שֶׁבֶר בַּת־עַמִּי 'they have healed the wound of my people' (Jer. 8.11), regarding the word as lacking an alef, but it seems that the word is regularly formed [עוֹמֶדֶת עַל מִשְׁפָּטָהּ]—whereas וַיְרַפּוּ is related to [מִן] תְּרוּפָה 'healing' (Ezek. 47.12) [this and following references not supplied by S-B or F], וַיְרַפְּאוּ 'they have healed' (Jer. 6.14 [||8.11]) is related to [מִן] רִפְאוּת 'healing' (Prov. 3.8).

And they commented similarly on כִּי נָצוּ גַּם־נָעוּ 'so they became fugitives and wanderers' (Lam. 4.15). They regarded the word as lacking an alef, but they distanced it from תְּנוּ־צִיץ לְמוֹאָב כִּי נָצֹא תֵּצֵא 'give wings to Moab, for she would fly away' (Jer. 48.9) and brought it closer to נֶאָצוֹת

'blasphemies' (Neh. 9.18, 26) and כִּי נִאֲצוּ הָאֲנָשִׁים הָאֵלֶּה 'that these men have despised' (Num. 16.30). But it is not correct to interpret thus, for נָצוּ clarifies נָעוּ and נָעוּ clarifies נָצוּ. The (correct) interpretation of them is 'they flew and also wandered'. And the interpretation of תְּנוּ־צִיץ לְמוֹאָב is 'give Moab wings [כָּנָף] that she might fly away'.

In the same way, they have emended [תִּקְּנוּ] פֶּן יִפְקֹד עָלֶיהָ 'lest any one harm it' (Isa. 27.3). They argue that the word has undergone a change of letters—they have replaced the yod by an alef, and interpreted the word accordingly (i.e. as אֶפְקֹד 'I harm'). But the word is not as they devise, nor its interpretation according to what they liken it. If an interpreter keeps coming to words (the meanings of) [ms: עִנְיָנִם] which he does not grasp [מַשִּׂיג], when knowledge of a word is hidden from him and he cannot find an explanation for it or establish its meaning without extracting from it or changing its letters or adding [אוֹ סְפוֹת; ms: אָז כְּפוֹת 'then extensions'] to its basic form [יְסוֹדָהּ; ms: יְצוּרֶיהָ 'its (basic) formation(s)'], its profundities are found to be flat and its terrors (or: obstacles [חַתְחַתָּיו]) become slight, and he creates an entrance for any dissembler [בּוֹדֶה; ms: בִּידָה '(anything) he concocts'].

But (in fact) the word is structured regularly and written regularly. The interpretation of its meaning is as follows, starting at the beginning.

(1.) 'In that day the LORD with his hard and great [S-B: הַגְּדוֹלָה; MT, F: וְהַ'] and strong sword will punish Leviathan the fleeing serpent, Leviathan the twisting serpent, and he will slay the dragon that is in the sea' (Isa. 27.1). (In other words.) And it will be when our God cuts off these enemies, that then they will cease from the earth.

(2.) 'In that day, A pleasant vineyard, sing of it!' (Isa. 27.2). (In other words:) Then, when the vineyard is fenced around with no breach, islands (and) nations [לְאֻמִּים; mss, F: וּלְאֻמִּים; ms: מֵאוּמִּים 'of peoples'] will pronounce her blessed and call (her) [S-B: וַיִּקְרְאוּ; F: וַיִּקְרְאוּהָ] 'pleasant vineyard'.

(3.) 'I, the Lord, am its keeper; every moment I water it. Lest any one harm it, I guard it night and day' (Isa. 27.3). (In other words:) I, the Lord, will guard it continuously lest the enemy visit it [יִפְקֹד עָלֶיהָ]; therefore I have attended to [פָּקַדְתִּי עַל] Leviathan, so that he will not destroy the vineyard.

This passage hangs on the interpretation of its beginning [סְמוּכָה לְעִנְיָן רִאשׁוֹן], (namely) that the vineyard [כֶּרֶם; mss, F: הַכֶּ'] will not be guarded and fenced around, except (until) [mss, F: כִּי אִם עַד] the might of Leviathan and the strength of the dragon be finished. But while we have found פֶּן יִפְקֹד עָלֶיהָ 'lest any one harm it' in all the readings (of Isa. 27.3) of Spain, in the documents corrected [הַמּוּגָּהִים] by them, which intelligent and knowledgeable people have illuminated [הִבְהִיקוּ; F: הִבְדִּיקוּ 'repaired'; ms: הִבְקִיהוּ 'tested'; הִבְקִיקוּ 'emptied'], in the readings of Tiberias (we have found) פֶּן אֶפְקוֹד עָלֶיהָ 'lest I harm it'. And there is none that knows which is correct apart from God.

אֶזְרָח ('native')
כְּאֶזְרָח מִכֶּם יִהְיֶה לָכֶם 'he shall be to you as the native among you' (Lev. 19.34), כַּגֵּר כָּאֶזְרָח 'the sojourner as well as the native' (Lev. 24.16, 22 Josh. 8.33), מִתְעָרֶה כְּאֶזְרָח רַעֲנָן 'spreading himself as a leafy tree' (Ps. 37.35). It is to be explained as a leafy tree that gives forth greenness and fresh growth [מִתְלַחְלֵחַ וּמַצְמִיחַ] like a tamarisk that is well-rooted [כָּאֶשֶׁל הַנִּשְׁרָשׁ], hence among human beings אֶזְרָח refers to people with roots [אַנְשֵׁי שָׁרָשִׁים].

אח (אָח 'brother', אָח 'brazier', אָח 'alas', הֶאָח 'aha', אָחוּ 'reed')
Divided into four. 1. הֲיֵשׁ־לָכֶם אָב אוֹ־אָח 'have you a father, or a brother?' (Gen. 44.19), הֲלוֹא־אָח עֵשָׂו לְיַעֲקֹב 'is not Esau Jacob's brother?' (Mal. 1.2).

2. וְאֶת־הָאָח לְפָנָיו מְבֹעָרֶת 'and the brazier was before him, burning' (Jer. 36.22*), וְהַשְׁלֵךְ עַל־הָאֵשׁ אֲשֶׁר עַל־הָאָח [L אל־...,אל־,] 'and he would throw them into the fire in the brazier' (Jer. 36.23). Its context illuminates its interpretation—as a vessel of coals which is made for fire [ms: vessels made for placing coals inside].

3. הֶאָח הֶאָח רָאֲתָה עֵינֵינוּ [S-B: ענינו F: עיננו] 'Aha, Aha! our eyes have seen it' (Ps. 35.21), יַעַן אֲשֶׁר־אָמְרָה צֹּר עַל־יְרוּשָׁלַםִ הֶאָח 'because Tyre said concerning Jerusalem, Aha' (Ezek. 26.2) [ms adds: וֶאֱמָר־אָח אֶל כָּל־תּוֹעֲבוֹת רָעוֹת (S-B: ואמרה), 'and say, Alas! because of all the evil abominations' (Ezek. 6.11)], אָח עֲשׂוּיָה לְבָרָק 'ah! it is made like lightning' (Ezek. 21.20). This word is not derivable like other words; it is used in its normal meaning [הִיא כְּמַשְׁמָעָהּ], and is said at times of great rejoicing [לְעֵת רִבּוֹת מָשׂוֹשׂ].

4. יִשְׂגֶּא־אָחוּ בְלִי־מָיִם [MT יִשְׂגֶּה] 'can reeds flourish where there is no water?' (Job 8.11), וַתִּרְעֶינָה בָּאָחוּ 'and they fed in the reed grass (Gen. 41.2)', כִּי הוּא בֵּין אַחִים יַפְרִיא [MT בֵּן] 'for he bears fruit among reeds' (Hos. 13.15). These are grassy, verdant places, flowing with water, at the sides of streams and pools.

4. *Miscellaneous Notes to the Translation*

אוּלַי. See above, 2b. Although M rightly notes the odd usage at Num. 22.33 (commonly emended to לוּלֵי 'unless'), he fails to register אוּלַי as a conditional, 'if', at Josh. 14.12 (perhaps also Jer. 21.2; Hos. 8.7) or in its most common meaning, 'perhaps'. In terms of morphology, M only cites אוּלַי followed by an imperfect (by far the most common construction) and with יֵשׁ, but not with the perfect (1 Kgs 18.27) or with noun predicate (Gen. 43.12).

All but one of the 22 occurrences of לוּ are cited, and M accurately makes the often subtle distinction between 'desiderative' and 'conditional' senses (*BDB* would place 2 Sam. 19.7; Mic. 2.11; Job 14.4 in the second rather than the first section, and Num. 22.29; Isa. 48.18; 63.19; Job 6.2 in the first section rather than the second), neatly connecting the conditional usage with the semantically and morphologically related particle אִלּוּ. Like *RSV* and *BDB*, M notes the oddity of Gen. 50.15, but does not, unlike *BDB*, provide an interpretation that has to assume ellipsis of an apodosis.

אָז. See above, 2b. Although M cites מֵאָז, the only collocation of אָז with preposition, and he includes all three instances of the by-form אֲזַי, the article as a whole is strikingly lacking in analysis when compared to that for לוּ and אוּלַי. The only lexicographical point of relevance in M's exegetical discussion—what does חֲתַן דָּמִים mean on each of the occasions that Zipporah says it: first 'bridegroom destined for death', second, 'bridegroom touched by blood of foreskin', and, thereby, brought back to secure life—is perhaps that אָז can sometimes mean 'only after this, consequently', rather than simply 'then'.

אֵזֵא. M's preference, against MT, for forms with final alef instead of he is also seen in his citation of Job 8.11 (אח, §4). Although M's argument about the interchange of alef with he, yod, and zero is hardly relevant to the meaning of אֵזֵא, he does at least include another example of a word related to אֵזֵא in the course of the excursus.

אֵזוֹב. M's three quotations cover all the 'encyclopaedic' information the Bible gives us about hyssop—it can be bunched, it is used for purification, and it grows out of walls—giving the reader a functional description—if you see a plant of which these things are true, then it might be hyssop—rather than a technical (botanical) identification. The lack of reference to Lev. 14.4, 6, 49, 51, 52; Num. 19.6, 18, where the use of hyssop in the sacrificial cult is described, is perhaps a further indication of the 'functional' nature of M's explanation—why should a reader want to know about the usage of a word in a context that he or she was never likely to encounter?

אֲזֵיק. See above, 2b5. M provides a singular form for his lemma here, although the only form that is attested is הָ/בָּאזִקִּים (contrast M's use of אֲדַרְכֹּנִים 'darics' as a lemma).

In his *Teshubot* to M, Dunash ben Labraṭ criticizes M for not realizing that the Masorah recognizes the alef in אזקים as written but not read—in other words, according to Dunash, there is no form אֲזֵיק at all, simply זֵק.

אזל. See above, 2b7.

אזן. In the first section, M treats Eccl. 12.9 as a unique example of the Pi'el of אזן I 'hear', not, as generally, of אזן II 'weigh'. The next two forms, an imperfect and an imperative only occur four times in all with M managing to cover three of these occurrences with just two quotations. The final two passages listed have perhaps been selected because of the oddity of their phrasing.

In the second section, M lists all three attested morphological forms.

אזר. M includes both Qal and Pi'el forms of the verb (though not the Niph'al at Ps. 65.7), as well as the cognate noun. The presence/absence of the verb in the parallel passage 2 Sam. 22.40 || Ps. 18.40 is used as a spring-board for an attack on those who treat forms, often in parallel passages, with or without an alef as mere variants of one another. The fact that the first three examples M chooses, אזר and זור, רפא and רפה, נצה and נאץ, relate to the alef in, respectively, first, third, and second root positions, indicates that he was coming close to a clearly structured triliteral root theory. But only in the case of the final example ('fly' is not the same as 'blaspheme') does his morphological acumen lead to an interpretation different from that of his opponents. In respect of the first example, M explicitly accepts that 'their meanings are the same', and in connection with the second example, under the lemma רף M lists Jer. 8.11 and Ezek. 47.12 together, saying 'they are (all) to do with healing'. In both cases, then, M's observations are somewhat inopportune in the context of a dictionary, where the presentation of meaning—and not grammar or morphology—should be the primary goal. Similar comments apply to M's discussion of Isa. 27.1–3, which has no strictly lexicographical value. (The yod/alef variant in this passage was still being discussed 650 years later by the Masoretic commentator J.S. Norzi.) As in the case of אזר 'gird' and זור 'encircle', M's harsh attack fizzles out in the end—'God only knows who is right'—although he does succeed in demonstrating how slipshod grammar can lead to wrong—and potentially blasphemous—interpretation.

אֶזְרָח. M's striking explanation, cited by Rashi, interprets the more common 'human' meaning on the basis of the 'botanical' one.

אח. See above, 2a (final paragraph), 2b1, 4, 5. Both examples of אָח 'brother' take the form of questions. Although under this lemma M cites nearly every instance of אָח 'brazier', the interjections אָח and הֶאָח, and אָחוּ 'reed', he fails to include אֹחַ 'owl' (Isa. 13.21), and does not seem to recognize—or believe there to be—a distinction between הֶאָח, expressing glee, 'aha', and אָח expressing grief, 'alas'.

RAMMOHUN ROY AND BISHOP HEBER'S VIEW OF THE TRINITY

Dermot Killingley

The Bengali brahmin Rammohun Roy (1772?–1833) claimed that the rational worship of one formless God was the essential message of all religious traditions, but was hidden by an overlay of irrational and superfluous doctrines which varied from one tradition to another. In Hinduism, he objected particularly to the multiplicity of gods, the mythology concerning them, the rituals used in their worship, and the elaborate rules of purity. In Christianity, he objected to the doctrines of innate human depravity, of the Atonement, of the Incarnation, and of the Trinity; the last is the one that most concerns us here. He therefore allied himself with the Unitarians, and corresponded with leading Unitarian ministers in England and the United States (Killingley 1993: 128-29, 135-37, 143-47).

In 1823, Rammohun published the fourth of a series of tracts entitled *The Brahmunical Magazine: or, The Missionary and the Brahmun*, defending Hinduism against the attacks of missionaries. This was not a periodical, but a series issued at irregular intervals; the first three numbers were published in 1821, and there were no more after the fourth. They were written in the name of Shivaprasād Sharmā, a pandit, but they are generally accepted as the work of his patron, Rammohun Roy. Rammohun frequently issued his works in the names of his associates; but since he was often widely recognized as their author, his use of pseudonyms and anonymity may be regarded as a literary device rather than an imposture (cf. Killingley 1993: 12-15).

By putting the name of Shivaprasād to the *Brahmunical Magazine*, he was able to express a more traditionally Hindu view than when writing in his own name (Killingley 1993: 121). He was also able to use the persona of a learned person from outside Western culture to show that the assumptions underlying Trinitarian Christianity were by no means as rational as many of his Christian contemporaries supposed, and were accepted by them only because they were 'imbibed...with their mothers' milk' (Ghose and Bose 1906: 188). He made the same point in a more satirical way in his *Dialogue between a Missionary and Three Chinese Converts*, published in the same year. There, his three fictitious Chinese characters misunderstand the Trinity in three different ways, because they have each taken literally a part of the missionary's teaching, and drawn rational but conflicting conclusions from it.

The fourth number of the *Brahmunical Magazine* begins with a defence of Advaita Vedānta, the system of Hindu theology on which Rammohun based his monotheistic teachings in many of his works. The defence is a response to an attack in Bengali which had been published by the Baptist mission at Serampore, a few miles north of Calcutta.[1] It opens, exploiting the device of anonymity, by expressing disappointment that Rammohun himself, represented as a friend of the author, has not replied to the missionaries' attack.

The second half of the tract turns from a defence of Advaita Vedānta to an attack on the doctrine of the Trinity. Although this attack is occasioned by a Baptist publication, it is directed against Anglican theology; perhaps Rammohun preferred to deal with a more prestigious adversary than the Baptists, who were regarded in Anglican circles as narrow-minded and intemperate. Still writing as the pandit Shivaprasād, he notes that the Christian writer accuses Unitarians of misinterpreting the Bible by rejecting the Trinity.

> I have consequently attentively read the Bible of the Christians; but to my great astonishment, I have been unable to find any explanation of the Trinity in that book (Ghose and Bose 1906: 187).

He then quotes the uncompromising statement of that doctrine from the Athanasian Creed:

> The Father is God, the Son is God, the Holy Ghost is God; and yet there are not three Gods but one God.[2]

1. This Bengali tract does not appear to be available; cf. D.K. Biswas and P.C. Ganguli in their edition of Collet 1962: 161.

2. The quotation differs slightly from the version in the Book of Common Prayer. Rammohun refers simply to 'their creed', though he must have been aware that the Apostles' Creed was far more familiar, at least to Anglicans, than the Athanasian Creed. As provided by the Book of Common Prayer, the Apostles' Creed was learnt in the Catechism and recited at Mattins on all but thirteen days in the year, and daily at Evensong, while the Athanasian creed was recited only at Mattins on those thirteen days. However, Rammohun's use of the name of Shivaprasād allows

After a series of analogies designed to show the absurdity of such a statement, he concludes:

> I regret that notwithstanding very great mental exertions, I am unable to attain a comprehension of this Creed (Ghose and Bose 1906: 188).

He then turns to various attempts to explain this doctrine, drawn from Anglican theologians. He explains:

> Exclusive of the writings of the ancient and modern Popish Theologists and those of Dissenters from the Episcopal creed, I find, to my still greater surprise, in the works of some celebrated Christian writers, who are held as the most distinguished members of the Church of England, the most palpably contradictory explanation given of this Trinity, some of which I here notice (Ghose and Bose 1906: 189).

He lists fifteen of these theologians, and attributes to them ten different explanations of the Trinity. He finds each of these explanations unsatisfactory, and all of them inconsistent with each other; some lean towards Sabellianism, regarding the three persons as modes or aspects of God, some to Arianism which regards the Son as not God by nature but created by the Father, while one seems to be a tritheist. But, he says,

> when the building is the mere creature of *fancy*, it is not to be expected that its architects should well agree in their description of its form and proportions (Ghose and Bose 1906: 191).

The fifteen theologians are named as in column 1 of the following table, and their doctrines are summarized, and in some instances their words are quoted, as in column 3. Sometimes two or three theologians are grouped together, as having the same doctrine.

1. Name as given by Rammohun	2. Identification from *DNB* and publications from British Library catalogue	3. Doctrine as given by Rammohun
Dr Waterland	Daniel Waterland 1683–1740; *Vindication of Christ's Divinity* 1719	three distinct, independent and equal persons constituting one and the same God
Dr Taylor	Jeremy Taylor 1613–67 Bp Down & Connor[1]	
Archbishop Secker	Thomas Secker 1693–1768 Abp Canterbury	

him a measure of ignorance of Christian matters where it helps his argument.

1. *DNB* also gives Dr Thomas Taylor (1576-1633), but he is considerably earlier than the others in the list, and has no relevant publications.

1. Name as given by Rammohun	2. Identification from *DNB* and publications from British Library catalogue	3. Doctrine as given by Rammohun
Dr Wallis	John Wallis 1616–1703, Prof of Geometry, Oxford; *Doctrine of the Blessed Trinity* 1690	Sabellian…three persons in the Trinity are only modes or relations, which the Deity bears to his creatures
Archbishop Tillotson 'probably'	John Tillotson 1630–94 Abp Canterbury; four lectures on Trinity 1693	
Bishop Pearson	John Pearson 1613–86 Bp Chester; *Exposition of the Creed* 1659; *On the Being and Attributes of God* 1661	suppose the Father to be an underived and essential essence and the Son to have received every thing by communication from God the Father
Bishop Bull	George Bull 1634–1710 Bp St Davids; *Defensio Fidei Nicaenae* 1685	
Dr Owen	?John Owen 1616–83; *Brief Declaration and Vindication of the Doctrine of the Trinity* 1669[1]	
Bishop Burgess	Thomas Burgess 1756–1837 Bp St Davids, later Salisbury; anti-Unitarian tracts 1814–20	supposes the three persons of the Deity to make one God, but does not allow that these persons are three beings
Dr Thomas Burnet	d. 1750; *The Scripture-Trinity Intelligibly Explained* (anon.) 1720	the Father…a self-existent Being, the Son, and the Holy Ghost dependent…which somewhat resembles the Arian Creed
Mr Baxter	Richard Baxter 1615–91	defines the three divine Persons to be Wisdom, Power, and Love…which resembles…Sabellius
Bishop Gastrell	Francis Gastrell 1662–1725 Bp of Chester; *Some considerations concerning the Trinity, and the ways of managing that controversy* (anon.) 1696; *Remarks upon Dr. Clark's scripture-doctrine of the Trinity* (anon.) 1714	'each…includes the *whole* idea of God and *something more.'*…a new axiom, *viz.*, that a part is greater than, or at least equal to the whole
Mr Howe	John Howe 1630–1705; *Calm and sober enquiry concerning the possibility of a Trinity in the Godhead* 1694[2]	three distinct, intelligent hypostases…make one God…as the corporeal, sensitive and intellectual faculties…form one man

1. Vice-Chancellor of Oxford University under the Commonwealth; refused to conform to the Church of England in 1664. *DNB* also gives David Owen, DD, fl. 1642; Richard Owen, DD, 1606–83; Henry Owen, 1716–95, medical doctor, clergyman and biblical scholar.

2. John Howe held Church of England and Presbyterian appointments, and favoured occasional conformity. *DNB* also gives his uncle Obadiah Howe, 1616–83.

1. Name as given by Rammohun	2. Identification from *DNB* and publications from British Library catalogue	3. Doctrine as given by Rammohun
Dr Sherlock	William Sherlock 1641?–1707 Dean St Paul's; *Vindication of the Doctrine of the Trinity* 1690; *Present State of the Socinian Controversy* 1698[1]	'three infinite minds are distinguished...by self-consciousness...Each...has the *whole* wisdom, power and goodness of the other two'...a system of perfect polytheism
Dr Heber, the present Bishop of Calcutta	Reginald Heber 1783–1826 Bp of Calcutta; *The Personality and Office of the Christian Comforter* 1826	the second and third persons...are no other than the angels *Michael* and *Gabriel*

Some of the fifteen are readily identifiable. There was only one Archbishop Tillotson and one Archbishop Secker, both of Canterbury, and the identity of Dr Heber is clear. The other names and titles are less distinctive, but since Rammohun describes these theologians as 'celebrated' and 'distinguished', we can assume that they are among those recorded in the *Dictionary of National Biography*. He also tells us that they are Anglicans, not Dissenters or Roman Catholics.[2] By these criteria enough of them can be identified to show a pattern into which the rest can be fitted; I have given the resulting identities in column 2 of the table, and mentioned some uncertainties or possible alternatives in endnotes.

Although Rammohun reports the views of these theologians almost entirely in the present tense, only two are contemporaries: Thomas Burgess, Bishop of St Davids and afterwards of Salisbury, and Reginald Heber, who had arrived as the second Bishop of Calcutta a few weeks before Rammohun published his tract. Of the rest, ten had been dead for more than a century.[3] Many of them, if not all, had contributed to the controversial exchanges over the Trinity which took place in three distinct periods: in the late seventeenth century culminating in the 1690s, in

1. *DNB* also gives his son Thomas Sherlock (1678–1761), Bp of London, but William Sherlock is more notable for his views on the Trinity.

2. The distinction between Dissenters and Anglicans was not always clear in the seventeenth century, when many clergy changed their allegiance or remained ambivalent. Baxter, though he sympathized with Dissenters and opposed episcopacy, remained in the Church of England until 1662, when he was offered the Bishopric of Hereford and refused it.

3. Nine if we identify 'Dr Owen' as Henry Owen (1716–95). But since his publications do not seem to deal with controversy over the Trinity, he is less likely to be meant than John Owen (1616–83).

the eighteenth from 1712 to 1720, and in the nineteenth from 1814 onwards.

George Bull wrote his *Defensio Fidei Nicaenae* in 1685, in answer to a charge of Socinianism—the term used for Unitarianism by its opponents; his aim was to establish that the ante-Nicene Fathers were not Arians but orthodox Trinitarians. Archbishop Tillotson was critical of the Athanasian Creed; as he wrote to Burnet, 'I wish we were well rid of it' (Wilbur 1952: 229). He had friends with Unitarian leanings, among them Thomas Firmin (1632–97), the London merchant who supported the Unitarians financially. In 1693, in response to a charge of Socinianism, Tillotson published four lectures on the Socinian controversy which he had given in 1680. John Wallis, Professor of Geometry at Oxford, was accused of Sabellianism because of his *Doctrine of the Blessed Trinity* of 1690, in which he explained the three equal persons of the Trinity by the analogy of a cube with three equal dimensions. While these laid themselves open to charges of Socinianism, Arianism or Sabellianism by subordinating the three persons to the unity of God, William Sherlock's *Vindication of the Doctrine of the Trinity* of 1690 was accused of tritheism, a charge which Rammohun repeats. In 1696 Francis Gastrell opposed Sherlock with *Some Considerations Concerning the Trinity, and the Ways of Managing that Controversy*, published anonymously, which led Sherlock to retreat from his tritheistic position, stating his revised views in *The Present State of the Socinian Controversy* in 1698 (see further Rupp 1986: 243–49; Wilbur 1952).

Controversy was opened again in 1712, when the latitudinarian Samuel Clarke (1675–1729), who is not included in Rammohun's list, published his *Scripture Doctrine of the Trinity*. By insisting that only the Father is supreme, while the Son and the Spirit derive their divinity from him, he came close to a Unitarian position. Gastrell, identifying himself only as the author of *Some Considerations*, published *Remarks upon Dr. Clark's Scripture-Doctrine of the Trinity* in 1714, asserting the orthodox view. Daniel Waterland's *Vindication of Christ's Divinity* of 1719, and Thomas Burnet's *The Scripture-Trinity Intelligibly Explained* of 1720, were contributions to the same exchange; Waterland upheld orthodox Trinitarian theology, while Burnet inclined towards Arianism.

Another resurgence of controversy came with the consolidation of Unitarianism in the early nineteenth century, armed with new developments in biblical scholarship and supported by funds and organizations which gave it an identity as a dissenting church; hitherto it had rather been a tendency which flourished among Dissenters and enjoyed some intermittent influence among Anglicans. Bishop Burgess wrote a number of anti-Unitarian tracts from 1814 to 1820, and Heber's Bampton Lectures of 1815 were devoted to a vindication of the third person of the Trinity against Unitarian views.

Leaving aside the question of the accuracy of Rammohun's account of these churchmen's views, we may ask where he acquired his knowledge of them. Since he was in correspondence with Unitarians at the time, and had formed the Calcutta Unitarian Committee with William Adam in 1821, he may have used some Unitarian source, either published or private. His argument has a partial precedent in Joseph Priestley's *General View of the Arguments for the Unity of God* (1785). Like Rammohun, Priestley gives a list of people who claim to believe the Trinity on scriptural grounds, and criticizes their views as either absurd or not really Trinitarian; his aim, like Rammohun's, is to show that the doctrine of the Trinity is incoherent. The theologians he mentions are Dr Waterland, whom he describes as a strict Athanasian;[1] the ante-Nicene Fathers, Bishop Pearson, and Bishop Bull, who claim that the Son is derived from the Father; Dr Wallis, whom he calls a Sabellian; and Dr Doddridge, whom he considers either a virtual Socinian or a virtual Arian. Any interpretation of the Trinity, according to Priestley, can be reduced to one of these versions. He gives only five names, as against Rammohun's fifteen; but all are in Rammohun's list except Philip Doddridge (1705–51), who would have been excluded from it as a lifelong Dissenter. The source of Rammohun's knowledge of the other Anglican theologians in his list is unclear, but the controversies of the late seventeenth century and early eighteenth century were well known to Unitarians, as were the arguments of contemporary Trinitarians.

Rammohun reports the view of his contemporary, Reginald Heber, as follows:

> Dr Heber, the present Bishop of Calcutta, maintains that the second and third persons of the Trinity are no other than the angels *Michael* and *Gabriel*. It was the Second Person, who conversed with Moses from Mount Sinai, and the third person, who constituted the Jewish Shekhinah (Ghose and Bose 1906: 191).

1. This designation is somewhat inappropriate, since Waterland himself, in his *Critical History of the Athanasian Creed*, had argued that it was not the work of St Athanasius (c. 296–373 CE) but of St Hilary of Arles (403–49 CE).

In his persona of a Hindu pandit, Rammohun claims that this doctrine must be 'gratifying to Hindoo Theologians', since it assumes the possibility of rebirth. The second person of the Trinity, he explains, is at first 'a mere spirit' (as encountered by Moses), then it becomes an angel (as Michael), and later it is born as a man 'by means of natural birth' (as Jesus). Heber's version of the Trinity thus

> countenances the doctrine of the migration of spirits from the bodies of superior to those of inferior creatures (Ghose and Bose 1906: 191).

Rammohun brings further discredit on Heber's understanding of the Trinity by stating that Christ's birth 'was effected, it is said, by the virgin Mary and the angel Gabriel', implying that Gabriel was the cause of Christ's birth and not merely its predictor. If the third person of the Trinity was indeed Gabriel, this is consistent with the statement that Mary was 'with child of the Holy Ghost' (Mt. 1.18). But to identify Christ with the archangel Michael seems to contradict the exaltation of the Son above the angels in the Epistle to the Hebrews (Heb. 1.4).

It would be strange if Heber, the author of one of the best-known hymns on the Trinity, should have held such a bizarre version of that doctrine. How did Rammohun come to represent him as doing so?

The answer lies in Heber's Bampton Lectures of 1815.[1] These lectures or sermons—the book uses both terms—were published under the title *The Personality and Office of the Christian Comforter* (Heber 1816). They uphold orthodox Trinitarian theology against Unitarianism, particularly mentioning the views of the Unitarian biblical scholar Thomas Belsham, Rammohun's older contemporary and one of his correspondents. It belongs, therefore, to the same period of Unitarian–Trinitarian controversy as Burgess's tracts.

The method which Heber follows in these lectures is based on the belief that the Bible is a unique source of divine truth, to be interpreted in the light of reason and of related literature, particularly Patristic and Rabbinic literature. The purpose of reason is to derive a coherent meaning from the different passages of the Bible. For instance, Heber argues that Trinitarianism and not Unitarianism is able to reconcile scriptural passages asserting the divinity of more than one person with those asserting the unity of God (Heber 1816: 213). But reason is not to be

1. The Bampton Lectures were endowed by John Bampton, canon of Salisbury (1690–1751); from 1780 to 1895 they were annual. Each lecturer gives a series of eight sermons in the University Church of St Mary the Virgin, Oxford.

allowed superior authority to scripture, since unlike scripture it is fallible. Heber draws an analogy between scriptural revelation and scientific truth: both may contradict what our senses tell us is possible, but both are to be accepted because they have more authority than our limited perceptions.

> That the sun is stationary, and that the earth is in constant and rapid motion, a motion more rapid than the swiftest bird, the dolphin, or the cannon-ball; some of us believe, because it has been demonstrated to us: but many more there are who acknowledge it against the testimony of their eyes and feelings, on no stronger ground than than that they have heard the fact from others, of whose information and integrity they entertain a better opinion than of the extent of their own knowledge and the accuracy of their own observation. Let but so much credence be given to the Omniscient, as we usually in facts beyond the limits of our own research accord to our fallible fellow creatures, and we shall hear no more of the impossibility of any doctrine which is explicitly revealed in, or correctly deducible from, those writings which we confess to be the oracles of God (Heber 1816: 216).

Rabbinic literature is quoted extensively in the notes appended to each sermon, to throw light on biblical words and passages. 'But', Heber warns us,

> we are obliged in all the Jewish writings to work our way through the endless contradictions and absurdities of all their several generations of expositors, and can generally find no better guide than the opinion of the majority (Heber 1816: 288).

In the primacy he gives to the Bible, as well as his use of related literature and reason as resources for its interpretation, Heber was following a well-established approach. Contemporary Unitarians used the same approach (Killingley 1993: 132-33), and Rammohun himself used it in the three *Appeals to the Christian Public* which he published in 1820, 1821 and 1823, interpreting the Bible in the light of reason and quoting rabbinical literature to elucidate Hebrew words. But those who relied on the Bible as 'the oracles of God' could differ greatly in what they considered a reasonable and philologically sound interpretation of it.

Heber's first sermon establishes what he calls in his title the personality of the Comforter—that is, the fact that the Holy Spirit is a person. The primary evidence for this lies in the saying of Jesus which Heber takes as his text for the whole series:

> Nevertheless I tell you the truth; It is expedient for you that I go away: for if I go not away, the Comforter will not come unto you; but if I depart, I will send him unto you (Jn 16.7).

These words promise not an abstraction but a person: not comfort but a comforter, 'not security but a guardian' (Heber 1816: 53). Heber, who does not habitually use scholastic language, describes the Holy Spirit as 'an ens, not an accident; an agent, not an action' (p. 54). Because the Spirit is a person, it is referred to by a masculine, not a neuter pronoun,[1] as in ὅταν δὲ ἔλθῃ ἐκεῖνος τὸ πνεῦμα τῆς ἀληθείας 'when he, the Spirit of truth, is come' (Jn 16.13). There would be no reason for this violation of Greek gender concord, Heber argues, if the noun did not have a male personal referent (Heber 1816: 59). He opposes 'the Sabellian who identifies his [the Holy Spirit's] person with that of the Almighty Father', and 'the Arian and Mohammedan who regard him as a created Intelligence' (Heber 1816: 54). Since angels are created intelligences, this rules out the identification with Gabriel which Rammohun attributes to Heber.

In his fourth lecture, Heber examines the Old Testament for references to the Holy Spirit, as well as to the Son. He is not, of course, claiming that the concept of these as persons of God was current in Old Testament times. As we have seen, he accepts the Bible as 'the oracles of God', but he holds that those through whom these oracles were revealed, such as Moses and the prophets, did not understand their full meaning; still less did their hearers. The Old Testament, in pre-Christian times, was in Heber's view a partially understood text to which the New Testament would provide the key. Part of this key is the doctrine of the Trinity.

Besides the many prophecies which were generally accepted in Christian tradition as referring to the future coming of Jesus, Heber found references in the Old Testament to the second person of the Trinity as active in salvation history. The being who directed Moses, guided the Israelites out of Egypt, delivered them in the Red Sea, and gave the law to Moses on Sinai, is the second person; for this identification, Heber claims the authority of the Church Fathers and the 'elder Jews' who identified him as the Logos (Heber 1816: 243). But this being also tells Moses: 'Behold, I send an Angel before thee, to keep thee in the way, and to bring thee to the place which I have prepared...

1. A person can also, of course, be referred to by a feminine pronoun, but Heber does not consider this possibility here.

my name is in him' (Exod. 23.20-21). This is what is referred to in post-biblical Hebrew as the *shekinah*—the presence or dwelling of God. Although called an angel, it is more than an angel; not a creature of God, but God himself. More precisely, Heber argues, it is the Holy Spirit. This is why the Israelites who rebelled in the desert are said to grieve God's holy spirit (Isa. 63.10; Heber 1816: 247). There is a discrepancy between this passage and 1 Cor. 10.9, which refers to the same event as an example of men testing Christ.[1] Heber explains the discrepancy by saying that Isaiah is referring to the Holy Spirit as the guide of the Israelites through the desert, while Paul is referring to 'that Jehovah who brought them out of the land of Egypt, and of whom the manna, which they sinned in refusing, was a type and bodily image'. Thus each is referring to a person of the Trinity, and therefore to God.

Heber thus finds that the two main stories of deliverance in the Bible present a common pattern in the functions of the persons of the Trinity. In the Old Testament, it is the second person of the Trinity who delivers the Israelites from bondage in Egypt, instructs Moses, reveals the law to him, and feeds the Israelites in the desert under the 'type and bodily image' of the manna. He also sends the third person as their guide into Canaan. In the New Testament, the second person delivers his followers from sin through his death, instructs his apostles and reveals the law in a new form, and feeds his people under the 'type and bodily image' of the Eucharist. He also sends the third person to be their guide.

We now have the source of Rammohun's second sentence about Heber's version of the Trinity: 'It was the Second Person, who conversed with Moses from Mount Sinai, and the third person, who constituted the Jewish Shekinah.' The preceding sentence, concerning Michael and Gabriel, is based on the latter part of Heber's fourth Bampton Lecture. This part is based mainly on the book of Daniel.

Daniel is the only book in the Old Testament in which any angel is given a name: Gabriel twice (Dan. 8.16; 9.21) and Michael three times (Dan. 10.13, 21; 12.1). From our perspective, we might think of this as a sign of the book's late date, along with its cavalier treatment of Mediterranean and Iranian history.[2] We are used to seeing apocalyptic

1. The King James Bible reads Χριστόν, where *RSV* reads Κύριον. Heber notes the variant, but says that the two words are generally synonymous in Paul.

2. Dan. 11.1 refers to an unhistorical 'Darius the Mede'; the prophecy of the four kingdoms (Dan. 2.37–40) implies an unhistorical succession of Babylon, Media, Persia, Greece. Nebuchadnezzar's officers have Persian titles (Dan. 3.2) and his

books such as Daniel and Revelation as products of particular historical situations, and as having been composed after the events which they predict. But Heber regarded the whole Bible as 'the oracles of God', and like many of his contemporaries took apocalyptic scriptures at face value, both as predictions of historical events and as having continuing relevance. For him, a prophet who knew heavenly beings by name was of peculiar importance.

Chapter 10 of Daniel, he says, is 'the clearest discovery of the existence and functions of God's Holy Spirit under the Mosaic dispensation'. This chapter describes a vision seen by Daniel when he was fasting on the banks of the Tigris: 'a certain man clothed in linen, whose loins were girded with fine gold of Uphaz' (Dan. 10.5). Daniel swoons, and is raised up by a figure, apparently the same as the one in linen and gold, who predicts some events in the history of Persia and Greece. He also refers to a helper whom he calls 'Michael, one of the chief princes' (Dan. 10.13), 'Michael your prince' (Dan. 10.21) and 'Michael...the great prince which standeth for the children of thy people' (Dan. 12.1).

Heber identifies Michael as 'one of the names ascribed to our Saviour in his preexistent state.' He claims authorities for this identification in the sermons of Luther and Calvin.[1] He also cites rabbinic texts which corroborate it, provided they are given Christian interpretations. One of these identifies Michael as the high priest in heaven,[2] whom Heb. 8.1 identifies with Jesus. Another describes him as pleading the merits of the Israelites against the accusations of Satan, and pleading that David be admitted to the heavenly Jerusalem despite his sins;[3] in a Christian reading, this intercessor for sinners is Jesus. In the New Testament, the defeat of the dragon by Michael and his angels (Rev. 12.7) is 'predicted in terms and under circumstances which can only suit the Messiah' (Heber 1816: 252). Again, in 1 Thess. 4.16 the Lord will descend 'with the voice of the archangel' to raise the dead, while Jn 5.25 says that 'the dead shall hear the voice of the Son of God'; Heber harmonizes these two passages by identifying 'the archangel' as Michael (for which he cites Jude 9), whom he identifies in turn as Christ.

musicians play Greek instruments (Dan. 3.4). Cf. Barr 1962: 591-92, 594; Porteous 1965: 45–51, 57-58.

1. Heber cites Luther's *Predigt über die Epist. am Feste Michaelis*, and Calvin's *Praelect. in Daniel.*

2. Heber cites *Sohar Chadasch* fol. 22.4.

3. Heber cites *Jalkut Rubeni* fol. 72.3.

If Michael is the Son, who is the man in linen girded with gold? Heber disagrees with Ephraim Syrus and other commentators who identify him with the Logos (cf. Jeffery quoted by Porteous 1965: 151), since this figure speaks of Michael as someone other than himself. Other commentators identify him with Gabriel, named in Dan. 8.16 and 9.21, and Heber accepts this identification.

Jewish writers say that Michael and Gabriel are the only ones in heaven who endure for ever. According to some rabbis, angels are literally ephemeral, being emanated daily from a celestial river and reabsorbed into it at night (Heber 1816: 266). Heber says that, while Christians have no concern with such fancies, they sometimes conceal truths such as the superiority of Michael and Gabriel to the other angels. He also notes the Jewish commentators' identification of the 'saviours' in Obad. 21 with Gabriel and Michael, and their identification of the destroyer of Sodom, the future destroyer of Leviathan, and the protector of the three in the furnace (Dan. 3.25; 28), with Gabriel.

His hypothesis is that the figure who is sometimes named Gabriel, and who ranks above the angels together with Michael who is Christ, is the Holy Spirit. Though he calls this his own hypothesis (Heber 1816: 285 n. k, 295 n. a), he claims a precedent in the view of Bishop Samuel Horsley (1733–1806) that the 'watchers' and 'holy ones' of Nebuchadnezzar's dream, mentioned first in the singular (Dan. 4.13) and then in the plural (Dan. 4.17), are the persons of the Trinity. He further suggests that the angel Gabriel who brought the annunciation to Mary (Lk. 1.26) was the Holy Spirit, and perhaps also the angel at the resurrection (Mt. 28.2).

However, he is careful not to claim too much for his hypothesis, and ends his sermon with a note of caution combined with a confident assertion of Trinitarian doctrine:

> These wilder and more fanciful speculations of theology, though, if correct, they may illustrate; if false or exaggerated, cannot, by their failure, affect the more solid columns of Christianity—those doctrines of the Atonement and Triune Deity against which the gates of hell are destined never to prevail; which, of whatever materials be the superstructure which we seek to rear on their basis, are themselves impregnably founded on the rock of eternal wisdom (Heber 1816: 274).

Rammohun's statement that Heber 'maintains that the second and third persons of the Trinity are no other than the angels *Michael* and *Gabriel*' is misleading, since it implies that Heber identified the Son and the Holy Spirit with figures who were thought of as mere messengers of

God, or leaders of his heavenly host.[1] On the contrary, Heber insists that on the biblical evidence Michael and Gabriel are not created intelligences, as the term *angel* would imply, and must therefore be manifestations of God. The man in linen and gold of Daniel's vision, he argues, excites greater terror than a merely angelical appearance does in any part of the Bible (Heber 1816: 264)—closely comparable, he might have added, to the effect of Ezekiel's vision (Ezek. 1.28), or that of Paul (Acts 9.4, 7-9). This man also claims to have strengthened Darius (Dan. 11.1). Heber tells us that Ephraim Syrus and 'all the Roman Catholic commentators' use this text to support the belief that angels guide the destiny of empires, each nation having received an 'Angel-Governor' when languages were divided at Babel (Heber 1816: 255, 288 n. m). Gabriel, on this view, is the guardian of the Persians, and Michael of the Israelites. But Heber refutes the doctrine of national angels with a reductio ad absurdum which exemplifies his application of modern knowledge to biblical material. Assuming that the division of nations is based on the division of languages, but using a historical view of language which was not available to the biblical writers, he asks what happens when a language splits? Do the Germans, the Dutch, the English and the Americans all have the same angel-governor? When a language dies out, what happens to the redundant angel? Besides, every time there is war on earth there must be war in heaven as well, so when can peace be found in heaven? But if we read the book of Daniel as Heber reads it, identifying the man in linen and gold as the Holy Spirit and Michael as the Son, 'the whole perplexed machinery of tutelary spirits fades away' (Heber 1816: 257-58).

Underlying this argument is a fundamental dichotomy between God and his creatures. Any being which appears to be on the borderline, such as the man of Daniel's vision, must be one or the other; and a being which inspires an enlightened mind with supernatural awe can only be God. Historical events may be guided by God, or they may be brought about by human agency, but to ascribe them to semi-divine beings is mere superstition. Heber finds a dilemma here in which to trap the Socinians, as the Unitarians were still being called by their opponents. Modern Socinians, he says, deny the existence of angels, so they cannot identify the man in linen and gold and Michael as angelic

1. Collet (1962: 142), paraphrasing Rammohun, quite explicitly misrepresents Heber as holding 'that the second and third persons in the Trinity are *simply* the Angels Michael and Gabriel!' (emphasis mine).

governors. But how can they do otherwise if they refuse to admit the distinction of persons in the Deity? (Heber 1816: 258). The whole thrust of Heber's argument is that the two figures in Dan. 10–11 are not 'finite created intelligences' as angels are supposed to be. When he says that the man in linen and gold is the Holy Spirit, he means that Daniel's vision is a manifestation of the Holy Spirit, in the same way as is a cloven flame, a wind, a dove, or the cloud over the Israelite sanctuary (Heber 1816: 262-63).

Heber does not tell us whether he himself believes in angels, but in his theology they seem to be an unnecessary category. The sermon which he wrote for the tour of his diocese which ended in his death says nothing about them, though, as befits a missionary sermon first preached on Whitsunday, it says a great deal about the Holy Spirit (Heber 1826). 'Cherubim and Seraphim falling down before thee' had their place, but it was not for them to instruct, guide or strengthen human beings. That was the function of God himself, and especially of the second and third persons of the Trinity.

Rammohun represents Heber as offering a novel version of the doctrine of the Trinity. But Heber's aim is rather to present a hypothesis about how that doctrine is revealed in scripture, especially the Old Testament, and how the second and third persons were occasionally and partially revealed even before the nativity and the first Whitsunday respectively. By identifying figures in the biblical narrative with persons of the Trinity, he extended the role of God in that narrative, thus glorifying God and making the narrative compatible with a world-view which saw no middle term between God and the world. But in Rammohun's view any identification of God with a being having name and form limited God and impugned his transcendence.

Of all Rammohun's Anglican versions of the Trinity, the one he attributes to Heber is the most unorthodox and the furthest from the actual views of the theologian in question. It is also the one that could most easily have been repudiated, but Heber does not seem to have done so; perhaps he thought it was beneath his notice. He had written in 1823 that the chief hindrance to his evangelistic work in Calcutta, besides the Dissenters, was a group of 'deistical Brahmins, who have left their own religion, and desire to form a sect of their own'[1]—an allusion to Rammohun and his followers, known as Brahmos or Hindu

1. Heber to his father-in-law Dean Shipley of St Asaph, 16th December 1823 (Collet 1962: 155).

Unitarians (Killingley 1993: 113, 128-29). In a similar context in another letter, he names 'an apostate Brahmin, Rammohun Roy'.[1]

But these remarks, both written within a week of his arrival in Calcutta, are unlikely to represent his own considered judgment. By contrast, in his Whitsunday sermon of 1825 he makes characteristically eirenical remarks both about Dissenters and about Rammohun:

> We rejoice that Christ is preached, even by those who hold not his faith in our own unity of fellowship;...we are content that the morality of the Gospel should be disseminated, even by those who rob Christ of his godhead and mediatorial attributes (Heber 1826: 23).

The last clause is a clear reference to Rammohun's Unitarian views, and in particular to his *Precepts of Jesus* of 1820, in which he had presented the moral teachings of Jesus as the essence of Christianity, indicating that the christological and soteriological doctrines are inessential, and even a hindrance to the propagation of Christianity. We have no record of any direct exchange between Heber and Rammohun, and perhaps none took place; but if it did, it would have been more courteous and constructive than Rammohun's well-known controversy with the Baptists.

BIBLIOGRAPHY

Barr, J.

1962 'Daniel', *Peake's Commentary on the Bible* (ed. M. Black and H.H. Rowley; London: Nelson): 591-602.

Collet, S.D.

1962 *The Life and Letters of Raja Rammohun Roy* (ed. D.K. Biswas and P.C. Ganguli; Calcutta: Sadharan Brahmo Samaj, 3rd edn).

Ghose, J.C., and E.C. Bose

1906 *The English works of Raja Rammohun Roy* (Allahabad: Panini Office, 1906; Reprinted New York: AMS Press, 1978).

Heber, Reginald

1816 *The Personality and Office of the Christian Comforter Asserted and Examined in a Course of Sermons on John XVI 7* (Oxford: Oxford University Press).

1826 *A Sermon Preached at Bombay, on Whitsunday May 22nd, at Colombo September 18th; and at Calcutta, on Advent Sunday, November 27th. MDCCCXXV* (Calcutta: Bishop's College).

1. Heber to Charlotte Dod, 15th December 1823 (Smith 1895: 168).

Killingley, Dermot
1993 *Rammohun Roy in Hindu and Christian Tradition* (Newcastle upon Tyne: Grevatt & Grevatt).

Porteous, Norman W.
1965 *Daniel: A Commentary* (London: SCM Press).

Priestley, Joseph
1785 *A General View of the Arguments for the Unity of God; and Against the Divinity and Pre-existence of Christ, from Reason, from the Scriptures, and from History* (Birmingham).

Rupp, Gordon
1986 *Religion in England 1688–1791* (Oxford: Clarendon Press).

Smith, George
1895 *Bishop Heber* (London: John Murray).

Wilbur, Earl Morse
1952 *Unitarianism in Transylvania, England and America* (Cambridge, MA: Harvard University Press).

JUDAISM TRADUCED: THE HOUSE OF LORDS AND THE WAR CRIMES DEBATE, 1989–1990

Jon Davies

In 1989 I transferred from the Department of Social Studies at the University of Newcastle upon Tyne to the Department of Religious Studies. One of the main reasons I moved was a guess that in the developing interests of John Sawyer I would find an approach to the study of religion that would complement my own—not that I had any particular proficiency in the study of theology or of the basic religious texts, but in the sense that both theology and texts seemed to me to be used in bewilderingly varied ways: and I wanted to know which of these ways was 'true'. I now know that this was a false quest! Still, knowing which road is not the right one gets you that bit closer to the true one; and I owe John Sawyer a great debt for so engagingly mapping out the many strange and wonderful ways in which human beings have sought to find and express religious purpose and meaning. This essay is as close as I can get to the Sawyer Style—a tracing of the contemporary uses of old and solemn ideas, in contexts in which, sadly, neither venerableness nor solemnity is much of a guarantee of probity. The essay is also, as it happens, about war and anti-semitism, areas in which John has always been deeply interested, and about which I have learned a great deal from him.

1. *Nuremberg, 1945–1946*

> 'Thank God we won the war, Neave', said the General, 'seems a shame to try men like Keitel and Jodl, both Generals, for losing it'. 'We are not trying them for losing it. We are trying them for mass murder, Sir!' 'Humph', said the General. He replaced his monocle to look at the girls on the dance floor. He did not speak to me again that night. The British general and I were very different. He had commanded a division against front-line German troops. He admired them with good reason. He felt a certain camaraderie with them. The British officers shut their eyes to the truth.

In this report (Neave 1978: 199) of an encounter in the Grand Hotel at Nuremburg at the time of the trial of Germany's war-time leaders, Airey Neave, the member of the British War Crimes Executive responsible for actually serving the indictments on the accused prisoners, gives a preview of the style and tone of the debate that was to take place in the House of Lords in 1989–1990. A *military* view of what happened in Germany overrode whatever sensitivity there may have been to the matter of 'War Crimes'. The military mind, properly enough, sees a war as fittingly and necessarily concluded when honourable soldiers and one-time enemies can come to a mutual agreement to forgive and forget. Voices, in particular those of 'the victims' (especially those who did not take part in the actual battles) are seen as vindictive disturbers of the virtuous peace between reconciled warriors. Such victims can be presented as agents of revenge and bitterness, all the more so because they themselves did not 'risk all' in the struggle for victory. The debate in the Lords differed very significantly from the debate in the Commons primarily because the Lords possessed many ex-servicemen and battle-experienced soldiers—whereas the Commons is practically devoid of such a contingent. When the War Crimes Bill was before the Lords, their Lordships saw the great Christian military and moral struggle and triumph of 1939–1945, not the terrible, non-triumphable, non-winnable matter of European Jews.

What one sees in the debates in the House of Lords is an extraordinary demonstration of selective remembering and selective forgetting, a recourse to and incantation of a semi-religious language whereby the representatives of the dominant culture (the House of Lords) contrived to create a version of 'Judaism' which set it apart, to *its* disadvantage, from the alleged norms of Eurochristianity, and then blamed it not only for being apart but also for being different and therefore religiously bigoted. That this 'Judaism' bore little resemblance to actual Judaism did not matter, however insistent and eloquent were the speeches of the Chief Rabbi, himself a member of the Lords. The Lords did not want obdurate vindictive victims, any more than Neave's General wanted to hear about the crimes of his brothers-in-arms, Jodl and Keitel. The debate, then, provided a good example of a *syncrisis*, 'a figure by which divers things are compared...a comparison of contrary things and divers persons' (*Oxford English Dictionary*, 1933 edition), a mobilization of religious categories for secular purposes, a remembering of the past to serve the perceived political necessities of the present, and a determined reinforcement of a many-centuries old Christian traducement of the Jews.

2. *A very old, very wise, very British, very Christian motto: the noblest vengeance is to forgive*[1]

In June 1990 Lord Longford drew their Lordships' attention to a book he had written in which he demonstrated, to his own satisfaction at least, that 'forgiveness was introduced by Jesus Christ' and that whatever happened in later Jewish writing, 'one cannot find forgiveness of man by man in the Old Testament...There is no explicit doctrine of forgiveness according to the best teaching of the rabbis made available to me' (Hansard, 4 June 1990, cols. 1177/8). Lord Longford had clearly not heard, or chose to ignore, the Chief Rabbi's comment in the earlier December 1989 debate that 'My faith abhors vengeance. The Law of Moses denounces (it) as a grave moral offence' (Hansard, 4 December 1989, col. 615). Lord Houghton, who had fought in the Great War, was 'acutely disappointed with the speech of the noble Lord the Chief Rabbi. It was a dreadful speech, dreadful in the literal sense, it was the voice of the Old Testament, the voice of the Old Testament as I was taught it, and Jehovah was not a kindly God' (Hansard, 4 December 1989, col. 633). Lord Hankey, with whose words this section starts, and who had in 1948–1949 been Head of the Russian and Eastern European desk at the Foreign Office and as such party to the British decision to stop all further war crimes prosecutions, was of the view that 'an eye for an eye and tooth for a tooth philosophy [i.e. a Jewish philosophy] was entirely against our good Christian upbringing...Nazism is dead...It is time for the new Europe we must absolutely create' (Hansard, 4 December 1989, cols. 671/2). Lady Saltoun explicitly contrasted the vengeful nature of the Jews with that of Christians: 'The Jews were not the only people to suffer during World War Two...What about the sufferings of our own prisoners of war at the hands of the Japanese? Most of them are Christians, and try to forgive and forget' (Hansard, 4 December 1989, col. 644).

Time and time again, not only were 'the Jews' defined as persons committed to seeking vengeance, but also as people without a moral code which could delimit that vengeance. In addition, of course, the definition of the debate as one between vengeance-seeking Jews and

1. Lord Hankey, Hansard, 4 December 1989, col. 672.

forgiving Christians created, or highlighted, or emphasized the almost total separation between the two religious groups. In the United Kingdom, it is quite common to identify minority groups by reference to their religious 'affiliation'; Muslims, or Hindus, for example. This has a double distancing effect: it separates such minorities from all other religious groupings, it clearly being impossible to be both a Muslim *and* a Christian, or a Jew *and* a Christian: and, in another distancing nuance, it separates people identified as 'religious' from the generally a-religious culture of the majority. Lord Halsbury, for example, was perfectly able to state that he did 'not expect the Jews to forgive', but 'vengeance cannot now be our duty', where by 'our' he clearly meant British-seen-as Christians, who were, he said, 'the least sinned against. We were never occupied and the worst we had to put up with was some bombing. Anyone under the age of 60 or thereabouts cannot remember what it was all about. That represents the majority of our nation' (4 December 1989, cols. 638/639). Presumably *British* Jews have simply to drop the issue because they are revenge-seeking members of an unforgiving minority.

It must be said, of course, that the implicit anti-semitism shown by a large part of the discussion in the Lords was not restricted to the Lords. In *The Sunday Times* (3 June 1990) Paul Barker pursued the image of Judaism as vengeance when he wrote that 'it was time to put the word of Moses back on the shelf and to take down the New Testament and the Book of Common Prayer. Even if some trespasses cannot be forgiven, there comes a time to draw the line across the account book of history and to turn another page'. *The Times* on 7 June 1990 printed a letter from an ex-serviceman who said that 'as someone who took part in the bombing of Germany, may I say that we took revenge enough to close the book for ever'.

There are a series of assumptions in this kind of comment, not least the implication in both letters that, since the end of the war, the British or the Allies had been steadfastly pursuing war criminals, which is very evidently not the case. There is, in the second letter, a larger confusion: the writer clearly assumes that the Bill in question was *aimed at Germany*. Lord Halsbury had also made this mistake. In the December 1989 debate he stated that he had read the report which lay behind the legislation (a report which he described as an 'historical pig's breakfast of man's inhumanity to man', in which 'everyone was beastly to everyone else in turn with one exception, which is that the Jews were beastly to no one but everyone was beastly to them' [Hansard, 4 December 1989, col. 637]), and then he went on (col. 638) to ask their Lordships to consider the hypothetical case of

> an old man who will be 70 years of age in 1990...He was born in 1920. At the age of 13 he entered his teenage years as Hitler took power. He joined the *Hitlerjugend* where he was brainwashed and indoctrinated in the belief that Jews, gypsies and Poles were subhuman. He was conscripted at the age of 19 and was footloose in the cauldron of Europe at the age of 25. Heaven knows what horrors he was party to. Has he since acknowledged his sins and repented? Heaven alone knows that, but if heaven alone knows, let us leave it at that. The judgement on that man in early time cannot be long delayed.

There is, of course, some sense in this: no doubt many a young German could and did find himself caught up in the Nazi evil in this way. However, neither Lord Halsbury (who had, as he said, read the background report) nor the writer of the letter to *The Times* referred to above seems to have grasped the fact that the legislation in question, the War Crimes Bill, *had nothing whatsoever to do with Germany* (which continues to prosecute its own war criminals under domestic legislation) or 'young' Germans, but was solely concerned with offences committed on the territory of the Baltic states or the Ukraine, and with offences which were offences at the time, allegedly committed by people then the citizens of those states but now citizens of and resident in the United Kingdom. There are no Germans involved, *Hitlerjugend* or otherwise; and as far as I know no RAF planes ever dropped bombs on Lithuania or the Ukraine, seeking 'vengeance' for the murder of Jews. The use of semi-theological expressions, and references to the vengeance of Jahweh, and the constantly reiterated view that revenge is not Christian (though it may well be Jewish) was so strong a self-convincing rhetoric as to rupture and then reorganize the very geographical and historical referent of the legislation and to present it as vindictive towards Germany and Germans. In so doing, the entire moral imagery of the Parliamentary debate was re-patterned into a debate about the nature of a war, the Second World War, in which the British and their Lordships, having done their duty, and brought about the defeat of a generally honourable military enemy—the battles on the *Western* Fronts at any rate were fought more or less according to proper rules of engagement—now wished to see an end to any further enmity with Germany. The title of the Bill—the *War* Crimes Bill—invited a discussion not so much of crimes, but of *war*: and for Christians the war in question, the Second War, was a just and Christian war, to be kept untainted by acts of (Jewish) vengeance.

3. *Cold War and Detente: 1948 and 1989*

> 'There must be an end to retribution. We must turn our backs upon the horrors of the past and look to the future.'
>
> Winston Churchill, September 1946.

> 'Retribution for these crimes must henceforth take its place among the major purposes of the war.'
>
> Winston Churchill, 25 October 1942.[2]

Several Lords invoked Winston Churchill. Lord Mayhew used the first quote (Hansard, 4 December 1989, col. 613). Only one, Lord Cocks (Hansard, 4 June 1990, col. 1152) used the second quote which prefaces Tom Bower's book (Bower 1981: 5), in which Churchill is clearly calling for 'retribution'. Lord Shawcross referred to Bower's book, instancing it as proof of his own determination, in the years of Nuremburg (where he was the chief British prosecutor), to press on with the increasingly unpopular war crimes trials (Hansard, 4 June 1990, col. 1097). Lord Shawcross did not mention the reasons for his failure to achieve his target of 2000 cases (Bower 1981: 205), which essentially derived from effective resistance on the part of British service chiefs and the Foreign Office, a resistance which led Bower to his full title, *Blind Eye to Murder: Britain, America, and the Purging of Nazi Germany—A Pledge Betrayed*. In essence, the developing Cold War created a new enemy, Russian Communism, and the old enemy, Germany, rapidly came to be seen as a vital political, economic and military ally in the years of the Cold War. This is amply documented by Bower (1981), Cesarani (1992), and Aarons and Loftus (1991).

Lord Mayhew, who in 1948 had been, as junior minister at the British Foreign Office, party to the decision to stop the war crimes trials, used the 1946 Churchill quote in his speech (and ignored the earlier one); and he expressly denied that that decision had anything to do with 'any wish to use war criminals for cold war purposes' (Hansard, 4 December 1989, col. 612).

For Lord Mayhew, who as a soldier had been at the 'liberation' of

2. Both in Bower 1981: 5.

Belsen, among the reasons for stopping the trials in 1948 was the fact that sheer numbers of possible war criminals made the job impossible; 'so huge was the number of war crimes suspects that it would never be practicable to deal properly with more than a tiny proportion of them' (Hansard, 4 December 1989, col. 612). He felt then, and felt now, that 'retaliation should end' (Hansard, 4 December 1989, col. 614). He later withdrew the word 'retaliation', but retained the word 'retribution'. He insisted that the 'overwhelming reason [for stopping the trials in 1948] was that we felt that retribution had gone far enough' (Hansard, 4 December 1989, col. 612); and he insisted that the reasons for stopping the trials in 1948 were doubly valid now, so many years after the event.

There is, of course, a considerable irony in the fact that the Cold War exigencies, which in the 1940s made it politic to seek reconciliation with the Germans in order best to contain the Russians, re-appear in reverse, as it were, when the fall of Communism in the USSR persuaded the Lords at any rate that it was politic to heap oblivion upon all war-time offences so as not to run the risk of creating further divisions in Europe. Several of the Lords specifically stressed the need to 'forget' the events of the war in order to create harmony in 'the New Europe'. Lord Halsbury, for example, was of the view that 'many evil men will be pardoned if we are to make progress towards a peaceful settlement of a new Europe which is probably already teetering on the edge of collapse' (Hansard, 4 December, col. 633); and Lord Macaulay of Bragar opposed the Bill because it might well produce something like a 'show trial' which would hinder the move to the new Europe in which 'retribution and summary execution' should have no part. 'The basic question' he said

> is whether we, as a country, should pursue persons reaching the end of their lives about events which happened 50 years ago, or whether, with the new Europe on the scene in 1992 and with the extraordinary events now happening throughout Europe, particularly in Russia and East Germany, we should adopt a charitable view that no good purpose will be served by any such prosecution and, indeed, that considerable harm might be done (Hansard, 4 December 1989, cols. 656, 657).

There seems little doubt that this view would carry support outside the House of Lords. In Britain in 1990 there was clearly a determination to wipe out the pattern of enemies inherited from both the World Wars and from the Cold War. In that year Nicholas Ridley lost his cabinet job for being rude about the Germans. In the same year, the Provost of

Coventry Cathedral (long the main centre for Christian reconciliation activities) announced that the Cathedral was to set the seal on our reconciliation with Germany and at the same time promote East/West relations by dedicating a new 'Chapel of the Stalingrad Madonna' at a ceremony in the Cathedral to be attended by the German President and the Bishops of Volgograd (Stalingrad as was), Berlin and Coventry (*The Independent*, 16 July 1990). At the actual ceremony, West German President Weizsacker spoke of the need 'to ask forgiveness of those who in the course of the second war were done injustice. The supreme honour that we can bestow upon the victims of the bombing of Coventry is that we follow and take up the law which binds all Christians, to try to forgive' (*The Guardian*, 15 November 1990).

Other events, such as the controversy about Bomber Harris, reinforced the idea that in war nasty things happened, on all sides. Harris's bombers had been responsible for about 600,000 German deaths and had in turn lost over 50,000 air crew. At the unveiling of the statue to him in May 1992, protestors compared him to Eichmann—although the *Daily Sport*, defending the Queen Mother for unveiling the statue, reported events as 'Hun Scum Boo Queen Mum' (*Daily Sport*, 1 June 1992). In the more dignified atmosphere of the House of Lords, Lord Campbell of Alloway asked, rhetorically, about the relative moralities of the Japanese and the Italians (should they not be prosecuted too?!), as well as about the nuclear and non-nuclear bombing campaigns of the Allies (Hansard, 4 December 1989, col. 621), while Lord Halsbury referred to Stalinist and other genocides (Hansard, 4 December 1989, col. 633). The net effect of such comments, summed up perhaps by Lord Houghton's comment that 'War is the ultimate atrocity' (Hansard, 4 December 1989, col. 636) is to blanket over any *particular* hideous events under the general horribleness of war, in which no one has a higher moral position from which to try or judge anyone else. If everything that happens in war is criminal, then there are no particularly culpable crimes, and the sensible thing is to forget it.

4. *My generation which grew up in the war, and whose fathers fought in it, knows that it was a just war*[3]

Christian just war doctrines arose in large measure because of the unfortunate propensity of Christian dynasties and states to fight each other,

3. Lord Irvine (Hansard, 4 December 1989, col. 676.

that is, under certain moral conditions, to kill. These conditions for war between states were amply fulfilled, as Lord Irvine pointed out, by the Allied prosecution of and victory in the Second World War. In just war language, the war was a great triumph for and of the military doctrines of Christianity. Lord Irvine was not alone in thinking this. 'Our moral worth rests in part', wrote Martin Wollacott in *The Guardian* (11 November 1989) 'on our role in the defeat of Nazism'. Mrs Thatcher, in her famous Bruges speech, referred to

> the concept of Christendom...for long synonymous with Europe...on which we base our belief in personal liberty. It was British help to resistance movements throughout the last war that kept the flame of liberty alive...It was from our island fortress that the liberation of Europe itself was mounted (*The Guardian*, 21 September 1988).

Lord Monson (who supported the Bill) said that 'no country did more than Great Britain to exorcise the vile creed of Nazism—an overpowering evil that threatened to poison the very soul of mankind' (Hansard, 4 December 1989, col. 649). Airey Neave, active in the prosecutions at Nuremberg, consistently contrasted Nazism with Christianity. He described the American judge John Parker as symbolizing 'all those Christian values which the Nazis had so ruthlessly destroyed' (Neave 1978: 234) and condemned Seyss-Inquart, SS General and Reichskommissar for Holland, as having 'embraced the most un-Christian features of national-socialism' (Neave 1978: 235). Neave was quite clear that the result of the Second World War was a Christian victory over Nazi evil. The Lords, in 1989 and 1990, were seeing things in much the same way—although forgetting that they were *not* being asked to deal with Germans, whereas Neave was. When seen in this way as a just and Christian war, it became relatively easy for the Lords, many of whom had been so closely involved in the war and in the post-war administration of Europe, to see the triumph as an end sufficient to itself, a self-evident proof of good faith and good practice, as an achievement which would be sullied by prolonged prosecution of the one-time enemy—again, it was Germany, rather than the real object of the legislation which kept appearing in their comments. Lord Houghton, for example, who had fought the Germans at Passchendaele (which he described as the 'biggest war crime' he knew of), raised the question of the 'Dam Buster' heroes. After the war, he said, he had gone to see the dams, and saw how the unleashed water had swept away people, farms and cattle: 'War', he said 'is the ultimate atrocity' (Hansard, 4 December 1989, cols. 634/635).

The very title of the Bill invited their Lordships to see it through war—*their* war. This war was either too Christian to be sullied with ignoble (Jewish) ideas of vengeance and vindictiveness, or too full of wrongs on all sides to make it possible to single out or 'grade' the offences and transgressions which took place during the war. There was a sense—see Lord Halsbury's jibe about everyone being 'beastly' but the Jews, or Lady Saltoun's comparison of the attitude of Jewish demands for 'vengeance' with those of Christian soldiers' forgiveness of their Japanese captors—that the Jews were overplaying their victim status. There was a rather telling moment in the June 1990 debate when Lord Shawcross, discussing the 1948 decision to stop all further war crimes trials, referred to the lack of help for arguments for continuing the trials from those like 'the Stern Gang and the bombing of the er er er...' 'King David Hotel!' shouted several of their Lordships, helpfully (Hansard, 4 June 1990, col. 1098).

Europeans in general, and old soldiers in particular, remember the past, and demarcate the various sections of this century by reference to war: the Great War, Inter-War, Post-War. War is an inevitably sacralized activity; and as it always involves death, it is difficult to see how it could be otherwise. Wars have the habit of shuffling and reshuffling small and larger loyalties, as well as of mobilizing and re-focusing religious and semi-religious sensibilities, and they can do this even in a culture relatively indifferent to formal religious practices. If there is such a thing as a 'European' identity, it lies in this century's experience and remembrance of war, refracted through religious categories of validation for the memory and example of *The Fallen*, seen as the prototypical Eurochristian warrior, dedicated to the steadfast performance of duty, motivated by an acceptance of self-sacrifice (the central Christian icon), and far removed from squalid thoughts of violence, or retribution—or even, to use a word employed (though later withdrawn) by Lord Mayhew, of 'retaliation' (Hansard, 4 December 1989, cols. 614 and 640). In placing the issue of what to do about 'a handful of old men' (Lord Home, Hansard, 4 December 1989, col. 627) or 'miserable old men' (Lord Houghton, Hansard, 4 December 1989, vol. 635) in the context of the country's war-memory, the Government let loose a whole set of sacralized experiences and memories which made it impossible (for the Lords at least) to pay too much attention to the Chief

Rabbi's statement that he 'declared an interest' (in British Parliamentary language he meant that he was personally involved)

> not as a Jew, or as a Rabbi, or as a refugee from Nazi persecution who had lost numerous close relatives in the Holocaust, but simply as a human being who felt that these monstrous crimes committed in our lifetime have diminished my own humanity and that of all my contemporaries (Hansard, 4 December 1989, col. 615).

Some, too few, of the Lords could get anywhere near thinking of humanity generally conceived, most of them being enmeshed in a particular reconstruction of the past—both ancient and modern—in which the very victims of Europe's wars become, somehow, the causes of dissension and enmity.

The Lords, who in no sense can be described as anything other than deeply decent people, unfortunately mobilized a vocabulary all too redolent of the long tradition of European anti-semitism. In Goebbels' film *The Jew Seuss* (1940/41), Seuss snarls at the 'Aryan' girl he is in the process of seducing or raping: 'Praying? Praying, eh!? Jews have a God too, the God of Vengeance, an Eye for an Eye, a Tooth for a Tooth.' In 1976, Roman Catholic Bishop Alois Hudal, Rector of the Pontifico Santa Maria dell'Anima, holder of a Golden Nazi Party badge, and one of the earliest 'rescuers' of Nazi asylum-seekers, reviewed his labours and commented that 'to help people, to save a few, without thinking of the consequences, working selflessly and with determination, was naturally what should have been expected from a true Christian. We do not believe in the eye for an eye of the Jew' (Aarons and Loftus 1991: 47). Clearly, members of the House of Lords neither were nor are people like Goebbels or Hudal: but too often they seemed willing to dip into the centuries-old vocabulary of Eurochristian anti-semitism. The construct of the alien and vengeful 'Jew' is the product of many years of Christo-cultural moralizing and proselytising, expressed and promulgated in prayer and pulpit, popular ballad and crude vernacular, and it appeared again and again in the course of the debate in the Lords and the comments in the national Press. Running in tandem with this pejorative and hostile view of 'The Jew' is the positive laudatory evaluation of 'The Christian', especially 'The Christian Warrior', seen as the repository of all that is chivalrous and decent in the culture and moral iconography and ethical codes of the West. The rejection by the Lords of the War Crimes Bill was proof of the continuing potency of this ancient antinomy, in which Jews and Christians are turned into two ontologically irreconcilable categories of European culture. These categories, this antinomy, this difference, was, as the debate in the Lords showed, massively reinforced by the experience and memory of war in this century, war in which so many of their Lordships had participated.

The sad thing is that there really was no need to conjure these little bigotries out of the historical undergrowth. There were, and are, perfectly good reasons for being dubious about the practicability of arresting and trying the 'miserable old men' who were the object of the legislation. This, of course, makes all the more interesting the recourse to the old, negative image of 'The Jew' and his vengeful 'Judaism'.

BIBLIOGRAPHY

Aarons, M., and J. Loftus

1991 *Ratlines—How the Vatican's Nazi Networks Betrayed Western Intelligence to the Soviets* (London: Mandarin Paperbacks).

Bower, T.

1981 *Blind Eye to Murder: Britain, America and the Purging of Nazi Germany—A Pledge Betrayed* (London: André Deutsch).

Cesarani, D.

1992 *Justice Delayed—How Britain Became a Refuge for Nazi War Criminals* (London: Mandarin Paperbacks).

Neave, A.

1978 *Nuremburg* (London: Hodder and Stoughton).

PROFESSOR JOHN F.A. SAWYER

1935	Born at Inchinnan, Scotland
1942–53	George Watson's College, Edinburgh
1953–57	Edinburgh University: MA Hons. Classics (First Class)
1957–59	National Service in Cyprus as military interpreter (Greek and Turkish)
1959–62	Edinburgh University: BD (distinction in Hebrew)
1962–64	Hebrew University, Jerusalem on Maclean Scholarship
1964–65	Assistant Lecturer in Hebrew and Biblical Studies at Glasgow
1965	Studied at Göttingen University
1965–78	Lecturer/Senior Lecturer in Religious Studies, Newcastle
1969	Completed PhD for Edinburgh: 'Language about salvation. A Semantic analysis of part of the vocabulary of the Hebrew Bible'
1978	Reader and Head of Department
1982	Personal Professorship in Hebrew and Biblical Studies
1993	Retirement

Learned Societies, etc.

1970–75	Secretary of Linguistics Section Newcastle University Literary and Philosophical Society
1974–79	Chairman of Tyneside Circle for the Study of Religion
1978–91	Chairman of North East Council of Christians and Jews
1984–86	President of British Association of Jewish Studies
1986–90	Joint Secretary of Association of University Departments of Theology and Religious Studies
1988–	Chairman of Tyne and Wear Racial Equality Council's Inter-Faith Panel
1989–91	Member of Newcastle's SACRE (Standing Advisory Committee on Religious Education)

Member of Society for the Study of the Old Testament
International Organization for Septuagint and Cognate Studies
World Union of Jewish Studies
British Association of Jewish Studies
Society of Biblical Literature
British Association for the Study of Religion
International Association for the History of Religion

Visiting Professorships, etc.

Guest Lecturer at Groningen University (1975), Emory University, Atlanta (1977), Witwatersrand University (1978), Catholic University, Leuven (1991)

1978	Visiting Fellow, Oxford Centre for Postgraduate Hebrew Studies
1985	Visiting Professor, Department of Middle Eastern Studies, Melbourne
1985	Visiting Lecturer, Oriental Institute, Oxford
1987	Special Public Lecture Series, University of Wales, Bangor
1988–	Editorial Board of *Abr Naharaim* (Melbourne)
1990–	Review editor of *Religion* (Lancaster and Santa Barbara)
1991	Annual Lecture (in French) at Institutum Judaicum, Protestant University of Brussels
1991–92	Leverhulme Research Fellowship

Publications

1. *Language and Linguistics*

1972	*Semantics in Biblical Research*, SCM Press, London
1976	*A Modern Introduction to Biblical Hebrew*, Oriel Press (RKP), London
1984	*A Modern Introduction to Biblical Hebrew*, 2nd impression
1986	*A Modern Introduction to Biblical Hebrew*, 3rd impression
1967	'Root-meanings in Hebrew', *Journal of Semitic Studies* 12, 37-50.
	'Context of Situation and Sitz im Leben', *Proceedings of the Newcastle University Philosophical Society* 137-47.
1968	'Spaciousness. An important feature of language about salvation', *Annual of the Swedish Theological Institute* 6,20.
1973	'Hebrew terms for the resurrection of the dead', *VT* 218-34.
1973	'The place of folk-linguistics in Biblical Interpretation', *Proceedings of the Fifth World Congress of Jewish Studies*, Jerusalem 1969.
1974	'A historical description of the Hebrew root *YS*'', *Hamito-semitica*, ed. J. & T. Bynon, 142-45.
	'The "original meaning of the text" and other legitimate subjects for semantic description', *Questions disputées de l'Ancien Testament*, Leuven, 63-70.
1976	'A note on the etymology of *sara'at*', *VT* 26, 241-45.
	Articles on *qbs*, *shaw'*, *ta'ah* in *THAT* II.
	'Response to three reviews of *A Modern Introduction to Biblical Hebrew*', in *JSOT* 1, 72-75.
1978	'The teaching of Classical Hebrew. Options and Priorities', in J.H. Hospers (ed.), *General Linguistics and the Teaching of Dead Hamito-Semitic Languages*, 37-50.
	'The meaning of *barzel* in Hebrew expressions for "iron-chariots" etc.', in J.F.A. Sawyer (ed.), *Midian, Edom and Moab*, 180-89.
1983	Article on *YS'* in *TWAT*, 3, 8/9, cols. 1035-59.
	'The role of Jewish Studies in Biblical Semantics', in H.L.J. Vanstiphout (ed.), *Scripta signa vocis,* 201-208.
1990	'Linguistics', in R.J. Coggins and L. Houlden (eds.), *Dictionary of Biblical Interpretation* (SCM Press), 398-401.
	'Etymology', *op. cit.*, 212-214.
	'Semantics', *op. cit.*, 616-618.

'The "original meaning of the text" and other legitimate subjects for semantic description', *Continuing Questions in Old Testament Method and Theology*, rev. edn Leuven, 63-70, 210-18.

2. *Biblical Studies*

1977 *From Moses to Patmos. New Perspectives in the Study of the Old Testament*, London: SPCK.

1982 (ed.) *Midian, Edom and Moab. Studies in Late Bronze Age History and Archaeology*, Sheffield: JSOT Press.

1983 *Isaiah*, Vol. I, Philadelphia and Edinburgh.

1985 *Isaiah*, Vol. II, Philadelphia: Westminster Press, Edinburgh: St Andrew Press.

1987 *Prophecy and the Prophets*, Oxford University Press.

1988 *Izaya-Sho* 1 (Japanese trans. *Isaiah* I) Tokyo: Shinkyo Shuppansha Press.

1993 *Prophecy and the Biblical Prophets* (rev. edn, Oxford University Press).

1964 'Notes on the Keret Text' (with J. Strange) *Israel Exploration Journal* 14, 96-99.

'The Qumran Reading of Isaiah 6.13', *Annual of the Swedish Theological Institute* 3, 111-14.

1965 'What was a *Moshia'*?', *VT* 15, 475-86.

1970 'An analysis of the context and meaning of the Psalm-headings', *Transactions of the Glasgow University Oriental Society* 22, 26-38.

'Those priests in Damascus (Amos 3.12 LXX)', *Annual of the Swedish Theological Institute* 8, 123-30.

'Literary and astronomical evidence for a total eclipse of the sun observed in ancient Ugarit on 3 May 1375BC' (with FR Stephenson), *BSOAS* 33, 469-89.

1972 'Why is a solar eclipse mentioned in the Passion Narrative (Luke 23.45)?', *JTS* 23, 124-28.

'Joshua 10,12-14 and the solar eclipse of 30 September 1131 BC', *Palestine Exploration Quarterly* 139-46.

1974 'The meaning of *be-selem elohim* "in the divine image" in Genesis 1–11', *JTS* 25, 418-26.

1975 'The ruined house in Ecclesiastes 12. A reconstruction of the original parable', *JBL* 94, 519-31.

1977 'David's treatment of the Ammonites in 2 Samuel 12.31', *Transactions of the Glasgow University Oriental Society* 25, 96-107 (reported in *The Times*, 9 May 1977, 1-2).

1978 'The proverb of the partridge in Jeremiah 17.11', *VT* 38, 324-29.

'The Old Testament and the Hebrew Bible', *Association for Religious Education Bulletin* 11, 17-19.

1979 'The authorship and structure of the Book of Job', in E.A. Livingstone (ed.), *Studia Biblica 1978* (Sheffield: JSOT Press), 253-57.

1980 'Types of prayer in the Old Testament', *Semitics* 7, 131-43.
'A note on Judges 5.20', *VT* 30, 87-90.
1982 'Was Jeshua ben Sira a priest?', *Proceedings of the Eighth World Congress of Jewish Studies*, Jerusalem 1981, 65-71.
1986 'Blessed be Egypt, my people. A commentary on Isaiah 19.6-25', in J.D. Martin (ed.), *A Word in Season*, 21-35.
1987 'Cain and Hephaestus. Relics of metalworker traditions in Genesis 4', in T. Muraoka (ed.), *J. Bowman Festschrift*, 57-71.
'Haggai', in C.C. Rowland and J. Rogerson (eds.), *Guidelines*, vol. 4, 2.
'Zechariah', *op. cit.*
1989 'Interpretations of Isaiah 45:8', *BETL* 37, 319-23.
'Daughter of Zion and Servant of the Lord in Isaiah. A Comparison', *JSOT* 44, 89-107.
1992 'The image of God, the wisdom of serpents and the knowledge of good and evil', in D.F. Sawyer and P. Morris (eds.), *A Walk in the Garden*, Sheffield: JSOT Press, 64-73.
1993 'Radical images of Yahweh in Isaiah 63', in P.R. Davies (ed.), *Among the Prophets*, Sheffield: JSOT Press, 72-82.
' "My secret is with me" (Isaiah 24.16): semantic links between Isaiah 24–27 and Daniel', in A.G. Auld (ed.), *Understanding Poets and Prophets: Essays in Biblical Interpretation*, Sheffield: JSOT Press, 307-317.
'Isaiah', in B.M. Metzger and M. Coogan (eds.), *Oxford Companion to the Bible*, New York: Oxford University Press, 325-29.
'Messiah', *op. cit*, 513-14.

3. *Religious Studies*

1982 (ed.) *Perspectives on Suffering* (audiocassettes with handbook) Audio Visual Centre, Newcastle University.
'Some Biblical views of suffering', in J.F.A. Sawyer (ed.), *Perspectives on Suffering*, 32-41.
'A change of emphasis in the study of the prophets', in R.J. Coggins *et al.* (eds.), *Israel's Prophetic Tradition*, 233-49.
1984 'Islam and Judaism', in D.M. MacEoin (ed.), *Islam in the Modern World*, 143-53.
'Biblical alternatives to monotheism', *Theology* May–June, 172-80.
1990 'History of Interpretation', in R.J. Coggins and L. Houlden (eds.), *Dictionary of Biblical Interpretation*, London: SCM Press, 316-320.
1991 'Combating prejudices about the Bible and Judaism', *Theology*, 94, 269-78.

In Press

1993 *Prophecy and the Biblical Prophets* (Japanese translation) Tokyo.
Prophecy and the Biblical Prophets (Spanish translation) Bilbao.
'Ethics of Comparative Interpretation', *Currents in Research: Biblical Studies* 1.

'Le serviteur souffrant dans les traditions juives et chrétiennes', *BETL*.

'Isaiah', article in *Dictionary of Biblical Interpretation* (ed. John Hayes; Atlanta: Abingdon Press).

1994 (ed.) 78 articles (90,000 words) in the field of religion by 69 authors for *Encyclopaedia of Language and Linguistics* (10 vols.; Pergamon Press/Aberdeen University Press).

In Progress

1991–93 *The Fifth Evangelist: Isaiah in the History of Christianity* (Cambridge University Press).

revision of *A Modern Introduction to Biblical Hebrew* (Sheffield Academic Press).

French translation of *A Modern Introduction to Biblical Hebrew* (Paris: Letouzey et Ané).

1992 Co-editor with D.F. Sawyer of a new series on 'Religion in the First Christian Centuries' (Routledge; 10-12 vols. initially planned).

1993–94 *Sacred Languages and Sacred Texts* (70,000 word volume for Routledge series).

1994 10,000 word article on 'The Semantics of Biblical Hebrew' commissioned for *Currents in Research: Biblical Studies*.

1994 Co-editor with C.C. Rowland (Oxford University) of new biblical commentary series (Oxford University Press).

Indexes

Index of References

Old Testament

PSEUDEPIGRAPHA

QUMRAN

TALMUDS

MIDRASH

PHILO

JOSEPHUS

OSTRACA, PAPYRI AND TABLETS

INSCRIPTIONS

Index of Authors

JOURNAL FOR THE STUDY OF THE OLD TESTAMENT

Supplement Series

1 I, HE, WE AND THEY:
A LITERARY APPROACH TO ISAIAH 53
D.J.A. Clines

4 THANKSGIVING FOR A LIBERATED PROPHET:
AN INTERPRETATION OF ISAIAH CHAPTER 53
R.N. Whybray

10 THE THEME OF THE PENTATEUCH
David J.A. Clines

14 THE FATE OF KING SAUL:
AN INTERPRETATION OF A BIBLICAL STORY
D.M. Gunn

15 THE DEUTERONOMISTIC HISTORY
Martin Noth

16 PROPHECY AND ETHICS:
ISAIAH AND THE ETHICAL TRADITION OF ISRAEL
Eryl W. Davies

17 THE ROLES OF ISRAEL'S PROPHETS
David L. Petersen

18 THE DOUBLE REDACTION OF THE DEUTERONOMISTIC HISTORY
Richard D. Nelson

19 ART AND MEANING:
RHETORIC IN BIBLICAL LITERATURE
Edited by David J.A. Clines, David M. Gunn & Alan J. Hauser

20 THE PSALMS OF THE SONS OF KORAH
Michael D. Goulder

21 COLOUR TERMS IN THE OLD TESTAMENT
Athalya Brenner

22 AT THE MOUNTAIN OF GOD:
STORY AND THEOLOGY IN EXODUS 32–34
R.W.L. Moberly

23 THE GLORY OF ISRAEL:
THE THEOLOGY AND PROVENIENCE OF THE ISAIAH TARGUM
Bruce D. Chilton

24 MIDIAN, MOAB AND EDOM:
THE HISTORY AND ARCHAEOLOGY OF LATE BRONZE AND
IRON AGE JORDAN AND NORTH-WEST ARABIA
Edited by John F.A. Sawyer & David J.A. Clines

25 THE DAMASCUS COVENANT:
AN INTERPRETATION OF THE 'DAMASCUS DOCUMENT'
Philip R. Davies

26 Classical Hebrew Poetry:
A Guide to its Techniques
Wilfred G.E. Watson
28 Hosea:
An Israelite Prophet in Judean Perspective
Grace I. Emmerson
29 Exegesis at Qumran:
4QFlorilegium in its Jewish Context
George J. Brooke
30 The Esther Scroll:
The Story of the Story
David J.A. Clines
31 In the Shelter of Elyon:
Essays in Honor of G.W. Ahlström
Edited by W. Boyd Barrick & John R. Spencer
32 The Prophetic Persona:
Jeremiah and the Language of the Self
Timothy Polk
33 Law and Theology in Deuteronomy
J.G. McConville
34 The Temple Scroll:
An Introduction, Translation & Commentary
Johann Maier
35 Saga, Legend, Tale, Novella, Fable:
Narrative Forms in Old Testament Literature
Edited by George W. Coats
36 The Song of Fourteen Songs
Michael D. Goulder
37 Understanding the Word:
Essays in Honor of Bernhard W. Anderson
Edited by James T. Butler, Edgar W. Conrad & Ben C. Ollenburger
38 Sleep, Divine and Human, in the Old Testament
Thomas H. McAlpine
39 The Sense of Biblical Narrative II:
Structural Analyses in the Hebrew Bible
David Jobling
40 Directions in Biblical Hebrew Poetry
Edited by Elaine R. Follis
41 Zion, the City of the Great King:
A Theological Symbol of the Jerusalem Cult
Ben C. Ollenburger
42 A Word in Season:
Essays in Honour of William McKane
Edited by James D. Martin & Philip R. Davies

43 THE CULT OF MOLEK:
A REASSESSMENT
G.C. Heider

44 THE IDENTITY OF THE INDIVIDUAL IN THE PSALMS
Steven J.L. Croft

45 THE CONFESSIONS OF JEREMIAH IN CONTEXT:
SCENES OF PROPHETIC DRAMA
A.R. Diamond

46 THE BOOK OF JUDGES:
AN INTEGRATED READING
Barry G. Webb

50 THE CHRONICLER'S HISTORY
Martin Noth
Translated by H.G.M. Williamson with an Introduction

51 DIVINE INITIATIVE AND HUMAN RESPONSE IN EZEKIEL
Paul Joyce

52 THE CONFLICT OF FAITH AND EXPERIENCE IN THE PSALMS:
A FORM-CRITICAL AND THEOLOGICAL STUDY
Craig C. Broyles

53 THE MAKING OF THE PENTATEUCH:
A METHODOLOGICAL STUDY
R.N. Whybray

54 FROM REPENTANCE TO REDEMPTION:
JEREMIAH'S THOUGHT IN TRANSITION
Jeremiah Unterman

55 THE ORIGIN TRADITION OF ANCIENT ISRAEL:
1. THE LITERARY FORMATION OF GENESIS AND EXODUS 1–23
T.L. Thompson

56 THE PURIFICATION OFFERING IN THE PRIESTLY LITERATURE:
ITS MEANING AND FUNCTION
N. Kiuchi

57 MOSES:
HEROIC MAN, MAN OF GOD
George W. Coats

59 CREATIVE BIBLICAL EXEGESIS:
CHRISTIAN AND JEWISH HERMENEUTICS THROUGH THE CENTURIES
Edited by Benjamin Uffenheimer & Henning Graf Reventlow

60 HER PRICE IS BEYOND RUBIES:
THE JEWISH WOMAN IN GRAECO-ROMAN PALESTINE
Léonie J. Archer

61 FROM CHAOS TO RESTORATION:
AN INTEGRATIVE READING OF ISAIAH 24–27
Dan G. Johnson

62 THE OLD TESTAMENT AND FOLKLORE STUDY
Patricia G. Kirkpatrick

63 Shiloh:
A Biblical City in Tradition and History
Donald G. Schley

64 To See and Not Perceive:
Isaiah 6.9-10 in Early Jewish and Christian Interpretation
Craig A. Evans

65 There is Hope for a Tree:
The Tree as Metaphor in Isaiah
Kirsten Nielsen

66 Secrets of the Times:
Myth and History in Biblical Chronology
Jeremy Hughes

68 The Triumph of Irony in the Book of Judges
Lillian R. Klein

69 Zephaniah, a Prophetic Drama
Paul R. House

70 Narrative Art in the Bible
Shimon Bar-Efrat

73 David's Social Drama:
A Hologram of the Early Iron Age
James W. Flanagan

74 The Structural Analysis of Biblical and Canaanite Poetry
Edited by Willem van der Meer & Johannes C. de Moor

75 David in Love and War:
The Pursuit of Power in 2 Samuel 10–12
Randall C. Bailey

76 God is King:
Understanding an Israelite Metaphor
Marc Zvi Brettler

78 Swallowing the Scroll:
Textuality and the Dynamics of Discourse
in Ezekiel's Prophecy
Ellen F. Davies

79 Gibeah:
The Search for a Biblical City
Patrick M. Arnold, S.J.

80 The Nathan Narratives
Gwilym H. Jones

82 Rhetoric and Biblical Interpretation
Dale Patrick & Allen Scult

83 The Earth and the Waters in Genesis 1 and 2:
A Linguistic Investigation
David Toshio Tsumura

84 Into the Hands of the Living God
Lyle Eslinger

85 From Carmel to Horeb:
Elijah in Crisis
Alan J. Hauser & Russell Gregory
86 The Syntax of the Verb in Classical Hebrew Prose
Alviero Niccacci
Translated by W.G.E. Watson
87 The Bible in Three Dimensions:
Essays in Celebration of Forty Years of Biblical Studies
in the University of Sheffield
Edited by David J.A. Clines, Stephen E. Fowl & Stanley E. Porter
90 Biblical Hebrew in Transition:
The Language of the Book of Ezekiel
Mark F. Rooker
91 The Ideology of Ritual:
Space, Time and Status in the Priestly Theology
Frank H. Gorman, Jr
92 On Humour and the Comic in the Hebrew Bible
Edited by Yehuda T. Radday & Athalya Brenner
93 Joshua 24 as Poetic Narrative
William T. Koopmans
94 What Does Eve Do to Help?
And Other Readerly Questions to the Old Testament
David J.A. Clines
95 God Saves:
Lessons from the Elisha Stories
Rick Dale Moore
96 Announcements of Plot in Genesis
Laurence A. Turner
97 The Unity of the Twelve
Paul R. House
98 Ancient Conquest Accounts:
A Study in Ancient Near Eastern and Biblical History Writing
K. Lawson Younger, Jr
99 Wealth and Poverty in the Book of Proverbs
R.N. Whybray
100 A Tribute to Geza Vermes:
Essays on Jewish and Christian
Literature and History
Edited by Philip R. Davies & Richard T. White
101 The Chronicler in his Age
Peter R. Ackroyd
102 The Prayers of David (Psalms 51–72):
Studies in the Psalter, II
Michael Goulder

103 THE SOCIOLOGY OF POTTERY IN ANCIENT PALESTINE:
THE CERAMIC INDUSTRY AND THE DIFFUSION OF CERAMIC STYLE
IN THE BRONZE AND IRON AGES
Bryant G. Wood
104 PSALM STRUCTURES:
A STUDY OF PSALMS WITH REFRAINS
Paul R. Raabe
105 RE-ESTABLISHING JUSTICE
Pietro Bovati
106 GRADED HOLINESS:
A KEY TO THE PRIESTLY CONCEPTION OF THE WORLD
Philip Jenson
107 THE ALIEN IN ISRAELITE LAW
Christiana van Houten
108 THE FORGING OF ISRAEL:
IRON TECHNOLOGY, SYMBOLISM AND TRADITION IN ANCIENT SOCIETY
Paula M. McNutt
109 SCRIBES AND SCHOOLS IN MONARCHIC JUDAH:
A SOCIO-ARCHAEOLOGICAL APPROACH
David Jamieson-Drake
110 THE CANAANITES AND THEIR LAND:
THE TRADITION OF THE CANAANITES
Niels Peter Lemche
111 YAHWEH AND THE SUN:
THE BIBLICAL AND ARCHAEOLOGICAL EVIDENCE
J. Glen Taylor
112 WISDOM IN REVOLT:
METAPHORICAL THEOLOGY IN THE BOOK OF JOB
Leo G. Perdue
113 PROPERTY AND THE FAMILY IN BIBLICAL LAW
Raymond Westbrook
114 A TRADITIONAL QUEST:
ESSAYS IN HONOUR OF LOUIS JACOBS
Edited by Dan Cohn-Sherbok
115 I HAVE BUILT YOU AN EXALTED HOUSE:
TEMPLE BUILDING IN THE BIBLE IN LIGHT OF MESOPOTAMIAN
AND NORTHWEST SEMITIC WRITINGS
Victor Hurowitz
116 NARRATIVE AND NOVELLA IN SAMUEL:
STUDIES BY HUGO GRESSMANN AND OTHER SCHOLARS 1906–1923
Translated by David E. Orton
Edited by David M. Gunn
117 SECOND TEMPLE STUDIES:
1. PERSIAN PERIOD
Edited by Philip R. Davies

118 SEEING AND HEARING GOD WITH THE PSALMS: THE PROPHETIC LITURGY FROM THE SECOND TEMPLE IN JERUSALEM
Raymond Jacques Tournay
Translated by J. Edward Crowley

119 TELLING QUEEN MICHAL'S STORY: AN EXPERIMENT IN COMPARATIVE INTERPRETATION
Edited by David J.A. Clines & Tamara C. Eskenazi

120 THE REFORMING KINGS: CULT AND SOCIETY IN FIRST TEMPLE JUDAH
Richard H. Lowery

121 KING SAUL IN THE HISTORIOGRAPHY OF JUDAH
Diana Vikander Edelman

122 IMAGES OF EMPIRE
Edited by Loveday Alexander

123 JUDAHITE BURIAL PRACTICES AND BELIEFS ABOUT THE DEAD
Elizabeth Bloch-Smith

124 LAW AND IDEOLOGY IN MONARCHIC ISRAEL
Edited by Baruch Halpern & Deborah W. Hobson

125 PRIESTHOOD AND CULT IN ANCIENT ISRAEL
Edited by Gary A. Anderson & Saul M. Olyan

126 W.M.L. DE WETTE, FOUNDER OF MODERN BIBLICAL CRITICISM: AN INTELLECTUAL BIOGRAPHY
John W. Rogerson

127 THE FABRIC OF HISTORY: TEXT, ARTIFACT AND ISRAEL'S PAST
Edited by Diana Vikander Edelman

128 BIBLICAL SOUND AND SENSE: POETIC SOUND PATTERNS IN PROVERBS 10–29
Thomas P. McCreesh

129 THE ARAMAIC OF DANIEL IN THE LIGHT OF OLD ARAMAIC
Zdravko Stefanovic

130 STRUCTURE AND THE BOOK OF ZECHARIAH
Michael Butterworth

131 FORMS OF DEFORMITY: A MOTIF-INDEX OF ABNORMALITIES, DEFORMITIES AND DISABILITIES IN TRADITIONAL JEWISH LITERATURE
Lynn Holden

132 CONTEXTS FOR AMOS: PROPHETIC POETICS IN LATIN AMERICAN PERSPECTIVE
Mark Daniel Carroll R.

133 THE FORSAKEN FIRSTBORN: A STUDY OF A RECURRENT MOTIF IN THE PATRIARCHAL NARRATIVES
Roger Syrén

134 TOGETHER IN THE LAND:
A READING OF THE BOOK OF JOSHUA
Gordon Mitchell

135 ISRAEL IN EGYPT:
A READING OF EXODUS 1–2
G.F. Davies

136 A WALK IN THE GARDEN:
BIBLICAL, ICONOGRAPHICAL AND LITERARY IMAGES OF EDEN
Edited by P. Morris & D. Sawyer

137 JUSTICE AND RIGHTEOUSNESS:
BIBLICAL THEMES AND THEIR INFLUENCE
Edited by H. Graf Reventlow & Y. Hoffman

138 TEXT AS PRETEXT:
ESSAYS IN HONOUR OF ROBERT DAVIDSON
Edited by R.P. Carroll

139 PSALM AND STORY:
INSET HYMNS IN HEBREW NARRATIVE
J.W. Watts

140 PURITY AND MONOTHEISM:
CLEAN AND UNCLEAN ANIMALS IN BIBLICAL LAW
Walter Houston

141 DEBT SLAVERY IN ISRAEL AND THE ANCIENT NEAR EAST
Gregory C. Chirichigno

142 DIVINATION IN ANCIENT ISRAEL AND ITS NEAR EASTERN ENVIRONMENT:
A SOCIO-HISTORICAL INVESTIGATION
Frederick H. Cryer

143 THE NEW LITERARY CRITICISM AND THE HEBREW BIBLE
Edited by David J.A. Clines & J. Cheryl Exum

144 LANGUAGE, IMAGERY AND STRUCTURE IN THE PROPHETIC WRITINGS
Edited by Philip R. Davies & David J.A. Clines

145 THE SPEECHES OF MICAH:
A RHETORICAL-HISTORICAL ANALYSIS
Charles S. Shaw

146 THE HISTORY OF ANCIENT PALESTINE FROM THE PALAEOLITHIC PERIOD
TO ALEXANDER'S CONQUEST
Gösta W. Ahlström

147 VOWS IN THE HEBREW BIBLE AND THE ANCIENT NEAR EAST
Tony W. Cartledge

148 IN SEARCH OF 'ANCIENT ISRAEL'
Philip R. Davies

149 PRIESTS, PROPHETS AND SCRIBES:
ESSAYS ON THE FORMATION AND HERITAGE OF SECOND TEMPLE
JUDAISM IN HONOUR OF JOSEPH BLENKINSOPP
Edited by Eugene Ulrich, John W. Wright, Robert P. Carroll &
Philip R. Davies

150 TRADITION AND INNOVATION IN HAGGAI AND ZECHARIAH 1–8
Janet A. Tollington
151 THE CITIZEN-TEMPLE COMMUNITY
J.P. Weinberg
152 UNDERSTANDING POETS AND PROPHETS:
ESSAYS IN HONOUR OF GEORGE WISHART ANDERSON
Edited by A.G. Auld
153 THE PSALMS AND THEIR READERS:
INTERPRETIVE STRATEGIES FOR PSALM 18
D.K. Berry
154 MINḤAH LE-NAḤUM:
BIBLICAL AND OTHER STUDIES PRESENTED TO NAHUM M. SARNA IN HONOUR OF HIS 70TH BIRTHDAY
Edited by M. Brettler and M. Fishbane
155 LAND TENURE AND THE BIBLICAL JUBILEE:
DISCOVERING A MORAL WORLD-VIEW THROUGH THE SOCIOLOGY OF KNOWLEDGE
Jeffrey A. Fager
156 THE LORD'S SONG:
THE BASIS, FUNCTION AND SIGNIFICANCE OF CHORAL MUSIC IN CHRONICLES
J.E. Kleinig
157 THE WORD *HESED* IN THE HEBREW BIBLE
G.R. Clark
158 IN THE WILDERNESS:
THE DOCTRINE OF DEFILEMENT IN THE BOOK OF NUMBERS
Mary Douglas
159 THE SHAPE AND SHAPING OF THE PSALTER
J. Clinton McCann
160 KING AND CULTUS IN CHRONICLES:
WORSHIP AND THE REINTERPRETATION OF HISTORY
William Riley
161 THE MOSES TRADITION
George W. Coats
162 OF PROPHET'S VISIONS AND THE WISDOM OF SAGES:
ESSAYS IN HONOUR OF R. NORMAN WHYBRAY ON HIS SEVENTIETH BIRTHDAY
Edited by Heather A. McKay and David J.A. Clines
163 FRAGMENTED WOMEN:
FEMINIST (SUB)VERSIONS OF BIBLICAL NARRATIVES
J. Cheryl Exum
164 HOUSE OF GOD OR HOUSE OF DAVID:
THE RHETORIC OF 2 SAMUEL 7
Lyle Eslinger

166 The Aramaic Bible:
Targums in their Historical Context
Edited by D.R.G. Beattie & M.J. McNamara

167 Second Zechariah and the Deuteronomic School
Raymond F. Person

168 The Composition of the Book of Proverbs
R.N. Whybray

169 Edom, Israel's Brother and Antagonist:
The Role of Edom in Biblical Prophecy and Story
Bert Dicou

170 Traditional Techniques in Classical Hebrew Verse
Wilfred G.E. Watson

171 Politics and Theopolitics in the Bible and Postbiblical Literature
Edited by Y. Hoffman & H. Graf Reventlow

172 An Introduction to Biblical Archaeology
Volkmar Fritz

173 History and Interpretation:
Essays in Honour of John H. Hayes
Edited by M. Patrick Graham, William P. Brown & Jeffrey K. Kuan

174 'The Book of the Covenant':
A Literary Approach
Joe M. Sprinkle

175 Second Temple Studies:
2. Temple and Community in the Persian Period
Edited by Tamara C. Eskenazi & Kent H. Richards

176 Studies in Biblical Law:
From the Hebrew Bible to the Dead Sea Scrolls
Gershon Brin

177 Text-Linguistics and Biblical Hebrew
David Allan Dawson

178 Between Sheol and Temple:
Motif Structure and Function in the I-Psalms
Martin R. Hauge

179 Time and Place in Deuteronomy
James G. McConville and John G. Millar

180 The Search for Quotation:
Verbal Parallels in the Prophets
Richard Schultz

181 Theory and Method in Biblical and Cuneiform Law
Edited by Bernard M. Levinson

182 The History of Israel's Traditions:
The Heritage of Martin Noth
Edited by Steven L. McKenzie & M. Patrick Graham

183 THE RELIGION OF THE SEMITES:
LECTURES ON THE RELIGION OF THE SEMITES (SECOND AND THIRD SERIES) BY WILLIAM ROBERTSON SMITH
Edited by John Day

184 PURSUING THE TEXT:
STUDIES IN HONOUR OF BEN ZION WACHOLDER ON THE OCCASION OF HIS SEVENTIETH BIRTHDAY
Edited by John C. Reeves & John Kampen

185 THE LOGIC OF INCEST:
A STRUCTURALIST ANALYSIS OF HEBREW MYTHOLOGY
Seth Daniel Kunin

186 THREE FACES OF A QUEEN:
CHARACTERIZATION IN THE BOOKS OF ESTHER
Linda M. Day

187 THE BOOKS OF ESTHER:
STRUCTURE, GENRE AND TEXTUAL INTEGRITY
Charles V. Dorothy

188 CONCENTRICITY AND CONTINUITY:
THE LITERARY STRUCTURE OF ISAIAH
Robert H. O'Connell

189 WILLIAM ROBERTSON SMITH:
ESSAYS IN REASSESSMENT
Edited by William Johnstone

190 THE PITCHER IS BROKEN:
MEMORIAL ESSAYS FOR GÖSTA W. AHLSTRÖM
Edited by Steven W. Holloway and Lowell K. Handy

192 BIBLICAL STUDIES AND THE SHIFTING OF THE PARADIGMS, 1850–1914
Edited by Henning Graf Reventlow and William Farmer

193 THE OPPONENTS OF THIRD ISAIAH:
RECONSTRUCTING THE CULTIC HISTORY OF THE RESTORATION
Brooks Schramm

194 PROPHESYING THE PAST:
THE USE OF ISRAEL'S HISTORY IN THE BOOK OF HOSEA
Else Kragelund Holt

195 WORDS REMEMBERED, TEXTS RENEWED:
ESSAYS IN HONOUR OF JOHN F.A. SAWYER
Edited by Jon Davies, Graham Harvey and Wilfred Watson